To Brita, Marion, and Pat

Preface

Nearly two decades of labor in the "vineyards" of employment policy convinced us that the integration of human resource development, labor market economics, and economic theory had been too long neglected. The third edition of *Human Resources and Labor Markets* is another step in rectifying that neglect.

This edition constitutes much more than an update and rewrite of the second edition. Human resource programs have experienced several sharp changes since this text was last revised, and new data bases have been developed that help to illuminate ever-changing labor market behavior and institutions. First, there have been many recent detailed investigations of basic labor force concepts and definitions. The economic and social environment has changed significantly since the Great Depression of the 1930s when these concepts were first developed and the Reagan administration promises further drastic changes.

The third edition shows why it is impossible to fully understand employment, the shifting work ethic, and changes in productivity without comprehending the basic fact that we live in a welfare state. For better or worse, this fact alters the nature of work, labor supply decisions, and the process of preparation for work. Consequently, this edition explores the issue of economic hardship in greater depth and shows how it differs from forced idleness.

Also this edition has been able to employ many new data sources such as longitudinal studies, which can provide more detailed and far richer information than most cross-sectional samples or time series. Using this type of added information, the book now contains entire chapters on youth labor problems and the difficulties faced by female workers in the labor market.

The economic and social climate has also changed since the last edition. We now have more than six years' experience with federal efforts to provide comprehensive assistance to the unemployed, and this edition presents an analysis and assessment of such employment and training programs, as well as a new chapter on human resource policy planning.

Lastly, inflation coupled with high unemployment has continued to plague the nation. Human resource policies are now viewed as the federal government's third means (along with fiscal and monetary policies) of dealing with these labor market pathologies. Any efforts to reduce inflation without massive unemployment, as well as efforts to increase productivity, must consider the basic human resource policy issues examined in this new edition. We do not claim that this text provides the right answers, but we have tried to ask the right questions.

The days when textbook authors needed only a quill and parchment to prepare a manuscript are long gone. Scholarship does not flow without logistical support from colleagues, research assistants, administrators, and secretaries. Financial support is vital. Our debts are many. Susan Appleman, Ellen Dodson, Curtis Gilroy, Robert Glover, Everett Kassalow, Marc Rosenblum, and Joyce Zickler made significant contributions. Cathy Glasgow and Gwen Luke moved the words from dictating machine or foolscap to manuscript, improving them in the process. Nancy Kiefer prepared the volume for publication. Recognition is given to all who have advised us or from whom we have adapted ideas and to the government officials who have borne our constant probing and querying, but their names are too many to list.

The Ford Foundation has been the major source of support for the activities of two of us over several years and a substantial supporter of the third. Most of the materials herein were prepared during the course of foundation-funded evaluations of federal employment programs. Though none of these institutions is in the business of subsidizing textbook writers, their support of other activities made this textbook possible. We offer our gratitude and absolve them of blame.

Sar A. Levitan
Garth L. Mangum
Ray Marshall

Contents

PART I
LABOR MARKET DYNAMICS

Chapter 1
Human Resource Development in Perspective

Economists traditionally have identified three factors of production: land, capital, and labor. In the preindustrial society agriculture was the major source of wealth. Production was based on rudimentary skills passed from parents to children, crude farming tools, and incremental improvements made by each generation on the "original and indestructible powers of the soil." Capital and labor were wedded to the land, and economic power belonged to those who could control its use.

With the Industrial Revolution, capital became the critical economic factor. It was capital that bought the machinery that, more than skill, accounted for rising productivity. The labor that operated the machines was relatively untrained and easily replaceable. Skill requirements increased as technology became more sophisticated, and workers gained more power by organizing, but capital remained the central factor in the mass-production economy. Government was concerned primarily with ensuring tranquil labor-management relations, and employers with maintaining a dependable labor force; neither displayed much concern with skill development.

In modern society the role of labor as a factor of production is becoming increasingly important. The world in which the bulk of the labor force was devoted to the production of goods is fading, just as did the world in which agriculture dominated the economic scene. The shift from manufacturing to service and information-processing activities and the increasing pace of technological change are making human resources the key ingredient to the nation's well-being and growth. In a service-oriented era the quality, quantity, and utilization of human resources are of central importance. Capital and natural resource endowments are vital factors in advanced countries, but it is the laborer—the human resource—who contributes most to the contemporary "wealth of nations." Human beings, according to the late Frederick Harbison, "are the active agents who accumulate capital, exploit natural resources, build social, economic, and political organizations, and carry forward national development."[1] Thus expansion and improvement of the work force are the *sine qua non* of continued increases in this output. Labor is the major beneficiary of, as well as the chief contributor to, prosperity and growth: The bulk of the national product is distributed in wages and salaries to individual workers, and expansion of the total product has improved the welfare of these workers.

THE SCOPE

Human resource development is the process of preparing people for a productive employment role, contributing to their maximum potential in producing the combination of goods and services preferred by the society. Investment in human resource development is, therefore, central to modern society. It embraces a broad range of areas that are of vital concern to all citizens, not only social scientists and policy formulators. Five main categories of interest can be identified.

• *Factors Affecting the Supply of and Demand for Labor.* Demographic forces determine the total pool of available workers, as well as their ages and, to a large extent, their distribution in the labor force. Cultural and economic as well as demographic factors affect the rates of labor force participation—that is, the proportion of able-bodied persons working or looking for work. Even broader social factors affect the worker's level of commitment and the willingness of those outside the labor force to enter the world of work.

• *Allocation of Workers Among Jobs and Jobs Among Workers.* Changes in the industrial and occupational distribution of employment, such as the massive decline in the agricultural sector, have important implications for the welfare of individuals and for public policy. In geographic areas or occupational categories where workers are in short supply, measures have to be taken to overcome shortages, and in areas or jobs characterized by an oversupply of workers, alternative opportunities may be needed. To the extent that any worker is "underemployed" in a job that does not fully utilize or develop that worker's abilities, measures that would tap the individual's potential would benefit not only the individual but also the whole economy.

• *Productivity of the Work Force in Its Various Economic Applications.* The level of total output and the standard of living it will support depend on the skills and abilities of the labor force. In order to realize the full potential of our nation's human resources and to ensure that workers reap a just reward for their labors, it is vital to understand the impact of education, vocational training, work experience, and related factors on the productivity of workers.

• *Efficiency of Labor Market Institutions in Utilizing Available Human Resources.* Many workers may be trapped in jobs for which they are over-qualified as the result of discrimination or arbitrary credentialing that qualifies workers for jobs on the basis of educational attainment that may be unrelated to performance. Other institutional imperfections may also limit the best match of supply and demand by placing arbitrary and discriminatory obstacles in the way of some workers to achieve their full potential.

• *Public Policy.* Government plays an important role in the labor market. Federal programs aimed at increasing the skills and employment and training opportunities of individuals disadvantaged by discrimination or lack of vocational preparation are one policy tool. Others include labor-management relations, educational programs, and monetary and fiscal policies. The goal of studying human resource development is to provide guidelines for public and private policy that will help develop and utilize the labor force as well as ameliorate related problems such as poverty and racial discrimination.

THE SETTING

Because human resource development deals with such a broad range of subjects, its study requires an understanding of the massive tides of change that are transforming our society and economy. Among the most important of these, at least in terms of their impact on the availability and use of human resources, are the following.

First, past gains in productivity have led to rising earnings and real incomes, which have been shared in some measure by almost all segments of the population. Affluence has significant implications for the utilization of human resources. For one thing, it means that monetary incentives are less powerful. The law of diminishing returns applies here as elsewhere, so that affluent workers can be expected to opt for leisure over work, to be less satisfied with wage gains alone, and to be unwilling to work in demeaning jobs. Affluence also means that society has greater opportunity and obligation to help those with special needs—to become concerned with the qualitative as well as quantitative aspects of life. As most people improve their incomes, poverty becomes less tolerable and increased welfare efforts more feasible. In turn, as the welfare floor is raised, the boundaries between work and dependence grow hazy, and low-wage earners may drop out of the work force if they can qualify for a more attractive income maintenance program.

More recently, productivity has not grown at the high rates the economy experienced in the past. Workers accustomed to steadily rising real incomes have insisted on a rise in money incomes beyond the slow or nonexistent rates of productivity increases, pushing up labor costs with inflationary consequences. Added to the effects of arbitrary energy cost increases imposed by oil exporting countries, the employed are more anxious to restrain their tax rates and less willing to share with the disadvantaged. The American solution to the classic dispute over income distribution has been to increase the total size of the pie without changing the proportions of the slices. With limited increases in real output, the potential for social conflict rises.

A second major development is the accelerated pace of technological change. Thousands of jobs are eliminated annually as new techniques of production or new patterns of demand emerge. Even more jobs are created, but such new jobs usually require a higher level of skill. Workers displaced by technological change do not necessarily qualify for the opportunities it creates. Overall, workers are increasingly pressed to demonstrate educational competence and flexibility in adapting to the job situation. But there persists a vast and probably growing number of repetitive and dull, though physically undemanding, jobs that have resulted from mechanization. Training efforts can cushion the transitions of displaced workers and help provide the skills to meet new needs. Efforts can also be made to increase the attractiveness of employment or at least widen the opportunities for upward mobility.

A third significant development is the drastic redistribution of population and industry. Urbanization has proceeded at a rapid pace, so that over two-thirds of the U.S. population now reside in metropolitan areas. Rural outmigration continues as agricultural employment declines, and this adds relatively untrained workers to the urban labor forces. Racial minorities and the poor tend to concentrate in the central cities, while the majority of people who have greater opportunities flee to the suburbs. Those who are locked in the central city by low income or racial discrimination face sustained job shortages. Employment and training policy can recognize and deal with these locational changes, so that workers can be matched with available jobs as effectively as possible. It has been more difficult to adjust to the flow of both capital and labor out of the older industrial cities of the Northeast and Midwest toward the South and Southwest.

Fourth, the progress of racial minorities toward equal employment opportunity has been significant over the past decade, but continued pressure will be needed to finish the task. Blacks, Hispanics, Indians, and others are still denied the full measure of opportunities to develop their abilities and to compete freely in the labor market. Education, employment, and training policies have played and can continue to play an important role in eliminating the problems of minorities and in implementing measures to assist them.

A final significant development is the rapid growth of government functions. Though questions may be raised about big government's accountability to the governed, its responsibilities continue to grow. Governmental support of programs designed to improve the employability and job opportunities of workers who experience difficulties competing for sustained employment have increased twentyfold during the 1960s and 1970s. The expansion in funding was accompanied by the decentralization of responsibility from national to state and local governments. But the millions left out of the economic mainstream continue to demand society's attention, and inflationary pressures only worsen their plight. Human resource policies must necessarily be integrated with other economic policies. These measures may become an increasingly significant factor alongside monetary and fiscal measures in determining economic policy.

HUMAN RESOURCES IN FLUX

These important transformations obviously affect the content and application of human resource development. Despite cutbacks in some areas, it is likely that this will continue to be a growth area affecting economic policy and resource allocation, both private and public. Theory and evaluation must adjust as new needs are perceived and new manpower efforts initiated.

Experiences with the educational and employment programs of the 1960s and 1970s and with broader human resource questions have provided practical and theoretical lessons. We know a great deal about the factors determining the supply of labor and the institutions affecting its quality. Theories of labor markets, including an increased focus on the operations of segmented markets, explain the allocation of labor among industries, occupations, and individuals. The productivity of labor has been estimated in a number of ways, and efforts have been made to measure the gains from remedial education and training. Special efforts have been made to provide compensatory aid to victims of discrimination in order to expand their opportunities and raise their productivity. The broader implications of human resource development not only touch on discrimination, economic development, and the persistence of poverty in an affluent society, but also affect the determination of national priorities and economic policies.

What further changes are likely in the nature of work, and what do they imply for human resource development and the labor market? Despite some increases in leisure time and some decline in labor force participation for marginal groups, most Americans will continue to work for a living.

Perhaps with rising female participation, the proportion of working Americans will rise. Goods are not free. The age of abundance has not arrived, and the individual who does not work, therefore, is considered a "free rider." Ours remains a work-achievement–oriented society. Even those who can afford to do otherwise are expected to contribute to the social welfare and to fulfill their own needs. The dropouts from society are few, although their number may be increasing. The challenge we face is not a redundancy of labor but the "human use of human beings to fulfill national goals."

The most important task at present is to draw together these diverse experiences and insights, blending theory with practical wisdom. The foundations must be strengthened so that we can learn from the past in dealing with the future.

Notes

1. Frederick H. Harbison, *Human Resources as the Wealth of Nations* (New York: Oxford University Press, 1973), p. 3.

Chapter 2
Work Life, Work Time, and Mobility

There is a myth about the nature and work life of the American worker. It projects the picture of a male family breadwinner working at his bench or desk 40 hours a week, year round from the time he leaves school until he retires. But the male, year-round, full-time workers, though still the largest group in the American work force, are no longer in the majority.

For one thing, Americans are moving toward a shorter work life. They stay in school longer, retire earlier, and live longer after they retire—somewhat over seven years, or double what it was at the turn of the century.

During the work life, leisure is assuming a greater role. Americans have decreased the number of hours they work weekly and annually, while earnings have continued to rise, though inflation and rising taxes may take their toll, and lagging productivity during the 1970s has sharply constrained the rise in real earnings. From one-third to two-fifths of the total rise in productivity during the present century has taken the form of increased leisure time rather than higher wages. Since World War II the share allocated to the latter has increased.

Mobility has also been a characteristic of American working life. Part of the American dream is that, regardless of persons' origins, they can move up to jobs requiring more skill and responsibility and offering more prestige and income than the ones they started with—or their parents held. More than other industrialized nations, the United States has been, and continues to be, a land of much upward social and occupational mobility of both an intergenerational and an intragenerational nature. Americans are also the most geographically mobile of industrial peoples.

These changes in work time, work life, and mobility have contributed to changes in how Americans view their jobs. For many workers the meaning of work and the work ethic has become less important as leisure time has increased and as individuals have realized greater freedom to choose where, when, and how much to work. The old images of the necessity of lifelong toil to support a family have been altered in modern society.

THE MEANING OF WORK

According to conventional wisdom, the work ethic was adopted by society at the beginning of the era of mass production. Because developing industries required willing and diligent labor, every agent of authority and education extolled the values of work. Wise men ranging from Luther to Ben Franklin and Horatio Alger fed workers a steady diet of exhortation and incantation from press, pulpit, and primer. All work was laudable; work well done would inevitably bring reward; work shirked led to degradation and ruin. Presumably, the naïve and malleable minds of eighteenth-century peasants were soon converted completely to this creed.

From this first flowering of the work ethic the path to the present has apparently been marked by the decay of the religious and secular props that supported the morality of work. Industrialization and urbanization, the church's loss of authority, and a gradual recognition that much of the work required by society was indeed tedious and unrewarding, slowly buried the notion that work was a good in itself. Stripped of its pious veneer, work once more became the accursed obstacle standing between men and the realization of a freer, leisured paradise.

Obviously, this abstract concept of the work ethic oversimplifies complex developments. It does not explain why people worked or worked hard or what they thought of their jobs. It is not clear whether the moralists' praise of work was ever accepted by the laborers or that it actually motivated their efforts much. Nor is it necessarily true that work before the Reformation was no more than unredeemed toil. Surely, many artisans had always taken pride in their crafts and had no need of a church-sanctioned morality to shore up the self-esteem they derived from their work. Similarly, it is questionable that people in the industrial era were much motivated by the morality that revered work, no matter what the attempts at indoctrination. Andrew Carnegie may have dedicated his empire to the glory of God, but the persons in his employ more likely worked for gold than grace.

The doubtful logic of tracing the history of the work ethic has shifted explanations of the changing meaning of work from philosophical to socio-logical or psychological models. These compare the kinds of work that peo-ple have performed in history and argue the effect of this work on attitudes and values.

Two classic idealized models are usually compared to work in modern society: life on the farm and the craft method of manufacture. Work on a pioneer homestead, it is argued, differed from industrial labor mostly in the relation of people to their environment, their needs, and their tools. The early farmer's work corresponded directly to the provision of the essentials for his survival. He ate from fields he sowed, wore clothes of homespun fab-ric, and slept in a house he built. He understood the tools he used and could usually repair them himself. He actually harnessed or dammed most of his power. Because of this close correspondence with work, its rewards, and the fabric of his life, the pioneer probably lacked equivalent concepts of work, opposed to leisure and recreation.

Similarly, the craftsman's work is imagined to have involved him more integrally than that of his industrial successors. Though he was removed from the direct production of all his necessities, he was still closely identi-fied with his work. He set his own pace, owned his tools, and probably sold or bartered his product. He could take direct pride in his skill and gain satis-faction from his completed products. The job still closely matched the abili-ties and psychological needs of its performer. His survival and prosperity were constant testimony of his skill. Again, work rather than leisure was the focus of his life and his chief satisfaction.

Industrialization, according to this reasoning, conflicted severely with the close correspondence between people and work in several ways. First, the urbanization attendant upon the Industrial Revolution removed most people from the direct production of the objects they needed for living. Though a village craftsman might not make his own shoes or grow his food, he was never far removed from these activities. The rapid expansion of transportation led to the production of many essential goods far from the site of their consumption and created a society that used commodities dis-embodied from the knowledge of how they were made.

Second, the rewards of work became less clearly attached to work itself by the introduction of objects of universal value and complex exchanges of goods and services. Silver coins, paper money, checks, and finally unseen credit balances became the goals of work rather than the goods that these objects represented.

Third, tools and processes of production became far more important, complex, alien, and powerful. Not only did the industrial workers not own the tools of their trade, but they also understood them imperfectly, could not repair them, and usually did not control their pace.

Fourth, the development of methods and scales of production that re-quired the coordinated efforts of tens or hundreds or thousands of persons meant that individual desires and rhythms were subordinated to imposed schedules. Labor began to be defined by time on the clock. At the same time, huge organizations removed most individuals many levels away from the center of responsibility and control. Men and women lost the clearly recognizable stake in production that they enjoyed as individuals or within small companies.

Fifth, and most important, the industrial process in its search for efficiency compressed the scope of individual jobs to the point that almost no production-line job required more than a tiny fraction of an individual's capabilities. Workers became, in Georges Friedmann's words, "bigger than their jobs."[1] Likewise, the results of an individual's efforts became less obvious. The satisfaction of the struggle, the outlet for creative energy in bending inert matter to human will were all but lost in many occupations.

These developments in purely industrial situations created the concepts of work that most of society came to accept. To some extent they were applicable to many nonindustrial enterprises in which size and complexity created similar conditions. But, legitimately, the critique applied most to the industrial mass manufacture of goods because only in this case did the requirements of efficiency mandate great size and organization and develop the minute specialization that created the conditions deplored by critical humanists.

According to the logic of the critics, these factors led to the radical separation of work and leisure and the decline of the belief in work for "work's" sake. Men and women lacking outlets for their capacities in the workplace sharply divided their lives into periods of work and leisure and sought self-realization solely in their leisure time, giving rise to the goal of working to escape from work. Unsatisfying jobs reinforced the idea that work consisted of anything that was unpleasant or undesirable but necessary and continuing. And as production became less a function of labor and leisure became an increasingly available fact, consumption took on a life of its own.

Shopworn as this version of the industrial transition is, it certainly reflects the changing status of some workers through the machine age. Obviously, though, not all of industrial society falls within the scope of these influences, for factories do not employ even a fourth of society's work force.

Evidently then, philosophical and sociological history fail to supply an adequate definition of work today. Work seems to include a host of things: Artists work on paintings; pensioners work in their gardens during the "leisure" years; volunteers work without pay. Identical activities are called work or recreation, depending upon who performs them. But though no useful definition is likely to include all the exceptions, some of the elements of our notion of work may be established.

From society's standpoint work is usually thought of as a person's job, an individual's productive activity and contribution to the economy. From this standpoint the opposite of work, which produces a good or a service, is consumption or any nonproductive or nonpaid activity. Conversely, from the individual's view work is the effort society exacts in return for the goods and services placed at the individual's disposal. Work is what society charges should or must be done, contrasted to voluntary activity. In this context the opposite of work is not consumption, but free time or leisure—time to do exactly as one chooses. But the cases of individuals whose work produces no good or service for exchange or the cases of volunteers who work because they wish to suggest that the traditional definitions of work may be outmoded. Work, redefined to account for these situations, is simply sustained and purposeful activity to accomplish goals. Work is the continuing struggle to bend the world to the human will and imagination, the natural urge to triumph over the limitations of the present.

The old notion of work—the drudgery required by society in order for it to function—is possibly becoming too narrow to be useful today. Work that is productive activity exchanged in the economy may be reduced to a mechanical concept in a future society in which all can be fed, clothed, and sheltered with barely any human effort. And work that is required "slavery" may vanish in a society in which affluence and leisure are widespread.

But would work disappear in such a world; would people cease to struggle against their limitations? Released from the burdens of producing goods and services to stay alive, would the human inclination to work atrophy and be replaced by a play ethic seeking no further development? Moreover, would a society that recognized that it no longer needed the work of most individuals in order to continue to exist release its people to allow them to choose what they wish to do? Would the requirement to work give way to freedom in leisure?

These questions are not nearly so vague and speculative as they might seem. To some extent the answers are already visible in the diversity of the present. Already one third of the working population produces all the food, power, clothing, shelter, and other goods by which society lives. Already great segments of the population enjoy amounts of leisure time that were formerly the sole prerogative of the few idle rich. And already there is argument over whether society is accepting the dead-end roles of the easy life in either work or leisure. Analysis of changes that are already taking place in work and workers can shed new light on these issues.

WORK LIFE: START LATER, RETIRE EARLIER

Men: Shorter Work Life Despite Longer Life

Men and women differ not only in the number of years they can expect to live, or life expectancy, but also, and much more significantly, in the length and pattern of their work lives.

Later entrance into the labor force and earlier retirement have arrested and reversed the long-term rise in the length of work life. (Table 2-1). The work-life expectancy of a man born at the turn of this century length-

Table 2-1   AVERAGE WORK-LIFE EXPECTANCY
FOR MEN IN THE LABOR FORCE, 1900–1970

	AVERAGE NUMBER OF YEARS AT BIRTH		
YEAR	LIFE EXPECTANCY	WORK-LIFE EXPECTANCY	OUT OF THE LABOR FORCE
1900	48.2	32.1	16.1
1940	61.2	38.1	23.1
1950	65.5	41.5	24.0
1960	68.8	41.1	25.7
1970	67.1	40.1	27.0

SOURCE: Howard N. Fullerton, Jr., and James J. Byrne, "Length of Working Life for Men and Women," *Monthly Labor Review* (February 1976): 32.

ened by about six years during the following five decades largely because average life expectancy rose. The best measure of long-term, work-life expectancy is gained by computing the average number of years spent in the labor force by males reaching adulthood. The average work-life expectancy for males rose from 32 years in 1900 to 40 years by 1980.

Many factors have contributed to later entry into the labor force. One is the vast decline in the farming population: farmers' children were put to work at an early age. Another is the impact of child labor laws and compulsory school attendance. In 1900, when about two-fifths of the work force were employed on farms, the average age of entry into the labor force was about 15. By 1980 the average age of young men entering the labor force had risen to about 18.

Income support from Social Security and private pension plans and compulsory retirement programs have dramatically increased the tendency to retire at age 65 or even earlier. The separation rate for working males rises sharply after age 64. Retirement continues to be a more important reason than death for separation from the labor force for several years after age 65, although the tendency to retire declines very sharply after age 65. Often, those who continue to work do so part time; in 1977 half of the 65-to-69-year-old male jobholders worked less than 50 weeks. This part-time and part-year employment may reflect the greater incidence of health problems, reduced opportunities because of discrimination, and the ceiling that Social Security puts on the retirees' earnings if they are to qualify for full-benefit payments.

The number of years males spend outside the labor force has increased nearly 70 percent during this century. A man born in 1900 spent, on the average, 16 years outside the labor force, compared with the projected 27 years for a man born in 1970. Despite later entry into the work force, the additional 11 years spent outside the labor force were added mostly at the end of life. Few could afford to retire at the turn of the century. In 1900 a youth of age 13 had a life expectancy of 35 more years, of which he worked 32 years and spent 3 in retirement. In 1970 the 30-year-old could look forward to 37 more years, of which the last 9 would be spent in retirement.

Women: More Work and Longer Life Expectancy

Women have accounted for three of every five additions to the labor force in the past 30 years. Unlike men, women have quite varied work-life expectancies, depending on whether they stay single, marry, give birth to children, or become the heads of households because of separation, divorce, or the death of their husbands (Table 2-2). Most women (95 out of 100) marry and half are married before they are 22. Whether or not they marry, about nine of ten women work outside the home at some time. Marriage and the presence of children tend to curtail employment, while widowhood, divorce, the decrease of family responsibilities, and changing attitudes tend to bring women back into the labor force. Women begin their careers at about the same age as men, usually after finishing high school. Frequently, they leave the work force a few years after they marry to have children; a growing proportion resume work before the children reach school age.

The small minority of women who never marry have the most continuous and longest attachment to the labor force; their work-life pattern closely resembles that of men. The 20-year-old woman who remains single will probably continue to work for about 45 years—slightly more than the average of 43 years for men. In general, however, women—especially those who can depend on their husbands' incomes—tend to work fewer years and to retire earlier than men. The Social Security option of retirement at age 62 may also play a part in encouraging women to leave the work force.

The one married woman in ten who does not have children has a work-life expectancy of 34 years—7 years less than single women—if she enters the labor force by age 20. The working life of married women with children is less predictable because of the intermittent nature of their careers. The average woman has borne her last child by age 35; after that her children enter school and her family responsibilities are considerably diminished. If she returns under these conditions, her work-life expectancy is nearly the same as for a newly married 25-year-old woman—27 more years. This means that a far greater portion of a woman's work life occurs

Table 2-2   AVERAGE WORK-LIFE EXPECTANCY FOR
WOMEN IN THE LABOR FORCE, BY MARITAL STATUS AND AGE, 1970

| | AGE | | | |
MARITAL STATUS	20	35	50	65
Single	41.2	28.5	15.0	4.4
Ever-married				
No children ever born	34.1	20.8	12.0	6.6
In labor force after birth of last child	[a]	26.8	11.9	4.5
Divorced, widowed, or separated	42.3	27.8	13.6	5.3

[a] Not applicable.
SOURCE: Howard N. Fullerton, Jr., and James J. Byrne, "Length of Life for Men and Women, 1970," *Monthly Labor Review* (February 1976): 33.

after she has reared her children to school age and has reentered the labor force.

Because the care of young children is a major factor preventing women from working, the decline in birth rates since 1958 has made it possible for larger numbers of younger women to enter or remain in the labor force. The more children a married woman has, the shorter her work-life expectancy. It is estimated that the first child reduces work-life expectancy by about ten years; each additional child reduces it by about two to three years. A relatively large percentage of widowed, separated, and divorced women return to the labor force, their work patterns often resembling those of men and single women.

WORK TIME: FEWER HOURS, MORE LEISURE TIME

Today's worker has about 1000 more hours of free time each year, or 2.8 hours each day, than did the worker at the turn of the century. This is in addition to the extra eight years of nonwork time the male has gained because he starts work later, retires earlier, and lives longer.[2]

Shorter working hours do not necessarily improve the quality of a person's life or necessarily enlarge the amount of leisure time. Part of the increase in nonworking time is used up in longer hours of commuting. Household appliances, convenience foods, ready-made clothes, and smaller families made possible by birth-control technology have given more women free time to take on paid jobs—and thus end up with the double load of work plus running the home and family.

The intrinsic value of leisure to a worker should, however, not be overlooked. Workers have not lost their zeal to reduce working hours. They wish to minimize the hours spent under supervision "to be masters of their own souls for as much of the day as possible."[3] A recent survey of wage and salary workers found that about half were willing to trade a pay increase for better retirement benefits or more paid days of leave.[4] Younger workers, especially, expressed preference for free time (away from the rigid discipline of the production line, which leaves no opportunity for personal business) rather than overtime work. Nevertheless, during the 1960s, there was a stronger emphasis on raising income; only 8 percent of the rise in productivity was allocated to reducing work time, with the balance being used to boost income.[5]

Whether future productivity increases will be adequate to provide a continuation of large increases in both leisure time and standard of living remains questionable. The goods-producing sector of our economy is not now growing as rapidly as the service-producing sector, in which productivity gains are smaller. Thus past increases in leisure time and standard of living cannot be sustained without technological breakthroughs in the service sector. The 20- to 30-hour workweek and a carefree abundance of goods are much further away than the prophets of cybernetics like to anticipate.[6]

The distribution of additional leisure time has taken several forms, and the emphasis has changed over the years from reduction in weekly hours of work to allocation of leisure time in blocks of days or weeks. Between 1900 and 1979 nonworking hours per year increased by 864, distributed as follows:

Reduction in workweek—744 hours (14.3 hours per week: from 53.2 to 38.9)

Increase in paid holidays—56 hours (7 days: from 2 to about 9.2 per year)

Increase in paid vacations—64 hours (8 days: from less than ½ to 2 weeks per year)

Much of the drop in workweek hours came in the first two decades of this century as social reformers citing health and fatigue factors crusaded for shorter daily hours of work. Another sharp decline toward a statutory 40-hour workweek took place in the Great Depression of the 1930s under the National Industrial Recovery and Fair Labor Standards Acts. Overtime pay was required for longer workweeks to encourage the sharing of work opportunities and to reduce unemployment. During World War II, of course, longer hours were worked, but in the postwar period the average declined slowly from the 40-hour norm to 38.9 by 1979—more because of increased part-time employment than a cutback in hours. The hours worked by full-time wage and salary workers barely changed in the post–World War II period. For example, in manufacturing where there are few part-time workers, the norm of 40 has been maintained through the period as the weekly hours of work ranged narrowly between 39.1 and 40.9. The Bureau of Labor Statistics (BLS) projects that the rate of decline in average hours paid for in all private industry will continue during the 1980s.[7] The BLS projections assume nearly full employment; higher unemployment would intensify pressures for reductions in hours and other work-sharing devices.

Although interest in the shorter workweek has continued, preferences for leisure shifted after World War II to increasing blocks of time off—vacations and holidays. Not only are more workers receiving vacations, but also the vacations are longer—4 weeks for workers with 20 years' service is not unusual. The United Steelworkers' sabbatical plan, which was negotiated in 1963 and was originally conceived of as a means of spreading work, allowed an extended vacation of 13 weeks, but the idea was not picked up by other industries. Paid holidays for wage earners were also a development of World War II and the postwar period: the average is about six paid holidays a year for all workers (including farmers), with workers in metropolitan areas getting more (seven for plant workers, about eight for office workers).[8] In the quest for more blocks of free time even legal holidays were rescheduled. More three-day weekends became a reality when Congress decreed that Washington's Birthday, Memorial Day, and Columbus Day were to be celebrated on Mondays.

Possibly a large share of future growth in productivity will be allocated to blocks of leisure time at the beginning and end of work life (especially the latter), in contrast to the earlier pattern of its absorption into shorter workweeks.[9] However, older workers might want to distribute their work and leisure differently, rearranging their total pool of work years so that they would not be forced to retire at a time when they might prefer to continue useful work. Whatever the individual preference, however, institutional arrangements and business conditions dictate the terms of nonwork time at both the beginning and end of work life. Part-time and part-year work opportunities for older and younger workers depend on the need for their services. Higher retirement benefits, though, would raise workers' options in choosing between work and leisure.

If given the choice, do workers prefer extra leisure or added income? It is difficult to generalize about this. Evidence seems to indicate that shorter hours are preferred by very young and very old workers, and by women, particularly if they are married and have household responsibilities. The bulk of part-time workers belong to these groups. More than four-fifths of the 15.2 million part-time workers in 1979 did not want full-time employment or were not available for it. In fact, some might have not worked at all if required to work regular hours.[10]

However, men with growing family responsibilities tend to maximize income instead of leisure, and many moonlight to supplement their income.[11] Moonlighting is more prevalent among married than single men, and it increases with the number of children. The primary motivation of all moonlighters appear to be financial pressure, with four of ten working to meet regular expenses and one of ten working to pay off debts. Further, there was no significant inverse relationship between moonlighting and length of workweek; thus among full-time workers, factors other than length of workweek determined whether they were moonlighting. Although moonlighting has risen rapidly among women during the 1970s, married women have had consistently lower rates.[12]

Workers Bypassed by Shorter Workweek

Despite the trend to shorter average working hours, a significant number of people—about one-sixth of all workers in 1978—are still working 49 or more hours a week. The bulk of these are persons with single jobs, not moonlighters with multiple jobs. Many of the long-hour workers genuinely enjoy their work or hold responsible positions and are either required or expected to work long hours; others who work long hours are paid low wages and frequently are not covered by minimum wage legislation requiring overtime pay after 40 hours.[13] In 1979 three-fifths of those who worked 49 or more hours a week were professionals, managers, or craftsmen, though these groups made up two-fifths of the labor force. By contrast, operatives, laborers, service workers, and clerical workers, who made up more than half of the nonfarm work force, were less than a third of those who toiled such long hours.

Free Time That Is Productive Work: Unpaid Volunteers

Free time is not synonymous with leisure. While much of the extra free time is consumed by coping with the more complicated mechanics of contemporary life, some is utilized in productive work that does not show up in national accounts. This is the contribution of volunteers doing good works for diverse social causes. Almost 37 million Americans—2 out of every 9 adults—contribute free labor to some health, educational, religious, or welfare service. Their contribution is equivalent to the work performed by a full-time regular work force of over 3.5 million. Voluntarism is apparently a function of being part of the Establishment. For example, people between the ages of 25 and 44—those with the most demands in terms of career planning and parenthood—account for over two-fifths of the volunteers. Three-fifths of the volunteers are women, and three-fifths also have paid jobs. The more schooling (and income) a person has, the more likely the individual was to do volunteer work.[14]

WORKERS' MOBILITY: THE AMERICAN DREAM OF MOVING UP THE JOB LADDER

Mobility has always been a characteristic of American working life, and few people hold just one job over a working lifetime. They change employers, though not necessarily the types of work they perform; or they may change jobs while staying with the same employer (sometimes by transferring to a different branch or plant). They move to new locations, though most employment shifts are within the same community or labor market area. They shift in and out of the labor force in response to changing economic or personal conditions.[15]

Perhaps most important is workers' mobility up the occupational ladder. Quite properly, Americans persist in the belief that, regardless of one's origins, economic and social opportunity should be open to all. Social mobility is of importance not only to individuals but also to the efficiency and well-being of society as a whole. As Lloyd G. Reynolds has pointed out:

> Geographic movement is apt to be a painful necessity, costly to individuals and the community. Movement from employer to employer may be simply an aimless wandering from one mediocre job to another. Real progress comes only through movement to a new job involving more in the way of skill, responsibility, independence, and income.[16]

Upward Occupational Mobility

Occupational and social mobility may be analyzed either in terms of changes that occur within a worker's own lifetime (intragenerational) or in terms of changes from parent to offspring (intergenerational).[17] More than most other industrialized nations, the United States is predominantly open and upwardly mobile. Extensive studies have documented that intergenerational and intragenerational upward occupational mobility have been and remain a fact of American economic life. In longitudinal studies of men between 45 and 59 years of age, Herbert Parnes reported that almost three-fifths had moved into occupations with higher socioeconomic status than those in which they began their work careers.[18]

Most of the upward mobility involves relatively short social distances rather than dramatic, long-distance, Horatio Alger–type leaps. Peter M. Blau and Otis Dudley Duncan found the usual move to be only 2 or 3 steps upward in their hierarchy of 17 occupational levels (ranging from farm laborers up to self-employed professionals).[19] Nonetheless, more of America's current business leaders have emerged from lower-class and middle-class origins than at the turn of the century (Table 2-3). Higher education appears to provide the ladder for upward mobility. But, at the same time, a college education remains largely a function of family income. In 1978 it was more than twice as likely that a young person would attend college if his family's annual income exceeded $15,000 than if the income were between $5000 and $7500. The number of children who must share a family's income also is a significant factor, and the steady trend toward family limitation should promote the chances of obtaining a college education.

Immigration and westward migration, and the continued growth of economic opportunities, have prevented locked-in social stratification in the United States. More American professionals have risen from the lower classes than in other nations. Blau and Duncan point out that about 10 percent of the sons of American manual workers moved into professional and technical occupations, compared with 7 percent for Japan and the Netherlands, 3.5 for Sweden, and 2.2 for Great Britain.[20] Comparing the United States, Great Britain, the Netherlands, and Japan, Joseph W. McGuire and Joseph A. Pichler concluded that there is more upward mobility into the middle class by craftsmen in the United States than in other industrial nations. They also found a lower rate of intergenerational downward mobility—from professional to skilled occupations—in America than in Great Britain and the Netherlands.[21]

Table 2-3 DISTRIBUTION OF
BUSINESS EXECUTIVES BY FAMILY STATUS, 1900–1964

ECONOMIC STATUS OF FATHER	1900	1925	1950	1964	1900–1964 DIFFERENCE
Wealthy	45.6%	36.6%	36.1%	10.5%	−35.1%
Medium	42.1	47.8	51.8	66.2	24.1
Poor	12.3	15.8	12.1	23.2	10.9

SOURCE: Joseph W. McGuire and Joseph A. Pichler, *Inequality: The Poor and Rich in America* (Belmont, Calif.: Wadsworth, 1969), p. 57.

The frustrations of blue-collar workers have received much public attention. One of their complaints is that men who start their careers as blue-collar workers have poorer chances of reaching a higher occupational status than those who start out in white-collar occupations (they already have achieved some status) or farm occupations (they are likely to benefit from mobility because of a low starting point).

But blue-collar workers may not be as hopelessly trapped in lower-rung occupations as has been assumed. As a group these workers are relatively better off than their fathers—whether they be native-born whites from low-income farm families, of foreign extraction, or blacks. Some advance to managerial or entrepreneurial ranks—as the carpenter who becomes a contractor or the truck driver who acquires a small fleet. Intergenerational upward mobility is enhanced by their children's greater access to longer education at publicly supported colleges and universities.

Upward mobility among blue-collar workers is not universal, however, and there are large groups of immobile and vulnerable workers in their ranks. Included in these sizable groups are men who hold blue-collar jobs similar to those held by their fathers or men who have even moved down the occupational scale; female heads of families who tend to be in low-paying, low-skill jobs; male heads unable to earn enough to allow their families to live much above the poverty level; and families whose children are unlikely to have access to college or other paths upward.

Just as blue-collar workers have difficulty moving up, so white-collar workers tend not to cross class boundaries into blue-collar jobs. White-collar workers who are unsuccessful in their occupations often move into retail trade, which, according to Blau and Duncan, still allows them to maintain white-collar status and to remain within the higher social scale, even though with relatively unskilled jobs.[22] Evidently, they prefer the status of a white-collar job, even though a job in coveralls or a hard hat may pay better, have shorter hours, and require more skills.

Government employment and training programs have allocated few resources to upgrading workers, though much rhetoric has been devoted to developing new careers to help the disadvantaged. Given the limitations of the job market, it may be unrealistic to hope that large numbers of workers can be simply upgraded from dead-end to upwardly mobile jobs.

Upward Mobility for Blacks

The upward mobility of blacks was a central issue of the 1960s and early 1970s. Past discrimination and hurdles built into our institutional structure have prevented blacks from utilizing opportunities that lead other minority or ethnic groups such as immigrants and their children to upward mobility.

During the past decade, however, extensive civil rights legislation and the widespread rejection by American society of discrimination in employment, at least in principle, boosted the status of American blacks, though the gaps between whites and blacks were not eliminated. The mean annual earnings of black males increased from 53 to 63 percent of those for whites between 1959 and 1978, and average black female earnings leaped from 62 to 93 pecent of equality with those of white females. In part, this was attributable to the fact that there was a steady movement of blacks out of the lower occupational groups (especially marginal farmers and farm laborers) into the categories of craftsmen and operatives, so that by 1979 four out of every five black blue-collar workers were in these latter categories. More striking was the fact that during the 1960s more than 300,000 blacks also gained entry into the preferred craftsmen category, although they remained underrepresented. More than seven-tenths of the increase in black employment between 1960 and 1970 was in professional, white-collar, and skilled occupations, while the lowest paid occupations—private household work and farm work—registered declines. Herbert Parnes and others have questioned the significance of these increases in black family income and occupational mobility. Parnes expected blacks to show upward occupational mobility because of their low starting position. His longitudinal studies, however, convinced him that the contrary occurred and that the relative disadvantages of black men when they begin "their working lives have become more pronounced during their work careers."[23]

Geographical Mobility

About 1 out of 7 Americans moves across county lines every three years, with about half of these migrating into another state. Counting also those who move within a county, the ratio goes up to about one in three.[24]

The character of geographic migration affecting labor mobility has changed. The flood of European immigrants has been curtailed, and western migration and the movement from the farm to the city have leveled off. A newer and more significant development is the movement from the inner cities to the suburbs. There are now more people in the suburbs than in the inner cities. This flight, initially of white and more recently black middle-class residents to the suburban rings, has been coupled with a relocation of plants and, particularly, retail and service establishments. Unemployment and transportation problems thus are compounded for those left in the inner city, as well as for suburbanites who still work in the cities. Energy shortages may reverse this fleeing from the cities.

Removing Impediments to Mobility

Society's challenge is to create conditions that will both optimize upward mobility and facilitate the process of matching workers and jobs. This suggests policies that open opportunities for upward movement, have sufficient clout to discourage wasteful or misdirected mobility, and maintain freedom of individual choice.

Socially beneficial occupational mobility can be achieved by providing better opportunities for education, training, retraining, and upgrading, while placing less emphasis on formal credentials such as a high school diploma.[25] Continued attacks on discrimination, and efforts to sustain and solidify the advances made in the past generation must be essential ingredients of any occupational mobility policy. In promoting occupational mobility, special provisions must be made for those left behind either because they are in depressed areas, are otherwise not mobile, or have been denied opportunities for upward mobility.

Discouraging wasteful mobility certainly involves a reexamination of social values and the status of various occupations. The quality of American life is not enhanced by worship of the diploma certifying that the recipient has completed a course in higher education, while public and private services are deteriorating because society considers the providers of these services to be inferior.

DISCUSSION QUESTIONS

1. "Workers are much better off today: They work less, make more money, and enjoy more leisure." Discuss.
2. There has been much talk in the public news media about discontent in the workforce. Show how changes in technology may affect work satisfaction.
3. Before the energy crises turned off other crisis, there was much talk about "worker discontent." How real do you think is the phenomenon of the alleged worker dissatisfaction? Evaluate the remedies proposed to alleviate worker dissatisfaction.
4. "Perpetual holiday is a good working definition of hell," George Bernard Shaw. Discuss.
5. What factors have been operating over time which have caused men to work shorter hours and women longer hours? Are these trends likely to continue?
6. Labor market mobility has always been a characteristic of American working life. Discuss.
7. Would reducing the standard workweek in manufacturing from 40 to 30 hours alleviate unemployment problems? Why or why not?
8. A recent bill introduced in Congress to combat unemployment would require double-time pay after eight hours of work. Do you think that the bill would achieve the goal of its sponsors?
9. Do you feel there has been a deterioration in the work ethic in the United States?
10. There are imperfections in the operation of U.S. labor markets that impede the mobility of some workers. What are they and how can they be overcome?

Notes

1. Georges Friedmann, *The Anatomy of Work: Labor, Leisure, and the Implications of Automation* (New York: Free Press, 1961).
2. Sar A. Levitan and William B. Johnston, *Work Is Here to Stay, Alas* (Salt Lake City, Utah: Olympus, 1973), p. 49.
3. U.S. Congress, House Committee on Education and Labor, *Hearings on*

Hours of Work (Washington, D.C.: GPO, 1963), p. 220, testimony by Eli Ginzberg.

4. Graham L. Staines and Robert P. Quinn, "American Workers Evaluate Their Jobs," *Monthly Labor Review* (January 1979): 7.
5. Geoffrey H. Moore and Janice Heipert Hedges, "Trends in Labor and Leisure," *Monthly Labor Review* (February 1971): 3–11.
6. Victor R. Fuchs, ed., *Production and Productivity in Service Industries* (New York: National Bureau of Economic Research and Columbia University Press, 1969), p. 10.
7. Norman C. Saunders, "The U.S. Economy to 1990: Two Projections of Growth," *Monthly Labor Review* (December 1978): 44.
8. Sar A. Levitan and Richard S. Belous, *Shorter Hours, Shorter Weeks: Spreading the Work to Reduce Unemployment* (Baltimore: The Johns Hopkins University Press, 1977), p. 13.
9. Juanita M. Kreps, "Time for Leisure, Time for Work," *Monthly Labor Review* (April 1969): 60–61.
10. Curtis L. Gilroy and Thomas F. Bradshaw, "Employment and Unemployment—A Report on 1973," *Monthly Labor Review* (February 1973): 6, and *Employment and Earnings* (January 1980): 165.
11. Vera C. Perrella, "Moonlighters: Their Motivation and Characteristics," *Monthly Labor Review* (August 1970): 57–64.
12. Carl Rosenfeld, "Multiple Jobholding Holds Steady in 1978," *Special Labor Force Report*, no. 221, U.S. Bureau of Labor Statistics (Washington: GPO, February 1979), and Edward Sekscenski, "Multiple Jobholders" (Spring 1980).
13. Peter Henle, "Leisure and the Long Work Week," *Monthly Labor Review* (July 1966): 721.
14. *American Volunteer 1974*, ACTION (Washington, D.C.: February 1975).
15. Major research on labor mobility in the 1960s is summarized by Herbert S. Parnes, "Labor Force Participation and Labor Mobility," in *A Review of Industrial Relations Research*, Industrial Relations Research Association Series, vol. 1 (Madison, Wis.: The Association, 1970), pp. 33–78.
16. Lloyd G. Reynolds, *Labor Economics and Labor Relations*, 4th ed. (Englewood Cliffs, N.J.: Prentice-Hall, 1964), p. 390.
17. Joseph W. McGuire and Joseph A. Pichler, *Inequality: The Poor and Rich in America* (Belmont, Calif.: Wadsworth, 1969), pp. 48 ff.
18. Herbert Parnes et al., *The Pre-Retirement Years*, vol. 1, U.S. Department of Labor, Manpower Administration, Manpower Research Monograph No. 15 (Washington, D.C.: GPO, 1970), p. 127.
19. Peter M. Blau and Otis Dudley Duncan, *The American Occupational Structure* (New York: Wiley, 1964), p. 420.
20. Ibid., p. 435.
21. McGuire and Pichler, op. cit., p. 52.
22. Blau and Duncan, op. cit., p. 421.
23. Parnes et al., op. cit., p. 128.
24. U.S. Bureau of the Census, *Current Population Reports*, "Geographical Mobility: March 1975 to March 1978," series P–20, no. 331 (Washington, D.C.: GPO, 1978): 1.
25. S. M. Miller, *Breaking the Credentials Barrier* (New York: The Ford Foundation, 1968).

Chapter 3
Labor Force Participation and Unemployment

Changing patterns of work life have been accompanied by dramatic shifts in labor force participation rates (the proportion of the working-age population employed or looking for work as opposed to working in the home, studying at school, or enjoying leisure) and in the composition of the work force. The key long-run shifts are greater participation of women and youth with declining roles for older workers. These shifts have resulted in an increased reliance on workers whose work-life patterns are different from those of workers who are employed full-time throughout the year.[1]

Underlying the changed composition in the work force is the rising level of expectations, which outstrips the sustained but relatively modest rises in productivity. This means that millions of families now need more than the male breadwinner can earn and that the added worker is far more likely to be the wife than a son or daughter. Moreover, the growth of consumer purchases on credit and inflation have heightened pressure on family income to meet the payments. In the three decades after World War II consumer indebtedness outpaced by more than six times the growth of all financial assets. Thus America is increasingly a nation of multiworker families "hooked" into working to maintain the desired standard of living.

Work, however, is no longer the only way to support a family. Income-support programs—including unemployment insurance, public and private retirement or disability benefits, and public assistance—provide money, limited as it may be. Income-support programs, including welfare, and work are increasingly interdependent. This is reflected in the movement of the 1960s toward providing assistance for parents who are capable of working but who are unemployed, and during the 1970s in efforts to design a system which would assure that work pays more than welfare. Traditionally, welfare had been aimed exclusively at helping persons outside the labor force—mothers and dependent children, the indigent aged, and the disabled.

The labor market has its pathologies, however, and not all persons who want jobs are successful in getting them, and many others who are employed fail to earn an adequate income to raise their families above poverty. Forced idleness, intermittent employment, and low-income jobs fall disproportionately to members of minority groups, females, and older workers. The American economy has not been successful in eliminating the ups and downs of business cycles; after nearly a decade of continued growth in the 1960s, the economy experienced in the next decade the worst recession since World War II.

OVERALL SHIFTS IN LABOR FORCE

A key change has been the sharp increase in the number of working women—especially married women. During the 1960s and 1970s women entered the labor force three times faster than men; for the first time, married men—the group that had previously constituted the bulk of the labor force—dropped to 40 percent of the workforce. A large share of newly married women are working; an increasing number of married women return to work after their children have entered school or grown up, and many do not wait that long. Since the beginning of the century, participation rates of married women have increased fivefold, and their share of the labor force has risen sixfold, to about one-fifth.

Until the 1970s, participation rates for youth showed a long-term decline, in part, perhaps, because their mothers add to the family exchequer, but more often because they encounter economic and legal barriers to work. Thus youngsters stay in school longer before starting their full-time work careers. In the first half of the century the participation rate for 14- to 19-year-old males has dropped by about a third, while their share of the labor force was cut in half—from about 10 to about 5 percent. After the post–World War II baby boom, however, the sheer numbers of young people increased. Until the 1970s, this was offset in part by reduced participation rates. Nevertheless, young workers aged 16 to 24 accounted for more than half of the labor force increase in the 1960s. In the 1970s, participation rates for youth began to rise again, and the proportion of this age group in the labor force rose from one in five to one in four.

The early work years are characterized by much part-time work (often combined with school) and fairly frequent job changes. The pattern changes as persons mature. Adult men reach a peak participation rate of about 96 percent in their mid-20s, and this percentage remains relatively stable for about 30 years. Job stability increases as the worker matures: A 55-year-old man can be expected to stay on a job over 7 years, or about 1½ times longer than a man of 20.[2]

At the other end of the age spectrum there has been a long-term decline in the participation rate of older males; for men over 65, the rate has dropped to less than half of what it was at the turn of the century. As in the case of youngsters, however, the sheer growth in the number of those 55 and older has offset their declining participation rate; there were more of these older workers in 1980 than a decade earlier.

These shifts have left overall labor force participation rates basically unchanged during the current century; the declines in some groups canceled out the increases in others. Since the end of World War II annual labor force participation rates have ranged between 59 and 64 percent of the total noninstitutional population in the United States. During the same period, male rates declined steadily from 87 to below 78 percent, while comparable rates for women rose from 32 to 51 percent (Table 3-1).

Of the 163.6 million noninstitutional Americans aged 16 or older in 1979, an average of 105 million were in the labor force. Excluding the 2.1 million in the armed forces, the civilian labor force averaged 102.9 million, of whom 96.9 million were employed. This left 58.6 million outside the labor force—including full-time students, housewives (mostly with responsibilities for raising children), retired workers, and some discouraged workers who stopped looking for work because jobs were not available. In addition to the unemployed, many of these who were "not in the labor force," as well as those who worked only part time, comprised part of the labor reserves, some of whom (especially nonworking wives and mothers, if day-care facilities were provided) might be induced to work in tight labor markets.

In 1954, when the civilian labor force stood at 63.6 million, the labor force participation rates of white and nonwhite males were just over 85 percent (Table 3-2). Both rates declined over the following quarter century, but that for nonwhites dropped off more sharply, falling to 73 percent by 1979. At the same time, the relatively high participation of nonwhite females in the labor force increased only slightly while the entry rate of white females increased significantly.

Concern has centered on the falling labor force activity among men, especially among nonwhites. On the positive side, increasing school attendance among the young and earlier retirement among those over 60 years old have drawn nonwhite males from the labor force. Nonwhites and whites alike may be changing their attitudes toward work and turning to other income support as an alternative to low-wage jobs. Another explanation for

Table 3-1   PARTICIPATION RATES AND
PERCENTAGE DISTRIBUTION OF THE LABOR FORCE, 1947 AND 1979

	1947		1979	
AGE-SEX	PARTICIPATION RATE	PERCENT OF LABOR FORCE	PARTICIPATION RATE	PERCENT OF LABOR FORCE
TOTAL	58.9%	100.0%	63.7%	100.0%
MALE	86.8	72.6	78.4	58.5
16–17	52.2	1.9	51.8	2.1
18–19	80.5	3.1	73.9	3.0
20–24	84.9	8.4	87.6	8.6
25–34	95.8	17.4	95.6	15.6
35–44	98.0	15.8	95.9	11.1
45–54	95.5	12.9	91.5	9.6
55–64	89.6	9.3	73.0	6.8
65 & over	47.8	3.9	20.0	1.8
FEMALE	31.8	27.4	51.1	41.5
16–17	29.5	1.0	45.8	1.8
18–19	52.3	2.0	63.1	2.5
20–24	44.9	4.5	69.3	6.8
25–34	32.0	6.2	63.9	10.7
35–44	36.3	6.0	63.6	7.7
45–54	32.7	4.5	58.4	6.5
55–64	24.3	2.5	41.9	4.4
65 & over	8.1	0.7	8.3	1.1

SOURCE: *Employment and Training Report of the President* (Washington, D.C.: GPO, 1979)
236–237; and *Employment and Earnings* (January 1980): 160–161.
Note: Detail may not add to totals due to rounding.

the lower labor force participation rates among minority workers is the fact
that they constitute a proportionately larger share of discouraged workers—that is, those who have given up the search for a job because they believe they cannot find one.

As noted in Chapter 2, a host of economic, political, social, and demographic factors have contributed to the changing composition of the work
force, as well as to its growth and size. These factors have been transforming
the United States, first from a rural, farm-oriented society to an urban,
blue-collar, goods-producing society, and now to a suburban, white-collar,
service-oriented people. But labor-force data do not support popular impressions that work is going out of fashion. While population nearly tripled
between 1900 and 1978, the labor force grew at a slightly faster pace (from
28 million in a population of 76 million, to 102 of 218 million).

The high birth rates of the post–World War II baby boom, following as
they did the low birth rates of the depression and war years, resulted not
only in a greater absolute number of youngsters but also in their higher
proportion in the population in the 1960s. In 1940 children under ten accounted for one-sixth of the population; by 1960 one of every five persons
was in that age group. As these youngsters reached work age in the mid-

Table 3-2 CIVILIAN LABOR FORCE
PARTICIPATION BY SEX AND COLOR, 1954 AND 1979

| SEX AND COLOR | 1954 | | 1979 | |
	PARTICIPATION RATE	PERCENT OF LABOR FORCE	PARTICIPATION RATE	PERCENT OF LABOR FORCE
CIVILIAN LABOR FORCE	58.8%	100.0%	63.7%	100.0%
MALES				
White	85.6	62.5	78.6	51.6
Nonwhite	85.2	6.6	71.9	6.3
FEMALES				
White	33.3	26.8	50.6	36.5
Nonwhite	46.1	4.1	53.5	5.7

SOURCE: *Employment and Earnings* (January 1979): 160–161.

1960s, they swamped the labor market even though their participation rates had been declining.

Because of lower infant mortality and better health conditions, life expectancy has risen by about 26 years since the turn of the century. The number of people 65 and over increased from 9 million (6.8 percent of total population) in 1940 to over 23 million, or 10.8 percent, within four decades. Therefore, even though their participation rates had plummeted, the number of workers 65 and older actually increased, comprising a nearly constant proportion of the work force.

During the first 15 years of the century, immigration added 10 million workers to a domestic labor force of 27 million. The immigration quotas of the 1920s and the severe unemployment of the depression sealed off U.S. borders, but illegal migrant workers are becoming an increasingly important part of the labor force. Excepting the heavy flow of Puerto Ricans to New York City, Cubans to Florida, Mexicans to the Southwest, and Asians to the west coast and other regions today, sons and daughters of the early immigrants are indistinguishable in the labor force, sharing with other workers rising expectations and expanded educational opportunities.

Military requirements, including the draft law between 1940 and 1973, have strongly affected labor force participation. Military needs remove large numbers of younger males as a source of civilian workers and generate demand for additional workers to produce goods to support the armed forces. At the peak of World War II over 12 million persons were in the armed forces, and about 8 million of those who were unemployed in 1940 were absorbed into jobs. Thus about 20 million more people were at work or in the armed forces in 1944 than were holding jobs four years earlier.

The Korean and Vietnam wars affected the demand for and supply of labor, though to a lesser extent than World War II. The expanded military requirements in Vietnam kept about a million young men out of the civilian labor force during the second half of the 1960s (about 900,000 18- to 25-

year-olds plus an undetermined number of draft-deferred students who might not have enrolled in college in the absence of a draft). The winding down of the war brought a large number of young men back into the civilian labor force during the early 1970s.

The armed forces plays an important role in human resource development for the 400,000 youth it recruits annually. About four of every ten male college bound youth enter the military which in many ways performs the same function as college for those who pursue longer education. For many persons in this age and educational attainment group, the military is the first work experience. Training and educational benefits accrued while in the military are bound to have a spill-over effect into civilian employment. The change to an all-voluntary armed forces in 1973 somewhat altered the military's role in human resource development. The special responsibilities assumed by the government to prepare servicemen for reentry into civilian life and to provide basic social welfare protections during and after service became less pressing in an all-volunteer force. The result has been a reduction in post-service benefits for volunteers. The armed forces have also been criticized for the narrow focus of training they offer in order to reduce costs. When economizing is required, extraneous activities are understandably the first to go. The decisions have apparently too frequently ignored the value of the potential long-run economic and social values that the education and training offered by the military may have upon the future of the military personnel when they return to civilian life, as well as upon the attractiveness of the military to potential volunteers.[3]

EDUCATION AND LABOR FORCE ACTIVITY

Labor force activity is generally greater among those workers who have attained additional educational credentials (Table 3-3). To the extent that

Table 3-3   PARTICIPATION RATES IN
THE CIVILIAN LABOR FORCE BY LEVEL OF EDUCATION, MARCH 1978

YEARS OF SCHOOL	LABOR FORCE PARTICIPATION RATE
TOTAL	62.2
less than 5	30.7
5–7	38.2
8	39.5
9–11	53.3
12	68.5
13–15	69.6
16	77.1
17+	84.3

SOURCE: Scott Cambell Brown, "Educational Attainment of Workers—Some Trends from 1973 to 1980," Special Labor Force Report, no. 225, U.S. Bureau of Statistics (Washington, D.C.: GPO, February 1979).

more education brings with it greater earning power, the better educated the worker, the more income the person foregoes by remaining out of the labor force. The attraction of additional income is especially great among married women who have invested in career training.

In 1900 the average worker had only a grade school education, and today's worker averages 12.6 years of school. Most of the gains have occurred among those who formerly were the least educated, bringing the majority of today's labor force to a level achieved by only a few in the labor force of the early 1900s.[4] Although much of the increase in education is a response to the demands of a service-oriented economy, a large part of the gain has occurred among workers independent of the jobs they perform. Educational advances, while enhancing worker motivation to strive for a better job, have been lost in many cases because the occupational structure of the U.S. economy continues to include a large number of jobs requiring only basic skills.

RISING EXPECTATIONS AND MULTIWORKER FAMILIES

Rising expectations have significantly affected labor market behavior. It appears that when wages are high and jobs plentiful, leisure may be deemed too expensive, especially if a still higher standard of living is sought. Thus an increasing proportion of families have more than one earner to enable the unit to achieve the desired standard of living. Once the multiworker families become accustomed to a higher level of living, the added earners are, in effect, obliged to continue to work in order to maintain the newly attained level, with inflation adding extra impetus. In 1979 over three-fifths of U.S. families had two or more gainfully employed workers—compared with about half in 1970 and less than two-fifths a decade earlier.

How are multiworker family members thus "hooked"? A standard of living clearly beyond the reach of the average wage earner is urged upon them, not only by manufacturers, retailers of consumer goods and suppliers of services, but also by the government, which publicizes appealing standards of living. The BLS city worker's budget (Autumn 1977) for a moderate or "intermediate" standard of living (one with few luxuries) for a family of four required $17,106. The "higher" BLS budget for the same family, one perhaps more in line with the popular conception of American affluence, carried a price tag of $25,202. The BLS budgets apply to an urban family of four; husband aged 38, wife not working, son 13 years old and daughter 8.[5] Average income for this particular type of family is estimated as adequate for the intermediate budget but not for the higher budget. In the average husband-wife family, the husband had a median income of $13,410 in 1977. In almost one out of every two cases the family attempted to make up the difference between his income and their budget expectations through the wife's work, raising the median income to $18,564 in 1977 for husband-wife families in which both were in the labor force.[6]

ADDITIONAL WORKERS AND THE BUSINESS CYCLE

The ready availability of jobs, a high level of economic activity, and inflation in the 1970s were major factors in increasing labor force participation and opening opportunities for multiworker families. The size of the labor force expands when jobs are plentiful, and persons who might otherwise not seek jobs enter the work force, a process facilitated by employers' making various accommodations to the needs of secondary workers. Inflation further spurs entry into the work force to maintain an accustomed standard of living.

Just as workers are lured into the work force by high demand, they can become discouraged and drop out of the labor force when they cannot find jobs. The hypothesis that the labor force expands in depressions, as wives and children of unemployed or underemployed workers try to find jobs to replace lost income, is not supported by evidence.[7] While some additional workers enter the labor force during recessions to bolster sagging family income, more workers withdraw in discouragement.[8] The additional worker is more likely to be a low-income person than the discouraged worker.[9]

The additional-worker hypothesis took on a slightly different meaning in the 1970s as the nation experienced a combination of historically high rates of both inflation and unemployment. The prospect of lower living standards for many families was brought on not necessarily by the unemployment of the principal breadwinner, but more likely by the erosion of the real value of the household's income due to rapidly rising prices. Many believe that these developments attributed to the rise in labor force participation among secondary family workers during this period. By 1979, three-fifths of both the unemployed and the employed were in families with at least one other member working. In more than half of all families where the husband was out of a job, someone else was employed.

LABOR MARKET PATHOLOGIES:
UNEMPLOYMENT, UNDEREMPLOYMENT, AND SHORTAGES

In the United States labor demand has tended to fall short of the available labor supply, except in times of war. At the same time, there have been frequent sustained shortages of highly specialized labor. Some unemployment and some shortages are to be expected in any dynamic economy, regardless of the level of labor demand. Job changes, plant shutdowns, the search for a first job, and seasonal swings all cause some temporary joblessness and underemployment; innovations (e.g., widespread use of computers) or extremely large changes in demand (e.g., rapid expansion and contraction of the space program) may result in temporary shortages or surpluses of skilled personnel. As long as labor market imbalances remain brief and moderate, they are only of passing social concern—a small price to be paid for free market operations. Above and beyond some frictional minimums, however, unemployment, underemployment, and labor shortages arising from longer-term imbalances have far-reaching implications for the well-being of individuals and for society as a whole.

The Historical Perspective

The levels of unemployment have varied widely over the past 40 years, encompassing long periods of massive waste of labor and considerably shorter periods of general shortages of labor (Table 3-4). Experience has shown that most of those gyrations could have been avoided or at least minimized by responsible and compassionate public policy, though complete cures for the ailments that plague the labor market remain elusive. The disaster of the 1930s, which brought unemployment rates of 25 percent or more, was eventually diagnosed as a shortage of effective demand. The crisis apparently developed mainly because economists and politicians lacked a clear remedy for the malady and relied too long on the response of automatic market mechanisms. The massive infusion of labor demand caused by World War II solved the unemployment problem, but at a cost of debilitating inflation. The jobless rate declined to just over 1 percent, a condition that could only be characterized as minimal frictional unemployment caused by excessive labor demand and strong social pressures against slackers during a national emergency.

The Great Depression left deep scars, and the prevailing view during the mid-1940s was that the high unemployment would return once the war

Table 3-4 AVERAGE UNEMPLOYMENT SELECTED YEARS, 1929–1978

YEAR	NUMBER (IN THOUSANDS)	PERCENT OF LABOR FORCE
1929	1,550	3.2
1933	12,830	24.9
1944	670	1.2
1948	2,276	3.8
1952	1,883	3.0
1954	3,532	5.5
1956	2,750	4.1
1960	3,852	5.5
1964	3,786	5.2
1968	2,817	3.6
1972	4,840	5.6
1973	4,304	4.9
1974	5,076	5.6
1975	7,830	8.5
1976	7,288	7.7
1977	6,855	7.0
1978	6,047	6.0
1979	5,963	5.8

SOURCE: *Employment and Earnings* (January 1980): 156. Data include 14- and 15-year-olds prior to 1947.

was over. Congress responded by enacting the Employment Act of 1946, affirming the national goal of an economic climate that would provide job opportunities to all persons "able, willing, and seeking work." The expected high level of unemployment did not develop in the immediate postwar adjustment period, largely because labor demand was sustained at high levels by a big backlog of consumer spending.

In the 1950s business contractions became more frequent, and recovery after each recession grew less and less adequate, leaving joblessness progressively higher. Although mass unemployment was avoided in the late 1940s and 1950s, the persistent rise of unemployment raised concerns of a progressive malaise that looked increasingly like secular stagnation. The policies of the federal government in the 1950s, primarily designed to aid and support normal market mechanisms, were not adequate in our increasingly complex, interdependent economy. In the 1960s they were replaced by diverse efforts to combat unemployment—aid to depressed areas, stimulation of business investment and consumer demand, and special employment and training programs aimed at improving the opportunities of the poor and unskilled to compete in the job market.

Policy orientation slowly shifted to the profound and continuing problems of persons who experienced difficulties in finding sustained employment in good times as well as bad or those who were condemned to a life of poverty even if they worked. Confined to the low end of the employment ladder by a lack of skills or special personal problems and living largely in big-city ghettos and rural slums, a small portion of the work force was living through a continuing cycle of intermittent unemployment and underemployment at low-paying jobs. Ultimately, these measures, coupled with the escalation of the Vietnam War, generated high employment. As the economy moved into the 1970s on a downbeat, concern shifted to the unemployment-inflation dilemma as unemployment remained persistently high during times of rapidly rising prices. Also, more careful attention was paid to the character of underemployment, subemployment, and inadequate earnings in attempts to define more clearly those workers who were failing in or are being failed by the labor market.

Unemployment and Underemployment

Underutilized manpower resources may be divided into four distinct groups: the unemployed; persons outside the labor force who want or need work; persons who are working fewer hours than they would prefer because of economic reasons beyond their personal control; and persons employed at jobs that are below their actual or potential skill level. No reasonable estimate of the size of the last group exists, although it must be large indeed. Data for the first three groups for the high-employment year of 1969 and during the downturn in the 1970s are summarized in the following tabulation:

UNEMPLOYED, UNDEREMPLOYED, AND DISCOURAGED WORKERS	NUMBER			
	1969	1971	1975	1979
Unemployed	2,831,000	4,993,000	7,830,000	5,963,000
On reduced workweeks, economic reasons	2,056,000	2,675,000	3,748,000	3,478,000
Discouraged because no job available	574,000	774,000	1,082,000	750,000

The estimates for 1969 relate to a period of strong demand, when underutilization was at one of the low points after World War II. In the 1970s, when labor demand was weaker, underemployment, unemployment, and discouragement were commensurately higher.

The Causes of Unemployment

Total unemployment is primarily a function of the general economic environment and is in large measure responsive to policy actions. Identification of specific forms of unemployment and their causes may be helpful in designing remedial policies for particular maladies. Economists have classified unemployment into four broad categories: cyclical, frictional, seasonal, and structural. Elements of each cause of joblessness usually can be found in each unemployment situation because they tend to reinforce and compound one another.

Cyclical Unemployment

Cyclical swings in business activity are the most commonly recognized (and probably most important) cause of unemployment and underemployment. The outstanding characteristic of cyclical unemployment in a modern economy is that the individual worker has little control over employment opportunities. Since the end of World War II, business recessions have been mild and of short duration. In each, unemployment stayed quite low until the peak of business activity passed, then rose sharply as the recession grew progressively worse. For some time after the trough had passed, unemployment tended to continue high. Policy response to cyclical unemployment has traditionally taken two forms—income-protection plans and attempts at stabilization of demand and production. In a marked downturn virtually no jobs are available in the sore spots most affected by the turn of activity. In the 1970s the federal government has added job creation programs for the unemployed as part of the counter-cyclical tools.

The economy has a basic productive potential that is a function of its resources—labor, capital, and natural resources—and the state of technology. A departure from the level of output appropriate to the existing resource base may result in continuing unemployment or overemployment, with neither being necessarily responsive to automatic correction by market mechanisms. In 1962 Arthur Okun estimated that for each 1 percent shortfall in the level of real output (GNP) from potential output, the overall unemployment rate would be higher by about 0.3 percentage points.[10] Okun estimated that potential GNP grew at an average rate of 4 percent a year, and the 4 percent figure became an accepted policy goal consistent with achieving full employment without generating inflation. More recently, however, updated estimates show that the economy's economic potential grew at about a 3.5 percent annual rate from 1968 to 1973 and 3 percent a year from 1973 to 1978.[11] The downturn revisions reflect, in large part, an assumption that the lagging productivity growth of the 1970s reflects not so much cyclical developments, but a lower secular trend. Many analysts believe this lower trend is the result of our nation's failure to add to its capital stock as fast as new workers have entered the labor force.

The overall unemployment rate consistent with Okun's calculations of full employment for the early 1960s was 4 percent. The comparable rate in 1978 was estimated by the Council of Economic Advisers to be over 5 percent; other estimates are closer to 6 percent. The change in this "benchmark" unemployment rate—the rate that could be reached if economic growth were to continue at potential—is due to the shifting composition of the labor force toward groups with higher frictional and structural unemployment rates. But others dispute the argument, charging that the higher unemployment estimates consistent with sustained economic growth reflect more the biases of the analysts than an objective analysis of labor market conditions.

Conventional policy prescriptions growing out of the potential GNP analysis call for aggregate demand policies to be used to stabilize economic growth at its potential. Policy tools include the stimulation or repression of consumer and business demand by the use of cuts or increases, higher government spending or retrenchment, and ease or restraint of money and credit. Even in the 1960s when tight labor markets prevailed, unemployment rates remained unacceptably high for some major groups of workers. Using aggregate demand policy to attack that structural unemployment is not always consistent with other economic goals for maximum price stability, minimum inflation, long-term growth, and a favorable balance of international trade and payments. In a relatively fully employed economy, structural unemployment can be reduced with policies and programs targeted directly at workers for whom there exist barriers to full participation in the labor market.

Other Types of Unemployment

The three remaining causes of unemployment—seasonal changes in activity, frictions in the job market, and structural imbalances—probably vary directly with cyclical joblessness and tend to be restricted to particular classes of workers.

Seasonal swings in activity—notably in outdoor work such as construction and agriculture—tend to result in temporary joblessness and contribute significantly to total unemployment. While precise measures are difficult—especially because a seasonal slack period may be extended by cyclical weakness or the slow obsolescence of an industry—the BLS estimated that seasonal unemployment accounted for about one-fourth of total forced idleness in the late 1950s; reexamination of comparable data for the late 1960s suggests a similar conclusion.[12] By the 1970s, however, seasonal unemployment decreased significantly. Using the same methodology, BLS estimated unemployment due to seasonal fluctuations to be about 14 percent of the total in 1978. In construction and agriculture the proportion was estimated at about 30 percent compared with 10 percent in transportation and trade. If seasonal joblessness could be reduced appreciably, it would benefit all sectors of the economy.

Seasonal swings recur annually, making it possible to measure in great detail their characteristics and predict their timing, amplitude, and cause (weather, institutional factors, and custom). Because seasonality is predictable within a relatively narrow range, employment and unemployment statistics are adjusted for seasonality, permitting closer identification of cyclical and secular trends. This adjustment, however, should not obscure the very sizable economic loss associated with seasonality. Much can be done to minimize these costs.[13]

Frictional unemployment results from temporary difficulties in matching available workers with available jobs. It arises mainly from lack of knowledge of opportunities and is marked by its relatively short duration. Such unemployment is unavoidable—as when women or younger workers enter the labor force or when skilled workers voluntarily quit.

Seasonal and frictional unemployment overlap, making clearcut distinctions impossible. Each June and July, for example, thousands of young people enter the labor market in search of temporary or permanent jobs. This vast inflow is partly seasonal—arising from the institutionally determined school year—and partly frictional—reflecting the time necessary to scour the market and find employment. As time passes, some of this unemployment can become cyclical or structural—that is, demand is not strong enough to absorb all of them (as in the summer of 1970), or demand is strong enough, but they are not adequately prepared for the available jobs.

Structural unemployment is more complex than seasonal and frictional unemployment and arises from basic changes in the composition of labor demand and failure of the labor supply to accommodate to new market conditions. Post–World War II examples include large cutbacks in the space program; the decline of the railroads, which combined with the switch to diesel locomotives to displace thousands of skilled railroad workers; the decline of coal mining in Appalachia; and the relocation of the New England textile industry in the South. These and other transformations left many skilled and unskilled workers stranded in areas with job deficits and urgently needing to learn a new skill or to relocate in exanding labor markets. Shifts in sources of energy are likely to be a major cause of structural dislocations in the 1980s.

Possibly a more subtle cause of structural unemployment is technological progress and automation. Productivity advances in agriculture displaced thousands of farmers; similar displacements have occurred in the durable-goods sector of manufacturing, where automation has reduced the need for some skills and sharply modified others. Because the structurally unemployed generally have a large investment in their skill and location, they are less likely than mobile young workers to find new jobs quickly. Thus structural unemployment tends to be of long duration and requires vigorous efforts at retraining, relocation, or infusion of new capital investment to create new jobs.

Unemployment can also be measured in terms of immediate causes that result in persons' joining the ranks of the unemployed; jobless workers can be identified as job losers, job leavers, reentrants, and new entrants. In 1979 the 6 million unemployed workers were distributed among the four categories as follows:

CLASSIFICATION	PERCENT OF UNEMPLOYMENT IN 1979
Job losers	41.6
Job leavers	14.1
Reentrants	30.0
Entrants	14.3

Job loss, accounting for the largest single group of unemployed persons, is generally either cyclically or seasonally induced, and it is most often the reason for unemployment among adult men. On the other hand, younger workers and women are most likely to be without jobs because they have recently entered or reentered the labor force. In conventional terms their unemployment is more likely to be frictional than seasonal. As involuntary idleness persists beyond a month, the probability that it is frictional diminishes; after 15 weeks or more it can no longer be considered seasonal, and a basic structural or cyclical problem becomes probable.

Comparing the duration of unemployment in two years, it is possible to classify the causes of unemployment (Table 3-5). Assuming, for example, that there was no cyclical unemployment in 1969—a year of strong demand and low unemployment—the data suggest that joblessness in a period of strong demand is essentially frictional and of short duration, though about one-eighth of the unemployment appears to have been structural. In 1975, at the trough of the recession, the relative significance of frictional unemployment was lower and long-term or cyclical unemployment became rela-

Table 3-5   DISTRIBUTION OF UNEMPLOYMENT
BY DURATION AND CAUSE, 1969, 1975, AND 1979

INITIAL CLASSIFICATION	LESS THAN 5 WEEKS LARGELY FRICTIONAL AND SEASONAL			5–14 WEEKS MORE SERIOUS PROBLEMS EMERGING			15 WEEKS OR MORE STRUCTURAL OR CYCLICAL		
	1969	1975	1979	1969	1975	1979	1969	1975	1979
TOTAL (ALL CAUSES)	58%	37%	48%	29%	31%	32%	13%	32%	20%
Job losers	51	29	41	32	32	34	18	39	25
Job leavers	61	41	50	28	30	33	12	29	18
Reentrants	62	48	55	26	30	29	11	22	16
New entrants	60	47	55	31	33	30	9	20	15

SOURCE: *Employment and Earnings* (January 1976), Table 11, p. 142; and (January 1980), Table 14, p. 168.
Note: Details may not add to totals because of rounding.

tively much more significant. By 1978 the economy recovered from the recession but cyclical and structural unemployment still accounted for one-fourth of total unemployment.

The majority of workers, however, remain without jobs for relatively short periods—that is, a large portion of unemployment is frictional or possibly seasonal. In 1979 only one-fifth were unemployed over 15 weeks, and close to half moved back into jobs after only 5 weeks or less of joblessness. The foregoing analysis assumes frictional unemployment affects all four classes of the unemployed. Seasonality, on the other hand, is more readily identifiable in the case of new entrants—students and graduates who swell the ranks of job seekers during the summer months. To a lesser extent the change of seasons also affects the job loss rate, which rises during the winter, when outdoor work is curtailed, and dips during the summer.

Job losers are the most likely to remain unemployed for longer periods of time; in 1979 they accounted for more than half of all jobless workers unemployed over 27 weeks. Since job losers are largely men in their prime working ages with strong attachments to the labor force, their numbers among the unemployed tend to increase disproportionately when cyclical unemployment is on the rise. Entrants and reentrants, in contrast, have the alternative of dropping out of the labor force again. Other factors, such as lower levels of educational attainment and the greater sensitivity of blue-collar workers to job loss, also may explain the greater likelihood of lengthy unemployment among job losers.

Characteristics of the Unemployed

Employability is a function of workers' preparedness for work, as well as employers' needs and prejudices. Thus the likelihood of being unemployed varies with workers' personal characteristics as well as with the more general economic factors that generate unemployment. Forced idleness is most likely to be visited upon those who are least able to cope with it—in general, the ill-prepared and the young. If the persons involved also happen to be black or female (or both), the likelihood of being jobless is multiplied by a factor of two or more.

Most men have historically had a full-time, year-round commitment to the labor force; among women the trend toward a more permanent attachment to the workforce is more recent, but is growing and has contributed in part to the rise in their labor force participation rate. In 1978 two-thirds of men who worked held full-time year-round jobs, about the same proportion as in 1960. For women, that fraction was 45 percent in 1978—up from one-third in 1960. Unemployment among male family heads, while appreciably lower than the national average, tends to be especially cyclically responsive, reflecting the heavy concentration of men in manufacturing and construction. In both 1975 and 1979, for example, married men accounted for 40 percent of the labor force. In the high unemployment year, 1975, they accounted for about 30 percent of total joblessness; that proportion fell to one-fifth by 1978, a year of rapid employment growth.

The incidence of unemployment is higher among women and is particularly severe for young workers even when high employment prevails. Frictional unemployment is higher for women and teenagers than for adult men, reflecting their greater likelihood of entering or leaving the labor force and the demands of school, marriage, and childbearing. These frictions are not the only explanations, however. Young workers and women are often restricted to entry-level jobs that are frequently sensitive to seasonal fluctuations or offer few opportunities for upward mobility. Employees have little to lose by giving up such jobs. The structural component of unemployment may also be important for younger workers and women. Mature women reentering the labor force after raising children may find their skills outmoded. Among younger workers the steady erosion of unskilled entry-level jobs probably has been very important, especially for school dropouts whose unemployment rates may be more than twice those of their peers who graduated from high school.[14]

Unemployment and its duration vary with educational attainment. In March 1978 just 2.5 percent of college graduates were unemployed. The high school diploma appeared to have a significant impact, since close to 11 percent of workers who had less than a high school education were unemployed compared to under 5 percent of high school graduates. These variations by education are also reflected in unemployment rates by occupation. Professional and technical workers—many of whom are college graduates—averaged 2 percent or less unemployed in each year between 1958 and 1970. Only in 1975 and 1976 did their unemployment rise as high as 3.2 percent when total unemployment was at 8.5 percent and 7.7 percent respectively. The rate for laborers—many of whom did not complete high school—has never averaged less than 6.5 percent and has been as high as 15 percent. The rate for laborers has typically been about five times greater than that for professional and technical workers and about two times greater for craftsmen. Obviously, inadequate preparation consigns a worker to the end of the employment queue and the top of the layoff list. The program implications are clear: Improved education and training can increase the supply of relatively skilled workers and rescue some of the unskilled from the cycle of recurring unemployment and underemployment.

In part, skill differentials and educational deficiencies are the cause of substantially higher levels of joblessness among blacks than among whites. The jobless rates of blacks have been consistently about double those of whites over the past two decades. Skill differentials are not the only explanation, however, Regardless of educational attainment, work experience, and sex, blacks are more likely than whites to be unemployed, to have extended periods of joblessness, and, when employed, to have lower levels of earnings. Discrimination doubtlessly accounts for a significant part of these differences.[15]

Discrimination also plays a role in the higher jobless rates of women and teenagers. A woman or teenager is more likely to be laid off than a man, more likely to be working part-time for economic reasons, and less likely to be in a high-income, high-status occupation. Of course, higher unemployment among women and younger workers should be expected, given lack of seniority, initial entry in the labor force, tendency to seek new jobs, or relative lack of experience.

Association with particular industries is often a cause of high jobless levels. Construction and agriculture are subject to seasonal swings in activity, while durable-goods manufacturing is very sensitive to cyclical changes. These industries tend to have higher unemployment rates and to be particularly responsive to changes in the growth rate of the economy.

Unemployment is also a function of geography. Industrial concentrations and occupational and racial distributions are largely responsible for this. Cyclical changes, for example, are greater in areas where manufacturing abounds, such as the Northeast and the North Central states. And structural problems have been evidenced in the experiences of Appalachian soft-coal regions and former New England textile and leather towns. In the early 1970s the declines in military-aerospace production boosted unemployment rates in southern California and Washington. Where minority workers constitute a larger proportion of the work force, unemployment and underemployment continue to be more severe, but occupational differences among regions have narrowed over the past decade primarily due to the upgrading of the Southern labor force and the proscription of discriminatory practices.

A more recent phenomenon is the persistently high unemployment in central metropolitan areas, reflecting the great migration of population from rural areas to big-city slums and the flight of industry from the inner city. The contribution of migration to unemployment in central-city areas has not been measured; but whatever the causes, the incidence of unemployment is greater in central cities than in their surrounding rings. In the nation's central cities—which contain four of every ten workers—the unemployment rate was 7.1 percent in 1979 compared with an average rate of 5.0 percent for suburban residents.

When these data are further broken down to measure specific poverty areas, the unemployment gap and extent of employment problems grow progressively worse. In 1970, when unemployment was 4.9 percent nationally, it was 9.6 percent throughout urban poverty areas.[16] Among family heads poverty area unemployment was more than twice as great as the national average. Six out of ten of the unemployed in these poorest areas were black; one-third had been unemployed for more than 15 weeks—twice the national rate. Race and lower educational attainment are no doubt important factors in the higher rates. A majority of poverty area residents were minority group members, and their median educational level was 10.2 years.

Unemployment is a problem faced by all industrialized countries, but, the United States seems to have tolerated a higher incidence of unemployment than many others (Table 3-6). Only in Canada, and, more recently, Italy, Australia, Great Britain, and France has unemployment been as persistent a problem as in the United States.

Averages tend to understate the actual number of people hit by unemployment at some time during the year. Monthly average unemployment for 1978 was 6 million, but work-experience data show that 17.7 million persons were among the unemployed for at least one week during 1978. The pressures of forced idleness on economic well-being, however, are greatest

---

Table 3-6   UNEMPLOYMENT RATES IN THE
UNITED STATES AND EIGHT INDUSTRIALIZED NATIONS, 1962 AND 1978

	1962	1978
United States	5.5%	6.0%
Australia	n.a.	6.3
Canada	5.9	8.4
France	1.8	5.6
Germany	0.4	4.3
Great Britain	2.8	6.0
Italy	3.2	7.2
Japan	1.3	2.3
Sweden	1.5	2.2

SOURCE: Constance Sorrentino, "Unemployment in the United States and Seven Foreign Countries," *Monthly Labor Review* (September 1970): 14; and Joyanna Moy, "Recent Labor Market Trends in Nine Industrial Nations," *Monthly Labor Review* (May 1979): 12. Note: Rates are adjusted to U.S. concepts.

when unemployment extends over a long period or is repetitive. In 1978, for example, 6.2 million persons were unemployed for 15 weeks or more, many because of repeated spells of unemployment.

Labor Shortages and Surpluses

While unemployment has been high for selected groups of workers, there have been continuing shortages of other kinds of workers—mainly those in the highly skilled, highly paid professions and those in the lowest-paid occupations. Amelioration of shortages in these groups is an important objective because skill bottlenecks create dislocations and obstacles to balanced economic growth. High employment levels are often erroneously identified by employers as shortages of general labor, largely because a tight market increases labor turnover, may reduce the rate of productivity growth, and usually results in higher unit labor costs. These concerns have surfaced only on rare occasions.

A more important problem exists, however, with respect to shortages of highly skilled workers. It may require several years of specialized training, not to mention huge costs, to develop skilled professional personnel. Filling these gaps should be a firstline national priority. Shortages of most unskilled jobs can usually be cured with a bigger dose of income and a dollop of prestige.

Some shortages result from restrictive practices designed to provide selected groups of workers with strong bargaining power. Some unions and professional associations engage in restrictive practices, not always successfully, to limit the supply of labor and raise income. Well-known examples include many construction craft unions, medical and dental associations, and university faculties that restrict the supply of new young Ph.D.'s. These special interest groups primarily restrict supply through arbitrary qualification standards, unduly extended training periods, limits on the number of apprentices per journeyman, artificially high licensing standards, and other techniques. Such practices are always defended as a means of maintaining high standards to protect the public from the "untrained" and "inept." A reasonable distribution of employment opportunities will not be achieved unless restrictive practices are corrected.

A major departure from the historically sustained demand for college graduates began during the late 1970s. By 1985 the supply of college graduates is anticipated to outstrip demand by 70,000 persons annually. Surpluses of college-trained manpower do not necessarily imply those persons will be unable to find work. In fact, the slowed growth of the economy may dampen the enthusiasm of youth to invest in college training, thereby correcting part of the imbalance in supply and demand for highly educated workers. Moreover, an overall surplus of college graduates masks continuing needs for workers trained in specialized occupations, many of which require other post–high school training, but not necessarily college.

UNEMPLOYMENT IS ONLY ONE DIMENSION OF INADEQUACY

Since the Great Depression labor market measures have focused on the availability of work, and policy makers have tended to react to these highly publicized barometers of economic conditions. The underlying assumptions have been that almost any job is better than no job and that employment is the sole means to obtain income essential for sustenance.

However, movement in and out of the labor force today is controlled by factors different from those in the 1930s, when the current labor force concepts were developed. For the bulk of the population a job remains the sole source of legitimate income, but transfer payments now account for nearly one-sixth of total disposable personal income. Large groups now have an income cushion provided by increased affluence and accumulated assets that can be used—in addition to transfer payments—when income is interrupted. Without in any way minimizing the individual's problems in search for gainful employment, developments such as the increasing number of working wives, the ability of families to support dependent children in school, and the economic padding provided for the aged and the temporarily jobless accent the need for a measure of economic deprivation based on an adequate standard of employment and earnings combined.

The policy makers who designed antipoverty programs during the 1960s recognized a need to measure low income among the employed as well as those forced into idleness. Seeking support for employment and training programs, then Secretary of Labor, W. Willard Wirtz, encouraged the preparation in 1967 of a subemployment rate. The measure added these groups to the number of unemployed: discouraged workers, full-time workers receiving wages insufficient to lift them above the poverty standard, and part-time workers who want to work full-time.

The need for new labor market indicators relating economic hardship to labor market conditions became pronounced in the 1970s as unemployment continued its upward trend and federal expenditures on employment, training, and income support programs increased. An index linking employment with earnings, serving as a supplement to the unemployment rate, could help determine appropriate policy measures by indicating the mix of needed counter-cyclical, structural, and income support programs in dealing with labor market related problems.

There are a number of important conceptual issues that are raised in designing an economic hardship index. Value judgments must be made as to what level of income provides an adequate standard of living, what criterion will be used to determine labor market attachment, and whether each individual's income should be used to measure earnings inadequacy or whether individuals should be considered in the context of their families. The time horizon used to measure both labor force participation and income also affects the level of the index. A year is usually considered an acceptable time framework. One measure of labor market pathologies that would include that section of the labor force that encounters difficulties in maintaining sustained employment as well as maintaining a predetermined minimum income level could be based on the following criteria:

1. Regardless of employment status of the people involved, the index would exclude persons with earnings above a predetermined level. The poverty threshold represents a minimal level of adequate earnings while family income at twice the poverty level is close to what the Bureau of Labor Statistics defines as a lower living standard. An index linking economic hardship and employment should be based on a household income between these two widely accepted standards. Families with adequate incomes normally have sufficient resources to adjust to adversity. They frequently have assets, in addition to transfer payments, to tide them over during their short-term unemployment.

2. Conversely, individuals whose earnings are inadequate to raise themselves and their families out of poverty and whose family incomes are less than the predetermined adequacy level would be included even if they work full-time. However, workers whose earnings are less than the poverty threshold but have family incomes above the predetermined level would be exluded from the hardship measure. To include all low earners would clearly disregard the economic realities of treating the family as a viable consumer unit.

3. An index that combines employment and earnings inadequacy would include both persons who want jobs even if they have become discouraged from seeking employment and workers who hold part-time jobs while looking for full-time positions. The income criteria applied to the unemployed would hold for discouraged and part-time workers.

4. Other criteria must be made to restrict the employment and earnings inadequacy measure to those whose economic hardship can be related to labor market conditions. Except for discouraged workers, persons must be in the labor force, working or seeking full-time work, say 40 or more weeks during the year to be counted. Discouraged workers would be included only if they have demonstrated sufficient attachment to the labor force by spending 15 or more weeks seeking employment. Voluntary part-time workers are excluded on the grounds that any deficiency in earnings is due more to personal choice rather than economic conditions.

The derivation of the index is illustrated in Table 3-7 based on March 1977 CPS supplement data. Using the criteria discussed above and defining labor market related hardship at twice the poverty level, the index measures 10 percent of all persons who were in the labor force for 40 or more weeks or were discouraged workers who sought employment for at least 15 weeks, and had insufficient income in 1976.[17]

The hardship index can also be derived for demographic subgroups. The incidence of hardship was highest among women and minorities. Fe-

Table 3-7   DERIVATION OF INDEX
LINKING EMPLOYMENT AND INCOME, 1976

	NUMBER (IN THOUSANDS)
Total in labor force, 1976	108,276
Less voluntary part-time workers	9,094
	99,182
Plus discouraged workers	+ 700
	99,882
Less those in labor force fewer than 40 weeks	−24,250
	75,632
Workers earning less than poverty line	15,526
Family income less than twice poverty line	7,563
Hardship index (percent of eligible labor force)	10.0

CHARACTERISTIC	HARDSHIP INDEX
All groups	10.0
Men	8.7
Women	12.1
Blacks	24.2
Hispanics	20.7
Other minorities	14.4
Whites	8.3
Age 16 to 19 years	26.4
20 to 24 years	12.9
25 to 64 years	8.7
65 years and over	15.8
Husband-wife family	8.4
Male head	11.8
Female head	24.2
Unrelated individuals	10.7

SOURCE: Special tabulations by the Bureau of Labor Statistics. National Commission on Employment and Unemployment Statistics, *Counting the Labor Force* (Washington, D.C.: GPO, 1979), p. 74.

male-headed families had a disproportionate share of workers in the hardship group.

Over time, the hardship index has moved in the same direction as the unemployment rate but with distinct differences. The index linking employment and earnings did not display the same upward trend as the unemployment rate and though the cyclical movements are in the same direction, the hardship index fluctuated much less. Unemployment is only one component of the hardship index, which is more reflective of structural employment problems than cyclical variations in employment opportunities. An increasing number of unemployed are buffered from hardship associated with unemployment by transfer payments and the incomes of other family members.

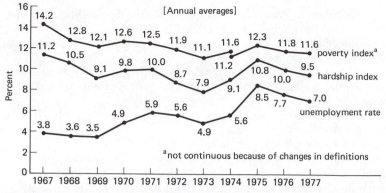

Figure 3-1   Unemployment rate, hardship index, and poverty index, 1967–1977. (Source: U.S. Bureau of the Census, *Current Population Reports,* Series P-60; U.S. Bureau of Labor Statistics, *Employment and Earnings;* and special tabulations by the Bureau of Labor Statistics. National Commission on Employment and Unemployment Statistics, *Counting the Labor Force* (Washington, D.C.: GPO, 1979), p. 76.)

Low earnings are clearly as much or more of a problem than unemployment, discouragement, and involuntary part-time work. Employment and earnings inadequacy is a continuing structural problem. Even when the official unemployment rate declined to 3.5 percent in March 1969, nearly one in every ten persons had inadequate employment and earnings according to this index. Policy prescriptions to combat these labor market problems must include long-run commitments to eliminate inequalities in wage structure and employment practices as well as countercyclical measures (Figure 3-1).

The Comprehensive Employment and Training Acts of 1973 and 1978 mandated that the Secretary of Labor develop an index of economic hardship. The National Commission on Employment and Unemployment Statistics, in submitting its recommendations to Congress in September 1979, strongly recommended that such a link between employment and earnings be developed and published annually.

DISCUSSION QUESTIONS

1. Outline the major shifts in the demographic composition of the labor force that have occurred in the post–World War II period.
2. Describe the traditional classification by economists of the kinds of unemployment that exist. How is each remedied?
3. Define the following types of unemployment in terms of their "cures" rather than their causes:
   a. Cyclical unemployment.
   b. Structural unemployment.
   c. Frictional unemployment.
4. How do changes in the overall level of economic activity affect labor force

participation rates? Be sure to include a discussion of the "additional worker effect" and the "discouraged worker effect."

5. What are the effects of the business cycle upon the size of the labor force and upon major specific groups?

6. How would you distinguish between *unemployment* and *underemployment?*

7. Discuss the relationship between the labor-force participation rate and levels of educational attainment.

8. Among what particular groups of workers is unemployment more likely to be the highest? Why?

9. Why is frictional unemployment unavoidable?

10. How successful has the unemployment rate been as a measure of economic hardship?

11. The monthly aggregate unemployment rate has been subjected recently to increasing criticism. According to the critics, what are the major shortcomings and strengths of the monthly unemployment rate as a social indicator? How would a subemployment or hardship index complement the overall unemployment rate?

12. Evaluate and analyze the charge that Current Population Survey monthly unemployment data fall short of identifying problems faced by workers in the labor market. What supplementary data would you favor, if any?

Notes

1. Herbert S. Parnes, "Labor Force Participation and Labor Mobility," in *A Review of Industrial Relations Research,* Industrial Relations Research Association Series, vol. 1 (Madison, Wis.: The Association, 1970), pp. 1–33.

2. Stuart H. Garfinkle, *Job Changing and Manpower Training,* U.S. Department of Labor, Manpower Administration, Office of Manpower, Automation and Training, Manpower Report no. 10 (Washington, D.C.: GPO, 1964), p. 1.

3. Sar A. Levitan and Karen Cleary Alderman, *Warriors at Work: The Volunteer Armed Forces* (Beverly Hills, Calif.: Sage Publications, 1977).

4. Scott Cambell Brown, "Educational Attainment of Workers—Some Trends from 1973 to 1978," Special Labor Force Report no. 225, U.S. Bureau of Statistics (Washington, D.C.: GPO, February 1979).

5. M. Louise McCraw, "Medical Care Costs Lead Rise in 1976–77 Family Budgets," *Monthly Labor Review* (November 1978): 33–36.

6. U.S. Bureau of Census, *Money Income in 1977 of Families and Persons in the United States,* series P-60, no. 118 (Washington, D.C.: GPO, March 1979), tables 63 and 64.

7. W. S. Woytinsky, *Three Aspects of Labor Dynamics* (New York: Social Science Research Council, 1942), part III.

8. T. Aldrich Finegan, "The Measurement, Behavior, and Classification of Discouraged Workers," in National Commission on Employment and Unemployment Statistics, appendix vol. I to *Counting the Labor Force* (Washington, D.C.: GPO, 1980).

9. Glen G. Cain, *The Net Effect of Unemployment on Labor Force Participation of Secondary Workers* (Madison, Wis.: Social Systems Research Institute, University of Wisconsin, October 1964).

10. Arthur Okun, "Potential GNP: Its Measurement and Significance," *Proceed-*

ings of the Business and Economic Statistics Section of the American Statistical Association (1962): 98–104.

11. *Economic Report of the President* (Washington, D.C.: GPO, 1979), pp. 72–76.
12. Seymour Wolfbein, *Employment and Unemployment in the United States* (Chicago: Science Research Associates, 1962), p. 293.
13. National Commission on Employment and Unemployment Statistics, *Counting the Labor Force* (Washington, D.C.: GPO, 1979), pp. 219–224.
14. Howard V. Hayghe, "Employment of High School Graduates and Dropouts," *Monthly Labor Review* (August 1970): 35 ff.
15. James Gwartney, "Discrimination and Income Differentials," *American Economic Review* (June 1970): 396–408.
16. U.S. Bureau of the Census, *Employment Profiles of Selected Low Income Areas,* Final Report PHC (3)-1 (Washington, D.C.: GPO, 1972).
17. National Commission on Employment and Unemployment Statistics, *Counting the Labor Force* (Washington, D.C.: GPO, 1979), pp. 72–77.

Chapter 4
Shifting Composition
of Employment

The dramatic enlargement in the role of women in the work force has coincided with other changes in the economy that have brought increased reliance upon workers who do not work full time year round but take intermittent or part-time jobs and tend to move in and out of the labor force. There have been important changes, too, in the types of work done—in the occupations and industries in which Americans are employed.

INTERMITTENT WORKERS

While the majority of workers still hold full-time, year-round jobs and account for the bulk of all hours worked, a very substantial number work intermittently. A total of 112.4 million persons were in the labor force during 1978, a year of healthy economic expansion, but only 55 percent were employed more than 35 hours per week (full time) for 50 weeks or more (year round). Employment averaged 94.4 million, or 15.9 million less than the total number of persons who worked during the year. There were 23 million part-time workers and 25.1 million who had full-time jobs but worked 49 weeks or less (Table 4-1).

These 48 million intermittent workers include many different groups

Table 4-1   WORK EXPERIENCE OF PERSONS 16 YEARS OLD AND OVER, 1978

	BOTH SEXES	MEN	WOMEN
TOTAL WHO WORKED DURING THE YEAR	110,290	61,917	48,373
PERCENT	100.0	100.0	100.0
FULL TIME[a]	79.1	87.9	67.8
50–52 weeks	56.4	66.3	43.7
48–49 weeks	2.3	2.4	2.1
40–47 weeks	4.9	5.3	4.4
27–39 weeks	5.3	5.0	5.7
14–26 weeks	5.5	4.9	6.2
13 weeks or less	4.8	4.1	5.8
PART TIME	20.9	12.1	32.2
50–52 weeks	7.0	4.0	10.9
48–49 weeks	.7	.4	1.1
40–47 weeks	1.9	1.1	2.9
27–39 weeks	2.8	1.5	4.5
14–26 weeks	3.7	2.2	5.7
13 weeks or less	4.7	2.9	7.0

SOURCE: U.S. Bureau of Labor Statistics.
[a] Usually worked 35 hours or more a week.

with diverse employment experiences. Many of those who work on and off during the year do so voluntarily; others are forced to reduce their schedules in the face of adverse economic conditions. Some are usually marginal workers who enter and leave the labor force as secondary earners. And, for the most part, they toil in low-paying, dead-end jobs.[1] For some of these workers the attractions of wage jobs are balanced against the lure of income alternatives such as welfare, unemployment compensation, crime, or "hustling" outside the regular labor market. For these groups there is a continual shifting in and out of the various activities depending upon economic conditions and the opportunities that are available.

Voluntary Part-Time or Part-Year Work

Voluntary part-time workers deserve separate attention because their number has been growing at a rapid pace, from roughly one-eighth of average full-time workers in 1960 to one-sixth in 1979 (Figure 4-1). This has not happened because of a shortage of full-time jobs, but rather because of a growth in part-time positions that are attractive to those who do not want to work full time.

To some degree, part-time work is cyclical; the number of persons working less than 35 hours a week or employed less than a full year rises and falls with the unemployment rate. However, the supply of part-time workers has increased with the number of married women and school-age youth

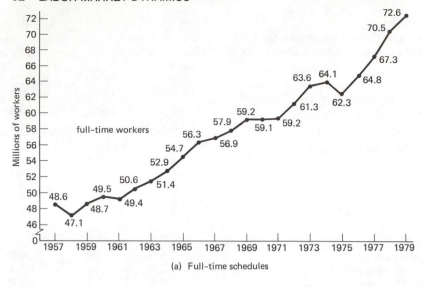

(a) Full-time schedules

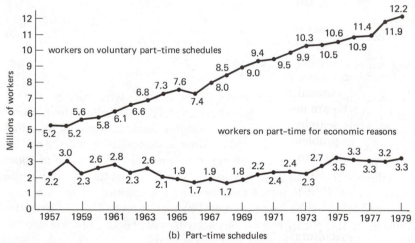

(b) Part-time schedules

Figure 4-1   Labor force in nonagricultural industries by full-time and part-time status, 1957–1979. (Source: U.S. Department of Labor, *Employment and Training Report of the President* (Washington, D.C.: GPO, 1979), pp. 282–284.

in the labor force.[2] Both groups must divide their time between nonmarket activities, like child care and studying, and work. Others, older and handicapped workers, face physical limits on the time they can spend working. Part-time work also is attractive to moonlighters, who hold other full-time jobs. Personal preferences for part-time work have been reinforced by public labor market policies that encourage students to enter work-study programs and place ceilings on the earnings of Social Security recipients.

The 12.2 million voluntary part-time workers comprised 14 percent of all employed persons in 1979. However, the proportion of workers in these positions differs by sex and age as do the reasons for preferring part-time employment. More than two out of every nine female workers choose part-time employment compared to one in fourteen male workers. Almost one of every four employed youth, aged 16 to 24, and one in two workers 65 years of age and older are in voluntary part-time positions. These are much higher proportions than those found for all workers. Seven out of ten workers on voluntary part-time work schedules are females; and four out of seven of these are married and living with their husbands. Youth, aged 16 to 24, account for over 40 percent of the voluntary part-time workers. Older workers are another 10 percent.

Overwhelmingly, their jobs are concentrated in the service and retail sectors, which accounted for almost three-fourths of the voluntary part-time jobs in 1979. More and more employers are restructuring their operations to use part-time personnel.

Variations in Labor Utilization

Involuntary reductions in labor utilization can result when some of those who are employed at full-time jobs have their work interrupted by periods of forced idleness or those who find full-time work is not available work at part-time jobs (discussed in the next chapter). Within these two groups are those who hold seasonal jobs in which unemployment is predictable and regular, those who are underemployed or unemployed for a comparatively short time while searching or preparing for new employment, and those who have serious problems in finding and holding jobs throughout the year.

Certain occupations and industries, especially agriculture and contract construction, have largely seasonal employment patterns. Agriculture is highly seasonal, and though migration can usually extend the working period, unemployment is still frequent. In 1977, 70 percent of farm laborers and overseers worked less than 50 weeks, and 28 percent held jobs less than half the year. Agricultural employment is becoming, however, a less important factor affecting labor force behavior. The number of farm laborers fell from 2.3 million in 1958 to 1.3 million in 1979.

Many of the 43 percent of all workers who held part-year or part-time jobs during 1978 found their employment interrupted by periods of forced idleness. To a large degree this type of underutilization of labor is cyclical, rising and falling with the unemployment rate.

The Secondary Labor Market

While part-time schedules have become widely accepted by many American workers and employers, some intermittent employment also reflects the existence of a secondary labor market where peripheral workers are generally employed in low-wage, low-skill, and low-status occupations. They are likely to be agricultural laborers, textile workers, and workers concentrated in the service and retail sectors with few earning more than the minimum wage and many earning less. Even when worked full time, these jobs usually yield an income near or below poverty thresholds. Because of unattractive working conditions and low pay, they are characterized by high absenteeism and rapid turnover.

Peripheral workers and the marginal jobs for which they are hired constitute a secondary labor market, which is different in many ways from the market for full-time, year-round workers. Intermittent work patterns are built into the secondary system. Employers act on the assumption that these employees are not committed to sustained work: Fringe benefits are minimized, little investment is made in training, and opportunities for advancement are closed off. On the other hand, employees feel little attachment to their jobs and tend to quit on a moment's notice. They have little interest in retirement plans or any long-range benefits because they expect their tenure to be limited; they tend to rely on job changes rather than advancements within the firm as a route upward.

This system has different effects on different people. While part-time job opportunities may fill the need of a wife to get out of the house several afternoons a week or of a college student to earn money over Christmas or during the school year, they are inimical to the migrant workers and their families who cannot find year-round employment or the ghetto family head who moves from one dead-end job to another.

The employment patterns of these peripheral workers are likely to continue in their recent trends. Seasonal unemployment will diminish as agricultural employment continues to decline, as construction becomes more stable through better planning and the introduction of industrialized methods, and as the number of teenagers looking for part-time or summer jobs declines during the 1980s. Some inroads will probably be made against frictional unemployment through improved labor market services; and human resource programs may help those with the severe employment problems. However, part-time employment will probably continue to grow along with expansion of the service sector, not to mention increases in the number of married women seeking part-time work as birth rates remain low. It appears that employment patterns will become more flexible; and, hopefully, the impact of adverse economic factors will be reduced.

Worksharing and Flexitime

Coincident with the trends in voluntary and involuntary part-time employment, there has been a growing interest in worksharing, flexitime, and other alternatives to the traditional workweek. The persistent high level of unemployment among minorities and other groups inevitably has generated pressures to reduce hours of work in order to increase the total number of available jobs. And the desire of workers to make the most of their leisure has led to demands for more flexible work schedules.

The most common work practice during a recession is to lay off workers based on seniority. However, a growing number of Western European nations, the state of California, and a few American firms, have tried the alternative approach of worksharing. Instead of laying off, say, 10 percent of the workforce due to a decline in the demand for labor, workers and employers participating in worksharing programs agree to reduce hours for all workers by 10 percent. Unemployment insurance funds have been used in Europe and in California to compensate workers for lost wages resulting from worksharing.[3]

The gains to society from worksharing—as opposed to layoffs—include: (1) a more equitable distribution of the severe impact of a recession; (2) continued job attachment, which keeps workers' employment skills fresh; (3) smaller gyrations in consumer spending patterns, which could soften the severity of an economic downturn as persons on reduced hours make smaller retrenchments in consumption spending than unemployed workers; (4) a reduction in public outlays for social welfare programs; and (5) maintenance of equal employment gains since minority and female workers often hold the least seniority.

Taking total number of hours of work as given, worksharing is an appealing solution to measured unemployment. If 10 percent of Americans employed full-time reduced their workweek to four days, nearly 2 million more four-day-a-week jobs would be created. Such estimates about worksharing, however, may be overlooking important factors that could vastly alter the desired result. Given existing government regulations and collective bargaining arrangements, an employer's best economic interests may be to resort to layoffs instead of to worksharing. Collective bargaining provisions may actually prevent an employer from opting for worksharing. In the United States one major roadblock to worksharing has been the fact that unemployment compensation is not generally available to workers who might reduce their workweek from, say, five to four days. Only California allows payment under the existing unemployment insurance system to a worker forced on a part-time schedule because full-time work is not available.

Besides worksharing, there also has been a growing interest in flexitime work alternatives. Under flexitime, a worker is most often required to be on the job for certain morning and afternoon "core" periods. These core periods could consist of, say, 10:00 A.M. to 12:00 noon and 2:00 P.M. to 4:00 P.M. Beyond these core periods a worker would have the choice of selecting remaining work hours. A flexitime system is designed to give workers more freedom to make jobs conform to their individual lifestyles.[4] While some studies claim that flexitime increases productivity, the sample data are still

too small to reach general conclusions. The increased participation of females in the labor force is likely to exert pressures in favor of flexitime.

YOUTH

In the course of U.S. economic history the age of first entrance into the
labor force has come later and later in life. Children once entered the
workforce before reaching their teens; today, some youth may reach their
mid-20s before entering the labor force on a full-time basis. Increased affluence, longer education, the steady decline of family farming, and child protection laws have contributed to this trend. These factors, in combination
with technological and socioeconomic changes, also have made it much
more complicated for young people to find jobs that provide an opportunity
to earn an adequate income and reasonable economic security. And the
transition from school to work is more difficult because young people lack
work experience, having spent their lives in an educational system that seldom provides the skills demanded by employers. Nor do government and
business expend much effort to smooth the way. As a result, some youngsters—especially dropouts—never find the bridge and are doomed to lives
of intermittent unemployment in low-paying, high-risk jobs. This problem
is particularly prevalent among minority youth.

    Young men and women show divergent trends in labor force participa-
tion. Young men's participation declined dramatically during the first half
of the century, largely because of increased school enrollment but has risen
again in the 1970s. Among young women, participation rates have risen
since the end of World War II, partly because of growing job opportunities
for part-time workers in retail trade and services and changing attitudes towards gainful employment by women. Labor force participation rates of
16-to 24-year-old men and women in 1947 and 1979 were:

	PARTICIPATION RATES			
	MALE		FEMALE	
AGE	1947	1979	1947	1979
16–17	52.2%	51.8%	29.5%	45.8%
18–19	80.5	73.9	52.3	63.1
20–24	84.9	87.6	44.9	69.3

At the same time, the extremely high birth rates of the post–World War II
era meant that the number of teenagers (aged 16 to 19) burgeoned from
10.6 million in 1960 to 16.7 million in 1978. As a result, their proportion of
the total labor force rose to nearly 10 percent.

    Pursuit of longer education to qualify for more complex jobs is the
main reason for late entry into the labor force. However, some young men
and women are discouraged. Overrepresented in this category are black
youth, many of them living in city slums, where the problems of drugs, de-

linquency, and crime have grown progressively worse in an atmosphere of idle hopelessness. Whatever their special job difficulties, these young people are prime candidates for lives of underemployment. Why are such youngsters outside the work force? Some believe that no one will hire them because they are too young. And judging from the unemployment rates of their peers who are in the labor force, this is probably true. Others have given up entirely or are engaged in illicit pursuits, and information is lacking whether they are counted among the unemployed. Some depend upon parental support and do not need or care to work. (Chapter 16 probes more deeply the nature and causes of youth employment as a perspective for current policy issues.)

Among the 16- to 24-year-olds going to school, almost one-half were in the labor force—mostly working at or seeking part-time jobs. Many young people in school and not in the labor force—close to 8 million in 1978—would probably like to have some additional income but feel that work is not available.

When employed, teenagers and men in their early 20s tend to be entry-level workers such as laborers, semiskilled operatives, and service workers. A large number work only part time. Teenagers are about three times more likely than mature men to be working in agriculture. The 1978 income of young men reflected their concentration in low-paying jobs:

TYPE OF INCOME	ALL MALES	14- TO 19-YEAR-OLDS	20- TO 24-YEAR-OLDS
Median income	$10,935	$1,135	$ 7,059
Year-round, full-time workers' income	$16,062	$7,074	$10,410

Joblessness and job turnover have always been relatively high among younger workers who are adjusting to new jobs. In 1979, a year of strong demand, the rate of unemployment for 16- to 24-year-olds was more than triple the rate for persons aged 25 and over. In fact almost half the unemployed were workers younger than 25 years. The unemployment situation for black and other minority group youngsters was much worse; their rates ranged upward to levels approximating depression conditions. Obviously, high unemployment and undesirable jobs are critical factors keeping large numbers of young persons outside the labor force, regardless of their school status.

In recent years the younger workers' normal liabilities have been reinforced by the great increases in the numbers of such workers and the continuing decline in the number of unskilled, entry-level jobs.[5] The proportion of jobs in the less skilled laborer, operative, and farming occupations has dropped substantially since the late 1940s—from over 4 of every 10 jobs to 1 in 4 by 1979; at the same time, white-collar positions have risen from 3½ in 10 to nearly 5 in 10—but youth normally fill the jobs requiring minimal skills. However, this does not necessarily mean that youth employment opportunities have been adversely affected, because education has kept pace with the increased demand for higher skills. Since 1940 the proportion of workers with high school diplomas has doubled, and the proportion with college degrees has tripled; the median number of school years completed has risen from 9.1 years to 12.6.

Economists disagree over the impact upon youth employment of rising federal minimum wages and broader coverage under the Fair Labor Standards Act (FLSA). Even without any minimum wage, econometric evidence indicates that the post–World War II period still would have seen high rates of youth unemployment. The general level of business conditions, demographic forces, population migration, the influx of undocumented aliens, the extension of the welfare state, and changing societal attitudes including more women in the workforce all appear to have influenced youth labor markets far more than minimum wages.

Just because the minimum wage involves some job losses does not necessarily damn the statutory wage rate. These social costs in most cases appear to be more than compensated for by the social benefits produced by the minimum wage in raising incomes for poor workers. Youth and the minimum wage, nevertheless, remain a continuing political issue. For example, during the 1977 round of congressional amendments, a proposal to establish a teenage differential wage rate lost in the house by only one vote. Students and certified learners may be paid 85 percent of the statutory wage rate. Despite a good deal of research into these difficult questions, social scientists have been able to produce very few hard conclusions about the impact of the minimum wage.

THE GOLDEN YEARS?

Turning to the other end of the age spectrum, older Americans, men and women alike, are faced with a bewildering and growing array of socioeconomic problems. Many lack the skills necessary to compete in a highly technical job market, relegating them to jobs below their potential skill levels; others have left the work force altogether. Our society takes pride in the recent increases in early retirement for what some call the golden years. This pride is partly misplaced; a large number of older Americans do not have adequate incomes to sustain a decent standard of living, and many have been forced by unemployment into premature retirement.

Older workers' employment problems spring partly from the failure of employers to recognize the vast accumulation of skill and experience currently being unutilized. Recent estimates place the number of healthy males aged 65 and over at 2.7 million,[6] and there were another 3.6 million men 45 to 64 outside the work force. Many of these men are voluntarily retired and have adequate incomes; however, many others have been forced out of the market and are living on substandard incomes.

As with younger workers, sheer population growth among older Americans has offset declining participation rates since the turn of the century, and especially in the post–World War II years. The number of older Americans (aged 55 and over) has increased by close to 75 percent since the end of World War II, rising to about 45 million. High birth and immigration rates before the Great Depression account for much of the increase, but the rise also reflects a longer life span brought about by better living, health, and work conditions. These same factors might be expected to stimulate participation by older people, and women seem to have benefited from them. However, men apparently encounter offsetting factors, for the proportion working has declined sharply—especially after age 65, though declining rates are also evident in preretirement years, especially for reasons of poor health.[7] Older men account for a steadily declining proportion of the labor force, even though their percentage of the total population has held quite steady. About 8.8 million men aged 55 years and over were employed in 1979. They accounted for 9.1 percent of total employment, down from 12.6 percent in 1960 and 13.7 percent in 1947. The number of older persons is expected to increase dramatically to a total of 49 million in 1985—a 90 percent jump from 1950. This increase also should be accompanied by further improvements in health care, permitting an extension of working life.

These large numbers of nonworking retirees would not constitute a serious social and economic problem if they had enough income to assure an adequate standard of living. However, many retirement incomes are inadequate: Almost 3.2 million older Americans (aged 65 and over) were living in poverty in 1978.

The pivotal retirement age is 65, reflecting the rapid development and liberalization of private and public pension plans. Many workers are retiring even earlier. More than half of those eligible are electing to draw Social Security benefits before age 65. Beyond that age, only one in five older men is in the labor force, and, of those working, more than one-third hold part-time jobs. Although these older men usually work part time by choice, they are twice as likely to do so for economic reasons as men in their prime working years.

Older workers are less likely than young workers to move among jobs. The benefits that accrue to seniority (especially job security) are important to older workers, who usually have considerable training, experience, community ties, and company loyalty. In addition, age barriers limit their opportunities for changing jobs. In part because they are less mobile, older workers tend to be concentrated in declining occupations and industries. Many are farmers or self-employed. As a result of this uneven distribution of employment, there are great disparities in the earnings of older men. On the average, however, their earnings are lower than for younger workers.[8] This difference is partly due to the tendency for some older workers to work only part time or part year; but there are also significant differences among full-time, year-round male workers, as shown in the following tabulation for 1978:

	MALES BY AGE IN YEARS		
CLASSIFICATION	45–54	55–64	65 AND OVER
Median income, all persons with income	$16,574	$13,624	$ 6,106
Median income, full-time, year-round workers	18,684	17,292	14,314
Percent of total with incomes of less than $3,000	5.6	7.3	20.1

The unemployment problems of older workers are somewhat unique. Because they have long job tenure, they are less likely to lose their jobs through layoff. But once set adrift from employment, they are apt to be shunted around among low-paying temporary jobs. Not only are there age barriers in hiring, but also older workers often lack adequate training for today's technical jobs. Older workers are thus much more likely than their middle-aged colleagues to spend many more weeks of fruitless searching for employment[9] (Table 4-2). Faced with this experience, many older workers simply withdraw from the labor force,[10] often without adequate income.

INDUSTRIAL AND OCCUPATIONAL SHIFTS

Shift to Service-Producing, White-Collar Employment

At the turn of the century 70 percent of all workers were in industries producing physical goods—in agriculture, forestry, fishing, mining, manufacturing, and construction; the rest were in service-producing industries. In 1979 the relative importance of the two was reversed, with two-thirds of all workers employed in service-producing industries—wholesale and retail trade, personal and business services, government, transportation and public utilities, finance, insurance, and real estate.

The most notable changes have been the persistent decline in farm employment, coupled with the burgeoning of service jobs. After 1950 farm employment declined by about 200,000 annually. In 1953, for the first time, the number of service workers—including cooks, janitors, barbers, practical nurses, firemen, and policemen—equaled the agricultural work force. The gap between the two continued to widen, and by 1979 there were over eight service workers for every farm worker.

The shift from goods-producing to service-producing industries was accompanied by a shift from blue-collar to white-collar occupations. In 1900 white-collar workers accounted for only 18 percent of employment. By

Table 4-2   FREQUENCY AND DURATION OF UNEMPLOYMENT
OF PERSONS WITH WORK EXPERIENCE BY AGE, 1978

AGE	PERCENT WITH UNEMPLOYMENT IN 1978	2 SPELLS	PERCENT UNEMPLOYMENT		
			3 OR MORE SPELLS	15 TO 26 WEEKS	27 WEEKS OR MORE
25–34 years	16.4%	16.3%	13.8%	20.3%	11.3%
35–44 years	11.8	14.0	14.3	22.7	14.1
45–54 years	9.7	17.4	16.1	26.1	17.3
55–64 years	7.9	14.7	17.4	23.6	19.7
65 yrs. & older	7.9	14.9	18.9	25.8	27.0

SOURCE: U.S. Bureau of Labor Statistics.

1956, for the first time, white-collar workers outnumbered blue-collar workers; now they account for half of all employment. The rising demand for white-collar service workers reflects higher standards of living, including better health care, more government services, and more luxuries.

The occupational and industrial shifts were accompanied by pervasive changes that have broad implications for the economic and social structure of the nation. The shifts favored occupations requiring more extensive skills and educational attainment. In 1900 laborers outnumbered managers and professionals. By 1979, 26 percent of all workers were managers or professionals compared to only 6 percent who were laborers. Profound occupational changes have also occurred within the goods-producing industries. Technological and organizational changes have enhanced the importance of nonproduction workers—for example, the white-collar jobs of executives, sales personnel, office workers, and engineers—as opposed to blue-collar positions. In manufacturing there were five production workers for each nonproduction worker in 1947. Today the ratio has been halved. While there may be disagreements about the net effects of technological advances—whether they have created more jobs than they have eliminated— there is little dispute that the occupational shifts have emphasized higher skills, both at the manual and intellectual level—definitely a step away from arduous, unskilled labor. The examples of coal miners displaced by automatic digging machines, stevedores by hoisting machinery, and clerks by automated billing and office machines are well-known, representative cases.

The movement of millions of workers from goods production to service production has not slackened the demand for labor. The fears or hopes of the prophets of cybernetics have not materialized, and instead of vast numbers of available but unneeded workers, the problem during the last half of the 1960s was more one of labor shortages in highly skilled occupations than surpluses, and even in the slack labor markets during the next decade the demand for labor continued to expand—not only in absolute numbers, but the ratio of employed workers to the total working age population continued to rise.

Industrial Distribution

Despite the reduced relative importance of employment in goods-producing industries, manufacturing remains the largest single provider of jobs (Table 4-3). Its share of employment grew from 21 percent in 1900 to 30 percent in 1947. Since then the relative importance of manufacturing as a source of jobs has declined to 23 percent of total employment. Nevertheless, manufacturing employment in 1979 stood at 21 million, not far below the all-time peak reached in 1969. The largest employers were the durable-goods industries, reflecting growing consumer demand for televisions, autos, and other consumer capital goods and, in the 1960s, the immense production of the American armaments industry.

The major growth in employment occurred in the service-producing industries, with the government sector growing faster than any other major industry since World War II. State and local governments account for the largest share of public employees (eight of ten in 1979) and most of the

Table 4-3   DISTRIBUTION OF
EMPLOYMENT BY INDUSTRY, 1900, 1947, AND 1979

INDUSTRY	1900	1947	1979
TOTAL EMPLOYMENT[a]			
Thousands	26,278	51,772	96,945
Percent	100.0	100.0	100.0
Goods-producing industries	69.7	50.9	32.2
Manufacturing	20.8	30.0	22.6
Durable goods	——	16.2	13.7
Nondurable goods	——	13.8	8.9
Mining	2.4	1.8	1.0
Construction	4.4	3.8	5.0
Agriculture	42.1	15.2	3.6
Service-producing industries	30.2	49.1	67.8
Transportation and utilities	8.7	8.0	5.6
Trade	9.5	17.3	21.7
Wholesale	——	4.6	5.6
Retail	——	12.7	16.1
Finance, insurance, real estate	1.2	3.4	5.4
Services and miscellaneous	6.6	9.8	18.3
Government	4.2	10.6	16.8
Federal	——	3.7	3.0
State and local	——	6.9	13.8

SOURCE: Data for 1900 are from C. G. Williams, *Labor Economics* (New York: Wiley, 1970), p. 1617; data for 1947 and 1979 are from *Employment and Earnings* (March 1971), 21, 49, and (January 1980), 178 and 204.
Note: Detail may not add to totals due to rounding.
[a] Agriculture includes wage and salary, self-employed, and unpaid family workers. Data for other industries exclude self-employed and unpaid family workers.

growth. The federal payroll increased by less than half between 1947 and 1979, while state and local employment more than tripled to almost 13 million. One-half of the state and local gains made during the past decade has been in education (schools account for half of all state and local workers).

Retail and wholesale trade, providing one of every five jobs in 1979, has doubled its share of employment since 1900. This growth has been an important source of employment for women and youth entering the labor force, and it came about despite the industry's increasing reliance on self-service techniques, automatic materials-handling equipment, and vending machines.

Employment in the heterogeneous service industry group—varied personal, business, health, and private educational services—almost tripled its share of total employment between 1900 and 1979. Private medical and health services experienced the largest gain, with private hospital employment accounting for about half that expansion; this reflects higher standards of health care and extension of private medical insurance plans as well as Medicare and Medicaid programs.

Occupational Distribution

Technological innovation, together with the shift from goods-producing to service-producing industries, caused significant occupational changes (Table 4-4). Among white-collar workers, professional and clerical workers have accounted for the bulk of the employment gains made during this century. Together these two categories grew from 2 million to 33 million. Managers and sales workers have grown less spectacularly; totaling 3 million in 1900, these groups accounted for 17 million in 1979. The wide variations in relative growth demonstrate that increasing white-collar employment has not been entirely an explosion of executives and experts. Rather it reflects the increase of a variety of information-based jobs, including numerous paper-pushing tasks.[11]

An analysis of specific occupations within these broad categories reveals more about the changing character of work. Among professionals and technicians, teachers have always been the most numerous group, and their numbers continue to increase rapidly. By 1970 there were more elementary schoolteachers than the total of all doctors, lawyers, and natural scientists in the nation. The fastest relative growth, though, has been among college teachers—from 7,000 to 545,000 during the century, having quadrupled since 1950. The increase in the number of teachers in the workforce has been slowing in the 1970s. The number of teachers other than college is actually declining.

Medical specialists are second in importance among professional and technical workers. Most of the employment increase in this field has come from occupations that have been added to the health-care field (for exam-

Table 4-4 DISTRIBUTION OF
EMPLOYMENT BY OCCUPATION, 1900, 1950, AND 1979[a]

OCCUPATION	1900	1950	1979
TOTAL			
Thousands	29,030	58,999	96,945
Percent	100.0	100.0	100.0
White-collar workers	17.6	36.6	50.9
Professional and technical	4.3	8.6	15.5
Managers, officials and proprietors, except farm	5.8	8.7	10.8
Clerical	3.0	12.3	18.2
Sales	4.5	7.0	6.4
Blue-collar workers	35.8	41.1	33.1
Craftsmen and foremen	10.5	14.1	13.3
Operatives and kindred	12.8	20.4	15.0
Laborers, except farm and mine	12.5	6.6	4.8
Service workers	9.0	10.5	13.2
Private household	5.4	2.6	1.1
Service workers, except private household	3.6	7.9	12.1
Farm workers	37.5	11.8	2.8
Farmers and farm managers	19.9	7.4	1.5
Farm laborers and foremen	17.7	4.4	1.3

SOURCE: *Employment and Earnings* (January 1980): 173; and U.S. Bureau of Census, *Historical Statistics of the United States* (Washington, D.C.: GPO, 1960), p. 74.
[a] Not directly comparable. Figures for 1978 are employed persons 16 years and older; for 1900, gainful workers; and for 1950, labor force figures.

ple, nurses, medical technicians, and paramedics) rather than from increases in the traditional medical professionals, such as physicians, dentists, and pharmacists. In fact, physicians and surgeons have declined as a percentage of the labor force and the population. In 1900 three of four medical professionals were either doctors or dentists. Today only one in five holds one of these titles.

Third in numbers, and one of the fastest growing of all occupations, are engineers, who numbered 1.4 million in 1979. Virtually all of these jobs have been added to the economy since 1900, when only 38,000 engineers were at work.

Except for teachers, most of the employment gains in the professional and technical fields have come in occupations that were unknown or numerically insignificant in 1900. This continues to be the pattern as technological, educational, and scientific advances determine the types of jobs created in the economy. Hundreds of thousands of accountants, computer specialists, draftsmen, social workers, and many others are employed today in professions that barely existed 70 years ago. The time-honored professional fields—doctors, lawyers, clergymen—are not only losing importance among the professions but are shrinking in proportion to the labor force as a whole. Occupations developed in the past 70 years have instead come to dominate professional employment.

In the burgeoning clerical field secretaries, stenographers, and typists are by far the most numerous, outnumbering teachers as the largest single occupational group. These occupations have grown to 4.8 million during the century, an increase of over 3,400 percent since 1900. This demand for secretaries shows no sign of diminishing. During the 1960s, 1.5 million secretaries were added to the labor force, a greater increase than the total number of assemblers in manufacturing. Other occupations that have gained dramatically in the past two decades are cashiers, bookkeepers, bank tellers, and office-machine operators. Each has more than doubled in the past 20 years.

The growth of clerical workers has paralleled the increase in the employment of women in the labor force. In 1900 the 212,000 women working in clerical occupations constituted 4 percent of all female workers and less than a hundredth of the total labor force. In 1979 the 14.1 million women in clerical occupations accounted for over one-third of workingwomen, one-seventh of the labor force, and four-fifths of all clerical workers.

The category of managers, officials, and proprietors has grown more slowly than either clerical or professional employment, and the patterns of growth have not been concentrated among a few occupations as is the case with professional and clerical work. But one trend operating through the past several decades has had an important effect on these jobs. Increasingly, managers are becoming employees rather than their own bosses. Since the advent of mass production and the demise of the handcraftsman, farmers and proprietors have been the last bastions of self-employment. But, evidently, both of these strongholds are under fire. In 1958, 3.5 million, or 52 percent of all managers, officials, and proprietors were self-employed. By 1978 the percentage of managers who were self-employed had fallen to 17. The entrepreneur and the small business owner are losing ground to bigger organizations, franchised outlets, and mass merchandising. The nation's managerial class is rapidly becoming a salaried group of employees, subordinate to larger organizational structures.

Similar factors have combined to slow the growth of sales occupations. Although the number of salesmen increased through the century, in the past two decades sales workers were a constant percentage of the labor force, despite a substantial rise in the dollar volume of products sold. The value of wholesale and retail real trade grew threefold from 1960 to 1979, but sales workers remained virtually unchanged at 6.4 percent of the work force. Trends toward larger sales units with self-service merchandising systems held sales employment back. Insurance and real-estate salesmen advanced more rapidly, but the bulk of sales positions—those in retail trade—expanded slowly.

Obviously, the facts of employment do not support the image of a white-collar economy peopled mostly with scientists and executives. Secretaries and typists outnumber all other occupations; clerical workers are the most numerous category by far. In the professional category noncollege teachers, paraprofessional occupations—draftsmen, nurses, and medical technicians—and artists and entertainers have accounted for more than a third of all new jobs. Though these workers indeed often wear white collars, it is misleading to add their jobs to the white-collar total and generalize about the changes in the quality of work.

Blue-collar work also disguises a multitude of barely related job experiences ranging from the proverbial tightening of bolts to handcrafting scientific instruments. Among skilled workers two occupational groups have accounted for most of the employment gains. First, repairworkers of all kinds have increased sharply in order to maintain the tremendous quantities of complex equipment and machinery needed in a postindustrial age. By 1979 repairworkers had displaced construction workers as the most numerous skilled workers. In 1900 skilled construction workers outnumbered repairworkers by nearly four to one. By 1970 repairworkers had multiplied ninefold to 2.8 million, representing nearly a third of all craftworkers and surpassing the 2.7 million construction craftworkers. The vast accumulation of fixed capital, equipment, machinery, and durable goods has shifted much of the employment of skilled manual workers to maintenance rather than initial construction.

A second development among skilled workers has been the increase of foremen. From 162,000, or 5 percent, of skilled blue-collar workers in 1900, foremen have increased to 1.7 million in 1979—13.2 percent of manual workers. This growth has been especially rapid during the past three decades. Production units of greater size and complexity and technology of greater sophistication have apparently raised the needs for first-level supervision in production. Together, foremen and repairworkers have accounted for 60 percent of the growth of skilled trades since 1900 and for 75 percent of that growth since 1940.

In contrast to craftworkers, semiskilled operatives are typically employed as machine tenders in manufacturing industries. In 1979 almost two-thirds of the 14.5 million operative jobs were in manufacturing industries. Two million of these workers operated various powered machines, while over a million were assemblers. Other large groups included 810,000 sewers and stitchers, 746,000 checkers, 185,000 painters, and 626,000 packers. However, during this century the greatest growth in operative employment has occurred in jobs associated with transportation rather than manufacturing: bus, truck, and taxi drivers and parking-lot and service-station attendants. These automobile-created occupations, nonexistent at the turn of the century, now employ 3.6 million individuals, one of every four operatives.

Evidently, beneath a surface of stable employment growth some significant changes have occurred in blue-collar work. Technology and economic growth have shifted blue-collar work toward repair, supervision, and transportation. None of these types of work conforms to the stereotype of blue-collar work—that is, the routine of the factory or assembly line.

The service category is even more diverse in skill and social status than the blue- and white-collar categories. Except for those with a clearly professional skill (for example, doctors), workers who provide health care, prepare and serve food, protect property, and clean or perform valet services are classed as service workers.

At the turn of the century, most service jobs were those of servants in private homes. That is, 60 percent of service workers were in private households. Today, private servants have given way to publicly available service workers shared by a broader group. In 1979 the number of private household workers dropped to 1.1 million, only 8 percent of the expanded service sector. Instead, restaurant workers have replaced personal butlers and cooks, and charwomen have supplanted live-in maids. The luxuries of personal attention are no longer loyally reserved to the few most wealthy but more often are sold to all comers in the open market.

This trend can be clearly seen in two of the fastest-growing sectors of the service industry: food service and cleaning occupations. Food service occupations (waiters, cooks, bartenders, and associated occupations) and cleaning jobs (maids, janitors, charwomen, dishwashers, etc.) numbered almost 7 million by 1979. The unpleasant daily tasks of cleaning and fixing food have been partly eliminated by machines, prepackaged foods, and throwaway containers, but the work that remains is more and more done by paid servants who perform these duties for many "masters."

The growth of institutional health care has stimulated the increase of nonprofessional hospital service jobs. As in the food and cleaning services, this development represents a shift away from work done at home to that paid for in the market. Care of invalids, once primarily the responsibility of the household and the visiting doctor, has now been almost entirely contracted out. Emptying bedpans, changing sheets, and taking temperatures, formerly the work of friends or relatives, now are paid occupational tasks occupying more than a million people.

These sharp rises in the demand for service workers are the logical outgrowths of affluence and technological advancement. With machine-supported production able to provide goods for all and with substantial purchasing power in the hands of many, desires for personal services have grown. Accenting this evolution has been the shift of women from the house to outside jobs, and the corresponding shift of the burden of many home and personal maintenance tasks formerly done by unpaid wives to hired, outside servants. To a large extent, former domestic services have been incorporated into the public domain. Though much the same type of work is being done, it is now less the private privilege of the few or the duty of the wife than service contracted to specialists. Because many people no longer wish to be burdened with these tasks, new institutions have been established to provide the services.

THE GROWTH OF PRODUCTIVITY

Though both the characteristics of the labor force and the occupational and industrial mix of the labor market have shifted substantially over the past several decades, the productivity of the workforce has continued to rise, although at a curtailed rate during the 1970s. Productivity is defined as the ratio of output (goods or services) to the inputs to production (labor, capital, energy, etc.). Most productivity measures, which are simply shorthand notations for the overall efficiency with which industry uses natural and human resources to fulfill society's needs, have trended upward and continue to do so, albeit at a slower pace.

There are many alternative productivity measures. One common index—output per workhour—measures the productivity of a single input—labor. The routinely cited figures concerning American productivity are such output-per-workhour measures, compiled by comparing the total value of all goods and services (in constant dollars) produced in the nation—the GNP—with the total number of hours paid. Other measures record output per unit of capital. Estimates for individual firms or industries are important in corporate investment planning, for example, in determining how many barrels per day a new refinery must produce in order to repay its cost of construction. Other more complete indexes combine and weigh all input factors to arrive at a single figure for overall productivity. There are also narrower measures that record the efficiency and usage of a single resource, for example, the board feet of salable lumber that a sawmill can cut from a given quantity of logs or the kilowatts of electricity that a power plant can generate from a certain quantity of fuel.

Each of these productivity indexes has specific uses. Output per workhour is useful for determining how fast wages can rise, since over the long run, real compensation per hour closely parallels output per hour. The overall efficiency indexes comparing output to weighted input of both capital and labor may be used to compare industries or national economies with each other. The relative strength of currencies, the need for new capital investments, or the impact of substituting capital and labor may be determined from such productivity indexes.

Despite the assumed certainty of published figures such as "productivity rose 0.5 percent during 1978," there are numerous problems with the measurement of productivity.[12] First, few of the data collected by federal or private establishments are designed specifically for measuring productivity. Production figures, workhour totals, or capital investment estimates are collected separately, by different statistical agencies and from different surveys.

Second, the measurement of various inputs presents difficulties. For example, though the concept of workhours seems straightforward, does it include coffee breaks, "downtime," paid sick days, or vacation time? And the more complex issue is: Are hours of labor by various employees of equal value—is the company president's time at $50 per hour equal to the janitor's hour? In general, most indexes count only hours actually spent on the job in productivity indexes, and some weigh workhours by wage differentials.

The measurement of capital inputs is even more difficult. The value of plant, equipment, land inventories, and other factors is greatly affected by accounting and depreciation methods. Moreover, the flow of capital—that is, the capital actually used in production—is even more difficult to gauge than the value of capital stock. The only truly accurate measure of capital input would be a record of the hours each type of capital is utilized, multiplied by the rental value. Obviously, such detailed and complex computations are seldom possible.

Third, the measurement of output can also be quite tricky. Though some physical outputs lend themselves to easy computation—for example, the number of bricks that a mason can lay per day—most are less clear. Issues of quality are important; for example, the production of a ton of tool steel is not equivalent to a ton of cast iron. Continuous changes in products and the introduction of new products make longitudinal comparisons difficult. When counting identical goods is not possible, productivity must be gauged by the dollar value of the output, which, of course, must be adjusted for price changes. Price deflators depend largely on components of the consumer and producer price indexes. To the extent that these indexes only adjust for quality changes associated with a rise in producer costs, real output and productivity may be underestimated.

The difficulties with measuring output are nearly insurmountable in the case of service industries, particuarly government, and in the construction industry. Since new buildings vary widely in purpose and value, construction output is usually approximated by the dollar value of the structures, adjusted for price changes. But structure value is largely a function of the labor and materials required in construction, so that productivity indexes for construction tend to be cost indexes that show little change in output per unit of input.

In service industries, where the output is often intangible, measures of productivity are usually based on the dollar value of services, deflated for price changes. As in the case of construction, this method depends on the adequacy of the price index. Government services, which are not bought and sold, must be approximated by wage rates and employment figures. These indicators, however, will reveal no change in labor productivity, since the output and input measures are identical. As a result, government is usually excluded from national productivity totals, which is unfortunate, since government directly employs about a sixth of all workers.

These limitations indicate that considerable research and data collection must be initiated before firm conclusions regarding changes in productivity may be drawn. Yet the most carefully constructed productivity indexes point up significant long-term trends.

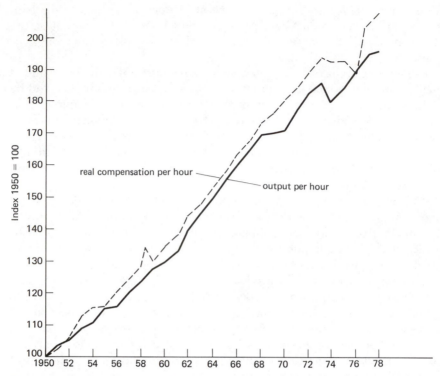

Figure 4-2   Output and real compensation per hour, private business sector, 1950–1978. (Source: *Economic Report of the President,* 1980 (Washington, D.C.: GPO, 1980), pp. 382–384.)

Since 1900 U.S. productivity has improved steadily (Figure 4-2). Annual fluctuations have been quite varied depending on the business cycle and the impacts of advances in technology. There was little improvement during the depression, for example, and quite rapid acceleration following World War II. From 1900 to 1950 the rate of increase averaged about 2 percent per year. In more recent years productivity growth has varied, averaging 2.8 percent from 1950 to 1960, jumping to 3.8 percent during 1960–1965, and receding to 2.3 percent for the next eight-year period. Productivity growth continued to decline to an average of 1.1 percent per year between 1973 and 1977. These figures for the whole economy smooth out wide differences in industries. Generally, agriculture and the goods-producing industries have made the greatest gains during the century, while service industries, which have been less able to substitute capital for labor, have shown smaller increases in output per workhour. Farming, in which productivity growth has averaged about 4.7 percent per year since 1950, has led the way, but other goods-producing industries have also registered sharp gains. Hosiery, radio and TV, household appliances, concrete products, and petroleum products all raised output per workhour by more

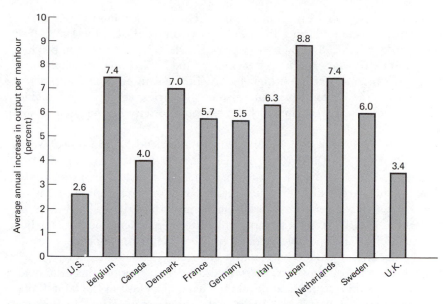

Figure 4-3   Annual productivity gains, 1960–1977. (Source: Keith Daly and Arthur Neef, "Unit Labor Costs in 11 Industrial Countries, 1977," *Monthly Labor Review* (November 1978):12.)

than 60 percent during the 1960s. Some goods producers, however, have registered slower gains, for example, auto, steel, and iron.

Some service industries have increased output at rates that equal goods producers. Air and rail transport and utility industries benefited by rapid growth that made possible great economies of scale. Each raised productivity by an average of 6 to 8 percent per year between 1950 and 1973. Most other service industries, such as trade, insurance, and banking, though they raised productivity some by applying technology, mass marketing, and self-service concepts to their enterprises, were unable to improve productivity as fast as the rest of the economy.

The decline in productivity gains after 1973 affected most sectors of the economy, goods-producing and service industries alike.[13] Mining, air and railroad transportation, and public utilities have experienced sharp declines in annual productivity rates. Still, productivity increases remained high in many industries, particularly hosiery, telephone communications, paints and allied products, and synthetic fibers. Auto, household appliances, metal cans, synthetic fibers, and petroleum pipelines were showing sharp increases in output per workhour with the economic recovery in 1977.[14]

Compared to other countries, U.S. productivity is still considerably greater, but this advantage has narrowed in recent years (Figure 4-3). In 1960 it was estimated that U.S. workers produced about twice as much per hour of labor as most other industrialized nations, including Japan, the U.S.S.R., and Western Europe. With growth rates of about 5 percent per year in Europe and 14 percent in Japan, however, foreign nations closed this gap appreciably during the 1960s, particularly during the last half of the decade, when U.S. productivity grew slowly. The slowdown in productivity after 1973 was experienced by most of the industrialized nations. Still, their growth rate remained higher than in the United States except for Sweden and the United Kingdom. In some industries, notably the manufacture of steel, West German and Japanese productivity has equaled or surpassed U.S. levels.

There have been various explanations advanced for the slowdown in productivity in the United States since the mid-1960s. Many believe that changing attitudes toward work are acting as a check on productivity growth, but there is little evidence for this hypothesis, although incentives to work may have eroded as a result of the growth of the welfare state. By the end of the 1970s, total government transfer payments nearly equalled one-sixth of total disposable income. Another factor presumed to account for the decline in productivity is that good old "Yankee ingenuity" is not what it used to be. However, there is also little to support this argument. Expenditures on research and development did level off in the later 1960s, and remained flat during the 1970s, but cannot account for much of the drop in productivity gains.[15]

The slowdown in productivity growth is a development that we should have expected. The reallocation of labor from agriculture to more productive sectors of the economy, a major reason for productivity gains in the 1950s and early 1960s, leveled off in the later half of the 1960s as surplus farm labor was depleted. Another factor behind the productivity track record is a less experienced workforce. In 1965, the proportion of the workforce under 25 years of age was 19 percent, compared to 25 percent in 1978. The labor force participation rate of women had risen from 39 percent in 1965 to 50 percent in 1978. The entry of new groups into the workforce most likely reduces productivity temporarily, until the labor market can adjust to the changing composition of the workforce. The increase in government regulations, diverting resources from measured production to promote clean air and water and safer work and living environments, has also reduced officially measured productivity. But from a social point of view, has real productivity fallen when accidents in the workplace are reduced and society also benefits from a cleaner and safer environment? Only as a country becomes richer can it think of spending scarce resources for these goods and services. The link between business cycles and productivity has been established. The sharp drop in productivity after 1973 coincided with the sudden increase in OPEC oil prices, the rise in the cost of other new materials, and loose labor markets. Capital investment has also slowed in recent years. With a surplus of workers and a decline in the capital-labor ratio, productivity either declines or grows very slowly because firms are not able to operate plants at optimum, efficient rates.

In the future, productivity growth in the United States should continue to improve at a more moderate rate than has prevailed in the two decades following World War II. Some have argued that an economy dominated by service industries may not be able to sustain past rates of growth in productivity that were characteristic of the goods-producing economy. Goods-producing industries were able to double their output between 1950 and 1970 with only a small increase in the number of workers. Based on extensive studies of the service industries Victor Fuchs concluded that the growth in productivity per worker since World War II in the goods-producing industries was twice as great as in the service industries; as the proportion of workers engaged in service industries increases, he argues, economic growth will necessarily slow.[16]

But the shift of employment to services in which productivity growth is slow will be offset by the continuing application of sophisticated technology to most industries. Though rates of advance will be uneven, the overall trend will continue upward. On the other hand, it may be expected that other countries' rates of productivity growth may be faster than that of the United States because of the increasingly rapid diffusion of technological know-how and the growing penetration of multinational companies in the world markets.

The continued growth of American productivity is crucially important if Americans are to continue to enjoy the improvements in standards of living that they have come to expect and if they are to sell their goods on a competitive basis abroad. Ultimately, improvements in the quality of life and increases in leisure time must stem from the productivity gains. Unless wage gains are backed by increased output, they merely inflate the money supply and result in no real gain. Thus productivity growth is one of the most important tools for controlling inflation. In the same way, as the productivity gap between the United States and other industrialized countries shrinks, the maintenance of foreign markets for U.S. goods will depend on productivity keeping pace with wages.

DISCUSSION QUESTIONS

1. What factors have accounted for the continual increase in the number of part-time workers? Is this trend likely to continue?
2. Since the turn of the century, there has been a long-term decline in the labor force participation rates of males and old people, and an increase in the participation rates of women below age 55. Examine the major factors responsible for these trends.
3. Youth and older workers experience unique employment problems. What are they and how can policymakers help to alleviate them?
4. Economists often speak of "primary," "secondary," or "segmented" labor markets. What do they mean?
5. Discuss the concept of secondary labor market(s) and its public policy implications.
6. What kinds of labor market adjustments are necessary as a result of the dy-

namic shift of demand by employers for workers with higher education and skills?
7. The rise of the "service economy" has increased the service industry's share of total employment, but has not increased its share of national output. Discuss.
8. Why do some economists feel productivity growth should decline as the U.S. economy becomes more dominated by the service industries?

Notes

1. Dean Morse, *The Peripheral Worker* (New York: Columbia University Press, 1969).
2. William V. Deutermann, Jr. and Scott Campbell Brown, "Voluntary Parttime Workers: A Growing Part of the Labor Force," *Monthly Labor Review* (June 1978): 3–10; and John D. Owen, "Why Parttime Workers Tend to Be in Low-Wage Jobs," *Monthly Labor Review* (June 1978): 11–14.
3. "A Cure for Unemployment?," *Business Week* (October 29, 1979): 163–164; and Sar A. Levitan and Richard S. Belous, *Shorter Hours, Shorter Weeks: Spreading the Work to Reduce Unemployment* (Baltimore, Md.: The Johns Hopkins University Press, 1977), pp. 61–66.
4. U.S. Department of Labor, *Employment and Training Report of the President, 1979* (Washington: GPO, 1979), pp. 81–83.
5. Edward Kalachek, *The Youth Labor Market* (Ann Arbor, Mich.: Institute of Labor and Industrial Relations, University of Michigan, January 1969), p. 55.
6. U.S. Department of Health, Education and Welfare, Public Health Services, *Health: United States 1976–1977* (Washington, D.C.: GPO, 1977), p. 12.
7. Herbert Parnes et al., *The Pre-Retirement Years*, U.S. Department of Labor, Manpower Administration, Manpower Research Monograph No. 15 (Washington, D.C.: GPO, 1970), (cf. p. 21, n. 17), vol. 2, p. 7.
8. U.S. Bureau of Census, *Current Population Reports*, "Money Income in 1977 of Families and Persons in the United States," series P-60, no. 18 (Washington, D.C.: GPO, 1979), tables 46 and 59.
9. U.S. Bureau of Labor Statistics, *Work Experience of the Population in 1977*, Special Labor Force Report 224 (Washington, D.C.: GPO, 1979).
10. Employment and Training Administration, *Employment Related Problems of Older Workers: A Research Strategy*, Research and Development Monograph 73 (Washington, D.C.: GPO, 1979).
11. The discussion is based on Sar A. Levitan and William B. Johnston, *Work Is Here to Stay, Alas* (Salt Lake City, Utah: Olympus, 1973), pp. 88–93.
12. Albert Rees, "Improving the Concepts and Techniques of Productivity Measurement," *Monthly Labor Review* (September 1979): 23–27.
13. Joint Economic Committee, *Hearings on Employment and Unemployment* (Washington, D.C.: GPO, June 1979), pp. 228–230.
14. Arthur S. Herman, "Productivity Increased During 1977 in a Majority of Selected Industries," *Monthly Labor Review* (September 1979): 54–57.
15. Edward F. Denison, "Explanations of Declining Productivity Growth," *Survey of Current Business* (August 1979): pp. 15–18.
16. Victor R. Fuchs, *The Service Economy* (New York: National Bureau of Economic Research and Columbia University Press, 1968), p. 47.

Chapter 5
Measurement and
Forecasting

Sophisticated measurement techniques and extensive data gathered over the years by governmental and private organizations have given us a clear picture of the changing patterns of American work. As a nation we have been fortunate in having such extensive data, although there is room for improvement. The challenge is to interpret the data wisely and apply the lessons learned to achieve societal goals.

COUNTING THE LABOR FORCE

The United States has one of the most comprehensive flows of labor market information in the world. Each month the Bureau of Labor Statistics and the Employment and Training Administration, working with other federal, state, and private organizations, collect and publish a detailed history of the previous month's labor market activity.[1] These analyses and statistical reports include estimates of (1) the size, marital status, and demographic composition of the population aged 16 years and over; (2) the number of workers by occupation, hours worked, age, sex, and color; (3) the number of filled jobs in industries and average weekly hours and earnings for nonsupervisory personnel; (4) the total number of persons actively seeking work and the number drawing jobless pay; the extent of strike activity, recent collective bargaining settlements, and pending negotiations; and (5) trends in wages, productivity, and unit labor costs.

Other federal agencies provide information on (1) total income flow earned from both past and present work or resulting from other transfer payments; (2) investments in training, especially formal education; (3) employment by industry (e.g., manufacturing) or by profession (e.g., scientific and technical personnel); and special analytical measures such as full-time equivalent employment and income.

Special data have been developed to supplement the recurring monthly and annual data. These special studies, which are designed mainly to portray labor market interactions at more detailed levels, include surveys of the poverty population, federal program participants, and longitudinal labor force participation and work-experience studies.

Because of the great expansion of labor market information and research in the past three decades, analysts can verify most labor market measures by comparison with an alternative, totally independent source. Until 1940 there were no reliable estimates of the current employment status of the population aside from the decennial censuses, and even that information had serious conceptual flaws for the analysis of labor market conditions.

This vast flow of labor force data, collected from thousands of individual households and firms, comprises a keystone for the formulation and implementation of monetary and fiscal policies and federal, state, municipal, and private training programs. These same data figure prominently in business research and planning and in private research.

Major Data Sources

The manpower statistics now in wide use originate from four major sources; (1) *household surveys,* including decennial censuses, monthly current population surveys, and special surveys; (2) *employer surveys,* including industry censuses, monthly payroll reports from individual firms, and special industrial studies; (3) *administrative statistics* drawn from the operating records of the Social Security Administration, the Employment and Training Administration, the Commerce Department, and various regulatory organizations such as the Interstate Commerce Commission; and (4) longitudinal surveys conducted by private organizations under government auspices. Each source has its own strengths, weaknesses, and unique conceptual and methodological properties. Together, however, these sources provide a network of labor force information. They differ in collection techniques and concepts, but are unmatched in detail useful for macroanalysis while providing a considerable body of microanalytical data.

Labor Statistics Before World War II

The decennial census, required by the Constitution, was not intended to provide labor force information. It did, however, furnish data on population, the human resource base from which all labor force analysis departs. By the mid-1800s the decennial census started to collect tidbits of economic intelligence, notably industrial employment estimates.[2] In each subsequent census the volume of employment information was expanded and refined as new departments and agencies sought to cope with the problems of a growing nation. Designed for other purposes (mainly political apportionment and tax assessment), the censuses became a vehicle for the collection of employment data and are virtually the only source of national socioeconomic information for the 1800s. Because of collection and definitional weaknesses, these early employment data are of limited analytical value.[3]

Employment figures gathered in the censuses of the early 1900s were based on the so-called gainful worker concept. Individuals were recorded as gainfully employed if they reported a trade (occupation) that provided money income or its equivalent. This concept had no time reference and tended, therefore, to exclude unemployment—most of the unemployed had held a job of one kind or another—and to inflate the employment figures further because those who had retired also had a gainful occupation. During the late 1930s, the gainful worker concept—which provided a useful inventory of occupational skills—was displaced by the more precise activity-oriented concept now in use.

SOCIAL PROBLEMS AND STATISTICAL DEVELOPMENT

Most present-day labor market information systems were byproducts of programs designed for other needs, or else thrown together in response to large-scale socioeconomic crises. As a result, available information has grown erratically, almost haphazardly. Major developments and improvements of labor force statistics closely followed and largely resulted from the Great Depression of the 1930s, the post–World War II recessions, the concern of federal officials with the nature and origins of poverty in the late 1960s, and federal policies in the 1970s aimed at the distribution of funds based on local labor force statistics.

The state of other arts also affected the evolution of the information network. Breakthroughs in communications, data processing, methods of statistical analysis, new methods of data collection, sampling techniques, and other factors played an important role in the growth of data systems, as did the consolidation of the reporting and analysis of labor market information in the Department of Labor in the late 1950s.

There has always been a certain ambivalence in the collection and analysis of employment and unemployment statistics, arising from differences in the objectives of the users. Some analysts, concerned with the welfare implications that may be drawn from the statistics, focus attention on the conditions and availability of jobs, with special reference to the impact of unemployment. Since the 1960s, the data have been used extensively in analyzing resource use, with a special view to the elimination of labor bottlenecks and the promotion of long-term growth. Oscillations between the two views have coincided with cyclical swings in unemployment.

Based on the old practice of blaming the messenger for the bad news, it was inevitable that the collectors of labor force statistics would be criticized by some when they reported unwelcome news. As the credibility of the employment and unemployment figures came under severe analytical and political attack, President Kennedy in 1961 appointed a panel of experts to appraise the employment and unemployment statistics.

The Gordon Committee

The presidental committee chaired by Professor R. A. Gordon—hence the Gordon Committee—interpreted its mandate widely. It examined and reported on the concepts, techniques, prospects, and problems involved in all major labor force data series then in existence.[4] The committee's report was significant mainly because it synthesized past statistical experience and clarified certain conceptual and methodological problems and recommendations for the future development of labor force information systems along resource-use lines. The report set the tone for the further development of labor market statistics in the 1960s and 1970s. Aside from its substantive contributions, the committee gave the collectors of employment and training data a clean bill of health and made special efforts to remove labor force data collection from the political arena.

Concepts and Sources: Their Current Status

The concept of employment used in labor force statistics is based essentially on remuneration, not work. The labor force statistics, therefore, exclude the work of homemakers, students, and volunteers. The service of homemakers provides the minimum equivalent of about one-fourth of the total GNP in unpaid domestic service annually. Volunteer work is also very important. A 1974 survey by the Census Bureau estimated that volunteer work equaled about 3,500,000 full-time, year-round workers.[5]

Also excluded from the statistics are groups engaged in illicit or otherwise unreported activities. The exclusions are based not on conceptual or moral objections, but rather on difficulties in obtaining such data. The subterranean economy is causing increasing concern as an estimated ten percent or more of total income remains unreported and eludes tax collectors. The persons involved are from all walks of life, ranging from lawyers and doctors to taxi drivers and roadside vendors. Illicit activities are estimated to generate roughly one-third of the unaccounted earnings.[6]

The inadequacy of statistics on undocumented workers, foreign-born workers who enter this country illegally, gained increased attention during periods of high unemployment in the 1970s. Estimates of the illegal alien population vary widely (from 4 to 12 million) and are based on the skimpy information available through immigration records of apprehended un-documented aliens. Fear of deportation has thwarted efforts to register illegal aliens.

HOUSEHOLD SURVEYS

The unemployment rate has an enormous impact on government policy and public opinion, but it is one of the least understood and most controversial statistics issued by the government. No single definition of what constitutes unemployment has ever been devised that is acceptable to all political and economic groups. The unemployment statistics used today are rooted in the Great Depression. When mass unemployment in the 1930s underscored the need for reliable current statistics, experiments with household (or population) surveys were begun. These efforts were sound in design but lacked the necessary objectivity because the definition of unemployment was based on a person's reported willingness and ability to work. The concept was dependent on the interpretation and attitudes of both the interviewer and interviewee. A more objective and rigorous standard had to be devised. A group of economists, statisticians, and sociologists in the Works Progress Administration developed a more objective measure based on actual activity during a specified week. Responsibility for the national sample survey (begun in 1940) was ultimately passed to the Bureau of the Census, and the survey (now the Current Population Survey, or the CPS) continues to utilize essentially the same concepts and methods today.

Although technical in detail, the concepts and definitions used in the CPS are very simple. The labor force consists of all employed and unemployed persons who are at least 16 years old. For purposes of the survey, people are counted as employed if they worked a single hour during the survey week for pay or profit or worked without pay 15 hours or more in a family enterprise. People who had regular jobs but were temporarily absent during the survey week for such reasons as vacation, illness, strikes, or bad weather are also counted as employed. Specifically excluded are those whose activity was confined to unpaid housework or to unpaid volunteer work for charitable organizations. Counted as unemployed are persons who were not working during the reference period, were available for work and had engaged in specific work-seeking activity within the prior four weeks, were waiting to be called back from layoff, or were waiting to report to a new job beginning within 30 days.

Excluded from official unemployment figures are discouraged workers, persons wanting employment but who are not looking for work because they feel none is available to them. The need for information on persons not in the labor force but who might be competing for new jobs was recognized by the Gordon Committee. The data are collected along with information on employment and unemployment by the CPS. To be counted as a discouraged worker, CPS respondents must state that the reason for not seeking work is because they believe no jobs are available to them due to economic conditions, employer biases, or lack of skills. Discouraged workers are classified among those not in the labor force rather than among the unemployed.

The CPS includes in the labor force civilians (16 years and over) who are not in institutions. Because it is useful to know the importance of defense demands on the labor supply, official figures from the Department of Defense on the size of the armed forces are added to the civilian work force to provide an estimate of the total labor force. Persons who are neither employed nor unemployed—mostly homemakers, students, disabled, and retired workers—are considered "not in the labor force."

Monthly employment and unemployment data are obtained by skilled interviewers from a sample survey of about 70,000 households. At the Bureau of the Census, data from the sample households (for the calendar week including the 12th of the month) are then "blown up" to national totals. Most data from this CPS are cross-classified by demographic characteristics such as age, sex, color, marital status, occupation, hours of work, and duration of and reasons for unemployment. The survey also provides data on the characteristics and past work experience of those not in the labor force.

Special CPS supplements also yield information on work experience in the prior year, income, marital and family status, and multiple jobholding. Since October 1978, the CPS has collected information on weekly earnings from households in their last month in the sample. The earnings information is reported quarterly. Other supplementary data are collected annually. Most contemporary labor market analysis is based on material drawn from CPS or the decennial census.[7]

EMPLOYER SURVEYS

The oldest continuous employment series is the *payroll employment* data, which date back to 1919. The monthly establishment survey data are derived directly from payroll records of participating private firms, government units, and nonprofit organizations. This monthly series is the best source of information on trends in wage and salary employment and a major source of information on hours of work paid for, average hourly and weekly wages of production and nonsupervisory workers. Compiled from mail questionnaires, the series covers a sample of firms employing nearly one-third of the work force.

Some kinds of work do not fit in the establishment employment definitions because they do not appear on a normal payroll record. Excluded are the self-employed, domestics working in private homes, unpaid family workers, and agricultural workers. Employment estimates for these groups are drawn largely from household surveys and administrative statistics. Information on agricultural workers is estimated from a limited number of establishments sampled by the Agricultural Establishment Survey.

Wage and salary employment is also measured in the *monthly household survey* (Current Population Survey, or CPS). Because of conceptual and methodological differences the count of persons with wage and salary *employment* differs from the number of jobs counted on payroll records.[8] The most important difference is multiple jobholding—a person may hold two jobs but is only counted once in the household survey. There are also differences attributable to unpaid absences from work. If no payroll entry occurs for a person, then no payroll job is recorded in the survey of firms. However, he is counted as employed in the household survey if he is away on an unpaid vacation, personal business, on strike, or for similar reasons. Another limitation of the employment survey is an underestimation of smaller firms. Workers in all occupational fields are sampled by the household survey.

The household survey is wider in scope than the establishment data. It covers all forms of employment, including self-employment, unpaid family workers, private household workers, and agriculture—all of which are excluded from the industry employment estimates based on employer reports. Each of these sets of data makes a unique contribution to the understanding of employment trends. The industry survey concentrates on industry and geographic detail, while the household data focus on characteristics of the employed, including age, sex, education, and occupation.

ADMINISTRATIVE STATISTICS

Administrative statistics tend to reflect the peculiarities of the program for which they are collected and, therefore, cannot be conveniently lumped into a simple classification scheme. Important labor market data are derived from Social Security files and from insured unemployment coverage and claims records. Both programs are limited in coverage but provide detailed data of considerable analytical significance. The Social Security figures cover employment by size of firm, geographic location of employment, and some earnings data. Insured unemployment claims—persons reporting a week of unemployment under an unemployment insurance program— comprise a cyclically sensitive cross-check of the total unemployment estimates and are available in considerable geographic detail. However, unemployment insurance data do not measure total unemployment because they exclude persons who have exhausted their benefit rights, who have not earned rights to unemployment insurance, and who have lost jobs not covered by unemployment insurance.

LONGITUDINAL DATA

Other sources provide longitudinal data on the labor force. Compared to the cross-sectional time series gathered by the CPS, longitudinal series or panel surveys trace the same individuals over time. The information gathered from repeated interviews can aid in identifying underlying flows in the labor market and behavioral patterns. The collection of longitudinal data on the labor market, primarily sponsored by government agencies other than the Bureau of Labor Statistics or the Bureau of the Census, has grown significantly over the last decade. In addition to the use of administrative records previously mentioned, there are a number of special surveys that have been developed for tracking samples of individuals.

A major source of such data is the National Longitudinal Survey (NLS) of labor market experience sponsored by the U.S. Department of Labor, and conducted by the Bureau of the Census and the Ohio State University's Center for Human Resource Research. The survey collects information on specific demographic groups considered to experience difficulties in the labor market. It includes data on current labor force status, wages, hours, family income and assets, health, training, work history, social-economic background, attitudes, and personality characteristics.

A Panel Study of Income Dynamics (PSID), sponsored by the U.S. Department of Health and Human Services, is carried out by the Survey Research Center of the Institute for Social Research at the University of Michigan. Information is collected from a national sample of 5000 families on labor market, family income, economic, social, psychological, and attitudinal attributes in order to understand the dynamics of change in economic status.

Another source, the Continuous Longitudinal Manpower Survey (CLMS) tracks a national sample of enrollees in federally supported employment and training programs. The survey is designed to provide information to assess the impact of efforts under the Comprehensive Employment and Training Act. The more recent Survey of Income and Program Participation (SIPP) planned for the 1980s by the U.S. Department of Health and Human Services and the Bureau of the Census, will generate longitudinal data on income linked to employment status and demographic information. The survey will also identify the source of family income which will aid in analyzing the impact of social programs on reducing poverty and their relationship to labor force participation.

In addition, the CPS has the potential for longitudinal analysis. Households selected for the CPS are interviewed for four months, dropped from the survey for eight months, and then interviewed for an additional four months before leaving the sample permanently. Under this 4–8–4 rotation, one-third of CPS sample households can be followed to the same month a year later, providing a very large longitudinal sample. However, the gross change data collected by the CPS are more susceptible to sample bias than the cross-sectional data. Because of these defects in the CPS longitudinal data, the Bureau of the Census has not made the information available to the public.

THE NATIONAL COMMISSION ON EMPLOYMENT AND UNEMPLOYMENT STATISTICS

Despite improvements brought about by the Gordon Committee report, there is always a need to periodically assess the adequacy of labor market statistics in light of changing economic trends and the use of data by policymakers. The activist role taken by the government since the 1960s toward combating poverty, discrimination, and structural unemployment has brought about a need to improve and expand available information on the labor market. A growing need to understand the dynamics behind aggregate employment and unemployment figures, to analyze local labor markets, to identify disadvantaged groups, and to evaluate progress toward policy goals contributed to the demand by users of the data for more detailed labor force information.

The structure and dynamics of the labor market had also changed. Women, particularly married women with husbands present, and teenagers, cohorts of the postwar baby boom, entered the labor force in unprecedented numbers. The increase in the number of families with more than one earner and the greater availability of unemployment benefits and other transfer payments reduced economic hardship caused by unemployment. It was also suggested that these factors contribute to a higher level of unemployment by allowing longer periods of job search.

The need to improve the data system became critical in the 1970s, as federal policies increasingly depended on unreliable state and local statistics as the basis for distributing funds. The demand by policymakers for reliable statistics for over 6000 political and geographic subdivisions was beyond the capabilities of the data system without additional research and funding. The question of biases in the distribution of funds became acute as federal allocations to local areas expanded to over $15 billion in some years.

Reflecting the need to review the labor force reporting system and to assess its relevance to current conditions, Congress established the National Commission on Employment and Unemployment Statistics (NCEUS). The commission presented 88 recommendations that, if adopted, would tighten labor market definitions, illuminate labor market dynamics, and enable Congress to establish sounder guidelines for allocating funds to states and communities to deal with employment and unemployment problems.

Labor market concepts would be updated and measured more objectively. Among the changes recommended, the commission advised including the military in the national—but not local—labor force count; changing the methods of identifying discouraged workers; and the collection of additional data on movements into and out of the labor force, including wages and occupations sought by the unemployed as well as job changes among employed persons. Possibly the most significant commission recommendation dealt with the need to link data on labor force status to income. The additional information would illuminate the dynamics of labor force experience, particularly for disadvantaged groups, and aid in measuring the extent of economic deprivation related to unemployment.

To derive more frequent and reliable state and local data, the commission recommended improvements in current techniques and expansion of current data bases. The Current Population Survey, if expanded, could provide more reliable annual data for states and major metropolitan areas, as well as for minority groups and rural areas throughout the nation. Expansion and improvements in the establishment surveys would also be helpful. Another potential source of information on local labor markets are the upcoming mid-decade censuses. Changes in the present techniques of estimating more frequent state and local statistics and those for smaller areas would offer only incremental improvements in their accuracy. Congress was advised to rely on annual data in distributing federal funds.

A review of the labor force count necessarily involves consideration of many highly technical issues. Among the most significant of these were seasonal adjustment and undercounting of the population, especially minorities. The commission favored changes in present practices for making seasonal adjustments on a more current basis. It also recommended changes in CPS estimates to compensate for the census undercount.

Despite the conceptual appeal of collecting job vacancy data, the technical difficulties and costs involved prompted the commission to recommend against collecting such data. In a related area, the commission emphasized the need for improving workforce data currently reported by employers including occupational data. Many important data series, including productivity, wage, and hours statistics, are based on employer reports.

FORECASTING WORK FORCE SUPPLIES AND REQUIREMENTS[9]

The Employment Act of 1946 stimulated interest in the size of the labor force for which jobs were to be provided "for all of those able, willing and seeking to work." In the 1950s creeping unemployment, often attributed to a mismatch between available and demanded skills, intensified the need to foresee changes in labor force supply and demand. The development of new employment and training programs in the mid-1960s and the 1970s increased demands for advance information about work force changes. At its best, forecasting is a critical ingredient in advance planning, encouraging the realistic appraisal of the likely costs and benefits of differing programs to facilitate a reasonable distribution of scarce resources. It is also used for individual career planning, market research, policy evaluation, and analysis of socioeconomic objectives.

The Nature of Labor Force Projections

Projections and forecasts are often differentiated, but in reality the difference lies in the confidence of the forecaster. After examining past trends, the projector develops a working model of the system. Assumptions about how the important variables are likely to behave in the future are developed and then applied to extend the past performance of relevant variables. Accuracy in projections is largely a function of the realism of the assumptions and the identification of all relevant variables; consequently, the cardinal sin of the projector is failure to make his assumptions explicit. Confusion also stems from failure to differentiate between descriptive projections (what is likely to be) and normative projections (what ought to be). Users of projections must take note of the underlying assumptions and appraise their validity; they should avoid reading into long-range forecasts an implied commitment to an imputed straight-line trend at intermediate points.

In the United States projectors generally emphasize descriptions that may enable decisionmakers to make more rational decisions. As various forms of public planning become more accepted in the United States, policymakers will be forced into a more serious consideration of the labor market implications of their decisions.

In summary, forecasts are based on implicit and explicit assumptions concerning the nature and direction of future trends. Because anticipated expectations are rarely met, forecasts should be regarded as "most likely" approximations. With all these caveats competent long-range labor supply and demand forecasts can, nonetheless, influence decision making because they (1) illuminate likely bottlenecks and imbalances in particular segments of the labor market, (2) indicate the likely consequences of instituting changes in existing programs or introducing new programs, and (3) provide an estimate of the total human resource pie by helping to price out societal goals in labor terms, to choose among these goals when necessary, and to move them along the least-cost path.

Projecting Labor Supplies and Requirements

Forecasts may be calculated in a wide variety of ways, ranging in complexity from simple linear extrapolation of past trends to complex econometric models. Each technique has its own special properties of detail, conditional restraints, and applicability to reality.[10] Because they are based on known population levels and longstanding trends in labor force participation, projections of the potential total labor supply are quite reliable as long as there are no radical departures from past practices. For example, labor force projections underestimated the increased entry of females into the workforce in the 1970s. No reliable base exists, however, from which to project labor supplies by skill level or any qualitative element other than educational attainment. Thus few attempts are made to project the supply of skills. However, this is not a serious loss, since few jobs have fixed skill requirements. Most employers vary their requirements to suit the state of the labor market, while the workers' mobility renders projections of supply by occupation and industry of little value.

Because employment levels in modern economics are in large part the consequence of public policy, levels of labor demand are subject to guess. Projectors have resorted to two major approaches with little practical difference between them. One assumes a level of unemployment based either on a normative or descriptive judgment. The other is to project GNP on the basis of assumed future growth rates and estimate the consequent employment. Neither method is very reliable, but in any event the purposes of the analyst are usually best served by projections of the *structure* of labor demand rather than the *level* of total demand.

When the structure of labor requirements is projected, total assumed GNP is distributed among industries on the basis of further assumptions regarding national economic goals. These are translated into anticipated patterns of consumption, investment, and government spending. Projecting requirements is especially difficult because the priorities assigned to national goals may change radically. The massive mobilization of scientific and technical personnel in the space program in the 1960s illustrates a radical alteration of national priorities that affected the composition of labor demand. Similarly, a rigorous pursuit of alternative energy sources may cause sharp departures in occupational and industry labor force projections for the 1980s. In addition, goals are heavily determined by private units, which may sharply and quickly change their demand patterns. Finally, innovations may alter the composition of labor demand and also modify the relative significance of different goals. Despite these difficulties, analysts are increasingly engaged in assessing the likely patterns of demand, relating these demands to work force requirements, and measuring the requirements against the anticipated supply.

Overall labor forecasts, therefore, usually involve a two-pronged effort. On one side, technicians—demographers, statisticians, and economists—develop detailed projections of the probable labor supply in its quantitative and even qualitative aspects. On the other side, policymakers articulate needs, specify goals, and establish a scheme of priorities. The broad estimates are then brought together, yielding a view of the likely future interaction of labor supply and demand.

Uses of Labor-Force Projections

A major concern of government is to avoid mismatches between labor demands and supplies. Clearly, the minimum level of unemployment attainable with tolerable inflation and the speed with which it can be achieved are affected by the degree to which open jobs match the qualifications of available workers. This requires more detailed and reliable short-term and medium-term projections of the labor supply by age, sex, race, and skill than are currently available. In fact, usable projections are largely limited to long-term forecasts of the total supply of labor. These projections may also provide warning, however. For example, projected age and race characteristics of the labor force for the 1970s indicated growing imbalances between demand and supply unless traditional demographic employment patterns were substantially altered.[11] Projections for the 1980s portend continuing worsening imbalance for young black workers if their participation rates in certain occupations fail to increase substantially. Providing warnings of projected shortages (or surpluses) of teachers, medical personnel, or scientists and engineers is also a familiar use of these long-term projections.

Less familiar is the increasing demand for employment and unemployment projections created by three policy developments. First, welfare-, employment and training-, and education-oriented programs require assessment of employment requirements as well as dollar costs so that potential labor market bottlenecks can be noted and efforts made to avoid them. Second, the expanded role of government in the economy has increased the need to foresee the impact on employment and unemployment of government decisions, especially those involving defense and space efforts. Changes in labor demand resulting from evolving governmental policies accentuated the need for contingency plans to generate jobs for the diverse groups that are victimized by federal policies. Third, the threat of major technological change has aroused some interest in projections of regional, industrial, and occupational employment fluctuations. Such early warning signals might stimulate advance planning to ease the adjustment to change. Recent recessions indicate that little progress has been made in this area.

Educational planners, involved in decisions concerning physical facilities, finances, and curricula, are among those most persistently demanding projections of the future. Fortunately, the required projections are not as difficult as might be assumed. Buildings have a long life, but they exercise little constraint on curriculum choices, and financial needs depend primarily on the number of students. Curriculum planning requires relatively little lead time or detail because curricula are relatively uniform in elementary schools and high schools and, even at the college levels, concentrations are sufficiently broad to require comparatively little detailed anticipation of occupational choices.

Vocational education and apprenticeship are oriented to specific occupations and thus require detailed projections of the employment outlook. But the number needed for replacement and industry expansion almost always exceeds the number trained, and the gap is flexibly filled by those who pick up the trade outside the formal channels. The more specific the occupational training required, of course, the greater the need for projections. But lack of projections is probably less of a barrier to planning than structural and institutional difficulties: (1) Budgetary constraints are more to blame than is lack of information for the oft-noted (but probably exaggerated) obsolescence of vocational school equipment and curricula; (2) more information is available than is used; (3) there are no overwhelming obstacles to reasonably accurate two-to-five-year projections of local labor requirements; and (4) planning should not be based entirely on local projections—from a national viewpoint, for example, it would make sense to allocate expenditures in declining regions for vocational education deliberately aimed at providing training for future outmigrants.

Projection needs for counseling and guidance parallel those of educational planning. Persistent youth unemployment has caused dissatisfaction with the information available for counseling and making vocational choices. The standard source is the *Occupational Outlook Handbook*, a BLS publication that projects, for roughly a decade ahead, general employment trends in some 300 specific occupations. These occupations account for the vast majority of workers in sales, professional and craft occupations, and smaller proportions of other workers.[12] The *Handbook* has gained wide acceptance by educational counselors.

Interest in improving the occupational projections of planners, counselors, and educators spurred several new efforts by the BLS and the Employment and Training Administration to collect additional labor market information. Based on census data, a national industry-occupational employment matrix was developed by BLS, covering 200 industrial and 400 occupational sectors. Similar state matrices are being developed by state employment service analysts. To help the states expand their matrices and improve their capabilities in occupational projections, the Employment and Training Administration is supporting the collection, in most states, of more detailed occupational employment statistics by employer surveys. BLS abandoned, however, in 1973, experimentation in the collection of data on job vacancy because of questionable usefulness of the data.

Labor Supplies in 1985–1990

The working-age population (aged 16 years and over) will total about 173 million in 1985 and about 180 million in 1990. There are three different projections for labor force growth by the BLS, based on differing assumptions of high-, intermediate-, and low-growth paths. All three predict a declining rate in the growth of the labor force. The projection that the labor force will reach 113 million in 1985 may be made with considerable confidence. This means an average annual increase in the labor force of nearly 1.9 million compared with average annual increases of about 2.1 million between 1970 and 1977.[13]

Labor force growth is expected to slow down after 1985 because the working-age population will increase by only 1.5 million annually between 1985 and 1990. This slowing of population growth is definite because all the people who will reach working age between 1985 and 1990 have already been born. However, this anticipated growth in the workforce must also include changes in participation rates, which tend to evolve relatively slowly, while population changes generally are more important over the longer run. Between 1970 and 1977 the labor force participation rate of men declined by 2.0 percentage points, and using the intermediate growth path, is expected to decline by 1.2 percentage points during the 1980s due to the increased number of prime working-age men. In contrast, the more rapidly growing labor force participation rate among women accounts for more of the projected growth in the labor force. The labor force participation rate of women increased 7.7 percentage points during the 1970s and is expected to increase by another 3.7 percentage points by 1985, then slow down to a more moderate increase of 2.3 percentage points by 1990. However, a reversal of current trends in birthrates during the next decade could slow the growth in labor force participation of females in childbearing years.

The labor force changes constantly, renewing itself as older workers retire and are replaced by younger workers and reentrants. These gross flows resulted in very large labor force increases between 1960 and 1970 when 2.4 million 16- to 19-year-olds joined the labor force. The growth in the teenage labor force continued in the 1970s as a high proportion of young women entered the labor market. In the 1980s, however, the number of teenagers in the labor force will decline, reflecting the reduced birthrates of the 1960s. In the late 1950s the BLS correctly projected rapid expansion in the teenage workforce and suggested a probable deterioration of their employment situation. The slow growth and ultimate decline in the labor force in the 1970s and 1980s may improve the job opportunities for teenagers. While one major labor market concern of the 1960s and 1970s was the mounting of efforts to bring youngsters into the mainstream of economic activity, the 1980s may bring greater concern for offering career opportunities to more mature workers.

Labor force increases for persons just over 25 years of age are one of the dramatic and productive labor force changes of the 1970s. The same persons who flooded labor markets as teenagers and young adults in the 1960s and early 1970s—and in many instances were not absorbed for a long time—now appear as highly educated, full-time, year-round workers. In particular, the number of 25- to 54-year-old workers will increase enormously between 1980 and 1990—by over 1.8 million a year, to more than 83 million in 1990. By 1990, workers in this age group will comprise 70 percent of the labor force compared to 60 percent in 1970.

The number of workers aged 55 years and over is expected to decrease by almost 1 million in the 1980s, compared to less than 200,000 in the 1970s. The decrease in the number of workers in this age group reflects the comparatively few people born in the depths of the Great Depression and earlier retirements induced by greater availability of pension plans and transfer payments.

Dramatic changes are forecast in the average educational attainment of the labor force. The entrance of better-educated young workers at the same time that older, less-educated workers are retiring continues to tip the balance toward a higher and higher average educational attainment for the nation's working force. By 1990 more than four of every five persons in the adult labor force (aged 25 years and over) will have graduated at least from high school, and almost one in four (about 22 million) will have completed four years or more of college work—compared with 64 percent high school graduates and 15 percent college graduates or higher of the early 1970s. The decline in the number of workers at the lower end of the educational scale is perhaps more dramatic. In the late 1950s one-third of the labor force had only an eighth-grade education or less; by 1990 only 1 of every 16 workers will be in that group.[14]

Labor force increases for blacks will probably continue to be relatively larger than for whites in the 1980s, especially among younger workers and adult males. The black labor force is expected to rise by almost one-third between 1977 and 1990, compared with an increase of about one-fourth in the white labor force. The rapid rate of growth—which reflects a sharp population increase—raises the possibility of exacerbating the already high unemployment rates for nonwhite workers. However, higher levels of educational attainment and progress toward equal employment opportunities may combine to produce further improvements in the employment status of blacks.

Some Implications

The major conclusions of the new labor force projections are that (1) the rate of growth of the labor force in the 1980s will be only slightly less than during the preceding decade; (2) the teenage labor force, with its myriad of special problems, will begin to contract during the 1980s; (3) the number of young adult workers, ages 25 to 55, will grow at a rapid rate during the 1980s; (4) the proportion of women in the labor force will continue to increase—totaling 46 percent of the labor force by 1990, up from 41 percent in 1979; and (5) despite a continuing trend of declining labor force participation of black males, the black share of the labor force will increase from 12.1 to 13.1 percent by 1990.

The expected overall growth of the labor force should provide more than an adequate base for sustaining the economic growth of the 1970s. Even the slower growth of the labor force during the late 1980s may not necessarily induce lower rates of economic growth because the long-term rise in the educational attainment of workers offers potential for increases in productivity. The increased supply of educated workers should help relieve skilled-worker and white-collar bottlenecks caused by a shortage of mature workers. Unemployment problems for the young should be reduced because fewer youths will compete for jobs. However, increased education and training do not automatically mean the end of skilled manpower short-ages or of youth unemployment. Sending more youngsters to college will not train the plumbers, electricians, or other skilled workers who are in short supply; overemphasis on college education for white-collar jobs—which may pay less, have longer hours, and require little preparation—pre-sents the real possibility that some young people are being overeducated. As a result, they may lack jobs commensurate with their education at the same time that skilled jobs go unfilled.

With concern focusing on the potential surplus of highly educated workers, the plight of workers at the opposite end of the educational spec-trum should not be overlooked. Although their numbers are declining, their relative disadvantage compared to the average worker is increasing as the average worker becomes better educated. Entry-level job requirements may be adjusted up as employers perceive the rise of the educational en-dowment of the work force. Thus, despite their dwindling number, the na-tion cannot be complacent about the undereducated and untrained; em-ployment, training and retraining programs will need to be expanded to correct these serious deficiencies.

Occupational Projections

Projections of labor requirements by occupation depend largely on differ-ences in the rate of growth of segments of the economy. One way the growth and decline of industries has been forecast is by analyzing national priorities. Although national goals are not exclusively set by the federal gov-ernment, legislation and federal budgets have a great deal of influence throughout the economy.

Relative price tags are usually the first consideration in deciding whether goals and priorities are feasible. The employment and skill re-quirements demanded, however, do not necessarily follow. Analysts at the National Planning Association converted the national goals for individual and social welfare set by a presidential commission in 1960 (plus space ex-ploration) into labor costs and related them to the likely configuration of labor supply in the 1970s.[15] They concluded that full achievement of the goals would require about 12 percent more workers than were expected to be in the labor force by the mid-1970s.[16] The commission appointed by President Carter to design a national agenda for the 1980s is likely to en-counter similar concerns.

Other factors affecting occupational projections are the changing tech-nology within industries and the productivity of workers. Patterns of em-ployment in American industries are altered in response to innovations, and since the turn of the century U.S. employment has changed from agrarian to industrial to white collar. New jobs are created, and some skills become ob-solete. For example, since 1950 the computer has resulted in a variety of new technical specialists. Occupational projections for the 1980s indicate that the demand for professional workers to develop and use the computer will continue to grow while some clerical occupations—payroll and inventory clerks, for example—will contract.[17]

While the occupational mix will be determined by the choices made among national priorities, industrial growth, and technological changes, the direction of long-term trends in the broad categories of workers—white collar, blue collar, and farm employment—is not expected to be reversed (Table 5-1). The demand for professional and technical workers will increase faster than total employment. The strongest demands for professional workers will be in the computer and health fields. The growth in clerical employment is anticipated to remain strong through 1985.

The rate of growth of blue-collar occupations will fall short of the overall increase in employment, and as with white-collar occupations growth will be uneven. The largest increases will be in the skilled crafts that depend heavily on construction and manufacturing activity. During the early 1970s, the number of skilled mechanics and construction workers grew rapidly and began to balance the shortage in construction and mechanical skills noted in some areas during the 1960s. The demand for semiskilled and unskilled workers is expected to increase very slowly during the next decade, reflecting the continued replacement of repetitive mechanical and manual chores with automated techniques. Due to rising productivity on farms, the number of farm laborers will continue to decline into the 1980s.

The most significant barriers to attaining our national goals are the potential mismatches of supply and demand. These projections illustrate the need to intensify human resource efforts, developing the capabilities to re-

Table 5-1   PROJECTED OCCUPATIONAL
EMPLOYMENT, 1985 (IN THOUSANDS)

OCCUPATION	1977	1985
TOTAL	90,546	103,400
WHITE COLLAR	45,187	53,200
Professional and technical	13,692	16,000
Managers and administrators	9,662	10,900
Clerical workers	16,106	20,100
Sales workers	5,728	6,300
BLUE COLLAR	30,211	33,700
Craftsmen and kindred	11,881	13,800
Operatives	13,830	15,200
Nonfarm laborers	4,501	4,800
SERVICE WORKERS	12,392	14,600
FARM WORKERS	2,756	1,900

SOURCE: Max L. Carey, "Revised Occupational Projections to 1985," *Monthly Labor Review* (January, 1976), table 1.

spond to shortages and surpluses in labor with education, employment, and training programs that will facilitate economic growth.

The State of the Art

National projections do not provide a blueprint of the future, but they do signal the warnings necessary for sound fiscal, monetary, and employment policies. It was not for lack of knowledge that inadequate provisions were made for teachers and classrooms to serve the postwar baby boom or that insufficient jobs were generated to absorb veterans returning from Vietnam or engineers laid off in the aerospace industry or workers displaced by energy shortages. Employment policy that takes seriously the goal of "useful jobs for all of those able, willing and seeking to work" will pay more attention to the age, sex, and racial structure of the labor force for which jobs must be provided, but here too there is no lack of reliable knowledge. Demographic projections provide adequate guidance for 10 to 15 years ahead on growth potential, employment needs, and quantitative educational requirements. It would be useful to have more advance information concerning the qualitative characteristics of the labor supply, but provision of better education and broader skills is an adequate substitute for detailed projections.

At local and regional levels, projections are more difficult because changes are less likely to be washed out by crosscurrents. The first need, of course, is a consistent national policy of full employment to maximize opportunity and provide a solid base for local projections. The second is to proceed with a program of making projections, so that experience can be gained.

Educational planners have all the enrollment projections and ample information about their students' employment prospects that they need for planning general education. The shortages of elementary teachers in the 1950s, of high school teachers in the early 1960s, and the excess supply of teachers emerging now were not difficult to foresee, given postwar birth rates and college enrollment figures for the 1960s. What was lacking was not forewarning but sufficiently flexible institutions.

Planners of more employment-oriented types of education and training—apprenticeship and vocational, technical, and to a lesser extent graduate education—need more detailed projections. Counseling and guidance people have less information than they need, but, all too often, more than they use.

Serious obstacles to satisfactory adjustment in the work force are still posed by lack of knowledge concerning job content, skill requirements, and transferability of skills. Employers tend to require excessive education and training, in part because they do not know what skills a job actually requires. And without knowledge about the transferability of skills, neither the detail required of projections nor the appropriate content of training can be satisfactorily determined. Manpower planning by individual economic factors—workers and firms—is increasingly important. In the past, firms have planned production, investment, and expansion but rarely their labor needs. Some firms have discovered the road to high profits may lie in their ability to attract and hold good employees. Also, increasing sensitivity to human distress and to criticism for failure to avoid displacement brought some commitment to the principle of planning to adjust to reduced labor needs through attrition.

On balance, although there is need for improvement in labor force projections, their deficiencies are not a serious limiting factor in program analysis and decisionmaking. Methodological improvements can and should be made, but steps to improve the presentation and dissemination of available projections are probably more important. In the end, the manpower problems of the past few years cannot be blamed upon the lack of information concerning the future. Action, not information, has been the absent factor.[18]

Effort and resources might be invested in the development of manpower projections within the region, the locality, and the firm. Many organizations and individuals are involved in the projecting, and all are not equally expert. The work of the BLS is the soundest available; less sophisticated agencies, usually involved in projections of specialized types of manpower, would be aided by government-wide projection guidelines. More intensive research effort needs to go into understanding skill requirements and transferability. In the end, however, the main burden is on the projection user: Accept the fact that even with the best of techniques, the future will remain opaque; use projections with patience and wisdom; and have faith in the far-from-perfect but reasonable flexibility of the labor market and the adaptability of human beings.

DISCUSSION QUESTIONS

1. Why is there felt to be a need to periodically reappraise the nation's labor market statistics? Are they not good enough?
2. Is it useful to attempt to forecast labor market trends? What kinds of forecasts do analysts make and what problems are encountered in making such projections?
3. What assumptions underlie forecast of occupational projections? What practical use can be made of such forecasts?
4. How are persons "officially" counted as unemployed? as employed? Are those reasonable definitions? If Tom, Dick, and Jane did not work during the "survey week," how is it possible that Tom could be classified as "employed," Dick "unemployed," and Jane "not in the labor force"?
5. "Statistics are no substitute for judgment." Discuss.
6. Social scientists turn increasingly to longitudinal data as a tool of analysis. What features of these data are unique and why are they particularly useful for labor market analysis?

7. What are the major sources for estimating national and local unemployment in the U.S.? Analyze some conceptual problems in measuring unemployment.
8. Why is it useful to conduct separate surveys of employers and households to measure the same thing, such as employment?

Notes

1. Among the more important statistical publications are the *Monthly Labor Review, Employment and Earnings, Area Trends in Employment and Unemployment, Employment and Training Report of the President* (annual), *Current Wage Developments,* and *Unemployment Insurance Statistics.*
2. J. E. Morton, *On the Evolution of Manpower Statistics,* Studies in Employment and Unemployment Series (Kalamazoo, Mich.: Upjohn Institute for Employment Research, December 1969), pp. 36–51.
3. Stanley Lebergott, *Manpower in Economic Growth* (New York: McGraw-Hill, 1964).
4. The President's Committee to Appraise Employment and Unemployment Statistics, *Measuring Employment and Unemployment* (Washington, D.C.: GPO, 1962).
5. ACTION, "Americans Volunteer" (Washington, D.C.: ACTION, February 1975), p. 3.
6. *U.S. News and World Report,* "The Underground Economy: How 20 Million Americans Cheated Uncle Sam Out of Billions in Taxes" (October 22, 1979): 49–52.
7. William G. Bowen and T. Aldrich Finegan, *The Economics of Labor Force Participation* (Princeton, N.J.: Princeton University Press, 1969).
8. National Commission on Employment and Unemployment Statistics, *Counting the Labor Force* (Washington, D.C.: GPO, 1979), pp. 206–208.
9. This section draws heavily on Garth L. Mangum and Arnold L. Nemore, "The Nature and Functions of Manpower Projections," *Industrial Relations* (May 1966): 1–16.
10. Herman Stekler, *Economic Forecasting* (New York: Praeger, 1970), pp. 3–15, 92–102.
11. National Commission on Technology, Automation, and Economic Progress, *Technology and the American Economy* (Washington, D.C.: GPO, 1966), pp. 54–55.
12. U.S. Bureau of Labor Statistics, *Occupational Outlook Handbook,* 1978–1979 ed., Bulletin No. 1955 (Washington, D.C.: GPO, 1978), p. 3.
13. Paul O. Flaim and Howard N. Fullerton, Jr., "Labor Force Projections to 1990: Three Possible Paths," *Monthly Labor Review* (December 1978): 26.
14. Denis F. Johnston, "Education of Workers: Projections to 1990," *Monthly Labor Review* (November 1973): 22–31.
15. American Assembly, *Goals for Americans: The Report of the President's Commission on National Goals* (Englewood Cliffs, N.J.: Prentice-Hall, 1960).
16. Leonard Lecht, *Manpower Needs for National Goals in the 1970s* (New York: Praeger, 1969), pp. 10–11.
17. Neal H. Rosenthal, "The United States Economy in 1985: Projected Changes in Occupations," *Monthly Labor Review* (December 1973): 18–20.
18. National Commission on Employment and Unemployment Statistics, op. cit., pp. 106–117.

Chapter 6
The Structure of
Labor Markets

In modern times labor, as other factors of production, is allocated partly by labor markets and partly by institutionalized arrangements that may or may not reflect market tendencies. It is, therefore, important to separate basic market forces from these institutional arrangements. A major objective of this chapter is to discuss the operation of labor markets, in terms of the applicability of economic theory. Before doing this, however, it will be useful to discuss the role that theory can play in illuminating the operation of labor markets and in prescribing remedies for market-related problems.

ROLE OF THEORY

Theory attempts to identify certain basic underlying causal relationships. As such, its usefulness derives from its ability to simplify otherwise complex phenomena. Theory, therefore, is not a mirror reflection of reality. It is a simplified abstraction from the complexities of reality so as to focus on the few essential causal relations. As an abstraction, a theory cannot be described as being true or false. The test of its quality is whether it is useful or not useful in understanding interaction among variables and in predicting how change in one variable will effect the performance of dependent variables. Indeed, the factors discussed in some theories might not even be observable in the real world, where the basic factors may be obscured by others that are more apparent than real. For example, people tend to infer that unions "cause" inflation when wage increases are followed by rising prices. However, rising wages and prices may, in reality, be caused by other, more fundamental forces that are less obvious or measurable. It might even be difficult to measure the results of underlying causal forces because of timing problems. When, for example, do we start measuring the impact of union wage pressures on prices? The wage pressures might actually be caused by price increases that occurred *before* we started our measurements.

The fundamental generalizations or principles about causal relationships are more important to our understanding of the basic factors at work than a detailed description of real situations. This is true because the facts change constantly. Indeed, excessive descriptions can obscure our understanding of basic causal relationships.

Theory can also play an important role in policy formulation. Indeed, with inadequate theories or conceptual frameworks, correct policies can be formulated only by chance. For example, combating inflation or unemployment requires an adequate theoretical underpinning. Similarly, a theory of wages is necessary to an understanding of the probable impact of minimum wages on employment.

Different theories of labor markets prescribe different policies for the resolution of the problems of unemployment and unequal employment opportunities. In vogue recently has been emphasis on a dual labor market theory that assumes some secondary markets more or less separated from primary markets (traditional analysis treats the whole economy as essentially one big labor market). Those who believe in dual markets argue that the problems of disadvantaged workers, who are employed mainly in the secondary markets, cannot be solved with general monetary and fiscal measures that assume some national queue for jobs.

Although theories are very useful for simplifying basic causal relationships, they also pose certain dangers that must be guarded against. It is particularly important to remember that theories are *abstractions* and, therefore, only a starting point to understanding particular situations. Because a theory is based upon certain assumptions, the predictions that flow from it are *theoretical* predictions, which means that they will obtain only so long as the basic assumptions underlying the theory are valid in the particular situations being examined. Policy makers, however, often are not interested in theoretical predictions but in *actual* predictions; that is, they are likely to be interested in more than the economic tendencies underlying a particular situation. Policy makers must, therefore, be concerned about the various noneconomic phenomena that influence the economic variable. In the case of racial discrimination, for example, the theorists can claim quite correctly that competitive markets would tend to erode racial discrimination, and this would be an accurate theoretical prediction. However, it might not be an accurate prediction of events in the real world because social events and institutions such as institutionalized racism make it very difficult for the tendencies to work themselves out. For the policy maker, therefore, economic tendencies that are counteracted by social forces are merely *theoretical*, but not *actual*, predictions of events. It is important for the policy maker to understand the theoretical economic tendencies in order to adopt proper policies, but he must know more than that. He also needs to know the institutional setting within which a particular problem must be solved.

We must also be careful, when using theoretical constructs, to avoid letting theories lead to rigid analysis. For example, the theories designed to explain labor markets at one time might be very useful because the theoretical construct reflected the basic underlying relationships at that time. However, there is a danger that the theory will be used long after the basic underlying relationships have changed, and the theory is no longer useful in explaining the labor market. For example, a labor market theory adopted during the Middle Ages clearly would not be valid in the twentieth century, primarily because during the Middle Ages the labor market was relatively insignificant and tradition was a much more important determinant of wages. The development of the free labor market, therefore, requires modification of the theory of wage determination. As we shall see, theory also causes people to generalize and, therefore, to ignore basic differences among labor markets. And theory might cause rigidity by focusing on certain phenomena at the expense of others. Because the theories cannot always be validated in the real world and because they frequently are based on events that cannot be observed, it is very difficult to keep theories flexible enough to adapt to changing circumstances.

In conclusion, therefore, theories are very useful in helping to simplify very complex labor market phenomena, but we must be very careful to be sure that the theory has indeed focused on basic causal relationships and that it does not induce such inflexibility in thinking that important variables in a particular situation are ignored as we move from the theory to the policy level. As we discuss some of the various theories which have been proposed to an understanding of labor market phenomena and to predict probable results from changing forces, we will resist the temptation to characterize them as true or false. We will ask only whether they are useful or not for the particular purpose for which they were devised.

DEFINITIONS OF LABOR MARKETS

A market is ordinarily thought of as a place where exchange takes place, where demand and supply work themselves out. However, the term "market" is used in somewhat different contexts. In some cases it means a specific place where buyers and sellers physically come together to arrange exchanges. An example of this would be the longshoremen's market in a port city where workers "shape up" every morning for hiring purposes.

Markets may also refer to buyers and sellers who are not necessarily brought together physically, as, for example, the market for college graduates. Workers from many different and widely separated places might compete for the same jobs, and workers in the same local labor supply might compete for jobs widely separated from each other. (It also should be observed that the terms "labor market" and "job market" are used interchangeably.) Clearly, in this latter sense the labor market concept is an abstraction and refers merely to the area within which exchanges frequently take place. Moreover, labor markets might be worldwide for certain highly specialized workers like deep-sea divers, or purely local, as it would be for construction electricians. One might therefore best define a labor market as encompassing all of the various means by which communication flows between employers and job seekers so that hiring and other related transactions can occur.

The main functions of labor markets are (1) to fix wages and other terms of employment and (2) to allocate labor among occupations, jobs and employers.

THE NEOCLASSICAL THEORY

The most widely accepted theory of the labor market is the neoclassical or orthodox theory. Neoclassical theorists emphasize certain common theoretical concepts, even though there are many differences among them. Proponents of this approach emphasize the abstract nature of their formulations. They attempt to focus on the most significant causal factors determining wages and employment and abstract from all others. These abstractions make it possible to reach conclusions about many different matters—income distribution, health, wages, the allocation of labor, discrimination, and many other matters—on the basis of a few abstract and simplified concepts. With modifications neoclassical economists use the same simple mechanism to analyze entrepreneurial behavior, general equilibrium for the entire economy, and international trade.

The basic neoclassical formulation ordinarily assumes perfect competition, although the model can be used to examine less-than-perfect competition. In a perfectly competitive labor market the following factors would exist on the supply side: (1) Workers have perfect knowledge of the market, including information on wage rates and available opportunities; (2) workers are rational and respond to differences in rates of return, including wages and noncash benefits; (3) workers are perfectly mobile; and (4) workers are not organized and make their own decisions on accepting jobs and wages offered.

On the demand side, perfect competition requires: (1) full and perfect

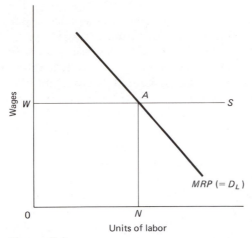

Figure 6-1

knowledge of the labor market by employers; (2) that employers are rational and attempt to maximize profits; (3) that no employer represents a large enough part of the total demand for labor to affect wages; and (4) that employers act individually, and not in concert, in fixing wages.

The competitive assumption is important to the neoclassical model because competition helps provide a rationale for universally applicable hypotheses. In the labor market, competition expresses itself in the form of actual and potential labor mobility.

The neoclassical model also assumes individual decisions to be stronger than group or class interests. Moreover, institutional arrangements are assumed to be constant and not to change while the system is moving toward equilibrium. This assumption is necessary in order to make the model determinant.

THE MODEL

The basic neoclassical model assumes that wages and employment are determined by demand and supply. According to the theory, demand is determined by the marginal productivity of homogeneous units of labor. Marginal productivity (or marginal revenue product [MRP]) is determined by the contribution to an entrepreneur's total revenue from selling the product of an added unit of labor. This becomes the demand for labor which for the firm can be depicted as shown in Figure 6-1.

The *MRP* curve slopes downward and to the right because of diminishing returns as additional units of labor are added. Under less than perfectly competitive conditions the *MRP* curve also will decline with additional units of labor because it is assumed that the price must be lowered if these units are to be sold, whereas under competitive conditions it is assumed that the entire output can be sold at existing market prices. Under competitive

Figure 6-2

conditions the supply curve of labor to the firm will be *WS*, as depicted in Figure 6-1, which means entrepreneurs could hire all of the labor they want at the existing wage. Equilibrium will, therefore, be where this supply curve crosses *MRP*, or the demand curve. At this point the firm's profits are maximized; at any lower level of labor utilization additional workers would contribute more to revenue than to cost ($W < MRP$), so that it would pay a firm to expand. At a level·of labor utilization larger than the equilibrium point, costs increase more than revenue ($W > MRP$), so profits must be falling. Where $W = MRP$, employment and wages of the firm are determined.

THEORY OF LABOR SUPPLY

Because it is based on marginal productivity, the demand side of the neo-classical wage-employment determining process is theoretically more de-veloped than the supply side. This presents some real theoretical problems, most of which are associated with the workers' inability to separate their labor from themselves. Workers might wish to work less and enjoy more leisure as wages rise (the income effect). On the other hand, there is a ten-dency for workers to want to work longer hours at higher wages in order to substitute the things higher wages can buy for leisure (substitution effect). If the substitution effect prevails, the individual's supply curve, showing how much labor will be supplied at different wage rates, will be shaped as shown in Figure 6-2, indicating a willingness to sell more labor at higher wages. On the other hand, if the income effect prevails, the individual labor supply curve will be as depicted in Figure 6-3, indicating a willingness to sell less labor at higher wages.

As a result of individual differences, a worker's utility function—which is determined by a combination of consumption goods purchased in the market, consumption goods purchased at home (paid for by sacrificed lei-sure or the amount that leisure could be sold for), and leisure—cannot be

Figure 6-3

determined. In other words, we have no a priori way of telling whether the income or substitution effect predominates.

Similarly, the aggregate supply curve for the whole economy cannot be determined, although economists commonly assume it to be as depicted in Figure 6-4, indicating a positive ratio between wages and labor at lower wages (the *P-S* segment of the curve in Figure 6-4) and a negative relationship between labor supplies and income at higher wages (the *S'-P* segment of the curve in Figure 6-4).

The aggregate labor supply curve is determined by labor force participation rate (LFPR), which will, in turn, be determined by the tendency for workers to enter the work force at various wage rates and labor market conditions. Unfortunately, however, there are countermovements in labor force participation rates that complicate the analysis. For instance, when unemployment rises, the involuntary loss of jobs by some family members

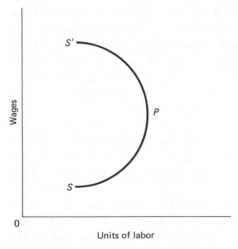

Figure 6-4

causes others to enter the labor force; this is the so-called additional-worker hypothesis mentioned earlier. If there are many additional workers in the work force, the official unemployment rate overstates the number of jobs needed to reach full employment because the additional workers will withdraw from the work force as unemployment rises. The presence of these discouraged workers causes the official unemployment rate to understate the number of jobs needed to restore full employment because presumably many of these discouraged workers would enter the work force in response to better job opportunities. The evidence suggests that during mild recessions, discouraged workers outnumber additional workers.

A number of implications grow out of the neoclassical theory. Some of these will be made clearer in Chapter 17 on the economics of discrimination. One implication of the theory is that workers are poor because of their low productivity. The obvious policy implication, if this is true, would be to increase workers' productivity through increasing their human capital, discussed in Chapter 7. Second, there is an assumption that income distribution tends to reflect differences in productivity, so that the theory tends to justify existing income distribution.

The marginal productivity theory also leads to the queue theory of the labor market, according to which employers are assumed to rank workers and potential workers along a single ordinal vector according to their respective productivities. Based on this concept, aggressive fiscal and monetary policies are advocated, increasing the demand for goods and services and, therefore, for successively less productive workers to produce that output. The theory can also support the use of training programs to enhance the productivity of various individuals, moving them ahead in the queues. In order for the queue theory to be valid it must assume fairly universal rankings throughout the economy. If different employers had different rankings, the relationships would be upset.

HUMAN CAPITAL AND BENEFIT-COST ANALYSIS

An extension of orthodox economic analysis into the human capital area has important implications for manpower programs. The concept of human capital, explored at greater length in Chapter 7, was adapted from physical capital investment theory by Gary S. Becker and Theodore W. Schultz during the later 1950s and early 1960s.[1] Human capital analysis was stimulated by concerns for poverty, economic development, the distribution of capital, and unemployment. Although the human capital concept had been around for some time,[2] it was not developed very much until the 1960s. It should be noted, however, that *the human capital concept depends heavily on the assumption that labor is in fact paid its marginal product* determined in factor and product markets. If labor is not paid its marginal product, human capital will not be a good measure of factor inputs. Moreover, the human capital concept forms the basis of benefit-cost analysis, which is widely used to evaluate human resource development programs. Benefit-cost analysis will, therefore, be limited by the theoretical defects in the neoclassical economic theory discussed in this and the following chapter.

EXTERNAL AND INTERNAL LABOR MARKETS

One of the first qualifications that must be made in the economists' traditional conception of a labor market is to distinguish the internal and the external labor markets. While the competitive neoclassical model concerns itself mainly with the so-called external labor market (that outside the firm or craft), the internal labor market concerns itself with the rules made within the firm or craft to fix wages and allocate labor among alternative uses. The internal labor market is controlled more by institutional rules that are not always compatible with the assumptions of the competitive labor market. For example, workers' wage rates and occupational positions within a manufacturing firm are much more likely to be determined by seniority than by relative productivity. These rules might be highly formalized if there is a union present, and they might be more informal if there is no union and the work group sets its own rules. In a very real sense, of course, there is no such thing as an unorganized work group because each group tends to be informally organized and to establish its own code of conduct and ethics, whether or not unions are present.

Because of these internal rules that govern the relationship between workers and employers, the employer does not necessarily act (in the internal labor market) as the competitive model assumes he will. For example, the employer is not very likely to cut wages in order to reduce costs as the labor supply schedule shifts to the right because he fully realizes that a wage cut could seriously damage the morale of his workers. Nor are employers always likely to increase wages when the demand for labor increases. To some extent, then, the internal labor market is isolated, at least in the short run, from the market forces of the external labor market. The main areas where internal labor markets are connected with external labor markets are what John T. Dunlop calls the ports of entry into the company.[3] These are defined as the points within the company at which the firm hires from the outside. Because labor market adjustments are not as volatile as the traditional theory assumes they will be, if employers equate wages with productivity, as competitive theory assumes, average wages must be equated to productivity for groups of workers over time because constant adjustments clearly are not made at the margin where marginal revenue equals marginal cost at any given time.

Clark Kerr has referred to the process of establishing institutional rules that structure labor markets as balkanization.[4] In Kerr's analysis institutional rules (among other things) cause labor markets to be structured. He cites Lloyd Fisher's description of the harvest labor market in California as a good illustration of a structureless market. Fisher defines a structureless market as possessing five conditions: "(1) There are no unions with seniority or other rules, (2) the relation between the employee and the employer is a transitory impersonal one, (3) the workers are unskilled, (4) payment is by unit of product, and (5) little capital or machinery is employed." In contrast to this, Kerr conceives of other markets as possessing various degrees of structure that can be caused by other things as well as the institutional rules. For example, many workers have skills that restrict their employment to particular occupations in which they seek work. Similarly, workers and employers form attachments for each other that are not lightly broken. Therefore, these customs and attachments tend to isolate the internal labor market from the operation of external forces.

The degree of isolation, or balkanization, to use Kerr's term, is increased with the establishment of internal rules that limit entry into the market and determine the movement of workers within those markets as well as their exit from them. In Kerr's words, once these institutional rules are established, "market forces seemingly impersonal in the aggregate, but exceedingly personal in individual situations, give way to personal rules which may seem exceedingly impersonal when applied to specific workers."[5] The main purpose of these rules is, of course, to establish control over the job territory for the people who are already in the market.

Kerr distinguishes two general systems of institutional rules, each with important subtypes. The first is communal ownership. This is the type of institutionalization typical of the building, printing, trucking, and similar trades. In this kind of labor market the workers assert control over all jobs in the labor market. The workers are likely to enter the market through unions rather than through employers because unions are likely to be the most stable elements in this labor market, partly because workers change jobs frequently in these casual markets. Moreover, the unions assert control over some traditionally managerial functions such as training. The unions will, therefore, establish fairly strict rules for admission into the market as well as the conditions under which people are allowed to work within the labor market. In this labor market the workers' loose tie to their employers is compensated for by a very tight tie to their occupation, and movement is, therefore, within the market and primarily horizontal rather than vertical. This is to say, workers can move about quite freely within the labor market once they gain entry into it. They have a strong identification with their craft, but they do not form strong attachments to particular employers. The significance of the union in the craft-type labor market is demonstrated by the fact that although the employer can remove workers from the job by discharging them, only the union can remove them from the market.

In the industrial situation, the second of Kerr's general systems, each worker tends to occupy his own job; when he vacates it, only one person is eligible to fill it. The group ordinarily establishes the rules, usually giving heavy weight to seniority to determine which workers will fill the job, although the workers' preference for seniority is often compromised by the employer's need to get the most productive people in particular jobs. In the industrial internal labor markets, therefore, seniority becomes much more important, and movement is largely vertical within families of jobs. The main contact of the internal and external labor markets is through the so-called ports of entry. Except for these ports of entry, competition among workers inside a labor market and those outside it tends to be very restricted.

> Competition among workers is reduced, the internal and external labor markets are joined only at restricted points, and within the internal market, craft jobs are likely to be fairly standardized and industrial jobs filled in accordance with seniority, so that workers are not actively contesting with each other for preference. Beyond this, the distribution of work opportunities by the craft union and the rehiring rights of the industrial contract tend to hold unemployed workers in a pool attached to the craft or plant and thus keep them from competing for jobs so actively elsewhere. . . .[6]

Reduced mobility is one of the main ways in which institutional rules isolate workers in the internal labor markets from external competition. The potential mobility of workers is the main sanction that makes wage rates interrelated. Once a worker builds up a certain amount of seniority in a plant, his mobility is undoubtedly restricted, and the penalty for his withdrawal from the internal labor market becomes greater and greater. It might, therefore, be very difficult for a worker to find another job with comparable pay and status if he withdraws from a particular labor market.

Peter Doeringer and Michael Piore developed the concept of the internal labor market more completely and related it more specifically to federal manpower policy.[7] Like Kerr, their concern is primarily with the formal and informal processes governing employment relationships and the forces that influence those processes. Key factors influencing internal manpower decisions include labor supplies in the external labor markets, the type of technology in the firm or industry, the value of the internal labor market to the firm's present work force, product market conditions, and customs.

A very important theme developed by Doeringer and Piore is:

> . . . that differences between the skills and abilities of the labor force are reconciled through a series of instruments which are controlled within the internal labor market. These instruments—recruitment procedures, training, compensation and the like—exist because a number of functions conventionally identified with the competitive labor market have been internalized to the enterprise. These instruments, individually and collectively, constitute a series of labor market adjustment processes by which the internal labor market adapts to changes in both production techniques and labor market conditions.[8]

As a consequence of these adaptive procedures, Doeringer and Piore tend to discount the argument that structural unemployment was a cause of rising unemployment rates during the 1960s. This, however, does not necessarily follow. Each firm can adapt labor forces of different skill levels to its own requirements and still avoid hiring large numbers of workers—like teenagers, women, and minorities—whose supplies have increased. Unless flexible wages or other benefits to entrepreneurs are assumed, there is no reason for employers to change their hiring practices to avoid hiring the workers they most prefer.

The internal labor market is generated by the specificity of skills to each firm, the prevalence of on-the-job training, and custom or unwritten rules based largely on past practices or precedent.

Doeringer and Piore challenge the neoclassical assumption that the internal labor market, which insulates workers from competitive markets, generates inefficiency. Many factors on which internal labor markets are based—the value of security and advancement to workers and savings to the employer in costs from recruitment, screening, training, and the reduction of turnover—cause efficiencies in labor utilization. However, there might be some inefficiencies resulting from attempts by workers to protect job security and ensure equitable treatment in internal labor markets. It has not been determined whether the efficiencies outweigh the inefficiencies, but there is a strong presumption that the internal labor market is, on balance, a force for efficiency.

Internal labor market analysis challenges the neoclassical assumptions that there are no fixed employment costs and that the employment relationship is temporary. Becker and Walter Y. Oi have worked out the implications of fixed recruitment, screening, and training costs within the framework of neoclassical theory.[9] It can be shown that these fixed costs create incentives for employers to establish more permanent relationships, but that profit maximization no longer requires wages to be equal to marginal products at any given time; workers can be paid more than their marginal products plus training costs at first and less than their marginal products plus training costs later.

According to Doeringer and Piore, however, Becker and Oi failed to emphasize

> ... the startling implications for neoclassical wage theory of the permanent employment relationship ... neither employers nor workers necessarily concern themselves with the connection between wages and marginal productivity at any point in time.... The disruption of neoclassical equivalencies between the wage and marginal product in each pay period ... involves the disruption of these equivalencies for a given job as well. The worker, therefore, may *never* produce enough in a particular job classification to cover his wages during the period in which he is employed in that classification.[10]

This means that wages are attached to *jobs*, not to workers as the neoclassical theory assumed. In a competitive society the wage for the job would reflect the marginal productivities of workers holding those jobs, but not in the internal labor market, which tends to be insulated from competitive forces. Moreover, the wage, even at ports of entry, is more likely to reflect the expected productivities of *groups* of workers than the productivity of *individuals.* Some workers are therefore paid more than their productivity is worth, while others are paid less. "In sum, the forces which in neoclassical theory yield a determinate wage establish, in the internal market, only a series of constraints."[11]

DUAL LABOR MARKETS

Another approach that has specifically challenged the neoclassical model is the "dual labor market" hypothesis. Economists have long known, that the labor market was balkanized or divided into noncompeting groups, but the dual labor market idea became more popular with scholars who were studying ghetto labor markets during the 1960s and early 1970s. These analysts at first studied ghetto labor markets in detail and then started reformulating some of the ideas of a segmented labor market developed by Kerr, Fisher, Charles Killingsworth, and others.[12] Although it is still more hypothesis than theory, the dual labor market concept is being developed more formally as a specific alternative to the neoclassical system.

Piore states the dual labor market hypothesis succinctly:

> The basic hypothesis of the dual labor market was that the labor market is divided into two essentially distinct sectors, termed the *primary* and the *secondary* sectors. The former offers jobs with relatively high wages, good working conditions, chances of advancement, equity and due process in the administration of work rules and, above all, employment stability. Jobs in the secondary sector, by contrast, tend to be low paying, with poorer working conditions, little chance of advancement; a highly personalized relationship between workers and supervisors which leaves wide latitude for favoritism and is conducive to harsh and capricious work discipline; and with considerable instability in jobs and a high turnover among the labor force. The hypothesis was designed to explain the problems of disadvantaged, particularly black workers in urban areas, which had previously been diagnosed as one of unemployment.[13]

Piore explains the separation of markets by a number of specific arguments, which he has refined and analyzed in some detail:[14]

1. Secondary markets are distinguished from primary markets by the behavior patterns, especially unstable employment, imposed on the workers in those markets. Employers and workers adapt to unstable conditions, and labor market institutions contribute to the perpetuation of these conditions. Welfare, for example, contributes to segmentation by providing such limited support that workers are forced into the secondary market. Unions operate mainly in the primary market and, therefore, contribute to the perpetuation of better wages, hours, and job protection in that sector. Unions have more difficulty in the secondary sector because the workers have

little power to win strikes. The Employment Service perpetuates secondary employment conditions by referring workers with the prescribed characteristics to secondary jobs. Workers tend to be barred from primary jobs not because of their lack of job skills but because they work intermittently and are not reliable.

2. Discrimination perpetuates segmentation by restricting certain workers to secondary markets not because of their education and skills but because they have superficial characteristics resembling most other workers in the markets. Doeringer and Piore emphasize that many workers in the secondary market have stable employment even though their jobs encourage instability.[15]

3. While technology influences the allocation of jobs between the primary and secondary sectors, many kinds of work can be performed in either sector and are where they are because of historical decisions to locate them there.

4. The behavior traits of workers in the various labor markets are reinforced by class associations. Jobs in the various sectors tend to be filled by people from particular classes. Piore defines mobility chains through which people pass. Workers enter these chains from a limited and distinct number of points that have economic and social significance.

   Thus people in a given job will tend to be drawn from a limited range of schools, neighborhoods, and types of family backgrounds; and conversely, people leaving the same school or neighborhood will move into a limited set of employment stations.[16]

5. A number of institutions and historical forces strengthen labor market segmentation. The importance of on-the-job training as a means of acquiring skills has increased the employer's incentive to hold some workers in more stable jobs, whereas other institutions have perpetuated instability. Migration of disadvantaged workers into urban areas perpetuates a supply of workers in the secondary markets. The lower-class subculture is mainly a function of the rate of migration into it by ethnic and racial groups already in a place relative to the new members.

The dual labor market approach deals with discrimination mainly as a factor in labor market segmentation, with no special theory of discrimination. Because of discrimination blacks have a high probability of being restricted to secondary labor markets. Moreover, once they get into these markets, the adaptive forces at work in that sector make it difficult for blacks to move into primary markets.

The dual labor market analysis is still in its formative stage and, therefore, it scarcely qualifies as a theory. So far, it is a classification system more than a theory. Moreover, the analysis and description apply to only parts of the economy and thus are not a complete system. Many labor markets, like those for craftsmen and independent professional and technical workers, do not fit neatly into the system. Moreover, the origin and causes of labor market segmentation are not satisfactorily formulated.

RADICALS

Evaluation of radical political economists is difficult because this group is not easily identified. Radicals apparently build on the work of multiple labor market analysts, but they add twists of their own. In particular, the work of radicals

> ... draws heavily on a precedent Marxist tradition, but it has molded and recast classical Marxism in response to modern social and historical developments; much of the classical Marxist methodology has been retained while some of the substantive generalizations of nineteenth-century Marxism have been revised to fit current realities.[17]

Like the dual labor market advocates, the radicals apparently do not have a well-developed theory of discrimination but assume, in addition to the technological and market forces producing labor market segmentation (especially the development of monopoly capitalism in the primary sector and competitive capitalism in the secondary sector), that capitalists segment labor markets in order to divide the proletariat and keep it from working as a unit in opposition to capitalism. Employers

> ... try to develop a stratified labor market in order to accomplish two complementary objectives. They were likely to seek, on the one hand, to minimize the extent to which those in jobs with less desirable working conditions could identify with those in more desirable jobs.... And employers were likely, on the other hand, to sharply segregate those blue-collar or secondary workers who could potentially identify with white-collar workers—and who might therefore develop class consciousness—from those blue-collar or secondary workers who were not likely to develop class consciousness, in order, obviously, to limit the potential costs of concessions to workers who made determined demands.[18]

Race enters radical analysis mainly as one means, among others, through which employers divide the working class. The radicals assume discrimination because of skin color to be mainly one form of discrimination by capitalists, who are motivated by a desire to maintain their power and increase the surplus value they can extract from workers.

The radical conception of discrimination is compatible with their overall purposes and methods. With respect to method, the radicals tend to apply global analyses, stressing the interaction of discrimination and what they consider to be the basic institutions of the capitalist system.

As a consequence of their systemic approach, radicals tend to concentrate on pervasive racism or discrimination. According to Raymond J. Franklin and Solomon Resnik, the "racist meaning of segregation in the American context derives from the fact that it is forced."[19] Moreover:

The legacy of white supremacy, as well as the legacy underlying the modes of black adaptations to a white-dominated society, are independent neither of each other nor of the present circumstances which define black-white relations. The white and black legacies—so frequently alluded to as independent streams of history—will not disappear until the present circumstances of inequality cease to operate in ways that parallel the slave and related conditions which gave birth to them.[20]

There appear to be a number of problems with the usual radical conceptions of exploitation. In the first place, these writers probably put too much emphasis on discrimination by employers and not enough on discrimination by employees. Moreover, it is doubtful that the assumption that a basic capitalist motive is to practice segmentation in order to divide the workers can be defended in every situation. It is true that employers used black strikebreakers, but this integrated rather than *segmented* labor forces in the long run. It also seems unlikely that employers always want racial division. We think employers are motivated mainly by profit maximization, and this might require segmentation to achieve such objectives as the prevention of unionization. On the other hand, with government pressures against discrimination and in favor of collective bargaining, employers would be foolish to promote racial conflict, which might prevent them from complying with the law or provisions in government contracts. In other words, profit-maximizing employers might use racial discrimination to increase their power and profits, but it is not possible to show that they always profit by racial strife. The radicals must strain, therefore, to build a model showing how employers always gain by conscious policies to divide the races. Employers in the primary sector, according to radical theory, are the main ones who refuse to hire blacks, while employers in the secondary market extract surplus value, or exploit them.

POLICY IMPLICATIONS OF INTERNAL, DUAL, AND RADICAL MARKET ANALYSIS

Recognition of the internal labor market supplies a number of useful insights. The concept suggests that training should be provided by each individual firm unless there are economies of scale. Most firms can do their own skill training, but they are not very well suited for general training in computational, verbal, or reading skills. Moreover, groups of firms, unions, individual workers, or governments must provide training that is not enterprise-specific because particular employers are not likely to incur the costs of training if they derive only partial benefits from it.

The internal labor market concept also suggests that the government should provide recruitment and training procedures to accomplish social objectives, like gaining greater employment opportunities for workers likely to be screened out by the firm's recruitment and screening procedures, but, if possible, firms will normally attempt to use the least expensive devices to recruit and screen their work forces. Employers will give heavy weight, for example, to procedures that will, with a given cost, maximize the probability of acquiring the kinds of workers they desire. If the public policy makers want to have blacks, the disadvantaged, or indigenous populations employed, they might adopt preemployment screening procedures to equalize the probability that employers will be able to obtain qualified workers from among these excluded groups. Indeed, to some extent manpower development and training programs accomplished this objective for employers by recruiting and screening workers who were reliable and trainable.

Internal labor market analysis suggests considerable flexibility in the processes whereby employers match workers and jobs. However, much of this information is specific to each enterprise, even though it would be useful to other employers and public policy makers. There is, therefore, a need for a clearing mechanism to collect information on the operation of internal labor markets, analyze this information, and disseminate it to labor market participants who can profit from it.

Internal labor markets also mean that many training, promotion, and wage-determining processes have powerful appeal to incumbent employees and employers. These internal processes are relatively isolated from external wage processes and labor market conditions. Increases in labor supply and unemployment in the external market will not necessarily reduce wages in the internal market. Similarly, unemployment in the external market will not necessarily prevent internal wages from rising. The internal market also influences the ability to reduce discrimination against blacks, women, or other excluded groups. The inclusion of new groups will be resisted because of the values of the internal processes even when there are no biases against the outsiders' personal characteristics.

But the interaction of the internal and dual labor market concepts supplies much more profound insights with strong policy implications.

Recent data have shown, for instance, that a dual labor market exists within the internal labor market as well as in the external market as many employers deliberately foster two separate labor forces in their establishments. They search extensively for, select carefully, and invest substantially in a core group of employees to whom they are prepared to make long-term commitments. For the rest of their work force, they prefer tenuously attached peripheral groups upon whom they can impose any fluctuations in demand. A major internal political struggle within unions as well as an issue between management and labor is the sharing of this job security and insecurity. For the peripheral worker, job search skills may be more important than the skill to do a particular job. As a result job turnover in U.S. labor markets is far greater than generally realized. For instance, the average nonagricultural job in the state of California has been shown to have 1.7 incumbents during each year while only 30 percent of those hired in the same state are still on the same job six months later.[21]

Within this selection process, employers treat quite differently the various labor supply sources. For those they recruit for the core employee group, or for whom union contracts or other institutional arrangements guarantee some degree of job security, they prefer sources with a great deal of qualitative certainty. Friends and relatives of current employees are a relatively known quantity somewhat guaranteed by employees' reluctance to accept the onus of having recommended an unsatisfactory new hire. Those who take the initiative to apply are accepted as more ambitious than those who wait passively for an offer. Academic credentials and membership in craft unions and professional associations are evidences of persistence and diligence as well as training and industry attachment. Want ads and public and private employment agencies are more likely to be used as sources of peripheral workers. Those who would become core employees or assist others to do so must know how to find access to the appropriate hiring stream.

The concepts of segmentation and shelters provide further insight into the external/internal relationship and the dual labor market.[22] Every incumbent employee who has a good job wants to protect it and those in casual labor markets whose attachment is to a craft but expect to circulate among the various employers in an industry want to protect and control access to all of those employers. Employees therefore seek to develop a variety of devices to shelter their jobs from external competition. They want a gate at the port of entry and they want to control the gatekeeper. Licensure, academic credentials, union and professional association membership are all examples of such sheltering devices.

Employers, on the other hand, want a screen, not a gate at the port of entry. They want to keep out high risk employees but provide maximum competition within the low risk group. They tend, therefore, to be ambivalent toward the segmenting and sheltering devices, sometimes embracing and sometimes seeking to circumvent them. Every shelter for an incumbent is a barrier for those not yet part of the in-group. The outs who would get in must learn the route at negotiating what is often a deliberately complex maze. Public policy makers must decide which sheltering devices are legitimate protections for the incumbents and which are unreasonable barriers to those without.

The dual labor market theory has undergone critical examination.[23] The barriers between the primary and secondary markets have been shown to be less impervious than originally thought. Most workers enter the labor force through the secondary market, but most eventually negotiate their way into the primary ranks. It is when particular age/race/sex and socioeconomic groups are found to be locked in and accumulating within the secondary labor market despite their attempts to break through the barriers that public policy must take a hand. Knowledge that such barriers exist is an important contribution to the theory but equally valuable is awareness that the barriers can be overcome with the assistance of appropriate policies and institutions.

The radical theories, on the other hand, appear to have made little contribution to the solution of either labor market or social problems. They theorize a world which does not exist. To hypothesize a world in which capitalist employers deliberately create a dual labor market for the explicit purpose of subjugating and exploiting a working class is to misread the dynamics and to formulate inoperative policies.

MULTIPLE LABOR MARKETS

The traditional economic theory and the dual labor market analysis must also be modified to account for broad differences among external labor markets. Within each broad classification, moreover, various submarkets could be analyzed, although we do not do so here. Public policy requires an adequate understanding of how these labor markets operate in order to avoid the mistakes that are likely to be made by assuming that the whole economy is a giant queue from which workers are hired on the basis of their productivity. If this were so, perhaps it would be possible to solve problems of unemployment and low incomes with aggregate economic policies alone. However, increasing aggregate demand by increasing the supply of money and spending through monetary-fiscal policies clearly has a differential impact on various types of labor markets. These aggregate measures might cause hyperinflation in some markets with no change in employment while leaving pockets of unemployment virtually undisturbed in other labor markets. The queue theory is, therefore, of some value *within* labor markets, but it has limited utility when applied to the whole economy.

Similarly, a dual labor market theory is deficient if it assumes that the economy can be neatly divided into two types of labor markets, in one of which workers have experienced considerable progress while those in the other lag behind. Similarly, it is not very useful to divide labor markets into such simple aggregate categories as agricultural and nonagricultural. There are many labor markets, but several broad classifications might be described as ideal types for purposes of illustration. Much more work needs to be done in order to identify and define types of labor markets and their interrelationships.

The Professional Labor Market

The first of these broad labor markets can be called the professional labor market. It comprises the various professions and is characterized by no tangible product and usually a high income elasticity of demand, which means that the demand for this kind of labor increases disproportionately with increases in incomes. Moreover, professional labor markets are characterized by very imperfect competition. Professionals often discriminate among clients according to their ability to pay, and often consider it unethical to compete either through advertising or price competition. The professional market also requires considerable formal education for entry. This market is imperfect compared with the competitive norm, not only because of the absence of competition but also because of the time lags for demand to adjust to supply and because professionals tend to control the supplies of labor in their professions through licensing and various forms of self-regulation.

The implications of this kind of labor market are clear. As national income increases, the income of professionals will increase, but there is no assurance that their productivity will go up, individually or in the aggregate. Indeed, there are very limited objective ways in which the performance of professionals can be measured by outsiders. Because of the imperfections in this market, professionals can raise their prices in accordance with their customers' ability to pay, need not be evenly distributed geographically, and are very difficult to regulate by indirect means. For example, how would a guidelines policy gearing salaries and wages to productivity operate in an industry in which there is no physical product?

Mainstream Labor Markets

The second market, which we shall call the mainstream, is characterized by extensive political and economic power, control of markets through product diversification and differentiation, considerable integration of production processes, the power to distribute products throughout a wide market, and ready or preferential access to credit and financial resources. Mainstream labor markets probably also have relatively high product-market concentration ratios, which means that a few firms account for large shares of total sales. The workers in this labor market usually require extensive training (either formal or on the job), have high skill requirements, are relatively well unionized, have considerable upgrading opportunities within the internal labor markets, and receive high wages. The firms in the mainstream also tend to be growth industries, with high ratios of capital to labor costs. Because of their political and economic power, the firms in the mainstream labor market are likely to have close interlocking relationships with various government agencies, particularly at the federal level but also at the state level, and account for a disproportionate amount of funds expended on government contracts. In short, the firms in the mainstream labor market are characterized by considerable power and prestige, and the workers in that labor market are likely to share that power and prestige through unions, which tend to be stronger in this labor market than in any other.

The Marginal Labor Market

A third labor market may be characterized as marginal. Firms in this labor market lack most of the advantages of those in the mainstream, are highly competitive, have low profit margins, and are characterized by a very high ratio of labor cost to total cost. Unions are weak or nonexistent, and both the unions and employers in this labor market have very limited power and prestige.

The working poor are heavily concentrated in the marginal labor market. Examples of the kinds of industries in this sector, whose employees' average hourly earnings are below the minimum wage: Southern sawmills and planing mills; nursing homes and related facilities; garment industries; laundries and cleaning services; synthetic textiles; cotton textiles; wood and household furniture; limited-price variety stores; eating and drinking places; hotels and motels; drug and proprietary stores; gasoline service stations; apparel and accessory stores; department stores; and miscellaneous retail stores.

Workers in these marginal industries have low wages and very limited upgrading possibilities. They also have relatively low levels of education and limited skills and training. Because the jobs they hold are relatively unskilled, they likewise have very limited opportunities for acquiring higher skills on the job.[24]

The Submarginal Labor Market

A fourth type of labor market can be called submarginal. This is a much more difficult market to define: Many of the people who work in it do not show up in the income tax or Social Security accounts because often they do not pay income tax or Social Security. Moreover, this labor market may be further subdivided into those engaged in legal and those engaged in illicit activities. This market contains a very large number of teenagers, adults with poor work histories, other adults with various obstacles to employment, and those who do not participate in the work force but are involved in various illicit activities or are on welfare. Many of the jobs in this labor market are characterized by very low entry requirements, low wages, high rates of turnover, informal work patterns, and work skills and competencies specific to ghetto life, which were acquired mainly through on-the-job training rather than through formal channels.

Many of the jobs in this sector have high turnover partly because they are very low-wage, dead-end jobs. Therefore, the employment disadvantages of this sector are due more to limited high-wage opportunities than to barriers to such job opportunities as exist in this labor market. Indeed, there apparently are many low-wage jobs in the ghetto that are readily available to ghetto dwellers. The clear determinant of the character of the jobs in the submarginal labor market is that the jobs there do not provide adequate security or wages to make it possible to stabilize employment. As a consequence, both employers and workers in the market have adjusted to this unstable routine. Many of the younger people in the ghetto are underemployed for long periods and spend their time hanging around on the street. This time is punctuated occasionally by exciting events, which the people of the street tend to recall with considerable relish. Indeed, one of the attractions for the submarginal labor market is its casual and sometimes exciting character. Employers adjust to this labor market because they expect to have workers who will be absent or late, and, therefore, they do not enforce discipline. Because the jobs are not very attractive anyway, it is no great tragedy for the worker to lose one, and it is very difficult to maintain high levels of work discipline and motivation. Of course, tragedies often occur when workers are forced to rely on submarginal labor markets to support their families. The main tragedy of submarginal ghetto markets is that they tend to be associated with factors—such as racism, poverty, low levels of education—that tend to be self-reinforcing and thus difficult to escape. Not all jobs in the submarginal labor market are necessarily characterized by low wages, and many of them have high wages per unit of time. However, these tend to be mainly the illicit and dangerous activities, such as prostitution or the sale of narcotics, which have a high risk attached to them. It probably is closer to the truth to say that most of the lawful jobs in the submarginal labor market are low-wage jobs but that many illicit activities carry very high returns per unit of time worked.

These four types of labor markets have important implications for theories of labor markets. For example, the equilibrating processes of traditional labor market theory are rendered inoperative by impediments to the movement of people among these markets. The first of these impediments might be *personal,* insofar as the worker might have inadequate education, training, work history, and motivation to move from the submarginal to the marginal labor market. But because workers in the submarginal labor market frequently have higher incomes than those in the marginal labor market, they have little incentive to aspire to the jobs in the latter category. Moreover, in order to reach even some jobs in the marginal labor market, it would be necessary for the workers to overcome the disutility of geographic and occupational mobility. This is true to some extent because the jobs in marginal labor markets are located outside the central cities, where many of those who work in the submarginal market are likely to reside. Residents of the submarginal labor market who want to reach marginal jobs must expend time and money to move from the central cities to the outer ring of metropolitan areas, sometimes a distance of many miles. It is, therefore, understandable that workers who have low-wage jobs readily available to them in their immediate areas will not be too interested in traveling long distances to get jobs at the minimum wage. Clearly, however, transportation costs would be more readily borne by these workers if they could acquire jobs in the mainstream. Ironically enough, many professional and mainstream jobs are located in the central cities not too far from the places where workers attached to the submarginal labor market are likely to live.

Certain *industrial* barriers may also impede movement of people among labor markets. Employers, for example, may discriminate against people from the submarginal labor market in general and racial minorities in particular. Moreover, some workers from the submarginal labor market or the marginal labor market may be barred from the mainstream by union discrimination. Unions, like employers, can discriminate against people with the values (e.g., dress, language, or life styles) held by those who work in the submarginal labor market. Historically some union members have discriminated against blacks regardless of the blacks' personal characteristics, place of residence, or geographical origin. Moreover, during periods when the mainstream labor market is relatively loose, employers are able to recruit adequate labor supplies without dipping into marginal and submarginal labor pools. Many workers in the latter two markets might have superior qualifications for the work that actually needs to be done but still be barred from mainstream jobs because employers have unrealistically high educational requirements.

Finally, there are various *social* barriers to the movement of people between labor markets. One of these is the cost of relocating from familiar to unfamiliar areas. Workers might incur considerable risk in moving from familiar areas that provide some security of income (however low) and personal relationships to other areas where there is some promise of higher wages but where a worker is required to enter at the bottom of a seniority line, where he has limited opportunities for advancement, and where he might be discriminated against because of race or culture. Moreover, the lack of market information about distant places makes many workers reluctant to incur the risk of moving. In addition, the income-earning alternatives of workers in the submarginal labor market might be superior to those in the marginal labor market. Indeed, the low wages in marginal and submarginal industries probably offer very limited incentives for people to even enter the labor market if they have welfare or other income alternatives.

We know much less than we should about the movement of people among these markets. The extent to which one can see movement among labor markets depends to a significant degree on one's overall theory of the labor market. Traditional economic theory has been based on a queue theory that assumes that people are lined up by employers on the basis of their productivity in relation to their wage rates. In this theory workers in the submarginal labor market have lower productivities than those in the mainstream, and it is assumed, therefore, that the personal characteristics of the workers themselves account for these limited employment and income-earning opportunities. Morover, the queue theory would recommend general economic policies to reduce the level of unemployment and give employers the incentive to move down the queue in order to hire disadvantaged workers.

The foregoing is meant to imply not that no mobility takes place among various types of labor markets, but rather that barriers among the labor markets are much more significant than those within each general labor market category. As labor markets tighten, of course, it is quite possible for firms in the mainstream to dip into the marginal and submarginal labor markets in order to meet their manpower requirements. When the labor market is slack, employers in the mainstream can use relatively inexpensive recruiting procedures and recruit internally or through referrals of outsiders by its own employees at the ports of entry into the internal labor markets. In the mainstream, employers can impose general restrictions that yield the results desired, primarily by recruiting people who are overqualified for available jobs. This can be done by imposing unrealistically high education and other requirements. But when the labor market tightens, employers achieve limited results from the traditional and less expensive recruiting and screening procedures and must, therefore, adopt new techniques that require them to recruit first from the marginal labor market and then from the submarginal labor market. They must also adopt more refined screening procedures and hiring criteria, and, as a consequence, the formal qualifications of the people hired probably tend to decline during these times. However, companies are able to continue to meet their manpower demands primarily through on-the-job training programs, supplemented by hiring new workers at the ports of entry.

Many people feel that the queue theory is inadequate to explain the operation of the labor market, particularly the movement of people among the professional, mainstream, marginal, and submarginal jobs. According to these critics, the labor market must be conceived of as coming in two, three, or maybe more noncompeting segments; therefore, the queue theory would apply mainly within the particular segment and not among noncompeting labor pools. The implication of this multiple labor market theory is that expansion of aggregate demand will not necessarily solve the problems of those in the submarginal labor market because it will simply exhaust the people in the professional or mainstream markets, bid up their wages and prices, and have relatively less effect on the incomes and earnings of people in the submarginal or marginal labor markets. Thus those who reject the queue theory argue for remedial labor market policies directed at the specific characteristics of each kind of labor market.

SUMMARY AND CONCLUSIONS

This chapter has emphasized the significance of theory for policy matters and has examined the traditional economic theory of labor markets. However, we have pointed out that even though the neoclassical model has some usefulness, its validity for understanding the operation of real markets is limited by a number of factors. Some of these factors—for example, the theoretical assumptions upon which the model is based—can be dealt with by refining the theory and relaxing the assumptions.

However, some of the other problems—for example, institutional rigidities that make it difficult for the market to operate, cannot be assumed away. Therefore, any realistic analysis of operational labor markets requires some understanding of these institutional forces. It is particularly important to understand the relationship between the internal and external labor markets and to know more than we presently know about the interrrelationships among such broad labor market types as the professional, mainstream, marginal, and submarginal labor markets discussed in this chapter. Moreover, there is an obvious necessity to have a better theoretical explanation of the interactions of the various kinds of labor markets and the adjustment of firms and labor markets to changing general demand and supply conditions. Without an adequate theory we will be hard pressed to come up with policies that overcome the imperfections and problems discussed in this chapter. It is particularly important to try to distinguish between the so-called queue theory and theories that view the labor market as being compartmentalized. It is our feeling that the truth probably lies somewhere in between these positions: That is to say, the queue theory operates, albeit imperfectly, within each labor market and with less speed and precision among the labor markets, but there is a great deal to be learned from studying the characteristics of different kinds of labor markets. Unfortunately, however, we know too little theoretically and empirically about labor market operations.

DISCUSSION QUESTIONS

1. Discuss the role of theory in understanding labor markets and other complex economic phenomena. Under what circumstances can a theory be considered right or wrong? What are the criteria for a useful theory?
2. How descriptive of reality is the neoclassical theory of labor markets? Does the usefulness depend upon its descriptiveness? What purposes does it serve? What useful insights does it offer?
3. What are the major determinants of the demand for labor? What are the major determinants of labor supply? How useful is their interaction in understanding wage setting and other labor market processes?
4. To what practical use could each of (1) a personnel manager, (2) a labor-management relations specialist, and (3) a public policy maker put knowledge and understanding of the following concepts: (a) the geographical, industrial, and occupational dimensions of labor markets, (b) external and internal labor markets, (c) the dual labor market, (d) segmentation and shelters?
5. Using the concepts of Chapter 6, assess the probable labor market consequences of (1) publicly financed skill training programs, (2) the minimum wage, (3) reducing the social security benefits of retirees by some portion of their postretirement earnings, (4) provision of a public employment service, and (5) a public service employment program for the unemployed and economically disadvantaged. Return to this question at the end of the course and see if your opinions have changed.

Notes

1. Gary S. Becker, *Human Capital* (New York: National Bureau of Economic Research, 1964); Theodore W. Schultz, "Capital Formation by Education," *Journal of Political Economy* (December 1960): 571–583, and "Investment in Human Capital," *American Economic Review* (March 1961): 1–17.

2. Lester Thurow, *Investment in Human Capital* (Belmont, Calif.: Wadsworth Publishing Co., 1970), pp. 2–6.
3. John T. Dunlop, "Job Vacancies Measures and Economic Analysis," in National Bureau of Economic Research, *The Measurement and Interpretation of Job Vacancies* (New York: The Bureau, 1966), pp. 27–38.
4. Clark Kerr, "Balkanization of Labor Markets," in E. Wight Bakke et al., *Labor Mobility and Economic Opportunity* (Cambridge, Mass., and New York: M.I.T. Press and Wiley, 1954), pp. 93–109.
5. Ibid., p. 96.
6. Ibid.
7. Peter Doeringer and Michael Piore, *Internal Labor Markets and Manpower Analysis* (Lexington, Mass.: Heath-Lexington Books, 1971).
8. Ibid., pp. 189–190.
9. Gary S. Becker, *Human Capital* (New York: National Bureau of Economic Research, 1964); Walter Y. Oi, "Labor as a Quasi-Fixed Factor," *Journal of Political Economy* (December 1962): 538–555.
10. Doeringer and Piore, op. cit., p. 76.
11. Ibid., p. 77.
12. Kerr, op. cit.; Doeringer and Piore, ibid.; Charles Killingsworth, *Jobs and Incomes for Negroes* (Ann Arbor, Mich.: Institute of Labor and Industrial Relations, University of Michigan, 1968).
13. Michael Joseph Piore, "Notes for a Theory of Labor Market Stratification," *Working Paper No. 95* (Cambridge, Mass.: Massachusetts Institute of Technology, 1972), p. 2.
14. Michael Joseph Piore, "Manpower Policy," in S. Beer and R. Barringer, eds., *The State and the Poor* (Cambridge, Mass.: Winthrop Publishing Co., 1970).
15. Doeringer and Piore, op. cit.
16. Piore, "Manpower Policy," op. cit.
17. David Gordon, *Theories of Poverty and Underemployment* (Lexington, Mass.: Lexington Books, 1972), p. 53.
18. Ibid., p. 76.
19. Raymond S. Franklin and Solomon Resnik, *The Political Economy of Racism* (New York: Holt, Rinehart and Winston, 1974), p. 13.
20. Ibid., p. 14.
21. Philip Hariman and Marged Sugarman, "Employment Service Potential," vol. I, II, and III. State of California, Employment Development Department, Employment Data and Research. U.S. Department of Labor, Employment and Training Administration, U.S. Employment Service (Washington, D.C., September 1979).
22. Marcia Freedman, *Labor Markets: Segmentation and Shelters* (Montclair, New Jersey: Allenheld Osman and Co., 1976).
23. Glen C. Cain, "The Challenge of Segmented Labor Market Theories to Orthodox Theory: A Survey," *Journal of Economic Literature* (December 1976): 1215–1257.
24. Barry Bluestone, "The Tripartite Economy: Labor Markets and the Working Poor," *Poverty and Human Resources* (July–August 1970): 15–37.

PART II
PREPARATION FOR
EMPLOYMENT

Chapter 7
Education in Human
Resource Development

Who would have thought in the 1950s and 1960s that the value of education as preparation for employment and as a major factor in economic development would ever be questioned? Yet that questioning, still a minority view into the 1980s, was a crescendo throughout the 1970s and into the current decade.

Given the intense interest and the tremendous investment in the years since World War II, it is too easy to forget that even the expectation of a tie between education and employability is a relatively new phenomenon. Even yet, there is no clear substantive relationship between the actual content of most jobs and most school curricula. In fact, the schools themselves seek employability for only a minority of their students. After two decades of lamenting the dropout rate and blaming lack of education for unemployment and low productivity, many began to argue in the 1970s that the U.S. labor force was becoming overeducated in relation to job requirements.[1] The more educated workers still had, on the average, higher incomes and experienced less unemployment than others but, detractors argued, this only indicated that those who had the inherent characteristics labor market success required also had what it took to succeed in school.

Education was strongly advocated during the 1960s as an instrument for lifting the poor and disadvantaged to a par with the mainstream of society. A decade later, in disillusion, it was argued that the schools had done little or nothing for equality.[2]

Given the controversies underlying a dissolving consensus, it is worthwhile to explore the issues and examine the evidence supporting such sharply divided opinions.

THE EMERGENCE OF EDUCATION AS A WORK PREREQUISITE

A hierarchy of the requirements for productivity and employability might include sound mental and physical health, a commitment to work as the most appropriate source of income, acceptance of industrial discipline, good human relations skills, basic communication and computation skills, technological familiarity, and job skills. The list hardly seems controversial, but when our grandparents entered the labor force, the last four items would have been included for only a fraction of jobs. As noted in Chapter 3, the median educational attainment of American workers is now 12.6 years compared to 8.7 years in 1940 and 10.4 years in 1952 (the rise seems to be flattening; the 1990 projections are for 12.7 years). At the turn of the century only 6 percent of the population remained in school after the 17th birthday, but it is doubtful that anyone would have blamed a person's unemployment on lack of education.

At what point did education and formal training become a critical determinant of employability? It has not been many years since most lawyers learned their profession by "reading" law as clerks. Formal training for physicians is less than a century old. The designation of engineer gained educational connotations only in this century. Formal credentialing of schoolteachers is also of relatively recent date, and a few states still do not require a bachelor's degree. Beyond the professions, bookkeepers, accountants, stenographers, and clerks obviously were required to read, write and cipher. Yet formal educational attainment had little relevance to employment for most of the labor force until after World War II.

The dramatic increase in the education of the American people surely is one of the most significant domestic developments of the past generation. In 1960, for example, 39 percent of the population 16 years of age and older had graduated from high school. By 1973 this proportion had risen to 68 percent. The total cost of education was about $9 billion in 1950, compared with about $66 billion in 1970, $98 billion in 1974, and $152 billion in 1979, reflecting both increased resources and inflation.

Though the time has been too short to be certain, a reversal or at least a flattening in trend for both enrollments and expenditures appears to be occurring. Enrollments are declining in absolute numbers because of declining births. Also, smaller proportion of high school graduates appear to be entering and graduating from college, and a reduced proportion are entering graduate school. Expenditures have been rising less rapidly than inflation, so that real resources are declining.

The faith of Americans in education as a ladder for upward social and economic mobility is deep seated and long term. World War II is properly designated as the event that transformed education from a minor to a major qualification for employment. The war itself imposed demands for skilled training. A 12-million-man military force was extracted from the prime labor force age group at the same time that war production multiplied the demand for technical and craft skills. In addition to those who learned new skills on the job, a vast increase in the public vocational education system allowed the training of 7.5 million persons before the war's end. Where skills could not be supplied fast enough, jobs were broken down into simpler tasks that could be performed by unskilled and inexperienced workers. Although the emphasis on vocational and skill training did not continue into the postwar period, formal education quickly emerged as a requirement for employment.

The emphasis on technology was accelerated during the war by the development of nuclear weapons and was continued with the space race. Much of the increased demand for college graduates following World War II was stimulated by the federal government, in part, as a consequence of the cold war emphasis on national prestige derived from scientific and technical achievement and the rate of economic development. America's development of the atomic bomb undoubtedly "persuaded" the Soviets to bridge the nuclear gap and develop their space technology, which, in turn, prompted the United States to attempt greater scientific achievements. Sputnik, the Soviet's first successful satellite, clearly elicited federal support for higher education—there was a space race to be won. Cold war strategy also involved economic development. A major Soviet goal was to become number one, and the competitive threat was an effective goad for the United States. Studies by economists attributing a significant part of economic growth to education therefore strengthened federal support for education.[3]

Postwar population developments also influenced the demand for education. First elementary, then secondary, and finally post-secondary enrollments were swollen by the postwar baby boom. The Vietnam experience was an additional incentive to stay in school.

Why education, in the post–World War II period, became a widely accepted prerequisite for employment is a matter of controversy. Of course, as long as professional and white-collar occupations were expanding as a proportion of all employment, education was certain also to become a necessity for a growing percentage of workers. But the emphasis went far beyond that, until a high school diploma was required for most apprenticeships, many semiskilled factory jobs, and even laborers' jobs at the bottom of a seniority ladder leading into semiskilled and skilled ranks. Perhaps these

Table 7-1   THE CHANGING EDUCATIONAL PATTERN OF MAJOR OCCU-PATIONAL GROUPS, 1952 AND 1977 (PERCENTAGE DISTRIBUTION)

MAJOR OCCUPATIONAL GROUP	8 YEARS OR LESS		9–11 YEARS	
	1952	1977	1952	1977
WHITE COLLAR				
Professional and technical	1%	0.8%	7%	2.3%
Managerial and officials	10	4.5	32	8.1
Clerical	4	2.3	25	9.8
Sales		3.9		13.5
BLUE COLLAR				
Craftsmen and foremen	18	13.0	48	18.8
Operatives	25	19.8	50	26.0
Laborers	43	19.3	41	29.9
Farm	43	31.5	38	18.6
SERVICE AND PRIVATE				
Household	31	15.5	43	27.7

SOURCE: Derived from several U.S. Department of Labor sources.

jobs, or at least those a few steps up the promotion ladder, were becoming more technical—and required an ability to comprehend written instructions, to read and record from gauges and graphs, and similar activities. But why assume that instructions are to be read and workmen are to keep records? In factories throughout much of the world safety and other instructions are given on picture signs, and clerks circulate to keep records. An alternative hypothesis is that as long as educated people were available, employers preferred to hire them, and emerging jobs were structured to fit them. The post–World War II GI Bill had no doubt played an important role in kicking off a spiral in which the supply of educated workers sparked the demand for them.

It is difficult to attribute to anything but supply the fact that 37 percent of laborers had a high school education or better in 1977, compared with 14 percent two decades earlier (Table 7-1). The interesting increases in the proportions with eight years or less of education for 1977 after years of steady decline probably illustrates the impact of immigration, legal and illegal. Beyond this category, the trend is clearly toward higher educational attainment in each occupational category. Of course, the proportion of educated people in the labor force would of necessity expand to accompany the growth of professional, technical, and clerical jobs. But it has been estimated that this accounts for only 15 percent of the rise in educational attainment in the work force. The other 85 percent represents higher educational attainment within the same occupation. In many cases the content of the job required more education. In others the employer selected those

12 years		13–15 years		16 years or more		MEDIAN SCHOOL YEARS COMPLETED
1952	1977	1952	1977	1952	1977	1977
16%	14.2%	21%	17.7%	55%	65.0%	16.5
34	33.6	13	22.4	11	31.4	13.5
50	56.3	15	23.2	7	6.8	12.7
	40.2		23.9		15.3	12.8
27	49.6	6	14.8	1	3.8	12.4
21	43.9	3	8.4	1	1.9	12.1
14	37.0	2	11.0	1	2.8	12.0
14	34.8	4	8.8	2	4.3	12.1
20	39.3	4	13.9	2	3.6	12.2

with more education because they were available and because he assumed that education was likely to correlate positively with productivity and promotability. In still others it was simply the fact that with educational attainment rising throughout the population, anyone hired at random was likely to have more education than his predecessor.

The apparent softening of the demand for and commitment to education is probably more a short- than a long-run phenomenon, with one exception. That exception is, of course, demographic. The downturn in birth rates, which began in the late 1950s and seems to have reached a low plateau approximately equal to the depression birth rate of the 1930s, has the earmarks of a long-term trend. The consequences have already passed through the elementary schools and high schools and are now affecting the colleges. Regardless of patterns in per capita education, the volume of education must inevitably decline. Since the education industry is one of the nation's largest employers, the employment impact of this dramatic demographic shift has been a major one, with teachers in surplus supply after years of shortages.

Accompanying this seemingly longer-run trend are several short-run factors. One is the very success of efforts to alleviate shortages. From about 1940 to 1970 the nation's stocks and flows of highly trained manpower lagged behind the growth in demand. Coincidentally, demand began catching up with supply just as the shift in space race commitments, a business recession, and the consequences of the falling birth rates all struck the labor markets simultaneously. The results were a short-term surplus of engineers, a longer-term redundancy in some scientific professions, and a considerable surplus of teachers. Over those years of seemingly endless demand, universities throughout the country had expanded their capacity enormously. That in itself was a great accomplishment. However, like the familiar inventory cycle in macroeconomics, each institution acted unilaterally, expanding without considering the expansion of others. Adding to educational capacity is a slow process involving bricks and mortar, equipment, teacher-training institutions, new faculty to train more new faculty, and so forth. Thus all the new capacity began coming "on stream" just as supply was catching up with demand.

Another result of the education explosion was the questioning of the conventional wisdom that a college diploma was a guarantee of labor market success. There was a reexamination of the relationship between education and job requirements and the discovery that only 20 percent of jobs were filled by and required college graduates. Since that was the very proportion graduating from college, there should have been no surprise in the discovery, but it clashed with the spreading myth of college for (nearly) everybody.

At the same time, education suffered from the overpromises of its enthusiasts. It had been proposed as a solution to almost every social and economic problem. It had done much to ameliorate many problems, but it could not do all that was promised—and disillusion usually brings overreaction. Later sections of this chapter explore the consequences of these developments.

EDUCATION OF THE LABOR FORCE: FUTURE PROSPECTS

Bureau of Labor Statistics projections promise a better educated labor force to 1990.[4] While the labor force is increasing from 105 million to 116 million between 1980 and 1990, the proportion of high school graduates will remain stable but the proportion of college graduates will increase from 15 percent to 22 percent. In the process the labor force will become much more homogeneous in educational attainment. Most of those who entered the labor force before World War II will have retired or died. The older workers will be the postwar GI Bill generation. Those born during the postwar baby boom will rise by 1990 to 34 percent of the workers aged 25 years and older. The younger adult workers will show a marked change. Even those in the labor force 65 years and over will have a median educational attainment of 12.1 years, compared with 9.6 years in 1970. A remarkable change during the 1970s was a shrinkage of the gap in educational attainment between blacks and other workers to 0.3 years from 3.3 years of a decade earlier. However, qualitative equality of education has yet to be achieved—perhaps it will be approached by 1990. That will leave a similar challenge to upgrade the education of Hispanics and Native Americans.

The traditional educational advantage of female workers over male workers will almost certainly have disappeared by 1990.

Of course, there will still be those having less than adequate education—22 million workers without high school diplomas in 1990 compared with 25 million in 1970. Despite minority group gains, they will still include a disproportionate number of those without a high school education. If present attitudes persist, these educationally disadvantaged workers will face relatively worse job prospects. But the overwhelming fact will be the decline in the educational differentials that have persisted so long.

Does this outlook for educational attainment match the expected educational requirements of future jobs? The question may be answered differently depending upon whether the criterion is the objective requirements of job content or the preferences of employers. Occupational trends promise to continue the positive correlation between education and employment. Projections discussed in earlier chapters are repeated here to estimate the future relationship. White-collar workers increased from 20 percent of all workers at the turn of the century to 48 percent in 1972. They comprised 51 percent of all workers in 1980. What links these occupations together is their reliance on intellectual and verbal rather than manual and manipulative skills. The fastest-growing occupational group in the labor market will continue to be professional and technical workers, and they, with the addition of clerical occupations, account for nearly all of the projected white collar increase. Sales workers and managers will remain constant or decline in number. The number of farm workers will continue its rapid downward trend; blue-collar workers will decrease slowly in number.

In the blue-collar category the number of craft workers will increase though falling slightly as a proportion of all workers, with emphasis on those craft skills likely to require the most formal education. Operatives and nonfarm laborers will continue their rapid proportionate decline while remaining stable in absolute numbers. Service occupations will grow with population, but the greatest growth will be in the number of those whose jobs have some educational content—police officers, hospital attendants, cosmetologists, and practical nurses. Only the professional occupations require college degrees. The labor force is growing more rapidly than employment for white-collar occupations, with the opposite being true in the blue-collar sector (Table 7-2).

College graduates probably will not experience rising unemployment relative to the less educated, but a "bumping back" process may occur, bringing the more highly educated into jobs not previously requiring this preparation. Many of the growth occupations have in common the need, if not the custom, of post-secondary but less than baccalaureate education. The half of all college entrants who drop out before graduation may help fill this need. The continued rapid expansion of two-year community colleges is probably a more functional approach. Enrollment in these institutions increased sharply between 1960 and 1980, rising to four million.

Table 7-2   COMPARISON OF PERCENTAGE
INCREASES IN LABOR FORCE AND EMPLOYMENT BY OCCUPATIONAL
STATUS GROUP, 1970 TO 1980

OCCUPATIONAL STATUS GROUP	LABOR FORCE INCREASE (1)	EMPLOYMENT INCREASE (2)	DIFFERENCE (1)–(2)
Group I, professional, technical, and kindred	45.3	39.0	6.3
Group II, managerial, clerical, and sales[a]	24.6	21.9	2.7
Group III, craft and kindred (part of)[b]	15.1	16.5	−1.4
Group IV, operatives (part of)[c]	11.0	16.9	−5.9
Group V, laborers (part of)[d]	4.4	10.6	−6.2

SOURCE: Harold Wool, *The Labor Supply for Lower Level Occupations*, p. 252, cited in *Manpower Report of the President* (Washington, D.C.: GPO, 1974), p. 111.
[a] Includes police, fire fighters, and related occupations. Does not include shipping and receiving clerks, messengers, and office helpers.
[b] Includes farmers; operatives in selected higher wage industries, e.g., transportation equipment, chemical, and petroleum; and barbers, bartenders, and practical nurses.
[c] Includes auto mechanics; construction painters, plasterers, cement and concrete finishers, and roofers; selected service occupations, e.g., hospital attendants.
[d] Includes most farm and nonfarm laborers, cooks and kitchen workers, cleaning and building service workers, domestic workers, and laundry and dry cleaning operatives.

EDUCATION AND EMPLOYABILITY

The higher a person's educational attainment, the more likely he is to be in the labor force, to avoid unemployment, to be unemployed only briefly when he enters or reenters the labor force or changes jobs, and to hold a better job (Table 7-3). There is a positive and significant correlation between level of education and lifetime earnings as shown by Figure 7-1. Studies have also shown that those nations that spend the highest proportion of their national incomes on education tend to experience the most rapid economic growth. All of this is discussed in more detail later in the chapter.

These should be strong testimonials to the value of education in developing the labor force and increasing the employment and earnings of the people. But the relationship is far from simple. Because the educational attainment of the work force rose from 8.7 years in 1940 to 12.6 years in 1978, one might expect unemployment to have steadily diminished. But, in fact, overall unemployment has fluctuated cyclically, with no evidence of upward or downward trend over time; and for teenagers there has been an upward trend in unemployment.

Similarly, a general shift toward the upper rungs of the occupational ladder might have been expected. Those occupations, such as professional and technical, which have always attracted people with the most educa-

Table 7-3   UNEMPLOYMENT RATES BY AGE
AND YEARS OF SCHOOL COMPLETED, MARCH 1978

YEARS OF SCHOOL COMPLETED (BOTH SEXES)	TOTAL: 16 AND OVER	16 AND 17	18 AND 19	20 TO 24	25 TO 34	35 TO 44	45 TO 54	55 TO 64	65 AND OVER
TOTAL	6.6	21.5	15.7	11.1	5.8	4.1	3.5	3.3	4.6
ELEMENTARY									
less than 5 years	7.7	a	a	a	10.0	7.7	8.0	5.5	9.1
5 to 7 years	8.1	a	a	14.7	11.2	8.5	5.8	6.3	6.2
8 years	8.8	36.9	25.2	23.0	14.8	9.0	5.8	3.8	5.1
HIGH SCHOOL									
1 to 3 years	12.4	20.8	20.9	18.9	11.9	6.6	5.7	4.5	4.1
4 years	6.2	11.5	13.4	11.3	6.6	4.1	2.8	2.5	3.7
COLLEGE									
1 to 3 years	4.6	a	9.2	8.5	4.1	2.2	2.2	2.5	4.1
4 or more years	2.5	a	a	6.1	2.6	1.8	1.3	2.4	3.1

SOURCE: Bureau of Labor Statistics.
[a] Less than 0.05 percent.

tion, have, in fact, expanded most rapidly. Yet the major effect of the rising educational attainment has been to raise the educational level within occupations. Therefore, it is not really clear whether individuals have climbed the occupational ladder as they achieved education or whether the steps of the ladder have become farther apart as better-educated people became available for the same jobs. Too many other factors influence unemployment to make this a meaningful statement. In the short run, education is more likely to determine who rather than how many are employed and unemployed. Whether the availability of an educated labor force sparks more rapid economic growth remains a topic of supposition and controversy.

People with more education earn substantially more over a working lifetime. Does this occur because their education prepared them for better jobs, because employers value and are willing to pay for their educational attainment, or because education has been pursued by those who possess more native ability, motivation, or better labor market contacts? Do employers prefer the better educated because job content requires such workers, because they are better disciplined or more promotable, because they have demonstrated persistence, or simply because employers have unrealistic views about the value of education? Does a better-educated labor force cause an economy to grow more rapidly, or is it that a more rapidly growing economy can afford the luxury of more education? What exactly is the contribution of education to employability? None of these questions can be satisfactorily answered, but they are worth exploring. That these questions are being asked increasingly is evidence of a reaction against the sacrosanct sta-

Estimated total income from age 18 to
death for males with varying levels of education —

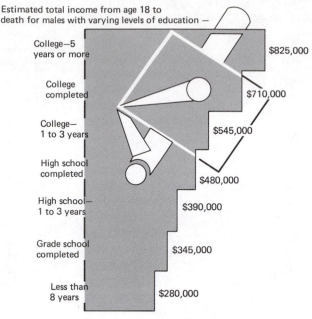

College—5
years or more $825,000

College
completed $710,000

College—
1 to 3 years $545,000

High school
completed $480,000

High school—
1 to 3 years $390,000

Grade school
completed $345,000

Less than
8 years $280,000

Note: Earnings are in 1972 dollars

Figure 7-1   The impact of education on a lifetime's earnings. (Source: U.S. Census Bureau.)

tus education has enjoyed as accepted preparation for employment over the past generation.

Studies comparing the lifetime earnings of high school and college graduates to that of those without either diploma have consistently shown a positive return to investment in education. However, as with any other investment outlet, as the amount of investment has increased the rate of return has decreased—the familiar economic phenomenon of diminishing returns. Calculations of the 1960s typically showed a rate of return of around 12 percent on educational investment.[5] Those in the 1970s tended to estimate a rate of return of around 8 percent. But in the earlier, inflationless period 12 percent was an extraordinarily favorable rate, while for most of the 1970s, 8 percent was below the inflation rate and prevailing rates of interest. If the only goal of an education had been an immediate monetary return, one would have been better advised to invest in treasury bills or money market certificates.

However, much of the controversy over rates of return to investment in education emerges from a failure to disaggregate and ask "what education for whom for what purposes." Civilization and individuals would certainly suffer if only such intellectual and skill preparation were undertaken as would pay off directly in wage and salary terms. Trained minds and hands are valued not only in labor markets. And the individual whose only rewards are found on the job is poor whatever the income. Nevertheless, for individual or community, economic return is one important factor in decision-making.

Disaggregating economic return by occupation and by personal characteristics provides a different set of insights as does exploration of the relative efficiency of alternative training methods.

Economic returns to education are really quite minimal for some 60 percent of the work force[6] primarily because the jobs they are in have no content to which education can contribute skills. In fact, overeducation may lead to frustration and lowered productivity. For the remainder, however, the connections are direct and the returns are substantial.

For many occupations, an educational credential, whether high school, college, or specialized training, has become the gateway. To the extent the individual wants entry to those occupations, education is immediately rewarded. If those are also high-paying occupations, the economic returns to attaining the credential will also be high. With the emphasis on higher education throughout the post–World War II years, the rising supply of college-educated workers has tended to shrink their differential relative to the ranks of skilled blue-collar workers and those with postsecondary but less than college-attained specialties and technical skills. For that reason, education pays off better in occupational than in income terms. Nevertheless, the returns to investment in education have been extraordinarily high for the professional, technical, and managerial ranks. Sales workers have been only slightly behind in their returns. For clerical workers, high school is a necessity but the returns to higher education are low. For other occupational categories, education carries a low return, except where a high school diploma is a prerequisite for entry. It should not be surprising, then, that the pattern of median years of schooling by occupation is as shown in Table 7-1. Neither should the lack of academic motivation of high school students headed for these occupations be criticized as short-sighted.

Given that relation between occupation and returns to investment on education, those whose access to the higher occupational ranks is limited could not be expected to profit greatly from education. Women and minorities are underrepresented in these occupations and, when they get in, their representation is biased toward the bottom range of those categories. In consequence, the rate of return to investment in education is substantially less for them than for white males. When they persist in pursuing education, they must do so for reasons which are not, on the average, totally economic.

Taking another cut at the same phenomenon, occupations have been divided into those which are enterprising, realistic, investigative, social, conventional, and artistic.[7] Even though several others of the types have higher proportions of those who have 16 or more years of education, only the enterprising category, which involves a quarter of all males and two-fifths of employed college graduates, offers substantial return to investment in education. The investigative, social, and artistic groups which are predominately college-educated receive a relatively low rate of return for their education. The realistic grouping, which provides over half of male employment and employs 10 percent of college graduates, has the lowest rate of return to education. The low rates of return often shown for vocational education, discussed in Chapter 8 is drawn into perspective by this analysis.

Another related analysis involves the relative efficiency of various methods of skill acquirement. Relevant variables are job content, personal characteristics, and economic conditions. Some occupational skills cannot be taught in a classroom setting because the working conditions cannot be simulated. For others, the risks to safety and costs are such as to require preentry preparation. Some workers have the background to learn on the job while others lack basic conditioning or preparation which is best supplied in a prejob entry situation. In times of high demand it may be best to learn on the job and in slack periods there may be no alternative to learning in an off-the-job setting. For any combination of occupation, personality, and economic condition, there must be some skill acquirement method more efficient than all of the others. Some rudimentary efforts have been made to develop rational criteria for choice, but the issue has been largely ignored.[8] Nevertheless, about one-third of the jobs in the U.S. economy appear to be doable by anyone with the equivalent of a high school education, average manipulative skills, and the ability to drive an automobile. Another third can be satisfactorily performed by those same people after a substantial amount of on-the-job training. The remaining third does require preentry training. One would not expect any significant economic return to investment in postsecondary education for those entering either of the first two groups of occupations.

EDUCATION AND THE TRANSITION FROM SCHOOL TO WORK

People who attain the most education, of course, also have other advantages that would have been present without the added education. A young person's educational attainment, for example, is also highly correlated with the education and income of his parents. Low-income families produce the highest proportion of dropouts and the lowest proportion of graduates. When socioeconomic status and ability are compared, low-ability students from high-income families are more likely to attend and graduate from college than are high-ability students from poor families. Yet school-connected difficulties such as lack of interest, poor grades, and disciplinary problems are more likely to be cited than money as the immediate reason when a low-income youth drops out of school. Most vital of all personal satisfactions is a sense of self-worth, normally reflecting one's judgments of the opinions of others. For the child of a nonverbally inclined family to be immersed in the usual academic environment is no way to develop that sense.

The child starts at a disadvantage, slips further behind, and either accepts a self-perception of failure or gains self-image from rebellion against social norms.

Those with the most education are most likely to have a job waiting for them when they leave school. And among those who look for employment, the better educated have more informal linkages and find jobs sooner. One of the realities of modern labor markets is that the workplace becomes more like the classroom and the skills which make for success in the latter carry over to the former. Education is also intertwined in many ways in the transition into the workplace.

Vocational training and academic education are often viewed as alternative ways of preparing for employment. However, rather than compensating for lack of education, skill training and educational attainment are positively correlated, largely because vocational training ordinarily becomes available only during the last two years of high school. By this time the compulsory school attendance age has been reached or passed, and most who are likely to do so have dropped out.

The cooperative work-study program, though still enrolling few students throughout the nation, is potentially useful in assisting the movement of high school students into the labor force. Under this program the student's day usually is split between school and part-time employment; special efforts are made to integrate the activities into a meaningful preparation for work. Because these opportunities also become available in the last years of high school, over twice as many graduates as dropouts have participated. Even of those high school graduates who do not go on to college, three times as many undertake some form of postsecondary training as do the dropouts.

Guidance from school or state employment service officials provides another bridge from school to job. Because most guidance is directed to students during their senior year in high school, dropouts tend to be excluded from this experience. Graduates are also more likely to have the self-confidence and interpersonal skills to seek help from labor market intermediaries.[9]

Not all students receive vocational guidance, and studies have shown that it usually is directed at those who seemingly need it least. Academic students are more likely to receive guidance than vocational students.[10] Only one-half of vocational students, compared with three-fourths of academic students, recalled discussing the selection of their courses with a counselor. Actual discussion of job plans was even less frequent, with one-fifth of the vocational and one-third of the academic students receiving assistance. If academic students receive more exposure to placement services beyond high school and are generally better equipped to make decisions, then the order of priorities in high school vocational guidance activities is obviously inverted. When it comes to self-directed job search, those with the most education are the most likely to have access to the all-important informal linkages, as well as to have a wider knowledge of the community and where and how to search.

In contrast to those leaving school at or before high school completion, the college-to-work bridge has been a reasonably secure one. The explanation may be that college students have been a select group that has demonstrated a commitment attractive to employers or perhaps because their backgrounds gave them better labor market access. However, the first postgraduation job is rarely the first work experience. The transition from school to work is likely to have been underway for a number of years. Now with college graduation a less unusual achievement and with supply catching up with demand for most college-trained occupations, successfully crossing the bridge is less automatic. Colleges are being pressed to clarify their dual roles in career preparation and in educating the whole person. If college is to fulfill its potential as a useful step in career preparation, labor market knowledge and career planning should be a part of that educational experience. Most faculty know only the academic market, yet the schools should accept an obligation to demonstrate the career application and the labor market demand for the academic disciplines.

The one-half of youth who, on the average, enter but do not complete college have an unknown variety of experiences. We know relatively little about the amount of schooling and training this group obtains, their reasons for failing to complete college, and their labor force experience. While those who complete a two- or three-year course probably find it a satisfactory bridge to their working career, those who fail to finish an intended four-year course are likely to be less well-prepared for a specific occupation. It may be significant that those who have attended college but have not graduated experience almost as much unemployment as high school graduates.

Now that most members of the labor force are high school graduates, a diploma offers little competitive advantage. The quality and content of the education received is becoming more significant. Chapter 8 discusses the potential of career education and the extent and role of vocational education as preparation for careers and the specific occupations of which careers are comprised. The proportion enrolled in vocational studies, the funds allocated to them, and the quality of vocational education all appear to be on the rise. The degree to which vocational education has been able to improve the employment and earnings experiences of its enrollees is debated but is generally perceived to be disappointing, perhaps because it concentrates upon those occupations showing little return for any schooling. If vocational schools concentrated on occupations which really required preentry preparation, the rate of return would probably rise.

The increasingly small proportion who fail to complete high school, of course, find themselves at the rear of any labor market queue. If one is looking for a simple formula for success in the transition from school to work, therefore, the statistics could be read as an endorsement for staying in school as long as possible, but observation of job content does not always explain why this is so.

EDUCATION AND WORKER DISCONTENT

If overeducation is a general phenomenon in the labor market of the United States, why do employers prefer better-educated people for subjective reasons and not for their potential productivity?

There are several possible explanations of this bias on the part of the employers. Some, concerned about promotability, may be looking ahead to the requirements of the job at the top of a promotion ladder. But relying upon past education for skills required by a future job suggests little faith in a person's ability to learn on the job. Racial bias has also been suggested as a cause of inflated educational requirements. Knowing that various minorities have lower-than-average educational attainment, employers may require education as a defensible shield for reducing the number of minority applicants. To the extent that education is a surrogate for all the advantages listed in the previous section, employers may be acting rationally and getting their money's worth. On the other hand, to the extent workers are overqualified for their jobs, the employer may be assuring a discontented work force. Various licensing and credentialing requirements, usually defended as necessary to protect the consumer, protect jurisdiction at the cost of overqualification. Just the fact that the educational attainment of the labor force has been more rapid than the upgrading of the objective educational requirements of jobs has a similar potential for discontent.

There is no necessary inconsistency in arguing both that the jobs requiring formal education are growing more rapidly than any others and that overqualification is pervasive in U.S. labor markets. The less physical and the more intellectual the production processes, the greater the need for formal education. Manipulative skills, such as typing, that are generally applicable, are taught more efficiently in the classroom than on the job. Given these trends, those without adequate formal education are at a technical disadvantage. Because education has purposes other than preparation for employment, the desire to consume education may lead to overqualification as a worker and overinvestment in the labor force. Yet society may profit from the nonlabor market contributions of the educated and the economy may experience greater vitality in the long run.

THE EDUCATIONAL INSTITUTIONS
FOR HUMAN RESOURCE DEVELOPMENT

Since "human resources" refers to the productive capacities of human beings, nearly every institution that affects our lives has an impact on human resource development. Consider the attributes of employability listed at the beginning of this chapter. The home is a key determinant of mental and physical health, commitment to work, acceptance of discipline, and human relations skills. The neighborhood and community are also involved. But because improvement in these basic institutions through public policy intervention is difficult, schools and other institutions are asked to provide remedies for any deficiencies. Thus elementary and secondary schools become the focus for the development not only of a general ability to understand and function in society, but also of discipline and human relations skills, as well as basic skills in communications and computation.

Labor market experts sometimes express dismay because the schools often do not accent and pursue their role as developers of human resources. These experts argue that basic labor force requirements would be better met if preparation for employment were specifically included among the priority objectives of education. Rupert Evans, several years ago, accused American education of concentrating on "school for schooling's sake."[10] The elementary schools prepare young people to go to high school, which concentrates on getting them into college, which is geared to meeting graduate school requirements. Only then, when the schooling potential is exhausted, is the emphasis vocational, but largely for education as a profession.

The pattern began in the days when elementary schools were assigned the job of producing literate citizens and Americanizing immigrants. Only the college-bound enrolled in high school as a preparatory stage. Vocational education was established as a separate system to protect it from the disdain of the academic educator. But with the high school providing mass education and education a growing prerequisite for employment, many feel that education needs a change of signals. One indicator is the growing interest in the concepts of career development and career education as described in Chapter 8; another is the large number of conferences directed to the issue of school-to-work transition. Finally, dissatisfaction with the way schools fulfill their employment-preparation role is a factor in the growing political criticism of education.

Whether viewed as a vocationalization of general education or a generalization of vocational education, there is growing interest in discovering techniques for integrating the two. The basic assumption is that preparation for a working career is among the most important of education's many objectives. Thus no one without the requisites for employability, including a salable skill, can be considered educated. At the same time, skill preparation should neither supplant other general education objectives nor be so structured that the individual will not be able to realize his or her full potential. It is from this premise that the concepts of career education have emerged. Some of the techniques for accomplishing this goal are elementary school orientation to the world of work, information and training in occupational choice, integration of academic and vocational content so that each serves as a vehicle for the other, and a more active role for schools in the placement process.

Community colleges, as we noted earlier, have been the most rapid growth components among educational institutions. The title is significant. While the term "junior college" indicates a college transfer emphasis and a desire to grow up to become a senior college, the community college is committed to serving the community's educational needs, whatever they might be. Most institutions that call themselves community colleges could have more honestly retained the "junior college" title. However, the generally recognized attributes, too often observed in the breach, are: (1) a truly open-door admissions policy for all persons over 18, regardless of past education, who can profit from instruction; (2) a service-oriented and student-centered philosophy that contrasts with the university's ambitions for a community of scholars; (3) a faculty that concentrates on teaching rather than research; (4) heavy emphasis on occupationally oriented two-year terminal programs; (5) a strong counseling and guidance program; (6) use of the campus as a community center for nonstudent activities and of the staff as a source of technical services to community institutions; and (7) an ambition to place one such institution within commuting distance of everyone in the population. A few community colleges have incorporated skills centers financed by the Comprehensive Employment and Training Act (CETA is discussed in Chapter 17) into their facilities; these centers offer remedial training and stipends to disadvantaged adults, who are not stigmatized as second-class citizens by being shunted to separate and less-than-equal facilities. Many community colleges accept individual referrals or whole classes of employment and training program enrollees on contract.[11]

Throughout U.S. history education has generally been considered an inherent good with more always better than less. Indeed, it was the major track bringing the children of immigrants and outmigrants from agriculture into the mainstream of the industrializing society. Education was essentially a sacred cow, deliberately shielded from partisan politics, decentralized, and characterized by professional autonomy. The 1960s saw federal support for education rise from $2 billion to $8 billion while all U.S. expenditures on education rose from $25 billion to $66 billion. Whatever the ills of society—and many formerly unrecognized ills were uncovered during the period—more and better education was the prescription. Because the products of education are difficult to measure, education administrators tended to measure the output by the input. Getting more education was simply a question of funding; quality was another matter.

Federal support for education reached a zenith of public support in 1965 with the Elementary and Secondary Education Act (ESEA). The act was designed to provide additional federal funds for school districts heavily impacted with poverty. Compensatory education was supposed to be the route to social as well as economic equality. Not only equal opportunity but equal results were expected.

Perhaps with the high levels of public expectation, disappointment and overreaction was inevitable. Peculiarities in the original ESEA distribution formula channeled moneys into high-income states with high levels of public assistance. Head Start began with great fanfare to prepare preschoolers from poverty families to compete in school with those from more educationally oriented families. Then a too early and too harsh evaluation declared it was not working. Progress was being made during the high-support preschool experiences, it was said, but was disappearing when the students were "dumped" into the standard (or substandard) environments of the regular schools in their neighborhoods.

Of course, results were never equal, but then neither were the opportunities. The widely publicized Coleman Report demonstrated that family and peer group influence was a more potent force in raising the educational achievement of disadvantaged students than was either the quality of school facilities or the competence of teachers.[12] Not only more money but a prescribed mix of high- and low-income and black and white students was a prerequisite for advance. Busing would be required to mix central city minority students with those from the middle class and white families who had fled to the suburbs, in part to escape substandard education—a new set of divisive controversies was begun.

Then at the end of the 1960s a period of debunking began, much of it based upon social science research. A replowing of the Coleman report data by Christopher Jencks and his associates concluded that all of the added expenditures had no effect on the desired socioeconomic equality.[13] Not noted was the fact that, while the federal government had been investing in compensatory education, the nondisadvantaged had been able to exercise the political power at both local and federal levels to see to it that the educational resources available to them increased even more. Compensatory education might or might not be a route to equality, at least in educational results. It had never actually been tested.

In the same environment, campus unrest was convincing the public that the college student recipients of taxpayer largesse were biting the hand that fed them. Human resource training programs also came in for their share of criticism. They were assailed because enrollees were trained for low-level jobs which, if available, left them in employed poverty—but at the upper rather than lower margins of the ranks of the poor.[14] And for too many, the problems of housing, transportation, racial discrimination, or isolation in a rural depressed area or central city slum stood in the way of employment.

Among the consequences of this disillusionment has been a rising rate of rejections in school bond elections and reduced generosity among legislators. Other public needs seem to take higher priority. Presidents of the United States now find vetoing education appropriations less than threatening politically. As previously noted, total educational expenditures had risen to $151 billion by 1978–1979, but that was only $94 billion if calculated in 1972 dollars and represents no real increase over that year. There is a demand for accountability. Granting a diploma is no evidence that education has done its job. Performance contracting in which public or private institutions are rewarded for demonstrated improvement in educational achievement has aroused considerable interest and some experimentation. Competency-based curricula and credit for experiential learning are other concepts aimed at measured performance. Increasing numbers of states require independent evidence of basic competencies before leaving high school. An alleged failure of our education system to prepare noncollege-bound youth (and many college graduates) for successful working careers has been an important factor in this discontent. Such are the penalties for the American faith in education as a key to both social change and social stability. Yet the practical result has been a slowing of upward trends in financial support, not a reversal. The total bill for all education in the United States still amounted in 1978 to 7.1 percent of the gross national product, compared with 7.3 percent at the beginning of the decade.

RETURNS TO INVESTMENT IN EDUCATION

For a variety of reasons, the economics of education has become a major field for professional economists. For many the subject consists of school finance. For most, however, the question has been: Does education pay? If so, how much of what kind for whom under what conditions?

The school finance approach emerged as school enrollments mushroomed following the World War II GI Bill and the postwar baby boom. Its emphasis was on how to get enough classrooms and teachers and funds to support them. The landmark in the education-as-investment approach was the American Economic Association presidential address given by Theodore W. Schultz of the University of Chicago in December 1960.[15] Titling his address "Investment in Human Capital," he noted the failure of his fellow economists to subject expenditures on education to the same rigorous analyses applied to investments in machinery, factories, and other forms of capital. The economic fathers—Adam Smith, David Ricardo, Thomas Malthus, Karl Marx, and Alfred Marshall, to name a few—had mentioned the importance of education and training in the improvement of labor as a factor of production, but none had attempted to specify a rate of return.

Schultz had been attracted to the riddle of economic growth. It had been supposed that adding greater accumulations of reproducible capital to a fixed supply of land and labor would result eventually in diminishing returns to such investments. When this did not occur in the United States, one logical explanation was that the supply of one or both of the other inputs must not be fixed. Improvements in the quality of human resources was a possible answer.

Related enigmas surrounded the persistent, relatively large increases in the real earnings of workers and the unexplained residuals in economic growth. Economists involved in the postwar recovery of Europe had found economies growing more rapidly than could be explained by the aggregate inputs of work hours, the stock and flows of reproducible capital, and natural resources. The residual had been explained as a product of technological change,[16] but the source had not been identified. A technological improvement could include any change in the quality of the inputs, including labor; hence education, health care, or any other investment in human beings could be a factor in that technological change.

Had the answer to the question "Does education pay?" been negative, interest among academic researchers might have died at birth. Because the preliminary results supported the predispositions of academicians and politicians, and the self-interests of the former, an immense literature emerged during the 1960s exploring and applying the concept of investment in human capital. Only the broadest outlines can be given here.

Measuring the Returns

Researchers into the returns to investment in human capital have tried a variety of approaches to measurement, both at the aggregate and individual levels. An aggregated approach has been to correlate indexes of educational activity with some index of national economic activity. Examples are inter-country comparisons of the relationship between per capita educational expenditures and growth in GNP.[17] In general, among underdeveloped economies those with the highest levels of educational expenditures experience the fastest growth. But does the country grow because of its investment in human resources or does it buy education because its favorable growth rate enables it to indulge its philosophical commitments? Or is it because well-paid workers demand better education for their children? Other studies have compared levels of educational expenditure to periods of country growth. The indications are supportive but leave the same question: Does the country grow because it invests or invest because it is growing and can afford it? Interindustry and interfirm comparisons have the same possibilities and shortcomings.

A number of researchers have attributed to investments in human beings the residual in economic growth rates unexplained by inputs of capital and land. Such approaches rarely show a direct cause-and-effect relationship to expenditures on education, on-the-job training, health care, or any other investment in human productivity, but they give strong support to education as a major factor.[18]

Given the difficulties of identifying the national rates of return from human resource investments, it has become the standard practice to measure the direct returns of education—that is, to compare the lifetime earnings of those with more or less education. The difference can then be expressed as an annual rate of return on the costs of education, discounted at some appropriate interest rate to measure the present value of a future stream of incomes.

Critiquing the Concept

This straightforward approach has its difficulties. First, as with any cost-benefit analysis, measurement of educational costs and benefits is not simple, and the choice of an appropriate discount rate can often predetermine the results. In calculating the returns to education or training, nonmonetary benefits, like the attractiveness of posttraining jobs, should be included, but these cannot be calculated in monetary terms. Training, education, and health increase a worker's satisfaction as a consumer of these things, but these contribute nothing to the measurable national output. These deletions would cause the internal rate of discount to underestimate the actual returns to training.

There are serious conceptual problems in determining costs as well as returns. For example, people must make expenditures for things such as food, clothing, housing, and medical care, which are maintenance costs of the human investment. But these things are needed in order for the worker to live. How much should we attribute to maintenance of the capital and how much to consumption?

There is a second difficulty with this approach. Most of the studies have looked at a cross section of people of different ages, races, education, and incomes and assumed that what was true of an age-income profile would be true of individuals over their life histories. Yet the many changes in educational costs and techniques, life expectancies, occupational structures, economic conditions, and other factors make this unlikely.

Another difficulty is that since labor cannot be separated from its owner, it cannot be sold. Therefore, it becomes more difficult than in the case of physical capital to borrow funds to make enough human investments to equalize costs and returns. The limited resources of the poor are an important constraint on their ability to make human resource investments.

A final criticism of this approach has been noted. The owners of physical capital maximize monetary returns from that capital. However, a very serious problem for human capital theorists is the fact that we cannot determine what those who make investments maximize. This is due to the fact that investors are assumed to maximize a utility function containing nonmarket factors like prestige, consumption benefits (both from the investment itself and from the nonmarket value of goods and services produced as a result of the investment), and earnings. Once we move from the assumption that all of these things (rather than only earnings) are maximized, it is not possible to tell whether or not an investor made an irrational choice.

However, these are only technical difficulties. The more serious ones are conceptual. Education is only partially approached as an investment by its purchasers (investors). It may be the parent who pays and makes the judgment of usefulness and purpose. Education, being a consumption good, may change the tastes of those who receive it, radically altering other consumption and investment decisions. At the elementary and secondary levels, attendance is a matter of compulsion, not choice. Society has decided it has an interest in the education of its citizens in addition to the individual benefits. If left to their own discretion and asked to pay for their own education, people, it is assumed, would meet their individual needs, but there would be insufficient education for social purposes. Measurements of return must differentiate between private and social benefits but neglect neither. If education is left to individual investment, those who can afford it will have it while those who need it the most to rise above their present circumstances will not be able to afford it. We often are forced to infer the future by the past, which is a very hazardous procedure in a dynamic society, as we shall see in connection with the argument that education or training cannot do much to improve the conditions of blacks or the poor.

If aggregate incremental earnings are taken as a measure of the national return from investment in education, the problem of conspicuous consumption emerges. As pointed out earlier in the chapter, if the employer hires those with educational attainment greater than required for the job, he may add to employee earnings without getting a commensurate increase in productivity. The most important criticism has also been identified earlier: the assumption that there is a direct relationship between a given investment (education) and productivity. There probably is a subrelationship, but it has not been satisfactorily demonstrated. We know that incomes and education are directly correlated, but we cannot tell which is cause and which is effect. The technique of arriving at the returns to education through regression equations that account mathematically for the influence on earnings of everything other than training or education is hazardous if there are important factors like differences in natural ability that are not accounted for.

There is no question that employers demand workers with education or training, but this is not identical with demanding workers with certain productive capacities. In other words, education might be used by employers to screen workers even though there is no necessary connection between education and job performance. Human capital theory is unable to specify precisely what it is that employers demand and what it is that workers supply, making the traditional demand-and-supply analysis much looser than many of its advocates imply. Insofar as there is a tendency for those with the greatest native ability and motivation to gain the most education, the education investment may be credited with what is really an economic rent on ability.

Usefulness of the Theory

For these and other reasons some economists have objected to basing human capital policy decisions on cost-benefit calculations. There is an assumption, for example, that the investment with the highest calculated rate of return would be the one decision makers should select. However, these calculations would be useful guides to action only if they were based on reasonably accurate measures of costs for achieving identical alternative objectives. Governments might decide to do nothing about the health of older people or training of any other than the brightest or youngest if decisions were made on the basis of human capital considerations alone. At best these calculations can only be used as an aid to decision making; they cannot become decision-making tools.

Even if we overcome the formidable obstacles to accurate calculation of human capital, this concept would be an imperfect guide to policy. We are still left with the problem of whose satisfaction should be maximized. Only value judgments could answer this question.

Human capital theorists have a way of meeting some of the objections to this concept by inserting new terms in their equations and proceeding as if that step solved every problem. And it is true that this procedure often helps solve theoretical problems, but it does not provide much policy guidance. For example, these analysts modify their equations for risk and uncertainty by adding probability terms. This procedure helps clarify some of the theoretical relationships involved in investment decision, but it is impossible to quantify all of these variables.

Despite its appeal, the human capital concept has many defects that limit its application to particular labor market problems. Some of these difficulties are due to ideological or political opposition to the concept. Some people oppose its use because it implies that differences in the distribution of income and wealth are due to the individuals themselves rather than to social institutions. Those who want to change social institutions will be less inclined to give weight to the human capital concept, which emphasizes marketable benefits, because it is very difficult to put a price on the value of social change. How much is it worth, for example, to eliminate or reduce racial discrimination or imperfections in labor markets? If earned incomes are due to differences in human capital, there is an implication that the poor simply were not interested enough in investing in themselves to improve their earning power, that they made bad choices relative to people who were better off, or that they simply had inferior physical and intellectual abilities. It is equally easy to argue politically that since earnings reflect productivity, taxes should not be progressive. It is not surprising, therefore, that whereas conservatives are the main champions of this concept, liberals and radicals are more likely to oppose it.

These considerations make the human capital approach an unsatisfac-

tory theoretical and practical way to make manpower or other human resource decisions. Few would argue against attempting to calculate crude
costs and benefits, but placing a great deal of reliance on them for decision-
making purposes is another matter. In the final analysis, policy makers must
make decisions on the basis of the weight of the evidence presented to
them. The human capital approach might provide better evidence for or
against a program, but the concept clearly should be used with great care.

   All of these criticisms notwithstanding, careful scholars have almost
uniformly concluded that the results of education and the rates of return to
investment in it are positive.[19] The gains appear not only in the lifetime
earnings of the recipients of education but also in the intergenerational impacts upon their children's earnings. Other rewards have been found in the
health of the recipients and their descendents, in the quality of family relationships, in job satisfaction, in voluntary service to the community, and in
the creativity and adaptability of the labor force. There can be little question that however difficult it may be to measure precisely, trained intelligence is the main hope for solving the world's social, environmental, and
economic problems. Moreover, trained intelligence clearly is an important
factor in improving the production of goods and services. However, intelligence can be and is trained in places other than formal educational institutions, and various places, procedures, and institutions undoubtedly have
advantages and disadvantages for various kinds of intelligence training. The
task of the future is to identify the unique role of each process and to improve it.

DISCUSSION QUESTIONS

1. How do you account for the rise in educational attainment of the average
   American worker from 10.2 years to 12.6 years in one generation? What have
   been some of the major social and economic consequences of that development? What do you foresee for the future of educational attainment?
2. To what extent is the rise of educational attainment a supply or a demand phenomenon? Explain. What are the alternative consequences for the wage structure? Have wages in fact responded as would have been expected under the
   circumstances?
3. Are Americans becoming overeducated? By what standards do you reach your
   conclusion? What are the consequences? What policies would you recommend
   for the future?
4. According to available evidence, do formal education, formal training, and informal training make for more productive workers, raise workers' salaries, and
   reduce unemployment? Why or why not? Why doesn't education "work"
   equally for all age/race/sex groups?
5. Explain the concept of "human capital." In what ways can education and
   training expenditures be considered an investment? What are the alternative
   ways of measuring returns to such investments? What are the major shortcomings of these measures?
6. Discuss the technical and conceptual issues and problems in measuring the

public and private returns to investment in human beings as an economic resource. What are the policy implications emerging from the current literature
on this topic? Of what relevance is the methodology of this literature to the
evaluation of current public programs designed to develop human resources?

Notes

1. Richard Freeman, *The Overeducated American* (New York: Academic Press, 1976).
2. Christopher Jencks, *Inequality: An Assessment of the Effect of Family and Schooling in America* (New York: Basic Books, 1972).
3. Edward Denison, *Sources of Economic Growth in the United States and the Alternatives Before Us,* supplementary paper No. 13 (Committee for Economic Development, New York, 1962).
4. *Employment and Training Report of the President* (Washington, D.C.: GPO, 1979), p. 363.
5. Richard Freeman, op. cit., pp. 26–27.
6. David Shea, "Education, Occupation and Earnings," Conference on Youth Employment, University of California Los Angeles, February 11–12, 1978 (U.S. Department of Labor), pp. 113–140.
7. Ibid.
8. Rupert Evans et al., "Criteria for Determining Whether Competence Should Be Taught on the Job or in a Formal Technical Course," *Journal of Vocational Education Research* (Fall 1976).
9. John T. Grasso and John R. Shea, *Vocational Education and Training* (New York: Carnegie Council on Policy Studies in Higher Education, 1979), chap. 2.
10. Rupert Evans, "School for Schooling's Sake," in *The Transition from School to Work* (Princeton, N.J.: Princeton University Press, 1963), pp. 189–209.
11. Garth Mangum and John Walsh, *A Decade of Manpower Development and Training* (Salt Lake City, Utah: Olympus Publishing Company, 1973).
12. James S. Coleman et al., *Equality of Educational Opportunity* (Washington, D.C.: GPO, 1966).
13. Christopher Jencks, op. cit.
14. Garth Mangum and John Walsh, *A Decade of Manpower Development and Training* (Salt Lake City, Utah: Olympus Publishing Company, 1973).
15. Theodore W. Schultz, "Investment in Human Capital," *American Economic Review* (March 1961): 1–17.
16. Denison, op. cit.; Robert Solow, "Technical Change and the Aggregate Production Function," *Review of Economics and Statistics* (August 1957): 312–330; B. F. Mossell, "Capital Formation and Technological Change in United States Manufacturing," *Review of Economics and Statistics* (May 1960): 182–188.
17. Frederick Harbison and Charles A. Myers, *Education, Manpower, and Economic Growth* (New York: McGraw-Hill, 1969).
18. Richard Perlman, *The Economics of Education* (New York: McGraw-Hill, 1973); Lester Thurow, *Investment in Human Capital* (Belmont, Calif.: Wadsworth Publishing Co., 1970).
19. These studies are summarized in Task Force on Education and Employment, *Education for Employment: Knowledge for Action* (Washington, D.C.: National Academy of Education, 1979): 64–71.

Chapter 8 Education for Employment

Chapter 7 explored in broad and general terms the role played by education in the development of human resources. This chapter gets more specific concerning educational activities specifically designed to affect people's employability—their attractiveness to employers and their productivity. The attributes of employability can be attained in the home, by life experiences in the neighborhood and community, in formal classroom training settings, or on the job. The latter is the subject of Chapter 10. This chapter is concerned with employability preparation in the classroom setting.

Schools and training institutions make three kinds of contributions to employability: (1) they assist in the development of general intellectual and manual skills essential to employment as well as to other aspects of modern life such as oral and written communication, computation, and the like; (2) they affect values, motivation, and personality involving the will to work and the necessary interpersonal relations which make most work possible; and (3) they offer training in specific occupational skills.

As pointed out in Chapter 7, education would have been considered a prerequisite for employment in very few occupations forty years ago. In the not too distant past, the phrase "education for employment" would have brought to mind vocational and technical education, and professional and graduate schools. Education at more general levels would have been considered relevant to employability but would have been assumed to have no direct responsibility for it. The flowering of career development theory and career education practice and increased efforts to link youth employment programs with the schools suggest a new phase concerned more with values and attitudes toward work than with the provision of occupational skills. This chapter reviews the current status of vocational education and ties it into broader issues related to the interface between education and employment. Chapter 9 is the locus of discussion of the contributions of higher education to human resource development.

VOCATIONAL EDUCATION

Vocational education is at a peak in funding and enrollments but has never been in more philosophical ferment. The data will be reviewed followed by discussion of the issues.

World War I was the immediate environment of the Smith-Hughes Act of 1917, the first federal support for vocational education. But that offered only a convenient timing for the interim resolution of a long philosophical and political struggle between the advocates of academic and manual education. Along with advocacy for training hands as well as minds was meeting the growing skill needs of an industrializing labor market. Three broad occupational categories were chosen—vocational agriculture, home economics, and trades and industry. The sum of $7 million a year was appropriated for matching grants to encourage states to provide training in these areas. Other occupational groupings such as distributive education, fishery occupations, technician training, and health care occupations were added over the years and federal appropriations rose to $55 million a year by 1963.

A new vocational education act in the latter year followed by amendments in 1968 and 1976 introduced a sharp change in philosophy. The emphasis was on the employment needs of various population groups rather than the skill needs of the labor market. The disadvantaged and handicapped were identified for special concern. A reallocation of funds from the secondary to postsecondary level was directed, reflecting the need for more sophisticated skills. Cooperative educational efforts between the employers and the schools were promoted. There was no longer a restricted list of occupations for training. In fact, any new or emerging occupation as well as any recognized one was eligible for funding, as was any general education necessary to facilitate the skill training. Guidance and counseling, teacher training, and instructional materials could also be supported from federal funds. Home economics and vocational agriculture were instructed to shift in the direction of gainful industrial employment. And congressional budget authorization multiplied from the tens of millions to the billions of dollars.

The popularity of vocational education was and is at the state and local

Table 8-1 PERCENT DISTRIBUTION OF ENROLLMENT
IN VOCATIONAL EDUCATION SELECTED YEARS 1961–1978

FISCAL YEAR	TOTAL ENROLLMENT (THOUSANDS)	AGRI-CULTURE	DIS-TRIBUTIVE	HEALTH
1961	3,856	20.9	7.9	1.2
1965	5,431	16.3	6.1	1.2
1970	8,794	9.7	6.0	2.3
1976	13,342	7.9	6.8	5.1
1978	16,705	6.0	5.7	4.5

SOURCE: Bureau of Adult, Vocational and Technical Education, U.S. Office of Education.
[a] Includes since 1970 a separate breakdown for occupation home economics as follows: 1970 1.7 percent; 1971, 2.1 percent; 1972, 2.6 percent; 1976, 3.6 percent; 1978, 2.8 percent.

level. In general Congress has been enthusiastic with the backing of a well-organized vocational education lobby, while each of the Johnson, Nixon, Ford, and Carter administrations has been cool to demands for expansion. As a result, appropriations have never neared the level of authorization and the federal proportion of total vocational education funding has shrunk. Out of a total expenditure of $131 billion for all education in 1978, vocational education received $5.6 billion in public funds.[1] Of that, state and local governments provided 91.2 percent, even though only a 50-50 match is required by federal law. Average costs per enrollee in the fiscal year 1978 were $334 with the federal government providing only $29. Given inflationary trends, federal resources allocated to vocational education decreased drastically during the last half of the 1970s while the state and local portion represented stability in real terms. Nevertheless, enrollments rose rapidly and consistently (Table 8-1).

New priorities established for vocational education during the 1960s experienced progress during that decade, but lost ground during the 1970s. Federal law established new priorities in vocational education on behalf of the disadvantaged and the handicapped but Congress failed to appropriate funds to implement those priorities. State and local governments, on the other hand, dramatically increased vocational expenditures for the handicapped but not for the disadvantaged. Yet enrollments of the disadvantaged increased substantially from 2.4 percent of the total in 1967 to 15.1 percent in 1972 before falling to 10.7 percent in 1978, while the physically and mentally handicapped have been persistently only about 2 percent of total enrollments. Another declared priority—to shift more vocational enrollments to the postsecondary level—failed as it stagnated at 11.2 percent in 1972 and 12.6 percent in 1978. Adults enrolled part time in vocational courses comprised 27 percent of total enrollments in both these years after falling from 42 percent in 1967.

By race, blacks, who were 15 percent of the relevant age group, were 19 percent of vocational enrollment in 1972 and 15 percent in 1978. His-

HOME ECONOMICS	OFFICE	TECHNICAL	TRADE AND INDUSTRIES	OTHER
41.8	—	3.2	25.0	—
38.6	13.5	4.2	20.0	—
29.2[a]	24.0	3.1	21.7	4.0
26.3[a]	23.4	3.6	23.3	—
21.9[a]	19.8	3.2	20.4	15.7

panics were proportionally represented while Native Americans and Asian and Pacific Islanders were underrepresented in population terms.

Occupationally, the vocational education trends have been as shown in Table 8-1. Beyond a consistent decrease in the proportions enrolled in vocational agriculture and home economics (which after 1970 was divided between consumer and homemaking, and occupational), there has been little change in proportions, despite labor market shifts. Of course the breadth of the occupational categories may hide major changes in enrollment proportions by specific occupation. Increasing the enrollment of women in vocational education became a goal of the 1970s but that did not change appreciably either, though female enrollments did decline proportionately in home economics and increase in agriculture, distributive, technical, and trade and industry occupations for a significant shift away from traditional stereotypes. The growing "other" category reflects the rise of activities related to employment but to no particular occupation such as guidance, remedial, or industrial arts programs.

In summary, it would seem fair to say that a substantial reorientation in policy and practice related to vocational education was mandated at the national level but had limited practical impact at the grass roots. Perhaps for that reason, federal funds were sharply restricted, but state and local taxpayers endorsed the status quo overwhelmingly, shifting funding from academic to vocational education to make that possible. However, underneath that indication of well-being festers the philosophical ferment considered later in the chapter. But first the groundwork must be laid by illustrating shifting patterns in thinking about the role of education in preparation for work.

CAREER DEVELOPMENT THEORY

Only over the past 30 years have educators undertaken to examine how schooling might best fit into the process of career preparation. The need for formal training in occupational skills has been recognized ever since occupations emerged which demanded preentry training. Consequent to the beginnings of such formal preparation for a few skilled trades as well as a few professions roughly a century ago, the issue arose of how to determine who should be trained for which occupations. Since freedom of occupational choice was assumed, the issue of how people were to make those choices was included. What emerged became known as the trait and factor approach to vocational guidance. Human beings had certain traits—talents, abilities, interests and so forth. Jobs could be analyzed to identify certain factors. If it could be determined which factor best suited which trait, happily-ever-after marriages between people and jobs could be achieved.

The trait and factor approach, though simplistic, was a significant contribution for its time and was the basis for much psychometric testing and task analysis. In fact, the massive psychometric testing relied upon as the basis for military assignments during World War II raised the questions from which modern career development theory emerged. It became obvious that career choice behavior, job satisfaction, and job success were much more complex phenomena than originally assumed. Occupational aspirations, stereotypes, and relative prestige interacted with social status, socioeconomic background, parental influence, and personal value systems in unexplored ways. Analysis of traits and factors might provide a basis for probability statements about success or failure but those might be little help in individual cases. Most important of all, it became apparent that human interests are never static. Individuals' preferences are constantly changing, including career preferences.

This experience sparked an area of research which still continues. Despite individual differences, psychologists found it was possible to generalize a process of human development and within it a process of career development.[2] There were stages of life through which most people passed at roughly the same ages and each stage was somewhat predictably the base for the next. Since work played a role in self-satisfaction and status as well as in material well-being, career development somewhat parallelled the human development of which it was part. Psychological as well as economic well-being might be enhanced if more attention were paid to that career development process. Since in the United States the schools tend to be the residual societal agency assigned to fill whatever gaps other institutions leave unfilled, career development became a concern of the schools. More recently, however, employers have begun to become aware of the significance of the concept to organizational well-being and career development has become an important component of research into organizational behavior.[3]

In general and in brief, interaction between biological and institutional influences carry most individuals through a set of developmental changes. Infancy is concerned primarily with survival and security, early childhood with learning a mass of simple survival skills and interactions within a limited social world. The focus is essentially on self, but in terms of learning basic skills without introspection. Then there is a growing awareness of a broader world and a learning of another set of survival skills, now social rather than physical. In later childhood there tends to emerge a time of introspection—of examining oneself in the context of the broader society to determine "Who am I and where do I fit into the scheme of things?"[4]

Considerable exploration is necessary over a substantial period of time to begin to find answers to those questions. Patterns of preference and ultimately of preferred lifestyle begin to emerge, shaped by environment and experience as well as self-direction. Choices are necessary throughout life but as time goes on more and more of them become irreversible and require more careful and explicit decision making. Maturity arrives when one knows who one is, can make a reasonable assessment of one's strengths and weaknesses and can accept and live with that knowledge, and can make decisions and accept fully the responsibility for one's own decisions and actions. But maturity is never fully achieved and even if it were, it would not be the end of human development. The popular book *Passages* is a fascinating portrayal of male and female adult human beings passing through all of the stages of life from leaving the home of parents to ultimate death.[5] Though its concerns are primarily interpersonal, all of those stages have obvious career implications.

Career development theories are attempts, based on observation and research, to provide a predictive pattern for the career-related aspects of this human development process. There is not the consensus upon which to base *a* career development theory but there are generally recognized categories of career development theories.[6]

One category emphasizes personality. It presumes that because of different personality structures, individuals are predisposed to certain needs. These needs direct the individual towards certain choices in search of either satisfaction or reduction of need. Certain types of occupations are more compatible with certain needs which predispose the individual toward those choices. Factors such as genetics, child-rearing practices, and early childhood experiences are likely to be stressed as the predisposing factors in these theories.

Others stress the sociological basis of career development. Social class horizons limit the range of experience, perception, and choice for all, regardless of socioeconomic level. A few may be confronted with alternatives so numerous as to make choice a source of overwhelming conflict. Others may be compressed to almost no choice. Poverty may precondition social responses, educational attainment, intellectual competence, and vocational ambitions. Parental ambitions and prejudice may be equally stifling to those at other levels. But in each case, the external environment is seen as the determining factor in these career development theories.

Others stress an information processing model. Limited information obviously limits and channels choice. But overwhelming amounts of unfiltered information may also lead to a premature career selection which is then defended by rationalization.

Economists have traditionally structured their theories on the concept of "economic man." That is, most people at most times can be expected to choose those occupations which will maximize the return to their own investments in themselves as human capital. Therefore, the interaction between the time and expense of training, on the one hand, and the expected lifetime income return from the occupation will predict occupational choice. But that theory is always prefixed by a *ceteris paribus*—all other things being equal, which they never are. It is useful in predicting how people on the average will choose under prescribed conditions but not in predicting or guiding the career choice of particular individuals. At the level of the individual, economists are more likely to stress the influence of the economic constraints of the person's environment, akin to those called sociological theories above.

Another category of career development theory emphasizes the importance of self-concept. One's career-related choices are shaped by the mental image one has of himself or herself in various settings and circumstances. One learns by experience and socialization the kind of person one is or prefers to be in terms of capabilities, values, strengths, weaknesses, and so forth and seeks occupations conceived as compatible with that image. As individual perceptions change, so do career preferences.

Each theorist would admit truth in all others but defend his or her emphasis. But all have in common some process of development from fantasy through growing realism to ultimate but not necessarily permanent choice. There is a stage of growing awareness of the role of work in the family, the society, and personal life. There is a stage of exploration, seeking compatibility among self-concept, preferred lifestyle, and occupation. But, until the age when actual employment experience is possible, that exploration must be vicarious and fanciful. Ultimately decisions are forced by the passage of time, at least in terms of whether or not to seek temporary jobs and which ones and whether to continue in school or search for full-time employment. Early jobs are part of the exploratory process. Later ones may represent decisions as to occupation but a continuing exploration for the preferred environment in which to pursue that occupation. For most, the occupational choice is probably momentary without consideration of long-range implications but there are still predispositions behind that choice and reasons for leaving off or continuing further search.

Vocational maturity, like personal maturity, never fully arrives but is approached and can be defined. Vocational maturity is achieved when one knows oneself, one's values and one's preferred life style, can pursue and process information for choosing a compatible occupation, can accept the responsibility and consequences of choice and can make objective judgments concerning the relative costs and benefits of continuance or change.

But; like human development, career development does not end with

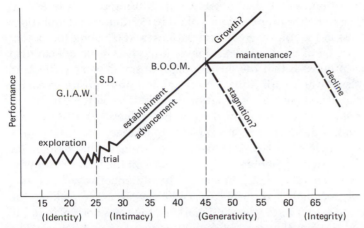

Figure 8-1   Stages in career development. (Source: Douglas T. Hall et al., "Research on Organizational Career Development," *Human Resources Planning*, vol. 1, no. 4, 1978:215.)

maturity. Psychologists have identified career development stages which parallel the "passages" of adult life (Figure 8-1). The teens and early twenties are periods of continuing exploration, a time of getting into the adult world (GIAW), according to one author.[7] The late twenties and thirties involve getting established or settling down (SD). During the forties, the individual arrives at mid-career with a career pattern pretty well set and predisposed to plateau, decline, or continual growth (BOOM or becoming one's own man [person?]). From there on it is a process of decline and coming to terms with one's inevitable mortality.

Study of the career development processes of children and youth have led to the conviction that career preparation in the schools should begin much earlier, not in terms of occupational training but in the development of values, the beginning of guided exploration and the development of decision-making skills.[8] That is the basis of the career education movement. These concepts of career development have also led vocational guidance and counseling away from simple testing and directed advice toward a process of guided self-discovery in career terms. Awareness of the continuance of the career development process throughout life is the motivation for the addition of career development planning to the processes of labor resources planning within the employing establishment described in Chapter 21.

CAREER EDUCATION

The direct operational consequences of the emergence of career development theory has been the various activities described as career education. Though specific programs and applications differ widely, there is a central concern and sequence which can be described briefly.[9]

Career education has the dual objective of (1) using the entire educational experience to better prepare youth of all backgrounds and ambitions for career success in the full range of occupations, and (2) using the potential career relevance of academic learning as a motivator for educational success. Its first premise is that the development of sound work values and positive attitudes toward work is more essential as a prerequisite to career success than the attainment of occupational skills. The latter can be attained at later stages in school or on the job, but values and attitudes are learned early and, if disfunctional, are difficult to change.

Therefore, career education is expected to begin in the elementary school simply because the school has little influence on the home during the preschool years when value development is already underway.[10] The elementary school assignment is primarily career awareness—making the child aware of the existence of work and workers, the roles both play in life and society, and the fact that the child will one day be one of those. The elementary stage coincides with the time in human development when the child is experiencing an enlarging awareness of the world outside the home and the neighborhood. Career awareness, therefore, merges into that growing social awareness.

Late childhood and early adolescence is the period for turning inward to examine oneself in relation to the broader society.[11] "Who am I?" "What am I like?" "What can I become?" Career exploration becomes the appropriate assignment for the middle school or junior high. The student explores his or her talents, abilities and interests, alternative lifestyles, and the occupations which are compatible with those lifestyles. It is impossible to become familiar with all of the 30,000 occupations in the *Dictionary of Occupational Titles* but they can be explored in broad categories such as those of the construction industry, office occupations, and so forth, a breakdown which lends itself to examination of life-style consequences.

At the high school age, there are decisions that the youth cannot avoid, including the choice of friends, personal characteristics, courses of study, continuance in school, and early jobs.[12] Decision-making skills taught at that point can help in personal and career choices. It is also a time of preparation for next steps—jobs, college, the military, marriage, etc. Career education shifts to that emphasis as well, with preparation for college, for full-time employment, for job search, and for placement.

Throughout, it is emphasized that school work is work too and the values, attitudes, and habits which make for success in the classroom are the same ones which will eventually make for success in the workplace. Career education is not expected to be taught as a separate course but is integrated into every subject. Each teacher in every classroom is expected to emphasize the career relevance of the subject matter. There is a preference for integrated projects which allow the student to learn the content of several academic subjects in a context of productive employment-related activities. Playing at operating and patronizing a grocery store, running a newspaper, or other community functions in an elementary classroom are examples.

Another key concept is collaboration between the school and employers, labor organizations, and other community institutions. The classroom is viewed as only one among many learning environments and not necessarily the most effective one. Thus considerable use is made of field visits, classroom visitors, and external community service projects. Linkages are also sought with the home with students learning of their parents' occupations as well as homemaking as an occupation. Considerable effort is put into breaking down occupational stereotypes by sex and race. The dignity of all work and workers is another concept usually emphasized.

Career education has become a substantial movement at the grass roots level with emotionally loyal adherents devoting tremendous efforts to develop and share their own classroom applications of the concept. Numerous trade and professional associations and service clubs have endorsed it and several state legislatures have made it a required priority. The response at the political level has been hot and cold, however. Each U.S. Commissioner of Education must have a new initiative to publicize and each has an average tenure of about 18 months. The career education term was publicized and given impetus by one commissioner during the Nixon administration, deemphasized by another under President Gerald Ford, and opposed by the Carter administration.

Initially, career education was financed from vocational education budgets and the American Vocational Association at first endorsed it and then began to advocate incorporation of some of its concepts into vocational education rather than divert the funds. The Carter administration opposed separate career education legislation and then, when Congress passed it anyway, opposed appropriations to fund the effort. Instead, it chose to put its own emphasis on remedial efforts on behalf of disadvantaged youth, emphasizing work experience rather than classroom activity. At the rhetorical level, "education and work initiatives" and "industry-education-councils" were preferred terminology.

Given a tradition in which educational change has generally been bought at the price of federal matching grants for specified purposes, the survival of the career education terminology may be in doubt. However, concern for the development of work values appears soundly grounded in theory and research and is likely to continue whatever the name.

WORK EXPERIENCE EDUCATION

The various cooperative work-study components of the Vocational Education Act, the Experience Based Career Education (EBCE) offshoot of career education, the work experience emphasis of the Youth Employment Demonstration Projects Act (YEDPA) discussed in Chapter 12, and a variety of locally sponsored programs represent another thrust in the effort to find better means for employment preparation. In vocational education terminology, work-study usually refers to work activities primarily directed to earning income to make study possible. Cooperative vocational education involves students sharing the day or week between schooling and employment under school supervision to assure that both are a linked learning experience. Though evidence is weak that subsequent employment and income progress is enhanced, such programs are widely endorsed.[13]

Experienced-based career education is a broader approach which emphasizes employment experience as a method of general as well as vocational education.[14] There are a variety of different models but one sponsored in Oregon by the Northwest Educational Laboratory is typical. The students in this program spend about 50 percent of their program time at learning sites, working directly with community instructors. The program uses a detailed task analysis procedure to identify the full learning potential of each employer or community site and to translate this potential into learning objectives. The objectives then become the basis for individualized projects which students complete in the community. The curriculum is divided into three content areas: life skills, basic skills, and career development.

The five life skills categories are (1) creative development, (2) critical thinking, (3) personal and social development, (4) science, and (5) functional citizenship. Lifelong learning, personal growth, and relationship of individuals to broader community, national, and world concerns are emphasized. The life skills content area also includes a set of "survival skills" such as knowledge of checking accounts, insurance, budgeting, auto maintenance, and so forth. The EBCE students must demonstrate competence in these areas as part of their program requirements. The basic skills components concentrate on reading, mathematics, writing, and listening and speaking skills. The career development component focuses on identifying career interests, understanding the world of work, general employability skills, and career knowledge.

Each year, individual students must complete ten projects, two in each life skills area. A set of 13 survival skills or competencies must be completed by all students in the program. Students must spend a minimum of fifteen hours a week at an employer or community site and complete a minimum of five career explorations per year. Students' progress in the program is carefully monitored and recorded. Individualized problem-centered projects which the students complete at community sites encourage them to manage their own learning and perceive the relationship among personal goals, career options, and specific knowledge skills. When students leave the program they receive a certification portfolio containing performance information as well as a standard high school diploma.

The Youth Employment Demonstration Projects Act starts from the premise that its economically disadvantaged clientele has already been "turned off" by the classroom. Yet it recognizes that intellectual as well as manual skills are essential to a successful career in modern labor markets.

Since YEDPA was designed as an experiment rather than an operational program, it has taken two separate roads to rehabilitation and labor market preparation. One has been to use work experience opportunities as motivation for return to the classroom; the other to supply alternative education opportunities during enrollment in work experience programs. With only limited success, its administrators have sought school cooperation in the assessment of experiential learning and the recording of academic credit for it to facilitate the attainment of educational credentials by those unwilling to return to the classroom.[15]

Representative of the variety of related experiments in alternative education, whether or not federally financed, is the career intern program developed by the Opportunities Industrialization Centers of Philadelphia.[16]

The interns (they are *never* called students) are either dropouts or those underperforming and on the verge of leaving regular central city high schools. They must have at least a fifth-grade reading level and not been characterized by major disciplinary problems. Essentially, they are self-selected for the program which moves them from a standard overcrowded city high school with overworked staff and minimum counseling to a unique school which accepts only 250 per year and has a high student-teacher/counselor ratio.

Each intern participates in a career counseling seminar and prepares a career development plan which leads to a series of one week "hands-on" experiences with employers in fields of the intern's interest. Meantime, the interns study a required curriculum and electives, all oriented around career applications and consisting of specially prepared individualized materials. The structure is essentially ungraded and students work at their own pace until they have completed the material required for graduation.

Careful records have been kept of interns and a control group. The clearest gains have been in the number of former dropouts and academic failures who have not only graduated from high school, but entered postsecondary education. The subsequent employment records of the interns are somewhat but not notably better than the controls, but the interns are much less likely to be out of school and out of work. About one-third of the interns drop out again, but that compares to 85 percent of those controls still in school at the time the interns entered the program.

Evaluators found that all school conduct of the interns improved: attendance, keeping appointments, initiative, completing assignments, test-taking skills, working well with peers and teachers, attention to classwork, willingness to repeat failed courses, reading and math skills (though the latter were still below national norms). As to employability, they improved markedly in career planning and career decision-making ability and in the behavioral protocols required by employers. Conclusions were that the success arose from a supportive atmosphere, ready availability and dedication of teachers, counselors and other staff, dealing with the intern as "a whole person," treating the school and program as a tool rather than an entity, providing a school experience congruent with realistic life goals, and expecting the interns to make their own decisions and to perform.

Whether such an approach is generally replicable is open to question. The costs beyond the preparation of curriculum, which could have served many schools, were somewhat greater per student than in general high schools but not above the standard for vocationally oriented high schools. The major problems would appear to be staff dedication and employer cooperation when generalized to large numbers. Nevertheless, the program seems to indicate that imagination, dedication, and clear and relevant goals can work when made available to youth who want a second chance.

Each of these work experience programs seeks to reverse the traditional advice to stay in the classroom longer as the best insurance for career success. But each is directed toward special populations which have not profited from the classroom approach. They leave unspecified the ideal role of education in employment preparation, if there is indeed one.

THE PHILOSOPHICAL BASE OF VOCATIONAL EDUCATION

These employment related educational developments bring us full circle to examine changes occurring in the philosophy underlying vocational education. Involved in the original Smith-Hughes Act and other early advocacies of vocational education was a complex of convictions that manual labor had an inherent dignity which had been ignored in an excessive concern for academic development, that equality of economic opportunity would be enhanced if manual and intellectual training were available side by side, that national productivity and international competitiveness would be promoted, and that individualism and enterprise would be fostered.[17] None of these objectives were ever accomplished but their echoes still ring in the debates of the 1980s.

The tradition of superiority of head over hand is too deeply instilled in too many cultures to be eradicated easily. Only when the wearing of a blue collar is rewarded with a higher income than that accruing to the white-collar worker is that shift in relative esteem likely to occur. Rather than equalizing opportunity, the advent of vocational education was followed by the introduction of tracking systems which identified in elementary schools who was to be cycled into higher education and who into vocational education. Productivity's rise and fall has been more the consequence of capital investment practices than of investment in human beings. A few vocational education graduates have become entrepreneurs. Nevertheless, the goals persist and, to a substantial extent, have been adopted by career education.

Perhaps the lack of clear evidence that vocational graduates experience more stable employment, higher incomes, or other advantages than students in alternative programs explains in part the negative stance of the federal government and the questioning by many of vocational education's strongest adherents. Evaluations of vocational education typically compare the subsequent employment stability and earnings of vocational students with those of students in the general education or college-preparatory curriculum who do not go on to college.[18] Girls in vocational courses do seem to profit significantly in comparison to girls in other courses. Those who receive vocational education in high school do better than others when they undertake further occupational training beyond high school. Otherwise, vocational students appear to do no better nor no worse than their comparison groups. That the vocational education students do not have superior employment and earnings is accepted as evidence that the vocational courses have not been worthwhile.

The ambiguous nature of the evidence concerning returns to investment in vocational education may be in part explained by studies differentiating income returns to all education by occupation and by social class.[19] Education was found to be substantially rewarded in income terms for those entering professional and technical employment or becoming employers and managers. That was not true for employees in lower levels of occupations. The occupations for which vocational education prepares one are in the latter categories. The fact that one can rarely obtain employment in the professional and technical ranks without the appropriate educational credential while few employers insist upon a credential for entry to the remainder of the occupational spectrum may be more telling than the actual educational content.

Whatever the cause, academic and national leaders in vocational education appear to be searching avidly for a new rationale and a new mission for vocational education. Noting that Congress has been willing to appropriate far greater sums for remedial work experience efforts on behalf of a relatively few disadvantaged youth than for occupational training for the entire population cohort, national leaders of the American Vocational Association advocate that vocational educators forego their concentration on classroom instruction and adopt work experience as an additional skill training mode.[20] Others argue simultaneously that most evaluations of vocational education are unfair and that vocational education has intrinsic benefits aside from preparation for employment.[21]

A college student can work in secondary labor market jobs for several years after high school with neither the student or the high school program marked as a failure. A vocational graduate the same age in the same occupation is a failure for the vocational program. If an academic student drops out of college, the student is blamed for failure to achieve. If a vocational student does not achieve in the training occupation, the vocational school has failed. Vocational education prepares for a range of occupations where the supply tends to exceed the demand more often than at professional and technical levels, and so on.

On the other hand, it is argued, the activities involved in vocational education are likely to be intrinsically interesting and enjoyable to those students. The motivations of vocational students at the high school level are admitted to be recreational and avocational, and:

> Play is an important factor in personal development. . . . Playing at being a homemaker, a farmer, a builder, a businessman, provides a testing ground for mature social action. . . . Play with tools and with the social relations inherent in productive work groups provide the context for learning complex social strategies and communication skills so necessary in adult life.[22]

Vocational projects, it is said, provide a sense of personal competence, the aesthetic pleasure of doing a job well, the integrity of sound craftsmanship, the development of cooperativeness in commercial enterprises, and a heightened sense of altruism from community service. Thus vocational education would be viewed as an alternative route to preparation for life rather than a specialized means for preparation for employment.

SUMMARY COMMENT

The ferment surrounding the concepts of career development, career education, education and work initiatives, and the underlying philosophy of vocational education suggest that we do not know as much as we thought we did about how people are best prepared for employment or even what role career success should play in our lives. Perhaps we lack answers because we have asked the wrong questions or asked them in the wrong way.

DISCUSSION QUESTIONS

1. What were the factors which led to the emergence of vocational education in the early years of this century? How many of those factors remain important considerations today? What are the major arguments for and against the provisions of occupational training within the public schools?
2. Testing your own impressions, what are the characteristics of those you generally think of as vocational students? What are your perceptions of their backgrounds and future prospects? What do those answers tell you about yourself and your labor market experience and views?
3. Using your own experiences and changing attitudes to this point in your life, what have been the stages you have gone through in career development? If you have made an occupational choice, what are the bases upon which it was made? Ask a number of people at mid-career or beyond how they came to choose their present occupation. Discuss the implications for employment-related education.
4. Looking back to your own childhood, what were the perceptions you had of your parents' work and its role in their lives? How important do you consider work within your value system? Is it a means to an end or an end in itself? How does your preferred occupation relate to your preferred lifestyle? What are the implications of your answers for career education?
5. Do your teachers often allude to the career relevances of the subject matter

they teach? What career relevance has this course? Does such knowledge affect your motivation to study and learn?
6. In your opinion, how extensively should career education concepts be applied throughout education? Why?
7. Remediation is a palliative at best. What can be done to better prepare people for employment and to change employing institutions and labor markets to prevent the development of employment problems? What are the relationships between education and employment?

Notes

1. *Summary Data, Vocational Education, Program Year 1978* (Washington, D.C.: Bureau of Occupational and Adult Education, U.S. Office of Education, U.S. Department of Health, Education, and Welfare, 1979).
2. Samuel Osipow, *Theories of Career Development* (New York: Appleton-Century-Crofts, 1968); John L. Holland, *Making Vocational Choices: A Theory of Careers* (Englewood Cliffs, N.J.: Prentice-Hall, 1973).
3. Douglas T. Hall, *Careers in Organizations* (Pacific Palisades, Calif.: Goodyear Publishing Co., 1976).
4. Helen Bee, *The Developing Child* (New York: Harper & Row, 1978).
5. Gail Sheehy, *Passages* (New York: Dutton, 1976).
6. Edwin L. Herr, *Review and Synthesis of the Foundations of Career Education* (Washington, D.C.: GPO, 1972).
7. Daniel Levinson, *Seasons of a Man's Life* (New York: Knopf, 1978).
8. Kenneth Hoyt et al., *Career Education in the Middle/Junior High School* (Salt Lake City: Olympus Publishing Company, 1973).
9. Rupert Evans et al., *Career Education, What It Is and How to Do It!* (Salt Lake City: Olympus Publishing Company, 1972).
10. Kenneth Hoyt et al., *Career Education and the Elementary School Teacher* (Salt Lake City: Olympus Publishing Company, 1973).
11. Rupert Evans et al., op. cit.
12. Kenneth Hoyt et al., *Career Education in the High School* (Salt Lake City: Olympus Publishing Company, 1976).
13. Irwin L. Herrnstadt et al., *The Transition from School to Work: The Contribution of Cooperative Education Programs* (Boston: Department of Economics, Northwestern University, 1979).
14. Kenneth Hoyt et al., *Career Education in the High School* (Salt Lake City: Olympus Publishing Company, 1976), pp. 335–340.
15. Joseph Colmen and Gregory Wutzberg, *Involving Schools in Employment and Training Programs for Youth* (Washington, D.C.: National Council on Employment Policy, 1979).
16. National Institute for Education, *The Career Intern Program: Final Report*, vol. 1 and 2 (U.S. Department of Health, Education and Welfare, 1977).
17. Willford W. Wilms, "New Meanings for Vocational Education," *UCLA Educator* 21 (1979): 5–12.
18. For a summary of these evaluations, see National Academy of Education, *Education for Employment* (Washington, D.C.: Acropolis Books, 1979).
19. David O'Shea, "Education, Occupation and Earnings," *UCLA Educator* 21 (1979): 39–45.

20. Gene Bottoms, "Executive Directions," *Vocational Education* (January 1979): 10–11; (April 1979): 12–13.
21. Harry F. Silverman, "High School Vocational Education, an Intrinsic Perspective," *UCLA Educator* 21 (1979): 46–51.
22. Ibid., p. 48.

Chapter 9
The Role of
Higher Education

Higher education, defined as all postsecondary education in colleges and universities, plays an important role in labor markets and human resource development. Postsecondary education also is a significant industry, providing employment to about 750,000 faculty members in more than 3,000 educational institutions. This system had total expenditures of $45.5 billion during the 1977–1978 academic year. About 10.1 million degree-credit students were enrolled in these schools in 1977. This represented a dramatic increase in college enrollments from 2.3 million in 1947 and 6.8 million in 1968.

Postsecondary schools supply a large proportion of technicians, managers, and professional workers. These institutions also advance knowledge, preserve cultural heritages, and facilitate upward social and economic mobility. The efficiency of the postsecondary educational system and the access to it by all sectors of the population are thus very important for human resource development and for political, economic, and social stability.

The importance of higher education is not vitiated by doubts about either the precise relationships between education and productivity, discussed in Chapter 8, or the fact that the higher-education system is necessary to provide the manpower to operate a society that becomes increasingly complex as it develops. It is clearly possible to exaggerate the importance of the scientific and technical requirements of an industrial economy. Most of the growth of demand for scientists, technicians, and other professionally trained personnel in the last 20 years has been sparked by governmental programs, by defense needs, and by population-related requirements for teachers and health-care personnel, not from the initiatives of the private industrial sector. Moreover, studies of output per worker and occupational skill mix do not indicate that those industries with the fastest rates of growth of output per worker increased their employment of skilled or white-collar workers faster than those whose productivity did not increase as fast.[1] Similarly, studies of developments in European countries found no significant relationship between productivity and educational changes.[2] The experiences of countries such as Japan demonstrate the possibility of operating a sophisticated industrial economy with average educational levels much lower than those prevailing in the United States.

There can be little question, nevertheless, that postsecondary education serves to increase the incomes of individuals, whether or not there is a causal relationship between this kind of education and GNP. The evidence shows workers with college degrees to have a number of employment and income advantages, such as higher beginning salaries, lower unemployment rates, higher labor force participation rates, and higher lifetime earnings.

COSTS AND RETURNS ON INVESTMENT IN HIGHER EDUCATION

Insofar as average returns to individuals are concerned, the net rate of return on education can be determined by calculating the discounted values of projected salaries (lifetime earnings) and deducting the costs (or investment) incurred in obtaining an education.

The costs of undergraduate higher education are not inconsiderable, even when controlled for inflation. The estimated average annual student charges (tuition, required fees, board, and room) in 1975–1976 constant dollars were:

	1965–1966	1975–1976	1980–1981
Public	$1,707	$1,748	$1,858
Private	3,483	3,667	3,916

However, the expenses of going to college vary considerably according to the type of institution. Of the total expenses incurred by colleges and universities, about 55 percent are for instructional services and 45 percent for housing and food services, organized research, extension, and other public services, student aid, and other student services. In 1980–1981 the tuition per average undergraduate student in American postsecondary schools ranged from $427 in public junior colleges to $3079 in private universities and $744 in public universities. To these costs should be added the approxi-

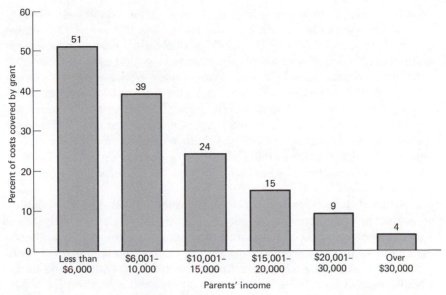

Figure 9-1   Financial aid by parents' income, 1975. (Source: National Center for Education Statistics.)

mately $8000 a year the average college student could have been expected to earn if not in school (less part-time and summer earnings). Thus, a 4-year college education in 1980–1981 would have cost about $35,000 if obtained in a public institution, and $50,000 if obtained in a private university. Because of rapidly rising costs in private higher-education institutions and a reduction in the quality gap between public and private colleges and universities, undergraduate enrollment has risen very sharply in public institutions (from 1.9 million in 1960 to 8.1 million in 1977), while enrollment in private institutions has increased relatively much less—1.3 million in 1960 to 2.1 million in 1977.

Costs of higher education influence the labor market in a variety of ways, but principally as they redistribute income among income groups and influence access to higher education. Because a much larger proportion of students from wealthy families attend college, as will be shown later in this chapter, the affluent are subsidized more heavily by higher-education expenditure than the poor. Nevertheless, the United States has steadily, as a matter of policy, increased the financial aids available to help students from lower income families attain to higher education (see Figure 9-1).

In the United States higher education has been perceived by persons from low-income backgrounds as an important means of upward social mobility. To some extent this belief stems from the observation that college-educated persons have had higher incomes and less unemployment, especially during depressions such as that of the 1930s, when many of those who suffered from unemployment and loss of income acquired strong motivations to educate their children in order to make them "depression proof."[3]

There seems to have been a similar rise in aspirations to go to college by low-income groups during the 1960s, undoubtedly because these groups suffered high unemployment rates during that period and because civil rights developments raised the aspirations of many blacks and other minorities. Before the 1960s the aspirations of high school graduates from all income groups increased gradually, but during the 1960s a new trend apparently set in, and the gap between the aspirations of the poor and those of the rich narrowed during the 1970s. Whether our system of higher education is a force for social stability clearly will depend upon the extent to which those rising expectations are matched by opportunities to acquire higher education.

Although it has clear economic significance, higher education cannot be evaluated in monetary terms alone. The higher-education system does much to preserve those cultural and intellectual traditions that influence the quality of life. In this role institutions of higher education provide benefits, such as extending the general base of technology, contributing to the advancement of knowledge and the arts, and providing support for public leadership. These benefits accrue to society as well as to individuals and, therefore, cannot be measured in benefit-cost or market terms alone.

The American emphasis on formal education undoubtedly was intensified by a number of developments during and after World War II, which strengthened the conviction that education was important for national security. The emphasis on technology during the war gave considerable impetus to higher education, an impetus accelerated by the development of the atomic bomb and the space race in the postwar period. Clearly, much of the increased demand for college graduates following World War II was stimulated by the federal government. This stimulation resulted, in part, from the cold war, which gave considerable emphasis to national prestige derived from scientific and technical achievements and the rate of economic development. Federal support for education initially concentrated mainly on the physical sciences and engineering, but it was extended to other areas as the federal government sought to strengthen educational institutions during the 1960s. In addition, as was mentioned earlier, the federal government stimulated college enrollments after World War II through the GI Bill and to some extent by granting draft deferments or exemptions to college students during the 1960s.

Postwar population developments also influenced the demand for college graduates. The college-age population declined during the 1950s because of the low birth rates during the depression of the 1930s and World War II. Indeed, there were fewer 16- to 24-year-olds in 1950 than there had been in 1930, even though the total population increased 45 percent during those years. As a consequence of these developments, there was only a slight increase in college enrollments in the 1950s, resulting mainly from a rising trend in the proportion of college-age people going to college rather than

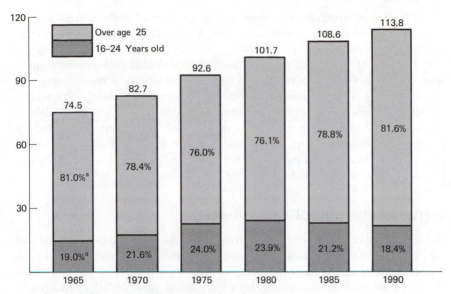

^a In 1965, 81 percent of the civilian labor force (74.5 million) were
over age 25; 19 percent were 16-24 years old.

Figure 9-2   16-24-year-olds as a proportion of the civilian labor force (age
16 and older). (Sources: U.S. Bureau of the Census, *Current Population Reports,* series P-23: no. 66, p. 42; series P-20: no. 324, p. 40; no. 292, p.
30; and Bureau of Labor Statistics.)

from an increase in the numbers of people in the college-age group. During
the 1960s, the number of college graduates increased greatly because of the
coming of age of those born during the postwar baby boom. The number of
bachelor's or equivalent degrees increased from 187,000 annually in the 1940s
to 287,000 in 1956, 505,000 in 1965, and 909,000 in 1975. The graduation of
the postwar baby boom generation and the lower rate of population growth
during the 1960s and 1970s caused that rate of growth to slow sharply
after 1975 and show signs of turning down as shown in Table 9-4 later in
this chapter. With the number of college age youth declining after 1980 a
continuation of that downturn is the expectation for the future (Figure 9-2).

ENROLLMENT IN HIGHER-EDUCATION INSTITUTIONS

There is great diversity in the American system of higher education. There
are over 11.5 million students at the postsecondary level in a great variety
of institutions. About 60 percent of the class hours offered to these students
are in the social sciences, humanities, liberal arts, and law; 17 percent are in
the physical sciences; 10 percent are in fine arts and applied arts; the remainder are in computer sciences and other fields.[4] About three-fifths of the
class hours offered by American postsecondary institutions are at the freshman and sophomore levels; 29 percent are in upper-division courses, and

about 8 percent are graduate courses. The number of college graduates at all degree levels sharply accelerated after World War II, but is now on the downgrade as noted above.

Because of the rising demand for vocational and technically trained workers, the lower cost of education in junior colleges and community colleges, and the decline in demand relative to supply for college graduates, enrollment in two-year colleges is expected to continue to rise in the 1980s. Between 1951 and 1969 enrollments in four-year institutions increased by 99 percent compared with 241 percent in two-year institutions. It is expected that two-year colleges will increase their proportion of college enrollments from about one-fourth in 1970 to 43 percent in 1990.[5]

OUTLOOK FOR COLLEGE GRADUATES

We should enter a word of caution about projections of the demand for and supply of college graduates. Although some aspects of these demand-and-supply conditions are fairly predictable, especially those that depend heavily on population projections, others are not as predictable, particularly those related to demand or to distant future events. In the long run, even population growth patterns change, as they did during the late 1960s and immediately following World War II. Projections also are complicated by biases in judgment, especially when those making the projections have vested interests in the outcome of those projections. Despite these uncertainties, however, projections of probable developments in the demand for and supply of college graduates provide better individual and public planning than would be possible without these projections.

The Supply of College Graduates

The most important factors influencing the future supplies of college graduates are the proportions of college-age people in the population and the proportion of these who complete college. On the demographic side, college enrollments can be predicted with a fair degree of accuracy by looking at the proportion of 18-year-old high school graduates who go to college. In 1975 49 percent of the white and 41 percent of the black high school seniors planned to attend college. Eighty-one percent of those whose families earned more than $25,000 planned to attend, 37 percent of those whose families earned less than $5000 planned to go to college.[6]

A major factor affecting college enrollments during the 1980s will be the declining fertility rates of the late 1960s; there will be fewer high school graduates in 1986 (3,158,000) than in 1975 (3,459,000), even assuming that the proportion of 18-year-olds who graduate from high school will continue increasing at about 1 percent a year so that about 90 percent of them graduate by 1982. The number of 18-year-olds was expected to have peaked at 4.3 million in 1979 (as compared with 3.6 million in 1969), and to decline

Table 9-1   ACTUAL AND PROJECTED EARNED DEGREES 1940–1985

ACADEMIC YEAR ENDING JUNE 30	BACHELOR'S AND FIRST PROFESSIONAL DEGREES	MASTER'S DEGREES	PH.D.S
1940	186,500	26,731	3,290
1948	271,000	42,000	4,200
1958	363,000	65,000	8,900
1970	772,000	211,000	29,000
1975	928,000	302,000	45,600
1976	997,504	313,001	34,076
1977	993,008	318,241	33,244
1978	1,028,400	334,100	36,200
1979	1,062,600	346,800	37,100
1980	1,090,700	373,200	38,900
1985[a]	1,025,000	405,000	42,000

SOURCE: National Center for Education Statistics.
[a] Projected.

to 3.5 million by 1986, and to rise gradually thereafter. The 16- to 21-year-old college-age population will peak in 1980 at 17.0 million, decline to 14.3 million by 1988, and increase gradually thereafter. As a consequence of these developments, college enrollments in full-time equivalents will increase from 5.8 million in 1968 to 9.8 million in 1982, and decline thereafter to 8.5 million in 1988.

The supply of college graduates increased sharply during the 1960s, rose more slowly during the 1970s, but it will decline in line with the previously mentioned enrollment trends during the 1980s. The number of bachelor's and first professional degrees increased from 667,000 in 1968 to about 1.1 million in 1980, or by approximately 60 percent. At that point a downturn began.

The outlook is for a continuous increase in graduate degrees, at least until the mid-1980s. The number of M.A.s awarded more than doubled between 1968 and 1980, from 177,000 to 373,000, and will increase to 405,000 in 1985. The number of Ph.D.s awarded grew from 23,100 in 1968 to 38,900 in 1980 and is expected to reach 42,000 by 1985. Altogether, 13 million degrees were awarded during the period 1968–1980—10.2 million B.A.s, 2.7 million M.A.s, and 400,000 Ph.D.s. Another 4 million college degrees can be expected during the first half of the 1980s.

The Demand for College Graduates

A substantial shift in the demand for college graduates occurred about 1970. Until then a college degree had been considered almost a guarantee of a good job. The space race slackened with men on the moon. The slowing birth rates began to impact upon the employment of teachers. Government research and development expenditures slowed down overall. Unemployment for professionals and technicians jumped from 1.3 percent in 1969 to 2.0 percent in 1970 and 2.9 percent in 1971 during a period when overall unemployment was rising from 3.5 percent to 5.9 percent. Journalists had a field day interviewing Ph.D.s holding jobs as taxi drivers and shoe clerks.

But the fears proved exaggerated. There had been a sharp break in the pace of growth but growth continued. By 1972 the number of professionals and technicians employed was rising again, reaching to over 14 million by 1978. Given the augmented supply, unemployment never fell to its old (levels below 2 percent) but fluctuated from 2.2 to 3.2 percent, depending upon the conditions of the national economy. Teachers, who account for three-fourths of the jobs requiring college degrees, seemed to be in a permanent slump. That also meant that the market stayed slack for those in the humanities. Specialties in physics and other sciences with a heavy government research and development dependence stayed in a permanent depression. Engineering rebounded and grew with the rise of the energy issue and the technician demand followed. Those social sciences limited primarily to the universities suffered but those with outlets into the business and consulting worlds did well. The health care shortages became less stringent with the slowing of population growth but jobs stayed plentiful.

The seller's market was gone but it was not totally a buyer's market, either. There was considerable "bumping back" with those with graduate degrees holding jobs for which a bachelor's degree had been considered sufficient and four-year degrees applying where a two-year degree had been enough. The market accommodated supply and demand but not without considerable disappointment for those who had built their expectations upon the demand and supply situations in effect when they had made their long-range decisions related to college and discipline. The salary structure also reacted with the premium for college graduation shrinking relative to other occupations.

Of the roughly 4 million graduates who entered the labor force between 1962 and 1969, 73 percent entered professional and technical occupations. About 17 percent entered managerial and administrative occupations. And about 3 percent entered sales, usually in the higher paying jobs. Less than 6 percent entered clerical, blue-collar, service, or farm occupations. Eight million graduated between 1969 and 1976. Of these, 46 percent found professional or technical jobs; 19 percent entered managerial and administrative jobs and 8 percent entered sales. Twenty-five percent entered jobs not previously sought or filled by college graduates; clerical, blue-collar, service, farm, or low-paying managerial jobs.

Looking ahead, the immediate outlook to 1985 involves little change in these patterns. It is estimated that about 10.4 million college graduates will enter the labor force over the 1976–1985 period, but only about 7.7 million job openings are expected in traditional occupations for college graduates. Employment of professionals and technicians is expected to reach 15.8 million by 1985, an annual rise of 1.9 percent. The number of

Table 9-2   DEGREES GRANTED TO WOMEN, 1969 THROUGH 1990

DEGREE	1969–1970		1977–1978		PROJECTED 1989–1990	
	TOTAL (000's)	PERCENT FEMALE	TOTAL (000's)	PERCENT FEMALE	TOTAL (000's)	PERCENT FEMALE
All bachelor's degrees	793	43.1	921	47.1	956	49.6
Business	106	9.0	161	27.1	N.A.	N.A.
Education	166	75.0	136	72.5	N.A.	N.A.
Engineering	45	0.8	55	6.7	N.A.	N.A.
Health professions	22	78.1	59	80.5	N.A.	N.A.
Physical sciences	22	13.8	23	21.3	N.A.	N.A.
Social sciences	155	37.3	113	40.5	N.A.	N.A.
All Master's degrees	208	39.7	312	48.3	375	47.5
Business	21	3.5	48	16.9	N.A.	N.A.
Education	80	55.3	119	67.7	N.A.	N.A.
Engineering	16	1.1	16	5.3	N.A.	N.A.
All doctor's degrees (except first professional)	30	13.3	32	26.4	34	31.0
First professional degrees	35	5.4	67	21.5	N.A.	N.A.
Medicine	8	8.5	14	21.5	N.A.	N.A.
Law	15	5.6	34	25.9	N.A.	N.A.

SOURCE: National Center for Education Statistics.

managers will increase by 2.2 percent per year. Sales and clerical workers, which will absorb a larger proportion of the college trained than had been traditional, will grow by 1.7 percent and 2.9 percent per year respectively. Given that total employment is expected to grow at 2 percent per year, the college graduate will have average prospects and will suffer only in comparison to the "salad days" of 1950–1970. Choice of disciplines and quality of training rather than simply a "sheepskin" will be essential to do better than the labor force average.

WOMEN AND MINORITIES

During the 1960s and 1970s the number and the proportion of women and minorities attending college increased substantially. The number of bachelor's degrees granted to women tripled between 1961 and 1978, compared with a doubling of the number granted to men, and the women's share of bachelor's degrees increased from 38 to 47 percent (Table 9-2).

Prior to 1970, however, the vast majority of women were educated for a limited number of female-dominated occupations, primarily elementary and secondary school teaching, nursing and related health fields, and social work. Many others studied liberal arts, which provided far less specific career orientation.

During the late 1960s and early 1970s, spurred by equal rights and af-

Table 9-3 ENROLLMENT OF WOMEN BY FIELD, 1970 AND 1978

FIELD	NUMBER		PERCENT CHANGE 1970–1978
	1970	1978	
Bachelor's degrees	341,276	433,857	27.1
Engineering	338	3,709	997.3
Business	9,515	43,760	359.9
MBAs	758	8,183	979.6
First professional degrees	1,908	14,311	650.1
Dentistry	36	566	1,472.2
Law	852	8,824	935.7
Medicine	713	3,069	330.4
Ph.D.s	3,980	8,473	112.9

SOURCE: National Center for Education Statistics.

firmative action legislation, significant numbers of women and minorities began to pursue careers in medicine, law, engineering, business, and other fields traditionally dominated by white males. The number of women preparing for these occupations increased much faster than the total degrees granted to women (Table 9-3).

One of the most dramatic developments of the 1970s was the enrollment of minorities in college education (Table 9-4). From 1968 to 1978, enrollment of minorities at the bachelor's level more than tripled, from 456,000 to 1,589,000. Data compiled by the Engineering Manpower Commission indicate that the number of minority students receiving bachelor's degrees in engineering increased by more than two-thirds between 1973 and 1978, from about 1900 to about 3200 (Table 9-5).

Office of Civil Rights data on minority enrollments for first professional degrees is shown in the following tabulation:

FIELD	NUMBER		PERCENT OF ALL ENROLLMENTS	
	1970	1978	1970	1978
Law	3,609	10,846	5.8	9.1
Medicine	2,903	7,886	6.8	11.7

These educational changes by women and minorities occurred at a time of declining employment prospects for college graduates. However, opportunities in many nontraditional occupations were still good, and were much better than teaching. Medical school enrollments increased significantly and the demand for medical doctors expanded. Employment opportunities for new engineering graduates were excellent, despite declining enrollments of white males and layoffs of aerospace engineers.

Employment opportunities for lawyers expanded rapidly, although by the mid-1970s sharp increases in law school graduates caused growing com-

Table 9-4   COLLEGE ENROLLMENT AS A PERCENT OF THE 18- TO
34-YEAR-OLD POPULATION, BY RACIAL/ETHNIC GROUP: 1970 TO 1977

	YEAR	WHITE	BLACK	HISPANIC ORIGIN[a]
ENROLLED IN COLLEGE AS A PERCENT OF THE POPULATION SUBGROUP	1970	15.8	10.6	N.A.
	1971	16.3	11.7	N.A.
	1972	16.0	12.0	8.3
	1973	15.2	10.6	10.3
	1974	15.7	12.7	11.5
	1975	16.8	14.3	12.7
	1976	16.6	15.5	14.2
	1977	16.6	15.6	11.8
ENROLLED IN COLLEGE AS A PERCENT OF HIGH SCHOOL GRADUATES IN THE POPULATION SUBGROUP	1970	19.9	16.5	N.A.
	1971	20.5	19.0	N.A.
	1972	19.9	18.5	16.9
	1973	18.6	16.2	20.4
	1974	19.0	18.7	21.9
	1975	20.1	21.6	22.9
	1976	20.0	22.3	22.8
	1977	19.8	22.4	21.2
HIGH SCHOOL GRADUATES AS A PERCENT OF THE POPULATION SUBGROUP	1970	79.4	57.4	N.A.
	1971	79.8	61.5	N.A.
	1972	80.4	65.1	49.5
	1973	81.8	65.9	50.5
	1974	82.7	67.7	52.6
	1975	83.4	66.1	55.3
	1976	83.0	69.5	53.3
	1977	83.9	69.8	55.5

SOURCE: U.S. Department of Commerce, Bureau of the Census, *Social and Economic Characteristics of Students*, P-20, and unpublished tabulations.
[a] Categories are not discrete (e.g., a person may be classified in both white and Hispanic categories).

petition for jobs. Opportunities for accountants, bank officers, financial managers, and certain other business and accounting areas remained strong.

Opportunities for women and minorities in college and university teaching remained bleak. Beginning in the early 1970s, a greatly expanded number of new doctorate holders competed for a stable number of academic positions, caused by a levelling off of college enrollments and research and development funding.

Reflecting the rapid increase in degrees granted, employment of women graduates grew even more rapidly from 1.7 million in 1959 to almost 3.2 million in 1970 and 5.7 million in 1978, increases of 87 and 80 percent over the two periods, reflecting both a more rapid growth in bachelor's degrees granted to women and their increasing labor force participation rates. Employment of minority graduates increased even faster, from

Table 9-5   BACHELOR'S DEGREES
GRANTED TO MINORITIES, 1975–1976

FIELD	TOTAL	MINORITIES	MINORITIES AS A PERCENT OF TOTAL
Total (All)	927,085	100,228	10.8%
Business	144,031	15,754	10.9%
Education	156,538	20,254	12.9%
Engineering	45,859	3,717	8.1%
Health professions	54,138	5,033	9.3%
Physical sciences	21,319	1,398	6.6%
Social sciences	126,990	17,041	13.4%

SOURCE: U.S. Department of HEW, Office of Civil Rights.

290,000 in 1959 to 635,000 in 1970 and 1,285,000 in 1978, increases of 119 and 102 percent over the two periods.

Surveys on job offers compiled by the College Placement Council indicate that in the mid-1970s women who majored in engineering, business, and the natural and computer sciences earned or had salary offers comparable to those received by men. National Center for Education Statistics data also indicate that women graduates were somewhat less likely to be underemployed than their male counterparts. Nevertheless, their reported underemployment (defined as those not working in professional and technical, or managerial and administrative jobs, and who reported that, in their opinion, their job did not require a college degree) was substantial. At least 24 percent of bachelor's degree recipients of June 1974–July 1975 were underemployed in 1976; no data are available by sex. Among 1976–1977 degree recipients, at least 22 percent were underemployed, according to preliminary data—24 percent of men and 19 percent of women.

The employment gains of college-educated women and minority group members also has been accompanied by growth in their unemployment, reflecting the competitive job market generally faced by graduates. As noted above, between March 1970 and March 1978, while the unemployment rate for all workers increased from 4.2 percent to 6.6 percent, the unemployment rate for college graduates grew from 1.5 percent to 2.5 percent; and the number of unemployed college graduates more than doubled. Unemployment rates for college-educated women similarly changed from 2.0 percent to 3.0 percent, reflecting a near tripling of the number of unemployed women college graduates. Unemployment of minority college graduates sharply increased from 1.4 percent in 1970 to 4.6 percent in 1978, their numbers growing sevenfold.

During the 1980s, barring dramatic and unexpected labor market changes, the general job outlook for college graduates is not likely to improve. Because of expected continued large numbers of bachelor's degrees granted and slower growth in professional and technical occupations, about a quarter of all graduates probably will have to enter jobs of the type not sought or filled by graduates during the 1960s. The fact that women and minorities are preparing, in increasing numbers, for occupations with good employment opportunities such as engineering, medicine, and business should improve their job prospects. Opportunities in nursing and related health fields, for which many women prepare, also are good.

Despite the favorable outlook in some fields, it appears that many women and minorities with college degrees may have to continue to enter fields not normally requiring college education or face periods of unemployment. In fields such as teaching and the careers resulting from a liberal arts background, the growing enrollments of women could lead to even greater problems for graduates than in the past. As in the past, college graduates, including women and minorities, will have an advantage over nongraduates, but in some fields they have had to compete with junior and community college graduates who have learned job-related skills.

RETURN TO INVESTMENT IN COLLEGE

With a slackening of demand outpaced by supply, it was only to be expected that the rate of return on investments in college education would fall. Earlier studies calculated a return of 14.5 percent per year based on 1939 data[7] and 10.1 percent for 1949.[8] Another study showed World War II veterans, controlled for ability and father's education, to have had a rate of return of 11 percent.[9] A study of 1959 census data showed a 12 percent return.[10] And all of that, of course, was in years when interest rates were low throughout the United States. More recent studies by Richard Freeman show the private rate of return to have slipped from 12.5 percent in 1968 to 10 percent in 1973 and the social rate of return for the same years to have slipped from 13 percent to 10.5 percent.[11]

With interest rates rising, college education is much less attractive in purely economic terms. But income differentials are not the only relevant measures. College graduates have also been shown to have better health,[12] more positive interrelationships with families, and to be more adaptive in responding to change.[13] There are indications of greater volunteer services and generally more satisfying lives.[14] But throughout, there is no really satisfactory way of separating the independent contributions of college education from the family and personal characteristics which have been the root cause of both college enrollments and the other achievements. One can only suppose that most people at most times, as long as they are not confronted with excessively serious obstacles, will add up all of the economic, personal, and social gains, compare them to the costs, and make a rational choice. A clear gain for society and the individual is the indisputable fact that many financial and social barriers have been removed over the past 20 years so that the choice is a freer and more realistic one for most Americans.

THE CHARACTER OF THE MARKET FOR EDUCATED LABOR

Despite widespread shortcomings, college-educated manpower labor markets do function in occupations in which much education is required and in which it takes considerable time for supply to adjust to demand. This is true not only because of the time taken for education but also because once young people do one or two semesters of work in their chosen fields in college, there apparently are very limited changes in direction possible. Moreover, the market for educated manpower is not one homogeneous market but many discrete markets with separate demand-and-supply characteristics. As a consequence of market imperfections, to be explored at greater length next, there is considerable waste of high-level manpower because of limited knowledge about the relationship between education and work requirements and overstaffing of college-educated manpower during times of manpower shortage.

The primary adjustment and allocative mechanism of college-educated manpower is its labor market. The terms "shortage" and "surplus" are essentially market-related, and it is natural for the economist to use the market as an indicator of either of those manpower conditions. Critical shortages in particular occupations should reveal themselves through relative salary gains; surpluses, through relative salary declines. During the mid-1950s, for example, when private and government voices were expressing deep concern about the critical shortage of engineers, engineers' salaries were actually lagging behind those of many professional groups—a kind of market behavior that would not suggest acute scarcity. Thus while the many different definitions of scarcity as applied to the labor market and other conceptual difficulties must be overcome, the market provides a frame of reference for verifying and quantifying conflicting statements concerning the value and utilization of college-educated labor.

The market for educated labor is complicated by a number of factors. First, demand and supply are interrelated to the extent that the amount supplied to the market (in the form of college graduates, etc.) determines, in part, the degree of utilization by those demanding the services of educated persons. Thus it becomes very difficult to predict and quantify the demand. The supply of highly educated manpower also tends to be inelastic in the short run, causing the burden of short-run adjustment to be placed upon salary increases or substitution of less-qualified personnel.

The labor reserve of an occupation—defined as "those persons who are trained and qualified to work in an occupation and who last worked in that occupation but are not currently employed"[15]—also is a means of adjustment, especially in those occupations such as nursing, teaching, and social work that employ a high proportion of women. The labor reserve has the advantage of being a potentially rapid form of adjustment—as much as 5 to 10 percent in several years' time. Salary levels are probably not as important in influencing those in the labor reserve as opportunities for part-time work and work schedules that fit children's school schedules.

The short-run forces that operate through the labor market determine the current salary level, and this is undoubtedly related to entry on the supply side of the market for educated manpower. But the relationship between salary and long-run supply is ambiguous and hazy. There seems to be no real consensus of opinion about the factors that affect entry into a given profession, although employment does seem to expand most rapidly in those fields with the highest lifetime earnings, after allowances have been made for costs and nonpecuniary benefits.

Analysis of supply-and-demand conditions is also complicated by the fact that few labor markets are closed. Because workers cross international boundaries, it is not possible to restrict market analysis to factors influencing domestic demand-and-supply conditions. In 1969, for example, approximately 10,300 scientists and engineers migrated to the United States, and about 14 percent of medical doctors were immigrants.

Career choices are also influenced to some degree by volatile events, such as the current social issues facing the nation. This would help to explain the increase in beginning students' plans to major in social sciences during 1961–1965, when there was considerable ferment over race, manpower, and poverty problems and in biology and other ecologically related courses during the rise of environmental interests in the early 1970s. Later in that decade, energy became a focus of both policy interests and enrollments. However, using intentions of students entering college to predict future supply is usually not very successful because as many as 50 percent of all undergraduates change their plans between their freshman and senior years.

In the past the response to short-run problems has been focused upon expanding the educational output, and this method of adjustment can do little to relieve manpower problems in the short run. This lack of adjustment results in large measure from the considerable time lags in adjustments of supply to demand for highly educated manpower. High current salaries seem to induce many people to enter a field, but when they graduate, the large supply tends to depress wages unless something happens to increase demand. The relatively low salaries then tend to reduce the supply of people entering the field.

Another reason for the rapid changes in this labor market is found in the accelerator concept. Such change is especially prevalent in higher education, where a relatively fixed ratio is maintained between faculty and enrollment. Marginal increases in enrollment can cause a large increase in the number of teachers required, just as decreases in the rate of increase in enrollment (as in the 1970s) can cause the demand for new teachers to fall rapidly.

Although the terms "shortage" and "surplus" are used to describe the demand-supply relationship in the labor market, these terms can be defined in a number of ways. Also, serious problems of interpretation of relative salary trends result from a labor market disequilibrium. In one sense, shortage means that the actual number is less than the number dictated by some social goal. However, this is a difficult concept to use because no objective measure of it is possible. A second type of shortage is the so-called wage-rise shortage, which occurs when demand increases faster than supply at the prevailing market wage, and, as a result, competitive forces increase wages. However, such an approach has its conceptual problems. If a shortage is never defined as anything other than a price rise and the analysis is always in terms of relative prices, the awkward situation is predicted in which there might be a shortage of engineers relative to teachers but not relative to medical doctors. For example, Blank and Stigler concluded that there was no shortage of engineers from 1929 to 1954 because the ratio of median engineering salaries to the average wage and salary of full-time employees had declined from 100 in 1929 to 67.9 in 1954.[16]

A third type of shortage is dynamic in nature and consists of job vacancies caused by salaries temporarily too low to clear the market. If, for example, employers do not raise salaries sufficiently fast in response to rising demand, dynamic shortages exist which ultimately would be eliminated by rising salaries. Kenneth J. Arrow and William M. Capron think that one of the causes of alleged shortages in various disciplines is caused by this reluctance (or inability to pay the necessary equilibrium rate). Using the postwar family-servant market as an example, they state:

> ... at the price they had been paying for household help, many families found they could no longer find such people (household servants). Rather than admit that they could not pay the higher wages necessary to keep help, many individuals found it more felicitous to speak of a "shortage." There is reason to think that at least some of the complaints of shortage in the scientist-engineer market have the same cause.[17]

Such dynamic shortages could take place readily in view of the very high skill requirements in many of the markets for workers with higher educations. In a short-run situation a drastic rise in going salary might entice only a few more entrants into the market. And the nature of the process of career selection, while definitely having some relationship to earnings, is sufficiently vague to warrant an opinion that a salary increase, even of a large magnitude, might not affect the supply of talent in the manner predicted by traditional economic theory—namely, a shift outward.

The final type of shortage involves what is called projected, or cumulative, supply shortfalls and excesses. In this instance the supply of a particular occupation is projected, based upon certain arbitrary ratios such as enrollments and student populations, and then the supply projections are compared with utilization or demand projections. The difference between the two projections enables the forecaster to predict either a supply shortfall or a supply excess. Although this approach is useful, it presents two difficulties. First, past trends must necessarily be used to determine ratios such as employment and enrollment, and there may be no basis for assuming that such ratios will remain the same in the future. But this is a problem faced by all future predictions. Second, there is the problem of determining demand because the supply of manpower will influence the degree of utilization.

Because the demand for labor is a derived demand, some of the market imperfections for educated manpower are caused by the nature of the product market. For example, private and public benefits from research, which is a heavy user of educated manpower, are apt to diverge in a market society. First, many of the benefits of private research activity cannot be capitalized in the market. Firms, for example, have great difficulty in extracting the full economic value of knowledge, that, once sold, can be resold in the market. This causes private benefits from research to be much less than the social benefits. As a consequence, the competitive market will cause inadequate basic research to be done.

Attempts to rectify this divergence by using patents or permitting royalties to be charged for private information do not solve the problem because such measures tend to impede widespread application of new and useful ideas. Moreover, R & D costs for a particular research project financed by private enterprise over a definite time period probably are subject to the law of diminishing returns, but because individual projects may complement each other, research expenditures as a whole may not be subject to that particular phenomenon. Thus the wide variety of projects undertaken yields total benefits that are greater than the sum of the individual project benefits.

The risk, uncertainty, and the length of time between project conception and fruition also may make it difficult to finance research entirely through market mechanisms. It is not always possible to anticipate the results of research. Moreover, more research might be desirable for purposes of general education and the advancement of knowledge unrelated to the *profitability* of the investments. In a sense, of course, the market might allocate research personnel after policy makers decided to expend funds for this purpose.

Conclusions on the Market for Educated Labor

As noted in Chapter 6, labor markets are basic economic institutions, although we need to know much more than we do about how they operate. There are many kinds of interrelated labor markets. For example, there are many differences among the markets for people with postgraduate and undergraduate degrees, and, within the professional labor market, the market for medical manpower is quite different from the market for economists or attorneys, although they have certain things in common and both fall into what we define as the professional labor market in Chapter 6. We have noted, however, that labor markets for educated manpower do operate in rough conformity with economic theory and undoubtedly could be improved considerably by reducing the barriers to market adjustments, including the barriers to entry to undergraduate and professional schools.

However, even if the labor market for educated manpower were perfected, we have noted that it would not perform such functions as basic research, preservation of cultural values, and the advancement of knowledge, all of which are essential to the quality of life, very effectively. These decisions, therefore, must continue to be made by public policy or private nonprofit groups.

CONCLUSION

This chapter has demonstrated the close association between higher education and personal occupational mobility. However, the reader is reminded of the difficulties involved in establishing *causal* relations between income and education discussed in Chapter 8. Regardless of the experts' reservations about the returns to education, there is no question that higher education plays and will continue to play an important role in determining occupations. Moreover, these choices are made for many reasons other than anticipated economic returns. Improving the effectiveness of higher education for labor market considerations will require not only the basic kinds of educational reforms suggested in Chapter 8 but also the means to make it possible to equalize educational opportunities among racial and socioeconomic groups more on the basis of ability to profit by higher education than on the ability to pay for it from private family income.

DISCUSSION QUESTIONS

1. An important book cited in the chapter's references was entitled *The Overeducated American*. What are the arguments for and against the proposition that we are overinvesting in higher education in this country?
2. Is a college education a good economic investment? For whom? Under what conditions? What other considerations than economic ones should enter into individual and public decisions concerning investments in higher education?
3. How nearly has the United States approached the ideal of equal educational opportunity for all?
4. One of the remarkable human resource developments of the last 20 years has been the marked shrinkage of the gap in years of education between men and women and blacks and whites. How do you account for that development? What are its likely consequences?
5. How effective have labor markets been in adjusting the supply of and demand for college educated workers? What has happened to the wage and salary differentials between the college educated and the noncollege educated in the process? Why?
6. Despite concern that the output of our institutions of higher learning may have been excessive in recent years, the unemployment rate of those with col-

lege degrees remains far below the rates for other groups. How do you explain that fact?

Notes

1. Joseph Froomkin, *Aspirations, Enrollments, and Resources: The Challenge to Higher Education in the Seventies*, U.S. Department of Health, Education, and Welfare, Office of Education (Washington, D.C.: GPO, 1969), p. 10.
2. Edward F. Denison, *Why Growth Rates Differ* (Washington, D.C.: Brookings Institution, 1967); see also idem, *Accounting for United States Economic Growth, 1929–1969* (Washington, D.C.: Brookings Institution, 1974), pp. 207–246; and *Accounting for Slower Economic Growth: The United States in the 1970s* (Washington, D.C.: Brookings Institution, 1979), pp. 42–46.
3. E. Wight Bakke, *The Unemployed Worker and Citizens Without Work* (New Haven, Conn.: Yale University Press, 1940).
4. Froomkin, op. cit., chap. 4.
5. Lawrence Southwick, Jr., "The Higher Education Industry: Forecasts to 1990," *Review of Social Economy* (April 1973): 1–19.
6. National Council on Educational Statistics, *The Condition of Education* (Washington, D.C.: GPO, 1978).
7. Gary S. Becker, *Human Capital* (New York: Columbia University Press, 1964).
8. W. Lee Hansen, "Total and Private Returns to Investment and Schooling," *Journal of Political Economy* (April 1963): 128–140.
9. P. Taubman and T. Wales, "Higher Education, Mental Ability and Screening," *Journal of Political Economy* (February 1973): 28–56.
10. Richard Eckaus, "Return to Education with Standardized Incomes," *Quarterly Journal of Economics* (February 1973): 121–131.
11. Richard B. Freeman, *The Overeducated American* (New York: Academic Press, 1976).
12. Victor R. Fuchs, *Who Shall Live? Health Economies and Social Choice* (New York: Basic Books, 1974).
13. R. T. Michael, *The Effect of Education on Efficiency in Consumption* (New York: National Bureau of Economic Research, 1972).
14. Alan Campbell, P. E. Converse, and W. L. Rodgers, *The Quality of American Life: Perceptions, Evaluations, and Satisfactions* (New York: Russell Sage Foundation, 1976).
15. John K. Folger, Helen S. Astin, and Alan E. Bayer, *Human Resources and Higher Education*, Staff Report of the Commission on Human Resources and Advance Education (New York: Russell Sage Foundation, 1970), p. 352.
16. David M. Blank and George J. Stigler, *The Demand and Supply of Scientific Personnel* (New York: National Bureau of Economic Research, 1957), p. 23.
17. Kenneth J. Arrow and William M. Capron, "Dynamic Shortages and Price Rise: The Engineer-Scientist Case," *Quarterly Journal of Economics* (May 1959): 307.

Chapter 10
Apprenticeship and
On-the-Job Training

The basic idea behind apprenticeship is to have trainees work with master workers on the job while they acquire the necessary academic, or job-related, training in classroom situations. Ideally, apprenticeship produces well-rounded skilled workers who master the theory and practice of their trade and who, therefore, can adapt to a variety of work situations. Well-trained workers not only should be more productive than those with less training but also should be less vulnerable to the technological changes that might render obsolete the skills of narrow specialists.

PUBLIC POLICY

The basic federal law establishing apprenticeship policy is the National Apprenticeship (Fitzgerald) Act of 1937, administered by the Bureau of Apprenticeship and Training (BAT) in the U.S. Department of Labor. The BAT has a field staff and offices in every state, and its main function is to promote apprenticeship programs by giving technical assistance to unions and employers, who determine their own requirements and administer their own programs within the framework of broad standards laid down by the BAT or state apprenticeship agencies.

The administration of apprenticeship is complicated by the fact that, besides the federal programs, 30 states, Puerto Rico, the Virgin Islands, and the District of Columbia have programs of their own, containing over three-fourths of the nation's registered apprenticeship programs. These state programs are administered by state apprenticeship councils (SACs). The SACs take major responsibility for the registration of apprentices and the administration of apprenticeship programs in SAC states. There is, however, no clear line of jurisdiction between the functions of the SACs and BAT's state and regional officials in SAC states.[1]

The BAT approves state programs that meet certain minimum standards. To receive federal approval a state apprenticeship program must be administered by a state's department of labor. Other federal standards for apprenticeship programs include:

1. A starting age of not less than 16 years.
2. A schedule of work processes in which the apprentice is to receive training and experience on the job.
3. Organized instruction designed to provide the apprentice with knowledge in trade-related technical subjects. (A minimum of 144 hours a year is normally considered necessary.)
4. A progressively increasing schedule of wages. Wages for apprentices ordinarily start at a certain proportion of the journeyman rate and progress to the journeyman levels over the period of the apprenticeship. Generally, the programs with relatively more applicants than openings (electrical, pipe trades, sheet metal workers) start apprentices at relatively lower proportions of the journeymen wages than those programs with fewer applicants relative to openings.
5. Proper supervision of on-the-job training with adequate facilities to train apprentices.
6. Periodic evaluation of the apprentice's progress, both in job performance and related instructions, and the maintenance of appropriate records.
7. Employer-employee cooperation.
8. Recognition for successful completions.
9. Selection of men and women for apprenticeship, without regard to race, creed, color, national origin, or physical handicap.[2]

If apprenticeship programs meet the standards set up by the Federal Committee on Apprenticeship and the state apprenticeship agencies, they can be registered by the BAT or the SAC, and those who successfully complete these programs are given certificates of completion either by the state agency or by the BAT.

Although some programs rely on correspondence courses for related instruction (and for keeping journeymen up to date), the public school system normally offers academic or job-related training and is financed by state, federal, and local funds. The Smith-Hughes (1917) and George-Barden (1946) Vocational Education Acts provided for partial reimbursement from federal funds for salaries of teachers and vocational administrators to states with approved vocational plans. Some joint apprenticeship programs supplement the salaries of apprenticeship instructors. Moreover, an increasing number of programs seem to have their own training facilities for related instruction.[3]

The local supervision of apprenticeship programs registered with the BAT usually is by Joint Apprenticeship Committees (JACs) representing labor and management. There are over 9000 joint apprenticeship committees; these committees may be national, state, or local in scope. Depending upon the trades, they usually are plant- or company-wide in manufacturing and nationwide in the crafts. These national committees do not impose standards usually or supervise individual training programs, although their standards usually are followed by the local committees. Local JACs might comprise a group of employers (as in the construction industry), a single employer and union, or an employer without a union. JACs sometimes merely advise employee and employer representatives who actually carry out the programs, but in a few states JACs actually direct the programs.

The number of apprentices peaked in 1949 partly as a result of the GI Bill, which provided stipends and costs for veterans taking apprenticeship training, and declined during the next decade. An upward trend was resumed in 1962, and by 1978 enrollment surpassed the earlier peak, but it remained subject to considerable cyclical variation (Table 10-1). One study found that more new apprentices were hired when unemployment was low, which probably reflects lenient attitudes on the part of both the employers and the unions.[4]

Apprenticeship is not only concentrated in a few industries but also varies considerably in importance within those industries. Overall, apprenticeship is not very important for some trades, viewed either in terms of the proportion of journeymen who acquire their training through apprenticeship or completion rates.

Moreover, within a given sector of an industry—usually the part that is most heavily unionized—apprenticeship is known to account for somewhat larger proportions of journeymen than it will in nonunion sectors.

The ratio of new registrations to completions varies considerably from trade to trade. The carpenters have by far the most new registrants but fewer completions than the electricians and the plumbers. The carpenters' programs have a high dropout rate partly because many apprentices are able to work at the trade without completing apprenticeships. The carpenters also have relatively low admissions standards as contrasted with the mechanical crafts.

Students of apprenticeship generally agree that among the construction trades, the electricians, pipe trades, and sheet-metal workers have the most extensive programs and rely more heavily on apprenticeship as a

Table 10-1   REGISTERED APPRENTICES IN TRAINING, NEW
REGISTRATIONS, COMPLETIONS AND CANCELLATIONS, 1947–1978

YEAR	IN TRAINING ON JANUARY 1	NEW REGISTRATIONS	COMPLETIONS	CANCELLATIONS	IN TRAINING ON DECEMBER 31
1947	131,217	94,238	7,311	25,190	192,954
1952	172,477	62,842	33,098	43,689	158,532
1957	189,684	59,638	30,356	33,275	185,691
1962	155,649	55,590	25,918	26,434	158,387
1967	207,511	97,806	37,299	47,957	220,151
1972	247,840	103,527	53,059	56,750	264,122
1974	280,965	112,830	46,454	56,292	291,409
1976	265,647	88,418	49,447	49,650	254,968
1978	262,660	131,139	50,464	54,111	290,224

SOURCE: U.S. Department of Labor, Bureau of Apprenticeship Training.

source of journeymen. This opinion is supported by studies of apprentices
per thousand journeymen, completion rates, and such indicators as attendance at related instruction classes and scores on the General Classification
Test for those entering the armed services in World War II.

The reasons for the size and quality of the mechanical crafts' apprenticeship programs seem to be (1) workers in these trades are employed by
subcontractors and, therefore, have steadier employment than workers
(carpenters, bricklayers, laborers) who work mainly for general contractors;
(2) their trades require more intellectual training as contrasted with those
learned primarily by on-the-job training; and (3) these are growth trades
compared with the carpenters, plasterers, and painters, whose employment
has been declining.

APPRENTICESHIP ISSUES

Limited Understanding of Apprenticeship

Concern over black employment, poverty, shortages of skilled workers, and
inflation—each a problem touched by apprenticeship—raises questions
about its practices. Nevertheless, this training system was not very well understood by those who were not a part of it.

Confusion results, in part, from considerable diversity in apprenticeship programs. Apprenticeship sometimes is a very informal system, with
little attention given to providing the trainee with a variety of work experience and academic instruction related to the requirements of the particular
craft. Other programs are better organized and provide all these things.
Some of the better programs are registered with either the BAT or various
state apprenticeship councils, while others are not registered with any governmental agency. Registered programs vary considerably with respect to
the ratio of applicants to openings, completion rates, duration of training,

employer participation in training, value and nature of related instruction, ratio of apprentice to journeyman wages. This diversity makes it difficult to generalize about apprenticeship.

The ideal or expressed apprenticeship standards and requirements are often confused with the actual system. The formalized apprenticeship programs depicted in the BAT brochures are likely to conceal considerable flexibility and diversity, particularly in the construction industry where more registered apprentices are employed than in any other industry. Some apprentices, in fact, become journeymen before completing the formal apprenticeship period—depending upon such factors as the relevance of the standards and procedures to job requirements, labor market conditions, and the degree of control exercised over the program by unions and employers.

While a formal statement of the craft structure in the construction trades might suggest rigid apprentice and journeyman classifications, there are, in fact, a wide variety of actual classifications, specializations, and statuses according to type and degree of skill. Moreover, there are regular flows of people between residential jobs (which are ordinarily the least desirable and require lower skills) and the better and more highly skilled commercial and industrial jobs. In this process, depending upon craft and industry, workers learn their trades by a variety of means, including (1) completing part of an apprenticeship; (2) picking the trade up on the job or in the armed forces; (3) working in nonunion jobs and transferring into unionized programs during organizing campaigns or during periods of full employment of union craftsmen; and (4) attending vocational-technical programs.

Adequacy of Apprenticeship

There is also some controversy concerning the adequacy of apprenticeship training to meet the nation's manpower needs. But because of technical difficulties in projecting manpower requirements, this is likely to remain an unresolved issue. The unions are suspicious of projections that would call forth supplies of labor beyond what the unions consider adequate to maintain steady employment. Government officials, however, often want to increase labor supplies in order to avoid labor shortages, which put upward pressure on wages and prices.

Another controversy results from a debate over the role apprenticeship plays in those trades in which it is concentrated. While the construction industry, for example, considers apprentice-trained journeymen to be all-round craftsmen with a knowledge of the theory and practice of their trade and affords such journeymen a special status, many construction workers have not served apprenticeships. Not all workers in the construction industry need to be as well trained as apprentices, but employers must have cadres of key workers who meet their manpower needs. These key workers, who often have served apprenticeships, supervise those who are not as well trained.

Many people question whether in every instance apprenticeship provides better training than informal means. Critics ask whether all workers need to serve apprenticeship of the same length, and some believe apprentices with the necessary academic training should not have to go back to school. Representatives of the apprenticeship establishment (unions, employers, and specialized government agencies dealing with apprenticeship) argue that workers who came into the trades through other means might be just as competent at particular tasks as apprentice-trained men, but they are less likely to have received systematic instruction. Moreover, the defenders of the system argue from the worker's point of view that apprenticeship makes it possible for trainees to acquire skills and enter supervisory ranks faster than through other means.

Although there is not enough to objective data to test the validity of all the claims made for and against apprenticeship, the available evidence suggests a number of conclusions:

1. The time required for training differs among individuals—a factor recognized by some crafts that permit apprentice dropouts to become journeymen before completing the period of apprenticeship. Moreover, other individuals take longer to complete their training than the prescribed standards because they fail one or more periodic tests and are required to repeat this phase of their training. However, many skilled workers enter their trades as "specialists" able to perform only part of the craft and are, therefore, restricted in earnings and upgrading opportunities relative to apprentice-trained journeymen.[5]
2. Little logical difference appears to exist between the methods of acquiring skills in terms of the competence of the worker; the important thing is that the skills and knowledge are acquired, not the method of acquisition. However, the evidence supports the conclusion that systematic training such as that provided by formal apprenticeship programs makes it possible to become an all-round skilled worker faster than informal types of training.[6]
3. The evidence also shows that workers who serve apprenticeships have higher earnings and are upgraded faster than those who do not.
4. Although many skilled workers have not served apprenticeships there was a trend in the 1950s for the construction crafts to place increasing reliance on apprenticeship.

There is no objective evidence concerning the relevance of admissions standards and procedures, and this question is not likely to be easily resolved. Because of the diversity of situations, highly specific tests would be required to clarify the issue. Moreover, to a considerable extent this judgmental question may not lend itself to precise determination. Industry representatives, who presumably have superior information, disagree among themselves. Resolution of this controversial question will, therefore, probably be in terms of agreement on the mechanism for determining qualifications and standards rather than in terms of precise determination of the standards and qualifications themselves.

Racial Discrimination

The issue of racial discrimination in apprenticeship has caused considerable controversy. Civil rights leaders attacked the apprenticeship system during the 1950s and 1960s, when demand for unskilled workers was declining, because these programs led to good jobs in skilled trades in which there were very few blacks. According to the 1960s census, only 2191 apprentices, or 2.52 percent of the total, were nonwhite. The lack of black apprentices was confirmed by many other studies.[7]

The reasons for the paucity of black apprentices seem to be clear, though it is more difficult to determine the relative weights to be assigned the various factors. Most of the reasons directly or indirectly involve racial discrimination—not only through specific and overt refusal to accept black applicants but also through the more pervasive institutional segregation that discourages blacks from applying for apprenticeship programs and apprenticeship committees from including black sources in their recruitment patterns. Institutionalized discrimination also results in a lower percentage of blacks meeting the qualifications for admission to many of the apprenticeship programs.

As a result of agitation for change by civil rights groups, there have been many efforts to increase the number of black apprentices and journeymen, especially in the construction industry. In 1963 Secretary of Labor Willard Wirtz approved new federal standards requiring all registered apprenticeship programs to select participants on the basis of "qualifications alone," to use "objective standards," to keep "adequate records of the selection process," and to "provide full and fair opportunity for application." Programs established before January 17, 1964, were not required to select on the basis of qualifications alone so long as they "demonstrated equality of opportunity" in their selection procedures.[8] In 1971 these regulations were strengthened to require outreach and positive recruitment by apprenticeship sponsors with deficiencies in the use of minorities.

These regulations had limited impact for a variety of reasons. Basically, few blacks applied for or could meet the qualifications and testing procedures of the JACs. This was not surprising because discrimination had become institutionalized and as a rule few blacks either knew about apprenticeship or thought they could gain admission. In addition, many blacks who meet the qualifications for apprenticeship do not aspire to manual trades. Moreover, the BAT, which administered the program, had very limited enforcement powers. Deregistration, the BAT's main weapon, apparently would be more of an inconvenience than a serious deterrent to discrimination.

In addition to the federal regulations, apprenticeship programs are subject to Title VII of the Civil Rights Act of 1964, the National Labor Relations Act, government contract committees (which require observance of the BAT's apprenticeship regulations as a condition of compliance with the nondiscrimination clauses included in government contracts), and various state apprenticeship regulations and fair employment practices laws. Policies for increasing black participation in apprenticeship programs include the creation of apprenticeship information centers and the funding of specialized programs to recruit, train, and tutor blacks to get them into apprenticeship programs.[9]

A number of organizations, especially the Recruitment and Training Program (RTP) and the National Urban League, have undertaken specific outreach programs designed to get blacks into apprenticeship programs. The RTP's approach in New York City was successful in increasing the number of black apprentices, and it has been used as a model in many other cities. It was endorsed by the AFL-CIO at its 1967 convention and by the Building and Construction Trades Department in February 1968.

By 1980 nationally funded outreach programs had been established in 114 locations and had registered over 45,000 apprentices. In addition, various types of outreach and preapprenticeship programs were funded locally by prime sponsors under CETA in an unknown number of locations.[10] In 1967 minorities had been less than 6 percent of all apprentices; by the beginning of 1973 they accounted for over 14 percent of all apprentices and were 17 percent of all new indentures for 1972–1973. By 1978, there were over 51,000 minority apprentices, constituting 17.7 percent of all apprentices (Table 10-2).

Apprenticeship outreach programs have been more successful than any other approach to this problem and have demonstrated the importance of a comprehensive approach that recruits and prepares black youngsters for apprenticeship programs.

During the 1970s, the movement for equal apprenticeship opportunity spread to women. In 1973, women constituted only 0.7 percent of all apprentices. As a result of the movement to get women into nontraditional occupations, the U.S. Department of Labor established goals and timetables for women in apprenticeship and funded outreach programs to recruit and place women in apprenticeship programs. As a consequence of all of these activities, the proportion of females among apprenticeship entrants increased from 0.8 percent in 1973 to 4.3 percent in 1978.

Table 10-2   REGISTERED APPRENTICES
BY TRADE, AS OF DECEMBER 31, 1978, UNITED STATES

	TOTAL	PERCENT MINORITY	PERCENT FEMALE
Total	290,224	17.7	3.1
Building Trades	175,303	19.3	1.9
Metal Working Trades	33,783	10.1	2.5
Service and Repair Trades	30,021	16.9	2.2
Personal Services Trades	8,413	21.2	19.2
Graphic Arts Trades	5,375	16.7	5.2
Miscellaneous Trades	37,329	16.7	5.7

SOURCE: U.S. Department of Labor, State and National Apprenticeship Systems (SNAPS)
Data.
Note: Characteristics data are not available for all apprentices. More specifically, characteristics data are not available for 8,926 apprentices or three percent of the total. Thus, percentages for participation of minorities and females are minimum figures.

Union and Employer Attitudes Toward Apprenticeship

Although there are a growing number of registered nonunion apprentice programs, the U.S. apprenticeship system is mainly a product of collective bargaining. A study of Wisconsin apprenticeship programs, for example, revealed that 96 percent of the employee members of joint apprenticeship programs in the building trades belonged to unions and 79 percent of the employer members belonged to contractors' associations.[11] However, the relationship between apprenticeship and collective bargaining undoubtedly is weaker in the South, where unions are not as strong as they are in other parts of the country.

As an extension of collective bargaining, programs reflect the interests of the parties at the table. Most students and practitioners seem to agree that apprenticeship training in the United States is primarily supported by craft unions because this training system satisfies a number of their important objectives—most significantly the maintenance of wages by controlling craft competence and therefore productivity. Control of apprenticeship also provides job security by giving unions some control over the supply of labor. Apprenticeship programs exist mainly in casual occupations such as the building trades in which job opportunities are characterized by seasonal and cyclical variations and periods of unemployment. A main union objective in these situations is to gain greater job security for members and to protect the skilled workers' investment in their skills. In the long run, it would be difficult for skilled union workers to maintain their wages unless their productivity made it possible for them to have unit labor costs at least as low as the alternatives available to an employer. Craft unions also see apprenticeship as a form of union security. In the absence of unions, employers have a tendency to fragment crafts by training narrow specialists in only part of the trade in order to reduce training costs and increase profits. Craft unions resist such fragmentation because it makes their members less adaptable to change and threatens the power of unions.

Unions also support apprenticeship programs in order to prevent the excessive use of low-wage workers in competition with their skilled members, as a means of controlling the supply of labor, and as a technique for providing job opportunities to friends and relatives. The unions' interest in apprenticeship is such, according to one authority, that "although some people feel that apprenticeship is moribund, many in organized labor feel just the opposite and so strongly that if the federal government discontinued its modest programs, these unions would continue to develop apprenticeship training as they have over the years.[12]

Employers' views on apprenticeship vary considerably, from industry to industry. Construction and graphic arts employers seem to share their unions' interests in apprenticeship though they are often willing to leave the administration of these programs to the unions. Employers in industrial plants are interested in apprenticeship training when they need craftsmen in identifiable and recognized classifications. Employers in the larger high-wage industries seem willing to support apprentice programs because they are less likely than lower-wage employers to lose their skilled workers once they are trained.

Unlike their counterparts in construction, printing, and some metal crafts, many industrial employers do not seem anxious to register their apprenticeship programs with the BAT or a SAC. Although registered programs do not have to be jointly administered by unions and employers, some employers consider the federal apprenticeship program to be too closely tied to unions. Others, including some government installations, are not interested in training well-rounded craftsmen with general skills that might be transferred to other employers or labor markets; rather, they seek primarily to train workers for the specialized tasks required in their particular operations. These employers are more concerned with maintaining flexibility of manpower utilization across several craft lines and thus are not interested in the comprehensive training in a particular craft provided by the apprenticeship system. Some large employers also have no interest in registering their programs because they want to avoid government regulation and red tape.

The wage and certification advantages to be derived from registering an apprentice program, therefore, seem to be more attractive to the construction and printing industries. While apprentice rates usually are above the minimums, federal and state minimum wage regulations often permit registered apprentices to be paid less than the minimum wage. The Davis-Bacon Act of 1931 provides for the establishment of prevailing wages on federal construction projects, allows apprentices to be paid less than journeymen, and requires the maintenance of journeyman-apprentice ratios. If a program loses its registration, apprentices must be paid the journeyman rates.

Another advantage to registered apprentices is the recognition that the certificate of completion bestows on the journeyman. The graduate of a registered apprentice program knows that his training is a passport to jobs in other geographic areas because of the standards to which his certificate of completion attests.

Standards, Qualifications, and Procedures

Qualifications, standards, and procedures used by apprenticeship sponsors vary considerably, though registered programs must meet the minimum federal standards listed previously. The specific standards are fixed by the particular joint apprenticeship committee. The numbers of apprentices usually are controlled by prescribing eligibility standards, fixing ratios of the numbers of apprentices and journeymen for each employer, and prescribing the duration of the apprentice training period.[13]

Characteristics of Apprenticeship Programs

Although there is considerable diversity in apprenticeship training programs, we can make some generalizations about the usual procedures involved in becoming an apprentice. Many youngsters get information about apprenticeship programs from friends or relatives. However, the traditional father-son relationship in many skilled crafts apparently is weakening because it discriminated against minorities and because many craftsmen with higher incomes send their sons to college. Aspirants who do not have friends and relatives in a trade can now obtain information from employers, unions, the employment service, apprenticeship information centers, or other sources.

The number of apprenticeship openings varies from trade to trade and city to city. Some trades—for example, electricians, plumbers, sheet-metal workers, and printers—typically have long waiting lists, while others—for example, roofers and carpenters—are more easily entered. The number of positions with any given employer depends upon how many journeymen he has; agreements between unions and employers typically specify a so-called journeymen-apprentice ratio. These ratios apparently have considerable influence in specific cases, but, in the aggregate, employers do not train as many apprentices as their ratios would allow. An applicant who otherwise meets the requirements for entry into an apprenticeship program usually must take an oral or written examination given by the employment service, a private testing agency, the employer, the union, or a JAC. The JACs traditionally have constructed and administered their own tests, but there appears to be a trend toward reliance on professionally developed written tests. The oral interview, usually administered by the JACs, is designed to determine the applicant's interest in the trade and whether he is likely to complete the apprenticeship successfully.

Critics of apprenticeship procedures contend that the oral interview should be eliminated or given little weight because it offers the JACs an opportunity to discriminate against blacks or others they wish to bar. But defenders of interviews counter that it is necessary to determine the applicants' motivation, since the JAC often allots scarce positions and devotes considerable time and resources to training. Unions also are fearful of flooding the market with partially trained journeymen. Moreover, the JACs are interested in getting the "right kind" of people into their training programs, which means persons who are socially acceptable as well as productive workers. There is a certain mystique and fraternal character about apprenticeship to which the JAC expects the new apprentice to conform. Part of the ritual in many trades takes the form of hazing and menial assignments designed to initiate the apprentice into the trade.

Once the apprentice is formally registered or indentured, he is paid a progressively increasing proportion of the journeyman wage scale. He gains the journeyman's rate when he completes his apprenticeship—at least one year and typically four years after he enters a program.

In some cases, the apprentice can enter the program by passing a simple aptitude test but must find his own job. In other cases, the JACs seem to be able to assure employment to the apprentice and assume responsibility for finding him a job. Many in the apprenticeship establishment are fearful that the "hunting license" approach, whereby the apprentice finds his own job, will bring too many people into the trade.

Some apprenticeship sponsors supplement the salaries of apprentice instructors and provide apprentice coordinators to supervise the training, but overall policy and guidance is established by the JAC or other sponsors. The apprentices' wages often are paid by the employer while they attend classes during the day, but this practice varies considerably. In some cases related training classes are held in the evening.

ON-THE-JOB TRAINING

On-the-job training (OJT) is the main way in which most workers acquire their skills. In spite of its importance, very little is known about OJT for a number of reasons. For one thing, OJT takes place during the production process, often is very informal, and occurs incrementally over a long period of time. Indeed, very often little identifiable instruction takes place, and the worker undergoing the training may not even be aware of the process. As a consequence, the process cannot be described by those who are undergoing it.

Nevertheless, some generalizations can be made about OJT. Much of our knowledge derives from special studies conducted during the 1960s, when efforts to train the disadvantaged focused general attention on OJT procedures. Although we do not know much about the magnitude of this form of training—in the sense of being able to measure the changes in skills accruing to workers per unit of time—OJT probably accounts for an overwhelming proportion of the skill gains in the work force. Indeed, some of the gains in income attributed to formal education probably are due to OJT.

To some extent, the use of seniority in promotion is tacit recognition by unions and employers of the importance of OJT. In many occupations seniority districts defining lines of job progression serve training as well as production needs. It is assumed that workers who have been in closely related jobs are in the best position to learn the next higher job in terms of skill. Moreover, the fact that workers in the line of progression have some assurance that they will fill higher jobs provides a motivation for junior workers to learn the higher jobs. But OJT is not limited to jobs in the line of progression. Some workers familiarize themselves with jobs outside their immediate seniority lines by talking with workers on those jobs, observing their operations, and perhaps operating the equipment during lunch breaks or other free-time periods. Because of the importance of these informal learning procedures, incumbents sometimes have considerable influence over which outsiders learn their jobs.

Apparently, OJT is very popular with workers and employers. Workers prefer this form of training because they can see its relevance and are not as likely to consider it to be as much a "waste of time" as classroom training. Indeed, some kinds of training cannot be learned in classrooms because it is difficult to simulate the actual conditions of the work place. Also, OJT has very limited wasted training because the worker uses the skills he acquires on the job. Moreover, he is paid a regular wage and not a stipend as under institutional training.

Employers prefer OJT because there is little question of its effectiveness and because it is more flexible and less expensive for many jobs than other types of training. Its impact is readily apparent to supervisors, who can observe whether the worker is learning the job. This form of training is flexible because it can be adapted to a wide variety of work situations and can be combined with all other forms of training. In some cases, for example, workers can be given minimal instructions and left to learn the trade on their own or by observing other workers who perform the same job. But OJT also can be supplemented with (1) formal demonstrations by other workers, instructors, supervisors, or engineers; (2) basic classroom training in theoretical or academic concepts that cannot be taught on the job; (3) vestibule training for new workers to familiarize them with the job; or (4) correspondence courses.

Also, OJT is flexible because it is a means whereby employers can adjust to technological changes and shortages of skilled manpower. As Doeringer and Piore have demonstrated, minor innovations are adopted by casual learning of the new process on the job, while major changes might require more changes in the normal training patterns. Innovations that create new jobs, for example, might require a period of relatively formal instruction by engineers, factory representatives, or others who have learned to operate the new equipment. Furthermore, OJT makes it possible for employers to adapt to a variety of labor market conditions.[14] For example, if there are shortages of skilled workers, employers can, through OJT and work rearrangements, utilize less-skilled workers.

Employers also like OJT because it seems economical. The training is a byproduct of production and, therefore, does not require the establishment of training staffs and procedures. The efficacy and importance of OJT undoubtedly account for the fact that very few companies have formal training programs.[15] Moreover, OJT can be carried out with craftworkers who would not be very effective in teaching formal classes but who might command considerable respect from trainees because of their demonstrated skills on the job. Similarly, OJT does not require the purchase of expensive additional training equipment.

In spite of its advantages, however, OJT is not suitable for all kinds of training, and, although less expensive than some other forms of training, it is not without its costs. Just as some skills are difficult to teach in classes, some kinds of knowledge cannot be taught very effectively on the job. For example, theoretical training is important to many kinds of jobs because it teaches the worker the basic causal relationships underlying the job. Workers who understand theoretical relationships undoubtedly are adaptable to a greater variety of work situations than those who only know how things happen but not why. Indeed, it can be argued that those who do not understand the basic theoretical aspects of their jobs probably have imperfect understandings of how things happen. Theoretical training is difficult to teach on the job because the basic causal relationships—for example, the forces conditioning the flow of current through electrical wires—usually are invisible and thus must be demonstrated with abstract models. The noisy hustle and bustle of the job rarely is conducive to instruction in these abstractions. And supervisors and other regular production workers might not be the best instructors for such abstract academic subjects. But the effectiveness of classroom instruction is not limited to theoretical training. Although academic subjects such as reading and computation skills probably can be more effectively taught off the job, the knowledge that those skills are useful for job performance undoubtedly is a powerful motivating influence, and motivation is very important to learning.

Moreover, OJT has costs that employers must consider. Employees' learning and working at the same time are not likely to be fully productive for a period, and the productivity of supervisors and skilled craftsmen might be impaired if they spend too much time teaching trainees. At the same time, craftsmen often make poor teachers because they resent having to train "greenhorns" or because they frequently have trouble explaining what they do or are reluctant to impart trade secrets that they feel give them an advantage. And there are possible economies of size and scale in a classroom where a number of workers must acquire the same kinds of training.

Although little emphasis was given to OJT during the first few years of the Manpower Development and Training Act of 1962, OJT became more important after 1965. Some MDTA-OJT programs were administered by so-called national contracts, while others were administered by individual firms. Under the national contracts an organization such as a union or the National Urban League was the prime contractor and subcontractor with individual trainees. After the passage of the Comprehensive Employment and Training Act (CETA) of 1973, OJT programs were shifted mainly to local prime sponsors. The CETA Reauthorization Act of 1978 gave greater emphasis to on-the-job training as part of a new private sector initiative to improve the linkages between the CETA system and the private sector. The private sector initiatives included a tax credit to encourage private employers to hire and train eligible workers and Private Industry Councils (PICs), made up of employers, union representative and other actors in the local labor market. The PICs serve as intermediaries between the CETA system and the regular economy.

Apparently, OJT has considerable support from political leaders, and, therefore, local prime sponsors are likely to want to continue OJT arrangements under CETA. There are a number of reasons for this, including both its low federal cost per trainee compared with institutional training and the higher posttraining employment built into the system. Not only is institutional training more costly, but also there is no assurance that its graduates will be able to find jobs.

In addition to the limitations discussed previously, OJT has a number of drawbacks for training the disadvantaged. For one thing, OJT requires the workers to find an employer willing to take him, which might be difficult to do because employers are extremely reluctant to train the disadvantaged, even when compensated by the federal government. During times of rising unemployment, it is difficult to place people in OJT slots because experienced workers are unemployed and there are likely to be very few job vacancies. Moreover, because employers select many of the workers to be trained under OJT, they tend to "cream" the available labor force, taking the best-qualified applicants and making it difficult for the truly disadvantaged worker to get training. Also, sometimes employers may abuse the OJT program by systematically failing to retain the trainee beyond the duration of the subsidy. However, if a disadvantaged worker acquires an OJT position, it is likely to do more than classroom training to help the trainee become and remain employed.

CONCLUSIONS

While the apprenticeship system in the United States is regarded by its supporters as a good training procedure that provides the academic and on-the-job training necessary to produce all-around skilled workers, it is criticized as being obsolete, inadequate to meet the nation's manpower requirements, and it is characterized by racial and other forms of discrimination against outsiders. The evidence suggests the following conclusions.

1. Apprenticeship in the United States is primarily an extension of collective bargaining.
2. Apprenticeship programs, while very diverse, are significant primarily in those industries and crafts in which employment is casual and in which the union is likely to be the predominant and most stable labor market institution.
3. The number of apprentices fluctuates with the business cycle, but the post-1962 trend seems to be upward. In the construction trades, unions placed much greater reliance on apprenticeship after the 1950s than they had previously.
4. Individuals who serve apprenticeships become well-rounded skilled workers in a shorter time, are upgraded faster, and have more regular employment than those trained informally.
5. Although apprenticeship outreach programs have been more successful than other efforts to increase the number of minority apprentices, these outreach programs are too new to give a clear indication of their impact on those institutional arrangements that have barred blacks and other minorities from apprenticeships. Moreover, outreach programs have been assisted by a number of other measures to reduce discrimination. In addition to outreach programs, an important determinant of entry into apprenticeship programs by blacks (and others) and their employment in the crafts will be the nature of the qualifications required to enter these training programs and work at these crafts. Because of their significance for economic and manpower policies as well as discrimination, apprenticeship qualifications, standards, and procedures undoubtedly will remain controversial issues for some time. But the outreach programs, according to the evidence available, have greatly increased the number and proportion of minority apprentices.

On-the-job training, which is part of the apprenticeship system, is the main way most workers acquire their skills. It has many advantages over classroom instruction. However, both classroom and on-the-job training are necessary for most crafts because mathematics, science, and other trade-related academic subjects cannot be learned very effectively at work sites.

DISCUSSION QUESTIONS

1. How do apprentice training and vocational school training compare with regard to preparation for work and occupations?
2. What industries and occupations seem likely candidates for expanding apprenticeship training?

3. How can entry into apprenticeships be made more equitable?
4. What would be the best way to inform high school students about apprentice training, especially students who have no relatives in apprenticeable trades?
5. Do vocational education curricula provide the needed classroom instruction for apprenticeship training?
6. How do cyclical economic fluctuations affect apprenticeship enrollment?
7. Preferential treatment of journeymen's sons in qualifying for apprenticeship has been defended as a property right passed on from father to son. Evaluate this view.
8. What should be the role of government—federal or state—in certifying apprenticeship programs? Or should the program be left to employer-union councils?

Notes

1. Lyndon B. Johnson School of Public Affairs, *Coordination of State and Federal Apprenticeship Administration*, Report of the Apprenticeship Project, vol. 2 (University of Texas at Austin, 1980).
2. *Apprenticeship Programs: Labor Standards for Registration*, 29 CFR 29.5, "Standards of Apprenticeship" (February 18, 1977).
3. Robert W. Glover, *Apprenticeship in America: Implications for Vocational Education Research and Development* (Columbus, Ohio: National Center for Research in Vocational Education, 1980).
4. David J. Farber, "Apprenticeship in the United States: Labor Market Forces and Social Policy," *Journal of Human Resources* (Winter 1967): 70.
5. Ray Marshall, Robert Glover, and William S. Franklin, *Training and Entry into Union Construction* (Washington, D.C.: Government Printing Office, 1974).
6. Morris A. Horowitz and Irwin L. Hernstadt, *The Training of Tool and Die Makers* (Boston: Department of Economics, Northeastern University, 1969).
7. Ray Marshall and Vernon M. Briggs, Jr., *The Negro and Apprenticeship* (Baltimore: Johns Hopkins Press, 1967); and *Equal Apprenticeship Opportunity* (Ann Arbor and Detroit, Mich.: National Manpower Policy Task Force and Institute of Labor and Industrial Relations, University of Michigan-Wayne State University, 1968); George Strauss and Sidney Ingerman, "Public Policy and Discrimination in Apprenticeship," *Hastings Law Journal* (February 1965): 285.
8. *Equal Employment Opportunity in Apprenticeship and Training*, 29 CFR 30, 1964.
9. Marshall and Briggs, *Equal Apprenticeship Opportunity*, op. cit.
10. Lyndon B. Johnson School of Public Affairs, *Preparation for Apprenticeship through CETA*, vol. 1, Report of the Apprenticeship Project (University of Texas at Austin, 1979).
11. Alan C. Feeley and Karl O. Magnusen, "A Study of Joint Apprenticeship Committees in Wisconsin Building Trades," in Center for Studies in Vocational and Technical Education, *Research in Apprenticeship Training* (Madison: University of Wisconsin Press, 1967), p. 84.
12. Felician F. Foltman, "Public Policy in Apprenticeship Training and Skill Development," in U.S. Congress, Senate, Subcommittee on Employment and

Manpower, *The Role of Apprenticeship in Manpower Development: United States and Western Europe,* volume 3 of *Selected Readings in Manpower* (Washington, D.C.: GPO, 1964), p. 112.

13. Marshall, Glover, and Franklin, op. cit.

14. Peter Doeringer and Michael Piore, *Internal Labor Markets and Manpower Analysis* (Lexington, Mass.: D. C. Heath, 1971).

15. John L. Iacobelli, "A Survey of Employer Attitudes Toward Training the Disadvantaged," *Monthly Labor Review* (June 1970): 51–55.

16. Stephen A. Schneider, "Apprenticeship Outreach Program," in Charles R. Percy et al., eds., *The Impact of Government Manpower Programs* (Philadelphia: Industrial Research Unit, The Wharton School, University of Pennsylvania, 1975), pp. 222–251.

PART III
GROUPS FACING
PROBLEMS IN THE
LABOR MARKET

Chapter 11
Economic Theory
of Racial Discrimination[1]

The theory of discrimination is important for human resource development because discrimination has been a basic cause of labor market segmentation and low incomes. A major objective of employment policy has been to improve the conditions of minorities. An adequate theory would promote this objective by facilitating our understanding of the causes and effects of discrimination.

An analysis of the economics of discrimination also makes it possible to examine the usefulness of labor market theories—especially the neoclassical theory—in dealing with this problem.[2]

According to Becker, "If an individual has a 'taste for discrimination,' he must act as if he were willing to pay something, either directly or in the form of reduced income, to be associated with some persons instead of others."[3] Becker makes the usual assumptions of neoclassical wage theory, especially perfect competition, homogeneous factors of production, and fixed institutional arrangements.

Becker defines a coefficient of discrimination in monetary terms for different factors of production, employers, and consumers, where it is assumed that the factors of production are equally productive. If an employer pays a money wage rate of W for workers, then $W(1 + d_i)$ defines a *net wage* rate, where d_i is the discrimination coefficient against this factor. If the employer has a preference for this factor, d_i will be positive; if he has a taste for discrimination against it, d_i will be negative.

The *market* discrimination coefficient (MDC) is defined as

$$MDC = \frac{W_W - W_B}{W_B}$$

where W_W is the equilibrium wage rate of white workers and W_B is the equilibrium wage rate of black workers.

The obvious implication of the discrimination coefficient is that the employer is willing to pay the favored workers ($W + d_i$) and the ones discriminated against ($W - d_i$), so that if W_W is the wage of white workers and W_B the wage of black workers and the employer prefers W's to B's, then $W_W > W_B$.

NEOCLASSICAL THEORY OF DISCRIMINATION

Besides the difficulties in making the model square with reality and the problems with the neoclassical model to be discussed next, the Becker-type model has other limitations for those interested in using the theory of discrimination to explain reality. For example, the long-run implication of the model is that employers with no discrimination coefficients would hire blacks because $W_B < W_W$, forcing their competitors to do the same, in which case the long-run equilibrium would be where the wages of minorities equaled the wages of whites either in integrated or completely segregated situations. If $W_W - W_B > d_i$ where d_i is the money value of the discrimination coefficient, employers would hire only B's; if $W_W - W_B < d_i$ employers would hire only W's; and if $W_W - W_B = d_i$ work forces would be integrated. This implies that employers would change their work forces in response to changes in wage rates. The implication of this analysis is that economic discrimination is mainly a reflection of market imperfections and monopoly power; otherwise, discrimination should tend to disappear in the long run.

Economists writing in the neoclassical tradition have attempted to modify Becker's model to make it conform with a reality in which racial wage differentials and employment patterns are perceived to be relatively stable. Barbara R. Bergmann utilized a Becker-type model to show how discrimination can cause wage differentials among equally skilled occupations.[4] Bergmann assumes two occupations requiring equal skills, one menial (M) and the other prestigious (P).[5] Her analysis suggests that discrimination can cause wage differentials among equally skilled occupations and that racial wage differentials may be maintained by occupation segregation rather than by overt wage discrimination. Her analysis also is useful in indicating that the discrimination coefficient differs among occupations because of status considerations. This is better than assuming that discrimination is a taste or distaste for physical association. Occupational segregation, or the crowding of blacks into a limited number of occupations, seems clearly to be a more realistic assumption than that equally qualified blacks and whites doing identical jobs in the same firms are paid different wages. However, the use of wage differentials and discrimination coefficients to explain how crowding occurs and how jobs get integrated seems unsatisfactory, a point soon to be developed at greater length.

Welch uses a model similar to Becker's to demonstrate that discrimination is caused more by employee preferences for working with members of their own race than by employers' taste for discrimination.[6] If a worker's wage is a decreasing function of the proportion of that worker's race in the firm's work force, it is possible to show that cost minimization in competitive equilibrium requires total segregation within a work force rather than combinations of black and white workers' receiving different wages, as implied by Becker's model.

Much of the work on the economics of discrimination assumes blacks and whites to be perfect substitutes. However, Welch and others point out that blacks might be complementary to white workers, making segregation impossible.[7] This would be the case, for example, if white foremen worked with all-black work forces and required a premium to do so equal to a coefficient of discrimination. This would increase the employer's cost of hiring blacks, who could, therefore, only be hired if $W_B < W_W$.

Arrow has developed the most complete statement of the neoclassical theory of discrimination.[8] His main objective was to explain racial wage differentials not based on productivity. He specifically sought "to develop Becker's models and to relate them more closely to the theory of general competitive equilibrium, though frequently by way of contrast rather than agreement."[9]

According to Arrow, the usual neoclassical assumptions would call for smooth rapid adjustments in employment to changes in relative wages. However, in the real world these changes do not occur, partly because of adjustment or personnel costs associated with hiring and firing workers. These costs are of training for specific jobs and administration costs associated with turnover. Personnel investments thus provide a cushion to prevent changes in employment with small changes in the relative wages of blacks and whites.

Arrow also prepared an alternative model to employer discrimination; in this case the employer's actions are based not on tastes but on perceptions of reality. If employers believe B workers are less productive than W workers, they will hire B's only if $W_B < W_W$, an idea also developed by Edmund S. Phelps.[10] This finding was based on three assumptions: (1) The employer can distinguish between B workers and W workers; (2) the employer must incur some costs before it is possible to determine the employee's true productivity; and (3) the employer has some conception of the distribution of productivities within the B and W groups of workers.

Arrow assumed two kinds of complementary jobs, skilled and unskilled. Some workers are known to be able to perform skilled jobs, while all are able to perform unskilled jobs. The employer does not know if any given worker is qualified but believes that the probability of a random W worker's being qualified is p_w, while p_B is the probability that a random B worker is qualified. If $p_B < p_w$, it follows that $W_w > W_B$. Arrow also noted that the wage rigidities that prevented W_B from falling much below W_w would lead to B's being excluded entirely.

Arrow recognized, however, that shifting from Becker's taste for discrimination (which is exogenous to the system and, therefore, not analyzed) to *beliefs* required some explanation for the beliefs. He considered one possible explanation to be the theory of cognitive dissonance, which argues that "beliefs and actions should come into some sort of equilibrium; in particular, if individuals act in a discriminatory manner, they will tend to develop or acquire beliefs which justify such actions."[11] Clearly, however, these beliefs would not persist if they were based merely on perceptions of reality that experience demonstrated to be erroneous, an argument made by John J. McCall.[12]

CRITIQUE OF THE NEOCLASSICAL THEORY

There is no commonly accepted standard for evaluating a theory of discrimination. For example, if Arrow's objectives to make the theory of discrimination compatible with competitive equilibrium theory and explain racial wage differentials are accepted, it can be concluded that he succeeded in achieving both objectives. But in accomplishing this he failed either to provide a satisfactory explanation of the basic causal forces at work in the real world or a guide to policy. On the other hand, a particular theory of discrimination designed to support policy might not adequately fit a general equilibrium model.

Conception of Discrimination

In order to make it fit the wage-theory mold, neoclassical economists define discrimination as a taste prompting an economic agent to act as if he were willing to pay something to be associated with some persons rather than others. This definition creates a number of conceptual problems. First, if it assumes discrimination to be a physical phenomenon—a desire by whites, for example, not to associate with blacks—it scarcely conforms with reality, because whites have been in close physical association with blacks. Clearly, discrimination is more a status or caste phenomenon, a concept that makes the theory more general because the physical phenomenon surely cannot be applied to sexual discrimination. Discriminators object to discriminatees partly because the latter are generally regarded to be inferior people who would lower the status of the discriminators.

Motives of the Economic Agents

But an economic theory of discrimination should show how discrimination interacts with the motives of certain economic actors. The neoclassical model does this, in part, by assuming that actors with discrimination coefficients modify the usual motives specified in the neoclassical utility functions. The model assumes that employers are motivated mainly by profits, but this motive is modified by a taste for discrimination or a perception of reality. If the model assumes physical association to be a problem, it is difficult to understand why employers, especially in large firms, would discriminate against blue-collar workers with whom top management would not be associating, at least in large firms. Some attempts to overcome this difficulty by assuming that employees are motivated by desires to maximize the incomes of white workers, which is perhaps a bit far-fetched. However, it is possible that the discrimination coefficients of employees could be transmitted to the employer, as Arrow specifies, causing behavior *as if* the employer had a discrimination coefficient. If the employer has a status motive for discrimination, there would be no objection to hiring discriminatees for inferior jobs, but employers would object to hiring them for higher-status jobs.

It cannot be proved that status motives are more realistic than benevolence toward white workers or the desire not to associate with blacks, but the empirical evidence seems to support this conclusion. Whites clearly have been more strongly motivated to bar blacks from status jobs such as mechanical craftworkers in the construction industry, railroad conductors and engineers, and managers and supervisors of integrated work forces than they have from jobs such as carriers (not a low-wage job), foundry work (also not low wage), cement masons, service workers, and laborers—all of which are considered to have lower status. This analysis of the empirical evidence is complicated by the fact that occupants of higher-status jobs also usually have more power to bar blacks, making it difficult to isolate motive from power.

It might be noted in passing that the neoclassical assumption of physical discrimination does not fit comfortably with the conclusion that competitive firms (which are likely to be smaller and have closer relations between employees and employers) are less likely to discriminate than those firms operating under conditions of imperfect competition; the latter type of firm is presumably larger and characterized by more impersonal employer-employee relations.

The model also proffers unrealistic assumptions about the motives of white workers, who probably are more responsible than employers for discrimination in blue-collar jobs. The neoclassicals assume that white workers with discrimination coefficients are motivated mainly by wage rates. This assumption leads to some curious results. First, white workers are presumed to demand higher wages to work with blacks who are perfect substitutes.

This is curious in view of the usual neoclassical assumptions that people act rationally, because surely white workers could see that such demands would be self-defeating, since blacks would displace whites, as the neoclassical model stipulates. White workers are more likely to demand that blacks be excluded entirely from status jobs than to demand racial wage differentials. As noted later, however, whether white workers succeed in barring blacks depends on the power relations between the parties. If employers are firm in hiring blacks and if adequate supplies of black workers are available, whites are not likely to quit good jobs because blacks are hired.

Moreover, the white workers' basic motivation is likely to be job control rather than wage rates. The wage rate is an important part of the job, but the job's status, working conditions, stability, opportunity for advancement, and the extent to which workers participate in the formulation of job rules also are important considerations. Discriminators are likely to desire to practice job control by monopolizing the better jobs for themselves, and they capitalize on race, sex, and other biases to achieve their ends.

Power Relations Among the Agents

However, a theory of discrimination should be able to say something about what gives discriminators the power to exclude discriminatees. The neoclassical model fails to do this because it does not deal with bargaining among groups and assumes wages to be the only objectives and wage differentials and wage changes to be basic causal forces. The neoclassical model also is silent with respect to the motives of black workers and the determinants of their power to overcome discrimination by white workers and employers.

INSTITUTIONAL DISCRIMINATION

The neoclassical model also fails to distinguish between specific overt acts of discrimination, when, for example, a worker is not hired or promoted because of race, and institutionalized discrimination, which pervades social and economic institutions. When discrimination becomes institutionalized, as it has for blacks, overt discrimination becomes a relatively less important cause of the disadvantages of discriminatees, because inadequate education, segregated labor market institutions, and other forces that deny equal access to jobs, training, or information greatly reduce the probability that those discriminated against will aspire to, prepare for, or seek to enter the status occupations. In neoclassical language institutional discrimination makes it less likely that black and white workers will be homogeneous substitutes. The same phenomenon has also been referred to as cumulative discrimination with regard to discrimination by sex.[13]

While the distinction between overt and institutional discrimination is useful, discriminators can practice overt discrimination while appearing to be objective. An example is the use of recruiting sources or screening devices that strongly reflect institutional discrimination.

The neoclassical theory does not deal with institutional discrimination because the model mistakenly assumes that institutions are fixed and do not interact, therefore, with the basic variables in the model. However, since the discrimination coefficient is itself considered exogenous to the system, the neoclassicals can hardly claim to have a *theory of discrimination*. A theory of discrimination should be able to explain the causes of discrimination and show how the economic variables in the model interact with the central phenomenon to be explained. The neoclassicists, because of the way they specify the model, must rely on competition operating through wage differentials to produce equilibrium. This probably requires that discriminators either be eliminated in the long run or change their tastes. But there is no indication of a relationship between competitive market forces and discrimination itself. It is unknown whether the taste for discrimination is irreversible and the persons of discriminatory persuasion are merely eliminated from the market in the long run or whether economic pressures cause discriminators to change their behavior and thus cause discrimination to be reduced or eliminated over time. These alternatives, while perhaps producing the same results in the model in the long run, are in fact substantively quite different.

Arrow realizes the need to deal with this problem in his alternative specification of the model, but his treatment raises questions for the model. To assume that the employer's discrimination is based on a perception of reality is a vastly different matter from assuming a taste for discrimination. This alternative formulation also raises the question of what happens when the employer's perception of reality is proved false by accurate information. It might be assumed in this case that the perception would conform with reality and that discrimination based on misinformation would disappear. Moreover, in this formulation, if the factors are really homogeneous, as the neoclassical theory ordinarily assumes, the congruence of perception and reality would reduce discrimination to zero, which would mean that there is no racial discrimination at all because the resulting discrimination would be due to reality and not to race.

A more realistic specification of the process of change would appear to be when some pressures (from government, the black community, or market forces) provide employers or employees with some motive to change black employment patterns with no necessary change in racial attitudes. Once the actors are required to cease discriminating, that part of their action based on inaccurate perceptions of reality changes immediately, but negative racial attitudes persist. The latter probably are eroded by a tendency for people to rationalize actions that their economic or other motives require them to take. Gradually, as discrimination declines, those discriminated against cease being regarded as inferior people, and status considerations for excluding them are reduced. Thus the line of causation probably is this: Overt discrimination is changed, attitudes change, and institutions change.

Wages and Competition

The assumption that wage differentials and wage and price competition are basic causal forces is necessary to make the neoclassical model compatible with competitive equilibrium theory, but this assumption also causes some problems for the theory. We have noted this problem as it relates to the behavior of white workers. But the assumption that racial wage differentials are important facts to be explained also creates some question of the model's congruence with reality. If it is correct to assume that job control and status are the workers' main objectives and that profits and status are the main objectives of employers, then discriminatory wage differentials for homogeneous labor in the same firms are not likely to be very significant forces in the real world.[14] There is indeed no evidence that such differentials exist for workers who are perfect substitutes. Because of the importance of job specificity and OJT, it would almost be necessary to show that blacks and whites in the same firms and occupations were paid different wages, and this seems to be a highly unlikely occurrence.

There is, however, considerable evidence of job segregation and the concentration of blacks in certain kinds of jobs. The larger supplies of blacks in these traditional jobs undoubtedly tend to cause wages in these jobs to be lower than otherwise, but there is at least a partial compensation on the demand side because the dependable supplies of blacks cause employers to prefer blacks for these jobs. The neoclassical model does not ordinarily deal with this problem because of its questionable assumption that demand is independent of supply.

To be sure, there are racial income differentials. But this is not the same as showing racial wage differentials for homogeneous units of labor, even though neoclassical analysts sometimes use incomes and wages as if they were interchangeable concepts. Incomes are influenced by factors such as nonwage income, occupation, hours worked, and method of wage payment, as well as by wage rates.

Neoclassical analysts could argue, of course, that hiring blacks who are more productive than whites would have the same effect as paying racial wage differentials, but this requires the homogeneous factor assumption to be relaxed. This in turn would disrupt the marginal productivity theory because it would not be possible to say whether productivity changes were caused by changing units of labor or by the addition of more or less productive workers.

The neoclassical formulation, therefore, approximates a theory of wages with an extra term, the discrimination coefficient, where the specification of the model predetermines the outcome, rather than a theory explaining the basic causal forces of discrimination. The results of this formulation are true by definition—blacks must accept lower wages than whites in order to get jobs.

The neoclassical competitive assumptions also ignore the importance of bargaining and group activity, which seem important in changing racial employment patterns. The usual neoclassical assumption is that decisions are made on the basis of individual motivations and that in the long run these will erode group rules that are incompatible with individual marginal productivities and wage- and profit-maximizing motives. However, there may be no way to test this assumption, for an employer may not be able to determine the productivity of an individual worker, especially when adding a black worker to a group of whites. He must calculate the costs of reactions of the whites as well as the gain from hiring a qualified black. This often will become a bargaining problem among groups of blacks and their supporters (black community, government agencies, etc.), white workers and their organizations, and employers. The power relations will determine whether or not blacks get hired. Within the institutional framework (including laws and prevailing race relations in the larger society) black power to gain access to jobs ordinarily will be determined by the ability to inflict losses on (or convey profits to) employers and their control of supplies of labor qualified to satisfy the employer's demands if whites boycott or strike to protest the hiring of blacks. Employers are motivated by net profits resulting from the racial employment bargain.

Black or white workers' power will not come from the marginal productivities of individual workers, therefore, but from the productivities of groups of workers. Moreover, the effect of change on the net productivity of work groups will determine the extent to which employers are likely to make new racial rules.

Employers will not only be influenced by the net effect of the employment decision but also by the impact of such external pressures as government, general employment conditions, and the nature of product markets. Product markets are important in bargaining situations because they influence the employer's vulnerability to consumer pressures—generally, consumer-oriented companies are more vulnerable to prevailing racial attitudes (negative or positive) than those whose main output is producers' goods.

A model of employment discrimination that ignores the power of unions is incomplete, but unions are generally ignored by the neoclassical model. A union's racial practices are determined mainly by the influence of race on the union's control mechanisms.[15] These control mechanisms are the procedures used by the labor organization to project and promote its basic objectives, which vary with the type of organization; and they will be explored at greater length in the outline of a bargaining model that follows.

On balance, a labor organization is not a basic force creating discrimination; it is a force to be used by its members to carry out their objectives whether one such objective is discrimination by whites or the eradication of discrimination. Orley Ashenfelter shows that craft unions have caused black wages to be lower than they would have been otherwise, while industrial unions have caused them to be higher.[16]

This suggests another major problem with the neoclassical model, namely, the assumption that competition necessarily erodes discrimination and group interests. Showing that competition does not play this role would cause considerable difficulty for the neoclassical model. Whereas the primary motivation for discrimination at the blue-collar level comes from white workers—which is a more realistic assumption than pointing to employers—oligopolistic firms might hire black workers faster than competitive firms in order, for example, to weaken the bargaining power of white-controlled unions. There is considerable historical evidence that blacks broke into nontraditional jobs in oligopolies like the steel and auto industries as strikebreakers long before they ever were hired outside menial classifications in more competitive industries like textiles, which avoided black areas in the South and has been known as a white man's industry.

It is true that blacks are concentrated more in industries with low product-market concentration ratios, but this does not prove that competitive industries are less discriminatory or that competition tends to erode discrimination. Blacks tend to be concentrated in competitive industries because these are low-wage jobs that hire mainly unskilled and semiskilled workers, consistent with black skill levels. Industries with higher product-market concentration ratios tend to have fewer blacks at least partly because they also have higher skill requirements than competitive firms and blacks generally have lower skill levels than whites.

There is no evidence showing—and considerable evidence to the contrary—that blacks have good employment opportunities in the white-collar and skilled jobs within competitive industries.[17] A major reason the neoclassical model can ignore the case in which blacks do not compete with whites in terms of wages is its assumption of full employment, which makes it difficult for employers to meet their labor requirements exclusively from one race. In reality, competitive firms have tended to locate in labor surplus areas, where their labor requirements were small relative to available labor pools.[18]

The neoclassical emphasis on competition also ignores the possible effects of bargaining on the racial employment practices of the large employer. Because of their low skills, white or black workers in small competitive firms have very limited bargaining power, but, by the same token, the competitive employer has less slack with which to respond to black demands for better jobs. These employers are more likely to be consumer-oriented and concerned that unpopular racial policies will reduce their sales and profits. Black consumer boycotts can be more effective against these firms than against the intermediate goods-producing oligopolists, who are less vulnerable to consumer boycotts but might be more responsive to threats of lawsuits or the loss of government contracts.

There is an important distinction between arguing, as neoclassical economists do, that competitive market forces tend to erode discrimination and that *industrialization* and the efficiency requirements of enterprises do so, as argued, for example, by Kerr, Dunlop, Harbison, and Myers.[19] These scholars rely on evidence from international studies to conclude that the logic of industrialism tends to erode discrimination. Industrial societies, in their view, tend to be open societies "inconsistent with the assignment of managers or workers to occupations or to jobs by traditional caste, racial groups, by sex or by family status."[20] This formulation emphasizes the interactions of employers' decisions with major institutions in the larger society, so that industrialization, rather than the neoclassical competitive market, causes changes that erode discrimination. Industrial societies not only tend to be open, but they also tend to produce urbanization and to be pluralistic, both of which increase the political and economic power of blacks to combat discrimination. Industrial societies also tend to give greater roles to governments and put a premium on using the political process to achieve economic ends.

The form in which the neoclassical model of discrimination is expressed impedes—if not precludes—empirical testing or use for policy purposes. As already noted, the model offers few suggestions for ways blacks might improve their employment patterns other than by accepting lower wage rates, improving their productivity, getting whites to change their attitudes, or enforcing antitrust laws. Because OJT is such an important method of acquiring skills, blacks also must find some way of gaining access to those jobs having skill development potential.

A number of features of the neoclassical model make it difficult to derive meaningful policy prescriptions from it. For one thing, the model is too simple and abstract to include enough relevant variables that can be tested empirically. Moreover, the model's assumption that institutions are given causes it to pay very little attention to specific measures to improve simultaneously black economic positions in the short run *and* initiate long-run reforms to eliminate institutionalized discrimination.

AN ALTERNATIVE FORMULATION

This critique of the economics of discrimination suggests at least the outlines of an alternative formulation that incorporates features of the neoclassical and other models but specifies the motives of the various actors and the contexts within which they operate on the basis of empirical evidence rather than a priori deductive reasoning. This alternative formulation could be called an industrial relations or bargaining model and is similar to that developed for industrial relations by John Dunlop in his *Industrial Relations Systems*.[21] However, it is not possible to present a definitive comparison of this alternative formulation with the neoclassical model because each model has different objectives and is formulated in different terms and at different levels of abstraction. The alternative formulation is less designed to be compatible with a general equilibrium model and, therefore, is less rigorous, but, hopefully, it can be tested empirically, is more relevant for understanding the basic forces causing and perpetuating discrimination, and affords more insight into appropriate antidiscrimination policies. Each group of actors in the racial employment process develops mechanisms to improve its power relative to other groups. In this formulation wages merely constitute one aspect of the job.

Also, a bargaining model assumes racial employment patterns in any given situation to be products of the power relationship between the actors and the specific environmental contexts within which they operate. These relationships and contexts can be empirically determined to some extent, and while relatively stable in the short run, they change through time and involve dynamic mutual causation rather than one-way causal relationships.

The Actors

The main actors involved in the determination of racial employment patterns are managers, white workers, black workers, unions, and government agencies responsible for the implementation of antidiscrimination and industrial relations policies. The main environmental features influencing racial employment patterns include: economic and labor market conditions, community race relations, the distribution of power in the larger community, industry structure and growth potential, the labor market skills and education of black and white populations relative to the labor requirements of various companies and industries, and the operation of labor market institutions.

Employers

It has been argued that the employer's main motivation is profit maximization and status. However, profit maximization must be considered in a much broader context than the effect of individual marginal productivities on wages.

Management hiring decisions also historically have been influenced by firm size, industry structure, and the nature of labor supplies. Assuming employer motives to hire blacks because of profit considerations, the strongest factor influencing the black workers' ability to combat discrimination is not marginal productivity of each worker but total labor supplies to meet management's requirements if whites strike or boycott. In the bargaining model the control of larger supplies of labor increases bargaining power. Although many other factors influence this relationship, whites will rarely be able to exclude large supplies of blacks qualified to take their place. Moreover, where there are adequate total labor supplies, employers frequently prefer minority workers for certain kinds of jobs because the limited job options available to blacks and their traditional employment in those occupations cause them to be crowded into these occupations and make them dependable sources of labor. Because blacks traditionally have been hired in certain occupations, employers have developed stereotypes that blacks are best suited for those jobs. Blacks have been preferred mainly for menial and disagreeable occupations but also for some higher-paying jobs such as musicians, athletes, trowel trades in the construction industry, waiters, and longshoremen. In short, unless their own status is threatened by hiring blacks, employers' profit motives will cause them to hire blacks when all-black work forces can be employed in particular occupations for less than all-white work forces and when dependable supplies of labor are available to perform particular tasks. The employers' demand for black workers may be influenced by pressures from governments or black communities.

However, employers maintain status motives for discrimination. Top management's status probably will not be adversely affected by integrating blue-collar work forces, but if members of management have racial biases, resistance to integration will increase as the integrated jobs come closer to their own in the occupational structure. This at least partly explains the lower representation of blacks in white-collar and managerial positions. Of course, partly because of institutional discrimination fewer blacks have the education, training, and skill requirements for managerial and white-collar jobs.

White Male Workers

This conceptual model assumes that white male workers are primarily motivated by status and job-control considerations in excluding minorities as well as women from "their" jobs. However, whether or not whites succeed in excluding minorities depends on whites' ability to bring pressure to bear on the employer. If whites are in sufficient supply to fill particular occupations, in the absence of countervailing powers, employers will find it profitable to hire only whites. However, if minorities are in sufficient supply to meet employers' labor requirements, employers might turn to minorities to weaken white unions. They will not necessarily pay the minorities or women workers a different wage, but their presence tends to moderate wage pressure unless minorities and whites form a united bargaining front. Similarly, the white workers' bargaining power would be weakened even if minorities are in helper or other mislabeled occupational categories while really performing the same jobs as whites. If they have inadequate bargaining power to prevent the entry of minorities or women into "their" jobs, bigoted whites are not likely to quit good jobs because of their racist attitudes, nor are they likely to demand wage differentials to compensate for their prejudices. Even assuming they have adequate knowledge of alternatives, prejudiced whites are likely to stay on their jobs if moving is costly in terms of loss of seniority, good wages, and the advantages of specialized nontransferable job skills in places where they have worked.

Unions

White workers will use the unions they control to preserve and ration job opportunities. On the other hand, black workers might use labor organizations to preserve or enlarge their own opportunities.

The race issue enters union operating procedures in a variety of ways. Different kinds of unions have different motives, procedures, and control mechanisms and, therefore, will react differently to the presence of black workers in an industry or trade. If there are few or no blacks in an industry or trade, craft unions have been motivated by job control and status considerations to keep them out. Whether or not these unions are able to bar blacks depends mainly on their control of entry into the occupation. Craft unions, for example, ordinarily have considerable control of the supply of labor. The main job-control instruments of craft unions are control of training, entry into the trade and union, and job referrals. In order to penetrate these crafts and unions blacks must ordinarily either threaten the unions' control instruments or inflict monetary losses on those organizations.

Because they confront different situations, industrial unions generally have adopted different procedures. Their members are not any more or less racially prejudiced than craftsmen, but job-status considerations seem to be weaker in the case of industrial unions. The main difference between craft and industrial unions is that the latter have little direct influence over hiring. In order to organize their jurisdictions, therefore, industrial unions must appeal to the workers hired by the employer. Thus if blacks have been hired in competition with white workers, the union's ability to organize and its bargaining strength will depend on its ability to attract blacks.

Union racial practices also are influenced by union structure. Since federations and national unions have broader political objectives than the locals, the motive for racial equality increases as we move from the local to the national level. Moreover, national craft unions also have stronger motives to take in blacks than their locals because the national unions' power depends to some extent upon the size of the membership, whereas the local often perceives its power to depend more narrowly on control of labor supplies in local labor markets.

Blacks

The blacks outside craft unions derive their power mainly from the strength of employer motives to hire them and the extent to which they can threaten wage rates and job-control procedures of discriminating white union members and their leaders; this in turn depends, primarily, on the number of blacks in a labor market who possess the necessary skills to compete with white union members and, secondarily, on the extent to which the black community and antidiscrimination forces are organized to overcome white resistance to the admission of blacks. Even if civil rights forces are well organized to achieve this objective, they will have limited impact unless they produce black applicants for employment, upgrading, apprenticeship, and/or journeyman status who meet the qualifications imposed by unions and employers or unless they successfully challenge the standards and specifications themselves. These considerations make it obvious that an effective strategy to overcome local union resistance ordinarily will require considerable attention to local labor market conditions and the control mechanisms used by the local union to regulate labor supplies and control jobs.

Environmental Factors

These specific and immediate forces affecting black employment patterns are influenced by environmental factors such as the relative amount and quality of education available to blacks, race relations in the larger community, the age and sex composition of the black work force, alternative income sources available to black workers and their families, housing patterns and transportation costs relative to the location of jobs, the physical and emotional health of blacks relative to whites, whether an industry is growing or declining in terms of employment, black and white migration patterns, the structure of industry in terms of its customers (blacks, whites, other employees, or government), general business conditions, skill requirements and job structures within industry, the black community's relative accessibility to job information, and the process through which employers and unions recruit and train workers for jobs.

While all of these factors are important determinants of black employment patterns, some are more important and measurable than others. General business conditions are very important because tight labor markets facilitate the employment and upgrading of blacks. However, this view must be qualified because experience makes it clear that tight labor markets are not sufficient causes of change. Many cities in the South have had low official unemployment rates, but they also had stable racial employment patterns between 1920 and the 1960s. Moreover, there is a difference between a labor market in which unemployment is declining and one in which unemployment is low and stable. Similarly, the overall unemployment rate obscures particular labor market conditions where blacks are able to get jobs. Finally, concerted efforts to change institutional arrangements can make it possible for black employment to increase in a particular category even when white employment is falling.

The bargaining model has some policy implications that are similar to those of the neoclassical model. The neoclassicals are correct in stressing measures to increase black productivity as a means of improving their economic positions. But they are wrong in assuming that market forces alone will gain blacks access to the jobs for which they qualify themselves. Policies must be taken to overcome employer and community opposition and white workers' control of jobs. Indeed, if blacks are unable to gain access to jobs, there is no effective way they can acquire the OJT so essential for access to many better jobs. Black workers certainly are not going to be able to gain access to many of these jobs and OJT opportunities by agreeing to work for lower wages than white incumbents.

The neoclassical model gives no place to group activities in changing employment opportunities, whereas the bargaining model stresses the need for group action to initiate changes in rules and laws to which individuals adapt. The bargaining model also stresses the need to build public policy (as well as group strategy and tactics) on an understanding of the responses of organizations and groups to various kinds of pressure, not merely on an understanding of market forces. However, there is an overlap between these formulations in the sense that market forces influence the power relations among groups.

The industrial relations model also stresses the need to explore the relationships among attitudes, overt and institutional discrimination, and market forces in order to determine how discrimination can be reduced or eliminated.

The policy implications of Arrow's formulations depend in part on whether we accept either the taste-for-discrimination or perception-of-reality formulation. The former would imply measures to reduce discriminatory tastes directly or indirectly through competitive forces. The latter would require more accurate labor market information to cause the probabilities of selecting qualified whites and blacks to converge.

CONCLUSIONS

This chapter outlines theoretical conceptions of racial discrimination advanced by neoclassical, radical, and dual labor market economists. It emphasizes these theories or hypotheses, especially the lack of agreement among the various proponents of the various systems and the formative nature of the dual labor market and radical approaches. These formulations also differ in their purposes. In general, discrimination does not occupy a central place in any of these formulations but is part of a broader conceptual framework. The neoclassical theory has been developed more systematically than the others, but, except in terms of compatability with competitive neoclassical general equilibrium theory, it seems to be inadequate in its definition and conception of discrimination, in treating discrimination as "given" and not to be explained by the model, in not taking into consideration the influence of groups and bargaining, in using deductive, rather than empirically derived, concepts that are difficult to test, in producing mechanical results that add little information about the forces increasing or reducing discrimination, in omitting significant factors impinging on discrimination, and in leading to inadequate policy recommendations. Given these limitations, progress toward integrating neoclassical theory and economic reality has been slow.[22]

For the purposes of understanding racial discrimination in employment and producing strategies, tactics, and policies for changing discrimination, a broader bargaining model is recommended. This model should distinguish between overt and institutional discrimination, call for an analysis of the motives of various actors impinging on the employment decision, emphasize the need to examine the power relations among these actors, and stress the need to examine the broader social and economic context within which the actors establish formal, informal, and institutionalized rules governing racial employment relations. There are clear overlaps among the neoclassical, radical, dual labor market, and bargaining formulations, but it appears that the last provides a better conceptual framework both for understanding the dynamics of racial employment relations and for formulating policies to improve black opportunities.

DISCUSSION QUESTIONS

1. "Discrimination represents a significant cost to employers. Consumers suffer for it, in turn, by paying higher prices for products they buy." Discuss.
2. Explain briefly the various "theories of discrimination." To which, if any, do you subscribe? Why?
3. "Labor unions, with their ability to control entry into a particular craft or trade, have been powerful agents of employment discrimination." Discuss.
4. Explain the meaning of: institutional discrimination; job segregation; "the crowding hypothesis"; wage and employment discrimination.
5. Why might employers who have in the past discriminated against minorities nonetheless have also favored antidiscrimination legislation?
6. Some economists have rationalized discrimination hiring practices as sound business practice using marginal revenue product analysis. Analyze critically their assumptions.
7. Briefly outline and critique the neoclassical theory of discrimination in the marketplace.

Notes

1. This chapter relies heavily on Ray Marshall, "The Economic Theory of Racial Discrimination in Employment," *Journal of Economic Literature* (September 1974): 849–871.
2. For a review of empirical research see Dale Hiestand, *Discrimination in Employment: An Appraisal of the Research* (Ann Arbor, Mich.: Institute of Labor and Industrial Relations, University of Michigan and National Manpower Policy Task Force, 1970).
3. Gary Becker, *The Economics of Discrimination*, 2nd ed. (University of Chicago Press, 1971).
4. Barbara R. Bergmann, *Occupation Segregation, Wages, and Profits When Employers Discriminate by Race and Sex* (College Park, Md.: Project on the Economics of Discrimination, mimeograph, 1970); "The Effect on White Incomes of Discrimination in Employment," *Journal of Political Economy* 79 (March/April 1971): 294–313.

5. This is our notation, not Bergmann's.
6. Finis Welch, "Labor Market Discrimination: An Interpretation of Income Differences in the Rural South," *Journal of Political Economy* 75 (June 1967): 225–240.
7. Ibid.
8. Kenneth J. Arrow, "Models of Job Discrimination" and "Some Models of Race in the Labor Market," in A. H. Pascal, ed., *Racial Discrimination in Economic Life* (Lexington, Mass.: Heath, 1972); "The Theory of Discrimination," in Orley Ashenfelter and Albert Rees, eds., *Discrimination in Labor Markets* (Princeton, N.J.: Princeton University Press, 1974).
9. Arrow, "Theory of Discrimination," op. cit.
10. Edmund S. Phelps, "Statistical Theory of Racism and Sexism," *American Economic Review* 62 (September 1974): 659–661.
11. Orley Ashenfelter, "Discrimination and Trade Unions" in Ashenfelter and Rees, op. cit., p. 26.
12. John J. McCall, *Racial Discrimination in the Job Market: The Role of Information and Search* (Santa Monica, Calif.: Rand Corporation, 1971).
13. Janice Fanning Madden, "Discrimination—A Manifestation of Male Market Power?" in Cynthia B. Lloyd, ed., *Sex, Discrimination, and the Division of Labor* (New York: Columbia University Press, 1975).
14. Lester Thurow, *Economics of Poverty and Discrimination* (Washington, D.C.: Brookings Institution, 1969).
15. Ray Marshall, *The Negro and Organized Labor* (New York: Wiley, 1965); Ray Marshall and Virgil Christian, eds., *The Employment of Southern Blacks* (Salt Lake City, Utah: Olympus Publishing Co., 1974).
16. Ashenfelter, "Discrimination and Trade Unions," op. cit.
17. Marshall and Christian, op. cit.
18. Welch, "Labor Market Discrimination," op. cit.
19. Clark Kerr et al., *Industrialism and Industrial Man* (Cambridge, Mass.: Harvard University Press, 1960).
20. Ibid.
21. John Dunlop, *Industrial Relations Systems* (New York: Holt, Rinehart and Winston, 1958).
22. Dennis J. Aigner and Glen C. Cain, "Statistical Theories of Discrimination in Labor Markets," *Industrial and Labor Relations Review* (1977): 175–187.

Chapter 12
Black Employment
and Income

Low income and inadequate employment opportunities were among the most important human resource development problems for blacks and other minorities in the 1960s and 1970s. Underutilization and underdevelopment not only deprive blacks of opportunities to improve their material welfare but also cost the nation the economic contribution they could make if they had better employment and income-earning opportunities, to say nothing of the costs of social instability.

Minority groups, particularly blacks, did much to stimulate human resource development programs. The civil rights movement's concentration on political rights during the 1950s gave way to greater demands for economic equality during the 1960s, when it became abundantly clear that abstract rights without economic opportunity had little meaning. Moreover, the institutional nature of racial discrimination came into even sharper focus in the 1970s as the adoption of programs to overcome specific overt acts of discrimination produced limited results. It became increasingly apparent that institutionalized racism was more deeply rooted and pervasive than more overt forms of discrimination and, therefore, that vigorous and comprehensive education, employment, training, and welfare measures would be required to combat it. Institutionalized racism affects all aspects of life—education, housing, jobs, social affairs—and causes the persons discriminated against not to aspire to or prepare for the kinds of jobs from which they are barred.[1]

POPULATION SHIFTS

Some of the nation's most significant race problems have come about in large measure because of the migration of blacks out of the rural South. Until roughly the time of World War I, almost all blacks were in the South and most of them were concentrated in the so-called black belt, a crescent of counties extending from Washington, D.C., through east Texas, each of which had a majority black population until the 1940s. Indeed, as late as 1940, over three-fourths of the nation's black population resided in the South. Because of the great outmigration since around the time of World War I, only about one-half of the nation's blacks remain in the South. Black outmigration appears to have been largely in response to job opportunities, which opened up initially because of the cessation of immigration from Europe into northern labor markets with the outbreak of World War I.

Black migration out of the South was accelerated by World War I, continued during the 1920s, slowed down some during the depression of the 1930s, speeded up again during World War II, continued until 1970, and reversed slightly during the decade of the 1970s. In 1940, 77 percent of the nation's blacks were in the South, compared with 60 percent in 1960 and about 50 percent in 1970. This black outmigration from the rural South has been one of the most significant developments of the past half century. In a relatively short time the black population has been transformed from predominantly rural and southern to predominantly urban and equally divided between the North and the South. Although segregation was not as institutionalized outside the South, racism has been a problem for blacks in the North as well as in the South. Moreover, because they were not very well prepared by training or experience for nonfarm jobs, blacks held mainly menial jobs in northern as well as southern cities. Indeed, in some ways the black's lot was worse outside the South. Blacks did not even hold the better jobs in black neighborhoods and were concentrated in central cities outside the South. In addition, those blacks who moved North during and after World War II found declining job opportunities in many of the industries that traditionally had absorbed large numbers of semiskilled and unskilled workers. Moreover, ghetto labor markets had characteristics that made it difficult for many young blacks to move into the mainstream even when discriminatory barriers were lowered. The ghetto labor market syndrome probably explains why blacks recently arrived from the South have better income and employment experience than blacks with similar characteristics who were born in Northern cities. The submarginal or marginal labor markets, which predominate in ghettos, have many job openings that ghetto dwellers find unattractive or occupy only for short periods. Blacks fresh from the South probably find these submarginal or marginal jobs more attractive than the opportunities that had been available to them.

Other problems confronted blacks outside the South. Indeed, although greater political power was available to them than had been the case in the South and they confronted less formal segregation imposed by law, nevertheless, blacks encountered discrimination and hostility from whites in other areas. The influx of southern blacks with different values and limited education or job training caused many northern whites to move out of central cities, leaving behind areas with larger black majorities, especially in the schools, and working-class or retired whites who had insufficient income to move out or who had such large investments in their homes that they were reluctant to move. These developments created racial tensions between black and white workers. Indeed, some observers believe that these tensions will upset the New Deal coalition, which included blacks and white ethnics, who had been concentrated in many of the neighborhoods into which blacks have moved.

Migration created problems for the South as well as the North. Those southerners who thought they could export their black welfare problems to the North were very short-sighted indeed. By not taking measures to retain blacks, the South aggravated its human resource development problem because the most productive part of its black population moved out, leaving behind the older, less well-educated blacks who have limited productive potential and, therefore, are not attractive even to the marginal industries that predominate in the region's economy. These industries have moved into the South in search of workers with higher qualifications who will work at lower wages. Because of the rapid displacement of southerners from agriculture and the lower level of industrialization, labor markets have been more attractive to marginal enterprises in the South than they have been in the North. In addition, lower welfare payments in the South forced more secondary workers in a family to work than is true in those areas where welfare payments are higher.

EMPLOYMENT CHANGES

The evidence reveals perceptible economic progress made by blacks during the 1960s, but it also shows uneven progress and the continuation of wide economic gaps between blacks and whites. Moreover, the economic gains of blacks relative to whites slowed down and in some cases were reversed during the 1970s. Discrimination and racial inequality remain very serious problems requiring the strengthening of antidiscrimination and other human resource development activities. Moreover, the causes of racial inequality are deeply imbedded in American society; therefore, progress will require sustained efforts and programs on numerous fronts.

For the nation as a whole there were some perceptible changes in black employment patterns during the 1960s and 1970s. Over both dec-

Table 12-1 OCCUPATIONAL DISTRIBUTION
OF BLACKS AND OTHER MINORITIES—1960–1979

	MINORITIES, ANNUAL AVERAGES		
OCCUPATION	1960	1970	1979
Total	100.0%	100.0%	100.0%
Professional and technical workers	4.8	9.1	12.2
Managers and administrators, except farm	2.6	3.5	5.2
Sales workers	1.5	2.1	2.8
Clerical workers	7.3	13.2	17.7
Craft and kindred workers	6.0	8.2	9.4
Operatives	20.4	23.7	19.9
Nonfarm laborers	13.7	10.3	7.4
Service workers	31.7	26.0	23.2
Farm workers	12.1	3.9	2.2

SOURCE: Bureau of Labor Statistics.

ades—particularly during the 1970s—total black employment grew proportionately faster than that for all workers. More importantly, nonwhites (who are over 90 percent black) increased their proportions of higher-status and better-paying white-collar jobs while they reduced their proportions in the service and laborer categories (Tables 12-1, 12-2).

Black women's relative employment gains were particularly striking, especially in professional, technical, managerial, clerical, and sales categories. Blacks, males and females, in the 25-to-34-year-old group improved their employment patterns relative to whites and relative to blacks in other age groups.

Despite these gains, however, blacks have a long way to go to gain employment equality with whites. Blacks account for over half of all private household workers and over a fifth of all laundry and dry-cleaning operatives, laborers, hospital attendants, janitors and sextons, maids and cleaners, and practical nurses. At the other end of the employment scale blacks represent very small percentages of managers, administrators, proprietors, sales workers, and professional and technical workers.

Blacks experienced dramatic percentage increases in some professional-technical jobs, but within these occupations they are heavily concentrated among the less-skilled, low-paying jobs such as social and recreation workers, registered nurses, medical and dental technicians, and elementary and high school teachers. Blacks traditionally have been concentrated in professional jobs serving black communities. When jobs are integrated, blacks appear mainly to get "new traditional" jobs, in which they replace whites who previously served black clients. Similarly, in the craft occupations blacks are underrepresented in the electrical, pipe, and printing crafts and overrepresented among brick masons, cement and concrete finishers, cranemen, derrick operators, painters, and roofers and slaters.

Black women advanced more than black men. Particularly impressive were the employment gains of black women relative to those of white

Table 12-2   EMPLOYMENT GROWTH OF ALL WORKERS
AND MINORITIES BY SELECTED MAJOR OCCUPATIONAL GROUP,
1960–1970 AND 1970–1979

| | PERCENT INCREASE 1960–1970 | | PERCENT INCREASE 1970–1979 | |
| | ALL | | ALL | |
OCCUPATION	WORKERS	MINORITIES	WORKERS	MINORITIES
Total	19.5	21.9	23.3	29.3
Professional and technical	49.2	131.4	35.1	74.4
Managerial and administrative	17.3	66.9	26.7	92.6
Sales	14.9	78.2	27.0	67.8
Clerical	40.5	121.3	28.4	73.5
Other	9.1	4.7	17.2	11.3

SOURCE: Bureau of Labor Statistics.

women, who also face discrimination. Moreover, black women have experienced employment gains in a narrow range of industries compared with black men.

UNEMPLOYMENT

Blacks also suffer more from unemployment than whites. Only about 50 percent of adult nonwhite males worked a full year in 1979, compared with 60 percent for whites. Over 20 percent of nonwhite males had no work experience, compared with 16 percent for whites; among those who found some employment, 38 percent of nonwhites, but only 29 percent of whites, experienced work interruptions during the year.

Because of these interruptions and the fact that they have more recently entered many nonagricultural jobs, blacks tend to have less tenure on the job than whites. Since seniority is an important determinant of job security, occupational upgrading, and other benefits, work interruptions and relatively short job tenure have long-run consequences beyond the immediate problems they cause.

Although black workers are about twice as likely to experience unemployment as white workers, the burden of unemployment shifts markedly over the course of the business cycle. During recessionary periods, the employment situation of blacks deteriorates relative to that of whites; when economic activity picks up, their conditions improve in relative terms.[2] Indeed, tight labor markets tend to be the most significant factors promoting improvements in black employment patterns. Nonwhites of all ages, especially males, benefit more than whites from tight labor markets during prosperity phases of the cycle. Even black teenagers, who as it was noted earlier suffer very high relative unemployment rates, were helped by these tight labor market conditions, although this only briefly offset the disturbing long-run trend of rising unemployment for this age group.

If past experience had prevailed, proportionately more blacks than whites should have left the unemployment pool during the recovery following the severe 1973–1975 recession. However, despite the fact that employment has increased considerably over the last half of the 1970s, the economy did not grow at a rate fast enough to absorb a large and growing workforce. Relative to their white counterparts, blacks made no gains in this period. Between mid-1975 and the end of 1979, the white unemployment rate declined slowly but steadily from 8.1 to 4.9 percent; the black rate hovered around the 13–14 percent mark for more than two years before falling to 11.4 percent by the end of the decade.

The higher unemployment rates of nonwhites are due largely to the fact that blacks are concentrated in occupations and industries such as nonfarm laborers, operatives, and service workers, in which unemployment tends to be both high and very sensitive to cyclical swings in economic activity. Although education tends to be correlated with unemployment, blacks of all ages and educational levels are more frequently unemployed than their white counterparts.

Nonwhite youths faced a particularly serious worsening of their employment prospects during the 1960s and 1970s. Unemployment rates of nonwhite teenagers rose from 15 percent in the mid-1950s to 20 percent or more during the 1960s. In the early 1970s, it climbed further to over 30 percent. By 1977, it had reached 40 percent, before abating slightly by the decade's end.

Nonwhites also suffer relatively high unemployment rates because they are more likely than whites to be concentrated in secondary labor markets, in which seniority means very little and in which wages and working conditions are barely preferable to street life and welfare.

Unemployment rates are imperfect indicators of nonwhite labor market disadvantages, however, because these rates only reflect those who are willing and able to work and actively seeking jobs—they do not reflect those working part time who would like full-time jobs, those working but not earning enough to raise them above the poverty level, or those who have become discouraged and ceased looking for jobs. There is some reason, therefore, to be concerned about the fact that the labor force participation rate of blacks has been below that of whites since the early 1970s (Figure 12-1). The trends are mirror images of one another, the white rate having risen steadily while the rate for blacks was falling through 1975 before rising until 1978.

Of added significance is the even greater decline in the black participation rate (in contrast with the rise in the white race) during recessionary periods. Many unemployed blacks leave the labor market when economic conditions deteriorate. They become discouraged with job prospects and withdraw from the labor force. Although these persons would like to work, they have given up looking for jobs and are not counted among the unemployed. There were over 200,000 discouraged nonwhites (75,000 men and

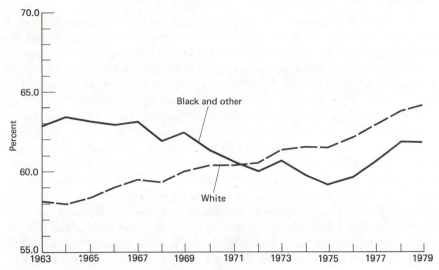

Figure 12-1   Civilian labor force participation rate, persons 16 and over, 1963–1979.

133,000 women) in 1979, accounting for almost 30 percent of all discouraged workers.

The extent to which blacks are overrepresented among the ranks of discouraged workers understates the black unemployment problem. Nonwhites share a disproportionate unemployment burden: 1 out of 10 in the labor force is black, but 2 out of 10 of the unemployed are black. When we observe, further, that nearly 3 in 10 discouraged workers are black, the plight of blacks in the labor market looms all the more serious.

PROBLEMS OF THE CENTRAL CITIES

Outside the rural South blacks are increasingly locating in large metropolitan areas, especially in the North and West. By 1975, 52 percent of blacks (compared to 30 percent of whites) lived in the South, and accounted for 19 percent of the population there. In the South the black population was about evenly divided between metropolitan and nonmetropolitan areas, but almost all blacks outside the South lived in urban areas, especially in the central cities of several large metropolitan areas. As a consequence of these population shifts, poverty—black and white—is mainly a rural phenomenon in the South, but outside the South it is mainly urban.

The concentration of blacks in central cities creates a number of serious social and economic problems. For one thing, the flight of whites from central cities as blacks move in leads to increasing racial segregation in housing and schools. Moreover, the flight of higher-income whites and the decentralization of industry to suburban rings create serious financial problems for the cities, making it difficult for them to render much-needed human resource development services to their populations. The decentralization of jobs creates special problems for blacks because of the transportation costs in money and time to reach jobs in outlying areas. The slum areas of many central cities are characterized by poor housing, crowding, high incidence of crime, poverty, and inadequate public services.

Because of the heavy concentration of blacks in the central city slums, there is a strong tendency to conclude that many problems associated with these areas have racial origins; this is no doubt true, but many also are due to the nature of the slum itself. For example, although much has been made of the disintegration of black ghetto families, presumably because of the legacy of slavery, the incidence of broken homes among Mexican Americans and Puerto Ricans closely resembles that of blacks today, and the incidence of broken families in Irish slums of westside Manhattan at the time of World War I was actually higher than the present black rate.[3] This and other problems of low-income slum dwellers are clearly more related to factors associated with ghettos than with race.

Nevertheless, there are important racial aspects to ghettos because discrimination in housing and employment contributes to the inability of many blacks to leave the ghetto, restricting them to employment within these areas, to "hustling" and other forms of illicit activity, or to welfare dependency. Discrimination in employment combines with inadequate education and other human resource development programs to trap many ghetto residents to lives of poverty and low incomes.

With respect to employment many central-city jobs are characterized by low incomes, limited upward occupational mobility, and high turnover rates. Unions in these occupations tend to be weak, so that workers have very limited job protection. Many employers and workers apparently adapt to these conditions, causing black concentration in these jobs to become self-perpetuating. Marginal jobs require limited skills or education, so that employers need only make limited investments in training and thus are not overly concerned about turnover. Many of the workers in these jobs are not motivated to discipline themselves to perform well and to avoid absenteeism and high quit rates. Surprisingly, however, many ghetto workers in these low-wage jobs have long job tenure and exemplary job performance.

There have been, in recent years, heated debates about how to solve the problems of the ghetto. Some observers argue for ghetto development, or "gilding the ghetto," while others argue for dispersing the ghetto through vigorous housing and employment antidiscrimination programs, increased job training, and improved transportation. However, these are not alternative solutions; both approaches should be used to increase the options available to ghetto residents—to either stay in the ghettos if they choose and improve their economic conditions or to work and live outside these areas. Currently, too many ghetto residents have no choice because they are trapped by low incomes and discrimination. It is particularly important to adopt measures to combat discrimination in housing as well as employment and public accommodations. There also is a pressing need to improve housing within ghetto areas.

CAUSES OF BLACK ECONOMIC DISADVANTAGES

Black income and employment problems are caused by a deeply entrenched constellation of forces that are difficult to overcome and that will require intensified and concerted remedies on a variety of fronts. Because these causal forces are so interrelated, it is difficult to assign weights to each of them. Our understanding of this problem is also complicated by the fact that many causal factors cannot be quantified, making it difficult for us to measure their intensity. Nevertheless, some consistencies are discernible.

Discrimination

While it might be argued that overt discrimination has declined, there is little doubt that institutional discrimination and statistical discrimination continue to be major problems. Nor is it a valid conclusion to say that enforcement of the Civil Rights Act of 1964 caused even overt discrimination to collapse. Direct studies of the impact of the act uniformly minimize its direct effect in changing black employment patterns.[4] For one thing, until 1972, the Equal Employment Opportunity Commission, the agency charged with enforcing the Civil Rights Act, had very limited enforcement powers. If discrimination collapsed before the relatively weak onslaughts of this agency, it was nowhere near as deeply entrenched as most students of this problem assumed it to be. But we suspect that the dynamics of the process of changing even overt discrimination are much more complex. The Civil Rights Act had limited direct impact on employment patterns because it was mainly aimed at combating overt discrimination, which could be proved in the courts, whereas institutional discrimination is a much more serious cause of black job disadvantage. Moreover, antidiscrimination laws operate mainly on the demand side of the employment process and do very little to change the supplies of blacks qualified to move into jobs when race bars are lowered.

Those who attribute the black employment changes of the 1960s to legislation probably confuse cause and effect and misread the processes involved in changing racial employment patterns. More probably, both the antidiscrimination legislation *and* the changes in black employment patterns were responses to the urban riots and other manifestations of black dissatisfaction with their rate of economic progress. It would be easy, therefore, to attribute to formal antidiscrimination measures the consequences of pressures for change from blacks.

Similarly, many of the changes apparently were due more to the direct effects of laws than to their enforcement. As noted earlier, many employers were motivated by profit considerations to hire blacks but were reluctant to do so for fear of adverse reactions from white employees or, probably, to a lesser degree, white customers. One of the most significant aspects of legislation is that it carries considerable moral force as representing the attitudes of a majority of voters. Thus many employers who faced limited opposition to change probably responded to legislation by adopting antidiscrimination policies. Even those employers who faced opposition from white communities and employees used the law to neutralize this opposition when they were inclined for profit or moral reasons to hire or upgrade blacks.

We suspect, for example, that the hiring or upgrading of blacks in many relatively low-wage industries in the South can be attributed to the fact that these employers were having trouble locating an adequate supply of whites who met their hiring standards, whereas qualified blacks, whose employment opportunities have been more narrowly restricted because of discrimination, formed more dependable supplies of labor for these jobs.

Thus the indirect effects of antidiscrimination laws clearly are most effective when they are compatible with employers' economic motives. Indirect effects will have less impact in higher-level jobs for a number of reasons. One is the limited supplies of blacks who meet the skill, experience, or education standards for these jobs. Second, whites in these occupations have more power to resist change because of their higher level of skills, their organizations, and their control of supplies of skilled manpower. These skilled craftworkers, within and without organized labor, have stronger status and job control motives for resisting the entry of blacks. Gaining greater entry for blacks into these occupations will require more direct measures to overcome white resistance, increase the supplies of qualified blacks, and overcome institutionalized barriers to entry.

Public policy also requires attention to the dynamics of the relationship between race bias and discrimination. The authors believe that race prejudice is changed mainly by reducing discrimination directly rather than the reverse. By changing discriminatory procedures, many of the myths influencing black-white relations are exploded. Moreover, people tend to modify their racist views as they are forced to rationalize their attitudes to make them conform with their nondiscriminating behavior. Thus it is more important to eradicate discrimination than to exhort people to change their attitudes, although both should be done.

Labor Market Conditions

There is almost universal agreement that tight labor markets—such as existed during World War II—generate powerful forces to improve black employment patterns. During such times, employers have stronger motives to hire, train, and upgrade black workers. At the same time, opposition by white employees to the hiring of blacks diminishes.

Nevertheless, tight labor markets alone will not guarantee improvements in black economic conditions, as seen from the fact that many occupations and skills remained closed to blacks despite tight labor markets during World War II. Similarly, many Southern cities have had very low levels of unemployment for years with no perceptible impact on black employment in particular trades or occupations. Clearly, therefore, tight labor markets must be supplemented by antidiscrimination, education, and training programs in order to produce changes in particular employment patterns. In the construction industry outreach programs have proved particularly effective in recruiting, tutoring, and placing blacks in apprenticeship and journeyman programs. Current demonstration projects to extend the outreach concept to other areas seem highly promising.

Transportation

The impact of transportation on black employment varies according to the characteristics of a place. In some cities the availability of housing is such that blacks live near job opportunities. In these places transportation is only a minor barrier to black employment. Similarly, transportation is less important as a barrier if blacks are able to get relatively high-paying jobs, even if these jobs are some distance from their homes. As noted earlier, however, transportation is much more important as a barrier to black employment in low-wage jobs because the net returns (wages less transportation) would be lower. Studies in major Southern cities show transportation to be a much more important determinant of black female than black male employment, probably because black females are more heavily concentrated in low-wage service occupations.

Labor Market Procedures

Blacks have more limited access than whites to labor market information about higher-paying jobs. Since blacks have tended to live in segregated housing, attend segregated schools, and work in segregated jobs, they are unable to acquire job information through informal means. Moreover, the widespread tendency for jobs to be filled through existing employees or relatives and friends perpetuates the exclusion of blacks from many jobs. Blacks tend to rely more heavily than whites on formal information sources like the employment service, although many employers do not use the employment service for skilled professional and technical jobs. Similarly, many employers have recruited professional, technical, and managerial employees primarily from colleges and universities which tend to be white dominated. Because these job search and industry hiring practices tend to be deeply entrenched, special efforts are needed to enlarge the labor market information available to blacks and others that tend to be disadvantaged by these procedures. Special consideration should be given to changing the employment service's image in black communities and making that agency a more effective instrument for improving black employment opportunities.

Industry Structure and Skill Requirements

A problem of considerable importance for black employment opportunities is the tendency for black employment to be inversely related to industry skill requirements and growth rates. Black employment is an increasing proportion of marginal, low-wage industries and a declining proportion of the high-wage, growth industries. In the South rapidly growing rural industries are avoiding areas with high black population densities and are not providing equal job opportunities for blacks even in those areas with heavy black population concentration. As noted earlier, much high-wage industry also is avoiding black population areas in the central cities. The inability of blacks to gain equal access to higher-paying jobs and employment in growth industries clearly limits their prospective economic opportunities relative to whites.

The causes of these black employment patterns are difficult to disentangle. Since blacks have lower levels of skills and education than whites, many employers practice statistical discrimination by recruiting from labor pools where the probabilities of recruiting employees who meet their standards are higher. Nevertheless, we cannot avoid the conclusion that some overt and much institutionalized discrimination is responsible for the low participation of blacks in growth industries and skilled jobs.

Improvements will require continued upgrading of black education and training, but other measures are also necessary. Antidiscrimination agencies must vigorously challenge discriminatory and unfair employment and selection procedures that deny blacks an opportunity to enter jobs having growth potential. Greater penetration of blacks into growth jobs would also be greatly facilitated by outreach efforts to recruit, train, and place blacks in specific growth jobs.

EMPLOYMENT AND TRAINING PROGRAMS

Studies of manpower programs adopted during the 1960s generally show that disadvantaged people as a group derived measurable benefits from participating in those programs. In general, blacks have benefited relatively more than whites from employment and training programs, but whites have made greater absolute gains and there is considerable variation among programs.[5]

In 1978, blacks accounted for one-third of the trainees under CETA and for one of every four employed in job creation programs. The impact of these programs on black employment opportunities and the implications of declining proportions of blacks in these programs should be given careful consideration. However, a detailed study of black employment in the South concluded that, despite considerable potential, the training programs had had relatively little impact on black employment patterns.[6]

INCOME

If blacks benefit more than whites from economic expansion, this progress should encompass income gains as well as increases in employment, and should have been particularly true of the expansionary decade of the 1960s. The trends in black and white family income do, in fact, provide some evidence of this. In 1960, black median family income was about 55 percent of that for white families. Black incomes rose considerably more in relative terms during the last half of the 1960s so that by 1970, income of the middle-class black family was 61 percent of its white counterpart.[7]

The absolute median family income for blacks continued to rise after 1970, but not as fast as that for white families, causing the black median to decline to 59 percent in 1978 (Table 12-3). The major reasons for the relative decline were noneconomic in nature:

1. An increase in the proportion of black families headed by women. Over the 1960–1978 period, the proportion has risen from 22 to 40 percent. Comparable percentages for white families were 8 percent in 1960 and 12 percent in 1978. Women, of course, earn on average considerably less than men, regardless of race, and black women earn even less than their white counterparts.
2. A decrease in the proportion of black working wives. Although the number of black wives who work has consistently increased, it has risen less than that among white wives, so that the black proportion of the total has decreased from 11 percent in 1960 to 8 percent in 1978.
3. A decrease in the proportion of multiple earners within black families. In 1969, 56 percent of black families had more than one earner. By 1978, this proportion had fallen to 47 percent, while the proportion of white families with more than one earner increased between 1969 and 1978—from 53 to 55 percent.

Data on incomes of *persons,* however—particularly for year-round, full-time workers—present quite a different picture. These data show that black individuals have made considerable progress relative to their white counterparts. In 1960, incomes of black male year-round, full-time workers was 66 percent of that of white men; by 1978, the income ratio was 77 percent (Table 12-3). For women, the change was even more dramatic: from 68 percent in 1960 to 93 percent in 1978. In terms of weekly earnings, blacks have made similar strides. In 1970, black full-time workers earned 74 percent of what white full-time workers earned. In 1978, their earnings rose to 80 percent of that of whites.

Table 12-3   CHANGE IN SELECTED INCOME AND
EARNINGS SERIES FOR WHITES AND BLACKS: 1960, 1970, AND 1978

| | | | | PERCENT CHANGE | |
| | | | | 1960– 1970 | 1970– 1978 |
STATISTICAL SERIES	1960	1970	1978		
MEDIAN FAMILY INCOME					
Whites	$5,835	$10,236	$18,368	75.4	79.4
Blacks	3,233	6,279	10,879	94.2	73.3
Ratio: black to white	.55	.61	.59		
MEDIAN INCOME: YEAR-ROUND, FULL-TIME WORKERS					
White men	$5,572	$ 9,447	$16,360	69.5	73.2
Black men	3,683	6,435	12,530	74.7	94.7
Ratio: black to white	.66	.68	.77		
White women	$3,377	$5,536	$ 9,732	63.9	75.8
Black women	2,289	4,537	9,020	98.2	98.8
Ratio: black to white	.68	.82	.93		
MEDIAN USUAL WEEKLY EARNINGS, FULL-TIME WORKERS					
Whites	[a]	$ 134	$ 232	—	73.1
Blacks[b]	[a]	99	186	—	87.9
Ratio: black to white		.74	.80		

SOURCES: The data on median family income, per capita income, and median income for year-round full-time workers were obtained from the March supplement to the Current Population Survey (CPS). The data on median usual weekly earnings were obtained from the May CPS.
[a] These data were not collected until 1967.
[b] Weekly earnings for blacks, as distinct from the "black and other" group, are not available for 1970. The figures for 1978 are also for the "black and other" group.

Although these data show progress, there is still a considerable gap remaining. Furthermore, the progress noted has occurred among a more select group of workers for whom one should expect the greatest gains—full-time workers employed year-round. Unfortunately, a considerable number of blacks are not among this group and are unable to find steady employment.

An advantage of concentrating on data for *persons*, however, is that it is possible to focus on changes affecting individuals rather than a group such as families, which is subject to changes in composition over time. Yet, it is the family which is the most predominant social and economic unit in this country. Since social policy has been directed toward the family unit, income data for families are the most relevant. Policymakers should be concerned most with the question of *adequacy* of income with which to support a family.

But to achieve and maintain an adequate income and living standard for black families is most difficult. More than half of all black families have

Table 12-4   FAMILIES BELOW THE POVERTY LEVEL,
BY RACE AND SEX OF HEAD, 1959–1978 SELECTED YEARS

YEAR	ALL FAMILIES BLACK	WHITE	FAMILIES WITH MALE HEAD[a] BLACK	WHITE	FAMILIES WITH FEMALE HEAD, NO HUSBAND PRESENT BLACK	WHITE
NUMBER (THOUSANDS)						
1959	1,860	6,027	1,309	5,037	551	990
1969	1,366	3,575	629	2,506	737	1,069
1974	1,530	3,482	506	2,185	1,024	1,391
1978	1,622	3,523	414	2,132	1,208	1,391
PERCENT BELOW POVERTY LEVEL						
1959	48.1	14.8	43.3	13.4	65.4	30.0
1969	27.9	7.7	17.9	6.0	53.3	25.7
1974	27.8	7.0	14.2	4.9	52.8	24.9
1978	27.5	6.9	11.8	4.7	50.6	23.5

SOURCE: U.S. Department of Commerce, Bureau of the Census.
[a] Includes male heads with or without wife present.

annual incomes less than $10,000, compared to one-quarter of white families. At the other extreme, one-fourth of white families, but less than 10 percent of black families, have incomes over $25,000 a year.

Not surprisingly, then, black families were much more likely to be below the poverty line than white families. The earliest data available on the poverty population (1959) show that 1.9 million black families were below the poverty level (Table 12-4). Although 6 million white families were poor, they accounted for only 15 percent of all white families. The poverty rate among black families was nearly 50 percent.

The number of poor black families declined during the 1960s. Although this number began to increase again in the 1970s, the poverty rate itself remained at the 1969 level—about 28 percent.

Despite the fact that there was a continual decline in poverty among black families maintained by men, it was more than offset by an increase among those families maintained by women. Furthermore, families maintained by women have comprised an increasing proportion of all low income black families. In 1959, about 30 percent of all poor black families were maintained by women; by 1978, this proportion had surged to 75 percent. A similar pattern was observed for white families, but it was much less pronounced. The increasing proportion of poor black families maintained by women is a reflection of the increasing proportion in the total black population of families maintained by women. In 1979, 41 percent of black families, but only 12 percent of white families, were headed by a woman (with no husband present). These families have had a consistently higher poverty rate than families maintained by men.

The official count of the poor, however, considers only money income and ignores in-kind assistance extended to the poor. If the true value of in-kind assistance had been included in total income, the number of poor would have shown greater declines than reported by the Census Bureau. This held particularly true for the 1970s when in-kind assistance continued to expand while cash assistance remained relatively stable.

The majority of poor families, regardless of race, receive earnings. Among poor black families, the proportion with earnings has declined from 68 percent in 1959 to 52 percent in 1977. By contrast, the proportion of white families receiving earnings rose from 50 percent in 1969 to 61 percent in 1977. The black women have a particularly difficult time in the job market, suffering the double jeopardy of both sex and race discrimination.

Relatively high poverty rates for black families (regardless of the person maintaining the family) are associated with those living in the South and in metropolitan areas, those with children under 18, and those maintained by persons with less than a high school education, or by a nonworking person. Poverty rates for individuals, both black and white, are somewhat higher than among families. Although the number of black persons below the poverty line outnumber whites by 2 to 1, blacks (31.3 percent) are over three times as likely to be poor as whites (8.9 percent).

CONCLUSIONS

Despite perceptible black economic progress since 1960, the racial gaps remain very large. Overt and institutional discrimination remain important problems, and antidiscrimination measures should be expanded and strengthened. Nevertheless, antidiscrimination measures alone will not do the job. Also needed are improved human resource development activities, including job creation, education, employment and training, and health, welfare, and income-maintenance programs. The causes of black disadvantage are deeply entrenched; therefore, they will be overcome only through concerted action on a variety of fronts.

DISCUSSION QUESTIONS

1. Black median family income rose relative to that for whites in the 1960s and declined during the next decade. Why? What accounts for the substantial income gap between blacks and whites?
2. Discuss the trends in labor force participation of blacks and whites over the last two decades. What are the reasons for the differences?
3. To what extent have population shifts in the post-World War II period affected the economic status of blacks in the United States?
4. Unemployment among black workers varies considerably more than among whites over the course of the business cycle. Explain.
5. Why are blacks more likely to be "discouraged workers" than their white counterparts?
6. Blacks have made substantial improvements in terms of their occupational distribution over the last two decades. Why do average family data fail to reflect these advances?

7. How do you account for the decline of labor force participation by black males aged 45–54 years?

Notes

1. Sar A. Levitan, William B. Johnston, and Robert Taggart, *Still a Dream* (Cambridge, Mass.: Harvard University Press, 1975), chapter 16.
2. Curtis L. Gilroy, *Unemployment in Recessions: Women and Black Workers*, U.S. Department of Labor, Women's Bureau, 1977.
3. Thomas Sowell, "Minorities and the City," paper prepared for the conference on Manpower and the Metropolis (Tarrytown, N.Y.: November 29–30, 1973).
4. Arvil V. Adams, *Toward Fair Employment and the EEOC: A Study of Compliance Procedures Under Title VII of the Civil Rights Act of 1964*, prepared for the U.S. Equal Employment Opportunity Commission (August 31, 1972).
5. Sar A. Levitan and Robert Taggart, *The Promise of Greatness* (Cambridge, Mass.: Harvard University Press, 1976), chapter 11.
6. Ray Marshall and Virgil L. Christian, Jr., eds., *Employment of Blacks in the South: A Perspective on the 1960s* (Austin: The University of Texas Press, 1980).
7. *The Social and Economic Status of the Black Population in the United States: A Historical View 1790–1978*, Current Population Reports, Special Studies, series P-23, no. 80, U.S. Department of Commerce, Bureau of the Census (Washington, D.C.: GPO, 1979).

Chapter 13
Hispanics

Next to blacks, the largest minority group in this country is that of Spanish origin (referred to hereafter as Hispanics). Hispanics live throughout the United States but are concentrated primarily in the Southwest.[1] Although they have serious employment and income difficulties, the problems of this group have not been as pervasive or intractable as those of blacks.

Overt discrimination against Hispanics has declined in intensity since World War II and never was as rigidly institutionalized as discrimination against blacks. Moreover, relatively few legal cases have been filed alleging discrimination against Hispanics. This undoubtedly is due, in part, to the fact that these groups have not been as vocal as blacks in demanding equality of employment opportunities. But this situation is changing as Hispanics become quantitatively more important and follow the example of blacks in demanding economic equality with whites.

The study of this group has been impeded in the past primarily by the paucity of data. Since 1973, however, reliable and current labor force data have been published by the Bureau of Labor Statistics, and detailed income and other demographic information has become available from the Bureau of the Census in recent years.

Table 13-1   TOTAL AND SPANISH-ORIGIN POPULATION BY THE TYPE OF SPANISH ORIGIN, FOR THE UNITED STATES, MARCH 1979 (THOUSANDS)

| | | PERCENT DISTRIBUTION | |
| | | TOTAL | SPANISH-ORIGIN |
ORIGIN	TOTAL	POPULATION	POPULATION
ALL PERSONS	215,935	100.0	N.A.
Persons of Spanish origin	12,079	5.6	100.0
Mexican	7,326	3.4	60.7
Puerto Rican	1,748	0.8	14.5
Cuban	794	0.4	6.6
Central or South American	840	0.4	7.0
Other Spanish	1,371	0.6	11.4
Persons not of Spanish origin[a]	203,856	94.4	N.A.

SOURCE: U.S. Bureau of the Census, *Current Population Reports*, Population Characteristics, "Persons of Spanish Origin in the United States: March 1979," series P-20, no. 347 (Washington, D.C.: GPO, October 1979), table 1.

[a] Includes persons who did not know or did not report on origin.

DEMOGRAPHY

Hispanics are a very difficult group to define. They do not all speak Spanish—some speak Spanish and English, some only Spanish, and some only English. Racially, this group may be black, brown, or white. They live in every state in the United States. In March 1979, about 12.1 million persons in the United States were Hispanic (Table 13-1). The majority were of Mexican descent (61 percent). Hispanics also included about 15 percent Puerto Ricans and 25 percent Cubans, South Americans, and other persons of Spanish origin. About the only thing Hispanics have in common is their Spanish language heritage.

Between 1973 and 1979, the Hispanic population grew at a rate 4 times greater than that of non-Hispanics. Increased immigration (legal and illegal) from Hispanic countries and a relatively high natural birthrate may result in the Hispanic population surpassing blacks as the largest minority before the year 2000.

In 1978 the largest concentration of Hispanics was in California, Texas, and New York. These three states accounted for two of every three Hispanics residing in the United States. Of the 2.7 million families of Hispanic origin in the United States, 85 percent lived in metropolitan areas. Furthermore, the majority of metropolitan-dwelling families resided in central cities. This contrasts markedly with residence patterns of non-Hispanic families. There were also noticeable differences among Hispanics: Mexican families were more likely to be residing outside metropolitan areas, whereas the opposite held true for Puerto Rican and Cuban families.[2]

INCOME

Hispanic families are not as well off financially as other families. Their median income was $12,566 in 1978, considerably lower than the median for whites ($18,368), but higher than the median for black families ($10,879) (Table 13-2). Further, a substantial proportion of Hispanic families was concentrated at the lower end of the income distribution: almost 25 percent of Spanish-origin families had incomes below $7000; for non-Spanish families, that proportion was only 14 percent. Puerto Ricans had a relatively higher incidence of people below the poverty level in 1978 than the other Hispanic groups:

	PERCENT BELOW POVERTY LEVEL
All persons	11.6
White	8.9
Black	31.3
Hispanics	22.4
Mexican	21.1
Puerto Rican	38.8
All other Spanish origin	15.8

Although recent reliable data are unavailable, Cubans are the only Hispanic group which has characteristically had lower percentages of people below the poverty line than the average for all people. Cubans have higher earnings in part because they are older and have higher levels of education. Cubans also have benefited from special aid from the federal government to help them settle in the United States. Many of those aided as refugees were persons with more wealth than other Spanish-origin people. In Miami Cubans have entered a broader spectrum of industries and occupations than blacks and are more likely than other Hispanics to be employed in higher-paying occupations. Relative to blacks in Miami, Cubans tended to have higher incomes and better employment opportunities.[3]

Puerto Ricans in New York generally have not fared as well relatively as Cubans in Miami. This is due in part to the better work experiences and higher educations and incomes of Cubans. Puerto Ricans in New York were concentrated in industries with unstable employment and suffered unemployment rates almost three times those of whites and twice that of blacks.[4]

Size of family, to the extent that it is related to the number of earners, can have a direct effect on family income. Larger families tend to have higher incomes primarily because they have more earners. On the average, families maintained by Hispanics were larger (3.9 members on average) than non-Spanish families (3.3 members on average). About 31 percent of Hispanic families, but only 18 percent of non-Hispanic families, had 5 or more members. Differences in size of families existed by type of Hispanic

Table 13-2   INCOME IN 1978 OF
ALL FAMILIES AND SPANISH-ORIGIN FAMILIES

FAMILY INCOME	TOTAL FAMILIES	SPANISH-ORIGIN FAMILIES					FAMILIES NOT OF SPANISH ORIGIN[b]
		TOTAL	MEXICAN	PUERTO RICAN	CUBAN	OTHER SPANISH[a]	
Total families (thousands)	57,804	2,741	1,620	434	208	479	55,063
Percent	100.0	100.0	100.0	100.0	100.0	100.0	100.0
Less than $4,000	5.6	9.6	9.3	15.8	5.0	6.8	5.3
$4,000 to $6,999	8.7	14.2	11.7	28.2	10.6	11.5	8.4
$7,000 to $9,999	9.7	14.0	14.3	14.0	13.9	13.0	9.6
$10,000 to $14,999	16.6	21.2	22.9	16.0	19.2	21.0	16.5
$15,000 to $19,999	16.9	16.7	17.4	12.1	16.6	18.4	16.9
$20,000 to $24,999	14.5	10.9	10.8	7.5	17.5	11.3	14.7
$25,000 or more	27.9	13.5	13.5	6.4	17.3	18.1	28.6
Median income	$17,640	$12,566	$12,835	$8,282	$15,326	$14,272	$17,912

SOURCE: U.S. Department of Commerce, Bureau of the Census.
[a] Includes Central or South American origin and other Spanish origin.
[b] Includes families maintained by persons who did not know or did not report on origin.

family: 19 percent of Mexican families had 6 or more persons in the family, compared to 11 percent for Cuban families and 8 percent for non-Hispanic families.[5]

Besides being larger, Hispanic families, due in large part to high birthrates, were also relatively younger, with an average of 1.7 persons under 18 years old in the family. About 40 percent of Hispanic household members were under 18 years of age. In 1979, the median age of Hispanic persons was 22, compared to a median of 30 for the non-Hispanic population. Moreover, 13 percent of Hispanic persons, but only 7 percent of non-Hispanic persons, were under 5 years of age.

Together, the relatively large size of Hispanic families and the young age of Hispanic persons contribute to the higher rates of poverty among Spanish-origin families. The average number of persons in Hispanic poverty families was 4.1 in 1979 (Table 13-3). Family size was even larger among Mexicans. As is true for families of every race, those maintained by a woman of Spanish origin were more likely than other Hispanic families to be below the poverty level. Females headed half of poor Hispanic families.

Educational attainment, too, is a determinant of income and poverty

Table 13-3 SUMMARY CHARACTERISTICS OF SPANISH-
AND MEXICAN-ORIGIN FAMILIES, BY POVERTY STATUS, 1978
(NUMBERS IN THOUSANDS)

| | | SPANISH ORIGIN | |
| | | BELOW POVERTY LEVEL | |
SELECTED CHARACTERISTIC	TOTAL	NUMBER	PERCENT
Families	2,764	591	21.4
Mean size of family[b]	3.88	4.09	—
With related children under 18 years old	2,057	520	25.3
Mean number of related children	2.23	2.62	—
Persons maintaining the family:			
65 years old and over	195	35	18.1
Not a high school graduate[c]	1,461	400	27.4
Worked last year[d]	2,185	285	13.0
Worked year round full time	1,495	92	6.2
Woman	561	301	53.6

SOURCE: U.S. Department of Commerce, Bureau of the Census.
[a] Includes families maintained by persons who did not know or did not report on origin.
[b] Mean based on persons of Spanish or other origin in Spanish origin families.
[c] Persons 25 years and over.
[d] Persons 14 years and over.

status. Persons of Spanish origin have not the educational level of their non-Hispanic counterparts. Whites completed a median 12.4 years of schooling in 1978, and among blacks, the median was 11.8 years. For Hispanics, however, the median was only 10.4. In 1978, about 17 percent of Hispanics 25 years and over completed less than 5 years of schooling; the corresponding proportion among non-Spanish was only 3 percent. Forty-one percent of Hispanics 25 and over, but 67 percent of non-Spanish persons, completed 4 or more years of high school.

Although the education gaps were particularly serious for all Spanish Americans relative to whites and blacks, considerable differences existed within the Spanish population. About half of all Cubans age 25 years and over completed 4 or more years of high school, compared to 34 and 36 percent for Mexicans and Puerto Ricans, respectively.

EMPLOYMENT

In 1979, 4.6 million Hispanics were employed, and accounted for 4.7 percent of total employment. Hispanics have benefited from both the general expansion in employment and federal economic stimulus programs after 1976. Between fiscal years 1976 and 1979, Hispanic participation in public service employment increased from 80,000 to 120,000. Over 500,000 Hispanics were served by CETA programs in fiscal 1979, over 70,000 of them in youth programs.

Between the fourth quarter of 1976 and the fourth quarter of 1979,

| MEXICAN ORIGIN | | | NON-SPANISH[a] | | |
| | BELOW POVERTY LEVEL | | | BELOW POVERTY LEVEL | |
TOTAL	NUMBER	PERCENT	TOTAL	NUMBER	PERCENT
1,623	306	18.9	54,451	4,720	8.7
4.06	4.44	—	3.31	3.62	—
1,236	267	21.6	29,581	3,562	12.0
2.33	2.85	—	1.97	2.43	—
113	20	18.0	8,016	674	8.4
917	221	24.1	16,513	2,470	15.0
1,375	198	14.4	43,313	2,282	5.3
924	65	7.0	32,588	820	2.5
252	116	45.9	7,675	2,309	30.1

Hispanic employment grew about 20 percent—from 3.8 to 4.6 million—which was double the rate for the total workforce. At the same time, the Hispanic labor force participation rate caught up with that of the population as a whole; in 1979 both rates were 64 percent. The rate for blacks stood at 61 percent.

Unemployment rates of Hispanics are characteristically higher than those of white workers, but significantly lower than those of blacks. This was true among adult men and women as well as teenagers.

Considerable differences exist in the employment situations of Hispanic groups. Cubans, again, are better off than their Spanish-origin counterparts. Their jobless rate averaged 7.8 percent in 1979, compared with 8.3 percent for all Hispanics (Table 13-4). Puerto Ricans were worse off with a labor force participation rate of only 51 percent and an unemployment rate of 11.5 percent. Puerto Ricans also had the greatest proportion of the unemployed who have lost their jobs.[6]

Occupational characteristics differed to some extent from the population as a whole. Hispanics, although to a lesser extent than blacks, tended to be concentrated in the lesser skilled, lower paying occupations. For example, only 8 percent of Hispanics, compared to 16 percent of all workers, held technical and professional jobs (Table 13-5). About 11 percent of all workers were operatives (garage workers and attendants, produce packers, manufacturing checkers, etc.), but 22 percent of Hispanics worked as operatives. Workers of Cuban origin had the most favorable occupational distribution; those of Mexican origin fared the worst.

Table 13-4   EMPLOYMENT STATUS OF THE CIVILIAN NONINSTITUTIONAL POPULATION BY SEX, AGE, RACE, AND HISPANIC ORIGIN, 1979 ANNUAL AVERAGE (NUMBERS IN THOUSANDS)

EMPLOYMENT STATUS	TOTAL POPULATION 1979	TOTAL HISPANIC ORIGIN[a] 1979	MEXICAN ORIGIN 1979	PUERTO RICAN ORIGIN 1979	CUBAN ORIGIN 1979
Total civilian noninstitutional population	161,532	7,901	4,721	1,065	592
Civilian labor force	102,908	5,019	3,119	543	391
Percent of population	63.7	63.5	66.1	51.0	66.0
Employment	96,945	4,604	2,864	481	361
Agriculture	3,297	221	197	4	4
Nonagricultural industries	93,648	4,384	2,666	477	356
Unemployment	5,963	415	255	62	31
Unemployment rate	5.8	8.3	8.2	11.5	7.8
Not in labor force	58,623	2,883	1,602	522	200

SOURCE: *Employment and Earnings* (January 1980): 191, 192.
[a] Includes persons of Central or South American origin and other Hispanic origin, not shown separately.

CHICANOS

Chicanos, or people of Mexican descent, constitute by far the largest group among Hispanics. In fact, those of Mexican descent exceed in number the combined total of all minority groups other than blacks (i.e., Puerto Ricans, Cubans, Native Americans, Chinese Americans, and Japanese Americans).

Despite their numerical importance, however, the definition, identification, and measurement of Chicanos has caused considerable debate. Many Mexican Americans are more American Indian in origin than Spanish. Most other terms commonly used to describe them are equally misleading.

Although there is some disagreement over its use, "Chicano," derived from the word *Mexicano,* is the term increasingly used by Mexican Americans to identify themselves. Younger Mexican Americans seem particularly to favor being called Chicanos, while some of their elders resist its use. The terms "Chicano" and "Mexican American" will be used interchangeably here.

The Mexican-American population is both a racial and a cultural minority; 95 percent of the Chicano population is part American Indian.[7] The Chicano concept of *la raza* (the race), however, does not refer to a set of racial characteristics, because Chicanos are a blending of Spanish colonists, American Indians, Anglos, and blacks. Moreover, the Mexican-American culture is significantly different from that of the majority of Anglos in language, religion, music, food, and literature.[8]

Although current and accurate statistics are not available, the Mexican-American population apparently is growing both relatively and absolutely. As noted earlier, the factors responsible for this growth include continued immigration (unrestricted until 1968, at which time a maximum of 120,000 from the Western Hemisphere was imposed), high fertility rates (fertility rates for Chicanos are 70 percent higher than those of Anglos in the southwest), and uncounted numbers of illegal entrants across the 1800-mile common border between Mexico and the United States. Most of the Chicano population is native-born of native-born parentage; less than 15 percent of Mexican Americans were born in Mexico.

The Border

The 1800-mile common border with Mexico has had a profound effect on the economic conditions of Chicanos. Immigration from Mexico since the 1920s has centered on agriculture, and Chicanos have been an important factor in the Southwest's agricultural labor supply. The original impetus to immigration from rural Mexico was the push of the Mexican revolution and the simultaneous pull of labor shortages in the United States during World War I. These shortages not only were caused by the diversion of American workers into the armed forces but also because immigration from Europe was stopped. After the war the demand for Mexicans remained, and because they were not covered in the quotas imposed by the National Origins Act of 1924, the supply was forthcoming to meet the demand. When the depression hit and displaced "Okies" and "Arkies" became the cheap labor supply, many Chicanos were forceably repatriated to Mexico.

There was another influx of Mexican farm workers during World War II, when an agreement between the United States and Mexico provided guarantees on working conditions and employment for short periods of seasonal farm work. This Mexican labor program was better known as the bracero program. It remained in effect until the end of 1964. The program was strengthened in 1951 with the passage of Public Law 78, which was strongly supported by growers as a means of meeting labor shortages induced by the Korean conflict.

This controversial program displaced many native Chicanos from the rural labor market. The proportion of Chicanos living in urban areas increased from 66.4 percent in 1950 to 79.1 percent in 1960.[9] In 1979, 81 percent of Chicano families lived in metropolitan areas as compared with 95 percent of Puerto Ricans, 97 percent of Cubans, and 86 percent of other Spanish Americans.

The bracero program is a good example of how public policy affects labor markets. The wages of agricultural workers relative to manufacturing workers declined sharply during the bracero period, forcing native Chicanos to migrate in search of jobs that paid them enough to meet living costs in the United States. Although growers complained of shortages of domestic workers during the bracero period, the labor market experience since the end of that program has clearly shown that domestic labor is available at competitive wages.

Table 13-5   PERCENT DISTRIBUTION OF
EMPLOYED PERSONS OF HISPANIC ORIGIN BY OCCUPATION AND SEX, 1979

| | TOTAL EMPLOYED | | WHITE-COLLAR WORKERS | | | |
ORIGIN AND SEX	NUMBER (IN THOUSANDS)	PER-CENT	PROFESSIONAL AND TECHNICAL	MANAGERS AND ADMINISTRATORS EXCEPT FARM	SALES WORKERS	CLERICAL WORKERS
Total 16 years and over	96,945	100.0	15.5	10.8	6.4	18.2
Total Hispanic origin	4,604	100.0	7.6	6.0	3.9	15.1
Mexican origin	2,864	100.0	5.6	5.2	3.1	13.9
Puerto Rican origin	481	100.0	9.8	4.8	3.5	19.0
Cuban origin	361	100.0	12.2	8.6	6.4	16.6
Other Hispanic origin	898	100.0	11.0	8.2	5.9	16.0
Men 16 years and over	56,499	100.0	15.1	14.0	6.0	6.1
Total Hispanic origin	2,848	100.0	7.2	7.4	3.2	5.8
Mexican origin	1,842	100.0	5.3	6.3	2.2	4.8
Puerto Rican origin	298	100.0	7.7	5.4	3.4	9.1
Cuban origin	208	100.0	12.9	12.4	5.7	8.6
Other Hispanic origin	500	100.0	11.4	10.2	5.8	6.2
Women 16 years and over	40,446	100.0	16.1	6.4	6.9	35.0
Total Hispanic origin	1,757	100.0	8.3	3.9	5.2	30.1
Mexican origin	1,022	100.0	6.2	3.2	4.7	30.3
Puerto Rican origin	183	100.0	13.0	3.8	4.3	34.8
Cuban origin	152	100.0	11.1	3.3	7.2	28.1
Other Hispanic origin	400	100.0	10.5	5.8	6.0	28.4

SOURCE: U.S. Department of Labor, Bureau of Labor Statistics.

Although the bracero program no longer exists, the problem of illegal or "undocumented" entrants workers remains. In 1968 it was estimated that 300,000 illegal entrants came from Mexico to the United States (a figure that is two-and-a-half times the official quota that year for the entire Western Hemisphere).[10] The number of illegal entrants appears to have increased dramatically since the bracero program was terminated, although there are no reliable statistics for this population.[11] In 1967, the last year braceros worked in the United States, 107,695 illegal entrants were returned to Mexico; in 1973, 609,673 illegal entrants were returned to Mexico, and their number was approximately one million in 1979.

There is considerable controversy over the relative merits of employing illegal aliens, braceros or domestics. Those who advocate the importation of Mexican nationals argue that domestic workers cannot be found to do the kinds of work performed by nationals. To some extent this is correct because domestic workers apparently avoid jobs in which many illegal aliens are employed because conditions there are likely to be undesirable. Illegal aliens have little protection from exploitation. Moreover, the aliens are likely to be more willing to work very hard for short periods of time because even low wages in the United States are much higher than those that they can earn in Mexico. Therefore, domestic workers consider it undesir-

| | BLUE-COLLAR WORKERS | | | | |
CRAFT AND KINDRED WORKERS	OPERATIONS EXCEPT TRANSPORT	TRANSPORT EQUIPMENT OPERATIONS	NONFARM LABORERS	SERVICE WORKERS	FARM WORKERS
13.3	11.3	3.7	4.8	13.2	2.8
13.9	21.5	4.0	7.8	16.3	3.8
14.9	21.9	4.4	9.4	16.1	5.5
9.6	24.0	4.2	5.4	19.2	.6
13.0	22.4	3.9	5.0	11.4	.6
13.4	18.8	2.8	5.4	17.3	1.1
21.5	11.6	5.9	7.3	8.5	3.9
21.0	19.2	6.3	11.9	13.0	5.1
21.7	20.1	6.6	13.7	12.2	7.1
14.1	23.8	6.7	8.7	20.5	.7
19.6	15.8	6.7	7.7	9.6	1.0
23.1	14.9	4.6	8.8	15.1	1.8
1.8	10.8	.7	1.3	19.8	1.2
2.4	25.1	.3	1.3	21.7	1.6
2.5	25.1	.4	1.6	23.4	2.6
2.2	23.9	—	.5	16.8	.5
3.3	31.4	.7	1.3	13.7	—
1.8	23.4	.3	1.0	22.6	.3

able to compete for sustained periods with workers who are "working scared" for short periods of time and limited objectives. However, apparently little difficulty was encountered in reverting to the use of domestic workers in many California industries after the bracero program was terminated.

Legislation has been proposed to make it illegal for employers to hire illegal aliens. The Immigration and Nationality Act of 1952 made it a felony "to import and harbor" illegal aliens but exempted employment and related services to employees (i.e., transportation, housing, and feeding).

There also are very weak penalties imposed on the illegal aliens who are apprehended. Almost all such illegal aliens are simply deported to their native countries at federal expense. They are rarely subjected to formal deportation proceedings that would make their future entry a felony. Apparently, the failure to utilize formal deportation proceedings is due mainly to the limited number of hearing offices.[12]

Commuters

Commuters who live in Mexico and work in the United States also depress wages and working conditions for native Chicanos. Commuters may be Mexican nationals or U.S. citizens. If they are aliens, they are either "green carders" (i.e., those who have been legally admitted as immigrants and are free to live and work in the United States) or "white carders" (i.e., legal visitors who can supposedly stay in the United States for only 72 hours at a time). White carders are technically not supposed to be employed, but that law apparently has never been very well enforced.[13] Similarly, it is an amiable fiction that many green carders reside in the United States, because many actually live in Mexico. Green carders must obtain labor certification specifying that a shortage of workers exists in their particular occupations in the United States and that their employment will not adversely affect wages and working conditions. The certification is made only once—at the time of the initial application as an immigrant. Once the green card is obtained, the holder is free to come and go as long as no absence from the United States exceeds one year or the holder becomes unemployed for longer than six months.

The exact number of green- or white-card commuters is unknown. However, in 1979 there were about 56,000 green cards issued permitting these commuters to cross the Mexican border *daily* to work in the United States. In addition, there were 9,000 more green cards issued to seasonal workers as of 1979. There are no figures available on the total number of white cardholders, although an estimate of several million is reasonable, as 180,000 white cards were issued in 1979 alone.[14]

A 1967 restriction bars green carders from employment as strikebreakers in places where the Secretary of Labor certifies that a labor dispute exists. However, the effect of this antistrikebreaker restriction apparently is nullified by the fact that employers usually have ample time to employ green carders before a dispute is officially certified.

After Congress permitted the bracero program to expire, the Secretary of Labor issued new regulations that made it clear that braceros would not be admitted under various subterfuges. These regulations specify wages and other conditions that employers must offer to domestic workers before foreign labor can be imported, and apparently they reduced the flow of Mexican nationals who applied for green cards after January 1, 1965. However, opinion differs as to the extent to which these rules really are enforced. Chicano and labor spokesmen still think too many commuters are permitted to enter, and thus they advocate tighter restrictions on entry, while employers complain of labor shortages.

The commuter system rests on administrative interpretation rather than statute. In 1927 the status of commuters was changed from alien visitors to immigrants by the Immigration and Naturalization Service. The justification for the perpetuation of this system is derived from a Board of Immigration Appeals decision in 1958: "The commuter situation does not fit into any precise category found in the immigration statutes. The status is an artificial one, predicated upon good international relations maintained and cherished between friendly neighbors."[15] Consequently, the U.S. worker who competes with Mexican commuters pays a substantial part of what the Secretary of State regards as foreign aid.

Although many commuters work in low-wage garment industries and retail shops on the U.S. side of the border, according to one estimate 60 percent or more of all commuters entering California and Arizona are farm workers; in Texas the figure is 18 percent. According to the U.S. Civil Rights Commission:

> The impact of the commuter is particularly acute in agriculture where mechanization is rapidly reducing job opportunities. Due to the high concentration of farms along the border and the fact that commuters often work in the lowest skilled, lowest paid jobs, farm workers, who are already underpaid, are the first to suffer competition from the commuter. Furthermore, the use of commuters as strikebreakers is especially damaging to this group's organizational struggles.[16]

Moreover, according to the Civil Rights Commission 88,700 South Texas farm workers were forced to migrate elsewhere in 1968 in search of employment, while commuters easily found jobs in the local economy. A VISTA (Volunteers in Service to America) worker summarized the difficult and ambiguous relationship of the commuter problem to migratory workers as follows:

> These people see the problem of the commuter as a very major one. They see that the people from Mexico, who are our brothers, come over on this side to work because the living conditions in Mexico are far worse than ours, they are poor. It is not their fault that they come and take our jobs, it is the fault of the U.S. government which exploits our brothers because they pay lower wages and at the same time the Mexican Americans on this side are left without jobs and they have to travel up North.[17]

Numerous proposals have been offered to terminate or to lessen the effects of the commuter system. Among these are its immediate termination; regularization of the labor certification process to require periodic reviews rather than simply the initial determination of the impact of the green carder; establishment of a nonresident work permit with regular review decisions; installation of a commuter tax on employers; purchase of tickets by those who cross the border for employment; a drive to give preference in employment to U.S. residents; the imposition of sanctions against U.S. employers who knowingly employ white carders; and specific limitations on the time a green carder can be employed in the United States before making it mandatory that he become a U.S. citizen. Moreover, it has also been argued that the current border employment practices violate Title VII of the Civil Rights Act of 1964, which bans discrimination on the basis of national origin, by favoring Mexican nationals.

Agricultural Employment and Public Policy

Because so many of them are farm workers, no discussion of Chicanos would be complete without looking at the special problems of agricultural workers. Regardless of race or national origin, many agricultural workers are disadvantaged.

Farm workers receive very limited coverage under state labor laws. No state minimum wage law would bring the worker up to the minimum poverty level even if it were possible to secure year-round employment. Only California provides workmen's compensation, despite the fact that agriculture is one of the nation's most hazardous industries. And the hazards of agricultural employment have become greater because of the increasing use of herbicides and pesticides—with their yet unknown effects on farm workers. No state provides unemployment protection.

Agricultural workers also have inadequate coverage under federal as well as state statutes. They are not covered by such laws as the National Labor Relations Act and do not receive unemployment compensation, mainly because the political power of agribusiness has been sufficient to prevent their coverage.

CONCLUSIONS

This chapter has explored the economic conditions of Hispanics. Although not as disadvantaged as blacks, Hispanics share a disproportionate amount of economic deprivation. Compared to their non-Hispanic counterparts, they have lower levels of education and income and higher rates of unemployment and poverty.

Among Hispanics, Chicanos are the most disadvantaged. Chicanos have worked primarily in agriculture and as migrants. Moreover, large families, inadequate education, cultural isolation from the dominant Anglo groups, language barriers, discrimination, poor health conditions, and political powerlessness have caused the Chicanos' conditions to be self-perpetuating. Besides all of these disadvantages, Chicanos face the added problems of competition from Mexican nationals. Ironically, under the bracero program these Mexican nationals had even better working conditions— guaranteed by the federal government—than were available to many native Chicanos. Their proximity to the border not only causes Chicanos to face competition with Mexican nationals, but successive waves of immigrants have made it difficult for Mexican Americans to be assimilated into American society as other groups have been. The Chicanos' conditions have improved during the 1960s and 1970s, although their employment and income conditions still lag behind those of Anglos.

DISCUSSION QUESTIONS

1. Do Hispanics have difficulties in the labor market that are noticeably different from those of other minorities?

2. What are the viable policy options for dealing with the growing illegal alien problem in the U.S.?
3. Discuss the relative economic positions of Cubans and Puerto Ricans. What factors have caused the differences between the groups?
4. By the year 2000 the Hispanic population may surpass blacks as the largest minority group. How could this happen and what are the implications of this?
5. Appropriate public policy to deal with the economic problems of Hispanics should be regionally based. Discuss.
6. Examine the claim that importation of foreign labor is needed to preserve United States agriculture because domestic labor would not do the work.
7. Estimates of undocumented alien workers in the United States have ranged from 3 million to 12 million. What data are used for these estimates and how do you account for the wide differentials?

Notes

1. This chapter relies heavily on Vernon M. Briggs, Jr., *Chicanos and Rural Poverty* (Baltimore, Md.: Johns Hopkins Press, 1973).
2. "Persons of Spanish Origin in the United States: March 1979" (Advance Report) *Current Population Reports*, series P-20, no. 347, U.S. Department of Commerce, Bureau of the Census.
3. Dale Truett, "Black Employment in Miami," in Ray Marshall and Virgil Christian, eds., *The Employment of Southern Blacks* (Salt Lake City, Utah: Olympus Publishing Co., 1974).
4. U.S. Department of Labor, Bureau of Labor Statistics, *The New York Puerto Rican* (New York: Middle Atlantic Regional Office of the Bureau of Labor Statistics), Regional Report no. 19, May 1971, p. 1.
5. "Persons of Spanish Origin in the United States: March 1978," *Current Population Reports*, series P-23, no. 339, U.S. Department of Commerce, Bureau of the Census.
6. Morris J. Newman, "A Profile of Hispanics in the U.S. Work Force," *Monthly Labor Review* (December 1978): 3–11.
7. Jack D. Forbes, *Mexican Americans: A Handbook for Educators* (Berkeley, Calif.: Far West Laboratory for Educational Research and Development, 1970).
8. Leo Grebler et al., *The Mexican-American People* (New York: Free Press, 1970), chaps. 13–20.
9. Donald N. Barrett, "Demographic Characteristics," in Julian Samora, ed., *La Raza: Forgotten Americans* (Notre Dame: University of Notre Dame Press, 1966), p. 163. The figures are from the U.S. census for the respective years.
10. John H. Burma, ed., "Economics," in *Mexican Americans in the United States* (Cambridge, Mass.: Schenkman, 1970), p. 144.
11. Clarise Lancaster and Frederick Scheuran, "Counting the Uncountable: Some Initial Statistical Speculations Employing Capture-Recapture Techniques," 1977 Proceedings of the Social Statistics Section, American Statistical Association; Leo Estrada and Manuel Garcia y Griego, "The Volume of Illegal Immigration into the U.S.: Too Much Speculation and Insufficient Data," University of California, Los Angeles, unpublished manuscript, 1978; U.S. Congress, House Committee on the Judiciary, "Illegal Aliens and Alien Labor: A Bibliography and Compilation of Background Material"

(Washington: U.S. GPO, August 1977), 95th Congress, 1st session; and U.S. Congress, Senate, "Temporary Worker Programs: Background and Issues" (Washington: U.S. GPO, 1980), 96th Congress, 2nd session.

12. Vernon M. Briggs, Jr., *The Mexican-United States Border: Public Policy and Chicano Economic Welfare* (Austin, Texas: Center for the Study of Human Resources and the Bureau of Business Research, 1974).

13. "The Commuter on the United States-Mexico Border," staff paper presented in *Hearings* before the U.S. Commission on Civil Rights, San Antonio, Texas (December 9–14, 1968), p. 983.

14. Statistics Branch, Information Services, Immigration and Naturalization Service, U.S. Department of Justice.

15. "The Commuter on the United States-Mexico Border," op. cit., p. 987. The original citation is Matter of M.D.S. & Immigration and Naturalization, p. 209 (1958).

16. Ibid., p. 998.

17. Ibid., p. 461.

Chapter 14
The Isolated
Native American

Native Americans residing on reservations have a long and well established, although frequently violated, treaty relationship with the federal government. The United States has taken on special responsibilities for the native Americans when they were forced to live on reservations in return for their "safety." Once covering vast land areas, the reservations still retain approximately 1 percent of the land area of the United States, much of it the most desolate terrain in the nation. The responsibilities toward reservation Indians have traditionally been carried out in a fashion that has promoted the dependence of the Indian community on the federal government. The Indian Self-Determination and Education Assistance Act of 1975 has set the goal of changing this policy by allowing tribes residing on reservations to contract with federal agencies for the design and operation of programs in their communities. But deep-rooted practices change slowly and it will take time before the goal of self-determination is fully realized.[1]

To enable reservation residents to carry out self-help programs the federal government has expanded assistance to native Americans. In 1979 federal outlays for Indians living in or near reservations amounted to $1,919 million, about $2,955 per person classified by the Bureau of Indian Affairs as a Native American (Figure 14-1).

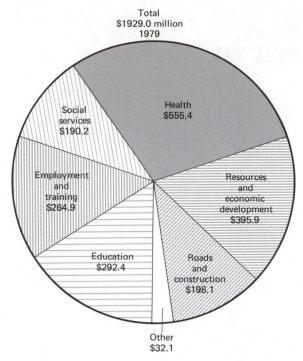

Figure 14-1   Federal assistance to Indians 1979. (Source: *The Budget of the United States Government: Fiscal Year 1981.*)

POPULATION AND DEMOGRAPHY

There is no universally accepted legal definition of an American Indian, or Native American, as many prefer to call themselves. Government agencies, depending upon their assigned functions, have used different measures of identification. The Bureau of the Census relies upon the individual respondent to decide his own race. Other government agencies cannot accept self-definition because eligibility to participate in their programs and services is normally determined by statutes or treaties. Eligibility under federal Indian laws was made dependent upon being half-Indian or quarter-Indian or being listed on a tribal roll. These various definitions make it easier to understand why estimates of the total American Indian population range from close to a million to twice that number.

It is important to stress that Indians are American citizens, free to move within the 50 states. Many have done so: next to the Navajo reservation, the largest concentrations of Indians are found in Los Angeles, Oklahoma City, Minneapolis, and several other urban areas. They share with other low income Americans the problems of living in central cities, but

Table 14-1   ESTIMATES OF INDIAN POPULATION ON OR ADJACENT TO
FEDERAL RESERVATIONS, TOTAL AND SELECTED STATES, APRIL 1979

STATE	POPULATION (THOUSANDS)
Total	653
Arizona	140
New Mexico	121
Oklahoma[a]	120
Alaska[b]	70
California	10
South Dakota	41
Montana	25
Washington	33
North Dakota	17
Minnesota	14
All other states	81

SOURCE: The Bureau of Indian Affairs, *Local Estimates of Resident Indian Population by States and Reservation: April 1977* (Washington, D.C.: The Bureau of Indian Affairs, 1977), p. 2.
[a] Includes former reservation areas in Oklahoma.
[b] Includes all Indians and Alaskan natives.

ironically Native Americans also have the unique difficulties common to immigrants facing pressures of adjustments.

By including only native Americans living on or adjacent to reservations, the Bureau of Indian Affairs (BIA) estimated in 1977 the total Indian population entitled to its services to be 652,700. This number included all Alaskan natives because the term "adjacent" in this case encompasses all of Alaska. The BIA also counts Oklahoma Indians who live on former reservations as its clients. Nearly nine of every ten Indians that the BIA considers in its jurisdiction live in ten states (Table 14-1). The total number of Americans claiming their roots here prior to the time when Columbus "discovered" their ancestors may be double that number.

There are 270 reservations, 24 other scattered land areas maintained in federal trusteeship for Indians, Eskimos, and Aleuts, and over 100 government-owned areas used by Indians and native people in Alaska.[2]

American Indians exhibit no single typical residential pattern: some tribes group into small villages; other tribes scatter themselves with miles separating the nearest neighbors; and others live in towns or familial groups or tribal enclaves of varying populations. By far the largest and most highly populated reservation is the Navajo, which spans part of Arizona, New Mexico, and Utah and covers an area the size of West Virginia. About 155,-000 Navajos live on this reservation. At the other extreme are 54 tribes with fewer than 100 persons each (Table 14-2). The thirteen most populated reservations account for more than half of the total Indian residents on or near the 277 reservations identified by the BIA. Some tribes are located near

Table 14-2   NUMBER OF INDIAN
RESERVATIONS BY SIZE OF POPULATION, 1977

POPULATION SIZE	NUMBER OF RESERVATIONS	TOTAL POPULATION
Total[a]	277	652,744
Less than 100	52	2,316
100–499	90	23,064
500–999	40	28,289
1,000–1,999	31	43,100
2,000–4,999	36	116,009
5,000–9,999	15	102,180
10,000–19,999	9	111,382
20,000–99,999	3	71,646
100,000 and over	1	154,758

SOURCE: The Bureau of Indian Affairs, *Local Estimates of Resident Indian Population by State and Reservation: April 1977* (Washington, D.C.: The Bureau of Indian Affairs, 1977), pp. 3–12.
[a] Includes former reservations in Oklahoma.

large cities, but more are located in isolated rural regions where there is no easily accessible transportation to urban areas. The 250 separate languages spoken by American Indians are evidence that these communities contain members whose traditions, values, and cultures vary as much among themselves as they do from other ethnic groups and the dominant white society.

Indians are a comparatively young and growing population. Despite a mortality rate higher than the national average, an unusually high birth rate results in a 3 percent annual population growth rate—twice the national increase. The median age of Indians living on or adjacent to reservations is only 18 years, compared with a median age of 30 for the rest of the nation. From all indications the Indian population will continue to increase substantially in the near future as preventive health and medical-care programs continue to reduce Indian death rates, especially in the younger age groups.

SOCIOECONOMIC CONDITIONS

With the exception of blacks living in rural areas, Indians on reservations suffer the worst economic conditions of any group in the United States. Median family income for all rural Indians is barely half that of rural whites. When the effects of large Indian families are added, per capita income comparisons are even more bleak. Among Indians on the 115 largest reservations surveyed by the census in 1970, per capita income was less than a third of the national average for all whites and only three-fifths of the levels reached by blacks and Hispanics.

The obvious explanation for this poverty is the lack of employment opportunities on reservations. Most Indian reservations contain few natural resources, are remote from large markets, have inadequate transportation systems, and lack trained and educated labor forces. As a result, the economic base on and near reservations is usually small or nonexistent, and the critical problem is joblessness.

In terms of occupational status Indians have been predictably concentrated on the lowest rungs. Surprisingly, however, the occupational status of Indian men is considerably better than that of blacks, with higher proportions of professionals, managers, salesworkers, and craftsmen, and with fewer operatives, laborers, and service workers. Another important but little-noticed aspect of reservation economies deserves attention: the limited and declining importance of agriculture and forestry. Though Indian lands comprise the chief natural resource on reservations, farming and forestry employ only one-tenth of Indian men. Since 1940 the decline in farm employment among Indian men has been dramatic:

	PERCENT OF THOSE EMPLOYED			
	1940	1950	1960	1970
Farmers and farm managers	46.7	24.2	9.5	2.3
Farm laborers and foremen	21.7	22.4	14.0	5.7

Though these figures are for all Indians, even on reservations only 12 percent of Indians were employed in farm occupations by 1970.

The job deficit and low incomes are further reflected in deplorable housing conditions. While half of Indian families live in unsanitary or dilapidated housing, it is estimated that less than 8 percent of all American families live in inadequate houses. Though federally funded public housing was initiated during the 1930s, a quarter-century elapsed before the federal government began to take steps to alleviate the poor housing on Indian reservations. But considerable progress was made in the 1970s. By 1980, the Department of Housing and Urban Development had completed over 29,000 housing units on Indian lands, the vast majority of which are available for homeownership.

Poverty and substandard housing conditions are reflected in the serious health deficiencies suffered by American Indians. Since the inception of the Indian Health Service (IHS) in 1955, there has been significant progress in improving the health standard of American Indians. By 1977, the infant mortality rate, though still 13 percent higher than that for the rest of the population, had been reduced by 74 percent. Maternal mortality and incidence of disease also has shown a significant decline. Between 1950 and 1970 the life expectancy of Indians increased by 5.1 years but was still six years shorter than for the average American. The ongoing efforts of IHS in providing health services to the Indian community through its hospitals, clinics, and visiting health workers will no doubt further diminish the incidence rate of disease among the Indian population. However, deficiencies in housing, nutrition, and health education must also be corrected.

EDUCATION

If Indians are to share in the high standard of living that surrounds their reservations, they must improve their educational attainment. Ever since whites settled on this continent, they have made attempts at, or at least paid lip service to, "civilizing" the native "savages." Nearly three centuries ago, the Virginia House of Burgesses established a "college for the children of the infidels." Concern with educating Indian children has been sustained ever since and, some would add, with possibly too little change in attitude until recently. Compulsory education applies equally to Indian as to all other American children.

In recent years responsibility for the education of Indian children on reservations has tended to shift from the federal government to the states and communities. But because Indians living on reservations are exempt from property taxes and contribute little to state or local taxes, the law provides for federal reimbursement to states and localities enrolling Indian children in their schools. More than four-fifths of the 215,000 reservation Indian children and youths attending school are registered in public schools. Mission schools, some dating to the colonial period, still enroll about 3 of every 100 of these children. The balance, 15 percent, attend BIA schools. Enrollment in BIA-operated schools ranges from a few children in an isolated Indian reservation to several thousand in a modern boarding school. In 1980 the BIA funded 64 boarding schools enrolling some 22,500 Indian children (including 5700 day students) and 95 day schools for another 11,500. The BIA also operated 15 dormitory facilities near public schools, housing 1,800 Indian students from isolated areas.

Whether an Indian child attends an integrated public school or a federal school for Indians depends primarily upon locational access. The policy of BIA is to encourage the child to attend public schools whenever possible. If there is no public facility within a reachable distance of the child's home, the bureau makes every attempt to allow him to attend a federal day school. In isolated areas where existing transportation is inadequate to allow school-age children to live at home, they are sent to federal boarding schools or to public schools near BIA operated dormitories. A child may also be referred to a boarding school by the BIA Division of Social Services or the Public Health Service. Many students who are placed in boarding schools away from their homes are delinquent, overage for their grade achievement, orphans, or children of imprisoned, hospitalized or separated parents. Students who have been unable or unwilling to adapt to a day school are transferred to boarding schools as a last resort with the mutual agreement of the youths and their parents.

Running the boarding schools for 16,800 Indian children is an expensive proposition—averaging more than $9000 per child during the school year, or more than three times as high as the cost per child in day schools and five times the cost per child in public schools. The boarding schools have been subjected to a great deal of criticism, and the news media have frequently played up unverified incidents of cruel discipline and the meager achievements that the BIA can show for the high costs. In response to public criticisms and to avoid high costs the BIA has tended increasingly to place Indian children in regular public schools or reservation day schools. During the 1970s the number of students residing in boarding schools was cut by half. But completely viable alternatives to the BIA boarding schools have not been devised. Although the BIA has been experimenting with mobile teaching units, it is not economically feasible to deliver educational services to the thousands of Indian families that live in utter isolation.

The schools responsible for the education of the nation's Indians are plagued by all of the problems confronting American education in general, but compounding the situation are conditions unique to Indian education. Like other school systems, especially those located in areas inhabited by other minority groups, they are troubled by the lack of continuity between teacher training and the actual school setting, language barriers, the lack of empathy of teachers and administrators for the children with whom they are entrusted, the shortage of qualified personnel and instructional materials, and the limited community involvement in scholastic affairs. Peculiar to schools serving Indian children are problems caused by the unique relationship of the tribes with the federal government and the distinct cultural heritage of the American Indian. Today, still one-fourth of the students entering school have little or no skill in the English language, and even more are totally unfamiliar with the ways of the white people that are perpetuated through the school system.

The effects of these problems can be seen in the statistics concerning Indian education. According to the 1970 census, the average educational attainment for American Indians was only slightly less than ten years of schooling. The high school dropout rate among reservation youths is considerably higher than for the rest of the nation. In 1970, 57 percent of Indian males aged 20 to 24 years had graduated from high school, a smaller proportion than the 63 percent of blacks and far below the 85 percent rate for whites. On reservations the dropout rate was even more severe, with less than half of rural Indian men aged 20 to 24 years having finished high school.

In recognition of these problems, many unique to reservation children, Congress established substantial supplementary educational programs for the Indian population. A variety of programs have been authorized by the Indian Education Act of 1972 and later amendments, including supplementary programs for Indian children in both public and BIA schools, basic education programs for adults, training programs for Indian teachers, as well as financial assistance for Indians training in other professions. Programs for Indian school children range from remedial reading and mathematics to bilingual education and cultural enrichment classes on the heritage of the American Indian. Efforts have also been made to involve Indian parents in the education of their children. In addition to the mandatory parent advisory committees, the Indian Self-Determination and Education Act of 1975 has given the Indian community the right to operate its own schools and to participate in the development of all programs. In 1979 Indian tribes operated 51 reservation elementary and secondary schools.

Increasing numbers of Indians who graduate from high school are going to college. In 1979, there were over 20,000 reservation Indians attending college on BIA scholarships. Another 1550 students were enrolled in the three Indian community colleges administered by the BIA. The BIA higher education office works with many public and private colleges and universities in efforts to increase the enrollment of Indian students, and it is estimated that the number of American Indians attending college is much higher than represented by the above figures. Once in college, however, Indian students are more likely to experience difficulties than other students which is reflected in an attrition rate twice as high as the national average. The problems faced by Indian students do not appear to be academic but rather are due to cultural differences that place obstacles to adjustments to living in a new environment.

LABOR FORCE PARTICIPATION AND EMPLOYMENT

Even though some reservations are endowed with valuable mineral resources and Indians receive substantial transfer payments from the government and from their tribes, the bulk of their income is earned through employment, much of it related to developing natural resources and administering federal programs. In the United States as a whole about 70 percent of personal income is derived from wages and salaries, and the proportion of Indian income is very nearly the same. But because their earnings are meager, more than half of the Indian population lives in poverty. As a rule, Indians work intermittently, if at all, and typically their jobs are low paying, unskilled, and unattractive. In 1977 three out of every 10 Indian workers living on or near a reservation earned less than $5,000, about 40 percent of the average wage received by full-time workers in American industry. There is a critical and chronic job shortage in and around most reservations, and Indians are usually ill-prepared for the few available jobs and are frequently discriminated against when they apply for work. A little more than half of Indians over 16 years of age living on or near reservations were in the labor force, compared with more than three-fifths of blacks and two-thirds of whites. With so few jobs available many of the nonparticipants in the labor force have evidently given up hope of finding a job.

These severe employment problems can be measured in many ways. Perhaps most striking is the fact that only 38 percent of reservation Indians over 16 years of age were employed in 1977 compared to 63 percent for the nation. Because far fewer adults have jobs and a much greater proportion of the Indian population is under 16, on the average only 23 persons out of each 100 on reservations work to support themselves and their dependents, compared with 44 for each 100 throughout the United States.

Unemployment is extremely high on the reservations, though technical problems make it difficult to apply the normal unemployment measures. Because jobs are scarce on or near reservations, many Indians are not seeking work even if they would welcome employment and are, therefore, not counted as unemployed under conventional government practices. To secure more realistic estimates the BIA compiles its own statistics. Its measure of the labor force excludes only those who cannot work because of ill health, child-care responsibilities, or school attendance; those who can work but are not seeking jobs are included among the unemployed. According to this definition, 40 percent of reservation Indians were unemployed in 1977. This rate overstates the problem if it is compared with national rates, which averaged 7 percent in 1977 according to the census definition. If the census measure were used, unemployment would be 26 percent among Indians on reservations, still nearly four times higher than the national rate. BIA local unemployment estimates ranged from 8 percent to as high as 77 percent in 1977.

	PERCENT WITHOUT JOBS
Pawnee	77
Santa Rosa	66
Apache	55
Hopi	48
Blackfeet	42
Navajo	39
Potawatomi	22
Quapaw	8

Underemployment and seasonal employment are also high. A study prepared for the Joint Economic Committee found that peak unemployment during the winter months is 70 percent higher than during the summer months when jobs are more plentiful because of agricultural work.[3] Farming and related occupations, which involve a variety of chores, generally do not afford much opportunity for complete idleness even on small or marginal farming units. For example, while the Navajo sheepherder is not completely unemployed, neither can it be claimed that he is gainfully employed or that the income from his occupation is sufficient to support himself and his family.

The jobs that are available in reservation economies reflect the dominant influence of government. Close to half of the jobs within Indian reservations are federal, state, or local government positions. This is more than three times the national average for government employment. By contrast, employment with industrial and commercial firms is far below proportions common in the rest of the economy and they provide jobs for a small fraction of the labor force on a full-year equivalent basis.

The federal government alone employs close to 26,000 Native Americans. In 1979 the Department of Interior employed an estimated 13,700 Indians full time including 8,600 Indians employed by BIA, and, an additional 5,930 by the Indian Health Service. The Department of Health and Human Services, the Economic Development Administration, and other federal agencies employed hundreds more. In addition, the Department of Labor funded some 15,000 temporary public service jobs.

Indians have been concentrated in low-level jobs and that was true until recently even when the government was their employer. But past practices are not easily corrected. Though Indians fill more than two-thirds of the jobs within BIA, they still hold less than half of the administrative, professional and executive jobs. In IHS, although three in every five of all employees are Indians, less than 3 percent of doctors and 20 percent of nurses are Indians. Shortages of qualified native American personnel rather than discrimination account for these conditions. However, strides have also been made in these agencies in recent years in training and upgrading native Americans for higher level positions. In 1973 only 1 percent of all doctors and nurses employed by IHS were Indians. These numbers have been increased partially by IHS's scholarship program for Native Americans entering the health field. The results can also be seen in the allied health occupations. In 1979, over three-fourths of the physician assistants employed by IHS were Indians. BIA does not have any special training or upgrading programs for American Indian personnel, though an Indian qualified for a position is preferred to other job candidates. The result has been a significant increase in Indian employment with BIA. In 1973 only a little more than half the total and only one-fifth of executive positions were filled by Indians.

Despite this progress made within federal agencies, the employment problems of Indians on reservations are severe. Though they cannot be attacked apart from the other Indian problems, two basic approaches must be taken. Efforts are obviously needed to increase the number of jobs available to Indians on or near reservations. More private firms must be attracted to the environs, and tribes and individuals should be assisted in initiating their own industrial and commercial enterprises. At the same time, efforts must also be expanded to improve the productivity of the Indian work force through training and to provide whatever other labor market services may be needed to put Indians to work. The challenge is to coordinate training and economic development programs to strengthen the economies and human resources of the reservations. These efforts should be combined with efforts on the part of Indians to exploit the resources available to them.

OBSTACLES TO ECONOMIC DEVELOPMENT

There are some very good reasons why more businesses are not located on reservations or near enough to hire substantial numbers of Indians. Most reservations are geographically inaccessible to product markets. With their low average income and typically widespread settlement, they provide only a limited market themselves for any products. The Indian labor force is generally unskilled, and because of their poor education Indians may be expensive to train. Though many on a reservation may be unemployed, only a limited number are available for work at a single geographical point because of the population dispersion. With differing cultural attitudes, many Indians find it difficult to adapt to sustained employment and job discipline, and the result is higher labor costs due to absenteeism and seasonal turnover, at least in the early stages of operation.

Capital for public and private investment is also in short supply. Financial institutions are unfamiliar with reservations and unwilling to take the high risks often involved in lending to Indians—especially because lands, which are the Indians' major asset, cannot be taken as collateral on loans. Public funds are equally limited, and the few tribes with substantial resources are sometimes reluctant to use them for commercial and industrial ventures.

Reservations generally lack the social overhead capital such as adequate transportation systems and sewerage and electrical facilities needed to attract businesses. In competing with many other localities for the limited number of new and relocating firms, they are usually at a disadvantage because they cannot offer the amenities available elsewhere.

To complicate matters, knowledge about conditions on reservations is scarce. Potential investors do not know what to expect because little information is usually available on labor supply, prevailing wage rates, skill levels, worker attitudes, and overhead capital. All of these factors can vitally affect the profitability of any operation. There is an equally severe shortage of trained personnel on the reservations to coordinate industrial development efforts; tribal leaders are sometimes unqualified or uninterested in planning and administering such programs. Faced with these uncertainties, businessmen understandably turn their attention to more predictable locations.

Improvement of reservation economies also depends on the health of the national economy. Even with special incentives, businesses may not flock to out-of-the-way reservations if labor is more readily available elsewhere. Federally sponsored economic development legislation attempted to cope with the problem. Although unemployment was more chronic on Indian reservations than in other areas in the country, Congress found it necessary to provide specifically for reservations to ensure that Indians would not be excluded. The program, however, was of little help to reservations while the labor market was slack generally. Tightening labor market conditions through the second half of the 1960s made reservations, with their abundant labor supply, increasingly attractive for expanding new companies, and carrots offered by the federally supported depressed-area programs added incentives to locate on reservations. Hardly any factories were located on reservations in 1960; 12 years later there were more than 200 factories employing over 7000 Indians, but this growth slowed down to a mere trickle during the 1970s, which were characterized by loose labor markets. An overall increase in unemployment has reduced the attractiveness of reservations for the location of new or expanding plants.

FEDERAL EMPLOYMENT AND TRAINING PROGRAMS

Unless more jobs are provided on or near the reservations, Indians will continue to have low employment rates; but Indians could hold many existing jobs if they were qualified. Without improvements in the labor force it is unlikely that industrial and commercial development can proceed; hence employment and training programs must be coordinated with economic development efforts.

Many cultural factors can impair Indian labor force participation. A major obstacle is that Indians often have a limited command of English and especially of industrial lexicon. Usually, Indians value landholdings and open spaces, preferring to live in isolated units rather than in congested areas. As a result, they are often scattered around the countryside and, with the poor transportation system, are unable to get to a place of work. Moreover, in a culture that emphasizes current needs, careful planning for the future is often neglected. For instance, Indians may abandon full-time, year-round jobs for attractive summer employment even though this means losing stable employment.

What is much more basic and much more difficult to overcome is the fact that Indians generally lack the skills and the knowledge to be productive workers. Their educational attainment, as noted earlier, is substantially below national norms, and the education they receive is often inferior. Because they have lacked job opportunities in the past and because outside training opportunities are limited, they have acquired few skills. As education improves, so will the abilities of the labor force, but more direct steps need to be taken through remedial training and basic education, along with the other services Indians may require to find employment and to improve their productivity and earnings.

BIA Programs

The BIA has provided employment and training services for Indians on reservations for nearly three decades. In the 1970s, Labor Department programs expanded these efforts. Close to 17,000 persons entered BIA's employment assistance and training programs in 1979 at a total cost of nearly $31 million, or over $1800 per person. Though BIA's efforts may be less extensive than those of the Labor Department, they are much more intensive.

The BIA has provided two categories of employment-related programs: job placement and adult vocational training programs. Under the first (and older) program Indians are employed on or near reservations or may be helped in finding jobs either within commuting distance or farther away where they may be relocated. Although there is no training component, some individuals who receive assistance may have participated in adult vocational training. Direct employment is designed to assist individuals who have a salable vocational skill. Based on individual needs, a wide variety of services—including interviewing, testing, counseling, placement, health care, and special equipment needed for employment—are available. Perhaps most important are relocation and subsistence grants until placement. The amount of assistance depends on the family size and whether the individual being assisted can commute to the job or must relocate. Total costs for the 9700 individuals and families who were provided direct employment services in 1979 averaged about $1500 per person.

The critical issue underlying the direct employment program is whether assistance should be used to relocate Indians to urban areas where jobs are more readily available or to help them find jobs on or near reservations. Fluctuations in the funding levels reflect a shift in national policy concerning the most appropriate method of serving reservation Indians. Preference for relocation was in line with the dominant philosophy of the early 1950s, which favored integrating Indians into the economic mainstream. Development of opposition from Indian groups resenting the loss of their best human resources and increasing job opportunities resulting from industrial and commercial development on reservations, not to mention the doubtful effectiveness of the direct employment efforts, resulted in the current policy emphasizing placements as close to the reservations as possible.

Almost all studies of the relocation effort have agreed that Indians working in urban areas can earn substantially more than those placed on or near reservations but that very few successfully adapt to urban life. For instance, a 1968 BIA follow-up of placements in urban areas during 1963, when relocation was heavily practiced, found that almost three-fourths had moved back to or near the reservation. Others have estimated that between one-half and two-thirds of all relocatees eventually return to the reservation.[4]

Given the limited success of relocation, the costs are not justified if clients return without gaining skills or saving money. However, those who want to leave the reservation should be helped because urban areas still offer greater opportunities. The BIA has, therefore, reversed its earlier preference for relocation and is trying to walk the tightrope of assisting without advocating relocation. Current policy thus seeks to make the reservations themselves viable economic units, and there is far more emphasis on locating jobs on or near reservations.

The adult vocational training program offers both institutional vocational instruction and on-the-job training through private schools, state vocational-technical schools, junior colleges, tribal-owned technical schools, BIA colleges, and special training programs set up in cooperation with other federal agencies, unions, tribes and private industry. Separate funds for on-the-job training were phased out in 1980, but OJT is still provided. The wage subsidies for OJT participants covering up to one-half of the minimum hourly wage have been used to attract employers to reservations and to induce them to hire Indians. Also the adult vocational training program funds are used to operate a residential training center which provides basic education and vocational training to entire Indian families.

In 1979 over 7000 persons entered the program, of which 75 percent received training on or near their reservations. This is a change from previous practice which favored providing the training in urban centers remote from reservations. Enrollees receive the same types of health and counseling services and grants as those in the direct employment program. In addition, however, they receive tuition and related expenses for vocational training plus subsistence payments throughout the training period so that costs run over $4000 per enrollee.

Evaluation of Indian institutional and OJT programs, though dated, did indicate that training results in significant increases in participants' annual earnings. Institutional trainees increased their pretraining earnings slightly more than did on-the-job trainees; however, the significantly higher costs of institutional training suggested that OJT may have been a more effective method to upgrade the skills of participants.[5] Also, OJT has been effective in providing jobs to Indians that may have not otherwise been available.

In 1979 the United Tribes of North and South Dakota provided intensive services to approximately 400 families in a residential training center in Bismarck, North Dakota. The center cares for the participants' whole family and offers adults a wide range of assistance, including intensive basic education, skill training, and home economics instruction, as well as job placement. Day care is provided for younger children. At one time there were four residential centers catering exclusively to extremely disadvantaged families. Current policy has broadened eligibility to the same requirements as for the rest of the adult vocational education program. The training center offers a unique opportunity to its limited number of participant families, however, its effectiveness has not been measured.

The mandate of self-determination has been used as leverage to get local BIA program administrators to involve the Indian community in programmatic decision making. In addition, in 1979 Indian tribes contracted to operate 26 local programs, including the residential center at Bismarck, North Dakota. One-fifth of total program funding went to tribally operated training projects.

Labor Department Efforts

Since the enactment of the antipoverty programs of the 1960s, the U.S. Department of Labor has provided employment, training, and related services to American Indians both on and off reservations. The Comprehensive Employment and Training Act qualifies all Native Americans, including Alaskan Eskimos and Aleuts, and Hawaiian natives, to receive assistance under the national programs authorized by CETA. Funds are awarded directly to Native American organizations on reservations and in urban areas. Additional funds under other CETA titles are given to tribal governing bodies on reservations, acting in a capacity similar to local and state CETA prime sponsors, for the operation of Indian employment and training programs. Indian tribes and bands, like other local governments, have been able to design employability development programs to meet their particular needs and individual goals in keeping with the theme of tribal self-determination. In 1979 over 100,000 Native Americans participated in CETA programs operated by about 180 different Native American organizations at a total cost of $222 million and an average cost of $2,200 per enrollee.

The native American grantees offered on-the-job training, classroom skill training, remedial education, work experience, public service employment, and supportive services such as medical services, child care, and transportation, depending on needs of each locality and the individual participants. The vast majority of participants were unable to earn sufficient income to pull their families out of poverty prior to enrollment. Over half the participants had not completed high school. A third of the participants received skill training and remedial education in a traditional classroom setting and nearly half increased their work experience through a variety of short-term subsidized employment positions. Though work experience offers little training opportunity, it focuses on developing good work habits and is considered effective by the Indian community. On completing the program, one in three participants returned to school or joined the military, and three of every eight found jobs.

American Indians on reservations are also eligible to receive a portion of funds allotted for CETA's job creation programs. In fiscal 1979, close to $120 million was allocated to native American tribes and organizations to develop public service employment projects employing some 15,000 persons. About one in every five participants found unsubsidized employment after participating in the program. Nearly one in four of the enrollees had difficulty in speaking English and more than nine in ten came from impoverished homes.

Approximately 27,000 young Native Americans from 14 to 21 years of age participated in CETA's youth programs at a total cost of $27.5 million, or a little more than $1000 per enrollee. The majority of young people in the programs participated in work experience projects although on-the-job training, career exploration, and other services were also provided. The 1979 summer youth program provided employment for about 18,000 youths. These youth programs have enjoyed widespread support among Indians, especially the summer youth program. The income provided, usually at minimum wage, is large relative to the low average family income. The problems are similar to those that apply to the programs nationally. Counseling and supervision are inadequate, and the jobs are often makework.

Increasing attention has been given to Indians under the employment and training programs administered by the Labor Department; and based on the relative size of their population, but not their needs, Indians receive a disproportionate amount of funds. For instance, Indian enrollment in fiscal 1979 accounted for 4 percent of all CETA program participants, well above the proportion of Indians in the population. But considering the concentration of need on the reservations, these shares still are inadequate; greater efforts must be directed toward making Indians employable, helping them to find work, and creating jobs.

In increasing the funds allocated for Indians, emphasis should be placed on upgrading, especially in public employment. Because so many Indians are employed by federal agencies, efforts to raise the skills and responsibilities of these workers should be encouraged. Despite recent improvements, Indians remain underrepresented in high level positions in government agencies such as BIA and IHS, which are intended to serve them. The tribally controlled employment and training programs, with the resources available to them, have the potential of making a contribution to this effort.

The vast resources that the federal government has recently allocated to Indian reservations have lacked coordination among related efforts such as employment, training, and economic development. Self-determination offers the potential to coordinate efforts toward a common goal. However, progress is often impeded by the lack of management and technical skills and by conflicts among the various interest groups on the reservations, as well as the frequently burdensome and unrealistic regulations imposed by the several federal establishments.

TREATING CAUSES RATHER THAN SYMPTOMS

A significant proportion of disease and premature death among Indians is a direct result of poverty, dilapidated housing, unsanitary water, and inadequate diets. A sound economy would mean that the necessary resources would be available to both the tribal community and individual families to build adequate housing, purchase nutritional foods, and construct sanitation facilities. Schools and communities could offer health education programs and individuals would have the financial ability to follow their advice for better health care.

With economic development the number of Indians dependent upon welfare would also decrease. For those not benefiting from increased economic opportunities, more intensive services and substantial assistance could be provided. Another potential benefit is that as Native Americans take on more responsibilities and are trained for meaningful jobs, they will become increasingly qualified for technical, managerial, and supervisory positions.

The primary goals of Indian programs are to increase Native American control over their own destinies and to improve their standard of living. Developing reservation economies is the *sine qua non* for achieving both of these goals. Past experience has indicated that a growing and productive economy is the single most important factor in the betterment of a population's social institutions. While this is not the only approach that can be taken to improve the conditions on Indian reservations, it does seem to be the most promising. And the right combination of Indian participation with federal assistance is the key to the development of Native American self-reliance and independence.

To meet the needs of reservation Indians, the federal government has increased substantially its contributions during the 1970s and improvements have been made. It is improbable that forthcoming funds will continue to increase sufficiently to meet all pressing demands. It will be necessary to make difficult choices among competing claimants and to determine priorities on the basis of needs determined by consensus of the Native American communities. Considering the underdeveloped reservation economy, the need to develop an adequate infrastructure remains a priority. Indian lands contain great potential wealth and developing these resources along with the technical expertise of Native Americans to manage their own operations can go a long way in furthering the economic progress on reservations as well as increasing the nation's ability to meet its expanding demands. However, not all tribes have these resources (about nine reservations receive 85 percent of the royalties from oil and gas), and the development of natural resources may conflict with Indian cultural values.[6] There is a lack of consensus among many of the Indian communities whether development of natural resources on reservations is compatible with other Native American goals and aspirations.

DISCUSSION QUESTIONS

1. Discuss the factors that have led the federal government to incur special obligations toward reservation Indians.
2. What changes have been brought about in Indian programs due to the Indian Self-Determination and Education Assistance Act of 1975?
3. Discuss the factors that impede economic progress on reservations. What strategies would you recommend to improve the economic base on Indian lands? What approaches have been tried? How effective have they been?
4. Discuss the pros and cons of relocating Native Americans in urban areas in order to find gainful employment.
5. Summarize the operations of the federally supported employment and training efforts on reservations.
6. How does the structure of educational institutions for Native Americans differ from that of regular public education?
7. In order to qualify for special assistance some federal agencies require proof of minimal Native American "blood," while other agencies qualify any person "who is regarded as an Indian by the community." What approach do you prefer? Indicate the basis for your preference.
8. "I have advised my people this way: When you find anything good in the

white man's road, pick it up. When you find something that is bad, drop it and leave it alone"—Sitting Bull. Reconcile Sitting Bull's advice with prevailing sentiments for self-determination.

9. "The goal of Native American self-determination should be the ultimate withering away of special federal programs." Comment on the realism of this advice.

10. Do you agree with the view that the crucial move involving federal assistance for Native American reservations is no longer the adequacy of funds, but who should control the design of the programs and the administration of the funds?

11. "The trouble with federal programs for Indians is that the assistance is offered by Big Brother with Reservations." Comment.

Notes

1. Sar A. Levitan and William B. Johnston, *Indian Giving: Federal Programs for Native Americans* (Baltimore, Md.: The Johns Hopkins University Press, 1975).

2. Bill King, "Some Thoughts on Reservation Economic Development," in U.S. Congress, Joint Economic Committee, *Toward Economic Development for Native American Communities*, 91st Congress, 1st session (Washington, D.C.: GPO, 1969), p. 68.

3. Alan Sorkin, "Trends in Employment and Earnings of American Indians," in U.S. Congress, Joint Economic Committee, *Toward Economic Development for Native American Communities*, op. cit., pp. 107–108.

4. Joan Ablon, "American Indian Relocation: Problems of Dependency and Management in the City," *Phylon* (Winter 1965).

5. Loren C. Scott and Paul R. Blume, "Some Evidence on the Economic Effectiveness of Institutional Versus On-the-Job Training," paper presented to the Forty-fifth Annual Conference of the Western Economic Association (Davis, Calif.: University of California, August 1970).

6. Alan Sorkin, "The Economic Basis of Indian Life," in *American Indians Today, The Annuals of American Academy of Political and Social Science,* March 1978, pp. 1–12.

Chapter 15
Women at Work

Women, especially wives and mothers, have played a key role in the changing composition of the labor force. Women workers are on the increase, not only in the percentage who work but also in their share of the labor force and in the variety of jobs they hold. Participation rates of women have doubled since 1900. With an average of 43.5 million women in the work force, women accounted for two-fifths of the total workers in 1979. Since the end of World War II about three-fifths of the total increase in civilian employment has come from women workers. Increases in the number of working wives and mothers in this period have been most dramatic. The number of working mothers almost quadrupled since 1950, while the total number of women workers more than doubled. In March 1979, 16.6 million mothers with children under 18 were working or seeking work, accounting for 55 percent of mothers with children that age. In 1960 only three of ten such mothers were working, and less than one in ten in 1940.

Half of the married women were employed in 1979, compared with one of every three in 1960 and only one of 20 in 1900. The 23.8 million working wives comprised close to one-fourth of the 1979 labor force. Between 1960 and 1979 more than a third of the increase in the total labor force came from married women. In addition, about one of every seven families was headed by a woman in 1979, and close to 60 percent of these women were in the labor force. Divorced, separated, and widowed women accounted for 11.2 percent of the labor force expansion since 1950. In 1979 three of every four divorcees worked but less than one-fourth of widows. The latter were generally older, and many received public or private pensions.

While women have made inroads into higher status and earnings occupations, the majority of the female labor force still hold jobs in traditionally female occupations with low pay and limited career opportunities. Though women now average about one-tenth of all lawyers and judges, doctors and industrial engineers, the highest growth in employment for women has been in clerical and service occupations. In 1979 about 80 percent of all clerical workers and 62 percent of all service workers were women, compared to 62 and 45 percent, respectively, in 1950. The increase of women in the labor force has transformed American society. But due to many still existing barriers, the needed changes are far from complete.[1]

FACTORS AFFECTING FEMALE WORK

American women of all classes have entered the labor market; black women and immigrants were the pioneers, followed by young single women, then wives reentering the labor force after their children have grown. The latest influx has been of young mothers. Many factors have led to the rise in female labor force participation, but several variables stand out. The ability to determine the number and spacing of children has been increased by advances in bedroom technology, while improvements in kitchen technology have facilitated household maintenance. This has reduced the amount of time required to carry out the woman's traditional role of running a household and raising children and freed more time to devote to other activities including gainful employment. At the same time, the opportunity cost of not working has increased for some women, as more women attain higher-paying jobs. Social and cultural factors have also played a role as the once held stigma associated with wives working has vastly diminished and concepts of the father's participation in child-rearing are being changed, albeit rather slowly.

For many women, however, labor force participation is a necessity and their earnings are an essential component of the total family income. Twenty-five percent of the female labor force are single and 20 percent are divorced, separated or widowed. Husbands' earnings have a major impact on labor force participation of wives, differing also by race. However, the husbands' occupations seem to have little effect on employment of their spouses. Over the last decade many women entered the labor market to maintain family real income that had been eroded by inflation. The availability of child-care facilities also is a factor and a major determinant of the ability of a mother to secure stable employment.

Table 15-1   INCOME OF HUSBAND, 1978

	TOTAL	UNDER $5,000	$5,000–9,999	$10,000–14,999	$15,000–19,999	$20,000+
		PERCENT IN THE LABOR FORCE				
All Wives	49	38	45	56	57	47
With children aged under 6 years	43	46	47	50	28	33
Black Wives	60	45	57	65	71	66
With children aged under 6 years	60	55	58	62	66	55

SOURCE: U.S. Bureau of Labor Statistics, Special Labor Force Report 219 (Washington, D.C.: GPO, April 1979).

Husband's Earnings

The level of their husband's earnings affect wives' labor force participation rates, although the relationship varies by race, age of wives, and presence and age of children. In 1979 participation of wives increased as husbands' earnings rose during the preceding year to $20,000. After that point the rate of wives' labor force participation generally declined. However, if pre-school-age children are present, participation rates are higher when husbands are in the lower earning bracket. Black wives not only have higher overall participation rates, but they also tend to remain in the labor force as husbands' incomes rise even if young children are present (Table 15-1).

Wives' earnings are important for achieving what many Americans deem a good living—say, $20,000 or more a year. The number of families at this income level would have been cut by half in 1968 if the families were to depend exclusively on the earnings of the husband alone rather than the income of the entire family.[2] An estimated 78 percent of families with incomes above $20,000 included more than one wage earner in 1977.[3]

However, sheer economic necessity, in the most basic meaning of the phrase, is the reason that more than half of the women in the labor force work. Women who accounted for about four of every nine working women in 1979 were either single, divorced, separated, or widowed. Many of these women are the sole supporters not only of themselves but also of children or parents. In addition, 42 percent of the 15 million women married to men who earned less than $10,000 annually worked. As Juanita Kreps has pointed out, these women do not have the luxury of choosing work at home over work in the marketplace.[4]

FEMALE FAMILY HEADS

Women—8.5 million of them—head one of every seven families. In 1979 six of every ten female-headed families included minor children. The female heads of these families reared 11.2 million children, and they provided for an additional 5.5 million persons in their families. In 1978, 29 percent of female family heads were widows, over half were divorced or separated, and close to 16 percent were single women who had never married—although three-fifths of them had children.[5]

Female-headed families have been increasing faster since 1960 than the total number of families—86 percent compared with only 27 percent. They account, moreover, for a growing portion of the remaining poverty in the United States. In 1979 three-fifths of poor families with children were headed by women. The growing number of female-headed families with children is one reason for the rise of welfare rolls in recent years.

The rising incidence of families headed by women is not due exclusively to increasing marital instability or illegitimacy. An estimated two-fifths of the 1.6 million additional female-headed families formed between 1940 and 1970 have been attributed to increased propensity to form separate households rather than sharing housing with other relatives. Income-support programs may also have boosted the growing ranks of female-headed families, as did declining childlessness and, of course, general population increases.[6]

Female-headed families can often count on very little, if any, income support from a divorced or separated father. Marital disruption is, therefore, often an economic catastrophe for women and children. One study found that only one in four divorced and separated women in 1975 was receiving alimony or child support. The average yearly payments these women were receiving totaled about $2400. For approximately half of the women getting child support, the payments constituted less than 10 percent of their total family income.[7] Roughly one white family in four becomes poor when a marriage ends in divorce or separation. The situation is even bleaker for black women.[8] One national survey that tracked the income of separated wives from 1967 to 1973 measured the average real drop in income at more than 29 percent for women who do not remarry.[9] These powerful economic realities have led more divorced and separated women into the labor force.

The median income of female-headed families was not quite half that of husband-wife families. When children were involved, families headed by women experienced much greater income disadvantages. The median 1979 family income of families headed by a mother with children was $8708, compared with $22,713 for two-parent families with children. Seven in ten children with both parents had family incomes of $15,000 or more compared with two in fifteen children living in female-headed families.

Many female family heads are prevented from working full time, year round by the presence of children, educational disadvantages, lack of salable skills, and residence in high unemployment areas. Although 66 percent of female family heads with minor children worked in 1979, only one in three worked full year, full time. Nor did full-time work guarantee an exit from poverty, since 5 percent remained poor despite full-time work efforts.

The proportion of families headed by divorced women has gone up by almost half between 1970 and 1978—to about 4.9 percent (or 2.8 million) of all families. The proportion of separated women has almost doubled to 2.2 percent of all families. The number of single women heading families has also increased, but not as markedly. Our mores seem to require that the mother assume responsibility for caring for the children. Though the father is not relieved of economic responsibility, the brunt of the support usually falls on the mother. Divorced and separated women are thus more likely to be found in the labor force than are wives, widows, or even single women. The proportion of divorced women who worked in 1979 was 74 percent, compared with 49 percent for wives and 59 percent for separated women. Divorced and separated women are also more likely than wives to be employed in full-time jobs. Further, the participation rates of divorced, widowed, or separated women with children under six are markedly higher than those of mothers with husbands present.

MARITAL STATUS OF MOTHERS WITH CHILDREN UNDER SIX	LABOR FORCE PARTICIPATION RATE, MARCH 1979
Total	45.4
Married, husband present	43.2
Single, divorced, separated, widowed	56.7

High participation rates, coupled with the generally lower income of female-headed families, indicate that day-care facilities at reasonable cost are particularly important to this group of women.

Day-Care Facilities

Although the presence of children, especially children under six, greatly reduces the chances of a woman's working, an increasing proportion of mothers with young children have remained in the labor force and others have shortened the interval of nonlabor force participation after giving birth to children. In fact, the greatest rate of increase in labor force participation occurs among mothers with children under three years of age. Trends of delayed marriage and first births and limiting family size resulted in a 25 percent drop between 1960 and 1978 in the under-five-year-old population despite the fact that maturation of the baby boom generation added over 11 million women to the 18- to 44-year-old population. Between 1965 and 1978 alone the number of working mothers with preschool-age children increased by 1.5 million.

Two-fifths of wives with children under the age of three work, as do almost half of those whose youngest child is between three and five and three-fifths of those with school-age children. In 1948 only 13 percent of all mothers with children under six were in the labor force; in 1979, 45 percent worked. Estimates for the future show a continuing rising trend. As already indicated, a group of mothers with children under six who have particularly high participation rates are those who are divorced, widowed, or separated, and their numbers are increasing.

As the number of working mothers with young children rises, day-care facilities become increasingly important. However, the types and quality of day care used by working mothers vary widely, with child-care centers accounting only for a minute proportion of day care. Nearly half of all children under 14 whose mothers worked part or full time in 1964 were cared for in their own homes, usually by relatives; about 16 percent were maintained in someone else's home. Only 2 percent of all children, and 6 percent of children under six, were in child-care centers. The rest were provided for under other arrangements or left to shift for themselves—"latchkey" children.[10]

For the most part child-care arrangements remain informal either in the child's or caretaker's home. Licensed child-care centers, serving primarily three- to five-year-olds, almost quadrupled between 1960 and 1979. The growth, resulting from stepped-up licensing of existing facilities as well as the addition of new ones, reflected federally backed efforts to ensure quality child care for low-income mothers engaged in government-sponsored job training or employment.

Day-care facilities are run by a variety of sponsors—including private, for-profit groups, unions, churches, and other nonprofit community or governmental organizations. In fiscal year 1977 federal programs contributed $1.8 billion for the purchase of 1.4 million child-care years through programs supporting welfare clients and other near-poor persons. The actual number of children whose care was subsidized was 2.8 million.

Regulations require higher quality, more formal, and consequently more costly arrangements than those obtained by most working mothers. In practice, arrangements meeting federal standards are scarce and enforcement is lax. If the regulations were to be met, costs of day care would rise. An estimate of the cost of day care in 1975 placed annual expenditures per child in a day-care center at $1425; services in family day-care homes cost $1350, and care in the child's home with a nonrelative costs $1325.

The fact that day-care facilities remain relatively scarce and costly has led to demands for further government outlays, not only to support more facilities but also to subsidize part of the costs to enable more working mothers to provide decent facilities for their children. Since the proportion of working mothers is highest among families in which family income is below $10,000, decent day-care facilities cost more than most are willing or are able to pay unless a subsidy is available.

In addition to direct subsidies for the purchase of child care, a limited tax deduction for work-related child-care expenses has been available since 1954. The Revenue Act of 1971 and the 1975 tax cut bill liberalized the law substantially allowing increasing proportions of middle- and upper-income families to take advantage of the provision. Starting in 1976 families with $35,000 annual income qualify for the maximum annual deduction of $4800 reduced 50 cents on the dollar up to an income limit of $44,600. In 1978, a tax credit was allowed for child-care payments to non-dependent relatives.

Education and Race

The more education a woman acquires, the more likely she is to work. Educational attainment is more a determinant of labor force participation for women than for men, who, once out of school, tend to stay in the labor force regardless of educational attainment. In 1978 the participation rate ranged from 26 percent for women with an elementary education to 66 percent for women with a college education.

Job opportunities for college-educated women have increased substantially. Better-educated women are able to take advantage of rising demand in the expanding professional and technical occupations. Though the number of women who are lawyers, doctors, scientists, and industrial engineers is still small, women have made significant gains in these fields in recent years. Women who have invested in a college education may also be reluctant to forgo the rewards from work in professional fields; their opportunity costs of staying at home are greater than for less-educated women. Women with four or more years of college who worked full time, year round in 1978 had twice the income of those with grade school education.

Race is also an important determinant of female labor participation. Black married women have had a history of higher labor force participation than white women. Their earnings, though low, have been needed to supplement the comparatively lower earnings of their husbands and to support larger families. More black married women than white work at some point during the year—63 percent of blacks had work experience in 1977, compared with 54 percent of whites. Black women are more likely to be forced into idleness, primarily because of the kinds of jobs open to them. The incidence of unemployment among white women—5.9 percent in 1979—was half as high as among blacks, and spells of joblessness were of shorter duration.

Although black women lag behind white women in educational achievement—11.9 and 12.4 years, respectively—the education differential among working women is minimal. Similarly, racial occupational barriers also persist, but professional and managerial opportunities available to college-educated black women have improved. In 1979 three of every eight employed black women with at least a high school diploma worked at blue-collar and service occupations compared with less than one-fourth of all employed white women with the same education. On the other hand, 74 percent of college-educated black women held professional or managerial jobs, the same percentage as whites.[11]

A contributing factor to the black wives' higher labor force participation is that they are better educated than their husbands; the reverse is true for whites. With more education, earnings potential and attractive work opportunities increase. Black wives who had some work experience in 1978 contributed more to family income than white wives—33 percent compared with 25 percent. When family income was over $20,000, black wives contributed 35 percent of the total compared with 25 percent by whites, suggesting that black wives play a greater role in helping their families reach middle class status.

PATTERNS AND AGES OF WORK FOR WOMEN

Wives and mothers more frequently move in and out of the labor market, either on a part-time or full-time basis, in response to their families' shifting needs, their own work desires, and labor market conditions. Over half of all wives worked at some time during 1977, but only four of every ten workers were employed full time, year round. About two of every three employed married women work at full-time jobs. Many did not work year round and others prefer part-time employment. Women accounted for over two-thirds of all voluntary part-time employment experience.

The distribution of women's employment rates by age has been bimodal. This M-shaped curve (Figure 15-1) reflected two peak participation periods: the first in early adulthood, when women were just out of school or were young wives earning money at the start of married life; and the second when mature women returned to work after their children have entered school or are grown. But in more recent years this distribution has tended to disappear as more young women are entering the labor force and remaining, even after childbirth. Comparison of 1947 and 1979 data suggests men are working less and women more.

For many years 18- and 19-year-olds had the highest participation rates among women; these were premarriage and prechildren years. After World War II many 45- to 54-year-old women entered and stayed in the job market, and the labor force participation rate of this group surpassed the younger group. But since 1964, participation rates of 20- to 24-year-old women have been rising most rapidly. In 1979 this age group had a participation rate of 69.3 percent, exceeding that of every other age group. The rising participation rates of younger women reflect higher levels of education, delayed marriage, deferment of first births, and smaller family size. These trends are especially pronounced among younger women. In 1967 slightly more than one-third of 25- to 29-year-old wives expected two or fewer births. A dozen years later, two-thirds of married women in prime childbearing years planned to limit family size to two or fewer children. Among younger wives the percentage desiring no more than two children was even higher.[12] If these expectations are realized, the bimodal labor force participation is likely to flatten further.

DISCRIMINATION

The recent interest in the women's liberation movement and the equal rights amendment has again illuminated the discrimination against women

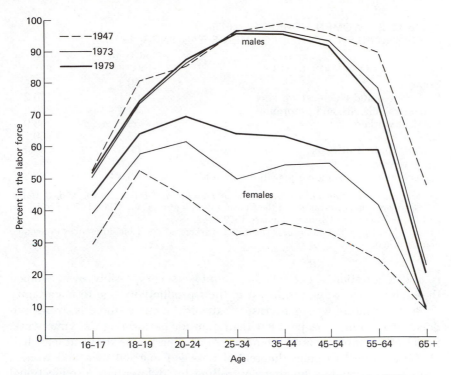

Figure 15-1 Labor force participation rates, 1947, 1973, and 1979.
(Source: *Employment and Training* Report of the President (Washington,
D.C.: GPO, 1979), table A-2; and *Employment and Earnings* (January
1980), table 3.

in the job market. Though the median level of educational attainment of
women equals that of men, women earn less than men, and the gap has been
widening. In 1955 the median wage for women who worked full time, year
round was 64 percent of what men earned; in 1978 only 59.4 percent. However, full-time women workers average fewer hours per week than men. If
one takes this factor into account, women's overall earnings ratio in 1978
was two-thirds that of men. Earnings disparities varied by occupation,
ranging from less than half in sales to almost three-quarters for professionals
(Table 15-2).

The earning comparisons give some idea of the disparity between men
and women, but they do not present a prima facie case of the exploitation of
women. The female labor force is heavily weighted with married women
whose attachment to the work force is often not as committed as that of
men. Though the practice may be changing, married women have experienced less occupational choice than men, by placing greater emphasis on
convenience of location or flexibility of hours above earnings. Their family
ties give them less geographic mobility than males, and some, indeed, give
up good jobs to follow husbands who decide to accept jobs elsewhere. There

Table 15-2 WOMEN WORKERS' MEDIAN
EARNINGS AS PROPORTION OF MEN'S EARNINGS, 1978

OCCUPATIONAL GROUP	ACTUAL RATIO	ADJUSTED RATIO[a]
Total	59.4	67.2
Professional and technical workers	64.1	70.2
Managers, officials, and proprietors	54.4	59.8
Clerical workers	59.9	63.9
Sales workers	45.4	50.7
Skilled/kindred workers	60.8	63.6
Operatives	58.6	64.3
Service workers, excluding private household	63.3	68.3

SOURCE: *Money Income and Poverty Status of Families and Persons in the United States: 1978* (Advance Report), Bureau of the Census (Washington, D.C.: GPO, 1979), pp. 18–19; and *Employment and Earnings* (January 1979), 184.
[a] Data relate to civilian full-time, year-round workers adjusted for differences in average hours worked.

is also a question about whether employers—or possibly even women themselves—are willing to invest in their productivity due to uncertainty about their future work patterns. Whatever the cause, there is strong evidence that women are paid less than men for performing the same work, laws to the contrary notwithstanding. According to one study, at least half of the one-third earnings differential between married men and women cannot be accounted for after controlling for differentials in educational achievements or work experience and continuity.[13]

The maldistribution of occupations by sex is a better indicator of the impact of discrimination (Table 15-3) and is an important factor accounting for the gap in earnings between men and women.[14] The majority of women are in clerical and service work (including domestic work), retail sales, teaching, and nursing. Even though women can now be found in virtually every occupation, most of the growth has been in these "women's" occupations, with the result that the bulk of women are still concentrated there. According to one estimate, almost half of the net increase in employed women between 1950 and 1960 occurred in occupations in which at least 70 percent of the workers were women, and almost 60 percent of the increase was registered in occupations that had a majority of women.[15]

Though slowly changing, women have been forced to concentrate in jobs that tend to have lower levels of responsibility and pay, while the better-paying jobs and occupations offering opportunities for upward mobility have frequently been foreclosed. Segregation of occupations by sex is especially pronounced in skilled blue-collar jobs controlled by unions. Few apprenticeships, which have the promise of upward mobility built in, have been open to women. The Department of Labor has taken actions to correct this situation, though much progress is needed. Women's share of professional and technical occupations actually declined since the 1940s from 45 to 43 percent in 1979, even though the absolute numbers of professional

Table 15-3 DISTRIBUTION OF
EMPLOYED WOMEN BY OCCUPATION, 1940 AND 1979

MAJOR OCCUPATION GROUP	PERCENT OF WOMEN EMPLOYED		AS PERCENT OF TOTAL WORKERS EMPLOYED IN OCCUPATION	
	1979	1940	1979	1940
TOTAL				
Thousands	40,446	11,920	—	—
Percent	100.0	100.0	41.7	25.9
WHITE-COLLAR WORKERS				
Professional, technical workers	16.1	13.2	43.3	45.4
Managers, officials, proprietors	6.4	3.8	24.6	11.7
Clerical workers	35.0	21.2	80.3	52.6
Sales workers	6.9	7.0	45.1	27.9
BLUE-COLLAR WORKERS				
Craftsmen, foremen	1.8	0.9	5.7	2.1
Operatives	11.5	18.4	32.0	25.7
Nonfarm laborers	1.3	0.8	11.3	3.2
SERVICE WORKERS				
Private household workers	2.6	17.6	97.6	93.8
Service workers (except private household)	17.2	11.3	59.2	40.1
FARM WORKERS				
All farm occupations	1.2	5.8	18.0	8.0

SOURCE: *Employment and Earnings* (January 1980), tables 22 and 23; and *Historical Statistics of the United States*, U.S. Bureau of Labor Statistics (Washington, D.C.: GPO, 1975), series D 182–232.

and technical women workers more than doubled. The relative decline reflected a change in the mix of professional jobs. For example, the increase in professionals included the spurt of engineering and related space-age occupations, which were predominantly male. Also, a greater percentage of the female labor force consisted of younger and less experienced women. The trend reversed in the 1970s as women's attachment to the labor force, educational attainment, and awareness of career possibilities increased.

Despite the gains made in career opportunities for women, most professional women workers are either nonpractitioner health workers or teachers, and women teachers are mostly confined to primary grades while men tend to teach in high school and college.

Many factors contribute to the high proportion of women in low-paying, low-status "women's" jobs. Not only does society place a low value on women's market services, but also many women themselves have tended to base their job choices on short-run needs rather than on long-run career considerations. Thus they are frequently willing to take these less desirable jobs because the hours and location are convenient, enabling them to combine family and job responsibilities more easily.

During the 1960s, rapid expansion of women workers in few occupations tended to depress women's earnings. However, Victor Fuchs views this as a short-run phenomenon, and he anticipates that earnings differentials will lessen in the long run.[16] In an era of increasing childlessness, declining family size, and delayed first births, careers have gained greater importance in women's lives, and demands for greater occupational opportunities are becoming more articulated and militant.

The low value given to housewives' nonmarket homemaking duties is reflected in the fact that this productive work is not counted in the gross national product or other national accounts, although such services are counted if domestics or others are paid to perform them. If, in 1964, the value of housewives' unpaid services had been counted in monetary terms—by using the wage rates of domestic workers—wives would have added about one-fourth to the GNP.[17]

IMPROVING THE EMPLOYMENT STATUS OF WOMEN

For many years legislation dealing with women workers was confined to state protective laws regulating minimum wages, maximum hours, and other standards of work concerned with promoting their health and safety. The Fair Labor Standards Act of 1938 (FLSA) was adopted to provide federal standards on wages and hours for both men and women. More recently, the emphasis has shifted toward curbing sex discrimination and providing equal pay and employment opportunities. While many states adopted equal pay laws, it was not until the 1960s that the federal government entered this field.

The Equal Pay Act of 1963 and Title VII of the Civil Rights Act of 1964 prohibit discrimination in employment based on sex as well as on race, color, religion, and national origin. In addition, Executive Order 11246 bans similar discrimination by federal contractors and subcontractors; and the Age Discrimination in Employment Acts of 1967 and 1978 proscribe discrimination on the basis of age up to the age of 70. The 1972 Equal Opportunity Act gave the Equal Employment Opportunity Commission the right to sue private companies for job discrimination. Throughout the 1970s, nondiscrimination clauses have been included in laws establishing federally sponsored programs. Of particular potential importance in gaining access to training for women are regulations prohibiting discrimination in apprenticeship programs registered with the U.S. Department of Labor and in federally funded employment and training programs. However, the number of women in apprenticeship programs remains small and the training obtained by women from CETA local prime sponsors is primarily in traditional female occupations.

The mere passage of legislation, of course, does not guarantee equal employment opportunities. The laws leave much to be desired in coverage, scope, and sanctions, and little is done to ensure compliance with existing provisions. It was not until 1972 that the Equal Pay Act, an amendment to the Fair Labor Standards Act, extended its coverage beyond that of the federal minimum wage law to include executive, administrative, and professional positions—the very jobs where discrimination appears most rampant and its elimination most crucial if women are to achieve an equal footing with men. The 1974 amendments to the FLSA extended coverage to low-skilled jobs, including domestic work and retail occupations, overwhelmingly dominated by women. Despite these legislative efforts to reduce discrimination, differences in pay for equal work continue and wage differentials between men and women have actually increased in some areas in recent years.

The most publicized and controversial attempts to improve the status of women is the pending Equal Rights Amendment to the Constitution. It states that "equality of rights under the law shall not be denied or abridged by the United States or by any State on account of sex," and it would make discriminatory laws unconstitutional. If it were adopted, women would presumably acquire the same rights as men in all areas of economic, social, and political life. However, some groups that favor improving the employment status of women oppose the amendment on the grounds that it would erode hard-won protective legislation. Charges that the amendment will adversely affect alimony and child-custody arrangements have been dismissed as invalid by supporters. Even without the ratification of the amendment, by 1980 a number of states had already undertaken extensive review of their laws for the purpose of amending or repealing sex discriminatory provisions.

DISCUSSION QUESTIONS

1. What factors have contributed to the consistently rising labor force participation rate of women in recent decades?
2. Women earn about 60 percent of what men earn. Why?
3. "Equal pay for equal work" is not necessarily in the best interests of women. Their lower wages are an attraction to employers and allow them to compete more favorably with their male counterparts. Comment.
4. Compare the earnings of black women with that of white women and black men.
5. While unemployment of women is higher than that of men, the data also show that unemployment rates of women increase less than those for men during business downturns; similarly, when economic conditions improve, the jobless rate of women declines less than men. Explain.
6. The majority of women are part of the so-called "secondary labor force" with relatively little attachment to the job market. How accurate is this allegation today? twenty years ago?
7. Do you agree with Professor Eli Ginzberg's statement that the rise of women entering the labor force is "the single most outstanding phenomenon of our century"?

Notes

1. Ralph E. Smith, ed., *The Subtle Revolution* (Washington, D.C.: The Urban Institute, 1979), pp. 46–48.
2. Herman P. Miller, *Rich Man, Poor Man* (New York: Crowell, 1971), chap. 12.
3. U.S. Bureau of the Census, *Money Income in 1977 of Families and Persons in the United States*, series P-60, no. 118 (Washington, D.C.: GPO, March 1979), table 26.
4. Juanita M. Kreps, *Sex in the Market Place: American Women at Work* (Baltimore, Md.: Johns Hopkins Press, 1971).
5. *Employment and Training Report of the President, 1979* (Washington, D.C.: GPO), p. 98; and U.S. Bureau of the Census, *Divorce, Child Custody, and Child Support*, series P–23, no. 84 (Washington, D.C.: GPO, June 1979), table 10.
6. Phillips Cutright and John Sconzoni, "Income Supplements and the American Family," U.S. Congress, Joint Economic Committee, *Studies in Public Welfare*, no. 12, part 1 (Washington, D.C.: GPO, 1973), p. 67.
7. U.S. Department of Commerce, Bureau of the Census, *Divorce, Child Custody, and Child Support*, series P-23, no. 84 (Washington, D.C.: GPO, 1979), pp. 3–4.
8. Howard Rosen, "Research Debunks Myths about Women Who Work," *Arizona Review* (Third Quarter 1979): 19.
9. Mary Jo Bane, *Here to Stay: American Families in the Twentieth Century* (New York: Basic Books, 1976), pp. 92, 132.
10. Seth Low and Pearl Spindler, *Child Care Arrangements of Working Mothers in the United States*, U.S. Department of Labor and U.S. Department of Health, Education, and Welfare (Washington, D.C.: GPO, 1968), pp. 15–16.
11. Scott Campbell Brown, *Educational Attainment of Workers, Some Trends from 1973 to 1978*, U.S. Bureau of Labor Statistics, Special Labor Force Report 225 (Washington, D.C.: GPO, 1979), table K.
12. U.S. Bureau of the Census, *Fertility of American Women: June 1978* (Washington, D.C.: GPO, 1979), series P–20, no. 341, pp. 26–27.
13. *Economic Report of the President, 1974* (Washington, D.C.: GPO, 1974), p. 155.
14. U.S. Department of Labor, Women's Bureau, "The Employment of Women: General Diagnosis of Development and Issues" (April 1979), p. 7.
15. Valerie Kincade Oppenheimer, *The Female Labor Force in the United States*, Population Monograph series no. 5 (Berkeley, Calif.: University of California, 1970), p. 160.
16. Victor R. Fuchs, "Short-Run and Long-Run Prospects for Female Earnings," NBER Working Paper Series, no. 20 (New York: Center for Economic Analysis of Human Behavior and Social Institutions, 1973), p. 14.
17. Ahmad Hussein Shamseddine, "GNP Imputations of the Value of Housewives' Services," *The Economic and Business Bulletin* of the School of Business Administration, Temple University (Summer 1968), pp. 53–61.

Chapter 16
Youth Employment Problems

The years 1963 and 1977 might be called the "Youth Years" on the national policy scene. In 1963 the first products of the postwar baby boom became 16 years of age and began entering the labor market. Chapter 17 documents the policy responses of that year. It is paradoxical that some of the same issues should arise again in 1977 when the pace of youth entry was about to decline as a result of the "birth dearth" of the 1960s. In part, the explanation was political. The 1974–1975 recession had pushed all unemployment rates, including those for youth, to extraordinary heights. A new Democratic administration was looking for new initiatives. Youth and veterans seemed the most likely candidates but the high veteran unemployment proved temporary as the post–Vietnam adjustment was completed. It was difficult to be against doing something for the nation's youth.

But viewing youth employment issues in that momentary focus is too narrow. The transition through adolescence from childhood to adulthood is generally considered to be the most difficult stage of life. That pattern has its labor market parallel as one makes the transition from the protected environment of home through the controlled environment of the school to the full competitive buffetings of the labor market. That transition has not become an easier one as the adolescent period has lengthened in our society. It is necessary, therefore, to consider youth among the special groups facing employment problems—teenagers 16–19 and young adults 20–24 years of age.

THE EXTENT OF YOUTH UNEMPLOYMENT

There are many ways of putting youth unemployment into perspective, among them its incidence, its intensity, and by interracial and international comparisons.

Incidence

In recent years, approximately one-half of all unemployment has been accounted for by those under 25 years of age. The unemployment rate of teenagers is presently triple that of the rest of the labor force. Since black unemployment is typically double that of whites, the unemployment of black teens is customarily six times the rate for white adults. Female unemployment rates being typically 1.5 times the overall average, the rate for black teenage girls hovers around 50 percent. (Living in a poverty area of a central city adds substantially to those rates.) In addition, labor force participation rates of black youth are about three-quarters of those for white youth of the same age.[1]

Stated another way, four out of ten black teenagers who seek jobs cannot find them; the ratio is five or more out of ten in some central city areas. But that formulation takes no account of the low labor force participation of disadvantaged youth. Only 22 percent of all blacks sixteen to nineteen years of age and 16 percent of those living in central city poverty areas have jobs, compared to 45 percent of the entire U.S. population of that age. More than 60 percent of all unemployed black teenagers reside in central cities with half of this group concentrated in poverty areas.[2] For these and other youths, there is a high correlation between their unemployment and their propensity to commit crimes.[3]

These are some of the hard facts of youth unemployment. However, one can choose another set of statistics to minimize the problem. Of the average of six million people unemployed during 1978, 1.6 million were teenagers, including 381,000 black teenagers, and 1.4 million were young adults. Half of unemployed teenagers are students. More than one-third of all unemployed teenagers are interested in part-time jobs. Less than one-tenth of teenagers and two-fifths of young adults are married with a spouse present. Most unemployed teenagers and a substantial proportion of young adults live with their parents. Only one-third of unemployed youth are from poor families. Most spells of teenage unemployment are short and most teenagers have little difficulty finding jobs. Every year the number of employed teenagers doubles between May and July, a remarkable labor market performance.[4] The bulk of youth unemployment is experienced by a relatively small group of school-dropout teenagers with long spells of unemployment.

Thus one has an ample field from which to choose data to maximize or minimize the youth employment issues.

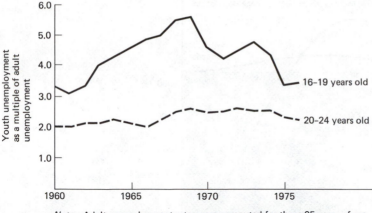

Note: Adult unemployment rates were computed for those 25 years of age and over.

Figure 16-1   Ratio of youth to adult unemployment rates, 1960–1976. (Source: *1977 Employment and Training Report of the President*.)

Intensity

A useful measure of the seriousness of youth employment problems which also supplies some basis for projection is the ratio of youth to adult unemployment (Figure 16-1). As new entrants to the labor force are involved in school and career exploration, youth unemployment has always been some multiple of the adult rate. During the late 1940s and 1950s that multiple was consistently around 2.8 for teenagers and about 1.8 for young adults. High birth rates having begun in 1947 and continued to a downturn in the late 1950s, an influx of youth into the labor market began in the mid-1960s, slowing down at the end of the succeeding decade. Thus the teenage/adult ratio climbed persistently to a peak of 5.5 to 1 in 1969 and then declined to its more historical near triple level by 1975. The young adult ratio rose moderately around 1967 but never experienced the spectacular change that characterized teenage relationships.

Since it is clear that the number of inexperienced youth the labor market has had to absorb has been a major factor in the level of youth unemployment, the number of teenagers in the population in the future is a key factor in projecting what will happen to youth unemployment rates. Figure 16-2 would suggest a sharp decline. Other factors in the rise of youth unemployment may have been the competition represented by the rising labor force participation rate for women and the influx of foreign workers, legal and illegal. That competition can be expected to continue. About 70 percent of all unemployed teenagers are new entrants or reentrants to the labor force and approximately 40 percent have never worked in paid employment. This suggests that youth unemployment will persist as some multiple of the adult rate.

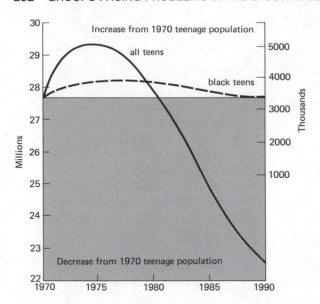

Figure 16-2   Relative population increase of black and all teenagers, 1970–1990. (Source: Garth L. Mangum, *Employability, Employment, and Income.*)

Black-White Comparisons

The gap between unemployment rates of white and black youth was small in the early 1950s but widened to 2.3 to 1 by 1966 and has persisted at approximately that ratio since then (Figure 16-3). Involved, undoubtedly,

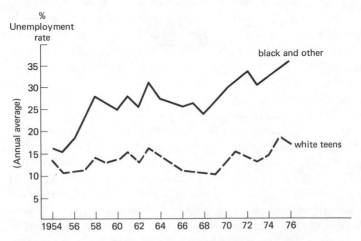

Figure 16-3   Teenage unemployment rates by race. (Source: *1977 Employment and Training Report of the President.*)

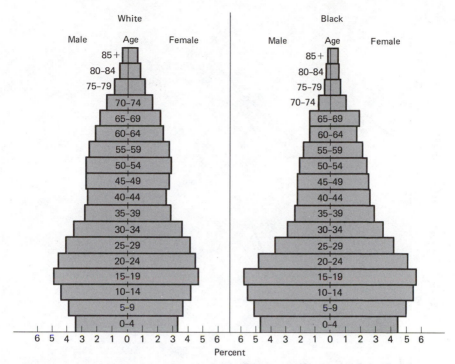

Figure 16-4 Distribution of the white and black population, by age and sex: July 1, 1977. (Source: U.S. Bureau of the Census, *Current Population Reports,* series P-25, no. 721, "Estimates of the Population of the United States, by Age, Sex, and Race: 1970 to 1977," (Washington, D.C.:GPO, 1978).)

vere a wide variety of developments; among them culturally different homes, substandard schooling, residence in areas with depreciating economies, inaccessibility of the informal linkages for job searches, the increasing availability of competing groups, and the fact that the birth rates have been even higher for blacks and other minorities than for whites. However, these are not adequate explanations within themselves. A combination of race and age discrimination is undoubtedly an important cause with other factors serving as vehicles for that discrimination. The demographic trends suggest that black youth unemployment will persist while that of white youth will decline (Figure 16-4). Nonwhites were 14.7 percent of the 18–24 age population in 1978; they will comprise 16 percent in 1983. By then the number of black teens will be declining, but less than the decline in white teens.

International Perspectives

A useful perspective can also be found by viewing international trends in youth unemployment. Until 1973, youth unemployment could be consid-

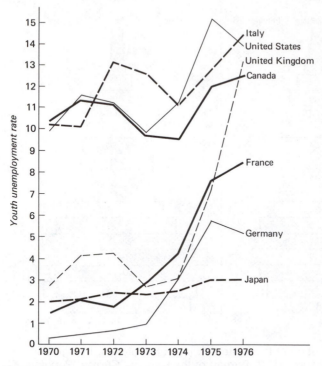

Figure 16-5 Trends in youth unemployment in seven member countries, 1970–1976. (Source: OECD, *Labour Force Statistics*. OECD, Statistics Division and National Sources.)

ered a uniquely American problem. Of the industrial countries that are members of the Organization for Economic Cooperation and Development, (OECD) only underdeveloped Italy and our sister North American nation, Canada, came near to matching U.S. youth unemployment rates (Figure 16-5).[5] There had been no immediate postwar baby boom in those nations which had suffered direct devastation during World War II. The tendency in most had been for youth to leave school early and go directly into a lockstep apprentice program.

The school to work transition had not been entirely painless. Youth unemployment was still some multiple of adult rates. But in most of Western Europe, economic growth had been rapid. Adults as well as youth had been in short supply relative to demand. With overall unemployment rates often under 1 percent as in West Germany and Sweden, a multiple of the adult rate still didn't amount to much.

But by the late 1960s, four or five years later than in the United States, a mini–baby boom began having some affects on the rate of new entrants to the labor market. More importantly the expectations of European youth were changing rapidly. They were less willing to accept the lockstep patterns of the past and began modeling their lifestyles after what they perceived that of U.S. youth to be. The youth riots in France in the late 1960s are an example.

But that proved to be only the beginning. The quadrupling of OPEC oil prices was much more devastating to other OECD members than to U.S. and Canada. The latter two still produced the majority of their own petroleum needs, the others practically none. Resulting inflationary pressures forced every OECD country to run its economy with considerable slack. And in Europe, there were few minorities and women to share the buffer position with youth. There were only the foreign "guest workers" to send home as a buffer before rising unemployment took its toll among youth.

Despite differences in the economic and social perspective, it is clear that the same phenomena essentially operate throughout the world as in the United States. Youth are in an exploratory mood. They are no more ready to settle down abroad than in the United States. Their unemployment does not tend to be long term. They tend to delay family responsibilities even longer than we. They are largely excused the race and sex differentials because of the lack of minorities and the limited labor force participation for women. Inevitably there will be considerable thrashing about at the entry to the labor market. Perhaps the added height of youth unemployment in the U.S. can be explained primarily by the interracial and inter-sex competition arising on the U.S. scene.

PATTERNS OF YOUTH EMPLOYMENT

To understand the persistence of youth unemployment, it is necessary to understand the patterns by which they make their way into the labor market, explore it, and finally settle down into relatively stable employment.

The School-to-Work Transition

At age 14 and 15 almost every young person is in school, neither seeking nor holding a job even in summer, except for traditional activities such as newspaper delivery, baby-sitting, and neighborhood lawn-cutting. Less than one-third look for work during these years. As Figure 16-6 illustrates, job holding begins to increase at 16 and 17 among both students and the few who will drop out of school at this age.[6] One-half work or look for work during the school year and three-fifths during the summer. Generally, these youth are not thinking in career terms but only looking for a source of spending money.

At age 18 and 19, most leave high school, either to enter the labor market or to continue into post-secondary education. One out of three will have completed their formal education. Of the rest about one-half (comprising 20 percent of the total population cohort) will ultimately graduate from four or more years of college. The rest will complete shorter programs or drop out without a post-secondary credential. Those 18- and 19-year-olds

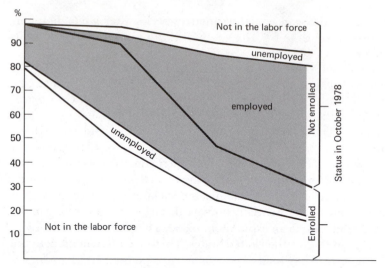

Figure 16-6   Youth in transition.

who continue in school will be primarily concerned with income and will rarely view the jobs they take as steps in a longer-term career plan. Those who do not plan on continued education will usually begin serious exploration of the job market, moving among various jobs in search of something they are willing to stay with. At this stage three-fourths of males and three-fifths of females either hold or search for jobs. A particularly devastating factor for the young women is that one out of ten 16- to 19-year-olds has borne a child.

By the early twenties, most young people are employed and self-supporting. Less than 30 percent are out of the labor force, about one-half of those still in school and the rest keeping house. Most have chosen or settled into an occupational area, though many have yet to find the job they will stay with. Family responsibilities rather than occupational preference may have been the stabilizing factor for some. Of the young adult group, 41 percent of the Hispanic males and 27 percent of the black males have become family heads. This is also true of 20 percent of the black females but only 4 percent of the white females.[7]

Involved in the shift from the search for spending money to career exploration and settling in is a transition from part-time to full-time jobs. Only one seventh of 16- and 17-year-old workers hold full-time jobs compared to three-fifths of employed 18- and 19-year-olds and four-fifths of workers 20–24 years of age. Conversely, one-half of the employable 16- and 17-year-olds hold part-time jobs for less than one-half of the year compared to one-fourth of the 18- and 19-year-olds and one-tenth of the young adults.

The occupational and industrial pattern of youth employment follows this transition process. Sixteen- and 17-year-olds are concentrated in sales, service, and laborer occupations. Young adults are more likely to be clerical, professional, or technical workers. A shift occurs from wholesale and retail to manufacturing and services. Mean hourly wages rise with age, as follows for May 1978:

14- and 15-year-olds, $1.00
16- and 17-year-olds, $1.36
18- and 19-year-olds, $1.72
20- and 21-year-olds, $2.04.

The labor market knowledge of the early teens tends to be limited to neighborhood odd jobs and the activities of adult role models. Career goals are vague, bounded by limited experience and observation, and frequently unrealistic. Through trial and error, increased networks of working friends and relatives, and through the broadening effects of education, most youth learn something about how to search for, find, and hold a job. A few catch an early vision of what they want to do with their lives but most do not do so into their twenties. Often before they know what they will want to do, most begin to stabilize their work patterns until they demonstrate sufficient dependability for employers to be willing to invest in formal and informal on-the-job training. Most emerge from high school with the basic skills of reading, writing, speaking, and computing so essential to modern job markets. Little occupational training is received in high school except such broadly adaptable skills as typing and the industrial arts. Beyond high school, a minority find specific occupational training in post-secondary education and the military but most depend upon on-the-job learning and experience. But by the early twenties most have an occupation they can call their own.

Employer perceptions of youths follow this same pattern, generally realistically. Young teenagers are considered unstable, untested, and undependable. Their productivity is in doubt, their tenure likely to be short, and their ability unknown. A good school record is reassurance but generally an employer will trust such youths only with rudimentary jobs requiring no formal or informal training unless they are personally known and have some kinship or friendship tie. By the late teens and early twenties, there will be enough evidence of stability growing out of school performance and early varied work experience for the employer to risk investment in the youth. With plentiful supplies of youths such as has been the case in recent years, and with the additional competitive factor of working women, employers could and did increase the age of acceptable career entry.

Thus both youth development and labor market demand parallel, intersect, and adapt. The youth's perceptions and intentions shift. The young person builds a pool of experience, credentials, and contacts. Each job tends to become more substantial and to provide greater exposure to other options. With a "track record" employers are more willing to hire and invest in on-the-job training. The young adult then moves from the external labor market into the internal labor market to progress within an establishment or onto a career pathway consisting of a series of jobs with various employers.

None of this is orderly. It is haphazard. The early jobs rarely have any connection with the later ones. There are many pitfalls, detours, dead ends, and points of discontinuity in this progression. Some of these discontinuities are positive. Leaving school with a credential to return after experience, more preparation, departure from the nuclear family, marriage, passing through the secondary to the primary labor market, the transition from part-time to full-time work and from youth to adult jobs are all necessary parts of the rites of passage. Most youngsters successfully negotiate these hurdles and find their way into a reasonably satisfactory working career.

Other discontinuities are negative: early school-leaving, early childbearing, drug or alcohol addiction, arrest and incarceration. These strike individually but they tend to be concentrated among certain socioeconomic groups: those from culturally and economically deprived backgrounds, minorities confronted by limited opportunities during critical developmental years, young women socialized into sex stereotypes, those with physical and mental handicaps. Certain geographical areas, rural and urban, impose their own barriers. Those who start from disadvantaged backgrounds generally face the greatest obstacles all along the path. They have less exposure to opportunity and more to negative events. Parental and peer influences are less positive and there is less institutional support.

The statistical evidence of the scarring effects of youth unemployment are clear.[8] For most, unemployment during youth is an incidental experience. It may even have positive effects if it leads to greater exploration and recognition of realities and requirements. But those who experience the most unemployment as youth continue to do so as adults. If their very sense of self-worth is damaged they may withdraw into failure or build their self-image in less socially desirable ways.

Thus, though youth unemployment overall is a declining problem, the career entry process is sufficiently fraught with difficulty and danger to require sustained attention.

Ghetto Youth Unemployment[9]

The inner cores of the nation's largest central cities pose a special labor market problem for those growing up there. A combination of deteriorating economies, perverse population trends and disfunctional lifestyles compound the standard difficulties of maturation and career entry. Every major city in the United States has experienced in the past 35 years a massive outflow of jobs in manufacturing, construction, wholesale and retail trade—the industries traditionally supplying most of the entry jobs for those without advanced credentials. Only finance, insurance, and real estate showed consistent growth in the first half of the 1970s in the central cities of metropolitan areas of one million or more. And these were primarily white-collar jobs requiring substantial education. Among occupational categories, only managers and administrators grew in those metropolitan areas during the same time period.

At the same time that jobs were fleeing the central cities, so were the populations. But for the most part, the leavers were the successful and the stayers were the unsuccessful. Between 1970 and 1974, for example, some 11 million people moved out of U.S. cities while 5 million moved in for a net loss of 6 million. But almost all of the outmigrants were white as were 4 million of the 5 million immigrants. During that same period, the net outflow of blacks was only one-half million out of the 12 million living in central cities. In 1960, 52 percent of blacks lived in central cities; 58 percent did so in 1974. Adding the growing concentration of Hispanics gave the big cities a minority ratio of 37.5 percent in 1974, 27 percent black and 10.5 percent Hispanic.

And within these minority social groups, it was primarily the economically more successful who moved out or stayed out. Tending to concentrate in the central cities were those families of least financial success and those most prone to various forms of social disorganization. It is in the family circle that most children and youth receive the acculturation that more than anything else determines their ultimate success or failure in the labor market. Family influence is probably still more positive than negative in the central city, but, since the incidence of failing parents is greater, the home environment is less likely to overcome the negative aspect of the external environment. In the nation as a whole one family in six is headed by a woman. One child out of two spends part of his or her life in a single-parent family. The former approaches one-half and the latter near universality in the central city.

Not only do central city youth tend to come from the less successful populations and be surrounded by the least favorable employment opportunities, those life styles necessary for survival tend to be least attractive to employers. This is not to say that these youth are unsuccessful. They tend to do a remarkable job of adapting to the circumstances and surviving and even excelling in terms of their environment. But each youth wants peer acceptance and respect; all want a sense of self-worth. But all too often those are available only in terms of language, grooming, and conduct which are unacceptable to most employers.

Research has not yet clarified whether employers are more likely to avoid hiring the youth or whether the youth in those settings are more likely to reject the kinds of jobs available to them. Despite the outflow of jobs as well as people, it is not clear whether or not there are enough jobs fillable by youth without extensive formal preparation if it were not for competition from central city and commuting adults. It is known that many youths become involved in and even relatively successful in the irregular or subterranean economy. They find alternative income sources from income maintenance programs and illicit activities. But how many are able to earn from these activities the equivalent of the income available from employ-ment is another unknown. Central city youth appear to be reacting ration-ally to their environment. The critical issue is whether the environment can be improved, the youth be removed from the environment or the youth be prepared to surmount the environment in socially acceptable ways.

YOUTH EMPLOYMENT PERSPECTIVES

One might summarize the hemorrhage of literature on youth employment and unemployment with the following premises:

1. Young unemployment, as a general phenomenon, does not appear to be a critical issue. Relative to the unemployment of adults, it ap-pears more favorable than during the low unemployment years of the latter 1960s. For youth as a whole, it is highly likely that unem-ployment relative to that of adults will decline.

2. Unemployment rates are not a very useful measure of youth labor market problems. They equate the unemployment of the 17-year-old scion of a well-to-do family attending school full time and seek-ing a part-time job to buy gas for his Porsche, without letting Dad know how many miles he drives, with the unemployment of a fam-ily head with six dependents, few skills, a big mortgage, and no in-come. Half of those youth out of school and out of work are not ac-tively seeking a job and, in fact, evidence little interest in having work offered. A few years ago, 14- and 15-year-olds were dropped from the unemployment measures. It may be time to do so with the 16- and 17-year-olds. At any rate, some indicator is needed which measures the present pain and long run deterioration of employabil-ity consequent to unemployment.

3. The haves gain and the have nots lose in the youth labor market. It is those from relatively affluent homes and with the most education who also have the best access to the formal and informal labor mar-ket intermediaries which make job search rewarding. Test of career development among 12-year-olds show that white youth have a greater understanding of the world of work, are capable of a more logical analysis of work-related situations and have a more varied prevocational experience than blacks on the average.[10] Those whose parents had post-secondary education do better on all such tests than those whose parents had not more than high school education. That is also true of in-school youth versus out-of-school youth. These differences permeate job searches and contribute heavily to who wins and who loses.

4. Substantial numbers of teenage youth evidence little interest in em-ployment. This is true of both those whose parents can afford to support them and those who have found more attractive sources of

income than work. Positive work attitudes and adequate labor market knowledge have been shown to be crucial factors in the establishment of stable and successful employment careers.[11] The attitudes and desires of youth related to work are remarkably like those
of adults. Most have strong work ambitions and reasonably clear
career goals. But blacks, females, and poor white males possess the
least adequate knowledge. Unsatisfactory labor market experience
early in their work history is the most debilitating factor.

5. For most youth, unemployment has no long-term scarring effect and
   may even provide some positive experience. Adding a few years to
   age is all that is necessary to solve their employment problems.
   However, those who experience the most unemployment as youths
   also tend to do so throughout their working lives. Damage to one's
   sense of self-worth may be permanent and that is more likely to
   happen to those whose opportunities have been more limited to
   begin with. Unemployment for youth as some multiple of adult unemployment is a universal experience. But the multiple is much
   greater when youth comprise a higher percentage of the total population, when labor markets are slack, and when there are major differences in race, ethnic origin, and education among groups of
   youths.

6. The serious problems of youth unemployment are concentrated
   among a relatively small group who are triply impinged upon by
   being poor, a minority, and without education. Their most apparent
   mark of identification is school dropout status. For instance, the 30
   percent of teenagers who are not in school account for 57.5 percent
   of the unemployed and 58 percent of those out of the labor force.[12]
   For high school completers, attaining the age of 20 is followed by
   an average drop in the incidence of unemployment of 38 percent.
   High school drop-outs experience an improvement of only 20 percent in employment as they leave their teenage years behind. As
   young adults, those who did not complete high school have double
   the unemployment incidence of those who did. Yet it is unclear
   whether the lack of schooling is the cause or whether that is merely
   a symptom of differences that emerge largely from socioeconomic
   and family status. The total numbers involved in these debilitating
   circumstances are small—no more than 500,000 in total. It is a
   toss-up whether that makes the problem easier to solve or easier to
   ignore.

SUMMARY

For demographic reasons, youth employment problems appear likely to decline overall. The policy emphasis directed to those issues during the late
1970s is not likely to last. Nevertheless, the transition from dependency in

home and school to independence in the labor market will always be a difficult one for most youth. For youth trapped in the deprived environments of central cities and rural depressed areas (not discussed in this chapter), there is no apparent reason to expect easing of their social and economic problems. Temporary access to the policy spotlight may be helpful in at least setting in motion programs which might make a significant improvement for a few over time.

DISCUSSION QUESTIONS

1. Youth employment problems currently receive a high priority within public policies. Is that concern justified? Why or why not?
2. In your opinion, why does the unemployment rate of teenagers persist at a level three or more times as high as the rate for adults? What might be done to lower that multiple? Should it be done?
3. Looking ahead, do you expect youth employment problems to ease or grow worse? Why? For what youth groups?
4. In your judgment, why have unemployment rates for youth persistently been higher in the United States than in any other developed country?
5. Using your own experience and that of your acquaintances, trace year by year from age 16 to age 24 the labor market objectives of the average youth. What insights does this exercise provide for understanding the problem of and the potential solution to youth unemployment?
6. From experience and from evidence, including that in this chapter, to what extent do you think unemployment as a youth has a permanent "scarring" effect on subsequent labor market experience? What are the implications for policy?

Notes

1. Arvil Van Adams et al., *The Lingering Crisis of Youth Unemployment* (Kalamazoo, Mich.: The W. E. Upjohn Institute for Employment Research, 1978).
2. Garth Mangum and Stephen Seninger, *Coming of Age in the Ghetto* (Baltimore: Johns Hopkins University Press, 1978).
3. Daniel Glaser, "Economic and Sociocultural Variables Affecting Ratio of Youth Unemployment, Deliquency, and Crime," *Conference Report on Youth Unemployment: Its Measurement and Meaning* (Employment and Training Administration, U.S. Department of Labor, 1978).
4. Martin Feldstein and David Ellwood, *Teenage Unemployment: What Is the Problem?* (Cambridge, Mass.: National Bureau of Economic Research, working paper 393, September 1979).
5. *Youth Unemployment,* Report on the High Level Conference, 15–16 December, 1977 (Paris: Organization for Economic Cooperation and Development, 1978).
6. *Youth Employment Policies and Programs for the 1980s: Analysis and Proposals of the Department of Labor* (U.S. Department of Labor, October 1979), mimeo.
7. Carol Jusenius, *Young Adults Out of School and Out of Work* (Washington, D.C.: National Commission for Manpower Policy, September 5, 1978).

8. Adams et al., op. cit.
9. Mangum and Seninger, op. cit.
10. *Career Development Needs of Seventeen Year Olds* (Washington, D.C.: National Advisory Committee for Career Education, 1979).
11. Paul Andrisani, "The Establishment of Labor and Successful Employment Careers: The Role of Work Attitudes and Labor Market Knowledge," *Conference Report on Youth Unemployment: Its Measurement and Meaning* (Employment and Training Administration, U.S. Department of Labor, 1978).
12. Feldstein and Ellwood, op. cit.

PART IV
PURSUING SOLUTIONS
TO LABOR MARKET
PROBLEMS

Chapter 17
The Emergence of Employment and Training Programs

The Employment Act of 1946 made it a responsibility of the federal government to influence the supply of employment opportunity. To that there was added in the 1960s and 1970s concern for the distribution of the supply of jobs. Among the means for doing so have been employment and training programs designed to improve the employability and to enhance the employment and earnings prospects of persons and groups suffering various disadvantages in competition for jobs. An exploration of the economic and social context in which these programs evolved is essential to identify their objectives and to assess their achievements.

THE FORCES INVOLVED

The forces leading to the emergence of something approaching a human resource policy in the United States during the 1960s can usefully be examined in long-, intermediate-, and short-run time frames.

The Long Run

Economic historians often find it useful to divide economic history into an agrarian or preindustrial phase and our present industrial society, and some sociologists have begun to talk of a new stage—a postindustrial society. This formulation is especially useful for understanding the growing attention given to human resource concerns.[1]

The primary characteristic of the economic stage before the industrial revolution was the involvement of most of the labor force directly or indirectly in agriculture. The Civil War marked the close of that period in this country. It was replaced over the following fourscore years by the industrial stage in which most of the labor force was engaged in the production and distribution of manufactured goods. In that world capital resources were the most important, and the "shakers and movers" were the owners of industrial capacity.

The term "postindustrial society" has become so intertwined with spectacular projections of wealth and technological advances that realists often reject its use.[2] Whether or not we are living through a transition to a new social stage or only the maturing of industrialization is not important for our present purposes. What is significant is that the number of white-collar workers in the U.S. labor force has exceeded those with blue collars for a quarter of a century, while the number providing services, governing, and processing information far surpasses those engaged in producing and distributing foods and fibers and manufactured goods. Human resources are becoming the critical ones.[3] The wealth, power, and prestige of individuals in society are more and more determined by what these individuals know and what educational credentials they have rather than by what they own. Both the farm and the factory are controlled less and less by owners and more by professional managers. Highly trained people move freely among posts in education, government, and industry, and the boundaries between these sectors and between the private and the public sectors increasingly blur.

The Intermediate Run

Long-run trends often seem to accelerate during wartime, and efforts to meet the manpower requirements of World War II produced consequences that have shaped the manpower problems and policies of the entire generation that has passed since that time. To feed and arm ourselves and our allies, as well as meet the demands of our civilian population, while sending more than 11 million of our prime-age, male workers off to war, required exigencies that turned out to be irreversible. Excess rural labor was transferred to urban production, and the process of capitalization in agriculture was speeded to free still more. The rate of increase of output per workhour in agriculture leaped from 1 to 6 percent a year and has averaged around 5 percent for the past quarter-century. The pace of technological change throughout the economy was speeded, and that process continued at the new pace during the postwar period. Women entered the labor force in unprecedented numbers and never returned exclusively to the kitchen.

The postwar baby boom, referred to in Chapter 2, assured a surfeit of new entrants into the work force 16 to 18 years later. Birth rates maintained a high plateau throughout the late 1940s and the 1950s then declined to roughly the same low rates that prevailed during the depression of the 1930s. With 2.5 million youths turning 16 in 1962 and 3.5 million in 1963, the policy emphasis of the years that followed was predictable.

Also, during the postwar period, the GI Bill sent unprecedented numbers to college, and an educational cycle began in which, since educated people were available, almost everyone needed education to compete. A new technology was created that assumed a well-educated labor force and, therefore, demanded it.

Important shifts occurred in the patterns of migration and the structure of cities. Throughout industrialization the movement had been from farm to city, but the cities grew largely due to the influx of European immigrants. As poor people, they sought the cheapest housing. The tenements were in the central cities, but so were the unskilled and semiskilled jobs. After World War II the migration was internal, from farm to city. By now, many of the immigrants were black and, later, of Spanish-speaking background. They still sought the oldest and cheapest housing in the central cities. However, the new technology demanded single-floor, continuous-process factories, and the necessary land at reasonable prices and acceptable taxes was in the suburbs, as were the skilled and technically trained workers. Public policy—agricultural price supports at one end and federally insured housing at the other—stimulated the trends. The new immigrants could not afford housing where the jobs were, and all too often they were denied, through prejudice, the opportunity to rent or purchase what they could afford. Transportation systems were designed to bring the white suburbanites to downtown white-collar jobs rather than distribute central city dwellers to suburban employment opportunities. Schools that had contributed to Americanization of European immigrants did not successfully incorporate the American minority poor into the postwar society.

All these trends seemed to converge during the 1960s. A more rapidly growing labor force and rising productivity required economic growth rates 50 percent above the traditional norm. A growing proportion of teenagers and women made the labor force more volatile, leaving the labor market when jobs declined and returning with a rush as jobs became available, seeking jobs in June and abandoning them in September, and often preferring part-time jobs and those with odd hours. The combination of increasingly sophisticated technology, the growth of white-collar jobs, and the competition of rising educational attainment created a demand for remedial employment and training programs. The objective was to improve the employability of those experiencing a variety of disadvantages in the competition for jobs. But the remedial emphasis was largely unaccompanied by preventive measures. The effect was to siphon off the disadvantaged from the labor market pool without staunching the flow of underprepared people into it.

The Short Run

The immediate forces involved in the emergence of employment and training programs were unemployment and race relations. Following the Korean conflict, unemployment crept persistently upward, fluctuating over the business cycle, but climbing higher during each downturn and leaving a larger residual with each recovery until it reached over 8 percent of the labor force (unadjusted for seasonality) in February 1961. The trend had been underway for some time before public policy makers absorbed with inflation, budgetary imbalances, and balance-of-payments disequilibrium awakened to its implications. Thus it became the major domestic policy issue in the 1960 election with the challenger Senator John F. Kennedy advocating "let's get America moving again" and the defender Vice-President Richard M. Nixon proclaiming "this is just a rolling readjustment." But when the new administration took office, it was sure of neither the problem nor its solution. There were essentially three schools of thought: (1) those who blamed unemployment on the displacement effects of automation and expected the rising unemployment trend to persist ever upward; (2) the structuralists, who defined the problem as round pegs and square holes—there were allegedly enough jobs for all those seeking them, but the job seekers lacked the education or the skills or were located in the wrong places; and (3) those who attributed the problem to a deficient rate of economic growth.

THE PROGRAMS

Without a consensus, within as well as without the government, there was little initial action from the Kennedy administration, but Congress was better positioned to move decisively, since the leadership in the House and the Senate remained unchanged. There were bills already "in the hopper" that had been discussed in previous sessions of Congress and even passed and vetoed by the previous President. The legislators were feeling direct pressure from the voters. The fact that initiative was left to Congress predetermined the policy choice. The structural issues were readily apparent—particular people unemployed in particular places; few senators and congressmen were trained to look beyond their constituencies to the pervasive but impersonal influence of overall rates of economic growth. With limited information as to who and where the unemployed were, the initial attentions went to the more vocal of constituents, adult male family heads with considerable labor market experience—coal miners, steelworkers, factory hands—now without jobs and complaining that machines had replaced them. A retraining program appeared to be the answer. The Manpower Development and Training Act (MDTA) became law in March 1962.

No sooner did recruiting for the new program begin in the fall of that year than it became apparent that the demand was less for retraining than for the training of those who had never obtained skills. In 1961, when MDTA was first proposed, the overall unemployment rate was 6.7 percent and the unemployment rate for married men was 4.6 percent; but the latter indicator dropped to an average of 3.6 percent throughout 1962 while the program was getting underway, and the tendency was to call back the experienced workers. Those left out of work were primarily new entrants to the labor force, and the recruits for the training program were primarily those who had never achieved substantial skills. Despite the abrupt fall in the unemployment rates for the adult male family head, the overall rate actually rose to 5.7 percent for 1963 after dropping to 5.5 percent for 1962. The negative offsetting factor had been youth unemployment rising to 17 percent.

The swollen 1947 birth cohort was now 16 years of age—the end of compulsory school attendance in most states—and the dropouts were striking the labor market in rapidly growing numbers. The 1963 national legislative effort was a response to those facts. A Youth Employment Act encompassing a Home Town Youth Corps and a Youth Conservation Corps, modeled after the National Youth Administration and Civil Conservation Corps of the 1930s, passed the Senate but failed in the House. Instead, MDTA was amended to allow its youth component to expand from 5 percent to 25 percent of total enrollment.

Modernizing Vocational Education

In addition, in that year Congress completed the first real reexamination of the basis of vocational education legislation since 1917, based on the work of a presidentially appointed study commission, consolidating reforms in the Vocational Education Act of 1963, which was briefly discussed in Chapter 11. In essence the Smith-Hughes Act of 1917 had responded to the needs of an adolescent industrial society. The assumption was that only a few needed specialized skills, so the act had offered federal matching money to states for training in the particular occupational areas designated by Congress. Additions of other occupational areas had been made over the years, but the underlying approach had not changed. In other words, the Smith-Hughes Act focused on the skill needs of the labor market. The Vocational Education Act of 1963 assumed that nearly everyone needed specific occupational preparation. Its emphasis was the employment needs of people. It was more than coincidence, however, that it became law during the year of youth in manpower legislation.

Declaring War on Poverty

Other emphases, gathering force over time, were to come to legislative fruition in 1964. A civil rights movement had gained momentum during the 1950s and early 1960s. That movement's demands began shifting from equal access to public facilities to the economic arena—jobs and income. Simultaneously, journalists and a few academic economists, influenced heavily by President Kennedy's experiences in Appalachia during the 1960 campaign, discovered that poverty was still extensive in affluent America.

The product was the Economic Opportunity Act (EOA) of 1964.[4] It represented a declaration by a new President, Lyndon B. Johnson, of total war on poverty. However, its weapons were neither new nor powerful. The administration's rhetoric against poverty was stronger than its will to commit resources or its knowledge of poverty's causes. The rejected Youth Employment Act of 1963 with its New Deal antecedents became the source of the Neighborhood Youth Corps and Job Corps conservation centers. The participation of the Defense Department in the internal government task force that designed the antipoverty program and the fact that a number of military bases, surplus since the Korean conflict, were slated for closing was the impetus for the Job Corps' urban centers. They were, in fact, residential vocational schools for youth whose home and neighborhood environments were considered too debilitating for successful rehabilitation. The Department of Labor recommended a large-scale work relief program modeled on the Work Projects Administration (WPA) of the 1930s, but had to settle for a small-scale Work Experience and Training Program for adults based on an even smaller program sponsored by the Department of Health, Education, and Welfare to allow public-assistance recipients to work for their benefits.

A Ford Foundation program aimed at combatting juvenile delinquency was the precursor of the Community Action Program designed to pull together all public and private antipoverty agencies in communities heavily impacted by poverty to coordinate and govern them by elected boards including representatives of the poor. Other pieces of the EOA had similar antecedents. Throughout, the emphasis was on youth and on breaking the poverty cycle by preparing for and providing jobs. Underlying the effort was growing awareness that nonwhites experienced double the unemployment of the rest of the labor force, that teenagers suffered three times the average level of unemployment, and therefore, that black teenage unemployment was six times the average.

Equalizing Employment Opportunity

Even more direct impact of the civil rights movement was Title VII of the Civil Rights Act of 1964, which forbade discrimination in employment on grounds of race or sex. Added to a previous executive order aimed at federal contractors, a strong national consensus on equal employment opportunity seemed to be emerging. Discrimination on grounds of sex was added as an obstacle by opponents of the bill to make the act more difficult to administer. Chapter 19 explores the consequences of those legislative and administrative decisions.

Whence the Jobs?

The year 1964 was also the time for another important attack on unemployment. The unemployment rate had fallen from its 1961 peak of 6.7 percent but persisted at 5.5 percent and 5.7 percent respectively during 1962 and 1963. The Council of Economic Advisers (CEA) diagnosed the economy's ills as the consequences of an inadequate rate of economic growth. An accelerating pace of labor force growth, added to rapidly rising productivity, demanded a rate of economic growth and job creation substantially above the historical pace. Yet a war-borne tax burden and absorption with anti-inflation efforts during the 1950s was slowing the pace of the economy below its potential. An economic education for a relatively conservative president was also a prerequisite, but in 1962 and 1963 Kennedy's economic advisers first sold him and then introduced to the Congress a tax reduction package designed to "get the economy moving again." President Kennedy's death intervened, but President Johnson's persuasive powers with his former colleagues and the sympathy for the unfinished program of the late president combined to spur passage of what was, at the time, a startling proposal: Cut the federal government's income without reducing expenditures at a time when the budget deficit is already large, and the result will be not a larger but a smaller deficit, plus an acceleration in the rate of job creation and a drop in unemployment.

The result, of course, was that unemployment did fall to 3.8 percent in 1966 and it was not just Vietnam. Unemployment had already declined from 5.7 percent to 4.5 percent before that event and was declining sedately without creating inflationary pressures.

Despite fears of automation and other structural changes, unemployment could be reduced by purely fiscal means. A few years more had to pass before the limitations of this approach were tested.

Education for Equality

The next year, 1965, might well be called the education year. Economists were making much of discoveries concerning the returns to investment in human capital, discussed in Chapter 7. There was growing faith that education, concentrated in those schools and areas impacted by poverty and low educational achievement, could compensate for social and familial handicaps and promote equality of economic and social opportunity. This was the aim of the previously mentioned Elementary and Secondary Education Act (ESEA) of that year, the largest single input of federal aid ever made to predominantly state and locally financed public education.

The Job Creation Issue

MDTA implied that the causes of unemployment were inherent in the unemployed. They lacked skills and, given them, could be placed in jobs. Job Corps carried the same implication, but it indicated an environmental source for the lack of skills and productivity. The Community Action Program and Civil Rights Title VII indicated an institutional source for unemployment and poverty. The issue was becoming clear, if the answer was not: When certain individuals and groups are found to suffer more than their proportionate share of unemployment and poverty, is the cause more likely to be found in their own lack of skills and motivation, or in biases built into societal institutions including labor markets? Operationally, would it be more effective to concentrate on changing the people or on changing the institutions?

Training programs appeared to work well for those living in suburban areas and modest-sized cities where jobs were available to those for whom skills were provided. Those in central cities and rural depressed areas too often seemed to graduate from the training programs with only a hunting license to search for jobs that did not exist. The rural depressed areas had no jobs, and the central city jobs tended to require education and life styles beyond the reach of many of the inner city residents or to offer only limited opportunities and low wages unattractive to those with any income alternatives.

Among labor economists there was emerging the hypothesis of the secondary labor market—discussed in Chapter 6—that there was a primary market of good jobs with favorable wages, fringe benefits, and opportunities for advancement separated by an impervious wall from a secondary market of low-paid, dead-end jobs of little worth and characterized by high turnover, and that most employment and training programs could offer no ladder to surmount that wall. At the same time, the central cities were heating up with a growing number of riots across the country, and a search began for ways of diverting federal funds and methods of cooling the flames. A few programs were added by amendment of the Economic Opportunity Act. But the great emphasis was on recruiting the cooperation of private employers in the war on poverty. After all, they had the handle on most of the jobs in the economy. In late 1967, particularly frightening riots had occurred in Detroit and Newark, following upon those in Watts, San Francisco, and elsewhere, and the nation's capital exploded upon Dr. Martin Luther King's assassination. Labor markets were tight, and general levels of unemployment were low as a result of fiscal policy and the Vietnam involvement. Yet not enough jobs seemed to be seeping into the central city areas, and it was becoming clear that not just any job would do, particularly for the young without heavy financial responsibilities. President Johnson, in a major message in January 1968, announced organization of a National Alliance of Businessmen (NAB), under the direction of prestigious national business leaders, to administer a Job Opportunities in the Business Sector program (NAB-JOBS).[5]

The initial results were beyond expectation. The plan was for the Labor Department to supply funds from MDTA and EOA to compensate the employers for any additional costs incurred by hiring initially less competent people. Approximately one-third of those who responded accepted such compensation, but the remainder pledged to hire the disadvantaged at no cost to the government. The combination of presidential publicity, widespread labor shortage, and dramatized reality of the problem was temporarily effective. However, a new administration the following year shifted its attention to war-born inflation, and rising unemployment followed the shift in policy. Employers could not hire the poor, the disadvantaged, or minorities while laying off long-term employees with recall rights.

For the first time since 1964, unemployment was not merely a problem of the disadvantaged. It struck more politically potent groups, particularly returning veterans. Congress responded with proposals for a large-scale public service employment program to offer jobs in the public sector of the economy to those not absorbed by the private sector or by existing levels of public employment. The jobs, it was hoped, would be useful and not essentially different in kind from those existing, but they would increase in number from temporary subsidization. The act was vetoed by President Nixon in December 1970, but when the economy failed to respond to either policy, a somewhat similar bill became law the following August as the Emergency Employment Act of 1971.[6]

The Act extended for two years and offered state and local governments $2.25 billion to place 150,000 unemployed persons on their payrolls. It was generally conceded to be a success, providing a new increase in employment, doing so rapidly with a minimum of waste or fraud, giving jobs to those who needed them, and providing useful public services. Nevertheless, the administration again opposed its extension as its expiration neared. Despite the evidence of success, the administration's commitment to the concepts of decategorization and decentralization (discussed later in this chapter) had intensified. If public service employment was the need in a particular locality, let that locality allocate money for that purpose from the decategorized funding provided it for decentralized decision making, while those with differing needs and priorities made other choices. Nevertheless, the commitment of Congress to the public service employment approach to job creation was growing, while its trust in the administration was shrinking.

REJECTION OF THE GREAT SOCIETY

Despite some 1968 campaign rhetoric rejecting concepts and programs of President Johnson's Great Society, President Nixon and his new administration in their first term made remarkably few changes in training and related policy programs. But beginning early in 1973, wholesale rejection of the Great Society and the elimination of its residue seemed suddenly to become administration policy.[7] It had become apparent as early as the 1968 election that social welfare policies that favored the disadvantaged and minorities were not endorsed by the mass of lower middle class workers. An effort had been made to weld together a new Republican majority, and the election returns evidenced success. A major governmental reorganization was underway, removing the previous term's appointees, who had been primarily nonpolitical experts in the various fields, and replacing them with appointees whose primary qualifications appeared to be loyalty to the White House. Employment, training and other Great Society programs came under increasing attack.

Not only administration stalwarts but members of the academic community, some who had been among the architects of the same programs, recanted and joined the critical chorus, arguing that the problems had been misread and the programs misguided. Because the programs' supporters had often been unrealistic in their rhetorical advocacy and claims for the programs, it was not difficult to prove that they had not achieved all they had promised.

However, the revelations lumped together categorically under the term "Watergate" reduced administration credibility, eliminated from positions of influence some of the strongest opponents of social welfare programs, and turned public attention elsewhere. More temperate examination of evaluative data restored a consensus that, though the programs had not achieved what they had promised, their benefits had generally exceeded their costs. Reform rather than rejection became the watchword.

The Emergence of State and Local Expertise

By 1971 MDTA, EOA, the 1967 Amendments to the Social Security Act, the Emergency Employment Act, and the Civil Rights Act of 1964 had introduced an institutional and an on-the-job skill training program for unemployed persons of all ages, a residential vocational skill program for youth (Job Corps), separate work-experience programs for in-school and out-of-school youth and for the adult poor, a community action program, the beginnings of efforts to enforce equal opportunity in employment, an employment and training program especially for welfare recipients, and a fairly large scale public service employment program. The initiative had been necessarily national. No lesser jurisdiction had the know-how or resources, and few had the interest to serve unfamiliar and often unpopular margins of the population. As illustrated, programs did not emerge from a careful exploration of problems, conduct of research, and experimentation with solutions; they were rarely based on experience. With various legislators putting their own brand on special gimmicks to serve essentially the same clientele, there were soon competing federal agencies and a proliferation of programs and service agencies at the local level. The services available among the numerous programs represented a smaller number than the programs themselves; classroom skill training, limited basic education, subsidized public and private employment, minimal work experience as an excuse for transfer payments, supportive services, placement, and enforcement of antidiscrimination measures.

As early as 1966, Congress began lamenting the interagency competition at the national level and the proliferation of programs at the local level. The Labor Department responded to the criticism in two ways: (1) by demonstrating rising concern for the increasingly restless central city minority disadvantaged, and (2) by intensifying the efforts it was already making to wrest from the Department of Health, Education, and Welfare and Office of Economic Opportunity their hold on pieces of the employment and training action.

Alarmed at growing signs of unrest and sporadic rioting in central city black ghettoes across the country, the Labor Department conducted special surveys which documented frightening levels of unemployment and endemic underemployment. Available MDTA and EOA funds were reallocated to fund Concentrated Employment Programs (CEP), eventually in 82 areas. The separate legislative sources prohibited commingling of funds but the concentration offered a significant administrative innovation: access to all of the programs was made possible through a single office in each area. Applicant needs as well as eligibility could be reviewed and, within the limits of available "slots," they could be assigned to the program most compatible with their needs.

Meanwhile, many involved in the administration of the federally supported employment and training programs were complaining of a straitjacket effect. Local economies varied by the industrial and occupational structure of employment and by state of economic activity, yet the fixed categories of the federal programs limited the adaptations possible in response to local conditions. Enrollees were required to fit into the restrictions of programs rather than the program being adaptable to the enrollee need. Responding to these complaints, the Department of Labor, with the Department of Health, Education, and Welfare (which had a partnership role in MDTA), and Housing and Urban Development (operating at the time as a Model Cities Program) and the Office of Economic Opportunity (for EOA) introduced a Cooperative Area Manpower Planning System (CAMPS). State and local program administrators were to meet in joint planning sessions and prepare joint local and area CAMPS plans for federal approval.

The experience was a difficult one. The various agencies were not accustomed to communicating. The arbitrary funding boundaries between programs still had to remain inviolate. Congress often did not complete its appropriations until well into the fiscal year, leaving the planners without advance knowledge of the resources to be available. The federal agencies continued to launch new programs and issue directives without advance consultation. Nevertheless, the experience whetted the local appetite for autonomy. Governors and mayors also came to the realization that substantial sums of money were coming into their jurisdictions through direct relations between federal, state, and local bureaucracies without involvement of the elected officials.

Congress, in December 1967, responded to some of the pressures for decentralization and decategorization by amending EOA, allowing local "prime sponsors" to commingle all EOA manpower funds in Community Work Training Programs (CWTP) adapted to local needs. However, Congress did not designate who should head those CWTPs. The Department of Labor and the Office of Economic Opportunity were unable to agree, the first advocating primacy for the public employment service and the latter for the community action agencies. The concept stayed on the books but never became a reality. Nevertheless, a consensus had emerged that federal manpower moneys should be allocated to the local level for discretionary use with a minimum of constraint. The only details to be worked out were the appropriate local leadership and the specific federal role. As it turned out, six acrimonious years were to pass in getting the decision made.

Community Human Resource Programs[8]

The decentralization–decategorization consensus was widespread within the Johnson Administration by its close and the Nixon Administration came in with that commitment. Not only was there continuity at the congressional, administrative and advisory levels in the human resources field between the two administrations, but the notion was in accord with a "New Federalism" concept which endorsed unconditional federal revenue sharing, providing reduced funds but giving maximum discretion to state and local governments in its use. Numerous legislative proposals emanated from both Congress and the administration between 1968 and 1972, but all foundered over various disagreements, most involving the role public service employment would play in the new approach.

A decision was made during the period, however. State and local elected officials would have the leadership role within their own jurisdictions. That reflected both administration preference and state and local initiative. A few governors and mayors initiated their own human resources planning operations, building on the CAMPS base. They were still unable to transgress program boundaries, but they were dedicated to coordination and to exploiting whatever discretion was available. Then, intoxicated by its overwhelming 1972 victory and frustrated with its inability to attain agreement from Congress, the administration resolved in early 1973 to decentralize and decategorize by administrative fiat without awaiting congressional approval. Thus by the autumn of 1973 every state, 126 cities, four counties, and 19 Indian tribes had federal grants to support human resources planning staffs and were designing their own programs.

Accelerating Welfare

The Social Security Act of 1935 had been well designed to meet the income maintenance needs of an emerging industrial society. In the agrarian world the extended family had supplied economic security but now the nuclear family prevailed. Old Age and Survivors Insurance enabled wage earners, primarily male, to earn during their active years rights to a pension when their working years were done. A temporary Old Age Assistance program would fill the gap until retirees would have had time to earn a pension. Unemployment compensation insured the regularly employed against the inevitable consequences of the business cycle. There was Aid to the Blind and Totally Disabled. Children of wage earners would be insured by the OASI and unemployment insurance was available to their parents. However, industrial accidents or disease might leave the family without a wage earner before age 65. Aid to Dependent Children (ADC) would take care of those few cases.

It really worked that way until the 1960s. Then the nuclear family weakened before the pressures of advancing urbanization and industrialization. The subsequent attempts to lump employment with welfare are detailed in Chapter 18.

THE COMPREHENSIVE EMPLOYMENT AND TRAINING ACT

As Watergate weakened the White House influence, greater autonomy could return to the Labor Department for compromise and negotiating with the Congress. The resulting Comprehensive Employment and Training Act (CETA), passed in December 1973, largely endorsed, legitimized, and extended what was already commonplace in many areas. The major addition was authority for counties as well as states and cities to become prime sponsors. The 1970 census had shown that about two-thirds of the nation's unemployment was in the suburban and rural counties, and unemployment, not poverty, was the concern for 1973. A new allocation formula, based primarily on unemployment, pulled moneys out of the central cities and distributed new funds to suburban areas without previous manpower program experience.

Any unit of local government with a population of 100,000 or more could apply to become a prime sponsor, receiving a formula allocation of funds to be spent according to its own employment and training plan. When two governmental units, say a city and a county, were eligible for funds for the same area, the preference was to be given to the smaller unit. Areas not eligible for prime sponsorship or which chose not to participate would become a "balance of state" prime sponsorship. The prime sponsor in each case would be the chief elected official—governor, mayor, or county official. A bonus was available to those units which would join together in a consortium more nearly representing a labor market.

The act was to fund the decategorized programs within which prime sponsors could decide, subject to regional DOL plan approval, who to serve, what mix of services to provide, and what organization to contract with for delivery of services. Another section of the act represented congressional preference for public service employment. Additional funds for that purpose were to go to jurisdictions with high and persistent unemployment. However, the language allowed prime sponsors to shift moneys between job creators and training projects.

A third section supported national programs beyond the reach of local prime sponsors such as migrant labor programs, Indian reservations, or contracts with national organizations. A separate section integrated the Job Corps into CETA. Finally, the act also provided for a joint government/private commission to study manpower policy issues.

Only MDTA and EOA were merged into and replaced by CETA. The Wagner-Peyser Act supporting the public employment service, WIN, and other manpower-related components of the Social Security Act, vocational rehabilitation, vocational education, veterans' programs, and a variety of other employment and training programs were left intact. It was not politically expedient to confront the powerful congressional committees with jurisdiction over these programs. But even the limited decentralization and decategorization proved to be task enough.

Unemployment with Inflation

In retrospect, CETA became law perhaps one month before the beginning of the deepest recession since the 1930. That recession was remarkable also because inflation continued to rage throughout it. Until 1966, the U.S. had enjoyed a remarkably sanguine price level experience. There had been a brief burst of inflation when the World War II wage and price supports were removed, another mild one at the beginning of but not on through the Korean conflict, and some price pressures from a capital goods boom in 1955. Otherwise, prices were almost totally stable.

Then with Vietnam the trouble started. Wars are inherently inflationary. Incomes are generated producing goods and services which are not placed upon the market for sale—too much money chases too few goods. Fiscal restraint has lower priority than pursuing the conflict. Employment rises and labor markets tighten. Added in 1966 was unwillingness to recommend standard wartime tax policies to sop up the excess purchasing power. A congressional election year was not considered the appropriate time to admit an undeclared war of substantial proportion was underway. Restraints thereafter were too little and too late and inflation accelerated.

A new administration at the beginning of 1969 successfully slowed the inflationary spiral but at the cost of rising unemployment. Then, with the 1972 election looming, policies were reversed so that the unemployment rate was declining nicely as the election approached. The inflationary aftermath waited until after a landslide victory.

Other international factors now entered the scene.[9] Successive bad crop years in several nations tightened world food supplies. The Japanese and Germans retaliated against a devaluation of the U.S. dollar by flooding the world with yen and marks. Economic booms in those and other countries and the U.S. recovery put heavy pressure on raw material markets. Above all, the Organization of Petroleum Exporting Countries quadrupled crude oil prices. U.S. prices, already on the rise, shot up to double digit levels. Prices rose more rapidly than incomes, with heavy outflows of purchasing power which was not available for recycling into demand within the American economy. Americans could no longer buy as much in the domestic markets and foreigners who were customarily heavy purchasers of U.S. goods were experiencing the same loss of purchasing power. Production plunged and unemployment soared, yet inflation declined only slightly.

With unemployment at its highest level since 1940, Congress was under heavy pressure to take action, despite considerable reluctance within the Ford Administration. The congressional answer was public service employment building on the Emergency Employment Act model. A new title was added to CETA, providing $2.5 billion designed to create 300,000 jobs in state and local government—jobs for any unemployed, not just for the disadvantaged.

The administration had a different priority. It foresaw a threat of permanence in the new approach. The executive branch preference was temporary extension and broadening of unemployment insurance, from an average benefit duration of 26 weeks for steadily employed workers primarily in private industry to a maximum of 65 weeks with practically all workers eligible. The argument was that the program would automatically and permanently cease when unemployment declined. Under the emergency atmosphere, Congress endorsed both approaches and unemployment insurance benefits rose from $8 billion in 1970 to $22 billion in 1975.

The recovery was slow coming. Unemployment, which peaked at 9 percent in May 1975, still averaged 7.7 percent one year later during a presidential election year. Yet the inflation pace never receded below 6 percent. It is generally conceded that the slow decline in unemployment amplified by a temporary rise just before the election (in part, a statistical fluke related to the seasonal adjustment factor) was an important factor in the loss of incumbent Gerald Ford to challenger Jimmy Carter.

The incoming administration chose initially to focus its attention on unemployment, reassured perhaps by the modest slowing in the pace of price increases and politically indebted to the group suffering the most from joblessness. The vehicles chosen were further augmentation of public service employment, special programs for unemployed veterans, and a major new youth employment crusade.

CETA's budget jumped from $7 billion to $11 billion and its public service employment slots from 300,000 to 725,000. Heavy pressures were imposed on prime sponsors who responded by overfilling those new slots by 25,000 in a mere nine months. The veterans' programs were only getting underway when the unemployment rates for Vietnam-era veterans declined sharply.

The choice of a youth emphasis in 1977 was an interesting one. Fourteen years had passed since the 1963 "year of youth." The influx of youth was still rapid but had passed its peak. The number of white teenagers in the United States was already on a rapid decline, though the number of blacks of that age was persisting. Teenage unemployment was nearly five times as high as adult unemployment in 1969 and only three times as high in 1977. However, five times an adult unemployment rate of less than 3 percent was much less frightening than three times 7 percent. And with the typical doubling of black unemployment over white, the black teenage rate was over 38 percent and, in the central cities of the nation, 43 percent.[10]

The Youth Employment Demonstration Projects Act was passed in 1977 with a $1 billion budget. Included was a Youth Employment and Training Program allocating funds to CETA prime sponsors by formula to increase their youth services, a Youth Community Conservation and Improvement Program to which prime sponsors could submit competitive proposals for funding, a limited number of Youth Incentive Entitlement Projects, also funded on a competitive basis to test the effectiveness of job guarantees in improving school retention, a Young Adult Conservation Corps, and an expansion of the Job Corps. The history going back to the Civilian Conservation Corps and National Youth Administration of the 1930s and continuing through the Neighborhood Youth Corps was obvious.

Recentralization and Recategorization?[11]

Despite the temporary consensus on decentralization and decategorization during 1967-1973, those concepts had natural enemies. Congress found it less than satisfying in practice to appropriate federal funds to governors and mayors who could then take the credit for dispensing them for services designed and delivered by their designees. Much better to have identifiable federal programs with categorized services for which they could identify the beneficiaries and take their share of the credit. The public employment service and the vocational education community had enjoyed a guaranteed role under MDTA whereas under CETA they had to compete for their piece of the action dispensed at mayoral discretion. Community-based organizations had been able to negotiate annual national contracts at the Washington level, backed by congressional influences. Now each local affiliate had to negotiate, often from a position of weakness, with the staffs of local elected officials. It was not surprising, therefore, that each time Congress addressed CETA it seemed to erode the local discretion which was its key concept.

As unemployment soared in 1974–1975, Congress could have added money which would have allowed prime sponsors to determine the needs of their labor markets. Instead, Congress added funds limited to public service employment. Again in 1976, it tightened the eligibility requirements to qualify for public service employment (PSE) and in 1977 again added funds to that program rather than to those titles which maximized local discretion. It addressed youth unemployment with a program restricted to youth with only one component, the Youth Employment and Training Program (YETP), leaving to the prime sponsor the basic choice among alternative services to youth.

Meanwhile, the rapid, pressurized growth of PSE had resulted in substantial numbers of instances of violations of law and regulation. Journalists were able to find sufficient instances of nepotism and political favoritism in the dispensing of PSE slots, shifting of regular city or county employees onto CETA payrolls, use of CETA funds to support services that would otherwise have been paid for through increased taxes and even theft of funds to make CETA, as one journal put it, "a four letter word."

In 1978 when CETA required reauthorization, therefore, it was feared by some and hoped by others that further recentralization and recategorization would occur. However, a defending constituency had also been created—governors, mayors, county officials, and their staffs—who were able to mount a substantial defense. The result was a revised CETA which retreated only mildly from the broad discretion of 1973.[12]

All CETA services including public service employment were limited to the economically disadvantaged and long-term unemployed. Ceilings were placed on individual enrollment duration for both public service employment and work experience. The allowable salaries for public service employment were lowered sharply. For the contracyclical public service employment title, the authorization was open-ended, promising enough funds to support jobs for 20 percent of the number unemployed in excess of a 4 percent unemployment rate, rising to 25 percent when the overall unemployment rate is above 7 percent.

The major new direction was a $5-billion program of private sector opportunities for the economically disadvantaged, the new Title VII. To participate prime sponsors must form a private industry council (PIC) and propose for Labor Department approval specific initiatives they intend to undertake to promote private employment of the disadvantaged. The wide variety of nonlimiting alternatives listed in the Act do not include, but do not specifically prohibit, wage subsidies. For the state and local administrators of CETA, the major change was a growth in detailed regulations and paperwork.

CETA had survived with its central approach only slightly eroded. What no one knew for sure at the end of the decade in which decentralization and decategorization emerged was whether it had made any difference. MDTA and EOA had been extensively evaluated; a decentralized and decategorized mix of services, different in every jurisdiction, was extraordinarily hard to evaluate. And besides, who had either the responsibility or the incentive to do the evaluation? One could test whether a group undergoing a skill-training program experienced a greater increase in annual income than did a control group who experienced no training. But how can one test whether a choice of target groups, service mix, and service deliverers made by the staff of a mayor or county officials provided greater positive impact upon the employability, employment, and incomes of the disadvantaged than a group of services categorized by congress and delivered according to federal fiat?

1980—A Hiatus?

Thus, the second decade of employment and training programs ended with neither a bang nor a whimper. One could well argue a continuing process in which demographic and socioeconomic developments in the 1940s and 1950s created problems which were responded to imperfectly during the 1960s and 1970s. Events during those decades have been creating new conditions which will thrust themselves into visibility; new sets of problems will in turn demand new policies—which will also be less than perfect. But if we have learned anything from the experience, these will be better than having no policies at all. At least that is the faith that sustains the makers and practitioners of human resource policy.

DISCUSSION QUESTIONS

1. What were the major socioeconomic and demographic forces which led to the emergence of employment and training programs in the 1960s and 1970s? How responsive were the programs to those basic causes?
2. Reviewing the controversy over inadequate economic growth or structural rigidities in the labor market as explanation of employment disadvantage, what are your judgments about the relative importance and interaction of each?
3. Why did reform of the AFDC program become a high priority after 1967? Since the program had been on the law books since 1935, what had happened to call it to public attention? Why has reform been so difficult to accomplish? What type of basic economic security program is required for the 1980s?
4. What were the factors leading to the demands for decentralizing and decategorizing employment and training programs? To what extent does the Comprehensive Employment and Training Program seem to have accomplished those objectives?
5. What has been and should be the role of private employers in employment and training programs? How can they be motivated to participate?
6. The programs of the 1960s and 1970s emerged in response to problems gen-

erated in the 1940s and 1950s. What types of employment and training programs will be required in the 1980s to respond to the problems generated during the 1960s and 1970s.

Notes

1. Garth L. Mangum, *The Emergence of Manpower Policy* (New York: Holt, Rinehart and Winston, 1969).
2. Daniel Bell, *The Coming of Post–Industrial Society* (New York: Basic Books, 1973).
3. Frederick H. Harbison, *Human Resources as the Wealth of Nations* (New York: Oxford University Press, 1973).
4. Sar A. Levitan, *The Great Society's Poor Law* (Baltimore, Md.: Johns Hopkins University Press, 1969).
5. Sar A. Levitan, Garth L. Mangum, and Robert Taggart, *Economic Opportunity in the Ghetto* (Baltimore, Md.: Johns Hopkins University Press, 1970).
6. Sar A. Levitan and Robert Taggart, *The Emergency Employment Act: The PEP Generation* (Salt Lake City, Utah: Olympus Publishing Company, 1973).
7. Sar A. Levitan and Robert Taggart, *The Promise of Greatness* (Cambridge: Harvard University Press, 1976).
8. William H. Kolberg, *Developing Manpower Legislation: A Personal Chronicle* (Washington, D.C.: National Academy of Sciences, 1978).
9. Garth Mangum, *Employability, Employment and Income* (Salt Lake City, Utah: Olympus Publishing Company, 1976).
10. Arvil Van Adams et al., *The Lingering Crisis of Youth Unemployment* (Kalamazoo, Mich.: The W. E. Upjohn Institute for Employment Research, 1978).
11. Bonnie and David Snedeker, *CETA, Decentralization on Trial* (Salt Lake City, Utah: Olympus Publishing Company, 1978).
12. Garth Mangum et al., *Job Market Futurity: Planning and Managing Local Manpower Programs* (Salt Lake City, Utah: Olympus Publishing Company, 1979).

Chapter 18
Work and Welfare

Traditional welfare policy assumed a clear-cut dichotomy between those who could not or should not work (the disabled, aged, and widows) and were, therefore, deserving of public support and persons who were able-bodied and should make their own way. To discourage the employable from seeking aid, assistance payments were generally kept at rock-bottom levels.

More recently, as an affluent society has provided rising support to the poor, the sharp distinction has blurred between those who should work and persons for whom society should provide. It has become ever more difficult to define and identify employability and employable persons or, for that matter, productive employment. As the boundaries between work and welfare have become increasingly vague, public policy has recognized a new obligation—to assist the working poor to receive a decent income.

THE GROWTH OF WELFARE

The Social Security Act of 1935, passed in the depths of the Great Depression, was the federal government's first general attempt at income maintenance on a sustained basis. The act established two groups of programs. First, social insurance programs—including old age, survivors, disability, and unemployment insurance—distribute income payments on the basis of prior earnings and tax contributions. Because benefits under the social insurance programs depend on past work and level of earnings, those most in need may be excluded. Second, public assistance programs—Supplemental Security Income for the elderly, the blind, the disabled; and Aid to Families with Dependent Children (AFDC)—provide income support on the basis of need alone. Public assistance payments were initially designed to help only the unemployable.

When the Social Security Act was passed, female household heads with small children were usually considered to be unemployable. The prevailing assumption was that they should remain in the home to take care of their children instead of entering the labor force. Because of a persistent job shortage, few women had the choice between gainful employment and support at home. But even when jobs became more plentiful, the structure of the law discouraged work by some who might have been able to earn at least partial support. Benefits were often deducted dollar for dollar from any earnings, and this "100 percent tax" discouraged any work effort.

Moreover, because the only jobs most welfare recipients could find offered little stability, income from employment was uncertain. A mother on relief who succeeded in finding a job and achieving economic independence was likely to experience difficulty in returning to the welfare rolls if her income fell or even if she lost her employment. There was often no financial gain in working, and frequently the efforts to achieve self-support could be undertaken only at a risk of losing even the meager sustenance provided by public assistance. Not until 1969—more than three decades after the beginning of federal public assistance—did the federal government provide incentives to recipients who sought partial or complete self-support.

The problem of persons preferring welfare to work was small in the first years of the act because relatively few individuals qualified and the majority on public assistance rolls were disabled or too old to work. Profound changes have occurred, however, in Aid to Families with Dependent Children (AFDC), which became the major public assistance component. The number of AFDC recipients approximately doubled each decade between 1936 and 1966, and again by 1970. Since then, however, there has been relatively little growth in the welfare rolls (Table 18-1).

The rise of AFDC during the 1960s was puzzling because it was not congruent with other trends of that decade. Between 1960 and 1969 the number of Americans below the poverty level dropped steadily from 40 million (or 22 percent of the population) to 24 million (or 12 percent) (without transfer payments, 27 percent of American families would still be living in poverty);[1] the unemployment rate, after a spurt up to 6.7 percent in 1961, fell to 3.5 percent in 1969. But the number of AFDC recipients rose from 3.1 million in 1960 to 8.3 million in 1969. In the 1970s the program expanded only moderately, peaking in 1975 when unemployment reached 9 percent.

Table 18-1 NUMBER AND BENEFITS OF
AFDC RECIPIENTS, SELECTED YEARS 1936–1979

DECEMBER OF YEAR	NUMBER OF RECIPIENTS (THOUSANDS)	BENEFIT PAYMENTS (MILLIONS)
1936	546	$ 22.9
1946	1,190	173.1
1956	2,270	616.4
1966	4,666	1,849.9
1970	9,657	4,857.2
1973	10,815	7,291.9
1976	11,203	10,140.4
1977	10,780	10,603.1
1978	10,325	10,729.2
1979 (May)	10,312	888.7

SOURCE: Department of Health, Education, and Welfare, National Center for Social Statistics.

Originally planned as a transitional program that would wither away as the contributory insurance components were broadened, AFDC grew for many reasons. First, population growth could be expected to expand the welfare rolls over time, other things being equal. Between 1940 and 1973 total population increased by 62 percent, and the population aged 14 years and under grew by more than 39 percent.

Second, federal legislation extended coverage to groups not previously eligible. In 1961 children who were dependent because of the unemployment of an employable parent were included in the unemployed-father component (AFDC-UP), in mid-1969 a foster-care component was added, and most states also have adopted a provision that permits children to receive assistance after age 18 if attending school.

Third, the Supreme Court struck down two typical state provisions that prevented many households from receiving AFDC. In 1968 the Court ruled unconstitutional the "man-in-the-house" rule, which made a man living in an AFDC home responsible for the children's support; the decision precluded cutting off aid because the mother lived with a man not obligated by law to support the children. The following year, the Court invalidated residence requirements for public assistance, then in effect in more than 40 states. Also, a 1970 Court ruling specified that a stepfather is obligated to support his wife but not her children by another marriage, who remain eligible for benefits.

Fourth, the addition of health coverage for AFDC clients and an increased knowledge of available benefits induced many poor families to apply for assistance who previously had not done so. Medicaid was passed in 1965, providing medical assistance to indigent persons, including public assistance recipients. Families who had not wanted to be on the public dole but who could not otherwise provide needed health care for their children could no longer turn down assistance. Also, the growing number of social workers and anti-poverty volunteers working in poor communities encouraged eligible families to apply.

Fifth, at least as important as the foregoing have been alterations in family structure. Divorces, desertion, and illegitimacy have risen sharply since the mid-1930s. All such changes, which leave a mother as head of her household, increase the number of potential AFDC clients. The incidence of poverty is six times as high in families headed by females as in families where both parents are present. While the rate of marriage per 1000 population has been virtually unchanged since 1935, the divorce rate has increased by 155 percent. Illegitimacy has increased even faster. Between 1940 and 1976 the proportion of all births that were illegitimate rose from 1 in 25 to 1 in 7. The structure of AFDC itself has been criticized for encouraging female-headed families. For example, an able-bodied man who cannot earn enough to support his family, may not qualify for AFDC-UP. To provide income for them he may desert and thus enable them to qualify for assistance. Similarly, the father may not marry the mother so that she may qualify for AFDC.

The foregoing developments substantially expanded the number of persons who qualified for AFDC benefits. But at least as important was the greater availability and attractiveness of AFDC relative to earnings—which induced those eligible to apply for aid. As the federal government assumed a larger share of the costs, states became less reluctant to qualify individuals for aid; as the level of aid grew, participation in the program became increasingly preferable for those eligible. Between 1963 and 1970 AFDC became increasingly attractive as welfare payments rose faster than spendable earnings and the AFDC rolls grew about 20 percent annually. Increased administrative curbs on overpayments or inappropriate payments, plus the fact that there are more AFDC adults per family and more are working, have kept payments per recipient relatively stable.

In 1978 a mother with one child would have had to make a considerable work effort in many states to equal AFDC benefits. A mother with three children generally would have had to work one and one-half times as much. For example, to equal California's AFDC benefits a mother with one child would have to work over 12 full days out of an average of 22 work days per month at $2.90 an hour—before taxes; a mother with three children, 18 days. In New York a mother with one child would have had to work more than 14 days; a mother with three children, over 20 days. In Ohio a mother with one child would have to work 8 days; a mother with three children, more than 12 days. Any income or Social Security taxes and work expenses would require additional days of work

In many cases a mother can benefit not only from AFDC cash payments but also from food stamps—which increase her purchasing power at the supermarket. Taking into account both AFDC and food stamp benefits, federal income and Social Security taxes, and modest work expenses, it has been estimated that a family of four had to earn over $5,800—$2.90 for 40

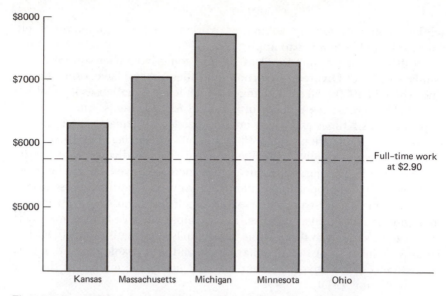

Figure 18-1 Earnings needed to equal AFDC and food stamp payments in selected states, 1978. (Source: U.S. Department of Health, Education and Welfare, *President Carter's Proposal for Welfare Reform,* May 23, 1979 (revised June 6, 1979), p. 24, table 1.) Note: Benefits are for a family of four; earnings are net of federal income and social security taxes and modest work expenses.

hours a week for 50 weeks a year—in a number of states to equal welfare benefits (Figure 18-1).

Additional benefits would further increase the level of wages needed to equal welfare benefits. As previously mentioned, many welfare families also benefit from Medicaid—which pays doctor and hospital bills. Some also live in public housing—which subsidizes their rent. An increase in family size would act similarly to boost welfare benefits and the level of earnings needed to equal them.

To determine eligibility for AFDC, states specify "standards of need" for various family sizes. As the standard is increased, more families fall short of it and hence are eligible for assistance. However, states are not required to pay in full what they designate as the full standard. In July 1978, for example, only 26 states and Puerto Rico paid 100 percent of needs and 2 states paid less than 50 percent.

The amount of income disregarded in calculating assistance payments has become increasingly important. Since mid-1969 states have been required to exempt earnings of $30 each month, plus one-third of all additional income and work expenses, in determining an AFDC family's needs. States that pay benefits below the standard of need may elect to disregard part or all earned income up to the needs level. States are also required to exempt full earnings of a child who is a full-time student or a part-time student not working at a full-time job. In addition, several states have adopted a provision that permits earnings of some children in any family to be disregarded in determining eligibility. Because the disregards now in effect apply only to families already receiving AFDC, they will not add more persons to the rolls; however, they do allow many recipients to remain who otherwise would have been disqualified.

THE REVOLVING DOOR

There is little opposition to paying public assistance to the disabled, blind, and aged. Few of these people could work even if jobs were available. By contrast, most heads of AFDC households are of working age and without physical handicaps, including women with school-age children and unemployed male family heads eligible under provisions offering assistance to such families in 26 states, Guam, and the District of Columbia. As the number of AFDC recipients has increased, so has the proportion of those on welfare who could be supplementing their income through employment or could leave relief rolls altogether.

The distinction made by the Social Security Act between those who can support themselves and those who cannot has been challenged, as work and welfare are closely intertwined. AFDC family heads need not make an all-or-nothing choice but may select the best combination of the two.

Contrary to common misconceptions, welfare recipients are not unable or unwilling to work, nor do they languish on the rolls forever. AFDC turnover is high as many families join and leave the AFDC rolls. In recent years close to 50 percent left within a year.[2] Changes in the earnings of family members are prominent among the reasons for opening and closing cases. Families headed by men tend to go on welfare because of loss of jobs; women tend to join welfare rolls because of loss of support due to divorce, desertion, or husband's illness. Moreover, about one current welfare family in three had previously received assistance, some more than once. It is probably not an overstatement to suggest that for certain socioeconomic groups receipt of public assistance at some time is a normal occurrence.

Nor is it true that AFDC recipients avoid work. In recent years a substantial and increasing proportion of welfare mothers was consistently in the labor force:

	1961	1969	1973	1977
Total in labor force	19%	20%	28%	29%
Employed full time	5	8	10	8
Employed part time	9	6	6	6
Unemployed	5	6	12	15

A closer examination of these data reveals wide variation among states. A 1977 survey reported 14 percent of AFDC families had some income from earnings; state rates ranged from 5 percent in West Virginia to 41 percent in Missouri. An estimated 40 percent of AFDC mothers worked at least part of the year, and many more may have worked without reporting their earnings to the authorities.

Not until the 1960s was there any significant change in the structure of the AFDC program. But, as the burden of the rolls rose, as the welfare population became less "deserving," and as the AFDC-UP component allowed relief for the first time for employable men, public assistance for dependent children came under increasing criticism. Moreover, few married women, and especially mothers, were in the labor force when the Social Security Act was passed. But in the succeeding four decades AFDC outlays continued to rise while a growing proportion of wives and mothers in all income levels were entering the labor force, as discussed in Chapter 5. The work force participation rate for mothers jumped from 9 percent in 1940 to 50 percent in 1979, including one of every three mothers with children under six. Exempting welfare mothers from employment when two-fifths of all married mothers were working no longer seemed justified.

THE EMPLOYABILITY OF WELFARE MOTHERS

The public debate dealing with AFDC frequently has been concerned more with rhetoric than reality, focusing on whether they *should* work, and failing to recognize that work and welfare are not mutually exclusive. The ability of welfare mothers to enter the labor market and earn some money has been confused with their ability to achieve complete economic self-support.

Employability is a complex balance of economic, social, and psychological factors. The presence of young children is the most obvious barrier to the employment of most welfare mothers and one that normally figures prominently in surveys of barriers to their employment. Even though it is increasingly acceptable for mothers to leave their children in another's care while they work, the limited supply of day-care facilities may be a severe constraint.

Over one-third of welfare mothers in 1977 had a child under 3; another 23 percent had no child under 3 but one under 6; 40 percent had only 6- to 17-year-old children. This means that 56 percent of the mothers probably needed full-time, year-round day care if they were to find steady employment.

According to Department of Health, Education, and Welfare estimates, the total capacity of licensed day-care centers and family day-care homes in 1977 was about 1,200,000. In the same year there were 2.7 million AFDC children under 6 (who required full-time care if their mothers worked) and another 2.7 million between 6 and 12 (who presumably needed part-time care). Licensed facilities fall far short of being able to accommodate the children of welfare mothers. And, of course, over 5.6 million working mothers with children below age six are competing for existing facilities.

Largely because the potential demand is far greater than the available supply, organized child care facilities have been frequently considered crucial for the employability of welfare mothers. Emphasizing the scarcity of licensed child-care facilities, however, may divert attention from the ability of these mothers to locate such services on their own. A woman's willingness to bear the costs of leaving her child(ren) depends largely on the expected benefits of doing so, especially on the potential earnings.[3] A survey of mothers in ten cities found that seven in ten mothers "said they could make 'arrangements' to work if a good job were available."[4]

The problem of dependency is less one of the lack of jobs or of child-care services than the lack of *good* jobs. Even if welfare mothers were not limited in their labor force activity by child-care, health, and other problems, their earnings ability would be quite limited.

By virtually every available criterion, welfare mothers are concentrated in the most unfavorable occupations, and their job status is likely to deteriorate in the future. About a quarter of all AFDC mothers had never been employed. Only 2 percent of those who were ever employed were professional, technical, or managerial workers, and less than a quarter were clerks, salespersons, craftsmen, or operatives. About half had worked in private households, in other services, or in unskilled work. The unfavorable occupational mix of AFDC mothers is due in large part to deficient education. In 1978 over three-fifths of welfare mothers had not completed high school, compared with one-fifth of all persons 25 to 44 years of age.

In addition to the difficulties of child care, poor health, unfavorable occupations, and lack of education, nearly half of the welfare mothers must contend also with economic discrimination because of race. Although the AFDC rolls were predominantly white during the program's early days, by 1961 nonwhites comprised nearly half of the caseload. This proportion changed little over the next decade:

	1961	1969	1973	1977
White and Hispanic	51.9%	50.5%	48.7%	52.6%
Nonwhite	48.1	49.6	51.3	47.4
Black	43.2	47.5	47.6	43.0
Indian	1.6	1.4	1.1	1.1
Other	3.2	0.7	2.6	3.3

A final consideration is the structure of work incentives. The treatment of income earned by AFDC recipients is a crucial variable in the choice between, or combination of, work and welfare. The factors just reviewed provide an indication of the extent to which welfare recipients *can* compete for employment and earnings in the labor market. But in the absence of a work requirement, their decision to enter the labor force—whether they *will* compete—hinges on the incentives offered for work effort. The employability of AFDC recipients depends frequently upon the incentives offered for work.

WORK AND TRAINING FOR RELIEF RECIPIENTS

Beginning in the early 1960s, the federal government implemented a series
of work and training programs for AFDC recipients. These schemes alter-
nately promised economic independence for those on welfare and relief
from the welfare burden for the nation's taxpayers.

"Working-Off" Public Assistance

The presumption that AFDC recipients were "unemployable" and outside
the work force became untenable in 1961 when the federal government extended coverage to families headed by an unemployed parent. The need for
the new law was clear: because the original Social Security Act denied assistance to families headed by an able-bodied male, the whole family was
penalized if the father could not find employment. The presence of employable parents on relief prompted Congress, in 1962, to amend the Social
Security Act to subsidize employment programs for relief recipients; until
1962 all AFDC recipients were presumed to be outside the work force, and
public assistance funds could not be used to provide work. States were encouraged to adopt Community Work and Training (CWT) programs designed to offer work relief rather than handouts and hopefully also to help
recipients to achieve economic independence.

The purpose of this amendment was twofold: to allay public criticism
of relief payments to persons able to work and to create work-relief projects
that would train and "rehabilitate" recipients. "Working-off" relief was
justified as being better for the recipients' morale and providing useful
public services under safeguards to prevent exploitation or the displacement of regular workers. The formal emphasis of CWT on training and rehabilitation reflected the nascent movement in the early 1960s toward more
organized employment and training programs for the disadvantaged.

Although the 1962 amendments were hailed as a vehicle for encouraging work and training for persons on relief, the provisions of the law tended
to reinforce the more traditional social services associated with public assistance. Only 50–50 federal matching funds were provided for the administration of CWT projects compared with the 3–1 ratio (75 percent federal–25 percent state) to cover the costs of social services. Project sponsors
also had to contribute all of the costs of supervision, materials, and training
on CWT projects in addition to their regular matching share of public assistance. It was, therefore, not surprising that, in order to obtain the maximum federal contribution, most states and localities chose to expand "social
services" rather than set up CWT projects.

CWT projects provided little training that would improve the employability of participants. Nor did recipients have any monetary incentive for
participating in CWT. A consistent feature of all projects, which varied
considerably otherwise, was a prohibition on additional income for partici-

pants in return for work performed (other than work-connected expenses). Instead, participants were required to work-off the amount of assistance they received, usually at the prevailing wage for comparable work performed in the community.

Antipoverty Work and Training

The Economic Opportunity Act of 1964 expanded the CWT program. In addition to unemployed parents on relief, other needy persons, including single adults, were declared eligible. The program reached its peak enrollment of 71,000 in 1967. The additional funds allocated to this effort and the broadening of eligibility reflected an increasing realization that low national unemployment rates might not be sufficient to assure a job for everyone who wanted work. Even though unemployment dropped throughout the 1960s, certain groups continued to experience considerable joblessness. A basic tenet of the antipoverty effort was an attempt to reach out, even beyond the welfare rolls, to help persons who could not compete in the labor market—to remove the structural barriers to their employment.

The challenge to the sponsors of the work and training programs was to provide useful training and work for participants. This proved to be a formidable task; most enrollees had multiple handicaps and little attachment to regular work. While the enrollees' work assignments featured a certain amount of informal vocational instruction, the bulk of these assignments was limited to low-paying, unskilled occupations. This phenomenon was understandable in light of the trainees' limited skills and educational attainment. Furthermore, work experience assignments were limited almost exclusively to government agencies and nonprofit organizations, and few trainees were assigned to private employers.

Despite laudable goals of rehabilitation and uplift, the Work Experience and Training (WET) program remained primarily a work-relief and income maintenance program. Few participants moved on to become self-supporting through private sector employment. The limitations of the program's training and rehabilitative services were partly to blame, but of greater importance was the lack of incentives and the failure of participants to find jobs that paid above the poverty income level. There were some rewards for participation, however, because enrollees could receive the full amount of the state's minimum standard welfare payment and allowances for work-related expenses; but neither of these was available for former participants with private jobs. Without any "sticks" or "carrots," few chose to leave welfare rolls.

The Work Incentive Program

In an attempt to induce public assistance recipients to seek "worthwhile" employment, Congress enacted the Work Incentive (WIN) program, as part of the 1967 amendments to the Social Security Act. By providing work and training incentives, Congress affirmed again the interdependence of work and public assistance, even though the incentives left much to be desired.

Rather than including persons not on AFDC, WIN consolidated its target population by aiming only at public assistance recipients in order to stem the burgeoning welfare rolls. This strategy also assisted WIN administrators. Because clients already received income maintenance, there was less pressure to place them quickly; instead, more thorough training could be provided. Moreover, funds did not have to be siphoned off for maintenance payments but could be concentrated to increase employability.

During training, participants received $30 per month along with continued welfare payments and the social services needed for successful completion of training. Along with the inducements for participation to entice welfare recipients to enter training or to find work, WIN also featured a work requirement. Most adults in AFDC families were required to register with a local welfare agency for referral. But because registrations far exceeded available positions, a list of priorities was used to ration the flow in decreasing order of job readiness.

To make these persons employable WIN offered a wide range of services, presumably adapted to each individual's needs. These could include orientation, job tryouts, basic education and other prevocational training, institutional and on-the-job training, follow-up, and day care for children. In theory an employability development plan was to be developed for each participant, detailing the package of services appropriate to individual needs.

An ostensibly more ambitious program than its predecessors, WIN emphasized institutional training, including basic education and day care. But the appropriations did not match congressional rhetoric. Most WIN enrollees received either nominal instruction or no instruction at all, and many were provided little besides orientation and placement counseling.

Day care is a necessary ingredient and sometimes crucial to increase the employability of AFDC mothers. Meager day-care expenditures have limited program performance, although WIN has made more extensive provision for day care than earlier programs.

WIN underwent a major policy change after Congress enacted in December 1971 a series of amendments introduced by Senator Herman E. Talmadge of Georgia. The objective of the Talmadge amendments was to induce welfare recipients to seek gainful employment. The Talmadge amendments exempted from participation any person who was under 16 or attending school; ill, incapacitated, or aged; too remote to participate effectively; caring for another household member; caring for a child under six; or a mother in a family in which the father has registered. All other adults were required to register for work or training as a condition of receiving assistance. The amendments, too, specified that unemployed fathers be referred first; next in line were mothers who volunteered (regardless of

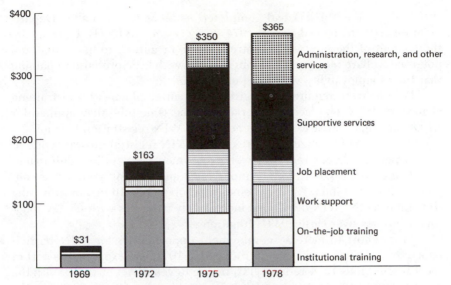

Figure 18-2   WIN expenditures emphasize on-the-job training and job placement instead of institutional training. (Source: U.S. Department of Labor.)

whether required to register); they were followed by other mothers and pregnant women under age 19; and, finally, came youths age 16 and over who were not in school, at work, or in training.

Dissatisfied with progress in moving welfare recipients into jobs, Congress mandated that the training components focus even more on job placement. The financial burden on states was eased as their share of training costs was halved from 20 percent to 10 percent. The Labor Department also decided to shift emphasis from training to direct placement, but the Labor Department experienced difficulty in arranging on-site training.

The complexion of WIN was drastically altered by these amendments (Figure 18-2). Funds for institutional training were cut considerably, while expenditures for on-the-job training and public service jobs increased. The largest component, however, was for labor market services—to place WIN enrollees in jobs, especially unsubsidized employment, and to provide follow-up services for 90 days.

In order to sweeten the prospects of employing welfare recipients, the 1971 Revenue Act provided a special tax credit to employers equaling 20 percent of wages paid to former WIN participants during the first 12 months. Employers in 1973 collected tax credits for 25,000 hires, but utilization of the program remained low for several reasons. Employers do not like the red tape, some harbor fears that the government will interfere with business operations, and some are prejudiced against welfare clients. Also, some welfare recipients do not want to be identified as such to employers because of the associated stigma.

Even before WIN II had completed its second year, Labor Department officials announced in mid-1974 its successor—WIN III. Once again, the content of the program was streamlined, or gutted, to get actual and potential welfare recipients into jobs quickly, with little pretense remaining that their employability was being upgraded.

Persons were required to register with an employment and training agency for WIN job placement services at the same time they applied for AFDC benefits from a welfare agency, with WIN registration becoming a condition for AFDC eligibility. Previously, WIN registration was required only of persons already receiving welfare payments, except for adult males.

This earlier exposure to the employment and training agency was coupled with a more intensive requirement for job search. In lieu of providing training directly, WIN developed increasingly close ties with CETA sponsors, who took over earlier WIN functions.[5]

In an effort to increase employment opportunities for WIN participants, the WIN tax credit, first introduced in 1971, was expanded as part of the Targeted Jobs Tax Credit (TJTC) by the Revenue Act of 1978. With the increased incentives authorized for 1979, a tax credit of up to $3,000 in the first year of employment was offered to private employers as an inducement to hire eligible participants, including welfare recipients. The effectiveness of the employer tax credit in stimulating employment for the economically disadvantaged is still not proven. Though 36,000 participants had utilized the WIN tax credit in 1978, there is doubt whether it was a significant factor in hiring decisions.

Program Operation and Assessment

WIN has suffered considerable attrition, as fewer participants remain at each successive stage. The problem is no longer as severe as it was in the first years of WIN, as policy directs more emphasis on employing welfare recipients. The initial stage of the funnel—determining who is appropriate for referral—is necessary to weed out persons with obvious problems. WIN staff were able to assess three-fifths of more than 1 million registrants in 1978, of which over 500,000 were found appropriate for referral. But the weeding out at later stages continued to whittle down the number of potential participants. Whatever the reasons for these leaks—that those referred were deemed unsuitable, failed to cooperate, or could not be accommodated—a great deal of wasted motion was involved. Of those found appropriate, about four of every five were placed into unsubsidized jobs directly or after intensive job search and counseling services. Less than 53,000 WIN participants in 1978 found unsubsidized employment after completing government sponsored employment and training programs.

On average, male participants fared better than women, largely because men had better work histories, fewer work impediments, and broader job opportunities. Those participating in WIN were far more likely to complete job entry and command higher wages than women. Women's comparative lack of success in finding employment through WIN stems from several reasons—including inadequate job skills and work experience, job discrimination, and a generally soft labor market for unskilled women workers. Because WIN personnel realized from past experience that women with many service needs have low potential for steady employment, they concentrated efforts on likelier candidates.

A woman's mandatory registration status was apt to change due to pregnancy or collapse of child care arrangements, and female volunteers could terminate participation in WIN at any time without fear of sanctions. A continuing problem confronting women in WIN is the lack of adequate child care facilities. In 1978, about 200,000 children were in WIN-funded child care arrangements with one-half of these arrangements in licensed day-care facilities.

Child care is costly. In 1978, a general estimate of annual cost of group day care meeting federal standards for three- to five-year-olds was $2,200. After-school and summer-care centers for children aged 6 to 13 cost an estimated $1,500 per year. These standards of acceptability and estimates of cost may be high; in many cases cheaper arrangements could have been made with relatives or friends—but the price tag would still have been substantial.

WIN's training and other services were inadequate to raise the earnings of employed graduates significantly above the minimum wage. In 1978 when the minimum wage was $2.65, the median hourly earnings of WIN recipients was $3.32. Clerical, sales, and services occupations, which attracted a disproportionate number of women, paid relatively low wages; semi-skilled and skilled manufacturing jobs, in which men were overrepresented, paid higher wages. These levels were generally sufficient to reduce welfare payments, but in a number of states even employed WIN completers were still entitled to partial benefits.

WIN has made special efforts to reduce employment barriers for female participants and open up job opportunities for them in better-paid, traditionally male occupations. Some success has been noted, but the small scale of these special projects still leaves a large wage differential between male and female participant graduates.

With the recent changes in WIN, public policy has virtually abandoned earlier rhetoric about helping welfare recipients to achieve financial independence, opting instead to move beneficiaries into any job as soon as possible. By reaching deeper into the barrel of welfare recipients and providing them less substantive services, WIN denies enrollees the opportunity to acquire skills that would contribute to sustained employability and an opportunity to escape poverty.

Whether inducements and training will prove effective depends on how easily the obstacles impeding those with higher employment potential can be overcome. Given the limited earnings potential of most AFDC recipients, the obvious strategy is to concentrate on those who are most employable and face the fewest obstacles to work. This means that male family heads, female heads with access to free or low-cost child care facilities, or those whose children no longer need day care would be served first.

This emphasis has been criticized as short-sighted. Some have argued that WIN should concentrate on helping young female family heads to encourage them to escape a life of dependency. According to this argument, long-run impacts should be considered secondary to substituting "workfare for welfare." Few would deny that a working family head sets a better example than one who lives on the dole, and it is probable that welfare begets welfare, but there is much debate about the degree of such effect. It has been demonstrated, however, that lack of education, poor diet, and crowded housing also generate dependency. There is a need, therefore, to balance the impact of WIN with income maintenance expenditures. The money used to create work, if a positive cost is involved, could be applied to helping young mothers, even if the per capita costs are higher than in helping older welfare recipients. Little is known about intergenerational effects of receiving welfare, or the impact of putting the family head to work and the children in day care. Without evidence those arguing for jobs at any cost cannot be proved wrong, and the price to be paid in substituting welfare for workfare must be resolved politically.

ALTERNATIVES FOR THE FUTURE

The CWT, WET, and WIN programs tried with scant success to solve the welfare problem by rehabilitating AFDC recipients. Despite these efforts, relief rolls—and criticism of the public assistance system—continued to grow.

One of the thorniest problems that all welfare reform proposals must confront is the overlap of cash and in-kind assistance. This overlap is inevitable under the current welfare structure with a large number of separate categorical programs, and in many cases it is desirable to the extent that it results in increased well-being for welfare recipients. Virtually all AFDC families nationwide are eligible for some medical benefits; three of every four receive food stamps and in some cases commodities; and one in seven lives in public housing.

This multiplicity of benefits tends to discourage AFDC families from seeking economic independence. First of all, as an AFDC family's earnings rise, it is confronted with a decrease in assistance of 67 cents for each dollar earned, above $30 plus work expenses, a social security tax of 6.65 percent on all covered earnings, federal income tax of 14 percent or more on income above $6200 for a family of four, and possible state income tax—all of which severely limit the net cash rewards for working. Moreover, a family that also receives food stamps loses another 30 cents for each dollar of earnings after certain deductions are made. And most perverse is the structure of Medicaid, whereby a family qualifies either for full benefits or for none—and can lose several hundred dollars' worth of benefits when its earnings exceed the eligibility level. Child-care assistance is deterring many single parents from getting off the dole and bringing back others who cannot pay the expenses of child care on their meager earnings.

Because of the multiplicity of benefits and cumulative tax rates, earnings were not always profitable to households receiving several benefits. In 70 percent of a sample of urban households, a dollar of earnings yielded no more than 32 cents in additional economic welfare.[6]

The work disincentive for AFDC-UP recipients also cannot be ignored. No matter what the earnings inadequacy of the head of household, the two-parent family loses total benefits if hours worked exceed 100 hours in any given month. Though aid to two-parent families is extremely limited in eligibility and benefit levels, unemployed parents under AFDC-UP suffer a heavy penalty for working.

Once off the welfare rolls, a former recipient does not qualify under the same income guidelines as during enrollment. Allowable deductions on earnings incur the possibility of higher incomes for welfare recipients than for families whose total income disqualifies them from assistance. The inequalities created by this system act as an additional incentive to stay on welfare in case of possible hardships in the future.

During the past decade, several schemes for reforming the welfare system have been proposed. Three broad criteria can be used to compare the wide variety of proposals: the extent of coverage and the levels of assistance; provisions made to enhance the employability of recipients (including work incentives and work requirements, provisions for training, and supportive services); and the costs involved. The proposals can be grouped into three basic categories: guaranteed income, or negative income tax; family allowances; and employment guarantees, including wage subsidies.

Income-Maintenance Strategies

The simplest and yet most comprehensive welfare proposal is the guaranteed income, or negative income tax. This would maintain an income floor for all persons by granting cash assistance to those whose earnings fall below that level. To encourage low-income workers not to drop out of the labor force, a percentage of earnings would be disregarded in calculating subsidies. Out of each dollar earned, the low-income family could keep some fixed amount without an equal reduction in its guaranteed minimum income.

Proposals vary widely as to the minimum floor and the percentage of income that could be retained. The lower the floor and the proportion of income retained as a work incentive, the lower the cost of the program. If the guaranteed income was higher and incentives were lower, costs would multiply and more people would be likely to drop out of the labor force and live off the dole. However, a lower floor would be injurious to those families whose head could not work and for whom incentives are meaningless. The basic problem of the guaranteed income is that it leaves such families at a minimum level of subsistence because their subsidy could not be raised without increasing payments to all those who work and supplement their subsidies.

Another method of providing cash assistance for the poor would be to pay all families with children a regular allowance to supplement their own income and meet some portion of the costs of child rearing. This proposal recognizes that the wages are based on productivity or on tradition, ignoring family size of the earner. While the principle of equal pay for equal work is desirable as a protection against discrimination based on color or sex, it ignores the differing needs of families and tends to deprive children in large families of basic necessities. The underlying justification for family allowances is that a child's well-being should concern society at large. Family allowances, accounting normally for a small part of the budget of even low-income families, are now paid in one form or another in most industrial nations.

The United States adopted an indirect and limited form of family allowance in 1975. The earned income tax credit (EITC) entitles families with dependent children and with annual incomes of less than $10,000, a refundable tax credit of 10¢ on each $1 earned for a maximum yearly benefit of $500. For incomes above $6000, the credit is gradually reduced and phased out when annual income reaches $10,000.

Family allowance programs are not a complete alternative to a guaranteed income because many poor do not have children; still family size is closely correlated with poverty and, depending upon their level, the allowances would lift many adults out of poverty along with their children. As with the guaranteed income, family allowances make no distinction based on labor force status. But a family allowance plan that is not needs-tested would reduce administrative costs and would interfere relatively little with work incentives. Because the program offers benefits to all children, it would probably find broader political support than any other alternative.

Gaining increasing attention, but less heralded than the guaranteed income, are proposals to guarantee employment and to subsidize wages. Large countercyclical job creation efforts under CETA have paved the way for similar endeavors targeted exclusively to welfare recipients. Immediate drawbacks are that only employable persons would benefit and that the government's role in the economy would be much increased. If the federal government became employer of last resort, for example, it would expand greatly both as an employer and as a provider of goods and services. Furthermore, unless wage levels in the public sector jobs were low, workers might be induced to leave private employment to accept public employment. But low wages would not lift many, especially large families, from poverty. Similarly, wage subsidies would assist only the employed and might result in serious distortions of the market mechanism.

Combining Work and Welfare

Crucial to welfare reform is to design a plan that would induce the needy to work while giving due consideration to the needs of long-term unemployed and unemployable poor. In August 1969 President Nixon proposed such an approach in the Family Assistance Plan (FAP). If passed it would have established a guaranteed minimum income for all families with children throughout the nation. In addition to the traditional clients of public assistance, FAP would have included almost 1.3 million families whose head worked full time, year round and another 650,000 families whose head worked substantially during 1969 but remained in poverty.

The plan would have doubled the number of persons eligible to receive assistance and income supplements. The purpose of boosting work incentives, expanding training, and providing day care was to replace welfare with workfare. The intent was to avoid greater outlays in the future and to arrest the growth of public assistance by moving all those able to work off welfare rolls and onto payrolls.

Congress did not adopt FAP and President Carter revised the welfare reform issue in 1977 under the Program for Better Jobs and Income (PBJI). The Carter plan dealt more directly than FAP with the lack of job opportunities for welfare recipients by recommending the creation of 1.4 million jobs earmarked for WIN participants, coupled with other changes designed to increase work effort. PBJI also proposed a major overhaul of the welfare system, combining AFDC, Supplemental Security Income programs and food stamps into one administrative system, and adding 2 million persons to the recipient list.

The Carter plan, like FAP, attempted to eliminate the anomaly of welfare recipients receiving higher incomes than those who work regularly at low wages or intermittently. By establishing minimum standards on a nationwide basis, the welfare reform bill would have significantly decreased the fragmented provision of public assistance. Similarly, by reducing interstate differentials, it would have diminished incentives to move to areas offering higher levels of assistance.

The Carter proposal presented a different set of drawbacks. In attempting to put more welfare recipients to work, the issues raised under WIN become more critical. Are private sector jobs available? If not, is it worthwhile to subsidize employment? Are the high costs of day care, training, and subsidies justified? The answers to these questions are not clear cut.

Many people feel that jobs are available for those who really want to work. They point, for instance, to the unfilled needs for domestic workers in most upper-class neighborhoods or to openings for dishwashers. In fact, however, such jobs are limited in number, pay, and accessibility. Graduates of WIN who find jobs usually earn little more than the minimum wage, and frequently these jobs offer little opportunity for upward mobility. But even dead-end jobs are in limited supply, and if those welfare recipients who are not now seeking work were to find jobs, the job shortage might become even more acute.

A more incremental approach to welfare reform was embodied in the proposed Social Welfare Reform Amendments of 1979 (SWRA). Taking one more step toward a guaranteed income for all poor families with children, the bill proposed changes in benefit levels and eligibility criteria that would reduce inequalities in the present system providing for a minimum support level for combined AFDC and food stamp benefits equaling 65 percent of the poverty threshold income in every state. In addition to making AFDC-UP mandatory in every state, the proposal would have qualified four member families with a monthly income of less than $500 to receive assistance. Also, families currently not eligible for assistance would be allowed the same deductions in earnings as families already on the rolls.

The proposal for welfare reform was two-pronged. While taking steps to insure minimal adequate benefit levels and to reduce inequalities in the system, the administration favored providing jobs and training to welfare recipients. This would allow them to become self-sufficient or at least not completely dependent on welfare payments. Starting initially with a proposal that would have been close to guaranteeing jobs to all welfare recipients capable of work, the administration retreated to a less ambitious program that would provide work opportunities to only a portion of welfare recipients and potential recipients.

An integral part of the reform measure is the requirement that all WIN participants intensively search for unsubsidized employment with the assistance of WIN and CETA staff. A proposed increase in the tax credit on earned income, along with the stipulation that individuals employed in publicly subsidized jobs would not be eligible to receive assistance, was included as part of the plan anticipating that the criteria would act as additional inducements to find unsubsidized employment.

Advocates of the incremental approach argue that the more ambitious plans linking employment with welfare would eliminate many of the problems encountered by the early Nixon and Carter proposals by reducing the eligible population and minimizing disruptions in the present system. Though work disincentives would be reduced, work incentives, to a large extent, would be dependent on intensive job search requirements and job creation. Anyone turning down a suitable job offer would be temporarily disqualified from receiving further assistance or receive reduced benefits.

If passed, the incremental welfare reform approaches would make many improvements in the welfare system. However, these plans failed to commit adequate dollars for training and supportive services. Past experience suggests that employment opportunities for welfare clients are limited and, too frequently, will not bring families out of poverty.

The various proposals for welfare reform pose the additional problem of determining the minimum income floor and appropriate incentive formulas. These are critical because all low-income families, not just those on welfare, would be eligible. If the income floor were raised or the work incentives were increased, the cost of the program would be significantly magnified as those with a higher income became eligible for assistance and they retained a larger share of the guaranteed minimum. Payments to those who cannot or do not work could be raised only by increasing the subsidies to those who do work. Thus the welfare of those at the bottom would probably suffer because they could not be helped without vast increases in costs. But if the income floor were raised and work incentives were kept low, it is likely that persons able to work would be willing to remain in dependency.

Neither widespread combining of work with welfare, nor complete welfare dependency, is compatible with our work-oriented society. Nonetheless, provision for the needy and poor is now widely accepted in our society. A gamut of strategies has been proposed to reform welfare and almost all share the goal of making work more attractive than welfare. But while the present income security has fulfilled its immediate goal of providing for the needy, the score for this more structural reform is less than perfect.

Private employers and consumers will have to accept that if enough workers are to be attracted to the available low-skilled, dead-end jobs, the remuneration for the work must be substantially increased. The alternative is growing welfare rolls and taxes. Employing all the poor will inevitably be a costly endeavor to which the affluent majority will have to contribute in one way or another.

DISCUSSION QUESTIONS

1. "The passage of the Social Security Act of 1935 marked the end of *laissez faire*, and paved the way for the United States to become a welfare state." Discuss.
2. "The negative income tax is the most efficient and equitable means of dealing with the poverty problem in the United States. With such a scheme, most welfare programs would become unnecessary." Discuss.
3. "Inequality of family income is an inevitable characteristic of our economy." Discuss.
4. Do you agree with the charge that while WIN may open short-run jobs, it offers little in the way of training for permanent positions with potential for upward mobility?
5. "The myriad of social welfare schemes to alleviate poverty is not only costly, but is a disincentive to work. The only way to get people off of 'welfare rolls'

and onto 'payrolls' is to work through the market place by offering businesses tax incentives to hire disadvantaged workers most in need." Comment.

6. "It is undesirable to provide poor families with food, housing, medical care, and other 'in-kind' payments at cut-rate prices. When subsidies are desirable, the government should provide cash subsidies and allow people to spend them as they wish." Discuss.

7. "Rehabilitation not relief" has been an implicit and explicit credo in U.S. antipoverty efforts. It is largely this emphasis that has so intertwined employment and antipoverty efforts. To what extent are employment and training policies and programs useful as antipoverty tools?

8. Our present welfare system has been described as a mess. Outline and evaluate the elements of a plan needed to reform the system.

9. Summarize what you believe are the salient facts concerning the impact of welfare upon labor force behavior and sketch your favorite scheme for reducing conflicts between work and welfare.

10. A significant phenomenon of recent years has been the increasing overlap between the wage structure and the benefits available from public assistance programs. What are the reasons for this development? What do you see as the consequences? Appraise the political prospects and potential effectiveness of proposals designed to deal with this phenomenon.

Notes

1. American Enterprise Institute, "The Administration's 1979 Welfare Reform Proposal" (Washington, D.C.: 1979), p. 20.

2. Sar A. Levitan, *Work and Welfare in the 1970s* (New York: The Ford Foundation, 1977), p. 34.

3. Sar A. Levitan and Karen Alderman, *Child Care and ABC's Too* (Baltimore: Johns Hopkins University Press, 1975), pp. 26–29.

4. Andrew K. Solarz, "Effects of Earnings Exemption Provision on AFDC Recipients," *Welfare in Review* (January–February 1971): 19.

5. U.S. Department of Labor and U.S. Department of Health, Education and Welfare, "WIN: 1968–1978; The Work Incentive Program, Ninth Annual Report to Congress" (Washington, D.C.: GPO, 1979), p. 6.

6. Joint Economic Committee, Subcommittee on Fiscal Policy, *Studies on Public Welfare*, "Additional Materials for Paper No. 6: How Public Welfare Benefits Are Distributed in Low-Income Areas" (Washington, D.C.: GPO, 1973), p. 109.

Chapter 19
Combating Discrimination
in Employment

Many black and other minority workers are situated in lower occupational positions and more frequently earn lower incomes than whites. They also incur higher unemployment rates and have lower labor force participation rates than whites. Moreover, they suffer disproportionately from long periods of unemployment. The causes of minority economic disadvantages clearly are deeply rooted in social and economic institutions that cause them to be at the end of the line when it comes to obtaining jobs.[1]

Overcoming the complex constellation of forces causing many minorities to be economically disadvantaged will require a variety of programs, the most obvious of which are measures to combat overt discrimination. The chapter will analyze these measures.

LEGAL AND ADMINISTRATIVE REMEDIES

Since World War II, enforceable laws against racial discrimination have been passed in all states except Alabama, Arkansas, Louisiana, Mississippi, and North Dakota. Generally, these laws are administered by part-time commissioners who ordinarily have powers to: (1) receive, investigate, and pass on complaints; (2) use conferences, conciliation, and persuasion in an effort to resolve complaints; (3) conduct public hearings, subpoena witnesses, and compel their attendance under oath as well as requiring the production of records relating to matters before the hearings; (4) seek court orders enforcing subpoenas and cease-and-desist orders; and (5) undertake and publish studies of discrimination.

Before the Civil Rights Act of 1964 blacks also used the courts to overcome discrimination in employment, although most court cases dealt with unions because, in the absence of statutes or nondiscrimination clauses in collective bargaining contracts, employers had no legal obligation not to discriminate. However, unions acquired legal rights and duties as a result of the National Labor Relations and Railway Labor Acts. Specifically, the Supreme Court ruled that the Constitution imposed upon unions, which acquired the privilege of exclusive bargaining rights, the duty to represent all members of the bargaining unit fairly. Aggrieved minorities have, therefore, brought legal action for injunctions and damages against discriminating unions. Moreover, in the 1964 Hughes Tool case the National Labor Relations Board (NLRB) held violation of the duty of fair representation to be an unfair labor practice, giving aggrieved minorities a measure of administrative relief because they can file charges with the NLRB instead of with the courts.[2]

The Civil Rights Act

Title VII of the 1964 Civil Rights Act outlawed discrimination on the basis of race, color, religion, sex, or national origin in hiring, compensation, and promotion. The law applied to all private employers, employment agencies, and labor organizations employing or serving 25 or more persons; an Equal Employment Opportunity Commission (EEOC) was created to enforce its provisions. Initially, this commission's role was limited to information gathering, mediation to encourage voluntary compliance, and "friend-of-the-court" legal support in antidiscrimination suits brought by others. Amendments in 1972 extended coverage to smaller organizations (15 or more people) and to state and local governments, government organizations, and educational institutions. More significantly, the EEOC was empowered to act as a plaintiff bringing civil actions in federal court seeking remedies on behalf of those who had suffered from discrimination. The 1972 amendments also shifted functions from the civil rights division of the Justice Department to the EEOC. Title VII initially had authorized the Attorney General to bring suit against respondents referred by EEOC after it had been unable to obtain voluntary compliance.

The basic compliance procedure remained unchanged throughout the period prior to March 1972, when the expanded powers became law. However, as court decisions broadened the definition of discrimination and the employers' liability for such acts, the EEOC gained leverage. In 1971 the Supreme Court ruled (*Griggs* v. *Duke Power Co.*) that Title VII "proscribes not only overt discrimination but also practices that are fair in form, but discriminatory in operation."[3] Preemployment tests that were not job related were ruled illegal, since arbitrary achievement tests were more likely to exclude blacks and other minorities. The precedent was expanded to include other job requirements that were not business necessities. For example, a company's policy of refusing to employ people with a number of arrests, but no convictions, was held to be discriminatory because blacks are statistically more likely to be arrested than whites.[4] More significantly, a landmark case in 1971 (*Robinson* v. *Lorillard Co.*) established the principle of monetary relief in class action cases.[5] This led some employers to reevaluate their potential liability to a class of employees that might be awarded damages by a court, and to opt for settling grievances out of court. The combination of EEOC's new potential for pursuing class actions, along with the standing of private groups of plaintiffs to obtain substantially greater levels of monetary relief, caused considerable concern among employers.

Many who feared conciliation activities might be abandoned in favor of litigation became much more amenable to the former. In 1973 the American Telephone and Telegraph Company (AT&T) signed a consent decree providing $15 million in restitution and back pay for several classes of female employees and a $23 million promotion package for women and minorities.[6] When the AT&T consent decree expired in January 1979, the federal government found the company in "substantial compliance" with its agreement to end job discrimination against women and minorities. Over the five years, AT&T had paid over $12 million in one-time back payments and $40 million a year in promotional adjustments. Nevertheless the government did not believe all equal employment opportunity problems of AT&T had been forever put to rest. In particular, it was noted that (1) women had been slow to move into certain skilled jobs that often require strenuous work, and that (2) minority women had made greater progress than minority men. The case illustrates the slow and complex process required to modify a major company's employment practices.

The increasing number of EEO complaints during the first half of the 1970s caused a growing backlog of cases reaching over 100,000 by 1977. Improved management procedures and more resources instituted in that year reduced the backlog by 41 percent by October 1979.

Most of this improvement, which was the first permanent backlog reduction in the EEOC's history, came as a result of the commission's new charge-processing system which permitted rapid "no fault" resolution of complaints during the early stages through negotiations between EEOC representatives, respondents, and complainants. This new procedure also caused the remedy rate for new cases to increase from 14 percent to 52 percent.

More importantly, the agency's administrative reorganization led to establishment of an Office of Systemic Programs (OSP). This unit specializes in systemic or pattern-and-practice charges of discrimination covering entire facilities or company-wide policies. This affects the employment of large numbers of persons, compared with the individual complaint process. By early 1980 almost 100 systemic charges had been filed against employers charging discrimination on the basis of race, sex and national origin. These actions reflect EEOC's increased effort where the potential exists to open more employment opportunities for persons and groups protected by Title VII.

THE CONSTRUCTION INDUSTRY

The civil rights movement's assault on racial employment practices in the construction industry increased in intensity during the 1950s and 1960s, when black employment opportunities were declining in major Northern metropolitan areas. In a number of cities coalitions of black organizations, formed especially for that purpose, closed construction projects through demonstrations in order to press their demands for more jobs for black workers.

Simultaneous programs were launched to increase the supply of black construction workers to fill jobs once they opened up. One of these efforts was a program to provide assistance for black contractors, who have traditionally been unable to acquire sufficient labor and capital resources and technical competence to perform large-scale commercial and industrial projects.[7] Organizations of black construction workers also were formed in a number of cities to challenge the building trades unions.

The Apprenticeship Problem

Civil rights leaders have concentrated on apprenticeship programs because they lead to good jobs in the skilled trades and because there have been very few blacks in them, in part because few black youngsters attempted to enter apprenticeship programs before the 1960s. Moreover, the craft unions' recruitment patterns excluded most black youngsters from any opportunity to enter the system. Blacks also have been disadvantaged in meeting the qualifications for entry into apprenticeship programs. Many programs require a high school diploma or GED, and not only does the education level of nonwhites still lag behind that of whites, but many blacks have been handicapped by what Kenneth Clark calls "the massive inefficiency of the public schools where the masses of Negroes go."[8]

In 1963 Secretary of Labor Willard Wirtz approved new federal apprenticeship standards designed to "provide full and fair opportunity for application." These regulations had limited impact for a variety of reasons, but basically it was because few blacks applied for or could meet the qualifications and testing procedures.

In addition to the federal regulations, apprenticeship programs are subject to Title VII of the Civil Rights Act of 1964, the National Labor Relations Act, government contract clauses (which require observance of the Bureau of Apprenticeship Training's (BAT) apprenticeship regulations as a condition of compliance with the executive orders), and various state apprenticeship regulations and equal employment opportunity laws.[9]

Legal sanctions have not been especially successful, although they have perhaps had the effect of creating among apprenticeship sponsors a climate conducive to change; apprentice standards and programs have raised their qualifications. The possibility of sanctions also seems to have strengthened "voluntary" compliance programs. Although sanctions have been used very rarely (because relatively few formal written complaints have been lodged against discrimination in apprenticeship training and because discrimination is difficult to prove), antidiscrimination agencies have succeeded in making investigations that have clarified the extent of black participation in apprenticeship programs and have focused attention on some of the problems involved in increasing the number of black apprentices.

The limitations of legal sanctions led to the creation of apprenticeship information centers to give information about apprenticeship programs and outreach programs to recruit, tutor, and place apprentices. These programs were discussed in Chapter 10, so that one need only note here that they were fairly successful in increasing the number and proportion of minority apprentices. Successful outreach programs have been operated primarily by the Recruitment and Training Program (the RTP was formerly the Workers Defense League), the National Urban League, Building Trades Councils of the AFL-CIO, the AFL-CIO Human Resource Development Institute, and other local organizations in some places. Largely as a result of these outreach programs, the proportion of all apprentices who are members of minority groups has increased steadily since 1960 from only 2.5 percent to 8 percent in 1969, and 18.2 percent in 1978.

Although apprenticeship outreach programs have been more successful than any other approach to this problem, it remains to be seen whether they can cause the kinds of changes throughout the country that will replace institutionalized discrimination with institutionalized equal opportunity. So far, however, they have demonstrated the importance of a comprehensive approach to recruiting and preparing black youngsters for apprenticeship programs. Moreover, this approach has demonstrated its effectiveness in getting blacks into other jobs more effectively and at lower costs.

QUOTAS AND PREFERENTIAL TREATMENT

Various programs to increase black employment opportunities in the construction and other industries have raised the highly controversial legal and moral issue of quotas and preferential treatment. To date, the Supreme Court has not fully resolved the issue, but in two major rulings in 1978 and

1979 held that at least some situations permitted preferential treatment on the basis of race in medical school admissions and company-sponsored apprenticeship training.[10]

As yet the high court has not squarely faced a situation of preferential treatment in the absence of any findings or suggestions of improper employer conduct. In each instance where it has ruled, the order was specific and narrowly drawn. For example, in the *Bakke* case, a majority concluded that the University of California had illegally practiced reverse discrimination by denying admission to Allan Bakke, a white.[11] At the same time, however, the Court ruled that race could be taken into account as a factor in the medical school's special admissions program.

Government policy over the past decade reflects the belief of agency officials and civil rights leaders that progress in eliminating employment discrimination requires compensation for past discrimination against blacks and other minorities. The Supreme Court has, however, set some limits as to the practices considered compensable violations. Events that occurred before the effective date of Title VII, July 2, 1965, and the present effects of bona fide union seniority provisions that may somewhat perpetuate prior discrimination do not constitute unlawful behavior by employers or labor organizations. Many unions and employers continue to distinguish between providing equal opportunity, their statutory obligation, and preferential treatment, which they continue to resist on the grounds that such programs discriminate against white workers and cause inefficiency.

Affirmative action plans have been judicially sanctioned for the past decade where exclusionary practices were found to have kept blacks and other minority workers out of job opportunities. The first major cases were in construction, but the legal principle is now well established in all areas of employment.

An early legal battle that contributed to resolution of this issue revolved around Labor Department efforts to impose local area affirmative action plans covering government construction contracts. The Philadelphia Plan was challenged by local building contractors, but upheld by trial and appellate courts.[12]

Similarly, construction craft unions in New York City, Ohio, New Jersey, Seattle, Washington, and many other locations were ordered to admit and train minority group members. In fact, Justice Brennan, writing for the majority in the famous *Weber* reverse-discrimination case in 1979, said: "Judicial findings of exclusion from crafts on racial grounds are so numerous as to make such exclusion a proper subject for judicial notice."[13]

The case arose out of a 1974 agreement between the Steelworkers union and Kaiser Aluminum & Chemical Co. that set up training programs to teach unskilled production workers the skills necessary to upgrade into craft jobs at the Gramercy, Louisiana plant. To help overcome the historic absence of black craft workers in that area, Kaiser set aside fifty percent of the training slots for blacks.

Admission to the program was by seniority, from each list by race. Brian Weber, a white man, sued because this system resulted in his nonselection for training while several blacks with less overall seniority were admitted.

The 5–2 decision (two justices not participating) states that:

> Congress did not intend to limit traditional business freedom to such a degree as to prohibit all voluntary, race-conscious affirmative action. . . . the Kaiser-USWA plan for the Gramercy plant falls within the area of discretion left by Title VII to the private sector voluntarily to adopt affirmation action plans designed to eliminate conspicuous racial imbalance in traditionally segregated job categories.[14]

Of course, what many people fear is that quotas and preferential treatment will cause blacks with less-than-minimum qualifications to be hired ahead of more-qualified whites in order to compensate blacks for past discrimination. Regardless of its short-run consequences, this kind of preferential treatment has serious long-run implications. No better statement of this point can be made than the following comment by the noted psychologist Clark:

> I cannot express vehemently enough my abhorrence of sentimentalistic, seemingly compassionate programs of employment of Negroes which employ them on Jim Crow double standards or special standards for the Negro which are lower than those for whites.
>
> This is a perpetuation of racism—it is interpreted by the Negro as condescension, and it will be exploited by them. Those who have been neglected and deprived must understand that they are being taken seriously as human beings. They must not be regarded as peculiar human beings who cannot meet the demands more privileged human beings can meet. . . . I suspect that the significant breakdown in the efficiency of American public education came not primarily from flagrant racial bigotry and the deliberate desire to create casualties but from the good intentions, namely, the sloppy sentimentalistic good intentions of educators to reduce standards of low-income and minority group youngsters. . . .[15]

SEGREGATED SENIORITY ROSTERS

Efforts to desegregate or integrate seniority rosters have involved many issues similar to those raised in the construction industry, as well as some that are unique. Indeed, in many ways the seniority question is more complex than the issues raised by minority participation in the construction industry. This is an important area because of the prevalence of job segregation, especially in the South, where institutionalized discrimination confined blacks to agriculture and the most menial or undesirable nonagricultural jobs, and because desegregation is essential to significant improvements in black employment patterns. The main issues raised by this question relate to whether blacks are to be compensated for past discrimination when seniority rosters are merged; whether company or plant seniority will be used for blacks alone or for blacks and whites; and whether such impediments as wage reductions, time limitations, and loss of pay will be permitted to deter integration.

Considerable attention was devoted to the segregated seniority issue by various government contracting committees during and after World War II. However, the impact of the contracting committees was limited by their inherent weaknesses and the fact that they concentrated on industries in which blue-collar employment was declining.

By the time of the Civil Rights Act, only token integration of blacks had taken place in major southern manufacturing plants. In addition to the factors previously mentioned, seniority integration was impeded by the fact that many blacks hired as laborers lacked the education and experience to move up. Conversely, many senior blacks would have been forced to accept lower wages and lose job seniority in order to enter the bottom jobs in previously all-white lines of progression. Because seniority is a jealousy guarded right and influences the profitability of industrial plants, it is not surprising that the terms under which seniority rosters are desegregated are such a controversial and complex issue.

An important pre–Civil Rights Act decision came in the 1959 *Whitfield* case, in which the U.S. Court of Appeals for the Fifth Circuit ruled that it was legal for unions to permit blacks to transfer to the bottom of the formerly all-white line of progression.[16] However, the Whitfield decision was, in effect, made obsolete by judicial interpretation in post–Civil Rights Act cases.

In the 1968 *Quarles* case departmental seniority at the Philip Morris plant in Richmond, Virginia, was held not to have been illegal per se. However, a system based on previous discriminatory practices was not legal, if employers "maintain differences in employee operations which were the result of discrimination before the Act went into effect."[17] In this case "the restrictive departmental transfer and seniority provisions . . . are intentional, unlawful employment practices because they are imposed on a departmental structure that was organized on a racially segregated basis." The court also concluded that Title VII of the Civil Rights Act "does not require that Negroes be preferred over white employees who possess employment seniority. It is also apparent that the Congress did not intend to freeze an entire generation of Negro employees into discriminatory patterns that existed before the Act." The court required the company to permit permanent black employees who had been discriminated against to transfer into formerly all-white departments on the basis of company seniority. However, the Quarles decision, which has been relied on widely in other cases, reduced the seniority rights of temporary black employees and did not disturb the departmental seniority system.[18]

The *Crown Zellerbach* ruling is viewed by many civil rights leaders as the next link in the historic chain of landmark decisions.[19] In this case, brought by the Justice Department under Title VII and Executive Order 11246, it was held that a departmental seniority arrangement at the company's plant in Bogalusa, Louisiana, violated the Civil Rights Act. As in *Quarles*, the court held that blacks who had been discriminated against could be promoted to jobs that they were qualified to perform on the basis of company and not departmental seniority. Moreover, the court held that "institutional systems or procedures which deny to Negroes advancement to jobs held by whites with comparable mill seniority and ability consistent with [the] employer's interest in maintaining [the] skill and efficiency of [his] labor force . . . must be removed." These institutional arrangements included prohibitions on promotions of more than one job slot at a time in instances when intermediate jobs did not afford training necessary for the next higher jobs or when employees had acquired the necessary training through temporary assignments; requiring black employees to enter the previously all-white lines of progressions below those steps necessary to provide training for the next higher jobs; limiting time intervals for promotion to periods longer than necessary to learn the job before promotion; and "deterring Negro employees from transferring to formerly all-white lines of progression by requiring these employees to suffer a reduction in wages and a loss of promotional security as a condition of transfer."

In the 1970 *Bethlehem Steel* pattern-and-practice case, a U.S. district court in New York found that a multiple-unit seniority did not itself violate Title VII if that system "was not and is not designed or motivated by racial discrimination." However, because of the company's discriminatory hiring and assignment practices, the seniority system "operates in such a way as to tend to lock an employee into the department to which he is assigned."[20]

In 1977 the Supreme Court ruled in *Teamsters* that only past-act discrimination was actionable, defining the latter as excluding present effects on bona-fide seniority systems entered into prior to passage of the statute. The court also held that the employees who suffered only pre-act discrimination are not entitled to relief, and that retroactive seniority cannot be awarded to a date earlier than July 2, 1965, the effective date of the Civil Rights Act.[21]

Thus, at the outset of the 1980s, the Supreme Court has sanctioned both retroactive remedies for employment discrimination based on race and sex, and placed an emphasis on present obligations of employers to hire women and minorities in areas where they have previously been underutilized. The basic tenets of equal employment opportunity are now firmly embedded in our legal system.

There can be little doubt that the legal remedies have played a role in combating discrimination, especially as these remedies have been strengthened during the 1960s and 1970s. However, legal procedures are incomplete tools in the fight for equality for a number of reasons. For one thing, under our system the evolution of the law and legal principles is a slow process. Experience to date suggests that there is little hope of avoiding a case-by-case approach, especially in the seniority cases, in which different racial histories, technologies, and skill requirements make it very difficult to generalize.

Legal sanctions, moreover, can do more to strike at overt forms of discrimination than they can to change the patterns that permeate social, political, and economic institutions. Hopefully, of course, measures that curtail overt discrimination also will initiate changes in the institutionalized patterns; but by generating conflict, legal approaches also can cause a hardening of racial positions, thus stiffening resistance to change.

Legal approaches also are limited because, in the economist's language, they operate only on the demand side of the problem and do little to change supply. Lowering the racial barriers does not ensure a supply of qualified people to take advantage of new opportunities. Positive approaches such as the outreach programs are required for this. Affirmative action programs, which tacitly recognize this, can change supplies where they are established by consent decrees or by voluntary programs. However, under Title VII, employers and unions can be compelled to stop discriminating against blacks, but they apparently cannot be compelled to recruit actively and to train them.

Experience with antidiscrimination programs seems to support the following conclusions:

1. Antidiscrimination measures are necessary but not sufficient to eliminate institutionalized discrimination in employment. These measures must be supplemented on the supply side by outreach programs. In the sociologist's language the legal remedies do not directly affect the institutions which tolerated, if not encouraged, discrimination in the first place.

2. While there is considerable apprehension by the collective bargaining establishment about the detrimental effects of the civil rights challenge, government agencies and courts seem, in general, to have strained to preserve traditional collective bargaining procedures. However, federal courts apparently are in no mood to permit subterfuges that perpetuate discrimination under the guise of legitimate business practices. Courts have ordered unions and employers to adopt measures to cure racial discrimination through reducing the unions' control of apprenticeship, referrals, and the determination of standards and qualifications.

3. The outreach programs suggest that collective bargaining can yield, however reluctantly, to demands for greater participation by minorities in rule making.

4. The establishment of fair and relevant qualifications and standards is essential to the resolution of many conflict areas in collective bargaining. Fair procedures for establishing standards and qualifi-

cations, with outside participation, would go a long way toward closing the credibility gap between the collective bargaining establishment and minorities and others outside the system.

5. The segregated seniority question is complicated by considerable diversity in technology and local realities. However, it will be difficult to continue practices that were designed to discriminate because of race and that deter job integration. Federal courts have preserved employers' rights to demand that upgraded workers be qualified and have not eliminated job or departmental seniority per se.

CONTRACT COMPLIANCE PROGRAMS

The Office of Federal Contract Compliance Programs (OFCCP) in the Department of Labor is responsible for enforcing equal employment opportunity and affirmative action requirements by federal contractors. Principal groups protected are minorities, women, handicapped workers, and disabled and certain other eligible Vietnam era veterans. In 1978, responsibility for all enforcement under Executive Order 11246 was consolidated into the Labor Department from eleven other federal agencies.

The contract compliance approach has several unique characteristics which enhance its capability to promote equal opportunity and affirmative action. First, OFCCP has the authority to initiate compliance investigations *independently* of discrimination charges. Routinely, a certain number of firms holding government contracts are selected for annual review, much the way that IRS monitors federal income tax returns.

The second distinguishing feature of contract compliance is that it places an affirmative action responsibility on federal contractors which goes beyond merely refraining from discrimination. This process also promotes systemic changes in contractor employment practices which have long-term effects on that employer and its workers.

Third, the contract compliance process relies upon administrative law in its enforcement proceedings, with resort to federal courts only when disagreement persists after an initial ruling by the administrative law judge.

Under Executive Order 11246, OFCCP investigates complaints which allege class or group discrimination by companies working for the federal government. In general, complaints of an individual nature are referred to the Equal Employment Opportunity Commission, which can also initiate charges independently. This practice is by mutual agreement with EEOC. Both individual and class complaints are investigated by OFCCP. When possible, complaints are investigated in the course of a compliance review to obtain maximum use of available resources.

During fiscal year 1979 OFCCP conducted more than 2,400 compliance reviews. At the end of December 1979, 403 affected classes were under investigation; of the 97 closed cases, two-thirds were found to be in favor of the complainants. In 1979 OFCCP obtained almost $9.3 million in settlements with 176 employers, excluding a $5.2 million settlement reached with Uniroyal, Inc. That award, made to 750 female employees, led to the reinstatement of Uniroyal as a government contractor. The firm, with at least $36 million in federal business, had been the largest employer in OFCCP's history to lose contract eligibility when it was debarred in June, 1979.

CONCLUSIONS ON MINORITY EMPLOYMENT

The causes of unequal employment opportunities and patterns are very complex and, therefore, will require that remedies be taken on many fronts. Antidiscrimination measures have an important role to play, but they are not sufficient to cause changes to take place. Tight labor markets alone will not solve the problem if discrimination and unequal access to education and training bar blacks from meeting job requirements. In the final analysis, all of these conditions coupled with special remedial programs such as the apprenticeship outreach programs seem to offer some chance for success.

Statistics on actions, successful settlements, and policies of the EEOC and OFCCP provide only some of the clues to their real impact. There may be, for instance, important spillover effects as employers change their practices in fear of government sanctions. Voluntary affirmative action efforts may also result from appeals to corporate consciences. If even small marginal changes are widespread, the impacts can be very beneficial for minorities.

DISCUSSION QUESTIONS

1. What do you interpret the term "affirmative action" to mean?
2. "Quotas and preferential treatment are an unfair means of increasing employment opportunities of minorities because they interfere with the efficient operation of labor markets." Comment.
3. Has the Civil Rights Act of 1964 lived up to its "landmark" status? Discuss.
4. The seniority system is one of the most important institutions for job security and the upward mobility of workers. Would you favor tempering the seniority system in order to compensate minorities for past discrimination?
5. What do you think would help the most in reducing employment discrimination:
   (a) More legislation?
   (b) Better enforcement of existing legislation?
   (c) Social and cultural changes that occur naturally over time?
6. Discuss the basic features of the AT&T consent decree. Do you think that this is a satisfactory solution to past discrimination practices? Why or why not?
7. Do you believe that the government should consider company personnel practices in awarding contracts?

Notes

1. Lester C. Thurow, *Poverty and Discrimination* (Washington, D.C.: Brookings Institution, 1969), chap. 12.
2. *Independent Metal Workers* (Hughes Tool Company), 147 NLRB 166 (1964).
3. *Griggs* v. *Duke Power Co.,* 401 U.S. 424 (1971).
4. *Gregory* v. *Litton Systems, Inc.,* 472 F.2d 631 (9th Cir. 1972).
5. *Robinson* v. *Lorillard Corporation,* 444 F.2d 791 (4th Cir. 1971), *cert. denied,* 404 U.S. 1006 (1971).
6. *EEOC* v. *American Telephone & Telegraph Co.,* 365 F.Supp. 1105 (E.D. Pa. 1973).
7. *Social and Economic Implications of Integration in the Public Schools,* seminar on manpower policy and programs, U.S. Department of Labor, Manpower Administration, Office of Manpower, Automation and Training (Washington, D.C.: GPO, 1964), p. 6.
8. Robert Taggart, *The Manpower System in the District of Columbia: At a Critical Juncture* (Washington, D.C.: National League of Cities–U.S. Conference of Mayors, March 1973), pp. 80–87.
9. Sar A. Levitan, William B. Johnson, and Robert Taggart, *Still a Dream* (Cambridge, Mass.: Harvard University Press, 1975), chap. 13.
10. *Regents of the University of California* v. *Bakke,* 438 U.S. 265 (1978); and *United Steelworkers of America* v. *Weber,* 440 U.S. 193 (1979).
11. *Regents of the University of California* v. *Bakke,* op. cit.
12. *International Brotherhood of Teamsters* v. *United States,* 431 U.S. 324 (1977).
13. *United Steelworkers of America* v. *Weber,* op. cit.
14. *United Steelworkers of America* v. *Weber,* op. cit.
15. Kenneth B. Clark, "Efficiency as a Prod to Social Action," *Monthly Labor Review* (August 1969), pp. 55–56.
16. *Whitfield* v. *United Steelworkers,* 263 F.2d 546 (5th Cir. 1959), *cert. denied,* 360 U.S. 902 (1959).
17. *Quarles* v. *Philip Morris, Inc.,* 279 F.Supp. 505 (E.D. Va. 1968).
18. Herbert R. Northrup, *The Negro in the Tobacco Industry.* (Philadelphia: University of Pennsylvania, 1970), pp. 78–80.
19. *United States* v. *Local 189, United Papermakers and Paperworkers,* 301 F.Supp. 906 (E.D. La. 1968), *affirmed,* 416 F.2d 980 (5th Cir. 1969), *cert. denied,* 397 U.S. 919 (1970). Also *Hicks* v. *Crown Zellerbach Corp.,* 49 F.R.D. 184 (E.D. La. 1968), 310 F.Supp. 536 (E.D. La. 1970), and 321 F.Supp. 124 (E.D. La. 1971).
20. *United States* v. *Bethlehem Steel Corp.,* 312 F. Supp. 977 (W.D. N.Y. 1970), *modified and remedied,* 446 F.2d 652 (2d Cir. 1971).
21. *International Brotherhood of Teamsters* v. *United States,* op. cit.

Chapter 20
Lessons from Employment and Training Programs

The Employment Act of 1946 declared it a responsibility of the national government to do something—it does not specify what—about seeing to the supply of employment opportunity. The Manpower Development and Training Act of 1962, the Economic Opportunity Act of 1964, and Title VII of the Civil Rights Act of 1964 all committed the nation to worry about the distribution of employment opportunity with special concern for those at the rear of the labor market queue. Amendments to the Social Security Act of 1967 were more concerned with getting people off welfare than with guaranteeing them opportunity. The Emergency Employment Act of 1971 was again concerned with the supply rather than the distribution of opportunity. The Comprehensive Employment and Training Act of 1973 was more concerned with who was to make decisions than with what decisions were made. Amendments to CETA have vacillated between the latter issue and temporary additions to the supply of jobs.

After some 20 years of experience, what lessons have been learned from employment and training programs?

DO EMPLOYMENT AND TRAINING PROGRAMS WORK?

That employment and training programs have survived the vagaries of economics and politics for two decades through wars and recessions, through the administrations of five presidents of sharply divergent philosophies, through substantial demographic shifts and dramatic changes in international relations must mean that either (1) they work and are retained because of their contributions, (2) they do not work but the problems are real so they are continued for lack of any better remedies, or (3) sufficient vested interest has been developed to protect them from political attack regardless of success. Whether or not the programs have been successful depends upon one's perception of their goals, the viewpoints of the evaluator, and what one is willing to count as success.

What Success for Whom?

Much depends upon the expectations and social philosophy of the observer. Paradoxically, one must look back to the earlier pre-1973 programs for evidence as to how well individuals and groups have been served by employment and training programs. By the very nature of its decentralization, CETA is extraordinarily difficult to evaluate.[1] Evaluation techniques are usefully divided between process and outcome evaluations and CETA evaluation has concentrated on the former. How many people of what personal characteristics were enrolled by what dates? What services were provided? Did performance correspond to plans? What proportion completed various components and how many were placed? Did public service funds merely replace appropriations the state and local jurisdictions would have made in the absence of federal grants? Answers to those questions have absorbed nationally sponsored evaluations. Local CETA prime sponsors have little interest in evaluation and what they have is also process oriented. How well have the various installations assigned the responsibility of service delivery fulfilled their tasks? Has their performance been in accord with their plans? Should they be refunded or should funds shift to other services and service deliverers? Outcomes can only be evaluated by long-term followup of treatment groups and comparison groups to test the incremental impact on employment stability, upward mobility, and annual income. For that type of evaluation, one must hearken back to the pre-CETA "categorical programs." These were national programs under federal responsibility which had to be defended as entities.

Despite the passage of years, there is still no consensus on the success of those programs. However, it is expectation rather than evaluation that is at fault. There is ample evidence that benefits exceeded costs for most enrollees in most programs.[2] On the average, people were brought from the lower reaches of poverty to its upper levels. Few were able to break through into the ranks of the nonpoor, but the majority were certainly more comfortable in their poverty. The reason was primarily the nature of the jobs available to the program completers. A full-time job at the federal minimum wage brought an income well below the poverty line for the urban family of four which was the norm among participants. In addition, nothing in the programs could make a permanent contribution to the alleviation of problems of housing, transportation, health, child care, or personal disorganization which might also stand in the way of employment success.

Thus for the social reformer out to build a new society or for those who took seriously the rhetoric of the crusade to eliminate poverty in the United States by its 200th anniversary, the results were disappointing. Those with instincts for tinkering at the social margins and who were satisfied with the finding that benefits exceeded costs by some small degree were prepared to defend the programs' results. For persons without overwhelming problems of child care, ill health, or alcohol or drug addiction, yet with sufficient family responsibility and income need to maintain them in entry level jobs, and who lived where private sector jobs were available, the programs were successful. A few experienced spectacular successes, primarily by becoming involved in program administration and rising in public agencies or consulting firms. The rest resorted to income maintenance programs, illicit income sources, or bare subsistence. Those were the results of MDTA and EOA funded services. There is no reason to think the results of CETA are any different. Those who had higher expectations have written off employment and training programs. Those with more modest expectations remain at the task of helping individuals step by step up a rickety ladder which is at least pointed in the right direction.

The Macroeconomic Impacts

Employment and training programs have now been in effect while unemployment rates ranged from 3.2 percent to 9 percent. There is no firm evidence that they have done anything to either restrain or reduce unemployment. Certainly everyone enrolled would have been either out of the labor force, unemployed, or employed at jobs less attractive to them than program enrollment. Just as an expansion of job opportunities attracts people from outside the labor force to compete with the unemployed, so does the availability of programs which offer either salaries or stipends. A direct correspondence between program enrollment and unemployment reduction is reasonable to assume but by no means proven. To the extent public service employment jobs are not a substitution for those local governments would have provided anyway (substitution, as discussed later in the chapter probably offsets about one-fifth of the PSE employment), employment is increased and unemployment is reduced to some lesser degree during the period that PSE slots are available.

Other programs can have little macroeconomic effect. They remove potential competitors from the job market during the enrollment period. Those which improve employability increase the recipients' postenrollment ability to compete for whatever jobs are available. In that sense, they are equal employment opportunity programs. But whatever competitive jobs the enrollees get are at the expense of those who would have otherwise held those jobs. That is the nature of a competitive society.

The strong public service employment emphasis of 1976–1978 and the youth enrollment and employment projects of the Youth Employment Demonstration Projects Act (YEDPA) after 1977 undoubtedly reduced overall unemployment for the period of enrollment. There is no reason to think that reduction will outlast the availability of program slots.

That does not mean that temporary public job creation is undesirable. In the unique conditions of stagflation, the traditional expenditure-increasing, tax-cutting, interest-rate-easing methods of recession fighting may no longer be available. Nothing among the causes of current inflation appears to emanate from the labor market, yet everything done to contain inflation impacts negatively on employment. Any public sector job creation tends to be inflationary in that incomes are paid without goods and services being placed on the market to buy with the added purchasing power. But that effect is minor beside the inflationary impacts of the budget deficits and easy money of the traditional tools.

Probing the Labor Market's Lower Margins

One clear lesson of the employment and training program experience has been the sponge-like nature of the labor market's lower margins. The whole New Deal period of the Great Depression passed without touching the lives of the primarily black, minority lower class. The pressures of all-out war were sufficient to involve nearly everyone. The applauded "Affluent Society" of the 1950s again ignored the fact that all were not sharing in that wealth.[3] Simple income statistics could identify 40 million people as of 1960 below an arbitrarily set poverty line. But it took employment and training programs seeking to enroll them to find out who and where they were and what the barriers to their successful employment were.

The Great Dichotomy

Out of that probing has arisen a basic issue never resolved after 20 years of program experience. When an individual or group suffers more than its proportionate share of unemployment and poverty, does the shortcoming reside in the individual or the group—that is, does the individual or group lack skill, experience, motivation, or some other prerequisite of employability—or are the labor market and its institutions biased against that individual or group? The policy implications are clear—if personal behavior is at fault, take action to change the people and if institutions are biased or ineffective, reform the institutions. The answer, obviously, is varying combinations of both. But what combination for whom and when? And how is it to be achieved? Earlier programs—MDTA and the Job Corps, for instance—opted for changing individuals. The Civil Rights Act of 1964 and job creation programs argued that institutions needed reform. CETA, it was hoped, would allow examination, diagnosis, and tailored and individualized prescriptions to emerge at the local level. That resolution has not come but awareness of the issue has had much to do with the formulation of the various service components which will be discussed later in the chapter.

The Nature of the Poverty Labor Market

The demand side for that dichotomy introduces the concept of the dual labor market, discussed earlier in Chapters 3 and 6. Clearly, some people are stranded in locations where there are no satisfactory jobs. Less frequently, there may be people unwilling to accept permanent employment. Whereas earlier it had been assumed that it was enough to ensure a sufficient quantitative supply of jobs, attending to the *quality* of jobs available is now recognized as being necessary. Evidence does not support the dual labor market hypothesis that those programs and services that attempt to change people can have little effect, though the institutions are probably more at fault than the people. Institutions often impose unnecessary barriers to employment through discrimination by age, sex, race, and more subtle factors and through recruitment, selection, and hiring practices unrelated to potential to perform the job. It is a rare person who does not want to be self-supporting and who cannot be used effectively in some kind of job. Nevertheless, people and systems are not as inflexible as suggested by the dual market thesis. Except for perhaps the native Americans on reservations, more members of demographic groups designated as difficult to employ "make it" than do not. For instance, twice as many blacks as whites suffer unemployment, but nine out of ten of the former who are in the labor force are working as are seven out of eight of the teenagers, who suffer triple the average unemployment. Even though institutions may pose the basic obstacles, most people can be prepared and supported to surmount those obstacles. Even though some people may be difficult to employ, a committed institution can absorb and use them productively. It may be more efficient to directly attack the basic causes, but it is not the only way.

THE USEFULNESS OF THE EMPLOYMENT AND TRAINING TOOLS

Out of the program experience has come the knowledge that, even under the best of economic conditions, there are still millions at the labor market's lower margins without adequate economic opportunity. Not only is more known now about who they are, but there is a greater familiarity with the nature of the barriers which bar them from successful labor market experiences. In seeking to overcome those barriers, a variety of program components have been designed and tested to become well-accepted components of an employment and training program package.

Outreach, Intake, and Assessment[4]

Outreach, intake and assessment were inherent needs in earlier programs but CETA has accentuated the need for at least the latter two. Outreach is rare despite its obvious relevance. Experience has demonstrated that there are those who are so isolated and alienated from the existing social and labor market institutions that they must be sought out and offered or convinced to accept human resources services and opportunities. But at most times and places the eligible persons who sought out the programs and applied for their services have exceeded the capacity of those programs. Outreach would have required rejecting eager applicants in order to seek out, at some expense, those not anxious to be served and this was rarely done. The exceptions to the general rule of applicants exceeding slots have been (1) programs offering no long-term gains beyond minimal income support (the news of who got what out of a program spreads quickly), (2) situations of overallocating funds to the wrong programs in rapidly expanding local economies, and (3) services so encumbered by red tape and deliberate hurdles that only those least in need can find their way through the maze.

A single program with broad eligibility and a range of services such as CETA requires some common intake point to see that the whole smorgasbord of services is considered as options for the individual applicant. To the extent that multiple programs and services are available to the same clientele, a common intake point facilitates coordination and minimizes gaps and duplications among services. CETA prime sponsors normally provide or contract for a common entry point but less progress has been made in providing unified and coordinated entry to WIN and to income maintenance and other programs available to the same populations.

If individualization of service under CETA is to be accomplished, assessment is a key. There is little advantage in a range of services unless there is some way of determining who needs what. Assessment is still at a rudimentary state but progress is being made. There has been a wholesale rejection of culturally biased tests, which is in itself progress. The current challenge is to replace them with assessment measures which can identify needs and predict results.

There are essentially three levels of assessment in employment and training programs. The first level simply involves determination of eligibility. To provide services to those who do not meet the admissions criteria is no loss to society but may bring down legal sanctions on the program operator. The second level of assessment cannot be avoided. As long as there are multiple services, eligible clients must be allocated to them. Random assignment or client choice are possible approaches but the basic concept of CETA entails something more. Most program operators have some criteria for deciding who should be assigned to what component.

Level three is the ideal of the assessment process—a diagnostic system for the individualization of services. Considerable progress has been made in designing and testing diagnostic tools for level one and level two assessments. Discussion of each is neither possible nor appropriate here. Only a few prime sponsors and other program operators have chosen to take the issue seriously but the progress they make will likely spread to others.

A critical controversy related to assessment is the role of the client in the process. Many by deliberation or default accept what might be called the "medical model." The patient is sick and they are the doctors to diagnose and prescribe treatment. Others reject this model with strong emotion. Their "humanistic model" assumes that the client is mature and capable of wise choice. In this model, the counselor acts as a resource to inform the client of the alternatives available for the client's decision. The rebuttal is that if the client were that wise, he or she would not be in trouble. Some form of joint decision will likely emerge from the conflict.

Classroom Education and Training[5]

Two overriding lessons have been learned from the training program experience: (1) no one now expects, as many did in 1967, a training program to reduce the overall rate of unemployment and (2) there are substantial numbers of people who can be prepared through training in some combination of basic education, coping skills, and job skills to compete successfully for jobs—if those jobs exist. Much has been learned of training methods and learning styles. The first lesson was that those with cultural and educational disadvantages could not be as successfully trained by the same institutions with the same methods as the more general population. Some institutions did change, and where they did not, skills centers were developed to specialize in the training of the disadvantaged. The latter did an impressive job of training but created another problem. The facilities were too often substandard in relation to the available postsecondary vocational-technical institutions, tending to stigmatize their enrollees and isolate them from the training mainstream. Better results seemed to occur when special services to the disadvantaged were provided within a more general training institution.

Those special services contributed as much to postsecondary vocational-technical training as those institutions did to the disadvantaged. Though not unique to or invented for training programs, a number of important innovations were developed and advanced through the programs: (1) prevocational orientation to help with personal problems and occupational choice; (2) on-site counseling, which involved intervention and client advocacy as well as self-discovery; (3) open-entry-open-exit training, which allowed a trainee to enter without prerequisite, move at his own speed, train in modular fashion, and leave with a salable skill even if he did not complete the full course; (4) the use of people with proved job and teaching skills but without necessarily having formal teacher education and teacher certification as instructors; (5) basic education integrated with skill training; (6) coupled institutional and on-the-job training; (7) on-site placement services, and (8) follow-up job coaching. It was also made clear that many only needed job skills accompanied by training stipends and could be referred individually and enrolled directly in regular vocational-technical courses.

Mistakes have been made and continue to be made. Training programs have tended to concentrate on those occupations for which turnover is high and training costs low, avoiding others having more promise for stability and income. These could guarantee a high placement rate and maximize the number of enrollees from any given budget—both understandable political objectives. However, higher cost alternatives might have proven more cost effective.

Training in institutional settings has been provided for occupations that are ordinarily learned on the job. Justification has been that disadvantaged workers needed the extra edge to compete with others who are available to the employer. In fact, vocational education in this country is usually designed to provide primarily entry-level training. Everyone at every level must ultimately learn on the job how to do the job. Only for a few can the work atmosphere and the full range of required tasks be simulated in the classroom or laboratory. A good guide would seem to be to consider what employers do when left to their own devices. For which occupations do they appear to consider OJT appropriate or preferable? For which do they customarily look to the schools? Every training style has its advantages and disadvantages, its benefits and costs. More careful study is needed of what works best for whom.

An alternative to the skills center under MDTA was the referral of individuals to regular postsecondary vocational and technical school programs. But to survive in that atmosphere, the enrollees had to have academic and personal skills equal to those of the regular students. To avoid the complications of operating separate institutions, CETA prime sponsors have gone over heavily to the individual referral approach. As a result, the better prepared appear to end up in skill training and are prepared for the labor market. The less well prepared are relegated to work experience programs where little improvement in their employability is possible.

The lessons learned from the training experience are summarized as follows: (1) Basic literacy is an essential prerequisite to employment in the United States, and techniques for teaching it to adults in conjunction with skill training had to be and have been developed. (2) Training is also useful and often essential to those whose work experience is unusually limited and for jobs for which employers expect some experience or exposure before hiring. (3) A variety of supportive services and a sympathetic but challenging atmosphere are necessary to train the really disadvantaged. (4) Training will be taken seriously when it is evident that it leads to attractive jobs but is a frustrating waste when it does not. A direct linkage to employment or a demonstrated high placement rate in desirable jobs is essential.

OJT and Apprenticeship[6]

Chapter 10 has explored OJT and apprenticeships as techniques of human resource development. However, it is worth some extra space to identify what was learned about them through manpower programs. It is difficult to analyze OJT in employment and training programs separately from subsidized employment. Employers are reimbursed for training costs or for some proportion of wage costs as an incentive to hire disadvantaged workers. Job placement rather than training has been the objective, and there has been little attention paid to the latter by administrators as long as the former occurred. Nevertheless, most jobs are learned on site, whether formally or informally, and either formal OJT or informal learning under the direction of a supervisor or a fellow employee must occur. The outstanding examples of on-the-job training have occurred where the program administrators have insisted on maintaining quality control to see that training occurred. Often these have been coupled with programs where classroom training alternated with OJT to the advantage of both employee and employer.

Employment and training programs have underwritten preapprentice training and coaching to prepare minorities for apprentice tests. Outstanding progress has been made, but in most cases the target has been entry to apprenticeship rather than the content of training. Preapprenticeship and apprentice outreach efforts have now expanded to the point that they threaten to swamp the capacity of existing apprentice programs. The challenge now is to expand that capacity.

Work Experience Training[7]

Among the pre-CETA manpower programs were several which promised work experience training for both youth and adults. It was assumed that just the discipline of showing up to work, being part of a work crew, and doing something useful would make an enrollee more employable. Despite some success, it was difficult to make the experience realistic and too often the program only became an excuse to keep the enrollees off the street and provide them money.

CETA emerged on the eve of the most serious recession since 1940. With jobs in short supply, the tendency was to stack the overwhelming number of applicants into work experience programs with little attempt at quality control. However, a few prime sponsors took work experience seriously, coupled it with remedial basic education programs, supervised it carefully, and insisted on discipline and productivity. The lesson was that work experience really could be training, could provide realistic job experiences and a reputation for productivity, and could lead to high placement rates and good job retention and advancement. But this was only possible if preparation, counseling, discipline from sympathetic but firm supervisors, and productivity were maintained.

Subsidized Private Employment[8]

President Lyndon B. Johnson in 1968 personally launched a major effort to persuade employers to hire minority and disadvantaged workers. The timing was propitious. Businessmen had seen their cities burning around them in the riots of the late 1960s. Yet the Vietnam War was at its peak and unemployment was at its lowest since the Korean conflict. They needed new labor sources. The National Alliance of Business was launched to promote the concept. The Labor Department was assigned to contract to pay the added costs of training disadvantaged workers. The majority of employers chose to hire without subsidy.

The concept was having promising results when the beginning of a recession removed one of the main stimulants to the program. Subsidized private employment, except for limited subsidized OJT, disappeared from the lexicon. An overdose of public service employment in 1976–1978 sent attention back to the private sector. The 1979 amendments to CETA added a private sector initiative title. Private industry councils are being developed to launch these initiatives with emphasis on youth employment. A targeted jobs tax credit program now offers tax advantages for hiring the disadvantaged. The only lesson possible to draw at this writing is that this tool is still untested.

Public Service Employment[9]

Public service employment proved to be a useful but overworked tool during the 1970s. It turned out to have three potential uses: countercyclical job creation, structural targeting, and employability development.

Under the Emergency Employment Act of 1971 and again in the 1976 amendments which added Title VI to CETA and the Carter economic stimulation in 1977, the objective was essentially jobs for any unemployed anywhere as an antirecession measure. Reaching peak numbers of 750,000 jobs nationwide, the effort proved that: (a) the number of such jobs could be created and expanded very rapidly (over 400,000 in nine months on top of a base of over 300,000); (b) in most jurisdictions there were always more applicants than slots; (c) the funding and employees were welcomed by state and local governments; and (d) useful work was performed by the great majority. There had been great concern that the public service employment funds would simply be used by local governments as a replacement for support by their own taxpayers with no net increase in the number of public jobs. A careful evaluation found this to be true for less than one-fifth of the PSE jobs.[10]

As originally written, CETA had in it a special title for only structurally targeted PSE. The funding was available only to those jurisdictions having high and persistent levels of unemployment and then only for the economically disadvantaged in those areas. During the depth of the 1974–

1975 recession almost every jurisdiction had high unemployment and it proved nearly impossible to keep the structural and countercyclical efforts separate. Nevertheless, those jurisdictions which had high unemployment even before the recession had no difficulty generating all of the PSE jobs they were eligible for and it proved no more difficult to develop jobs for the economically disadvantaged than the others, even though the types of jobs were very different.

The employability development objective was only implied rather than explicitly stated by the legislation. PSE enrollees were to experience transition into unsubsidized jobs within a prescribed time span. Since the continuance of high and persistent unemployment was presumed for the structural component, the transition requirement implied that, following the work experience, the PSE enrollees would be better able to compete for whatever jobs existed. The recession prevented an adequate test and transition was largely neglected. However, the 1978 reauthorization of CETA re-iterated the time limitation and extended it to all activities. It also specifically authorized such training and other services which might be required to make the transition possible. It is at least a reasonable presumption that a period of PSE experience, properly administered, could be as effective in developing employability as a stint in on-the-job or classroom training.

Nevertheless, the experience was not entirely positive. The heavy federal pressure to fill this rapidly expanding number of slots did cause many prime sponsors to pay less attention than they should have to the quality of the job experience or the usefulness of the tasks. Eligibility for the nondisadvantaged coupled with high salary ceilings supplementable by local funds resulted in many going into PSE jobs who, with a little more effort and time, could have found unsubsidized employment. Both by accident and deliberation, many ineligibles appeared on PSE rolls. Some local governments did take advantage of the system to use PSE as a form of federal revenue sharing. Despite the usefulness of the tasks performed, they were, by definition, those which local taxpayers had not considered as sufficiently important to spend their own tax money on. Assigning the unemployment to low priority tasks is not misallocation of labor but some would have found other jobs and there could have been other alternatives such as subsidized private employment.

All in all, the PSE experience was positive but not unsullied. Because of its lessons, future experiences should be even more positive.

Supportive Services[11]

An important lesson of the Great Society social welfare effort was that everything is related to everything else. The worker must get to work, and that fact depends upon the transportation system and the availability and location of housing. Poor health can be a serious limitation. Child care can be an almost absolute bar to employment of female family heads. Even where any of these may not be a complete bar to employment, they may cause sufficient absenteeism to make it difficult to keep or advance in a job.

Some are in such condition in their personal finances that even the acceptance of a training stipend brings an influx of creditors upon them. Many have legal trouble but cannot afford professional advice. The incidence of drug addiction and alcoholism may be high among target groups. Employment and training programs are often used as therapy in alcohol and drug rehabilitation programs, which is all right if it works; but those programs should not be held to the same placement and retention standards as others. Recently and about-to-be released prison inmates are especially in need of help.

Each and all of these supportive services, it has been demonstrated, are essential for some of those needing services as prerequisites and accompaniment for program enrollment and for successful employment. Contrary to the traditions of the counseling field, which advocates primarily nondirective counseling and client self-discovery, the counselor in the employment and training program tends to perform as the "hustler" of these services, most of which cannot be purchased with employment and training program funds.

Nevertheless, the attractiveness of supportive services is its own trap. The services are not inexpensive. They can always be mounted and delivered whereas job placement and retention is never assured. It is too easy to be enticed into supportive services as an end in themselves to the neglect of the real objective of job placement. Not every employment and training enrollee needs supportive services and none needs all of them. Careful analysis is necessary to determine when and what services are needed on an individual basis. Only when there is reason to think success will be unlikely without and likely with supportive services is the expenditure of employment and training funds for that purpose justified.

Placement and Job Search Services[12]

Chapter 24 deals at length with placement and other services provided by the public employment service and other labor market intermediaries. That chapter emphasizes that the employment service, though the most ubiquitous and complete in its services, is only one intermediary among many. It has no power over the supply of jobs or workers, but can play an important facilitative role that will differ according to the structure and needs of labor markets. Employment and training programs have demonstrated the usefulness of job development—that is, an advocate of the job seeker works to find jobs that fit a particular individual or group and convinces the employer to accept the individual or group. By the same token, the programs have demonstrated the need for placement officers assigned to a particular program and representing its enrollees. From an overall economic viewpoint one might argue for more global judgments in the allocation of the work force. But if the disadvantaged are to have their needs redressed, they must have special advantages. The planner's role is to consider the entire labor force and labor market in recommending policy and priorities within that scope. The administrator should administer according to the priorities set.

The newest tool in the employment and training tool box is job search training. Effective job search is a skill and any skill can be taught. Successful job search consists primarily of the communication skills to impress an employer, a knowledge of grooming, how to fill out applications, how to obtain labor market information, how to decide on an occupation and identify employers who have such jobs, how to contact them, and the motivation to persistently do so. Job search training programs are emerging at an explosive rate in CETA and WIN. The employment service is reluctant because self-placement brings no budgetary rewards, but that can and should be changed. Outside the employment and training world, the number of books commercially published on job search instruction and the number of fee-charging workshops are multiplying rapidly. The usefulness of job search training has been demonstrated. What is needed now is an assessment to determine the most productive techniques.

Equal Employment Opportunity[13]

Perhaps the best evidence of effectiveness in equal employment opportunity efforts is the backlash from those charging reverse discrimination. But what are the specific lessons? Pursuing and accepting employees of unfamiliar race and sex does have its costs. A realistic threat of higher costs from failure to accommodate is necessary to offset understandable reluctance to change. Yet that reluctance can be even further reduced by supportive efforts to provide qualified job applicants at low cost to the employer. Linkages between employment and training and affirmative action programs can be productive. Examples are the apprenticeship outreach efforts which have supplied minority applicants fully capable of scoring high on apprentice entry tests and the minority women employment program which has recruited and supplied minority women with all of the credentials and skills necessary for managerial and professional jobs.[14] If the employee is to fulfill a public goal like equal employment opportunity, there is no reason the public should not assume most of the cost.

Another lesson is an obstacle. It is difficult to enforce equal employment opportunity until one knows how to measure its presence or absence. Knowledge of labor markets is still too rudimentary to know what the geographical boundaries and legitimate entrance requirements are in a particular instance. Is the proportion of black women Ph.D. economists on a university faculty to be determined by the proportion of women in the total population, the percentage of blacks in the local community, the ratio of the university's economics faculty to all economists as compared to the ratio of black women Ph.D. economists to all economists or some other alternative? It is difficult to judge affirmative action until it can be measured.

Perhaps the final lesson is that though progress has been made, only the easiest heights have been conquered. As overt discrimination lessens, the hard core of firmly institutionalized, unrecognized practice becomes more obvious. Future gains will be more difficult than those of the past; yet public support is not expanding apace with the difficulty of the task.

Welfare Recipients[15]

One group of human resource services deserves further comment, even though it is treated fully in Chapter 18. The public maintains an antipathy toward public assistance recipients. It refuses to recognize that the beneficiaries are in reality largely dependent children, that welfare is not an economic problem but a social one, primarily caused by family breakup in the urban society. The problem will not diminish while the number of female headed families is rising. Not only child-care problems but the wage structure of those jobs available to women, particularly those without education, militates against self-support. The evidence is that welfare recipients and their children have the same ambitions as most everyone else but less opportunity to fulfill them. For example, WIN has no difficulty in enrolling welfare recipients for training and other services and it can even place them. Retention is the problem, and that problem has its roots in work expectations and the family. Welfare reform will be expensive. Guaranteed jobs will be effective for a few if the wages are sufficiently subsidized. But the basic problem will not yield to labor market solutions.

Youth Services[16]

Youth employment is another intransigent problem. All of the program efforts of the past 20 years have had no impact on its aggregate level. Only the decline of teenagers as a proportion of the population has caused the ratio of teenage to adult unemployment to decline. The passage from adolescence to adulthood has always been rocky and has lengthened in our time. The peculiar problems of the central city, stressed in Chapter 16, add to those difficulties. Yet some lessons have been learned concerning what does and does not work after 20 years of youth program experience:

1. One lesson is the ultimate importance of the development of strong work values, good work habits, and the normal coping skills that go into good interpersonal relations. No youth or adult will be successful in the labor market without them. These are best incor-

porated in the process of growing up, but for those who arrive at the
end of adolescence without them they can be taught—but only with
difficulty.

2. The best way to learn to work is to work, but most work experience
    programs have failed because the work situation was neither realis-
    tic nor taken seriously by either the youth or the administrators.
    Work experience programs can make a positive contribution when
    the jobs are real, where productivity is required, and the program is
    not overloaded with unmotivated youth. There must be positive
    peer influence. The staff must combine rapport with firm discipline
    and production requirements but must consider employability de-
    velopment the end and output the means. The coping skills of good
    attitudes and good conduct must be stressed as heavily as job skills.
    Career exploration should be considered an important by-product
    and good performance should be documented as a source of recom-
    mendation for placement. Public service employment is as good as
    private employment if these criteria are met.

3. Classroom skills training has been productive for youth when sev-
    eral requirements have been met. All that was said earlier for class-
    room skill training holds true for youth but several factors proved
    especially important when addressed to this group. Young trainees
    were more likely than older ones to have herd instincts. Therefore,
    it was most important to avoid grouping those of limited ability and
    ambition together. Positive peer pressures were needed from either
    motivated youth, or even better, a mix of adults with youth. For re-
    lated reasons, youth were more sensitive than adults to the quality
    and image of facilities. They needed to take pride in the institution
    in which they were being trained. Age made a great deal of differ-
    ence in the nature of the training needed. No matter how good the
    training or how high the placement rate was, the turnover of teen-
    agers was high. Therefore, an opportunity for career exploration
    and development of good work habits and general tool skills appli-
    cable to a number of occupations were more productive than the
    skills of a specific occupation. It was those who were in their early
    twenties and ready to settle down who profited from training in a
    specific occupation. They tended to be most motivated by a reputa-
    tion for high placement or promise of a job guarantee following
    completion.

4. Subsidized on-the-job training has had limited use with youth, prob-
    ably because of the reluctance of employers to invest in them. How-
    ever, it should be valuable as a career exploration route for teen-
    agers and a direct tie to longer-term employment for young adults.

5. Counseling as part of employment and training programs has
    proven useful as an adjunct to employability development and
    placement when designed to help youth come to a better self-

understanding, recognize the type of conduct expected by employers, and understand the need to improve school and job performance and to develop a reputation for stability and diligence. Un-
structured, sensitivity-type sessions and personal counseling
unconnected to employment concerns seemed to have no measurable impact upon employability or work performance.

6. The teaching of job search skills as a component of youth programs
   had limited testing. However, the evidence to date suggests that job
   search skills can be effectively taught and that, when accompanied
   by information as to where to search, can have a significant effect on
   placement rates. However, successful job search does not imply retention. All of the pre-YEDPA youth program experience attests to
   the short tenure of teenagers, the exploratory tendencies of those in
   their early twenties, and the need for either a few more years or the
   assumption of the responsibilities of marriage before continuous
   employment becomes attractive.

Planning and Managing Local
Employment and Training Programs[17]

The underlying assumption of CETA was that local officials were better
able than those in far off Washington to design a mix of employment and
training services adapted to the needs of disadvantaged workers and the
realities of the labor market in each community. It was also assumed that
those same local officials were in the best position to choose among the alternative service deliverers and elicit from them the most effective performance. The potential political consequences of failure would provide the
motivation. Experience of the first five years seems to give the CETA prime
sponsors good marks for program management but either an "incomplete"
or a "withdrawal" for planning. Few seek to establish priorities among target groups in any but political responses. Occupational targets are set more
by postplacement rates than by knowledge of present or future labor market demand. Practically no attempt is made to get specific about the barriers impeding the job success of individuals or groups. What worked reasonably well last year is expected to work next year and usually does. Low
retention, completion rates or placement rates are evidence of unsatisfactory performance and lead to change, but those changes are more likely to
be best guesses than the results of analyses. Whether prime sponsors are unwilling or unable to plan remains unknown. The whole system of delayed
information and constant changes of signals from the national and regional
level militates against planning.

On the other hand, prime sponsors have shown themselves highly
adept at program management. In a relatively short period of time, they
have taken on an untried and unfamiliar program directed at deepseated
economic, social, and psychological problems. In an atmosphere of un-

known budgets, constantly changing signals, and crash expansions and contractions, they have enrolled the people and delivered the services with remarkably few failures. Management is a daily persistent demand whereas
the pro forma filling in of blanks can always be a stopgap substitute for
meaningful planning. And sound planning can never really be enforced because it can never be recognized by outside observers.

Research, Demonstration, Evaluation, and Staff Development[18]

Employment and training programs have profited throughout their history
from a constant accompaniment of research, demonstration, and evaluation. At any specific moment, administrators are likely to feel that those
funds could be more productively spent on the delivery of services. Research is of such a nature that one never knows what, if anything, the policy contribution of any specific project will be; yet over time new insights
are gained which become the basis of experiments and demonstration.
These can fail as well as succeed. Proving what does not work is also a contribution. Better to have failure in a small experiment than in a full-scale
program. And most successful programs were once demonstrations. No one
likes to be evaluated, and there is no universally acceptable model. However, those who object to being evaluated are quick to grasp favorable evaluations when attacked by the press or by funding sources. Continual improvements have been made in the art of evaluation. No single evaluation
can be taken totally at face value. The complexities of life without the controls of laboratory experiments are too great. Nevertheless, consensus
among independent evaluations has proven, over time, to be highly dependable. There has been constant carping from the researcher that "the
policymaker ignores me" and from the latter that "they never research the
right question" or "the research results always arrive after I have had to
make the decisions." But it is almost certain that the employment and
training programs would have been less innovative and less effective without the research support.

Perhaps staff development has been the area of greatest weakness. A
few universities, motivated by federal funding, have put together meaningful professional programs for the preservice or inservice training of staff.
Short-term workshops have been numerous but with little evidence of last-
ing contribution to staff competence. By and large, program staff have been
left to themselves to derive their own competence from experience. The
turnover is so high that this is a constant race. But then the same rates of
turnover, if they persisted, might negate the usefulness of any staff training
effort.

QUERY

Are these lessons worth the billions spent on employment and training programs over the past 20 years? The answer need not be yes. The programs

were not undertaken for the experience but for the impact of the services on the working lives of those chosen by social consensus to be the recipients. Their worthiness must be assessed in terms of improvements in family incomes and career satisfaction. In a sense, any learning is a bonus. But unless lessons are identified, recorded, and applied, there is likely to be little progress or improvement. Throughout the years there has been a great deal of learning and application by those who had the experience, but little recording and dissemination. What one administrator has learned has not defended another against making the same mistakes. And each generation of policymakers seems determined to rechart the paths their predecessors have pioneered without leaving an adequate log behind.

DISCUSSION QUESTIONS

1. What does current evidence allow us to say about the relative success of employment and the training programs? What are the relevant criteria for determining success? By these criteria, how would you rate the overall success of such programs?
2. Discuss the problems of evaluating employment and training programs. Who has an interest in evaluating such programs? What criteria would you expect each to use? How dependable do you consider evaluation efforts to date? What suggestions would you have for an affordable, yet effective evaluation system?
3. What is your estimate of the macroeconomic effects of employment and training programs? To what degree and under what circumstances might they be effective in reducing the tradeoff beteen unemployment and inflation?
4. What is your answer to the "great dichotomy" posed in this chapter? How would you appraise the relative importance of behavioral and institutional factors in explaining the phenomenon of economic disadvantage? How consistent have the various employment and training programs been with your judgment as to causality?
5. Make your own assessment of each of the various service components found most frequently in employment and training programs: classroom training, on-the-job training, work experience, public service employment, supportive services, job development, and job search training.
6. What labor market related services can you conceive of that ought to be added to the kit of employment and training tools to aid disadvantaged workers to improve their employment and income experience? What would be the major obstacles to supplying these services?

Notes

1. Garth L. Mangum et al., *Self Evaluation of CETA Manpower Programs*, Employment and Training Administration, U.S. Department of Labor, 1976; and Garth L. Mangum et al., *Job Market Futurity: Planning and Managing Local Manpower Programs* (Salt Lake City: Olympus Publishing Company), chapter 9.
2. Charles R. Perry et al., *The Impact of Government Manpower Programs* (Philadelphia: Industrial Research Unit, University of Pennsylvania, 1975).

3. John Kenneth Galbraith, *The Affluent Society*, 3rd ed. (Boston: Houghton Mifflin, revised, ·1976).
4. Lee Bruno, *Intake and Assessment: CETA Program Models*, Employment and Training Administration, U.S. Department of Labor, 1978.
5. Garth Mangum and John Walsh, *A Decade of Manpower Development and Training* (Salt Lake City: Olympus Publishing Company, 1973); Sar A. Levitan and William H. Johnson, *The Job Corps: A Social Experiment that Works* (Baltimore: Johns Hopkins University Press, 1975).
6. James Bromley and Larry Wardle, *On the Job Training: CETA Program Models*, Employment and Training Administration, U.S. Department of Labor, 1978.
7. Marion Pines and James Morlock, *Work Experience Perspectives: CETA Program Models*, Employment and Training Administration, U.S. Department of Labor, 1978.
8. Sar A. Levitan et al., *Economic Opportunity in the Ghetto: The Partnership of Government and Business* (Baltimore: Johns Hopkins University Press, 1970).
9. Ray Corpuz, *Public Service Employment: CETA Program Models*, Employment and Training Administration, U.S. Department of Labor, 1978.
10. Richard Nathan et al., *Job Creation Through Public Service Employment*, report no. 6, National Commission for Manpower Policy, Washington, D.C., 1978.
11. Susan Turner and Carolyn Conradus, *Supportive Services: CETA Program Models*, Employment and Training Administration, U.S. Department of Labor, 1978.
12. Miriam Johnson and Marged Sugarman, *Job Development and Placement: CETA Program Models*, Employment and Training Administration, U.S. Department of Labor, 1978.
13. Sar A. Levitan et al., *Still a Dream* (Cambridge, Mass.: Harvard University Press, 1975).
14. Robert W. Glover et al., *Stepping Up: Placing Minority Women into Managerial and Professional Jobs* (Salt Lake City: Olympus Publishing Company, 1979); Ray Marshall and Vernon Briggs, *Equal Apprenticeship Opportunities* (Ann Arbor: The Institute of Labor and Industrial Relations, University of Michigan, 1968).
15. Sar A. Levitan et al., *Work and Welfare Go Together* (Baltimore: Johns Hopkins University Press, 1973).
16. Garth Mangum and John Walsh, *Employment and Training Programs for Youth: What Works Best for Whom?*, Employment and Training Administration, U.S. Department of Labor, 1978.
17. Garth Mangum et al., *Job Market Futurity: Planning and Managing Local Manpower Programs* (Salt Lake City: Olympus Publishing Company, 1979).
18. Garth Mangum, "A Review of Manpower Research," in Benjamin Aaron et al., *A Review of Industrial Relations Research*, vol. 2 (Madison, Wis.: Industrial Relations Research Association, 1971).

PART V
LABOR MARKETS
AND ECONOMIC POLICY

Chapter 21
Human Resource Planning

As human resources have taken on a more crucial economic role in the firm, the community, and the nation, the cost of failure to foresee needs and meet impending problems has increased apace. In response, the larger firms in private industry and many public agencies attempt to foresee crucial human resource needs and prepare for them, insofar as it seems profitable to do so. Government statistical agencies strive to provide better projections and attempt to forecast total employment needs and, qualified by other goals, seek an acceptable and achievable level of employment. Local governments use federal funds to plan for delivery of remedial services to those facing various disadvantages in job market competition. Nations facing critical surpluses or shortages of labor are guided by international agencies in formulating long-range plans to meet those problems. Thus, though there is no overall integrated framework for human resource planning, its fragmented pieces add up to an impressive range of activities which can be described and assessed.

But understanding the role of planning is often impeded by a confusion of tongues. This chapter provides a brief definition of planning. It then identifies and briefly surveys human resource planning activities as they exist within employing organizations and among national and local governments world wide.

THE PLANNING PROCESS

Planning pervades all human activity. Every decision—to build a house, start a business, launch a public program, or even to take a drink of water—involves an explicit or implicit plan. And every plan consists of and every planner goes through essentially the same set of steps. (However, to cast the net that broadly deprives the planning process of meaning.) More formally, a planning process is a series of logical conclusions concerning future actions that are prepared by planners and recommended to decisionmakers for approval and action. The planners may also be decisionmakers and actors but the functions are conceptually separable ones.

Every planner goes through essentially the same set of steps in interaction with decisionmakers and implementers, regardless of the subject of the plan. There is first a recognition of a problem. All is not as it should be and planning might make it better. Next comes the statement of a goal—the ideal to be attained. But goals are generally broad and nonspecific—good health, full employment, higher profits, and so forth. These must be transformed into specific objectives which are doable, achievable, and measurable in order to derive programs for their attainment and determine whether progress is being made. There is usually more than one way to skin a cat but all are not equally desirable. All reasonable alternatives for the accomplishment of the objectives are examined in search of the one which promises to be most cost effective. A program is designed around that most promising alternative and is implemented. But planning does not end there. No one yet knows whether the program will really work. The program is monitored for its performance and evaluated for its progress and outcome. Information from the monitoring and evaluation is fed back to the planners and decisionmakers and the program is modified, dropped, or replaced as indicated by the results.

Those planning processes discussed in this chapter have in common a concern for the development, allocation, and utilization of human resources. They vary widely in purpose and nature but they all have in common, even if their participants do not realize it, the standard set of planning steps:

1. Problem identification
2. Goal setting
3. Derivation of objectives
4. Examining alternatives
5. Program design
6. Implementation

7. Monitoring and evaluation
8. Feedback and modification

MICRO HUMAN RESOURCE PLANNING

Microeconomics is the theory of the firm. Hence planning to meet the staffing needs of a particular business firm or public agency is frequently described as micro human resource planning.

The Incidence of Micro Planning

Obviously, any organization must do some planning related to staffing its activities. However, no one knows the number of firms engaged in formal internal personnel planning. No comprehensive survey has ever been made.

The Bureau of National Affairs polled a sample of personnel officials representing 300 large companies in mid-1968 to ascertain the extent of labor utilization and planning.[1] Five of every six companies had some formal procedure for meeting future personnel needs. Three out of four firms conducted audits for managerial personnel, two-thirds for professionals, 70 percent for clerical employees, and 56 percent for blue-collar workers. Nearly one-half of those conducting work force audits used projections ranging from six months to five years. Over one-half conducted formal periodic audits or reviews of personnel supplies and needs. Instruction in work force analysis or planning was given to first-line supervisors in 44 percent of the firms. More than half had some plan for coordinating staffing requirements so that surplus labor in one subdivision could be loaned to others experiencing shortages.

A proprietary private survey in 1976 found 150 major firms with human resource planning activities sufficiently structured and institutionalized to merit analysis. The number of practitioners involved in such micro-level planning became sufficient by 1978 to establish a Human Resource Planning Society and to publish a journal. Leaving aside the consultants, academics, and vendors among its membership, the Society identified 300 members directly engaged in the planning function for companies and government agencies.[2] Thus, the number of organizations involved is not known but the number is clearly on the increase.

Motives for Planning

Planning is not a cost-free activity and any organization facing cost-restraining pressures will undertake and maintain over time only those activities which appear to contribute more to accomplishing the organization's goals than those activities cost. Motivation appears to involve demand and supply factors, cost and profitability factors, and legal and social pressures.

The persistent shift in the occupational mix from laborers, semiskilled operatives, and—to a lesser extent—skilled craftsmen to more highly trained managerial, professional, and technical personnel has required more forethought in recruitment, internal staff development, and retention. The generally high levels of education in the United States, the mobility of the work force, and the availability of training institutions make actual skill shortages rare. Nevertheless, people at these more advanced levels are never as readily available as the lesser-skilled groups; fewer make those high investments in their own preparation, there is rarely a ready pool of unemployed workers, and there may be actual shortages in some locations.

Demography has been a factor. Low birth rates during the 1930s and 1940s meant that the college trained would be scarce in the 1950s and 1960s, mid-career managers, professionals, and technicians in short supply in the 1970s and 1980s and, perhaps, top management beyond there. From the mid-1980s on, recruiters may have a difficult time finding applicants for entry level jobs.

Industry has become more mobile and public agencies have experienced more fluctuations as well as growth. Plant relocations, expansions, contractions, and new product lines all are more difficult without planning. Firms must assure that personnel are available in unfamiliar locations, that new facilities are staffed in the proper sequence as various divisions come "on line," that attrition phases out unneeded employees as much as possible to avoid cost and criticisms, that the skill mix required by new product lines is recruited to meet production targets.

Major construction firms which undertake sophisticated projects in isolated areas have special planning problems. Increasing pressures and requirements on top management make executive succession a key planning assignment involving years of anticipation. Among the most impressive planning activities are those of consulting firms with computerized rosters that can immediately identify available personnel with unique characteristics; firms in high technology industries considering a major investment or change of direction; and international construction firms considering a bid or negotiation for a project in some remote area, for all of whom personnel planning is at the heart of corporate decision making.

Profitability factors relate to the costs of not doing planning. The more biased the skill mix is toward professional, technical, and skilled employees, the harder they are to find, the broader the geographic market over which recruitment search must be extended, the more the employer must invest in training and development as well as recruitment, the longer term the commitments that employer must make to employee, the more that is lost by delay in finding the right person, and the greater the risk of hiring the wrong person. The rising costs of fringe benefits, the strengthening of job guarantees, and the high costs of training and of further recruitment make employee turnover something to be strenuously avoided. It is important to have the right person in the right place at the right time.

Finally, equal employment opportunity requirements that the employer take affirmative action to have the right mix of sexes and races while not discriminating by age or handicap require a considerable degree of planning. One could follow a nondiscriminatory hiring policy with no planning whatsoever. However, as long as some expected relationship between payroll proportions and population proportions is the necessary defense against large back pay awards, planners will be important people.

Techniques of Micro Human Resource Planning

Private firms, especially, are not likely to continue planning activities which do not at least appear to pay. Since every organization's problems are different, so are its planning processes. Nevertheless, they all follow something like the steps of the paradigm above. The unique aspects of microplanning are:

1. An employee information system. The typical personnel planning activity within a business firm begins with an employee information system which adds to the standard personal data further information about education, training, skills, experience, language proficiency, mobility, performance appraisals, promotability appraisals, and job preferences. This provides a base for filling needs from within the firm and facilitating career development and progression for the employee.
2. A forecasting capability. The second component is forecasting capability, occasionally using sophisticated computer analysis and mathematical models but more often relying on simple counts of vacant positions, estimates of losses from turnover and retirement, and analysis of operating and project plans and expected productivity. Forecasting is preliminary to a programming response which may be in the form of increased recruiting, plans for executive replacement and succession, or additional training and career guidance for current employees.
3. And, increasingly, career development programs. Especially notable is the growth of career development programs within the firm to dissuade valued employees from leaving the firm to speed their career progression. Individualized career plans, jointly prepared between the employee and a counselor, assess the employee's prospects, specify goals to be accomplished, and, if upward progression is unlikely, reduce unrest by letting the employee know why and what can be expected in current status.

A generalized planning model presented by the American Society for Personnel Administration and following the flow chart of Figure 21-1 is a

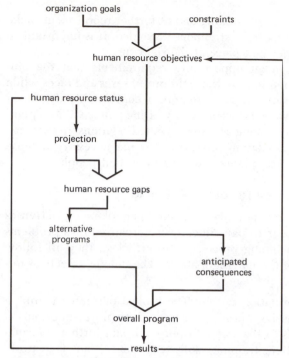

organization goals

constraints

human resource objectives

human resource status

projection

human resource gaps

alternative programs

anticipated consequences

overall program

results

Figure 21-1   Human resource planning approach. Reprinted by permission from ''Human Resources Planning and PAIR Policy,'' by George T. Milkovich and Thomas A. Mahoney, Chapter 2.1 of *ASPA Handbook of Personnel and Industrial Relations,* copyright 1979 by The Bureau of National Affairs, Inc., Washington, D.C.

useful illustration.[3] The figure stresses the important point that personnel goals are not ends in themselves but are means to the accomplishment of some broader organizational mission to which they must be subordinate and contributory. For a business firm, these organizational goals will relate to production, sales, or financial performance; for a public agency, to the achievement of some specified mission. Similarly, every organization operates in the framework of some set of environmental constraints set by legal, economic, and social conditions. Being clear as to what the organization is trying to accomplish, the human resource requirements and implications of those goals, and what is possible within the environmental constraints (or what is necessary to circumvent some of those constraints), a set of specific objectives can be derived. These will involve numbers, skills, and a sequence of availability.

A quantitative and qualitative inventory of current personnel by number, skill, mix, and productivity extended by a projection of where present policies and programs will take internal human resource availability by the action date allows the planner to identify gaps which will then exist between the status quo and what will be necessary to accomplish the objectives. Programs are then designed to close the prospective gaps before they can emerge. These programs may involve recruitment, training, redeployment, motivation, job redesign, reorganization of work processes, changed compensation practices, delayed or earlier retirement, or any other combination to attune staffing to mission and goal achievement. This program design stage presupposes the examination of alternatives as indicated by the generalized planning paradigm earlier in the chapter. This step is illustrated in Figure 21-1 in part by the anticipation of consequences. The relative cost-effectiveness of the alternatives is not known but can only be predicted by considering the most likely costs and consequences.

Anticipating consequences may also have another connotation. No set of actions is without its unforeseen consequences. Examples are given later in the chapter of the unforeseen labor market consequences of public policies and programs with quite different objectives. The same phenomenon is pervasive at the micro level. The planner never knows what all of those consequences will be but should seek to anticipate them. Work rules changes will affect labor-management relations. Changes in the wage structure will affect retention, turnover, morale, and so forth.

But finally some program must be chosen and implemented. It must be monitored to see how it works out in practice. Its results must be evaluated to see if they are consistent with the objectives, within the range of projected costs, and as productive as possible. Since nothing is ever as good as it might be, a feedback loop carries the evaluation results back to the origins for modification. A new status quo now exists. Some objectives have proven unrealistic. But in light of those experiences, a new iteration of the continuous planning process begins.

Considerable sophistication is often addressed to the projection stage, to the neglect of more important steps. Projection is, after all, a fairly mechanical process. The future is inherently unknowable. One can only project into the future what is known about the past and present. A computer is a convenient paper shuffler and can do nothing a sufficient quantity of clerks could not do. Mathematical techniques bend trend lines in directions predetermined by the formula. Their major contribution is to offer more alternatives for judgmental choice more cheaply.

Who Plans?

The key step most often neglected is careful specification of objectives—both the organizational objectives and the derived personnel objectives. Having clearly defined the mission, all else tends to fall in place. Yet there is a persistent tendency to confuse means and ends and to specify misleading objectives. The objectives also predetermine the organizational structure of the human resource planning function. Who plans and where they are located in the organizational hierarchy tends to be determined by the nature and focus of objectives.

The literature speaks of "top down" and "bottom up" approaches to micro human resource planning. The top down approach, illustrated by

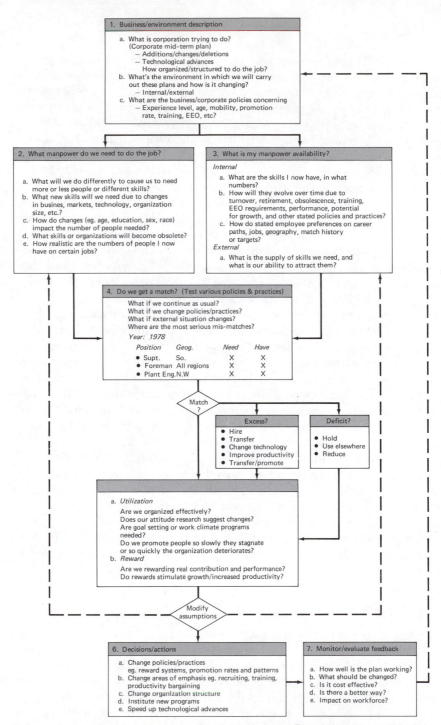

Figure 21-2   Human resource planning process. Reprinted by permission from "Human Resources Planning and PAIR Policy," by George T. Milkovich and Thomas A. Mahoney, Chapter 2.1 of *ASPA Handbook of Personnel and Industrial Relations*, copyright 1979 by The Bureau of National Affairs, Inc., Washington, D.C.

Organizational unit	Date	Page of

Block (top-left)

Position		
Incumbent	Age	yrs.
	Empl.	yrs.
Promotable to	When	yrs./mos.
Replacement no. 1	Age	yrs.
	Empl.	yrs.
Present position	Promotable	yrs./mos.
Replacement no. 2	Age	yrs.
	Empl.	yrs.
Present position	Promotable	yrs./mos.

Block (top-right)

Position		
Incumbent	Age	yrs.
	Empl.	yrs.
Promotable to	When	yrs./mos
Replacement no. 1	Age	yrs.
	Empl.	yrs.
Present position	Promotable	yrs./mos.
Replacement no. 2	Age	yrs.
	Empl.	yrs.
Present position	Promotable	yrs./mos.

Block (middle-left)

Position		
Incumbent	Age	yrs.
	Empl.	yrs.
Promotable to	When	yrs./mos.
Replacement no. 1	Age	yrs.
	Empl.	yrs.
Present position	Promotable	yrs./mos.
Replacement no. 2	Age	yrs.
	Empl.	yrs.
Present position	Promotable	yrs./mos.

Block (middle-right)

Position		
Incumbent	Age	yrs.
	Empl.	yrs.
Promotable to	When	yrs./mos.
Replacement no. 1	Age	yrs.
	Empl.	yrs.
Present position	Promotable	yrs./mos.
Replacement no. 2	Age	yrs.
	Empl.	yrs.
Present position	Promotable	yrs./mos.

Block (bottom-left)

Position		
Incumbent	Age	yrs.
	Empl.	yrs.
Promotable to	When	yrs./mos.
Replacement no. 1	Age	yrs.
	Empl.	yrs.
Present position	Promotable	yrs./mos.
Replacement no. 2	Age	yrs.
	Empl.	yrs.
Present position	Promotable	yrs./mos.

Block (bottom-right)

Position		
Incumbent	Age	yrs.
	Empl.	yrs.
Promotable to	When	yrs./mos.
Replacement no. 1	Age	yrs.
	Empl.	yrs.
Present position	Promotable	yrs./mos.
Replacement no. 2	Age	yrs.
	Empl.	yrs.
Present position	Promotable	yrs./mos.

Figure 21-3   Employee replacement chart. Reprinted by permission from "Human Resources Planning and PAIR Policy," by George T. Milkovich and Thomas A. Mahoney, Chapter 2.1 of *ASPA Handbook of Personnel and Industrial Relations,* copyright 1979 by The Bureau of National Affairs, Inc., Washington, D.C.

Figure 21-2 drawn from the ASPA handbook, begins with overall organizational goals and objectives and derives the work force implications from them. In a top down approach, the human resource planners will generally be attached to the top corporate planning staff where they will play a significant role in both determining and facilitating corporate directions. The bottom-up approach illustrated by Figure 21-3 is a problem-solving approach. Its locus is the personnel office. It begins with the analysis of individuals and units, identifies problems, and puts in place less global programs to solve these problems with the intent of preventing disturbance rather than redirecting more global plans. Both have their place and every organization, whether planning implicitly or explicitly, will have some evidence of top down and some of bottom up human resource planning. But the emphasis will differ considerably by the nature of the organization, its environment, and the personalities of its leadership.

Career Development Planning

A third broad area of personnel planning within the employing organization—and one currently the focus of considerable attention—is career development planning.[4] Chapter 8 discussed theories of career development as applied to individuals, across a cradle-to-grave pattern. Career development within the organization is based upon that knowledge, though limited to those stages following entry into full-time employment. However, though the career development efforts of the organization serve the individual, that is means rather than end. The objective is to serve the needs of the organization and, therefore, only those career development efforts survive which prove to be useful in furthering organizational objectives at a reasonable cost.

Because of the relative scarcity of highly competent executives, professionals, and even technicians, and because of the investment the employer ultimately makes in recruiting and training them, turnover can be very costly. The best and the brightest tend to leave for greater challenge if they perceive their career progress being blocked. Career development planning consists of: (1) assuring that viable career paths do exist within the firm; (2) disseminating knowledge of those paths; and (3) undertaking a joint planning process between employee and organization to assure that a path is open that is attractive and to the mutual benefit of individual and organization and that the employee is launched on that path.

Initially, at least, it is necessary to study and modify the organization to provide career path opportunities. Then each individual must be brought to see realistic alternatives for progress, including the performance requirements of each path. Even the valuable employee who has "peaked," performs well at current status, but has not the attributes to move further up the ladder, is aided by a career development planning process. Uncertainty breeds frustration and dissatisfaction. To know that one is valued in the present assignment and is assured of tenure and improvements in standard of living without promotion is generally sufficient for those of whom the assessment is truly realistic. Others, in a joint planning exercise, have alternatives identified along with a clear and preferably written statement of the performance required for each path. Contingencies beyond the control of either individual or company which may impede the desired progress are also posed to guard against overexpectation.

Such activities are generally undertaken only for the level of staff sufficiently valuable and irreplaceable to justify the expense. A few firms even make such counseling available at all levels as a service to employees. Those faced with contractions, plant closings, and other retrenchments have also used a similar process to ease transition and reduce animosity and discontent. Affirmative action programs are facilitated by planning to prevent accumulation of target groups at or near the entry point and to defend against subsequent criticism of tokenism. Planned replacement of key executives is also aided by linkage with a well-structured career development program. Whatever its particular application, career planning within the organization tends to be an activity compatible with the interests of both employee and employer.

Space will not allow further illustration or explication of micro-planning techniques. That can be found in literature listed at the end of the chapter.[5] Our purpose here is to alert the student to an increasing area of human resource activity.

MACRO HUMAN RESOURCE PLANNING[6]

Labor force planning at the national economic level is a worldwide phenomenon of which there are essentially four models, two each for developed and developing countries. The developed countries can be divided between those with primarily private enterprise and those with primarily socialist economies. The developing countries are best dichotomized in this context between the labor surplus and labor shortage nations, the latter primarily oil exporters.

Developed Market Economies

The United States is not atypical of the human resource planning approaches generally followed by countries which depend primarily upon the market system for allocation of economic resources, including human resources. Conceptually, at least, it is useful to think of economic planning as labor force planning, so long as its primary goal is employment. The Employment Act of 1946 implied the task of estimating the number of persons likely to be seeking work and devising policies for sufficient economic growth and job creation to absorb them. Though this is not a very explicit process, the Council of Economic Advisers always has available to it labor force projections made by the Bureau of Labor Statistics. The employment outlook is a key consideration in economic and political policymaking, and despite the need to temper the employment goal with other goals, some action is always recommended. However, political tension is inevitable among those who would place varying degrees of priority on full employment, inflation control, and other interacting and conflicting economic priorities.

Advocates of a more intensive and extensive economic planning effort generally are inclined to put a higher priority on employment than some alternative and often conflicting goals such as stable prices. The history of the Humphrey-Hawkins Full Employment and Balanced Growth Act of 1978 is an example. As originally introduced, it would have set a specific low unemployment rate target and required the administration to achieve it, including guaranteeing public service jobs to all unemployed. To gain acceptance, however, it became necessary to make the prescribed unemployment rate a goal only, with no requirement or strategy to achieve it. In fact, the bill's sponsors had also to accept a large number of conflicting goals such as a specified inflation constraint and full parity prices for farmers, which reduced the act to a relatively meaningless expression of congressional and administration concern.

Similarly, the federal budgeting process could be considered in part as an exercise in human resource planning. Decisions to spend various amounts on defense, aerospace, atomic energy, agriculture, education, or any of the myriad of federal budgeting allocations are also decisions for sectoral allocations of labor resources. Tax decisions are also decisions to allow or discourage private activities which allocate labor within the private sector and between it and the public sector. Economic development activities, such as those to aid depressed areas, are in reality designed primarily to affect the spatial distribution of employment. Availability of federal aid to education influences the labor force participation rates of some marginal and potential members of the labor force, Social Security benefits impact upon the participation rates of older persons, and large-scale public job creation brings the discouraged worker back into labor force activity. Nationally made projections of labor requirements both aid and influence individual choice among occupations, planning for educational facilities and other resources, and the actions of employers.

Though not the purpose of this book, the immense impact on human resource policy of national decisions outside the labor policy field should be noted. A few examples can illustrate the economic and social costs of failure to foresee and compensate for the manpower impact of national policies. Agricultural price support programs introduced in the 1930s were major factors in encouraging consolidation and mechanization of farms, forcing (or allowing) millions to leave the land, to migrate successfully or unsuccessfully to the cities, or to remain as the rural nonfarm poor. Federal housing and highway-building policies encouraged the demand for labor to shift to the suburbs, without aiding substantial portions of the supply to follow. Medicare imposed greater burdens upon an already short supply in health occupations. Aerospace decisions encouraged large supplies of expensively trained personnel to invest their careers in that field, then abandoned them. Availability of retirement benefits continually encourages earlier retirement in a population characterized by increasing longevity, while Social Security restrictions on continued earnings discourage second careers and create a new social class, the elderly poor. Raising the compulsory retirement age is one small and weak countermove against these economic disincentives.

Some human resource planning has been addressed to such special needs. Both the Atomic Energy Commission and the National Aeronautics and Space Administration during the 1960s made some attempts to forecast the requirements their programs would generate for college-educated employees and gave some grants to universities and to individuals for scholarships to expand the output of such personnel. Similar scholarship programs were made available for counselors as veterans' education and antipoverty programs expanded demand. The Bureau of Labor Statistics, the National Science Foundation, and the National Institute of Health contribute a sporadic flow of projections of occupations expected to experience relative shortages, giving some indicative guidance to private decisions.

These are sufficient examples to illustrate some need for comprehensive human resource planning at the national or total economy level. That a political demand for such has never intensified is *prima facie* evidence that either the current system works reasonably well or that distrust of planning exceeds the threat of the unplanned.

The European experience follows a similar pattern. The major differences over the post–World War II period have emerged from the fact that the democracies of Western Europe have been dominated primarily by labor governments. High employment had higher priority than stable prices in that inevitable conflict of interests. Maintaining high levels of employment, and also dealing with more homogeneous labor forces, racially and educationally, Western European policies were less concerned with providing opportunity for the disadvantaged and more with preparing marginal groups to take advantage of plentiful opportunity. Lower labor force participation rates for women, a smaller and longer-delayed youth employment problem, and the cushion of migrant workers who could be sent home to southeastern Europe in times of slack also accounted for this difference in policy. Only with the OPEC price increases in totally oil-dependent nations did prices rise to preeminence over employment among public policy concerns.

Japan represents another modest departure. Facing the consequences of population growth in a resource-short economy, stringent and successful population control measures were undertaken. Then, unexpectedly, the economy boomed, causing extreme labor shortages and requiring an emphasis on high productivity to meet production demands. But with those and other national and area differences, the general objective of maintaining high employment levels while minimizing inflation, along with specialized planning when particular projects confront skill obstacles, well describes the policies of the industrial democracies. Their human resource planning is incoherent and fragmented but it fills gaps in relatively well-operating systems.

The Socialist Economies

The Soviet Union can serve as an illustration for countries which indulge in more directive planning than the United States and rely less on labor market forces. Soviet human resource planning starts from the bottom. Each enterprise submits its labor requirements to the regional economic council. The council works out a budget to meet the needs of all its establishments for all types of labor. Administrative and government agencies work out the combined balance of work forces for the cities, regions, and republics. A tendency for establishments to overestimate their needs to avoid shortages is a significant problem.

To meet the labor requirements of a planned economy, education at almost all levels is tied to the skills required in the labor market. Education and training are centrally planned. The number of students and number of educational institutions are determined by the USSR Council of Ministers. Plans for technical training in schools or universities are the responsibility of the Ministry of Higher and Specialized Secondary Education, state committees are responsible for planning and organizing state vocational training, while on the local levels enterprises together with educational and planning authorities work to relate education to the needs of the local economy.

A government-manipulated wage structure is the primary tool for allocating labor in the Soviet Union. There is no coordinated local job information and placement service. People generally find jobs for themselves through notices at factory gates, street bulletin boards, newspaper and radio ads, and word of mouth. The vast distances of the Soviet Union are a major problem. A special agency is responsible for handling the huge flow of the labor force from villages to cities and from one region to another.

Unlike free economies, wages in the Soviet Union are manipulated by government edict to affect the movement and distribution of the labor force. The structure of wage rates consists of the base rates for the lower wage grade and the schedules of percentage increase for the higher grades for each occupation. The structure of differentials is designed to compensate for differences in training and for difficulties or dangers in working or living conditions. In addition, differentials are used to promote employment in occupations, industries, and regions of special national significance. Recognizing the low productivity of dissatisfied workers, the Soviet worker is free to choose his or her occupation, industry, and region, However, this freedom is undermined by the fact that, if one wants to increase earnings and acquire a claim to a larger share of the still-scarce consumer goods, one must work where the government wants one to work. To ensure conformity all over the country, the wage systems established in the plants are expected to conform to central standards.

To induce entrance into specific occupations of high demand, especially during the take-off period of the Soviet economy, wage differentials between skilled and unskilled occupations were intended to be large. However, as education and skills improved, such extreme differentiation became unnecessary. Industrial and regional differentials have persisted in order to attract workers to priority areas.

The Labor-Surplus Developing Countries

The Second World War brought the industrial and nonindustrial countries of the world into a continuing contact of differing magnitude than had ever happened before. Not just a few but millions of Americans and Europeans spent years in the less-developed world, often in situations which made allies of those peoples. At the same time, in the technology and living standards of the developed countries, the underdeveloped obtained a taste of the wealth and power of industrialism. Since the wealthy nations were the industrial ones, both concluded, the answer was to industrialize the underdeveloped world.

Economic development became a major field within the economics profession, and every economic development team sent out under the auspices of nations or international agencies had its human resource planner. A multi-year economic development plan would be derived spelling out the specific industries and facilities to be introduced and their capital, raw material, and human resource requirements. The skill requirements of the facilities to be constructed and operated were derived from the staffing tables of comparable facilities in developed lands, in both quantitative and qualitative terms. These were then generally translated into broad educational categories in terms of: (1) science-based college degree, (2) arts-based college degree, (3) two or three years of postsecondary schooling, (4) secondary completion, and (5) less than secondary. A skill survey of existing establishments generally followed, stressing the educational attainment of the incumbents. Those not employed in some recognizable establishment could be assumed to be without education. The outlook for those establishments, added to the personnel requirements of the economic development plan, comprised a forecast of labor requirements by education level.

Since most of the higher level jobs were filled by immigrants, the speed with which they were to be replaced by native workers was an important supply factor. Only the modernizing sector of the economy was considered, and unskilled labor and semiskilled labor were assumed to be no problem. Education was to be tied directly to development needs. Since the education system was generally rudimentary and elitist, designed only to give a classical education to those who would become subsidiary administrators to colonial authorities, a whole new education system would then be designed to meet the practical emphasis.

The approach was well-intentioned but soon ran into trouble. Improved sanitation cut death rates while leaving traditional birth rates unchanged. Populations exploded, overwhelming both the food-producing and job-creating capacity of the economies. Word-of-mouth exaggeration of the opportunities and incomes generated by industrialization attracted a flood of rural to urban migrants, for whom there was neither housing or jobs. The abandonment of traditional agriculture cut food production in the face of population growth. Following the developed industrial models, the new industries were capital-intensive. Sufficient capital was not available, despite foreign aid to create the needed jobs, even had the markets been available.

Now a new objective controls human resource planning in the less developed countries: maximize the income of people where they are. Since capital is in short supply, emphasize labor-intensive technology. Industrially, the emphasis has shifted to agriculture in pursuit of both self-sufficiency in food supplies and of labor-intensive employment. Education programs have shifted attention to literacy and its linkages to problems of health, community development, homemaking, and employment. Work force planners continue to ply their trade but with more realism and less enthusiam.

The Labor-Short Developing Countries

A final international model is provided by the labor-short, oil-exporting, less-developed countries. Experiencing explosive, high-technology growth, they have by and large abandoned, at least in the short run, any hope of primary reliance on domestic labor. Some form of income guarantee is typically provided the undereducated native population which is generally small.

Saudi Arabia with foreigners comprising over 50 percent of its labor force, Kuwait 75 percent, and the United Arab Emirates over 90 percent, are not atypical. The United Arab Emirates is an extreme case with a native population of only 200,000 and a labor force of over one million in 1978. Remarkably, despite endemic labor shortages, development and production have never been seriously impeded in these circumstances. The labor surpluses of other less developed nations, combined with modern communications and transportation, have made it possible to meet most personnel needs. Labor agents have appeared to scour the world as commission-earning headhunters. Lands with excess populations have workers as their major export and source of foreign earnings. Each such country has its specialty in skill export, depending upon the nature of its education system, usually inherited from colonial nations. Egypt exports teachers and civil servants. Jordan exports technicians of Palestinian origin. India and Pakistan provide engineers, technicians, and skilled craftsmen; Yemen and Bangladesh, among others, unskilled labor.

In these environments, expatriate human resource planners ply their trades, usually under the auspices of international agencies. The mass labor requirements are not their concern. That is left to contact between expatriate employers and labor agents. Native populations are either employed by government, become entrepreneurs, or are pensioned off. Foreigners staff the private sector. The tasks for planners are (1) to foresee and guard against shortages of specific critical skills, (2) to assist in establishing procedures for controlling immigration, (3) to alert those nations to the possible consequences of overreliance on foreign labor, (4) to supply policy alternatives for achieving various targets of reduced reliance on foreigners, and (5) designing programs for preparing and motivating native populations to assume a larger share of labor force activity.

In both less-developed models, work force planning is much more specific than in either of the developed models, perhaps because of the importation of internationally sponsored planners. Because it is their job, they prepare detailed plans, but that does not mean those plans are carried out with any less fragmentation than in the developed cases.

LABOR MARKET PLANNING

Somewhere between macro- and micro-planning lies labor market planning. It is *macro* in that it encompasses a major economic function and can only be approached by a public authority. It is *micro* in that it is concerned with particular employers and specific job seekers rather than broad aggregates.

Labor markets are multidimensional. The term can apply to all of those who work or seek work, or to all workers in an occupation (e.g., the clerical labor market), in an industry (the construction labor market), or in a geographical area (the metropolitan labor market). The occupational, industrial, and geographical markets overlap (college professors in a national market, ironworkers in a regional labor market, and taxi drivers in a local labor market). Planning could occur within any of these dimensions.

A labor market must incorporate and bring together both the supply of and the demand for labor. The domain of human resource policy is generally conceived of as encompassing all supply-side concerns; but on the demand side, it is conceived of as including only the concern for particular employment opportunities for particular individuals. As such, it serves as a bridge between, and overlaps to some degree, economic development policy on the one hand and social welfare policy on the other (the social welfare concept being broader than the human resource concept in that the former involves all factors related to the welfare of individuals and groups in society, while the latter is limited to their productive attributes and activities). The labor market planner, therefore, must limit the field so that it is manageable, but must be familiar with and able to relate to, contribute to, and use policies, programs, and resources outside but closely related to his or her field of concern. Clearly if there is no economic activity, there are no jobs; but an array of social services and amenities is necessary to make employability possible. The labor market planner must know the economic system which creates the jobs; the employers who control them; the unions which represent the employees; the roles of the families, churches, schools, and other institutions of the labor market which match or fail to match supply and demand.

The geographical dimensions of a labor market are determined by the range over which employees and potential employers communicate and workers move to obtain employment. Those with high investments in their occupational skills often prefer to abandon their residence rather than change occupations. They operate in regional, national, or international labor markets. But most workers would change occupations as well as jobs rather than move; that is, most people live and work, and jobs occur, primarily in local labor markets. The basic premise of planning for local labor markets is that each differs significantly and that problems are best identified and solved at the labor market level by those knowledgeable about conditions there.

However, in the United States there are no available organizations to plan for industries, occupations, or regional labor markets. Political jurisdictions are hardly ever contiguous with labor markets, but standard metropolitan statistical areas (SMSAs) usually are. Therefore, what little labor market planning occurs emphasizes local labor markets, i.e., the geographical area which encompasses both the residences and places of employment of most workers within normal commuting patterns.

Planning for a local labor market might encompass enhancement of the full career potential of all labor market participants and assuring that the full human resource needs of the local economy are optimally met. No one has that responsibility, however. Most labor market relationships work out reasonably well without intervention. Planning is required only if intervention is to follow. For that reason, local labor market planning in the United States is generally limited to concerns of either (1) economic development, or (2) meeting the employability, employment, or income needs of those finding it difficult to compete successfully for available employment opportunities. Economic development requires labor market planning. Planning for programs which focus upon the needs of disadvantaged workers is much less than labor market planning. Still, if it considers the full range of potential opportunities and the full range of resources available to aid the target groups, it is a reasonable approximation of labor market planning.

The target groups of federally funded programs are only a small minority of the actual and potential labor force. Problems range across the entire spectrum of skills and occupations on both the demand and supply sides of the labor market. A planning process similarly dedicated to improving labor market functioning would concern itself with relationships across industries and occupations, population groups, generations, and institutions. In that exercise, federal program budgets would be viewed as only one important source of funding. The response would be a search for ways to fit federal programs and funds into the pursuit of labor market objectives without violating federal objectives. But that is a level of political sophistication yet to be realized.

EMPLOYMENT AND TRAINING PROGRAM PLANNING

The most comprehensive employment and training program planning activity is (as the name implies) required by the Comprehensive Employment and Training Act (CETA). In addition, formal plans are required as a prerequisite for federal funds in the Work Incentive Program (WIN), the public employment services, and for social services under Title XX of the Social Security Act. An annual prime sponsor plan is required identifying the target groups to be served, specifying the mix of services to be supplied and designating the organizations assigned to deliver the services as authorized by CETA's various titles. At the heart of the CETA concept is the notion of decentralized planning for the delivery of a decategorized range of services, dependent upon local and individual need. The remainder of this chapter illustrates how CETA planning is conceived to work and comments on how it actually works out in practice.

The Planning Steps Applied to CETA

In the context of a public program on behalf of the economically disadvantaged the generalized planning steps set forth at the beginning of the chapter emerge as essentially six planning tasks: (1) out of the population eligible for service (always many times greater than the number who can be served with available resources), establish priorities among and within target groups; (2) identify present and potential job openings accessible to the client groups after receiving program services; (3) identify the barriers that currently impede access of the target groups to those jobs; (4) design a mix of employment and training services capable of removing or overcoming those barriers for members of the service group; (5) choose an agency or combination of agencies and organizations capable of delivering the needed mix of services; and (6) monitor the performance of the service delivery agencies, evaluate their results, and feed back learnings from the evaluation step to improve this and other programs. Each of these tasks deserves brief comment.

Calculating the Universe of Need

Very little detailed data are systematically collected specifically concerning the economically disadvantaged on a subnational basis. To compensate for this lack, local program planners can either make use of proportions derived from national surveys or develop their own sources. For example, the simplest methodology uses a multiplication factor that varies with the area's unemployment rates. Similar factors of proportionality are used to account for low-income full-time workers, underrepresentation of specific groups in the labor force, the census undercount, near-poverty unemployment, and several other key components employed in building universe-of-need estimates.

This approach has been widely criticized for its narrow orientation, the use of national relationships in the methodology, and the lack of estimates of sufficient specificity to enable planners to use it as a basis for mix-of-service prescriptions at the local labor market level. The use of national factors of proportionality is especially serious when estimates must be prepared for smaller cities and areas. Questions also have been raised as to the applicability of the same set of factors to both inner-city and rural planning areas.[7]

In response to these criticisms, attempts have been made to classify the planning area population by race, sex, age, specific labor force status, educational attainment, income levels, and several specific target group indicators drawn from census data. While census data rapidly become dated and are limited in a number of other ways, the effort has helped to standardize the base data available to state and local planners. Efforts are continuing to update the census materials and develop additional data on the assessment of the need for employment and training services. A mid-decade census of population has been approved, but the scope has not been determined. The search is for data which will reveal not only who and how many are in need of services, but what services they need.

Despite the increasing availability of data in more usable forms, little real impact has yet been made on actual program operation. The present planning process still largely ignores decisions about whom to enroll and why. Age, race, and income guidelines are used to screen in and screen out applicants who, within broad categories of eligibility, are enrolled basically on a first-come, first-serve basis. Program operators are faced with the problem of serving an almost endless variety of enrollee interests, aptitudes, and needs. Rational planning is most difficult under these circumstances.

Planning tools are needed that group prospective clients by the specific types and degrees of service needs they have in common. The incidence of barriers to employment for these homogeneous groups must be identified, and the barriers must be related to specific employment requirements. The planner should identify which barriers are amenable to modification by what services. Resources can then be allocated to services in proportion to the incidence of the relevant barriers in the group to be served. These tasks require an overall construct that relates the population to the labor market and allows the use of static measures in what is actually a very dynamic environment.

A great deal of research and experimentation will be required before this essential first task of program planning can be accomplished satisfactorily. Even then, since needs always exceed resources, choice of whom to serve must be made largely on political grounds among the groups needing services, but the decisions could be made more rationally with relative costs and effectiveness in mind.

Accessible Job Openings

The ultimate payoff for employment and training planning, as long as it has a social welfare orientation, is a better job and a higher and more stable income for members of the chosen target groups. A first principle for any labor market planner to remember is that the demand for labor is a derived demand. No one buys labor for its own sake. Jobs come into existence only when someone spends (or is expected to spend) money for the purchase of a good or service and an employer hires someone to produce what is demanded. The only exception to that market orientation is when a public agency charged with responsibility for employment opportunities spends public funds directly for the hiring of a target individual with the job as the product and the production as a byproduct.

Given the number of jobs that do now and will exist, the next question is the relation of demand to supply. At a moment in time, the concept of job vacancy would provide the answer. Just as a person without a job and actively seeking one is unemployed, a job vacancy would be a situation signaled by active efforts of an employer to fill a position. Because of conceptual and technical problems, the government does not collect job vacancy statistics. The next best measure is one of relative tightness: For which occupations is unemployment low? And for which occupations is it high?

Over a longer period, net growth in employment in occupation, and replacement needs resulting from termination, retirement, and death, measure the accessible demand. Accessible supply is more difficult. For jobs requiring specific skills, the output of the training system—academic education, vocational education, apprenticeship, OJT, and so on—provides an indicator. However, relatively few jobs have very specific skill requirements. Many jobs can be satisfactorily held without previous training, and skills learned on the job are often easily transferable to another job. However, labor market planning can never be an exact science. The planner deals in probabilities. Data, though weak, can provide guidance to the alert planner knowledgeable in the workings of the labor market, in identifying those occupations in which a client is more likely to be able to find jobs than in other occupations.

Finally, the planner must be knowledgeable about employer recruitment, selection and hiring practices, and the objective requirements of jobs. Vital concepts are the relationship between the external labor market and the internal labor market and the ports of entry through which persons are hired from outside the establishment and then move through transfer and promotion within the internal labor market as described in Chapter 6. Only then can the planner judge which jobs might be accessible under what conditions to which job seekers and then prescribe measures to prepare people for the jobs or aid them to remove or surmount barriers to job access.

Barriers Assessment

Having established priorities among the target population and identified accessible jobs, the planner must next assess the barriers confronting particular groups or individuals among the chosen clientele. That task in turn is followed by prescriptions of a mix of services to surmount the barriers. Barriers assessment is at a very rudimentary stage, however.

In general, barriers can be divided into two groups: (1) those inherent in the individuals themselves—lack of skills, experience, motivation, and so on—requiring some change in the individual and (2) those incorporated into the institutions of the labor market and the society—discrimination is a prime example—and requiring institutional change.

Little is known currently about the relative incidence of barriers to stable employability within population subgroups. The individual assessment of program clients requires gathering accurate information about the aptitudes, skills, attitudes, personality traits, life and work histories of enrollees. The potential exists for the use of such individual assessment data in making estimations of handicaps or barriers within the entire population groups, but substantial effort is still required to develop usable techniques.

Therefore, the first concern of the planner employed under the CETA system is the availability of jobs. But that is not sufficient. The planner must assure that (1) a job is available and (2) the client has realistic access to that job. Also, since planning is a future-oriented activity, the planner must be sure not that the job is there now but that it must be accessible at the end of whatever preparation process is involved. This requires a knowledge of the current employment structure and the relations of supply and demand, an ability to project that relationship, and a knowledge of the entrance requirements and access routes to jobs and an ability to manipulate them.

The primary tool for planning job access is (1) an industry-occupation employment matrix, current and projected for the future and (2) some indicator of the relative accessibility of available jobs to particular clients. National data may not be much help to the planner for a local labor market. Therefore, the Department of Labor and the state employment security agencies are cooperating in an Occupational Employment Statistics program now in operation in 44 states. As a measure and a base for projections, it is an invaluable tool for the employment and training program planner.

The most serious problem encountered in the projection of such data is the fact that traditional methods of assessment are quite inappropriate for use with the seriously disadvantaged. Newer, specially designed methods are coming into use, but they have yet to be tested adequately for validity and acceptability. Some methods of assessment have been designed for specific local purposes such as the assignment of individuals to training programs geared to specific labor market opportunities, but their data may lack flexibility for more general estimating purposes. Nevertheless, some form of individualized assessment of service needs is inescapable, whether done by some formalized system or casual judgment. To identify or develop an orderly and consistent system for making such assessments the planner must be aware of the various methods under use or experimentation, the rationale behind their usages, and their limitations.

Assessment tools need to be validated under varying circumstances in various types of labor markets with different subgroups of the disadvantaged if they are to be useful in the planning and administration of decentralized manpower programs. At present, the state of the art permits few well-supported generalizations based upon assessment data. As promising assessment tools are administered to larger groups of clients, a data base for improved understanding should emerge. Until that time, however, it is at least possible at present to categorize particular groups in relationship to particular jobs as being job ready and immediately placeable, subject to modest employment barriers, or faced by high barriers to placement, and to identify for each of those groups generally the most persistent and serious barriers to their employment.

The Mix of Services

Given identification of the barriers faced by target groups in assessing available jobs, prescription of the type of service or services needed to avoid or surmount those barriers is a logical next step and is usually indicated by the barrier itself. Two decades of program experience have identified a long list of different services useful for some people under some conditions. The challenges are (1) to identify who needs what and (2) to deliver that "what" effectively. Essentially, these services can be categorized under six headings:

1. Entry services to recruit and enroll clients and to assess their needs.
2. Employability improvement: to improve the basic employability of individuals.
3. Job access: to remove obstacles that impede access to available jobs.
4. Job creation: to create jobs for the target individuals.
5. Supportive services—services other than employment and training to facilitate participation in programs or jobs.
6. Income maintenance to provide income through transfer payments sometimes attached to some work activity short of a recognizable job.

A critical task of the planner is adjusting the mix of services to changing labor market conditions. Changes in local economic conditions have two basic impacts on the mix of services. First, changes can alter the universe of need. For example, the characteristics of the unemployed change as the unemployment rate changes. A rising unemployment rate will generally decrease the proportion but not the numbers of the unemployed having serious barriers to employment. The second major impact of rising unemployment on the appropriateness of the service mix is the obvious decrease in accessible jobs. Not only does the absolute number of job openings decrease, but the selection criteria of employers is likely to rise. Competition for available jobs increases, and workers are generally willing to settle for lower wages than their skills and education would warrant at other times. Placement rates from skill training programs fall off. Opportunities for OJT are harder to obtain. Referrals tend to become less and less disadvantaged. Job creation begins to look more attractive. The program operator and the planner begin to question the appropriateness of the service strategies.

There has been need throughout the employment and training experience for a set of criteria to determine which mix of services is likely to be most effective and efficient for which people, for which jobs, under what conditions. In developing such criteria, the planner needs reliable estimates of the relative incidence of specific barriers to stable employability within the chosen subgroups. Those barriers, once identified, can become the basis for prescription: What mix of services are most likely to be successful in removing or overcoming those barriers?

The problem, of course, is that present methods for predicting the existence of barriers within population subgroups are inadequate for the purpose of prescription. Until techniques are available for identifying the barriers faced by individuals and aggregating them into proportions among groups, planners and practitioners will be left with only the most general notions of barriers and how they relate to particular occupations and service strategies. Nevertheless, decisions must be made, and the planner will make them on the basis of the best information and judgment available.

Choosing Among Alternative Service Deliverers

The freedom implied by the decentralized and decategorized planning model would allow the planner working for a governor, mayor, or county executive to choose, with the advice of a planning council, which of the available public and private agencies should have the assignment of delivering to the chosen clients which components of the service mix. Available in every community are the public schools and the public employment service. There are also public welfare agencies, vocational rehabilitation agencies, private schools, community action agencies, community-based organizations representing various minority groups, private organizations, both profit and nonprofit, and other alternatives. The choice is a mix of response to political forces and objective judgment concerning the relative effectiveness of various agencies for various tasks. The planning unit may either contract separately with each agent for performance of a particular task or may choose one as prime contractor to subcontract to others. Whatever the choice, the planner under this new system is in a politically sensitive but potentially powerful position to influence both the relative welfare of agencies and their staffs and the effectiveness with which services are delivered.

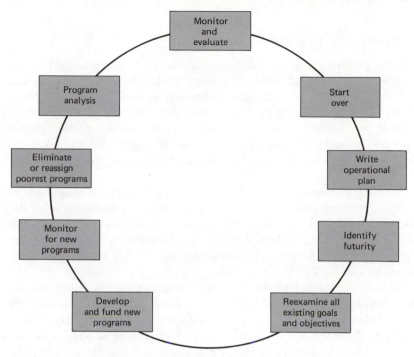

Figure 21-4   Continuous planning model. (Source: Garth Mangum et al., *Job Market Futurity: Planning and Managing Local Manpower Programs* (Salt Lake City: Olympus Publishing Company, 1979), p. 128.)

Monitoring and Evaluation

Whether or not the plan accomplishes its objectives depends in part on its appropriateness under prevailing circumstances and in part on the efficiency and effectiveness with which it is carried out. Therefore, to test the plan, the planner must be able to monitor performance to assure efficiency on the part of the service deliverers and evaluate the results to determine whether the prescriptions worked—that is, did an improvement in the employment and income of the clients result that would not have happened in the absence of the services? The evaluator at the national level asks: Was the effort worthwhile? Could the funds have been better spent on something other than employment and training services? The labor market planner asks: Could a more effective mix of services have been provided, or could they have been delivered more efficiently?

As the only purpose of monitoring and evaluation at this level is service improvement, it is followed by feedback and modification in subsequent planning cycles. In fact, in a continuous and ongoing program, the evaluation of the results of current activities can be viewed as its starting point of each cycle as in Figure 21-4 rather than the general paradigm suggested earlier in the chapter.

CETA Planning in Practice

That is the planning approach around which CETA was designed, along with some of the practical problems confronted by the dedicated planning staff. And many there are with the dedication to use the data and techniques available and search for better. But they are not in the majority. There is no way to require people to plan. They can always go through the motions and submit the appropriate number of pages with the required blanks filled in, but they may just be spreading next year's budget over last year's plan.

There are a discouraging number of barriers. Congress is frequently so late in its appropriations that the planning year begins without knowing the resources to be available. Labor Department instructions may be equally late. Data are rarely available in the form in which they are needed and for the area over which the planner has jurisdiction, though reasonable surrogates can be created by the innovative.

Planners are subject to the final determination of the policymakers, whose sense of political acceptability may overrule the planners' seemingly objective judgment. Most discouraging to good planning is the fact that so few can recognize it when it occurs. A shoddy plan and an admirable one are equally likely to survive the approval process. Then once a plan has been submitted and approved, frequent changes in legislation, regulation and funding availability require continuous modification. Motivation to sound planning must emerge primarily from the professional commitment of the planner and from the respect of colleagues. For the true professional, that is enough.

THE FUTURE OF PLANNING

Every planning process has its frustrations. The future is always uncertain. A bad plan may be worse than no plan. The best of plans may be ignored by the decisionmaker who has overriding priorities. All planning has costs and is worthwhile only when the costs of failure to plan are greater in probability terms than certainty of the planning costs. There is no comprehensive human resource planning but a great deal of fragmented planning where the situation meets that cost-benefit test. Perhaps it is the growing complexity of the world which has foreordained that planning is on the increase and, usually, on the improve in each of the types discussed in this chapter.

DISCUSSION QUESTIONS

1. Test the planning steps outlined in the chapter against your own experience. Apply them to some tasks you have undertaken: did you go through all of these steps? Were there other steps? What changes in the list would you advocate?
2. Have you ever been involved in an organization which undertook planning to meet its own internal personnel needs? If so, what was the motivation? What

were the techniques? What were the problems? How useful was the exercise?
If not, was there a need for such planning in any organization with which you
have been involved? What would it have accomplished? Why was it not undertaken?

3. The U.S. society seems to be characterized by an extensive range of private
planning and a minimum, though growing, amount of public planning. However, the public planning is primarily planning for the administration of public
programs rather than planning for the achievement of broader social objectives. How do you explain this apparent preference? What are the arguments
for and against an expansion of public policy planning relative to U.S. labor
markets?

4. What is your impression of the effectiveness of human resource planning in
those nations which attempt to guide their policies by a series of five-year
plans? What kinds of problems might be susceptible to resolution through such
planning efforts? What kinds of problems are unlikely to bend to such treatment?

5. The Comprehensive Employment and Training Act (CETA) probably incorporates the most extensive program planning process in the United States. Every
community is within the jurisdiction of some CETA prime sponsor. Inquire
what unit of government has responsibility for CETA in your area. Interview
someone engaged in the CETA planning process. Discuss the nature of that
planning and the extent to which it influences the workings of local labor markets. What evidences exist as to CETA's results in your community?

Notes

1. Bureau of National Affairs, "Effective Utilization of Manpower," *Personnel
   Policies Forum,* survey no. 83, August 1968.
2. James W. Walker and Michael N. Wolfe, "Patterns in Human Resource Planning," *Human Resource Planning* 1 (1978): 189–202.
3. George T. Milkovich and Thomas A. Mahoney, "Human Resources Planning
   and PAIR Policy," in Dale Yoder and Herbert G. Heneman, Jr., eds., *ASPA
   Handbook of Personnel and Industrial Relations* (Washington, D.C.: Bureau of
   National Affairs, 1979) pp. 2-1–2-30.
4. James W. Walker, "Personal and Career Development," in Yoder and Heneman, op. cit., pp. 5-57–5-74.
5. Milkovich and Mahoney, op. cit., Elmer Burack and James W. Walker, eds.,
   Manpower Planning and Programming (Boston: Allyn & Bacon, 1972); Douglas
   T. Hall, *Careers in Organizations* (Pacific Palisades, Calif.: Goodyear Publish-
   ing Company, 1976); Lee Dyer, ed., *Organizational Careers Research and
   Practice* (Ithaca, N.Y.: Cornell University, 1975); Herbert G. Heneman, Jr., and
   George Seltzer, *Employer Planning and Forecasting,* U.S. Dept. of Labor, Manpower Administration, Manpower Research Monograph no. 19, 1970.
6. The remainder of this chapter is based on Garth Mangum et al., *Job Market
   Futurity: Planning and Managing Local Manpower Programs* (Salt Lake City:
   Olympus Publishing Company, 1979).
7. National Commission on Employment and Unemployment Statistics, *Counting
   the Labor Force* (Washington, D.C.: GPO, 1979), chap. 15.

Chapter 22
The Employment and Training Connection with Macroeconomic Policy

The goals of employment and training programs fall into four general categories. First, the programs seek to help match the supply of and demand for labor, increasing the efficiency of the labor market mechanism. Second, they are aimed at helping workers who suffer particular disadvantages in competing for available jobs. Third, during periods of slack business activity, they seek to directly create jobs that will provide an appropriate countercyclical balance and, at the same time, generate needed public services. And finally, in the broadest sense, they are designed to provide every worker the vocational preparation needed for occupational choice, while at the same time ensuring that societal labor requirements will be met.[1]

Given restricted resources, only limited progress can be expected in the realization of these ambitious goals. Some frictional unemployment will always remain—when workers search for new jobs and are temporarily unemployed or when employers relocate or close their businesses. Seasonal factors will continue to generate temporary joblessness. Cyclical imbalances, which appeared to have grown more intense and unpredictable in the 1970s, will continue to be a prime problem. Some structural unemployment will exist as long as technology and changing tastes continue to make some skills obsolete, as long as many entrants to the labor force are ill prepared, and as long as the supply and demand for labor do not match perfectly. Workers will never have complete freedom of choice nor will industry's needs be exactly met when the future is uncertain, and particularly when those needs are not the same as workers' preferences.

Nonetheless, employment and training programs can lessen labor market imperfections. Through improved labor market services—such as better reporting of current and expected job vacancies, testing, outreach, and counseling—the duration of unemployment and the number of unfilled jobs may be markedly reduced. Through special rehabilitation and training programs for disadvantaged workers, combined with increased efforts to break down discrimination and restructure jobs for those with few skills, workers with deep-seated and long-lasting employment problems can become more productive and self-sufficient. With increased education and training for work and with better vocational guidance, workers can increasingly be placed in occupations of their choice in which their skills will be used productively.

Measures to increase the productivity, reward, satisfaction, and availability of employment are potentially far-reaching. Such improvements would affect all those who are in, can be drawn into, or will eventually enter the labor force, especially those who can expect to face barriers to employment during their work lives. Because of potential value, employment and training programs must be recognized as increasingly important economic factors which must be put to work in concert with other government economic policies, if the programs are to achieve optimal effect. Therefore, the relationship between employment and training policies and other economic policies of the government should be carefully examined and articulated.

MONETARY AND FISCAL POLICIES

During the post-World War II period the major objective of national government economic policy has been to regulate the aggregate demand for goods and services, which, in turn, affects the level of total output. Monetary and fiscal measures are the major tools. By changing the quantity of money in circulation (monetary policy), the government can stimulate or cool down business and consumer spending. As more money is made available, interest rates fall, consumption increases, profits rise, and investment is stimulated, but prices also tend to rise. Conversely, as the quantity of money is reduced, money incomes rise less quickly, so that consumers spend less and funds for investment are more difficult and expensive to acquire, decreasing aggregate investment and reducing pressures on prices. By changing its taxing and spending (fiscal policies), the government can change the amounts of cash in the hands of consumers and adjust its own demands for goods and services. Tax increases and reduced government spending will reduce demand, while tax cuts and increased government spending will add to demand.

One of the major reasons for regulating demand is to balance the economy's production of goods and services with consumption and investment demands and, in turn, to generate an economic climate in which the labor needed to produce these goods and services will be fully employed. This was articulated in the Employment Act of 1946, which exhorted the federal government to assume a continuing policy to promote maximum employment, production, and purchasing power. These goals were reiterated with somewhat stronger emphasis on the achievement of high employment in the Full Employment Act of 1978, which requires explicit reports to the Congress on the policies designed to achieve national economic goals. Monetary and fiscal policies can be used to alter the level of unemployment by affecting the demand for final products, which, in turn, changes the demand for labor. Arthur Okun, one-time chairman of the President's Council of Economic Advisers, estimated in 1962 that for every 1 percent increase in real gross national product, beyond normal growth arising from an expanding workforce and productivity gains, unemployment is reduced by 0.3 percent.[2] "Okun's Law" has sometimes been taken as suggesting a rather straightforward relationship between monetary and fiscal measures regulating aggregate demand and the level of unemployment. This oversimplification ignores the prime role of price change in the translation of nominal spending into real output changes. Indeed under some circumstances stimulative actions will have perverse outcomes. For example, when the economy is running near or at full capacity, a sudden increase in spending can pull prices upward; demand-pull inflation is the result. A policy contracting the money supply is one way to attempt to control this type of inflation.

A more difficult type of inflation to treat is the cost-push variety because it may occur while unemployment is associated with less than full employment and while production is below capacity. It arises largely from imperfections in the market that allow unions and corporations to push prices up in response to rising costs, which, in turn, generates rising costs and prices in a continuing spiral. Aggregate demand policies are not likely to cure cost-push inflationary ills, and policymakers may be forced to consider some form of market intervention.[3]

Attempts to regulate prices may have significant side effects throughout the economy. Maintenance of full employment is, of course, not the only goal of monetary and fiscal policy. By affecting the domestic price level, these policies change the relative attractiveness of exports and imports, altering the balance of trade and the balance of payments. By regulating the pattern of business, consumer, and government spending and by changing aggregate economic conditions, these measures affect the level of investment and production in the short run and the rate of economic growth in the longer run.

Structural Versus Demand-Deficient Unemployment

The relationship of employment and training policy to monetary and fiscal measures has been a source of controversy in recent years. Some economists claim that structural unemployment has increased markedly, as the skills of more and more workers have become obsolete because of technological change. According to their theory, there has occurred a twist in the demand of labor, so that educated and skilled workers are in short supply while large numbers of unskilled and poorly educated workers are no longer needed. If this is the case, an increased demand for goods and services will lead to wage increases in the occupations with a deficient supply of labor and to subsequent price rises. Though less skilled workers also will be hired, a high level of inflation may also result, rendering impractical the necessary monetary and fiscal policies. Employment and training programs, it is argued, are needed to train and retrain workers for available jobs and to employ those who cannot be trained.

There is continuing debate over the magnitude of such structural changes in the economy—and, consequently, over the policy implications. In the early 1960s argument raged openly between structuralists and those who urged a cut in taxes to increase aggregate demand and thereby reduce unemployment.[4] A tax cut, combined with the Vietnam build-up, did cut unemployment sharply. The 4 percent unemployment rate reached by the end of 1966 temporarily weakened the case of the structuralists, who had argued that such expansionary fiscal policies would have unacceptable inflationary consequences.

Low unemployment after 1965 postponed debate for some time, but with high unemployment in the 1970s, the arguments resurfaced over proposals for an enlarged public employment program. Such programs permit detailed targeting—on socioeconomic, regional, or industrial/occupational groups—and structuralists claimed that such a measure was needed to provide for an ever-increasing number of workers whose skills were no longer required by the industrial system.

The late R. A. Gordon suggested that part of what was previously thought to be structural—unemployment among teenagers and blacks, for example—was due to high turnover rates among those workers rather than prolonged periods of unemployment.[5] Although vacancies may exist in a low-wage sector, workers displaced in the high-wage sector may choose not to switch to low-wage sector jobs due to the potential high wages or other attractions of the high-wage sector; in this case unemployment may more accurately be called "differentially high-wage frictional unemployment." True structural unemployment only exists when workers wish to, but cannot, move to fill job openings in other areas, sectors or occupations. This type of structural unemployment calls for a breakdown of discrimination based on age, sex, and race which segments labor markets, as well as enlarged training programs. Efforts leading to the reduction of labor turnover and improvement in job search techniques would decrease long-term frictional unemployment.

A review of the labor market experience of disadvantaged workers during the sustained prosperity of the 1960s lends credence to both structuralist and demand-deficiency arguments. Expansion of demand brought unemployment rates to the lowest levels ever achieved with absence of wage and price controls. Yet the unemployment differentials between the labor force as a whole and those experienced by the various disadvantaged age-sex-race groups actually increase. Unemployment rates for those with poor education declined, for example, but their labor force participation rates went down even more. These developments highlight the fact that monetary and fiscal measures must work along with manpower programs and antidiscrimination policies to train, retrain, and give the structurally unemployed greater mobility in the labor market.

EMPLOYMENT AND TRAINING
PROGRAMS AS A COUNTERCYCLICAL TOOL

Until the implementation of the Emergency Employment Act in 1971, employment policy played little or no role in efforts to control economic fluctuations. As shown in Chapter 17, employment and training expenditures and programs expanded continuously throughout the 1960s but were applied without any countercyclical intent. With the passage of the 1971 act, however, and the massive jobs effort stimulated by the Comprehensive Employment and Training Act, public employment was added to the arsenal as a new tool for countering business downturns. From these efforts a number of lessons have been learned concerning the effectiveness of different strategies during periods of varying economic conditions. (An overall review of lessons learned from employment and training programs was presented in Chapter 20.)

First, regular training programs oriented toward the private sector are most effective in tight or improving labor market conditions. Subsidies to hire and train disadvantaged workers, to induce business to locate in depressed areas, or to eliminate discrimination will have their greatest impact when qualified workers are in short supply and when firms are expanding and opening new plants. Conversely, when firms are forced to lay off employees because of declining demand, when they have excess capacity and are trying to eliminate all but their most efficient plants, and when fears of unemployment lead to employee hostility toward newly hired disadvantaged workers, OJT or locational subsidies will be less effective.

Second, public employment is an effective strategy for holding down unemployment during cyclical contractions and periods of inadequate economic growth. Analyses have indicated that public service jobs offer the greatest "bang for the buck" in terms of lowering unemployment with a given amount of federal investment and further have the property of creating useful services. Moreover, a substantial proportion of the workers hired came from the disadvantaged segments of the labor force, thus providing help to those who were hurt worst by the business cycle. Many thousands of public service jobs require little or no training and only a small capital investment, and people can be put to work on these jobs as a temporary measure with little prior notice. There are, however, clear limits on the extent and duration of these programs. The existence of about three-fourths of a million public service jobs during 1977 raised concerns about substitution and the consequences of future program reduction.[6]

Third, publicly supported training becomes more important and effective in slack times, if for no other reason than to fill the gap left by declining private-sector participation. Institutional training provides at least income maintenance and perhaps useful training and basic education. Loose labor markets reduce trainees' chances of opting for jobs instead of training and diminish pressures by employers on training institutions to speed the delivery of trainees. Under the circumstances trainees are more likely to complete training courses. Since placements, employment rates, and increased earnings potential are closely correlated with completion of training, institutional training programs probably become relatively more effective during slack times.[7]

Fourth, training programs serve a different clientele when unemployment is high than when jobs are plentiful. Increasingly during the 1960s, the more seriously disadvantaged workers were helped—to a large extent because of generally expanding employment opportunities. The labor queue moved forward rapidly, and the disadvantaged became next in line for employment and hence became most in need of services. The fact that these programs emphasized the needs of the unskilled, poorly educated, and members of minority groups subject to discrimination does not mean that the process cannot be reversed. In all programs there is a tendency to "cream" the available and intended clientele for those most likely to benefit from assistance. When demand slackens, less disadvantaged workers among targeted groups seek and are selected for programs, so that those with more severe problems receive less attention.

Fifth, labor market services should be adjusted to changing economic conditions. When jobs are plentiful, the employment service can not only function as a labor exchange, but can also expand services to the disadvantaged providing them with needed counseling and other assistance and induce them to seek and find employment. However, when unemployment is high, fewer employers turn to the employment service, and those that do can choose among recently employed and less disadvantaged workers. This is the time when job development efforts to upgrade skills should be increased, even though the disadvantaged will be less successful in terms of placement. While the recently unemployed should be aided in their return to the labor force, the hard-core unemployed should not be ignored. If private jobs cannot be found, they should be directed to institutional training or to public employment.

These five lessons suggest that, if employment and training programs are to be administered in a countercyclical way, there must be flexibility to shift among different programs and approaches as economic conditions change. Since control over most funds has been shifted more to the states and localities under CETA, this goal can only be met by concerted and coordinated efforts of local administrators, coupled with an incentive system of federal payments geared to business conditions. This has been partially accomplished both by appropriating additional funds to local programs during economic declines and by establishing standby federal public employment funding that is distributed when unemployment passes a certain level. This trigger mechanism provides that public employment moneys are released when unemployment reaches a predetermined level, say 4.5 percent. Public employment funds are added if unemployment climbs. For example, for each 0.5 percent increase in unemployment above 4.5 percent, an additional 10 percent increase in employment and training funds might be provided. Thus if unemployment rose to 6 percent, employment and training funds would rise by 30 percent. Alternatively, the public employment program might be designed to soak up a percent of total excess unemployment above a predetermined acceptable level. Using this approach, the 1978 CETA requires the President to report annually to Congress the amount of funds needed to employ 20 percent of all the unemployed in excess of 4 percent and 25 percent of unemployment estimated to surpass 7 percent. This would mean that when unemployment reaches the 6 percent level, it would require federal funds to hire about 400,000 unemployed workers and nearly 900,000 persons when unemployment reaches 7.5 percent. The formula might also be applied in determining allocations for each state and locality, to help depressed areas that are especially hard hit by rising aggregate unemployment.

While conceptually appealing and justified on humanitarian grounds, there are a number of formidable technical obstacles to the use of employment and training programs as a countercyclical tool. Difficulties exist in forecasting needs in local labor markets and in estimating current conditions. Planners often cannot estimate skill shortages, and since skill training takes some time, programs face a timing problem. Training programs also could aggravate unemployment by increasing the supply of labor and could contribute to inflation if their costs are not kept relatively low.

There are problems, too, in expanding and contracting public employment in a countercyclical fashion. With the exception of the 1974–1975 recession, economic contractions since World War II have averaged less than a year in length, barely enough time to initiate large-scale public employment efforts. The best that could occur in such periods is for existing programs to be expanded. Still, any reasonable expansion in employment and training programs would absorb only a small proportion of recession victims. At its peak, the Comprehensive Employment and Training Act provided public service jobs for as much as 10 percent of total unemployment. Thus, the application of employment and training programs is hardly a substitute for monetary and fiscal measures in controlling economic fluctuations.

These programs nevertheless have a vital, if limited, role to play. While aggregate-demand management can change the level of unemployment, the effects must spread throughout the economy. For instance, an increase in spending to reduce unemployment will lead to increased business profits and increased earnings for those already employed as well as to the hiring of some additional workers. Public service employment and training expenditures, however, are directed specifically to those who are most in need of help. For a dollar of expenditure, employment and training programs have more impact on unemployment than other types of spending, and expansion of such programs may be the best way to help the unemployed when demand slackens.

THE TRADEOFF BETWEEN INFLATION AND UNEMPLOYMENT

Other things being equal, as unemployment is reduced and the pool of employable labor diminishes, firms must pay higher wages and salaries and/or accept workers of lower productivity. This increases the labor cost per unit of output, and in order to maintain their profit margins firms increase their prices. The ultimate cost of goods and services to the consumer is raised, with the inflationary pressures intensifying as the supply of idle workforce decreases. Prior to the 1970s when the American economy experienced both high unemployment and rising prices, the accepted strategy for achieving greater price stability was to reduce aggregate demand—which was expected to lead to the termination of less productive workers, some reduction in wage and salary demands, and thus to falling labor costs per unit of output.

Although the relationship between price changes and the level of unemployment is not exact—as the high inflation and high unemployment of the 1970s regrettably demonstrated—it has tended, at least in the first two and a half decades following World War II, to be inverse to changes in consumer prices (Figure 22-1). Under those conditions, in determining the thrust of its macroeconomic policies, the government must balance the harm caused by inflation with the bitter consequences of unemployment—though the latter may be reduced by unemployment insurance payments and other forms of income transfers. The tradeoff is not made explicitly, but pressures mount for expansionary monetary and fiscal policies when unemployment grows, and policymakers in recent years appear to be more ready to accept the consequences of additional unemployment when wages and prices accelerate too fast. At any given time, there is some preferred point

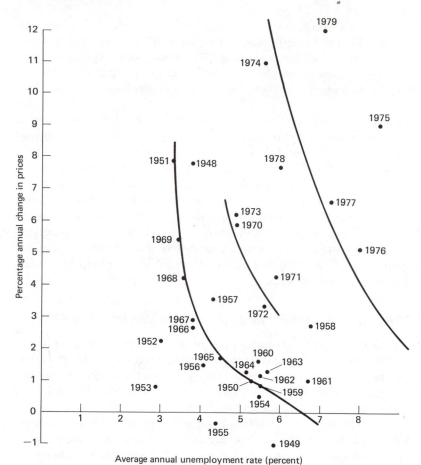

Figure 22-1 Annual changes in consumer price index and level of unemployment, 1949–1979. (Source: U.S. Department of Labor.)

on the curve toward which monetary and fiscal policies are directed. This is suggested in Figure 22-2 by a series of indifference curves, I_1, I_2, and I_3. All combinations of unemployment and inflation rates represented by a single curve are equally acceptable to the formulators of public policy. The curves are concave because at lower rates of unemployment policymakers will be more willing to trade off increased unemployment in order to reduce hyperinflation and vice versa. They would prefer both a lower rate of unemployment and inflation—that is, any point on I_1, to any point on I_3, but they are indifferent to the combinations represented by any one curve.

The attainable combinations are represented by the Phillips curve, the P-C line drawn in the chart. In choosing the goal of monetary and fiscal measures, policymakers will try to move to the lowest possible indifference

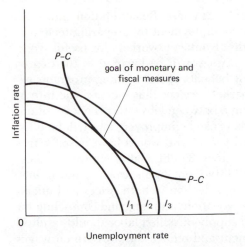

Figure 22-2   Inflation-unemployment indifference curves.

curve. This is the one that is tangent to the Phillips curve, or I_2 in the diagram.

During the 1970s, the observed tradeoff between price change and unemployment shifted (to the right in Figure 22-1) posing a much less favorable set of outcomes to any set of macroeconomic policies. This shift appears to reflect basic changes in the availability and prices of federal resources, in the structure of the economy and its institutions, and in the way labor market participants behave. While the activities of the Organization of Petroleum Producing and Exporting Countries (OPEC) and rising energy prices have received the most attention as the cause of concurrent high unemployment and rising prices around the world, the underlying causes extend beyond energy, involving a wide range of other factors including human and capital resources, technological changes and productivity trends. In these new circumstances, the high levels and long duration of unemployment necessary to reduce inflation pose unacceptable losses in social well-being and economic output. To ameliorate the dire consequences of high unemployment and inflation, policymakers have had to develop strategies designed to shift the Phillips curve to the left, to achieve some reduction in unemployment without unacceptable increases in prices.

Shifting the Phillips Curve

Employment and training policies of sufficient scope and adequate design should be able to alter the structure of the economy so that the tradeoff between unemployment and price changes is improved, or, in technical terms, the Phillips curve is shifted leftward and any given level of unemployment can be achieved with less effect on prices—or, in terms of Figure 22-2, society can move to a preferred indifference curve. Rehabilitation and train-ing programs can reduce structural unemployment by preparing technolo-gically displaced or educationally disadvantaged workers for useful work. Unemployment will be reduced and prices will be lowered to the degree that the productivity and placement benefits of the training programs ex-ceed their costs. Improved labor market services that increase the rate of placement and reduce the waiting time between jobs lower the level of un-employment. If the mobility of workers can be improved, jobs will be filled that would otherwise have remained vacant and would have raised wages and prices in the tight labor market areas. Traditionally, improved place-ment, counseling, outreach, and mobility-inducing measures could reduce frictional unemployment, resulting in a decline in both prices and unem-ployment. Finally, improvements for vocational training and counseling for all workers resulting in an increased supply of skilled labor should result in more personally satisfying employment and reduce the pressure on wages and prices from labor bottlenecks. Helping those with the most severe labor market problems and the highest rates of unemployment will reduce the disparities among the unemployment rates of various groups in the labor force and, in turn, lower the pressure on wages so that there will be less price rise at any level of unemployment.[8] After nearly 20 years of efforts in this direction we have not succeeded in creating an environment that is conducive to a significant narrowing of the range of unemployment rates among various groups in the labor force.

The impact of past employment and training programs on the tradeoff between unemployment and the rate of price change cannot be measured. Claims that training efforts have shifted the Phillips curve to the left (or at least slowed its shift to the right) are based on faith rather than empirical evidence. The effects of increasing expenditures are undoubtedly dwarfed by other changes in the structure of the economy. Also, their impact will probably be felt only in the longer run because the payoff on training ex-penditures comes in increased earnings and productivity of assisted workers over many years.

The Policy Mix

The fluctuations in price change and unemployment rates in the post–World War II period resulted not only from exogenous economic fac-tors but also from misapplication of monetary and fiscal tools and changing notions about the proper tradeoff between inflation and unemployment. During the Eisenhower years, more emphasis was given to fighting inflation than to lowering unemployment. The government's tight monetary and fis-cal policies were blamed for the recession of 1958 and 1959. The Demo-cratic victory in 1960 is frequently attributed to the high level of unemploy-ment, which reached 6.8 percent in December 1960. Promising to "get this country moving again," President Kennedy emphasized the need for full employment, proclaiming an interim goal of 4 percent unemployment. To this end he proposed an income tax cut, which was not initiated until 1964, after President Johnson assumed office. During the Johnson administration, increasing employment was still given priority over fighting inflation. Budget expenditures increased markedly without adequate monetary restraint or taxation, with the result that prices began to rise too fast.

In 1968 the Republicans were voted into office pledging to stop the rise of prices. Tacitly, GOP economic advisors acknowledged that this would probably be accompanied by a rise in unemployment to a level estimated at 4.5 to 5 percent; the rate actually rose to more than 6 percent, reviving charges of Republican insensitivity to unemployment. In the early 1970s administration planners reverted to expansionary monetary and fiscal policies, which stimulated renewed economic growth and trimmed unemployment. Again the inflationary push became severe, but half-hearted wage-and-price controls resorted to in 1971 did little to arrest inflation. While the shifts in policy were not always explicit—because both parties gave lip service to the incompatible goals of reducing unemployment *and* price stability—it is clear that there have been some major swings in public preferences over the past two decades. Following the OPEC oil embargo and world-wide crop failures over the 1973-1975 period, the nation faced the worst inflation and unemployment combinations of our experience. These problems were exacerbated by the public's loss of confidence in the ability of the government to deal with economic problems as the attention of one administration was diverted by the Watergate scandal and the subsequent resignation of the President, and succeeding administrations were unable to devise and implement policies to effectively address the more adverse inflation/unemployment situation. At this writing, inflation is running at a 13 percent annual rate and unemployment is above 6 percent, a circumstance that reemphasizes the urgency of looking beyond conventional macroeconomic policy for ameliorating the twin threat of high unemployment and the danger of accelerating inflation.

One reason for the unfavorable inflation-unemployment tradeoff is that our economy is not perfectly competitive. Most goods are produced by firms having some degree of control over prices, while labor unions and other associations of working people, such as professional associations, have some power to maintain or raise their wages or money incomes. There is a consequent rigidity in prices and wages because large firms are reluctant to lower prices and union bargainers will rarely accept wage reductions, even when sales and employment are slack. Even more serious, some firms with excess capacity and declining sales will raise their prices to bolster falling profit margins, labor unions press for wage increases despite rising unemployment, and service industries will take advantage of shortages that may persist even in a recession. Concentrations of market power can thus lead to rising prices, wages, salaries, and fees despite reductions in aggregate demand and rising unemployment.

Moreover, our experience in the 1970s has taught us that inflationary pressures are very slow to unwind even when aggregate demand slackens. Success in curbing inflation has been difficult to achieve because of the momentum of past inflation and the reciprocal relationship between wages and prices. For a large portion of the job market, wages are influenced strongly by bargaining power and equity considerations, which typically involve maintaining wages relative to inflation rather than to shifting conditions in the labor market. Supporting workers' desires to sustain real incomes are employers' concerns about declining morale and, consequently, productivity. Thus, many workers have been able to match the rise in prices with adjustments in their wage rates, albeit with some delay, either through some type of cost-of-living escalator or by large catch-up wage increases when contracts are renegotiated. The sensitivity of wage increases to high rates of past inflation has meant substantial wage increases during recent years despite historically high rates of unemployment.

The measured empirical relationship between unemployment and price changes reflects structural characteristics of the economy. To the degree that corporations and labor unions have market power that they use to maintain or raise prices and wages even when aggregate demand is falling, the tradeoff between unemployment and price rises will have worsened. And because market power implies discretionary behavior, the reaction of the economy to any monetary and fiscal measure has become less predictable. One method of attempting to gain greater control over the economy is to enforce some type of regulation over wage-and-price changes, instituting what is called an incomes policy.

Wartime Controls

Because the regulation of wages and prices involves the transfer of power from the private to the public sector, wage-and-price controls were historically a wartime phenomena prior to 1971. They have been used to allocate goods for military needs and to ensure that lower-income families get a fair share of scarce commodities, which otherwise would be available only to those able to pay inflated market prices.

During World War II, the National War Labor Board, made up of business, labor, and public representatives, was established to administer wages, while the Office of Price Administration was set up to stabilize prices and rents and to regulate the rationing of scarce goods. The mechanisms for controlling prices and wages were generally rated as successful. From 1914 to 1920, with only the very limited controls of World War I, average hourly earnings rose 142 percent and the cost of living 100 percent. From 1941 to 1945, when controls were in full effect, wages rose 40 percent and prices 22 percent despite more severe labor and consumer goods shortages.

Controls were also instituted during the Korean hostilities, which lasted from June 1950 until February 1953. Despite relatively mild inflationary war pressures, prices rose much more rapidly during the control period of the Korean War than during World War II. By the time wage-and-price controls were instituted, about eight months after the outbreak of hostilities, most of the inflationary pressures generated by the military action had run their course; and the wage-and-price controls administered by the Wage Stabilization Board and Office of Price Stabilization remained a holding action, providing insurance and standby machinery in case the limited Korean action spread into a full-blown war.

Though experience with these wartime controls is not directly transferable to peacetime conditions, it highlights several issues that are relevant under any circumstances. Most obviously, the almost universal rejection of controls after both wars raises questions about their effectiveness and the difficulties of substituting regulation for the allocative efficiency of the free market in the long run. For instance, the pent-up postwar consumer demands and the expressions of serious labor unrest after World War II suggest that distortions had occurred in the rationing process and that resumption of market functions was necessary to relieve them. There is also the basic issue of how to allow wages to adjust to the cost of living. The National War Labor Board rejected arbitrary freezing of wages and permitted wages to catch up to the increases in cost of living prior to the imposition of controls in October 1942. After that period the wage-and-price controls were maintained, and no general wage increases were permitted until the war was won. Despite the inflationary pressure, President Franklin D. Roosevelt insisted that no increases in prices and wages could be tolerated. "The only way to hold the line," he declared, "is to stop trying to find justification for not holding it here and not holding [it] there."[9] This meant that wages could not be adjusted to increases in cost of living and that values in consumer products deteriorated. The policy was effective as long as the support of the war remained universal. Such widespread support was lacking during the Korean period, and the inflationary pressures were milder; therefore, wage-and-price controls were much less stringent than in World War II.

Even though the Korean hostilities were marked by little change in money wages, wage controls raised problems concerning changes in hours of work, pensions, fringe benefits, shift premiums, vacations, upgrading, and merit or length of service increases. During both wars, these forms of remuneration increased markedly, frequently in lieu of general wage increases. Some of these resulted in deferred increases that were reflected in increased labor costs after controls were removed, and others raised unit labor costs immediately but did not show up in average hourly wage or salary schedules and, therefore, could be glossed over by the regulatory officials. Finally, there is the issue of raising the wages of workers receiving substandard earnings. Equity dictates that such increases should not be controlled, and even the rigid regulations of World War II permitted such increases. But raising wages of low-paid workers reduces wage differentials and encourages higher-paid workers and their unions to press for wage increases in order to maintain historical advantages.

The Guideposts

The problems inherent in wage-and-price controls argue persuasively against peacetime controls. However, when inflation combines with high levels of unemployment, the public becomes amenable to some degree of control. This was the case in 1962, when President Kennedy, through his Council of Economic Advisers, announced a set of voluntary guidelines for price and wage changes. They carried no penalty for violation and were intended to show business and labor the limits of good behavior compatible with price stability. The guideposts set forth by the Council of Economic Advisers coupled wage-and-price increases to overall productivity growth, suggesting that the rate of wage gain should follow the overall trend rate of output per labor hour and price adjustments for individual industries should match changes in unit labor costs.[10]

Many complications were concealed by these simple rules, and some exceptions were recognized explicitly by the council. Wage increases could exceed the guidepost rate in industries or areas that attracted insufficient numbers of workers. Prices could rise, or at least fall more slowly, in industries unable to attract capital to finance expansion, but they should rise at a lower rate where profits were being earned because of market power. Because almost every firm or industry could claim an exemption on one of these grounds, the guideposts were far from clear cut. Nevertheless, the central idea was that wage and price changes would depend on productivity changes.

From 1962 to 1964 these guideposts were enforced with varying enthusiasm and success. Though there were no sanctions imposed on industries or unions violating the rules, the government applied a variety of pressures from "jawboning" to market retaliation. Whether the guideposts had any impact outside the few cases of active intervention is debatable. Studies comparing wage and price changes during guidepost years with those of earlier years suggest that annual wholesale price changes were between 0.5 and 1.5 percent less than expected and that annual consumer price increases were reduced, on the average, by 0.5 percent. These reductions were probably due to the guideposts, though their significance has been questioned, since in the long run suppressed wage and price increases are likely to exert themselves. At most, the impact of the guideposts was not large, and it could not check the price increases that resulted from increased war spending.[11]

Peacetime Wage and Price Controls

The prolonged economic expansion of the 1960s, stimulated by government spending without tax increases, built up severe inflationary pressures in the economy that spilled over into the 1970s. The rate of inflation reached 5 percent in 1970 even though business conditions had deteriorated, with unemployment topping 6 percent in December. When consumer prices continued to rise during the first half of 1971, despite continued 6 percent unemployment, the administration elected to institute a 90-day wage-price freeze followed by nationwide wage-and-price controls.

Congressional sentiment for the adoption of an incomes policy had been building for some time. Indeed, the freeze action taken by President Nixon was based on legislative authority passed earlier by Congress—over the President's protest. Though the move was distasteful to the President and his economic advisers, there seemed to be few alternatives that would convince the public that the government was committed to combating inflation. Moreover, inflation aggravated the balance-of-payments situation. Fiscal and monetary policy alone no longer seemed capable of tuning the economy to a politically acceptable combination of inflation and unemployment necessary for both foreign and domestic confidence in American business.

From the initial freeze through three subsequent phases of wage and price controls, the impacts of controls were disputed. Some argued that controls were political window dressing that had little effect independent of business and credit conditions—Milton Friedman referred to the controls as cosmetics, at best. Others felt controls were too successful, creating distortions in the allocation of resources and hurting wage earners worse than employers. There was support for both sides. When controls were finally ended in 1974 with inflation racing ahead at more than 10 percent annually, there was a general consensus that, though controls might have accomplished some specific goals for a limited time, over the long run they were both ineffective in regulating powerful market forces and disruptive of the economic system.

The three-year experiment with regulated wages and prices did not produce unequivocal evidence about the impacts (or lack of them) of controls. It did, however, establish more clearly the parameters and limitations of incomes policies. Several conclusions stand out:

1. Controls are of little use in curbing the inflation caused by excess demand in an overheated economy. When controls are imposed under such conditions, they tend to create shortages and dislocations in the economy, frequently exacerbating rather than curing the problem.
2. Wage and price controls and/or freezes may have had some impact

in limiting the inflation caused by expectations or by the market power of large economic units. The initial freeze and the first period of controls apparently did temper inflationary expectations. When controls were lifted, the surge in consumer spending indicated that expectations of rising prices had been revived. The evidence indicates that controls can be of use in holding down prices and wages in sectors that are temporarily subject to excess demand. The rapid increase in subsidized medical care, the shortage of gasoline, and the rapidly rising construction wages in the surging housing market were three situations in which controls reduced what probably would have been excessive increases. For this purpose stand-by monitoring and stick-in-the-closet control mechanisms appear to be warranted.

3. The life of any control system is limited. If controls are not to be administered by a large enforcement agency, they must depend largely on voluntary cooperation. Public willingness to abide by the regulations quickly evaporates if controls are viewed as unfair. Less quickly, but just as surely, the usefulness of controls will diminish in time, even though the public accepts their equity. If controls are successful, there will be calls for their abandonment as unnecessary. If they fail, the arguments will be that they should be ended because they are useless. In a freely competitive economic system, all factions seldom agree that they are receiving their due; when the government is the arbiter, everyone soon feels cheated or tries to manipulate the system.

This was certainly the course of events during the early 1970s. Initially, bipartisan congressional sentiment, business, labor, and academic groups supported or at least were willing to try controls. Once controls were implemented, however, defections began quickly. By the time controls were ended in 1974, there was hardly a voice raised in their defense. Business claimed its profit margins had been unfairly crimped and its investments thereby curtailed. Labor claimed it had been the "patsy" accepting wage hikes within the guidelines while prices climbed far faster.

Controls aimed at curbing the market leverage of large economic units appear to be more effective in holding down wages than prices during cycles of business expansion. With unemployment remaining over 5 percent throughout most of the 1971–early 1974 control period, there was never any generalized labor shortage such as might be experienced in wartime and thus no natural demand pull on wages. At the same time, union bargaining power was compromised by the 5.5 percent guideline, and nonunion employee leverage was no doubt also hurt, as employers could claim a legal and moral right to limit salary raises. But controls were unable to check demand-induced inflation of prices. Under pressure, prices rose rapidly, while wages, in the absence of excess demand for labor, could not rise as easily. Initially, perhaps, during the slack, economic controls on those with market power may have been equally effective against both large corporations and large unions. The experience during the crest of the business cycle, however, indicated that labor was squeezed between continued wage guidelines and inadequate price controls.

The demise of the controls program was followed by six of the most turbulent years in the nation's economic history. The inflation rate soared to 11 percent in 1974 and posted an additional 9 percent rise in 1975. Prime movers in the accelerated rise of consumer prices were food and energy costs—costs which figure prominently in most families' budgets. At the same time, business activity soured as consumer spending and business investment declined in reaction to greater uncertainties about availability and cost of oil. Heavy layoffs in the hard-goods and construction industries drove the unemployment rate to its highest level since the Great Depression—8.5 percent for 1975 as a whole. Succeeding years brought highly unfavorable combinations of inflation and unemployment (Figure 22-1). During this period, there was considerable debate about policies to combat inflation and unemployment simultaneously. As mentioned earlier, public service employment programs were used as one weapon but little agreement could be achieved on an appropriate combination of price-wage restraints. As a consequence, it was not until the late 1970s that a formal guidelines policy was implemented under the Council on Wage and Price Stability (COWPS). As the program was initiated during 1979, the initial focus was on voluntary compliance with general goals which hardened as the year progressed. In any event, exogenous factors swamped any positive effects that the guidelines may have had on prices. In large part reflecting further sharp increases in gas, fuel oil, and in food prices, consumer prices rose at a double-digit rate.

Incomes policies and wage and price controls remain controversial. Apparently, the rising costs of raw materials, the changing mix of the labor force, the increasing skill requirements of the job market, and rising inflationary expectations have shifted the Phillips curve to the right, with ever higher levels of inflation associated with given levels of unemployment. Though wage-price controls have not been utilized, the Carter administration was persuaded by the potentially salutary impact of the monitoring device and general guidelines, but the Reagan administration pronounced these mechanisms as ineffective and abolished them. Clearly, neither income policies nor employment and training programs can be relied upon to solve the problem of the unemployment-inflation tradeoff in the face of the United States dependence upon foreign sources of energy and upon other imports. Controlling wages and prices, improving the workings of the labor market, retraining workers, and employing workers on public payrolls can be helpful in tuning the economy to the best possible point on the Phillips curve, but they cannot be relied on to solve the chronic problems associated with rising levels of unemployment and inflation.

DISCUSSION QUESTIONS

1. Probably the most difficult policy issue related to employment and training programs at the present time is the conflict between low unemployment and price stability. Which of the current programs appears least well adapted and which the most helpful to a situation in which unemployment is allowed to rise while pursuing policies to reduce inflationary pressures? Why?
2. How does the role of employment and training programs differ during various phases of the business cycle? How can it operate as a countercyclical tool? Has it been successful?
3. How can the adverse effects of inflation be most equitably spread among various parts of the economy and population?
4. Distinguish between short-term and long-term impacts of wage and price controls.
5. Explain how structural characteristics of the labor force are related to national monetary and fiscal policy.
6. Distinguish between: cost-push and demand-pull inflation; structural versus demand deficient unemployment; wage-price guideposts and wage and price controls.
7. Explain the underlying relationships inherent in the so-called "Phillips curve." What accounts for its location and shape? Is the curve shifting and what role, if any, do employment and training programs have in this movement?
8. Discuss the application of the Phillips curve to American experience during the past decade. Indicate the impact that appropriate training programs might have on shifting the curve. Specify the type of programs you would favor.
9. Consider two following situations: 6 percent unemployment with 10 percent inflation versus 10 percent unemployment with 6 percent inflation. Which of these situations would you prefer as a public policymaker? What kinds of questions would you want answered in choosing between these alternatives?
10. What do you believe is a realistic level of U.S. unemployment (as measured by CPS) that we should strive for by the end of next year? Explain the bases of your choice in light of the experience during the past two decades.

Notes

1. William G. Bowen, "What Are Our Manpower Goals?" in R. A. Gordon, ed., *Toward a Manpower Policy* (New York: Wiley, 1967), p. 59.
2. Arthur Okun, "Potential GNP: Its Measurement and Significance," *Proceedings of the Business and Economic Statistics Section of the American Statistical Association* (1962), pp. 98–104.
3. Charles C. Killingsworth, "The Development of Employment Policy," address delivered at the University of Notre Dame, 1980).
4. The opposing views are presented by Walter Heller and Charles C. Killings-

worth in Garth L. Mangum, ed., *The Manpower Revolution* (Garden City, N.Y.: Doubleday, 1965), pp. 97–146.

5. Robert A. Gordon, "Some Macroeconomic Aspects of Manpower Policy," in Lloyd Ullman, ed., *Manpower Programs in the Policy Mix* (Baltimore: Johns Hopkins Press, 1973), pp. 14–50; and *The Need to Disaggregate the Full Employment Goal* (The National Commission for Manpower Policy, Washington, D.C., 1978).

6. Martin Neil Bailly and James Tobin, "Inflation-Unemployment Consequences of Job Creation Policies," in John L. Palmer, ed., *Creating Jobs* (Washington, D.C.: Brookings Institution, 1978), pp. 43–86.

7. Robert Gay and Michael Borus, "Validating Performance Indicators for Employment and Training Programs," *Journal of Human Resources* (Winter 1980): pp. 29–49.

8. George L. Perry, *Inflation and Unemployment* (Washington, D.C.: Brookings Institution, 1970), p. 42.

9. Executive Order 9328, April 8, 1943.

10. *Economic Report of the President, 1962* (Washington, D.C.: GPO, 1962), p. 189.

11. John Sheahan, *The Wage-Price Guideposts* (Washington, D.C.: Brookings Institution, 1967), pp. 79–95.

Chapter 23
The Role of Unions and Collective Bargaining

Labor organizations have become important labor market institutions in all industrialized economies. It is important, therefore, to understand their role in labor markets. In order to do this, however, it is necessary first to outline the origin, development, and structure of unions. This will be followed by a discussion of the role of collective bargaining in labor markets. We conclude with an assessment of the impact of unions on employment and training programs.

THE NATURE OF LABOR MOVEMENTS

The term "labor movement" means different things in different countries. In most it refers to trade unions, political parties, and other cultural or educational organizations that represent workers. However, in the United States, "labor movement" refers almost exclusively to trade unions.

The differences between the labor movements in the United States and other countries are rooted in political, social, and economic institutions. The main reason American unions have not formed a labor party relates to our political and economic conditions, which have fostered less class consciousness than conditions in European countries. In Europe workers had to form political parties in order to gain the right to vote. The franchise became particularly important with industrialization and the growing importance of government in the lives of individuals. In the United States, however, workers were born free in the sense that they had the right to vote at an early date. It was not necessary, therefore, for the working class to organize itself in order to gain the right to vote. Moreover, unlike European workers, Americans did not conceive of themselves as a permanent working class. In part, this was because no political stigma was attached to them by denial of the right to vote. Moreover, the United States did not have feudal traditions as did European countries. Feudalism was a class system whose impact on social relations remained long after the system itself ceased to be important. No titles or other formal class distinctions existed in the New World.

Although American workers had serious problems, they were comparatively better off than their European counterparts. Their economic well-being was due, in large part, to relative labor shortages as the United States was being developed. Economic mobility made it difficult for socialists, who were active in the United States at a very early date, to organize workers on a class basis. As the twentieth-century American socialist leader Norman Thomas put it, socialists had difficulty gaining labor support in the United States because American workers found it easier to rise out of their class than to rise with it.

The American political system also has worked against the formation of a labor party. Because of the vast power of the presidency, a political party must have some chance to elect a president in order to become significant nationally. However, the manner in which the American president is elected gives great advantage to major national political parties and makes it very difficult for third parties to become established. In European parliamentary systems the chief executive is elected by parliament and not from geographic areas. Moreover, those systems sometimes have proportional representation. As a consequence, minority labor parties can exercise political influence in selecting prime ministers by participating in coalitions within the parliament and gradually building their political strength to become majority parties.

Another aspect of the two-party tradition in the United States that makes it difficult for third parties to get started is the ability of the major parties to incorporate popular features of third-party platforms, thus co-opting popular issues with workers and other voters. As a consequence of lack of class consciousness, relative economic mobility, and the American political system, the American labor movement was organized mainly around the job.

Although American workers were relatively better off economically than their European counterparts, they had serious problems that they sought to redress within the political system and through collective bargaining. Moreover, American unions had to overcome stiff opposition from employers and governments in order to achieve their status as generally accepted institutions. Before the 1930s employers generally were free to oppose unions by a variety of tactics, including discharging workers for union activity; requiring employees to sign yellow-dog contracts (agreeing, as a condition of employment, not to join unions); planting company spies in union ranks; blacklisting union members; making it difficult for those discharged for union activity to find new jobs in their localities, crafts, or industries; and intimidating union members and organizers with armed guards and physical violence.

Governments not only permitted use of these antiunion tactics, but actively opposed unions by a variety of tactics of their own. The courts interpreted many union tactics as being illegal and often nullified legislative attempts to outlaw yellow-dog contracts and other antiunion tactics. The Sherman Antitrust Act of 1890 was used against union activities and courts issued injunctions against strikes, picketing, and boycotts. Injunctions were particularly onerous to unions because they could be issued by proemployer judges without a hearing and could be sweeping in their prohibitions. Union leaders and members were subject to fines and imprisonment for defying these injunctions, however unfair their restrictions. Therefore, labor leaders had to spend considerable amounts of money and time defending themselves against hostile judges.

Also, at the state and local levels courts were hostile to unions as were legislatures and governors. Union organizing, strikes, picketing, and boycotts were actively counteracted by state officials, who used state and local police to curtail union activity.

Unions also suffered from periodic recessions and depressions before the 1930s. Even without government opposition rising unemployment made it very difficult for workers to win strikes. Recessions and the hostile legal environment made it difficult for any other than the strong craft unions in the transportation, printing, and construction trades to become very well established before the 1930s.

The social ferment of the 1930s created an environment much more favorable to union growth, though workers with limited skill—like those in agriculture, southern textiles, food processing, sawmills, and other low-wage industries—continued to have great difficulty getting organized. The main factors facilitating union growth in the 1930s and later were:

1. The depression, which was blamed in part on the private enterprise system, resulted in mass unemployment and economic hardship. Sentiment grew that it was good social policy to promote collective bargaining in order to make it possible for workers to protect themselves from arbitrary employer decisions and to combat future depressions by sustaining wages and, therefore, purchasing power.
2. As a consequence of growing acceptance of collective bargaining, new legislation curtailed some traditional antiunion tactics of gov-

ernments and employers. Courts, which had been particularly hostile to such union tactics as strikes, boycotts, and pickets, became much less hostile. The main favorable laws were the Norris-La Guardia Act of 1932, which limited the use of court injunctions against unions and outlawed the yellow-dog contract, and the National Labor Relations Act of 1935 (Wagner Act) which curtailed employers' antiunion activity, created the National Labor Relations Board (NLRB) as an enforcement agency, and provided for representative elections supervised by the NLTB.

3. Organizing activity was stepped up by intense rivalry between the American Federation of Labor (AFL), organized in 1886, and the Congress of Industrial Organizations (CIO), formed in 1935. The CIO challenged the AFL for leadership mainly around the question of organizing workers along industrial lines (e.g., steelworkers, rubber workers, auto workers, etc.) instead of around particular crafts (electricians, plumbers, sheet-metal workers, etc.). In general, the CIO adopted broader social objectives than the more conservative AFL. The CIO was actively supported by many intellectuals who saw the new federation as a vehicle to reform society. There can be little question that the CIO spurred the AFL to action, but both organizations agreed that rivalry ultimately caused more harm than good. They merged to form the AFL-CIO in 1955.

4. World War II greatly encouraged the growth of union organization, particularly among semiskilled workers. Organization was facilitated by tight labor markets, which made it easy for unions to exhibit gains for the members; a favorable government attitude because the government wanted union cooperation in the war effort; and the activities of the National War Labor Board, which had the power to compel employers—under threat of seizure by the armed forces—to sign collective bargaining contracts.

5. As unionism grew in general public acceptance in the decades of the 1950s and early 1960s, employees in the public sector also came to look upon unionism more favorably. This change in attitude, combined with action favorable to union organization on the part of the federal government, and some of the states and numerous local governments, has led to a great expansion of unionism and collective bargaining in the public sector. Bargaining is now about as extensive in the public services as in any other major sector of the economy.

6. By the beginning of the 1980s these generally favorable public attitudes toward unionism have declined, and many employers have also manifested less acceptance of unionism and collective bargaining. Also, as the economy has grown, many of the newly created jobs have been in occupational areas that the labor movement has traditionally found quite difficult to organize. These changes have

led to a significant decline in the relative rate of unionism (union membership as a proportion of the nonagricultural wage and salary force), as follows:

	UNION MEMBERSHIP (MILLIONS)	UNION MEMBERSHIP AS A PERCENT OF NONAGRICULTURAL WAGE AND SALARY WORK FORCE
1958	17.0	33.2%
1961	16.3	30.2
1964	16.8	28.9
1967	18.4	27.9
1970	19.4	27.3
1973	19.9	25.8
1976	19.6	24.7
1978	20.2	23.6

Despite changes in the political, social, and economic environment within which they operate, the basic character of the American labor movement—its emphasis on collective bargaining and disinclination to form a labor party—remains.

The Origin of Labor Movements

The role of unions and collective bargaining in American labor markets will be illuminated by looking at some of the major forces causing labor movements to start and to develop. Although they disagree over the roles and objectives of labor organizations, most authorities agree that labor movements originated with industrialization. Industrialization invariably creates a number of problems for workers. Chief among these is the fact that the workers depend on employers for jobs in a market often characterized by unemployment. It might be argued that demand and supply will protect workers, but these impersonal forces have little regard for workers' welfare. Industrial societies are characterized by economic instability because of difficulties in maintaining a balance between the production and the sale of goods. Because industrialization causes workers to be dependent on wages, workers have considerable insecurity unless they acquire some means to protect themselves from unbridled market pressures.

Producing units in industrial societies also tend to be larger and more impersonal than under preindustrial conditions. Impersonalization makes it necessary for workers to create machinery through which they can express their grievances to management. Also, very large corporations often have a great deal of power over the markets they engage in. Unionization has been viewed as one way workers can counteract in part this concentration of economic power.

Workers in industrial societies may also be deprived of income by factors such as industrial accidents, early superannuation, and illness. Economic security was much less of a problem in preindustrial societies because the family was the basic producing unit. The family took care of its own in time of distress, and in any event was much less dependent on the market than the industrial society family. Industrialization created needs for new social security procedures as the family ceased to be the basic producing unit.

The industrial society, therefore, created a need for workers to have some means of protecting themselves from market forces and of participating in the formulation of rules governing wages, hours, and working conditions. Every democratic, industrial society, therefore, has produced some kind of labor movement. In some cases, the movement is dominated by revolutionaries who believe that the workers' problems are inextricably bound up with the capitalist system and that that system must be eliminated if the workers' problems are to be solved. Other labor movements are socialist-dominated and hold that destruction of the system by revolution might not be necessary, but that solutions to the workers' problems will require considerable modification of capitalist institutions. Specifically, the socialists advocate the public ownership and/or control of all large-scale man-made and material means of production. Socialists believe that control of the socially necessary industries and considerable economic planning will be required to eliminate economic insecurity while maintaining individual freedom and initiative.

American unions have believed they can solve the workers' problems through collective bargaining and political action within the framework of the existing economic and political system. Although the movement's ideology is not necessarily immutably fixed, the forces that shaped it for the most part remain—the standard of living, the rate of economic growth, the absence of class consciousness, the nature of the American political system, and the relative success of collective bargaining.

However, it should be noted that the American and West European labor movements have drawn closer together ideologically since World War II. European socialist labor movements have de-emphasized radicalism and given greater emphasis to collective bargaining, while the American labor movement has become much more active politically since the depression of the 1930s. Indeed, American unions have actively backed much of the social legislation adopted in the United States since the 1930s and have participated formally or informally in every national campaign.

Labor Movements in the Developing Countries

The labor movements of the developing countries are quite different from those of the United States and Europe. Indeed, when examined from a Latin American or African perspective, the European and American movements appear to resemble each other closely. In Western industrial countries trade unions are likely to be more independent of political leaders and place more emphasis on collective bargaining and economic gains for their members. The labor movements of the developing countries, however, face unique pressures. They have greater difficulty establishing collective bargaining relations with employers, partly because their leaders are likely to be intellectuals whose talents and interests incline them toward political activities rather than collective bargaining. In some countries—for example, India, Ghana, and Israel—the labor movements were used to establish political independence. Collective bargaining also is impeded by the workers' weak bargaining power, caused by labor surpluses and limited skills. A major obstacle in the developing countries is opposition from political leaders who consider free collective bargaining to be incompatible with industrialization. The basic argument is that unions increase consumption at the expense of production, promote economic instability, and divert resources from capital formation. Political leaders in these countries, therefore, are likely to insist that unions play a productionist role until the economy is developed, when they can become more consumptionist.

The insistence on a productionist role for trade unions has been advanced by leaders with a wide variety of political persuasions. Countries led by dictatorships have greater power to hold down consumption through centralized planning and the military power of the state. Countries that try to follow democratic procedures have greater difficulty, but their industrializing elites also ordinarily insist on a productionist role for unions. It might also be noted in passing that where labor movements have been used to help countries achieve independence, political leaders have encouraged consumptionist roles for the labor movement before independence and productionist roles after independence.[1]

FACTORS SHAPING THE AMERICAN LABOR MOVEMENT

An examination of some of the factors shaping the growth of unions in this country will help to explain their current role in the labor market. One of the most important influences has been the spread of markets. Although some labor unions existed in preindustrial times, there was nothing that could really be called a labor movement because these local unions were isolated and rarely came in contact with each other. However, with industrialization and the widening of product markets, workers in formerly isolated labor markets came in direct competition with each other and, therefore, organized in order to protect their wages and working conditions. The spread of the market influenced wages by causing workers as well as goods to compete directly over wider areas. For example, before industrialization, shoemakers in Philadelphia could operate on the basis of the demand-and-supply conditions within the Philadelphia labor market; but with the spread of the market they had to be concerned with competition from shoemakers throughout the United States and foreign producers.[2] Transportation and communications improvements made it possible for merchants to buy in the cheapest market and undermine the wages and working conditions of workers throughout wide geographic areas. In order to prevent wage competition indirectly through the flow of goods or directly through the flow of workers, local unions in various parts of the country formed national unions and federations. The national unions were concerned mainly with the activities of a particular trade or industry, whereas the federations organized different local unions at the city or state level and different national unions (made up of affiliated locals) into national federations. The federations were concerned more with political and interunion matters than with collective bargaining directly. In other words, the spread of the market gave workers all over the United States common interests that they organized to protect and promote.

Another factor influencing the growth of unions in the United States has been the size of firms. In the manufacturing sector, particularly, unionism is directly related to the size of the firm. There are a number of reasons for this. For one thing, large firms are more easily organized by unions because the cost of organizing is less than it would be to organize the same number of workers in many smaller firms. But, more important, employers and employees in large firms rarely have close working relationships. Consequently, rules must be adopted to govern wages, hours, and working conditions. Workers, therefore, are likely to organize either into informal groups or formal trade unions in order to have some influence on the formulation of working rules and some means of redressing their grievances. Grievance adjustment is particularly important in a large firm because of the difficulties involved in communicating directly with management.

Skill levels are also important in determining union growth. The earliest unions to be organized usually were among the skilled workers in the printing and building trades or on the railroads. In such industries, the workers' investment in their skills gives them a common interest to protect. Moreover, a union of skilled workers has more bargaining power than one of unskilled workers because the skilled workers are much more difficult to replace in the event of a strike. The ability to inflict damage on an employer during a strike is an extremely important aid to the growth of unions that emphasize collective bargaining. Unions of skilled workers perpetuated their power by controlling the supplies of workers in particular crafts through control of entry into their unions and crafts.

Not all of the unions that acquired strength in American labor markets have had great skill. Unions of workers located at strategic points in the production or distribution process hold a strategic advantage. For example, teamsters and longshoremen have had very strong unions, mainly because of their strategic location rather than the amount of skill they possess. Their ability to win strikes has been due to the damage they cause by refusing either to move goods or to load or unload ships.

Business cycles have played an important role in the fluctuation of union strength in the United States. As a general rule, unions have gained membership and power during periods of prosperity and lost ground during periods of recession or depression. The reason for this is not difficult to find. During prosperity, the unions' power to win a strike is considerably enhanced because there are likely to be labor shortages and employers are likely to offer less resistance because they can usually pass wage increases to consumers in the form of higher prices. Moreover, employers are likely to lose sales if strikes occur when there are backlogs of unfilled orders. Conversely, during recessions and depressions, employers are under much less pressure to give in to union demands and are more likely, therefore, to offer more resistance. Moreover, employers might be able to win strikes when rising unemployment gives them a plentiful supply of strikebreakers. It should be observed, however, that unions sometimes have gained considerable membership during recoveries immediately following prolonged depressions. At such times workers have accumulated dissatisfactions stemming from the depression period but that could not be translated into union organizing because of their inability to win strikes. As noted earlier, depressions also cause public sentiment, and hence government policy, to become more sympathetic to workers and their organizations. When recovery starts, the workers' power increases relative to that of employers', and union membership thus grows very rapidly.

Wars also have played an important role in the growth of union membership. Indeed, many of the same forces influencing the growth of unions during periods of prosperity are present during war—particularly tight labor markets. Moreover, during wars the government is likely to adopt a more favorable attitude toward unions in order to gain cooperation with war production. Therefore, governments are likely to enhance the prestige of union leaders by appointing them to important positions in the war effort and to assent to other measures that will encourage union growth. Thus a combination of the government's favorable attitude and tight labor markets often causes union membership to increase considerably during and immediately after wars.

These great spurts in union membership are, however, ordinarily followed in the postwar period by counterattacks from antiunion forces that make it difficult for the unions to hold their wartime gains. For example, in the aftermath of World War I came the so-called open-shop movement of the 1920s in which employers all over the United States joined in a concerted effort to reduce union strength. The movement was so successful that this was one of the few prosperity periods when union membership actually declined after reaching a peak in 1920. By the 1930s only the strongest unions had survived. Somewhat similar to the period of the 1920s has been the latter part of the 1960s and 1970s. Partly because of employer resistance to unionism the labor movement's relative growth halted, despite the great expansion of employment and production in these years.

Public opinion also has an important influence on the growth of unions. Public opinion influences legislation and government attitudes toward unions, as well as the workers' willingness to associate with them as organizations. Ironically, there seems to be some inverse relationship between the unions' public image and their economic power. During the Great Depression of the 1930s, when the unions' economic power declined, their public image benefited from public sympathy for the underdog. Other factors were at work, then, too, of course. Similarly, during World War II and the immediate postwar period, when unions grew rapidly and increased their economic power, public support of them apparently declined because they were no longer considered to be the underdog.

Laws and court action also have influenced union growth. As noted earlier, before the 1930s governments—especially the judiciary—were generally hostile to unions and collective bargaining. The legislation and court decisions of the 1930s and 1940s created a more favorable environment. But the tide turned again after World War II. Congress passed the Taft-Hartley Act of 1947 and the Landrum-Griffin Act of 1959 (both of which restricted union activity and made organizing more difficult); many states, particularly in the South, passed antiunion right-to-work laws, which sought to prevent unions and employers from entering into contracts making union membership a condition of employment. Although courts restricted union activities more than during the late 1930s and early 1940, neither they nor other branches of government have returned to the antiunion stances they took before the 1930s.

It is very difficult to gauge the importance of these laws and court decisions for the growth of unions. There seems to be little question that early court hostility hurt unions, particularly those of semiskilled and unskilled workers who were not strong enough to withstand the employers' antiunion tactics. Discharging and blacklisting workers for union activity made it difficult for unions to organize. Moreover, the need to defend themselves in time-consuming and expensive litigation often sapped the strength of unions.

The more favorable legal environment of the 1930s made most of the employers' antiunion activities illegal and greatly reduced the use of injunctions against unions, but it did not necessarily make it easy for unions to organize. The Norris-La Guardia and National Labor Relations Acts reduced union-management relations more to a purely economic (instead of physical, economic, and legal) struggle but did not necessarily allow unions to win those economic struggles by striking or boycotting employers. As a consequence, unions in many industries—textiles, food, processing, and work clothes, for example—have not been able to organize extensively. Moreover, in spite of numerous organizing campaigns, unions remain relatively weak in the South. On balance, therefore, the evidence suggests that legislation is only a marginal factor in union growth and that the basic determinants are the economic, strategic, and skill factors influencing a union's ability to induce employers to bargain. A major effect of legislation is the moral climate it creates by crystallizing majority opinion.

Of course, to argue that labor laws have had limited impact on union growth does not mean that governments *could not* influence union growth. The activities of the National War Labor Board clearly stimulated membership in the weaker unions. Moreover, Presidents Kennedy and Johnson stimulated union membership among federal employees by encouraging collective bargaining between federal agencies and unions. The federal government *could* encourage union membership in countless other ways, especially by giving preference in contracts to employers who engage in collective bargaining.

Another factor influencing the growth of unions has been product market concentrations. Since the 1930s concentration of product markets controlled by a few firms has been directly correlated with union strength, as measured by contract coverage. To a very large extent, this relationship obtains because the larger firms tend to have the highest concentration ratios and, as noted earlier, are more likely to be unionized. However, the concentration ratio is a measure of market control as well as size, and those firms that have the greatest ability to control their destinies in the market can tolerate unions more successfully than highly competitive firms such as those in the textile industry that resist unions for fear that collective bargaining will undermine their competitive positions. Also, the change in public opinion during the 1930s apparently influenced the organizability of large firms with high concentration ratios. Before that time large and powerful firms were able to use their political, economic, and physical power to prevent unions from unionizing. With the change in public opinion during the 1930s, however, it became much more difficult for these companies to employ antiunion tactics. Under these conditions it was much easier for the unions to organize large companies.

Public Support of Collective Bargaining

Another force influencing the growth of unions in the United States has been the emergence of general public support for the concept of collective bargaining. When their employees were first organized, many companies dealt with unions as necessary evils, but as these relationships became established, a rationale for collective bargaining emerged that has become widely accepted among unions, employers, and the general public. Some of the main ideas supporting collective bargaining were embodied in the National Labor Relations Act of 1935 and reaffirmed in the Taft-Hartley Act of 1947. One of the reasons for passage of the former act was the belief that collective bargaining was a good anticyclical measure. The depression of the 1930s, it was argued, was caused in part by the workers' inability to organize and bargain collectively and thus maintain their wage levels.

Another rationale for collective bargaining is the assumption that rules governing wages, hours, and working conditions are best made jointly by workers and employers. Indeed, collective bargaining has been considered an extension of democracy to the work place. Rules based on participation, it is argued, are much better than those unilaterally imposed by employers on unions or by unions on employers. Moreover, this form of rule making is considered superior to government-imposed rules because it can be more flexible. The argument continues that the people who experience the problems are in a better position than anyone else to make the rules governing those problems. Collective bargaining, therefore, permits greater flexibility because the rules can be made to fit the circumstances. And collectively bargained rules can be changed more rapidly to fit changing circumstances than would be possible with government regulations.

The idea of participatory democracy, therefore, has been accepted by many employers as a force for social stability. This concept is based on the belief that by participating in the formulation of working rules and joining political organizations workers gain a stake in the system. For this reason many employers support efforts to extend the so-called free labor movements to the developing countries. They feel that collective bargaining will buffer the spread of revolutionary unionism in those countries. Supporters of this idea are impressed by the fact that revolutionaries never seem to make much progress in countries with advanced collective bargaining systems.

Another rationale for collective bargaining is equity. The National Labor Relations Act declared that governments had not only helped employers gain power by permitting them to form corporate and other forms of business activities but that the power of the state had also been used to impede union growth before the 1930s. Thus it was only equitable to protect workers in their right to organize and bargain collectively. This reflected the belief that individual workers had unequal bargaining power when dealing with individual employers and that it was unjust to enforce the freedom of contract between parties who were not of substantially equal bargaining power.

Problems of Collective Bargaining

Collective bargaining generates many problems. First, there is the problem of strikes, which become increasingly important as the economy becomes more interdependent. Strikes can inflict considerable inconvenience, if not damage, on the public. Therefore, much attention has been given to the problem of how to maintain collective bargaining while preventing the damage that might be inflicted by strikes. To date, no effective solution has been found, but a number of remedies have been attempted, including prohibition of strikes by certain workers, mediation and conciliation by outside government or private experts, fact finding by outsiders to narrow the range of disputes and influence public opinion, and labor court systems to settle disputes by judges. The problem with all of these approaches is the fact that they inject an outside opinion and power source into the collective bargaining relationship and thus nullify some of the benefits of participatory democracy discussed previously. In this as in many other matters there is no ideal or unique solution.

Another drawback of collective bargaining is that, because it is based on power and conflict, it does the most for the people who need it least. The stronger workers in the labor market, such as skilled electricians, could protect their incomes because of their skills; the weakest workers in the work force, like agricultural or textile workers, those in marginal and submarginal labor markets, have very limited ability to form unions because they have great difficulty winning strikes.

A third problem is the ability of an entrenched labor organization to exclude outsiders for reasons like race, sex, or national origin in order to monopolize labor markets. Moreover, the public interest might be ignored by collusion between strong unions and employers to fix prices. This is a particularly important problem with respect to discrimination against blacks, other minorities and women. If a union effectively controls the labor market, it can exclude minorities or women from operating in that market by refusing them admission to the union. This problem is discussed at greater length in Chapter 11 on the economics of discrimination.

A number of factors have tended to expand government's role in collective bargaining in the past decade or so: (1) The charges that unions as well as employers were occasionally an obstacle to fair treatment of blacks and women and other minorities in industry have led to government intervention in collective bargaining (Equal Employment Opportunity Commission) in an effort to eliminate such discrimination. (2) The fragility of many privately negotiated pension plans led the government to introduce legislation (Employee Retirement Income Security Act) which seeks to establish plans, as well as to provide reinsurance protection for the employees covered by them. (3) Growing public concern over safety and health in industry has brought about major federal government intervention (Occupational Safety and Health Act) to establish and police standards in this field.[3]

Added to these important areas of government intervention in the realm of private collective bargaining has been the intervention of almost every administration in the past thirty years to influence the determination of wages and prices (usually in the form of "guidelines"), in order to combat inflation. Moreover, there is the strong likelihood that these efforts to introduce some "incomes policy," as these controls over wages, prices, and other income flows have come to be called, will continue in the decade ahead. The role of government in collective bargaining seems destined to grow.

Union Structure

Union structure tends to define the power relationships among different levels of a labor organization. In the United States the basic labor organization is the local union, which is typically restricted to workers in a particular craft in a local area or a particular industry or group of related industries in a local area. For example, the carpenters in a local construction labor market might be members of a local carpenters union, whereas the workers in an automobile assembly plant might be members of the United Automobile Workers (UAW) local union, regardless of their particular craft or occupation.

Craft and industrial locals differ in several fundamental ways. Craft unions are ordinarily made up of workers who have very limited attachments to particular employers. In the building trades, for example, the craftsmen change employers quite frequently and, therefore, rely on unions for jobs, which gives the union considerable power in the labor market. If the union can control the supply of skilled craftsmen, employers must hire workers through the union. Moreover, labor organizations may have considerable control over training through their control, jointly with employers, of the apprenticeship system. Finally, some craft unions enhance their power in a labor market by influencing licensing arrangements.

The industrial union, however, has very limited control over hiring. Most of its power comes from control over the internal labor market in a particular firm. Its main impact ordinarily is to formalize arrangements that were already in existence. For example, the lines of progression, which determine promotion priorities within the internal labor market, are determined to a significant degree by the logical relationships among jobs, which reflect the technology of a particular process. The industrial union can formalize this relationship, help establish seniority as the main factor determining progression, establish grievance procedures, and exert some influence on wage rates, but these unions ordinarily have much less control of the labor market than craft unions.

Local unions are affiliated with national unions or, if they have locals outside the United States, with international unions. The internationals are combinations of locals within an industry or group of related industries or crafts or groups of related crafts. To follow up our early example with the locals, the local auto workers' union would be affiliated with the UAW nationally, and the local carpenters union would be affiliated with the United Brotherhood of Carpenters and Joiners of American (UBCJ). The UBCJ is an international based mainly on the craft principle, and the UAW is an international composed mainly of local industrial affiliates. A union is an international when it has affiliates outside the United States—in Canada, for instance—but the terms "national" and "international" are used interchangeably.

Power relationships between local and national unions depend largely on the scope of the market. If the market is mainly local, as in the building trades, the local union has more influence vis-à-vis international unions than would be true if the market were national in scope, as with the automobile industry. But relationships between the local and national unions also are influenced by factors such as the national union constitutions, the political power of the particular local leaders, the power and personality of the national leaders, and the collective bargaining alternatives available to the local if it secedes from the national union. If, for example, the local union can secede and affiliate with another national union, its power in dealing with a particular national union is enhanced. However, the local's ability to continue its collective bargaining relationships depends upon whether the scope of bargaining is national or local. It might be very difficult for a local to pull out and affiliate with another union if all other local unions in the same company in other areas are affiliated with the same national union and if all deal with the same company.

Public employee union structure follows a logic of its own. Power and bargaining relationships are largely influenced by the structure of the governmental unit in which the union is operating. Thus, in the federal government the federal unions generally include important bargaining agreements at the federal level. On the other hand, at the local government level critical bargaining generally occurs with county or city governments which largely control their own budgets and administration. The local unions at that same level are, therefore, largely free to make their own "bargains." Indeed, one of the reasons why so many local and state independent associations (independent, that is, of the AFL-CIO or any of its affiliated national unions) could flourish so long, is due to the fact that the initial focus of governmental power is at the state or local level. For practically all government unions (and associations) it must also be added that their wages and working conditions are critically affected by government action as well as by collective bargaining, which often makes these unions more heavily dependent upon lobbying and political action than are most unions in the private sector.[4]

The next level in the union structure is the federation. Federations might be city, state, or national. These organizations are comprised of groups of local unions at the city or state levels and groups of national unions and nonaffiliated local unions at the national level. Although their power is probably increasing somewhat, the federations are the weakest link in the American union structure. A city or state federation has very limited power over local unions because locals can continue to operate independently of the federation. Similarly, national unions can and have withdrawn from the AFL-CIO, which has been the main national federation in the United States since 1955, without seriously impairing their collective bargaining position. The United Mine Workers never joined the AFL-CIO, the UAW withdrew in 1967, and the International Brotherhood of Teamsters (IBT) was expelled from the AFL before that organization merged with the CIO. The federations' main functions are political and mediatory; that is, they represent the labor movement in dealing with public agencies and help settle disputes among the unions affiliated with them. Because the federations are the keepers of the labor movement's conscience, they ordinarily take broader positions on public issues than the national and local unions, which are mainly economic collective bargaining organizations. If the federation were a bargaining agency, as it is in many countries where federations deal on a more centralized basis with employers, its power over the local unions would be strengthened considerably, because expulsion from the federation would cause the national or local to lose bargaining rights. Similarly, the power of federations increases as the importance of the political and mediatory functions becomes more significant.

THE IMPACT OF UNIONS ON WAGES

Economists have differed sharply over the extent of the union's power to influence wages. Not surprisingly, this topic has received considerable public attention: The impact of unions on wages has significant implications for economic growth and stability as well as for the distribution of income between union and nonunion workers and between labor and other factors of production.

The layman may be surprised to learn that economists have questioned whether unions have much impact on wages. The role of unions generally has been exaggerated by employers, newspaper editors, and even union leaders, who take credit for wage increases that might have been caused by increasing productivity and rising general price levels. Because wages rise when unions negotiate contracts, many assume that unions cause the wages to rise; actually, some wage increases might have occurred in the absence of unions.

Economists, and particularly economic theorists, tend to minimize policy decisions, especially in the long run, and to emphasize market forces as determinants of wages and employment. The classical view has it that market forces are the only determinants of wages in the long run; but after the depression of the 1930s revealed such obvious "imperfections" in the market mechanism and spurred the growth of unionism and government regulation of wages and employment, few economists could deny the importance of nonmarket forces in wage determination.[5]

If one compares wages under union and nonunion conditions, economic theory would lead one to expect that the elasticity of demand for union labor would be an important determinant of the unions' impact on wages. If the demand is relatively inelastic, unions will be able to raise wages without greatly increasing unemployment. Elasticity of demand, however, is determined by derived demand, which means that the demand for labor is derived from the demand for the final product and the demand for other factors of production. Economic theory would also lead us to expect that the demand for labor would be more inelastic (1) the more essential union labor is to the production of the final product, (2) the more inelastic the demand fo the final product, (3) the smaller the ratio of the cost of union labor to t e cost of the product, and (4) the more inelastic the supply of other facto s of production.

Although this economic analysis is fairly straightforward, measuring the impact of unions on wages is much more difficult because it is not easy to isolate the unions' influence because this is a problem of multiple causation. For example, unions are influenced by factors such as the ratio of labor cost to total cost and economic conditions, which also influence wage levels. There is consequently a strong positive correlation between the percentage of workers organized in a given industry and wage rates in that industry. However, it is difficult to determine whether unions are strong because of the factors that make wages high or whether wages are high because of the unions. An empirical investigation also might find very little difference between union and nonunion wages because employers in nonunion sectors raise wages in order to avoid unions. If a union established a pattern that was followed by the nonunion sector, measurement of the differences between union and nonunion wages would fail to detect the impact of the union.

In spite of the measurement difficulties, a large number of empirical investigations have produced some consensus among economists concerning the relative extent of union influence. These investigations have been primarily of two types: (1) cross-sectional analyses at a given time to determine the difference between union and nonunion wages and (2) time-series analyses which attempt to study union and nonunion conditions through time.

These studies indicate that the union's relative impact is strongly influenced by business conditions. Unions seem to exert their greatest influence relative to nonunion control groups during the early stages of a recession or depression, in part by producing a downward rigidity in wage movements. If the depression is prolonged, however, the union influence tends to disappear because not even the strongest unions can withstand the adverse effects of a severe depression. Unions also seem to have an advantage during periods of high employment and stable prices, but the extent of the advantage depends upon the strength of the union. Strong unions raise wages by as much as 15 to 25 percent above what they would have been in the absence of unions. The strongest union influence seems to have come from unions of skilled workers and industrial organizations which have been able to organize large sections of their labor markets. Strong industrial unions such as the United Steelworkers probably have an impact in the range of 10 to 15 percent when employment is high and prices are stable. But even during periods of high employment and stable prices, some unions have very limited impact on relative wages because of adverse economic conditions that make it very difficult for nonunion sectors to organize or for unions to raise wages without generating substantial unemployment.

Albert Rees, a careful student of the impact of unions on wages, concluded in the early 1960s that "my own best guess of the average effect of all American unions on wages of their members in recent years would lie somewhere between 10 and 15 percent."[6] Rees also concluded that because unions enter into contracts for fixed time periods, their relative impact on wages is least during periods of rapid and unexpected inflation because union wages lag behind those in nonunion sectors and because employers, knowing that unions will resist wage cuts when labor markets slacken, resist union wage pressures during inflated periods.

In a detailed review of 20 empirical studies of the impact of unions on relative wages, Harold G. Lewis found some uniformity in the evidence concerning the union's advantage. The ratio of union to nonunion wages seems to have been greatest during the bottom of the Great Depression, when the union advantage might have reached 25 percent. With recovery from the depression the union advantage declined to between 10 and 20 percent by the end of the 1930s and almost disappeared during the 1940s. Lewis concluded: "I estimate that in recent years the average union/nonunion relative wage was approximately 10 percent to 15 percent higher than it would have been in the absence of unions."[7] Lewis thus agrees with Rees's estimate of the unions' relative impact.

As for the unions' impact on labor's share of the national income, empirical studies are highly inconclusive, although (as with relative wages) there are a number of measurement difficulties. It is not inconsistent to argue that unions influence relative wages but not labor's share, because it is possible for unions to redistribute income from the nonunion to the union sector. Recent research also indicates union wage policies tend significantly to lower inequality in the unionized sector.[8]

With respect to the size distribution of income, the evidence suggests that unions have raised incomes of more highly paid blue-collar workers, narrowed the income gap between the best-paid manual workers and more highly paid white-collar workers, and widened the gap between the best-paid blue-collar workers and the very poor. This is largely due to the fact that unions have had their greatest influence in mainstream labor markets and have done very little in marginal and submarginal markets.

One reason for the unions' concentration in the mainstream is that they are likely to have greater success in raising wages in the less competitive firms that predominate in that labor market. The unions' success in mainstream markets is due, in part, either to the fact that they have helped employers control their product markets or to the fact that they occupy strategic positions in the labor and product markets, as is the case with the teamsters. In assessing the significance of product market structure, it also is important to emphasize the multiplicity of causes influencing the determination of both wages and union structures. Of course to say that there is a strong correlation between market structures and wages is not to deny that other factors are at work.

The prevailing institutional arrangements must also be considered in assessing the importance of market structures on union strength. For example, as noted earlier, before the 1930s, unions undoubtedly had much less influence on wage determination in oligopolistic industries than they did after that time. In the institutional setting of the 1920s large employers were able to use their economic and political (and, in some cases, physical) power freely to prevent unions from organizing their employees, but this changed during the social ferment of the 1930s.

This is not to argue that oligopolistic employers conceded larger wage increases than if workers had not been organized, even though a number of factors might have caused higher wage increases in unionized oligopolistic firms. Because many of these companies had considerable monopsonistic power in the labor markets, traditional economic theory would hold that wages might be raised without reducing employment. However, if the monopsonists are making only normal profits (sufficient to keep firms in this industry) before unionization, raising wages might reduce employment in the long run because the firms could not continue to operate. The sudden reduction of monopsony power in the short run may explain the phenomenon commonly found in empirical studies. Unions have a sizable wage advantage over nonunion firms during the early stages of unionization, but the discrepancy disappears through time. Obviously, a continuing advantage to firms operating under oligopolistic conditions would require changes in the extent of the monopoly powers through time, which is hardly realistic.

Similarly, in oligopolistic firms whose product and labor demand curves are kinked at prevailing prices, increasing costs will not necessarily reduce employment (Figure 23-1a). It is assumed that employers will not gain much business if they lower prices (because their rivals are likely to follow suit) and will lose if they try to raise prices (because their rivals are not likely to follow). Since the demand for labor is a derived demand, it, too, will be kinked (Figure 23-1b). Prices are likely to be inflexible under this condition because employers lose total revenue when they lower or raise prices. In such cases unions might be able to raise wages within the limits of the discontinuity of the marginal revenue product curve without creating unemployment, as depicted in Figure 23-1b. Indeed, oligopolistic employers might offer less resistance to wage increases that they could shift to consumers in the form of higher prices. It is even conceivable that oligopolies that raise prices by some percentage amounts as they increase wages could actually profit from wage increases, depending on the ratio of labor cost to total cost and the elasticity of demand for the final product.

Other conditions exist in which wage increases will not necessarily lead to unemployment. One of these is the so-called shock effect, in which rising wage pressures cause employers to become more efficient and, therefore, able to absorb the wage increases without reducing employment.

The argument that union wage policies distort resource allocation does not necessarily assume that the labor market would be perfect without union influence; there are many market imperfections besides the operation of unions. Moreover, some unions perform functions—such as providing better job information and training—that improve the operation of some

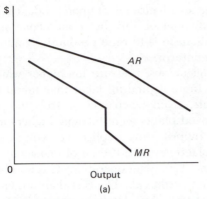
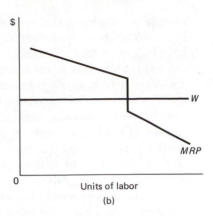

Figure 23-1

labor markets. Furthermore, the judgment that unions make for a worse allocation of labor implies that a higher GNP is better than, for example,
greater worker participation in the formulation of work rules. Finally, a
larger GNP is not necessarily better for all groups in the economy.

Other authorities doubt that the impact of unions on wages can be
ascertained through the uses of traditional economic theory. Reynolds, for
example, has advanced the proposition that "the effects of trade unionism
cannot be deduced from first principles and that on the contrary, simple
economic models of union behavior are likely to be quite misleading."[9]
Reynolds' survey led him to the following hypotheses:

1. Collective bargaining has reduced occupational differences within
   particular industries and has probably brought them closer to what
   they would have been under perfect competition.
2. Collective bargaining has reduced interplant differentials, on a national scale in industries characterized by regional or national competition and on a local basis in local industries. In this respect, also,
   collective bargaining has probably produced a closer approximation
   to the competitive wage structure.
3. Collective bargaining has probably widened interindustry differentials and in an anticompetitive fashion. Unionism has penetrated
   most effectively into the relatively high-wage industries and has
   tended to make the rich richer.
4. Collective bargaining has probably reduced geographical differentials, but this effect has been weaker than the first three effects and
   largely incidental to the reduction of interplant differentials. The
   reductions of geographical differentials have probably brought the
   wage structure closer to competitive standards than unions in a few
   industries that have overshot the mark.

Related to the unions' impact on wages are their possible effects on
productivity and other aspects of the employment relationship. Popular

opinion usually has it that unions have an adverse effect upon productivity. It is difficult to make a definitive judgment on this, but some economists have suggested that the impact of unionism is to raise productivity above the levels prevailing in the nonunion enterprise.[10]

This is true, in part, because the unions' pressure for higher wages tends to lead employers to substitute more capital for labor than might be true in most nonunion establishments. Even when one controls for the amount of capital per worker, unionized plants seem to show higher productivity. It is argued that the union by providing a collective "voice" enables workers to express their dissatisfaction and criticism of management and frequently brings about improvements in plant operation. This is unlike the case in nonunionized plants where the individual worker does not have a real voice, and has as his only alternative to quit. Higher turnover leads to rising costs of production.[11]

Aside from questions about the impact of unions on the relative wages of their members, there can be little doubt that unions influence the structure of workers' compensation significantly. The great growth of fringe benefits including private health insurance and pensions, as well as paid vacations and paid holidays for industrial workers, has been due, in large measure, to union bargaining efforts. The fact that nonunion companies have followed the lead of unionized firms in establishing similar plans for their employees is evidence that the unions have been articulating a need that individual employees are less able to express. Unions also can hire lawyers and actuaries to assist in negotiating various benefit programs. It is estimated that the cost of fringes is about 14 percent higher in union than in nonunion firms.[12]

Unions and collective bargaining also influence the patterns of wage increases, and with this the pattern of inflation. For example, with a view towards greater stability, many employers have tended to negotiate longer-term collective agreements with their unions (commonly for three years' duration in large companies). But to make them acceptable to their employees, employers have had to agree to significant periodic wage increases (at least once a year) during the life of these agreements. This tends, in a sense, to anticipate any inflation which might occur, as well as to insure employees a share in any increase in long-term productivity. At the same time, however, it tends to reduce the possibilities of downward flexibility in prices.[13]

As part of these many long-term agreements, too, unions frequently demand and negotiate the inclusion of so-called escalator or cost of living clauses, which adjust wages in keeping with changes in consumer prices. By January 1980, 5.5 million workers were covered by such clauses, compared to 2.5 million in 1968.[14] While these clauses generally do not initiate upward price movements, they certainly tend to reinforce them by placing a kind of compensation—labor cost floor beneath upward movements, once the latter occur.

Conclusion on Union's Impact on Wages

In conclusion, therefore, there is a consensus among those who have studied the problem that unions have had considerable influence on relative wages in the labor markets where they have gained strength. But their relative impact varies with business conditions, being greatest during recessions and least during inflation. The unions also tend to have a relative advantage immediately after becoming organized that declines with time. In general, the unions' ability to raise wages depends upon the elasticity of demand for labor, which is, in turn, influenced by the nature of competition in the product market. Unions have had their greatest impact in mainstream labor markets and thus probably have narrowed the income gap between the higher-paid blue-collar workers and white-collar workers, but they probably have widened the income gap between the well-organized blue-collar workers and those working in marginal and submarginal labor markets, who tend to be less well off.

UNIONS, EDUCATION, AND EMPLOYMENT AND TRAINING PROGRAMS

Trade unions vary widely in the interest they show in education and training. Craft unions such as those in the construction trades are interested in apprenticeship and other training programs as a means of maintaining wages (by limiting the supply of labor as well as improving its quality) and craft identity (by instilling pride in a particular craft).

Industrial or noncraft unions, however, have a different stake in education and training, which reflects their collective bargaining concern over maintaining wage rates, protecting wage rates from being undercut by trainees, gaining educational and training benefits for their members through collective bargaining, and using training programs to protect such vital collective bargaining interests as seniority. This last objective may be achieved by giving senior employees the right to be trained for jobs for which their seniority makes them eligible. Industrial unions might also use training as a means of protecting their members' jobs from technological changes or merging or relocating plants.[15]

Because of their special interests and functions, state, local and national federations are likely to take a broader view of education and training. For example, they are apt to favor general education that enables workers to participate in the political process. They have also been major supporters of free education for workers and programs to help the disadvantaged. Federations also are interested in education and training as a part of human resource programs and other policies designed to reduce unemployment. The federations' broader interests derive in some measure from their political role, which requires them to work actively with civil rights and other groups to achieve common economic, social, and political objec-

tives. Still, federations are likely to see social objectives in terms of their effect on the institution of collective bargaining. They tend, therefore, to insist that education, training and human resource programs be compatible
with such established collective bargaining procedures as union wage
scales, the apprenticeship system, job referral procedures, and seniority.
But more often than most national or local unions, federations attempt to
promote the interests of blacks and other minorities who sometimes are
barred from union benefits by racial discrimination.[16]

American unions played an important role in establishing universal
free education in the United States in the nineteenth century. The labor
movement realized that workers were not likely to make very much
progress in an industrial society without education, which in the early 1800s
was too costly for workers' children. Workers' demands for free public education were met with vigorous opposition from the conservative classes who
feared that educated workers would turn to radical politics and who simply
balked at paying taxes to educate the children of the working class. Selig
Perlman explained the situation in the following terms:

> That the education situation was deplorable much proof is unnecessary.
> Pennsylvania had some public schools, but parents had to declare themselves
> too poor to send their children to a private school before they were allowed
> the privilege of sending them there. In fact, so much odium was attached to
> these schools that they were practically useless, and the state became distin-
> guished for the number of children not attending school. . . .
> To meet these conditions, the working men outlined a comprehensive
> educational program. It was not merely a literary education that the working
> men desired. The idea of industrial education, or training for a vocation,
> which is even now young in this country, was undoubtedly first introduced
> by the leaders of this early labor movement. They demanded a system of
> public education which would "combine the knowledge of the practical arts
> with that of the useful sciences."[17]

Although the labor movement supported academic training in order to
prepare workers for citizenship, they were more interested in vocational
training. But their attitude toward vocational education was somewhat ambivalent. Unions were strongly committed to the apprenticeship system as a
means of preparing workers for the skilled trades, in part because apprenticeship systems usually were products of collective bargaining and thus
were controlled to a significant degree by unions, and also because apprenticeship training combined academic with on-the-job training—which
workers always seem to have favored. Hence even though unions endorsed
vocational education very early—Samuel Gompers supported both the
Smith-Hughes and George-Deen Acts, which established the vocational
educational system in the United States—they have rarely deviated from a
traditional belief that most trades cannot be learned in classrooms and that
vocational education by itself does not provide adequate preparation for
the skilled trades. Unions have, therefore, favored vocational schools that

provide instruction in academic subjects and otherwise prepare students for the apprenticeship programs.[18]

Union Concerns: Training and Education

The unions' attitudes toward education and training programs can be understood by considering their fundamental concerns. First, the American labor movement has always given top priority to collective bargaining as an institution. Unions, therefore, have strongly favored those forms of education and training that were most directly related to the collective bargaining system.

Second, the skilled trades derive their power in large measure from their control of labor supplies. They have, therefore, been very much interested in controlling the means of training skilled nonunion workers who might compete with them, and they have always taken a dim view of skill training outside the collective bargaining system.

Third, unions are very much concerned with the productivity of union members. Union leaders realize that they will not be able to maintain high wages unless unionized workers are more productive than the alternatives available to their employers—unproductive union workers give employers an incentive to substitute machinery for labor or to operate under nonunion conditions. In order to police their jurisdictions, unions have found it necessary to have an adequate supply of well-trained labor. Thus craft unions strongly favor the apprenticeship system not only because it is controlled by collective bargaining but also because they are convinced that it gives the worker practical on-the-job experience as well as some understanding of the theory of his trade. The unions believe that workers trained in both the theory and the practice of their trades will be much more flexible and able to perform a greater variety of jobs than would be the case if training were narrow and specialized. General training, they feel, makes workers less vulnerable to unemployment than specialized training, which employers are more likely to favor. Employers tend to retain the best-trained workers when demand for labor declines.

Although unions prefer training through apprenticeship, they admit members who are trained by other means. Indeed, a majority of craftsmen have not served apprenticeship. Unions are likely to admit such workers in order to maintain control of the labor market: They would clearly weaken their position if there were many workers the employers considered to be craftsmen who were outside union jurisdiction.

Unions have recently become interested in education and training programs because of the pressures to admit more blacks and other minorities to the skilled trades. Historically, craft unions on the railroads and in the printing and construction trades barred blacks from membership. In part, this practice stemmed from a monopoly instinct that caused local unions to exclude all except certain favored groups from their unions and thus from union-controlled crafts. But the civil rights movements of the 1950s and 1960s generated considerable pressure on unions to admit minorities to membership. The unions responded by insisting that blacks and other minorities come into the crafts primarily through the apprenticeship system. They realized that not many blacks could get into their crafts this way because apprenticeship programs graduate very few workers each year. But they argued that blacks who entered unions through apprenticeship would be well trained and, therefore, the markets would not be flooded with unqualified craftsmen.

Union Training Programs

A number of unions participate in joint union-management programs for training apprentices and journeymen. Journeyman training programs are necessitated in some crafts by rapid changes in technology and work procedures. For example, the International Typographical Union (ITU), which has long had an interest in education, has established a training center in Colorado Springs that specializes in short courses to teach journeymen new techniques in the printing and publishing trades. The ITU has attempted to ensure that members whose jobs are destroyed by technological changes are given first claim to jobs utilizing the new techniques.

The International Brotherhood of Electrical Workers (IBEW) and the United Association of Journeymen and Apprentices of the Plumbing and Pipe Fitting Industry of the U.S. and Canada (UA) also have maintained strong apprenticeship and journeyman-upgrading programs. The IBEW and the National Electrical Contractors Association established a national Joint Apprenticeship Committee in 1941; in 1947, when other training became more important, the name was changed to the National Joint Apprenticeship and Training Committee for the Electrical Industry. The national committee has adopted national standards for training programs administered by local joint committees. Programs are jointly financed, but a percentage of payroll contributions by employers was becoming the most widely used plan for financing during the late 1960s.

In 1956 the UA and the Mechanical Contractors Association of America, Inc. established a national retraining program for steamfitters and plumbers. In order to finance this program the union and employers established a national training fund to which the contractors contribute on the basis of the number of hours worked. The program is administered by a joint union-management committee that assists local joint training committees and provides equipment and national guidelines for journeyman-upgrading training. The UA has a staff of training coordinators and a program for training superintendents and instructors at Purdue University. The plumbing industry feels that training is necessary in order to keep journeymen abreast of new materials and methods.[19]

Union interest in education and training has not been restricted to the crafts; many industrial organizations also have established programs to educate and upgrade their members. The industrial unions are mainly interested in preparing their members to advance in the internal labor market. Some interest in education and training programs has been stimulated by federal education and training programs, which seek to help the disadvantaged, and by civil rights movement insistence that lines of progression be desegregated. Many older workers, already on the job but unable to obtain upgrading because of limited education, are apt to resent these efforts to help blacks and other minorities. Moreover, many black workers lack the necessary qualifications for upgrading. Finally, industrial workers face the threat of technological displacement and have attempted to use retraining programs to help them adjust to new jobs.

UNIONS AND EMPLOYMENT AND TRAINING PROGRAMS

It is difficult to generalize about the labor movement's attitude toward remedial employment and training programs.[20] Reactions have varied widely according to the multiplicity of motives and interests within the movement. The federations, which are mainly public relations and political organizations, viewed the new training activities more favorably than did national unions, which, in turn, viewed them more favorably than did their local affiliates. Many local craft unions feared that the employment and training programs would flood the labor market with partially trained craftsmen who would depress wages and generally undermine working conditions. They also saw the new training programs competing with the established apprenticeship activities. Union fears were aggravated by those who oversold these programs as a solution to the social and economic problems of the disadvantaged. It was understandable, for example, that a construction union in a labor market that ordinarily admitted no more than 100 new craftsmen a year would be alarmed by claims that 2000 or 3000 disadvantaged people were to be trained in these crafts. Fears were intensified by the civil rights advocates' attack on the all-white policies of many local unions. These unions, therefore, were persuaded that manpower programs would be used to channel blacks into union training programs from which they had been excluded.[21]

Labor opposition to the new programs was not restricted to the craft unions. Many members of industrial unions feared that the new programs would give preferential treatment to the disadvantaged and advance them ahead of workers already in factory jobs. A frequent complaint of union members was that the disadvantaged were being given opportunities that older workers had never enjoyed, even though these older workers also had limited qualifications for advancement. The AFL-CIO and its affiliates also have supported the new employment and training programs and have actively participated in a number of them. In 1980, for example, there were 14 national contracts with unions at a total cost of $54 million.

Organized labor also has supported the Job Corps concept of residential training for hard-core disadvantaged youths.[22] The first union to become involved with this program was the IUOE, which ran training programs for heavy-equipment workers at the Jacobs Creek Center in Tennessee. The instructors were journeymen IUOE members; the union agreed to place the trainees who completed the training course. Trainees were allowed to enter the IUOE apprenticeship program and ultimately to become regular journeymen. In 1980, nine international unions had Job Corps contracts with the Department of Labor.

Some of the OJT programs provide greater insight into the nature of the labor movement's involvement with this kind of training. One of the largest of these programs is Operation Manpower, which is sponsored by the AFL-CIO Appalachian Council in cooperation with the Departments of Labor and Education. The council's basic approach is to work through affiliated local unions or their employers. It has emphasized OJT as well as coupled programs that combine OJT with vocational and basic education. By 1980, the Appalachian Council had Job Corps and on-the-job training contracts totaling $15 million.

As a result of the apprenticeship outreach and other programs in which unions participated, it became apparent that a joint effort between the U.S. Department of Labor and the whole labor movement could produce beneficial results for employment and training programs. Such a cooperative arrangement, it was felt, not only would take advantage of the labor movement's network of affiliated organizations but also would overcome worker resistance to helping the disadvantaged. It was also considered to be important for the labor movement to (1) convince field-level government officials and employers that unions could participate effectively in employment and training programs and (2) establish its credibility with the hard-core unemployed—especially minority groups, which were assuming an increasingly antiunion stance because of publicity given to discrimination against blacks and other minorities by various unions.

In order to accomplish these objectives, the AFL-CIO executive council created the Human Resource Development Institute (HRDI) in September 1968. The U.S. Department of Labor has funded the institute to administer a "nationwide program to recruit, train, employ, and upgrade the unemployed and underemployed."[23] HRDI staff come from a wide range of backgrounds and involvements in civic and community organizations. The institute is particularly active in apprenticeship outreach programs—which it encourages and provides with local liaison and follow-up—and in preapprenticeship training programs.

HRDI expanded its activities into a variety of areas. One of the most significant of its new activities was to take over the coordination of apprenticeship outreach programs operated by local building trades councils in 21 cities. These programs are designed to recruit, tutor, and place minorities in unionized apprenticeship programs. HRDI is also involved in job

development and placement programs. Its staff cooperated with union officials in placing disadvantaged workers in jobs not ordinarily listed with the
employment services. Since these jobs were covered by union contracts,
they usually provided better wages and working conditions for the disadvantaged than were ordinarily available to them from other sources. In the
prisoner program, the institute works with local unions and correctional institutions to develop training programs for prisoners and helps released prisoners find job opportunities in unionized plants. Finally, the HRDI actively
promotes adequate union representation on state and local employment
and training planning councils. In 1980 HRDI had contracts with the Department of Labor for some $10 million.

Conclusions on Unions and Labor Markets

Although unions represent about 24 percent of all nonagricultural employees in the United States, their influence extends far and wide in American
labor markets because collective bargaining covers most of the blue-collar
workers in the mainstream transportation, construction, high-wage manufacturing, printing and publishing, and other industries. The unions' overall
impact on wages might be debated, but it is generally agreed that they have
influenced wage structures and have a significant impact on the wages of
their members—although the specific impact varies with the particular
labor market and general economic conditions. Therefore, unions are major
labor institutions in both the external and internal labor markets.

It should also be noted that unions and collective bargaining have
played an important role in education, employment and training programs.
Historically, the labor movement was a major influence for universal free
public education. Unions have been particularly interested in vocational
education, although union leaders generally consider it inferior to apprenticeship training. Reflecting the workers' preference for practical OJT,
unions feel that few crafts can be learned in the classroom. They also prefer
job training that is established under collective bargaining to that provided
unilaterally by employers. Labor leaders point out that collective bargaining makes it possible for training to reflect the interests and needs of employers and workers and also ties the costs of training to those who are to
benefit most from it. They argue, for example, that employers by themselves would not provide broad, general training to make employees more
"unemployment-proof" and adaptable to diverse job situations. Rather,
they argue, employers are more interested in minimizing training costs and
maximizing profits, which often dictate narrow, specialized job assignments. Moreover, employers tend to desire excessive supplies of workers in
order to meet peak labor requirements and minimize upward pressures on
wages. In contrast, the unions attempt to see that workers are well trained
and that supplies of labor are no greater than necessary to meet the demand
for workers at negotiated wage rates. Unions have used training programs

not only to provide general training but also to train members for the new jobs generated by technological changes that render older skills obsolete. Moreover, some unions—especially those in casual occupations in the transportation and construction industries—maintain job information and referral systems for their members.

The labor movement's training functions create problems for those who advocate comprehensive national programs. For one thing, some unions attempt to use their control of training and referral systems to monopolize job opportunities for their members. They are, therefore, very suspicious of government or other training programs that are not at least partly controlled by unions or that compete with union programs. Where unions are strong enough to impose closed-shop conditions (whereby workers must join unions *before* they come to work), they can prevent the employment of the workers trained in public programs by refusing to accept the trainees as union members. Although the closed shop is outlawed by the National Labor Relations Act, strong unions have been able to enforce de facto closed-shop conditions because of their control of labor supplies.

The AFL-CIO generally has given strong support to employment and training legislation, even when some of its affiliates and their members were unenthusiastic. With few exceptions unions participated only in employment and training programs that were compatible with collective bargaining. Unions can be expected to resist programs that are incompatible with that system—if they threaten to undermine union control of training or referral systems.

In view of the growing importance of public and private employment and training programs, education and training will undoubtedly become an increasingly important subject of collective bargaining in the future. Moreover, it can be expected that agencies such as the AFL-CIO's HRDI will be strengthened to link training programs to collective bargaining and that machinery will be established to resolve conflicts between union-controlled programs and public policy. Conflicts are particularly likely because of continued pressure to enlarge the employment opportunities of blacks, other minorities, and women who have not had adequate access to many training, upgrading, and referral programs controlled by unions. Government agencies probably will become increasingly concerned about the implications of control of labor supplies for price stability. To whatever extent these pressures threaten the sanctity of collective bargaining, they undoubtedly will elicit continuing and increasing resistance from labor unions.

DISCUSSION QUESTIONS

1. Trace the changing roles and functions of trade unions as an economic institution during the past four decades.
2. Is it true that workers in the South are less willing to join labor unions than workers elsewhere? Why or why not?

3. Conventional economic theory holds that an increase in wage rates results in a decrease in employment. How can unions reconcile these conflicting goals in the collective bargaining process? Discuss.

4. If the effects of the minimum wage on employment are adverse, what accounts for the union support for increases in the federally mandated minimum?

5. What limitations, if any, do you think the government should impose on the right to strike? Why does the United States have a higher level of strike activity than West Germany or the Scandinavian countries?

6. What are the advantages and disadvantages of strong control over local unions by national unions? Give examples.

7. It has become increasingly common for union-management contracts to include provisions whereby wages adjust automatically to changes in the cost of living. What effect does this have on relative differences in union-nonunion wages over the course of the business cycle.

8. Craft unions and industrial unions differ in the extent to which they can exert pressure in the collective bargaining process. Discuss.

9. "Union wage policies interfere with the free flow of resources in the labor market and result in a misallocation of resources. Society suffers by paying higher prices and accepting a lower level of employment than otherwise would occur." Discuss.

10. Why has the American union movement failed to develop its own political party?

Notes

1. Good discussions of labor in the developing countries can be found in Walter Galenson, ed., *Labor in Developing Countries* (Berkeley: University of California Press, 1962); and Everett M. Kassalow, *Trade Unions and Industrialization: An International Comparison* (New York: Random House, 1969), part II.

2. Benjamin Martin and Everett M. Kassalow, eds., *Labor Relations in Advanced Industrial Societies* (Washington: Carnegie Endowment for International Peace, 1980).

3. Gerald G. Somers, ed., *Collective Bargaining: Contemporary American Experience* (Madison, Wis.: Industrial Relations Research Association, 1980).

4. Daniel S. Hamermesh, ed., *Labor in the Public and Nonprofit Sector* (Princeton, N.J.: Princeton University Press, 1975).

5. Albert Rees, *The Economics of Work and Pay* (New York: Harper & Row, 1973).

6. Albert Rees, *The Economics of Trade Unions* (University of Chicago Press, 1962), p. 79.

7. Harold G. Lewis, *Unionism and Relative Wages in the United States* (University of Chicago Press, 1963), p. 5.

8. Richard B. Freeman, *Unionism and the Dispersion of Wages* (Cambridge, Mass.: National Bureau of Economic Research, working paper no. 248, 1978).

9. Lloyd G. Reynolds, "The Impact of Collective Bargaining on the Wage Structure of the United States," in John T. Dunlop, ed., *The Theory of Wage Determination* (New York: St. Martin, 1957), p. 220.

10. Charles C. Brown and James L. Medoff, "Trade Unions in the Production Process," *Journal of Political Economy*, June 1978.
11. Richard B. Freeman and James L. Medoff, "The Two Faces of Unionism," *The Public Interest* (Fall 1979): 69–93.
12. Richard B. Freeman, *The Effect of Trade Unionism on Fringe Benefits* (Cambridge, Mass.: National Bureau of Economic Research, working paper no. 292, October 1978).
13. Joel Popkin, "Incomes Policies," in Clarence C. Walton, ed., *Inflation and National Survival* (Montpelier, Vt.: The Academy of Political Science, 1979), pp. 163–175.
14. Edward Wasielewski, "Scheduled Wage Increases and Escalator Provisions in 1980," *Monthly Labor Review* (January 1980): 9.
15. Jack Barbash, "Union Interests in Apprenticeship and Other Training Forms," *Journal of Human Resources* (Winter 1968): 63–83.
16. Ray Marshall, *The Negro and Organized Labor* (New York: Wiley, 1965).
17. Selig Perlman, *History of Trade Unionism* (New York: Augustus M. Kelly, 1950; reprint of the original 1922 edition), pp. 14–15.
18. Sumner H. Slichter, James J. Healy, and E. Robert Livernash, *The Impact of Collective Bargaining on Management* (Washington, D.C.: Brookings Institution, 1960), p. 70.
19. Derek C. Bok and John T. Dunlop, *Labor and the American Community* (New York: Simon & Schuster, 1970), p. 347.
20. Carnegie Council on Policy Studies in Higher Education, *Giving Youth a Better Chance* (San Francisco: Jossey-Bass Publishers, 1980), pp. 236, 252.
21. Ernest G. Green, "Apprenticeship: A Political Weapon Against Minority Youth Unemployment," in National Commission for Employment Policy, *From School to Work* (Washington, D.C.: GPO, 1976), pp. 201–226.
22. Sar A. Levitan and Ben Johnston, *The Jobs Corps* (Baltimore: Johns Hopkins University Press, 1975), pp. 67–73.

Chapter 24
Institutions Providing
Access to Jobs

The primary actors in the labor market are employers and employees—those who hire and those who seek and accept jobs. To facilitate prompt and effective contact between primary actors, a variety of supplementary institutions have emerged which are commonly spoken of as labor market intermediaries. Some are public agencies, and others are nonprofit organizations supported by the taxpayers, but the majority are private institutions supported either by the users or by those who hope to make a profit from the services they provide. No one can adequately understand the workings of the labor market without familiarity with these institutions. Since some are publicly supported while the others compete with those that are not, knowing them is essential to understanding of public policy toward labor markets.

A matter which makes labor market intermediaries of special import in human resource policy is the role of all other intermediaries in relation to that of the public employment service. When the latter was established in 1933 under the Wagner-Peyser Act, few other intermediaries existed. A very few unions operated hiring halls in specific areas. An occasional political machine might dispense some patronage jobs. But, with minor exceptions, the public employment service had the field to itself. In subsequent years, other labor market intermediaries have burgeoned. The public employment service, while still the most ubiquitous, is one among many, often raising the question, "Why a tax-supported public service to compete with so many private organizations that appear available and anxious to do the same job?" This chapter describes a number of such organizations to acquaint the reader with their roles and functioning, but with the above query as an underlying policy issue.

THE ROLES OF LABOR MARKET INTERMEDIARIES

The matching of people with jobs may well be the most central of all economic activities. The entrepreneur combines human, natural, and capital resources in the production of goods and services desired by consumers and investors—but only human resources are essential to every productive process. And labor income comprises three-quarters of the entire national income and is the source of sustenance for all but a minor fraction of all of the individuals and families in any industrial society.

It is impossible for any employer to be directly aware of more than a smattering of the millions of potential employees nor the job seeker of more than a handful of the hundreds of thousands of employers. Without intermediaries there are limited ways in which each can signal wants to the other. The number of employers the job seeker can physically contact are exceedingly limited as are the number of potential employees reachable by the hiring employer.

Even knowing who wants work or who is offering jobs is to know little. Every job has its specific requirements and every employer has a set of expectations that go beyond the mere ability to do the job. Work habits, comportment, appearance, sociability, dependability, compatability, and numerous other criteria stand alongside a variety of job skill expectations. Similarly, jobs differ by pay, security, working conditions, supervisor conduct, and an equally large number of characteristics including the actual occupational content. Few of these are externally obvious. Without intermediaries, the worker would have access to only a minor range of the potential employment opportunities and the employer would be forced to choose from among a narrowly restricted supply of available workers. No wonder that both employees and employers have demanded the creation of labor market intermediaries and that those demands have been met.

Miriam Johnson has illustrated the relationships between employers, employees, and intermediaries (Figure 24-1).[1]

The employer is perceived as a broadcaster announcing the availability of jobs and the mass of potential job seekers as the intended audience. The hierarchy of broadcast audiences is that indicated by a BLS study of how workers seek and find jobs (Table 24-1).[2] As noted in Chapter 6, the employer functions in an internal as well as an external labor market. Upon recognizing a need for additional workers, the initial broadcast will often be

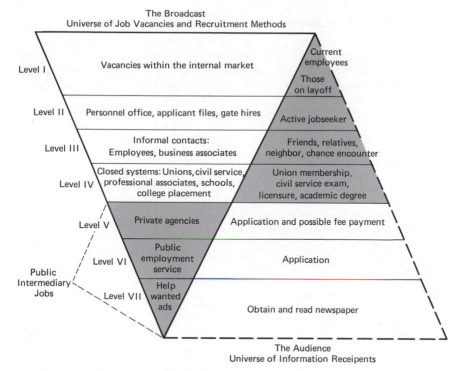

The Broadcast
Universe of Job Vacancies and Recruitment Methods

Figure 24-1   The recruitment job search model. (Source: Miriam Johnson, *A Bifocal View of the Labor Market* **(Washington, D.C.: Employment and Training Administration, U.S. Department of Labor, 1978).**

limited to the internal market of those already employed or on layoffs with recall rights. This will generally be the first source because the employer may have obligations established by union contract, tradition, or policy, or because those represent more familiar and, therefore, less risky employees. Having exhausted this source of supply, the employer, according to the BLS data, most often turns to those who make direct application, perhaps because of the low recruitment costs of that approach, perhaps because those who take the initiative to apply are viewed as more likely to be satisfactory employees than more passive job seekers.

Next the broadcast is beamed to friends and relatives, both of the employer and of incumbent employees. These are a familiar and therefore less risky audience than the labor force at large. The friends and relatives of employees are likely to be quite similar in characteristics to those employees and the latter are likely to be reluctant to submit to the onus of having recommended an unsatisfactory applicant.

Next in the hierarchy appears a wide range of intermediaries which are themselves of limited access and have been set up by groups of either employers or employees to exercise some degree of job control. Employers and

Table 24-1   METHODS USED TO SEEK AND FIND WORK (1972)

METHOD	JOB SEARCH		JOB FINDING	
	NUMBER	PERCENT	NUMBER	PERCENT
Total (thousands)	10,437	100.0%	10,437	100.0%
Applied directly to employer		66.0		34.9
Asked friends:				
About jobs where they work		50.8		12.4
About jobs elsewhere		41.8		5.5
Asked relatives:				
About jobs where they work		28.4		6.1
About jobs elsewhere		27.3		2.2
Answered newspaper ads:				
Local		45.9		12.2
Nonlocal		11.7		1.3
Private employment agency		21.0		5.6
State employment service		33.5		5.1
School placement office		12.5		3.0
Civil service test		15.3		2.1
Asked teacher or professor		10.4		1.4
Went to place where employ-ers come to pick up peo-ple		1.4		0.1
Placed ads in newspapers:				
Local		1.6		0.2
Nonlocal		0.5		a
Answered ads in professional or trade journals		4.9		0.4
Union hiring halls		6.0		1.5
Contacted local organization		5.6		0.8
Placed ads in professional or trade journals		0.6		a
Other		11.8		5.2

SOURCE: U.S. Department of Labor, Bureau of Labor Statistics, *Jobseeking Methods Used by American Workers,* bulletin 1886 (Washington, D.C.: GPO, 1975), pp. 4–7.
[a] Less than 0.05 percent.

their associations do not desire to limit the potential universe of job applicants but only to screen out those who may turn out to be high-risk employees in terms of skills, work habits, or personal attributes. Employee groups seek to limit competition for good jobs to those within their own associations. The public has chosen to create limited-access intermediaries in pursuit of higher-quality public services and limitations on the political spoils system. Thus in this range of intermediaries are found employer and trade associations, professional associations, union hiring halls, school placement offices, and merit systems.

Only after the job broadcast has been beamed at and picked over by these privileged groups, according to the Johnson thesis, does it become available to the public at large. The three intermediaries available to all are the want ads (available to all for 15 cents or a trip to the public library), the private employment agencies (eager to make placements for a fee), and the public employment service (available free to all applicants). But all three, according to this author, are the residual recipients of only the hardest to fill jobs.

This perception of the job search/recruitment process focuses on which groups the intermediaries serve. Additional insights are available through examination of the services performed. One dimension is the relative passivity/activity of the intermediary role. At one extreme is the passive labor market exchange role. Job orders and work applications are received, matched by criteria set by employer and job seeker, who are informed where to make contact with the other. The opposite extreme is the broker role in which the intermediary becomes advocate and salesperson for the employer or job-seeker client.

Related, but a somewhat different dimension, is that of services provided. The intermediary may accept the status and decisions of the labor market participant and pursue an employer or job seeker without seeking to change either. Going beyond that level, employer or employee may be counseled, assisted in decision-making, and provided with information to facilitate decision. Workers may also be taught job search techniques and employers may be shown improved recruiting procedures to better pursue their own match-up. Ultimately, job seekers lacking skills may be trained and employers assisted in restructuring their jobs to improve their attractiveness or the match with the opposite side of the labor market.

These two dimensions form a useful backdrop for reviewing the quantitative and qualitative roles of labor market intermediaries. However, this chapter is limited to consideration of those intermediaries which participate in the actual process of placing workers in jobs. Those primarily concerned with affecting the employability of workers and the attractiveness of jobs have been treated in other chapters.

THE EMPLOYER'S PERSONNEL OFFICE

Though it is not technically an intermediary because it is part of the employing establishment, the rising incidence and importance of the formalized personnel management function over the past thirty years or so is worthy of note. Not the least important reason for signaling this development is the fact that large numbers of the users of this textbook may be potential personnel managers.

Recruitment, selection, hiring, training, motivating, compensating, and directing the activities of employees are necessary functions which cannot be avoided by any employing organization, public or private. However, numerous factors have intervened to make this a specialized set of functions within any organization of sufficient size to have a relatively constant in- and out-flow of employees. Sheer size of employing establishments has been one obvious factor. Unionization has been another. There are the obligations within labor-management agreements to be administered. Unions are quick to take advantage of precedent and personnel departments must be the watchdogs of supervisory actions that may be precedent-setting. Production-oriented line officers are not always the best practitioners of human relations.

The growth of fringe benefits, some governmentally provided or required, some negotiated, and some unilaterally offered by employers, both add to the costs of hiring and turnover and require technically qualified administrators. More sophisticated technology and rising skill mix add to the necessity of careful selection and subsequent training. More recently, to the earlier wage-hour legislation have been added governmentally imposed requirements for equal employment opportunity, occupational safety and health, minimum standards for pensions, and so forth, all too technical and specialized to be administered by the line supervisor absorbed in production concerns. Added to this list of primarily private employer concerns are the technicalities of public personnel administration in the expanding public sector.

Though employed by the employing establishment, it is well to note an intermediary tendency in these personnel administrators. Though responsible for contributing to the output potential of the organization, they comprise a professional body trained to look out for the employee's welfare as well. Professional associations such as the American Society of Personnel Administrators (ASPA) and the American Society for Training and Development (ASTD) are constantly at work to enhance this professional stance. In addition to the varity of academic credentials in the field, ASPA promotes its own professional credentialing process to give a degree of standardization and collegiality to the field.[3] Professional personnel managers (or human resource managers, to use a term of growing popularity) thus function as intermediaries between the line managers of their own organizations and the current and potential employees, seeking to accommodate the long-term interests of both.

UNION HIRING HALLS

A union does not sell labor but represents those who do. Thus it is properly perceived as an intermediary between the employees whom its functionaries represent and the organizations which employ them. Every function of a union in negotiating the conditions of work, the rules which will govern the workplace, the compensation of the workers, and the enforcement of the labor agreement is an intermediary role. As noted in Chapter 23, union membership encompasses only about one-fifth of the labor force, but that membership of over 20 million certainly makes unions the largest category of intermediary.

Since this chapter is focused primarily on the function of matching workers and jobs, the other intermediary roles of unions can be noted and set aside. Unions intervene in the recruitment, selection, and hiring process in only a limited number of cases, but where they do, that intervention tends to be vigorous. The traditional goal of the trade union movement has been to take wages out of competition to prevent them from being driven down by workers willing to work for less than the union scale. The history of the labor movement has been the history of strife with management and government to establish and maintain sufficient control of the labor supply to enforce that noncompetitive behavior. Craft unions, having a community of interest in a common set of skills, pursued the closed shop, denying employment to those not of the group. Industrial unions, lacking the bargaining power of scarce skills, awaited the advent of government support under the National Labor Relations Act to require, not that the employer hire only union members, but that once hired all would join the union.

On the other hand, employer groups have consistently fought and lobbied against union control over the labor supply. Given that persistent tension between management and union, it is no surprise that union hiring halls exist only where they are as attractive to the employer as to the employee. The environment in which the union hiring hall is attractive to both employer and employee is the casual labor market. A casual labor market is one in which the relationship between the employee and employer is inherently temporary and tenuous. The worker may have a long-term attachment to the industry but only a short-term one to the particular employer. Examples are construction where job tenure tends to be limited to the participation of a particular employer in a specific component of a project, maritime where the worker signs on for one voyage, longshore where the duration of a job is the unloading of a ship, and in agriculture where it is the harvesting of a particular crop on a specific farm.

In all of these, the employer tends to be small and susceptible to business failure. None are large enough or stable enough to provide pension plans and other fringe benefits. There is no continuity of employment to accumulate seniority as a source of job security. The union has greater continuity than the management. Rotation of jobs on a longest-out-of-work first-placed basis substitutes for seniority. Cents per hour contributions establish industry-wide or union-run funds.

Union hiring hall arrangements cover only an estimated two million workers[4]—two percent of the labor force—but their coverage is high in particular industries. Involved are one million construction workers (one-half the unionized construction work force but less than one percent of non-union construction), almost all of the quarter of a million longshoremen and offshore maritime workers, and a smattering of teamsters and motion picture workers. The United Farm Workers has the need and the ambition but not yet the power to enforce similar practices. With the latter exception, the alternative to union job control was an oversupply of labor, considerable idleness, and the corrupting temptation for bribes and kickbacks. Employers resisted at times and places but ultimately concluded that they had as much to gain from the "decasualization" as the workers. Perhaps the need is best demonstrated by the fact that nonunion employers in some of the same industries and public agencies in similar but unorganized industries have established similar institutions.

Hiring hall procedures vary widely according to the conditions, needs, and customs of the industry and area. In general, hiring hall procedures call for employers covered by the labor-management agreement to list job vacancies with the hiring hall. Workers register with the hiring hall as they become unemployed. The hiring agent assigns the workers to the jobs in some prearranged order and the workers are expected to report to the employers to whom they are assigned. The order of assignment is determined by some combination of duration of unemployment, attachment to the industry, and seniority. Construction and maritime unions generally refer first those out of work longest but do so within classes of workers differentiated by period of attachment to the industry within the locality. In longshore work with its very brief duration, seniority on the pier or inverse order of accumulated earnings may prevail.

Whatever the formal rules, both employers and employees generally have considerable discretion. Employers retain the authority to hire workers directly once they notify the union, to reject those with inadequate skills or to discharge those who prove unsatisfactory; the workers may turn down undesirable referrals. However, these privileges remain limited and subject to denial if the result becomes too chaotic.

The existence of the hiring halls and the rules which govern them have developed out of the experiences and needs of the industries in which they exist. Typically, these are casual labor markets in which the attachment between the employer and employee is of relatively short duration, limited to completion of a particular construction project, voyage, or unloading of a ship. Frequently unemployed, the workers are anxious to minimize the length of those periods and the costs of job search. Similarly, the employer needs assurance that a telephone call can bring a flow of workers known to have experience in the industry. The hiring hall is also usually a component of a locally centralized industry arrangement making it possible for many employers to contribute in sequence to the types of fringe benefits the more stably employed enjoy from a single employer.

In addition, the high rate of turnover and frequency of job openings encourages an excessive number of workers to enter the industry in hope of getting a share of the jobs. The hiring hall is often part of a decasualization process designed to give employment priority to those of more permanent industry attachment. In that sense it also becomes the casual labor market's substitute for the seniority rules of more stable markets.

In limiting competition, of course, the decasualization process of which the hiring hall is a part does limit the accessible supply of labor and probably results in higher wage levels. The gains to the well-attached employee and the employer are obvious. The impact on economic efficiency would require comparison between the incremental wage cost and the benefits of reduced chaos and time lost in recruitment and job search. Currently, there appears to be more interest in the possibility of extending the hiring hall concept to the decasualization of agricultural labor than to limiting the process where it currently exists.

THE "CLOSED" INTERMEDIARIES

The union hiring hall is but one example of a wide range of labor market intermediaries having in common the fact that they are not generally available to all workers, regardless of affiliation or personal characteristics. The hiring hall is generally accessible only to members of a particular union, with preference for members from the local area. Federal labor laws once attempted to end this exclusivity by making it an unfair labor practice to require union membership or nonmembership as a criterion for employment. The expediency of shifting to length of industry attachment in long unionized industries and areas proved to be an effective substitute which could not be attacked without interrupting pervasive and long-standing seniority practices throughout the economy.

Though their control over labor supply is generally less pervasive than the hiring hall model, a number of other intermediaries of limited access are worthy of mention. One of these is the use of merit systems in public unemployment. All but the highest levels in the executive branch of the federal government are available only to those with prescribed educational and other credentials and the ability to pass prescribed examinations.

Most state and local government employees are also covered by merit system arrangements. These vary substantially by jurisdiction but are sufficiently alike for generalization. For broad levels of employment such as clerical, general administrative, and technical skills, a competitive examination is publicly announced. A roster is established ranking applicants by exam score. The federal and some of the state and local systems give preference to veterans. This is accomplished by adding a prescribed number of points to the score the veteran earns on a competitive exam (a practice objectionable to women's groups whose veteran numbers are few). The highest three scorers remaining on the roster are referred to the agency requesting personnel in a particular occupational category, with the agency allowed to select from those three.

At more specialized levels or managerial ones where intangibles play a larger role in choice, the employing agency carefully prescribes its requirements and selection criteria. The specific job is advertised publicly. Applicants are generally screened by a panel with final choice by an immediate supervisor but subject to challenge by unsuccessful applicants who feel they may have been discriminated against on any ground.

Professional and trade associations accept ads for jobs and workers in their official journals. They maintain formal labor exchange at their conventions, usually consisting of some means for potential employees and employers to advertise their availability, meet, and interview each other. However, these associations take no responsibility for job search, recruitment, or placement.

School placement offices represent another relatively closed intermediary, limiting service to present or former students. Nearly every four-year college or university and most community colleges have a placement office. The College Placement Council is a national trade association representing them. For the four-year and graduate institutions, the major function is to coordinate the campus visits of recruiters from business firms and public agencies. The smaller four-year institutions and the two-year colleges are more likely to maintain contacts with local employers.

Their degree of aggressiveness varies widely, some acting as only a passive contact point for employers, others pursuing employers to attract them to the campus. Many provide a career counseling function, assembling information on the occupational outlook and career choice materials. A few offer a clearinghouse of part-time and summer jobs. Most probably do not view themselves as a broker representing the students in pursuit of jobs but as providers of a convenient location for employers and students to contact each other.

In addition to whatever the school as an institution may do, technical and vocational instructors in all kinds of institutions have traditionally maintained an informal placement service through personal contact. After having come to the school from industry and maintaining those contacts, they call personal friends on behalf of particular students. However, they tend to restrict themselves to a few favorite or especially qualified students and do not represent an openly available resource, even for students.

In recent years, related to the career education movement discussed in Chapter 8, school placement offices have been appearing at the high school level. In a larger high school, the school may have its own placement office. In other cases, a school district may provide the service for several high schools. Most often the placement office will consist of one person and, perhaps, a full or part-time secretary. Generally, that individual will not be a trained or experienced placement officer but a reassigned counselor or perhaps an athletic coach nearing retirement. At times, the school placement officer may also be responsible for cooperative education and work study programs. The high school placement office generally does not depend upon employers to come forward with job orders. Instead, the placement office will seek opportunities to speak at business and service clubs to prevail upon employers to place orders with the school. Often, the contact will be in connection with a community-wide drive for youth employment opportunities. Rarely is there a relationship between the placement pursuit and any long-term career planning for youth. Part-time, summer, and entry-level jobs are more likely to be both the pursuit and the product.

Community-based organizations also serve as labor market intermediaries for their clientele. Since these are normally organized on racial or ethnic lines, they tend to be available primarily to those from those groups. They also tend to serve a primarily low-income population and restrict their activities geographically to locations where those groups are concentrated. The classic example might be the Opportunities Industrialization Centers (OIC).[5] A black Baptist minister in Philadelphia, Rev. Leon Sullivan, noted in the early 1960s the many employers with all-white work forces in a predominantly black community. He led other clergymen of his race in fomenting a consumer boycott to pressure for jobs for blacks. When employers responded that the available blacks lacked the necessary skills, Reverend Sullivan responded by organizing OIC as a self-help training institution which stressed race pride as well as acquiring job skills. "Build, brother, build" as opposed to "Burn, baby, burn," he argued, was the key to black progress. Impressed by the success in Philadelphia, foundations and federal agencies then provided the funds to extend the OIC concept nationwide. National and local advisory committees of businessmen provide access to job openings as well as advise on appropriate training occupations.

Operation SER, a primarily Hispanic organization growing out of a post–World War II and Korean pursuit of placement for Mexican-American veterans, the Urban League, the Japanese American League, and any number of other national and local organizations represent the same phenomenon. Classroom skill training, promotion of on-the-job training, basic remedial education, placement services, and various supportive services such as medical and child care are examples of CBO activities which vary widely by locality.

PUBLICLY ACCESSIBLE INTERMEDIARIES

Each of the above intermediaries have in common that they are not readily available to the general public but require some special affiliation. Another range of intermediaries are generally available at little or no expense to all job seekers. Almost anyone who cannot afford a newspaper can find access to the help wanted ads at a public library.

A private employment agency will charge a fee from either job seeker or employer, but not until a job is secured and a paycheck is earned. The public employment service is freely available to all who can reach its doors but it focuses on the needs of the unemployed. Somewhere between the limited-access and publicly accessible intermediaries is the temporary help agency which brokers the need of both workers and employers for part-time and flexible relationships into a growing industry. Because it is the key publicly supported intermediary available in almost every labor market, the public employment service is treated last in this chapter to provide the maximum comparison and represent its residual assignment.

The Newspaper Help Wanted Ad

Newspaper help wanted ads have intrigued policy makers far more than their potential as aids in job search and recruitment. The persistently high volume of ads even during recessions and in areas of persistently high unemployment have often been accepted as evidence of labor market mismatch. The *Conference Board* maintains an index of help wanted ads as a leading economic indicator. The assumption that help wanted ads could be taken at face value and indicated coexistence of high numbers of unfilled jobs alongside high unemployment was one of the arguments for the Manpower Development and Training Act of 1962. Only one major study has gone behind the want ad to assess its relation to labor market reality.[6] That study's findings are helpful in assessing want ads' role as a labor market intermediary.

The newspaper is a passive actor in the labor exchange process. The newspaper rents space to the advertiser without responsibility for the accuracy of the information nor the result. The interest of the newspaper is in selling advertising space and in selling newspapers. It merely provides a possible information source for employer-employee contact. The test of the help wanted ad as a labor market intermediary is the quality of the information purveyed.

Help wanted ads provide limited information regarding area labor markets. Nothing in the ad normally tells how many jobs are involved. The same ad may be duplicated in more than one newspaper and the employer and several private employment agencies may be listing the same job. Many employers having high-turnover jobs maintain permanent ads to generate a pool of applicants regardless of current needs.

The Johnson study found that approximately one-fifth of the total number of ads in the Sunday editions of major metropolitan newspapers were display ads from private employment agencies designed to attract walk-in traffic to the agency. One-third of the space in those newspapers was devoted to display ads from national advertising firms for high-skill technical jobs outside the area. Six percent of the ads advertised earning or training opportunities which were not jobs at all. Only one-third of the ad space consisted of employer-placed ads and 12 percent of these were for jobs outside the SMSA. Since most ads were placed for a number of days, to a daily reader only 30 percent of the ads each day would represent new jobs offered by an employer.

A relatively small group of employers were found to generate a high volume of ads. For instance, 16 percent of the employers were multiple ad users and they accounted for 38 percent of all employer placed ads. These heavy ad using employers also tended to be the ones who made extensive use of the other media as well, one-third having placed job orders for the same jobs at the public employment service, 25 percent with a union, and over one-half with private employment agencies.

Professional/technical/managerial jobs and those in clerical and in sales split about evenly approximately one-half of the ads, with services and a combination of blue-collar and farm jobs splitting the other half. A high proportion of the sales jobs were commission sales. Over 50 percent of the employer-placed ads did not give the employer's name. A quarter did not give enough information to identify the industry. Over 85 percent supplied no wage information and the location could not be identified for five percent. One out of four of the jobs listed were in the low-pay, low-status category even though those jobs comprised only 13 percent of the total employment in the labor markets studied. Use of want ads varies by industry and therefore by cities depending upon industry mix. However, about one-half of employers seemed to be help wanted ad users.

Of employer users surveyed, 60 percent claimed at least one hire from their ads. According to the BLS study of job search methods, 46 percent of job seekers had responded to help wanted ads and 14 percent claimed to have found their jobs that way.

Thus, the help wanted ad can be viewed as a widely used and cheap means of communication between recruiters and job seekers. It has a bias toward the lower levels of job attractiveness. The help wanted ad should not be taken at face value by either job seeker or labor market analyst.

The Private Employment Agency

Probably least known of the important labor market intermediaries are the private employment agencies. Because of the private, profit-seeking nature, they do not face the same reporting requirements as public agencies. They have also rebuffed most efforts to include them in labor market research. However, at least the outlines of the industry are uncoverable from the publications of the National Employment Association and state regulatory agencies.[7]

There are approximately 10,000 private employment agencies in the United States in comparison to the approximately 2000 local offices of the public employment service. The number of private employment agencies has doubled in the last ten years. They employ 50,000 people in comparison to the 30,000 staff of public employment agencies. The private employment agencies are of three general types: (1) general agencies covering occupations below the managerial level, (2) executive recruitment firms, and (3) search firms which operate on a retainer and pursue top managerial talent. The largest general employment agency has 500 offices nationwide but the average has one office, six employees, and annual gross receipts of $100,000. Approximately one-fifth are owner-operated. The average agency makes only 150 to 170 placements in a year. In total perhaps, 1.5 million to 3 million placements per year are made through such agencies.

The normal fee for a placement is about 10 percent of the annual starting salary. About 60 percent of such fees are paid by employers and 40 percent by employees. Generally, it is the higher level of occupations for which the employer pays the fee with the employee paying in the lower level occupations in which workers are in surplus supply.

The modus operandi of the private employment agency is a subject of debate and little information. Public employment service advocates argue that a reason for the rapid growth of the private agencies in recent years has been an ability and willingness to circumvent equal employment opportunity rules in making referrals. There is anecdotal evidence that this does happen but none as to the generality of such practices. It is also argued that the agencies make placements by persuading the job seeker to accept a job for which the applicant is overqualified. What is certain is that the private agency is much more active in a brokering role than other intermediaries. It has to be; survival depends upon it. Typically, the agencies appear to be highly selective in which applicant they invest time and effort. But having an attractive applicant, they do not wait passively for a matching job order. The counselors, who work primarily on commissions, get on the telephone to call employers with whom they may or may not have previous acquaintances and persist until they win agreement for a job interview.

Many feel strongly that a worker should not have to pay a fee to obtain anything as essential as a job. But that these agencies are growing rapidly, even though both employers and job seekers have readily available access to a free public agency, provides a direct market test of the value placed on their services.

Temporary Help Agencies

The temporary help industry emerged immediately after the Second World War with the two largest, Manpower and Kelly Services, established in 1947 and 1948 respectively. Tight labor markets, the growing costs of fringe benefits, the rise of female labor force participation, and rapid technological change were all factors. Employers needed access to personnel for emergency situations and peak work periods, yet wanted to minimize underutilization of regular workers. Entrepreneurs noted the potential demand and moved to meet it.

It is estimated that some 2000 firms, mostly small and geographically limited, now make up the industry.[8] Some are branches of larger firms, some are owner-operated, and a few are franchised. There seems to be no available information on the number of workers employed. From 65 to 70 percent of the firms provide primarily clerical help. Another 25 to 30 percent are in the industrial sector while perhaps 2 to 3 percent provide technical and professional help. Capital requirements are low and competition is intense. Profit margins as a percent of sales are low and the attrition of firms is high.

The temporary help services seem to meet the needs of the workers as well as the employers. Surveys have shown that the majority prefer the temporary help assignment because of its flexibility and adaptability to their available time and because of the variety of work assignments. Only a fraction work the temporary assignments because they cannot find a satisfactory regular job. In general, the temporary workers seem to be of a comparable socioeconomic status with the regular employees of the firms which they serve.

Most of the temporary help service employees learned of the opportunity through newspaper ads, with current temporary employees as the next most important source of information. About half were unemployed when they sought the temporary work assignment, with others out of the labor force, in school, and working at other jobs. Over one-third had not held a job during the previous five years. Perhaps one out of four express themselves as unwilling or unable to accept any other kind of job. However, a high proportion, perhaps one-quarter to one-third, complain that they are not offered as many hours of work as they would like. Some sign on with two or more agencies. Many also moonlight as temporary help workers in addition to a regular job.

Pay is generally rather low and fringe benefits are limited. Tenure in temporary help status tends to be relatively short, in the four- to seven-month range. About half leave for regular employment.

Surveys of companies using temporary help have shown that about two-thirds use them to replace employees on leave, three-quarters to assist with special projects, and 60 percent to augment during peak seasons. Availability on short notice was reported as the major advantage. Both employers and regular employees seem to be favorably disposed to the use of the temporaries. Only when the tasks are unique and complex requiring considerable training and supervision does there appear to be general dissatisfaction.

Though reports of abuses have been few, there has been advocacy for regulation of the industry. Organized labor in a few cases lumping temporaries into their opposition to contracting out of bargaining unit work has been one source of opposition. All in all, the temporary help phenomenon seems to be a good example of enterprise and adaptability with employer and employee need satisfactorily merged.

The Public Employment Service

The public employment service has been held to the last in this recital, not because it is of least (or most) importance, but because it is the primary representative of public policy among labor market intermediaries. It is best understood and assessed against the perspective of the others.

The public employment service was launched by the Wagner-Peyser Act of 1933, a broad charter which remains essentially unchanged after the passage of nearly half a century. The legislation mandated only an employment service in each state without defining the term. The concept which came to dominate over the years was the labor exchange—a relatively passive organization to which workers could apply for jobs and employers could direct job orders for the agency. The agency could then match capabilities to requirements and refer the worker for interview.

The failure of Congress to mandate a more active role for the public employment service may have been inherent in its beginning. Born at the low point of the Great Depression, there were few jobs into which to place anyone.[9] The initial role was to screen applicants for welfare and work relief projects. Then, with the advent of the Social Security Act, a work test for unemployment compensation eligibility was added. Depression merged into war and the employment service was federalized to assist in the allocation of scarce manpower to defense projects. The next assignment was demobilization followed by Korean War mobilization and demobilization.

Following those years of federal domination of the ostensibly state services, the organization subsided into the doldrums. Economy drives placed the 1960 budget below that of 1948. Maintaining a minimum staff in small towns and reducing staff in larger places added to the nonurban bias. Periodic recessions kept the unemployment insurance claim load high and pushed the emphasis in that direction. At the close of the 1950s, the gap between the employment service's primarily blue-collar clientele and the rapidly expanding white-collar and technical work force was noted and an effort was launched to retool to attract those workers and their employers.

Even while planning for this reorientation was underway, forces were gathering for another sharp shift in direction. The Kennedy and Johnson administrations' manpower programs and the War on Poverty stressed the problems of the disadvantaged and the minorities. Several years of constant hammering by the senior partner in the state-operated but federally financed system shifted the emphasis once again, only to discover that job orders and, therefore, placements were on the decline. The diagnosis was that employers were coming to view the employment service as a source of primarily ill-prepared workers. The new training programs provided new tools. If the workers were not attractive to the employers or no jobs were available, they could be referred to training programs for rehabilitation or to subsidized employment. But ultimately the need for placement had to be faced.

The 1970s were marked by another shift in policy, this time to an emphasis on service to employers. Attracting more job orders would be to the advantage of all applicants, including disadvantaged ones. Staff were assigned to make employer contacts. Expensive public relations drives began. The magic of the computer was expected to speed data processing, improve job matching, and represent modernization. Job banks computerized for quick recall and widespread dissemination gave access of current job order information to welfare agencies, community based organizations, and schools. Operating data were concentrated into Employment Service Automated Reporting Systems (ESARS) to assist federal reporting. A funding formula based next year's budget on last year's placements. And in most states the name was changed to Job Services.

But then another shock—decentralization. With the Comprehensive Employment and Training Act, mayors, county officials and, to a lesser extent, governors were to determine who should receive services, what services were to be provided, and which agencies should have the service delivery assignment. The employment service still had its traditional relationship with the mainstream of the labor market. But during the 1960s it had become substantially dependent on funds from employment and training programs and that could now be obtained only by pleasing local officials. A period of resentment and strife followed before accommodation began to emerge at the close of the 1970s.

Throughout these twists and turns of policy, a number of themes were consistent. Alone among public agencies, despite its free services, the public employment service is in the embarrassing position of begging a clientele to use it. It was launched in a 1933 world in which few labor market intermediaries existed. Unions were weak and limited primarily to a few skilled crafts. Private employment agencies were few and frequently of unsavory reputation. Few attended college so school placement offices were of little significance. There were few professionals in the labor force and little role for professional associations. The "spoils system" of political patronage had not yet been defeated by the strengthening civil service movement. All of these plus the community-based organizations and competing public agencies were on the scene a generation later. How to carve out a clear role and justify taxpayer support was a constant challenge.

Not that other intermediaries were notably more successful. Some, as noted, had their own restricted clientele. The proportion of job placements made through private employment agencies was not dissimilar from that of the public service. Help wanted ads figured in nearly three times as many hirings but that was only an information source, not a competing institution. The fact was simply that direct application and informal communications through current employees, relatives and friends met the needs of most employers adequately. And if few employers used the public employment service, then there was little incentive for job seekers to do so. Where the jobs are, there shall the job seekers be also. The hardest-to-place workers and the hardest-to-fill jobs are almost certain to be the residual lot of the public employment service—as it is of the other publicly available intermediaries.

Another theme has been federal dominance. The federal-state employment service has been accused of responding to the feds, "We can't obey your rules because we are a state agency," and to their governors, "We are sorry, Governor, but we run on federal money and are beholden to their rule." As a matter of fact, however, the federal purse strings have dominated throughout the history of the agency which has responded, with some lag, to every vagary of federal policy. Federal regulatory and enforcement responsibilities currently involve it in the administration of 22 laws, 14 executive orders, and 14 interagency agreements, few of which contribute directly to the task of getting jobs for people or people for jobs. Requirements that all federal contractors list their job openings and that food stamp and AFDC recipients register for work are the most relevant of examples. Masses of data are gathered and forwarded to Washington for compiling in national data banks but little is processed or analyzed in a form relevant to local labor market planning or administration.

There is presently no satisfactory way of comparing the relative cost-effectiveness of the various intermediaries. For most, there are no data on either placement costs. The private employment agencies make from 1.5 to 3 million placements a year at a cost to job seekers or employers of something like $900 apiece (in 1976). The public employment service in the same year placed 3.2 million (one-tenth of them for three days or less) at an average cost of $250. The average pay of the employment service placement was $2.91 per hour compared to $4.67 for the private agencies. Despite some considerable overlap, they do not serve the identical range of the market.

Job Service, as it is now called, faces its golden anniversary in a quandary. It can compete with every other intermediary, seeking to be all things to all people. It can continue as a local arm of national policy, responding to changing federal priorities. It can identify viable roles not being adequately filled by others, most likely varying widely by locality. It might become a major source of local labor market information to the aid of job seekers, employers, and public planners. It might expand research and understanding of local labor markets. It might identify those occupations, industries, and workers not adequately served by other intermediaries and concentrate on meeting their needs. It might become a more aggressive broker for those in greatest need, learning some lessons in aggressiveness from the private employment agency counselor. It might encourage self-placement by teaching job search skills and supplying labor market information to narrow the search for the most likely employer. Inertia being what it is in every organization, the most likely choice is the status quo. But that may mean slow starvation and institutions as well as people generally possess an instinct for survival. The pressures of the times may force this most ubiquitous of all intermediaries into a flexible but aggressive brokering role.

SUMMARY

Though employer and employee ultimately find each other, the loss of income and production consequent to the search has called forth a variety of intermediaries to facilitate a match between people and jobs. There is no way to compare their relative effectiveness. Each is a creature of its history and environment, and has its own niche in the labor market. The student of the labor market must understand them all. The practitioners and policymakers must assess the strengths and weakness of each and weld them into a viable system which, though not orderly, fulfills the needs of all who cannot meet their own needs through exercise of labor market power. Those which are private meet the market test of their worth; as long as their members or their customers are willing to foot the bill, it must be assumed that they get their money's worth. Only where they threaten to exploit the helpless or seriously violate public policy should there be government regulation or interference.

Job Service is a public entity, taxpayer supported. All such institutions should be persistently subject to comparisons of their costs and benefits. Clearly there is a role for a public employment service but that role is likely to be a changing one in changing labor markets and requires frequent reassessment.

DISCUSSION QUESTIONS

1. Name and describe the labor market intermediaries active in your community. Discuss with your classmates the experiences you and others have had with various of these intermediaries. What appear to have been their impacts on employers, job seekers, and the labor market?
2. Discuss the recruitment and job search model of Figure 24-1. Does it square with your experiences? Interview a few employers to see if it accurately describes their practices. What are the implications for policy makers?
3. A number of countries outlaw private fee-charging employment agencies. An Executive Order in the United States requires private employers doing business with the federal government to list all job openings with the public employment service. What are the pros and cons of these two policies? What differences are they likely to make in the workings of the labor market?
4. What, in your judgment, have been the factors resulting in the rapid growth of both private employment agencies and temporary help services in recent years?
5. Relate the various intermediary institutions discussed in this chapter to the labor market concepts discussed in Chapter 6. Which of these intermediaries provide examples for which of those concepts? What insight can the concepts of external and internal labor markets, dual labor markets, and segmentation and shelters lend to our understanding of the origin and role of intermediaries?
6. Job search training is described elsewhere in this volume as the newest tool in the employment and training tool kit. From your own job seeking experience, what, if any, training is needed to improve job search skills? In what institutional settings is this training best provided?

Notes

1. Miriam Johnson, *A Bifocal View of the Labor Market, Job Development and Placement: CETA Program Models,* U.S. Department of Labor, Employment and Training Administration, 1978.
2. U.S. Department of Labor, Bureau of Labor Statistics, *Jobseeking Methods*

Used by American Workers, bulletin 1886 (Washington, D.C.: GPO 1975), pp. 4, 7.

3. Personnel Accreditation Institute, *Study Guides for Accreditation Examinations*, American Society for Personnel Administration, Berea, Ohio (undated).
4. Robert Glover and William Franklin, "Hiring Halls as Labor Market Intermediaries," in National Commission for Manpower Policy, op. cit, pp. 255–282.
5. Bernard E. Anderson, *The Opportunities Industrialization Centers* (Philadelphia: Industrial Relations Unit, The Wharton School, University of Pennsylvania, 1977).
6. Miriam Johnson, op. cit.
7. Garth Mangum, "The Private Employment Agency as a Labor Market Intermediary," in National Commission for Manpower Policy, op. cit., pp. 283–308.
8. Martin J. Gannon, "An Analysis of the Temporary Help Industry," in National Commission for Manpower Policy, op. cit., pp. 195–226.
9. National Council on Employment Policy, *Wagner Peyser Act, Time for A Change?* Washington, D.C., 1979; Miriam Johnson, *Counterpoint: The Changing Employment Service* (Salt Lake City, Utah: Olympus Publishing Company, 1973).

Chapter 25
Industrialization and
Rural Development

Economists have attempted to explain the causes of the wealth and income of individuals and nations since long before the time of Adam Smith. That economic productivity has been due to the joint efforts of capital, human and natural resources, and entrepreneurs is well established, but the weights to be given each factor of production and the precise causal relationships among them are not as clear.

In recent years economists have devoted considerable attention to the economic development process. Some of this work has attempted to explain the role of human capital investments in economic development, especially in the developing countries. Others have been concerned with the differential rates of growth among regions, individuals, and sectors of the economy. Although the issues are far from settled, experience with the industrialization of either underdeveloped countries or lagging regions and sectors leaves little doubt that the development of human resources plays an important role in raising incomes.

AN OVERVIEW

Industrialization and human resource development (HRD) are closely linked because industrialization shapes people to its own requirements.

Economic development, or the growth of income-earning opportunities, influences education and training by providing the resources to support educational activities as well as means of acquiring on-the-job training experiences. The interaction among economic output and education and training is similar to the formation of nonhuman capital: HRD requires prior production to support education and training activities until those in whom these investments are being made can become productive.

However, the interactions between HRD and income-generating activities make it very difficult to establish with precision causal relationships between national incomes and investments in human resources. As noted in Chapter 7, such investments are unquestionably closely related to the growth of per capita income, but we do not know whether the HRD investments cause the incomes to grow or whether incomes cause HRD investments to grow. Moreover, there is some question over the extent to which joint returns to all factors of production can be attributed to human and nonhuman capital.

Similar linkages exist among training programs, economic development, and education. Programs that match people and jobs increase individual and national productivity by helping people to be more productive. For example, mobility of training programs to move people from labor-surplus to labor-shortage areas increases national income if the costs of making these moves are less than the incomes gained. However, measures to influence the supplies of workers assume that there are jobs available for them. Moreover, jobs are an important part of the training process because most of the skills and attitudes needed for modern industry are learned either on the job or by being exposed to economic activities.

However, our problem is complicated by the fact that HRD is not entirely economic. Education, for example, has consumption characteristics because it involves processes through which education improves noneconomic as well as economic aspects of life. Similarly, education and training might have social benefits by improving political processes and facilitating social order. Therefore, efforts to determine the economic returns to education and training encounter the problem of how to factor out these consumption and social benefits, all of which undoubtedly facilitate economic development.

An HRD strategy must also concern itself with programs to eliminate barriers to personal improvement that are not related to productivity. The major factor here is discrimination because of race, sex, age, or national origin (discussed at length in Part III).

Similarly, while industrial societies must provide for the maintenance of those who cannot or should not work, many health and welfare activities have no direct measurable relationship to productivity, even though they play important roles in shaping economic development. The manner in which these health and welfare services are rendered also has important implications for economic development. Ill-fed children suffer psychophysical damage that permanently affects their ability to be educated and trained for productive work. Moreover, income maintenance clearly is necessary if workers are to support themselves and their families while they are being trained. The interaction of education, income, health, and jobs is nowhere more evident than in the well-known vicious circle that makes it difficult for many poor nations and individuals to improve their positions.

INSTITUTIONS, HUMAN RESOURCE DEVELOPMENT, AND INDUSTRIALIZATION

Not only are there close causal interactions between the various components of HRD (jobs, education, training, antidiscrimination, and welfare) and industrialization, but industrialization itself interacts in a very significant way with political, social, and economic institutions. The nature of HRD programs is closely related to levels of economic development, national objectives, and the nature of the society in which industrialization takes place.

As Kerr, Dunlop, Harbison, and Myers show, industrialization requires increasing levels of technology, which have significant manpower implications. These levels of technology necessitate the development of a science and technology based upon a variety of research organizations, particularly in the advanced stages of industrialization. Moreover, industrial systems require wide ranges of skills and professional competence, which must be widely distributed throughout the working population. As a consequence, it is their view that the creation of a highly skilled professional and technical labor force is as important for industrializing societies as the accumulation of capital goods: "The professional, technical, and managerial component of the labor force, private and public, is particularly strategic since it largely carries the responsibility of developing and ordering the manual and clerical labor force."[1]

Because of the centrality of science and technology in the industrial society, technical competence tends to replace traditional ways of assigning people to jobs. Industrial societies tend to become meritocracies in which people are assigned to jobs primarily on the basis of their abilities, not on the basis of caste, racial group, sex, or family status. Moreover, the industrialization process has a profound impact on the family. In preindustrial societies the family is likely to be the producing unit, whereas industrialism tends to disintegrate the family and to make the business firm the primary production unit.

A nation or a region adopting HRD strategies must decide (1) which people within the population are to be educated and trained and (2) at what level of education. Moreover, decisions must be made about the kinds of education and training to be undertaken: Are resources to be devoted to scientific and technical training or to the arts and humanities? To some extent, these decisions might be made by the market because activities that are in greatest demand will provide the largest rewards and, therefore, induce people to enter them. But choices about HRD cannot be left entirely to the market.

Harbison and Myers have shown that the HRD strategies adopted clearly depend on the level of economic development, among many other things.[2] These authors identified various levels of economic development with corresponding HRD strategies. In underdeveloped countries, for example, the main national objectives tend to be national sovereignty and independence, and the rapid development of primary industries is likely to be considered an important means for achieving these national objectives. Because educational levels tend to be quite low in the underdeveloped countries, the development of primary education is usually an important HRD goal.

As societies become partially developed, they concentrate upon building the base for industrialization while increasing productivity in agriculture. During this stage, there are likely to be shortages of skilled and technical manpower. As a consequence, these manpower needs are met by importing personnel from more advanced countries. The important HRD objective during this stage of economic development is likely to be extension of universal primary education, which becomes attainable because of the resources made available by economic development. Secondary education, especially in science and mathematics, must also be expanded in order to meet the need for subprofessionals and technicians. Because of the shortages of skilled and educated labor, the extension of education and training requires improvements in educational technology in order to overcome critical shortages of teachers.

As the society reaches the third, or semiadvanced, stage, the national economic objective is likely to be rapid and massive industrialization. During this stage, large-scale unemployment of unskilled workers is likely to be coupled with continuing shortages of those with higher levels of education and skill. As a consequence of this imbalance, institutions of higher education, as well as those providing job training and adult education, are subjected to considerable pressures. It becomes particularly important for higher education to emphasize science and technology and for vocational and adult education to meet more closely the requirements of employers.

In advanced countries HRD needs tend to emphasize innovations in order to maintain a rapid rate of economic development. Concerted and sustained efforts are needed in advanced industrial societies to achieve full employment because of the difficulty of distributing the output of a highly productive economy. As productivity rises and the same output can be produced with fewer people, it becomes necessary to adopt specific measures to prevent rising unemployment. During this stage—when science and technology play an important role in continuing innovation—higher education, particularly at the postgraduate level, is given priority. At the same time, however, advanced societies experience strong pressures for universal secondary education in order to place higher education within the easy reach of all people. Measures also are necessary in advanced economies to eliminate inequalities among various segments of the population because these inequalities become increasingly apparent as incomes rise, and rising national incomes make it possible to reduce inequalities. Moreover, dynamic changes make skills obsolete and lead to knowledge explosions, all of which require perfection of education and training in order to prevent maladjustments and to promote equality of economic opportunity.

Attitudes of Political Leaders

Strategies for HRD are influenced not only by the stage of economic growth but also by the nature of the institutions and the attitudes of the political leaders in the areas undergoing industrialization. For example, revolutionary intellectuals tend to harbor quite different attitudes about the role of education and training than political leaders with middle-class values. The revolutionaries are likely to conceive of education as a primary means of achieving national objectives—as a means of developing human resources for the state and not for personal enjoyment. Moreover, the educational system is likely to be more specialized and functional, with a high priority on science and technology. In the Soviet Union, for example, science and education have become important instruments for state power. Max Lerner has explained:

> For the Russians, science has become mainly an instrument of state power, part of their Grand Design for world domination, indeed part of their political religion. This is something that we need to understand; for the Russians there is a political mystique of science. There is a belief that nothing is impossible for man once he has the weapons of science.[3]

Pluralistic societies such as the United States, however, are less likely to have unified educational objectives. Education, like other institutions, is apt to reflect the divergent interests and influences of different groups within the society. However, the society as a whole tends to emphasize widespread public education as a means of making political democracy more effective. Education in the United States also tends to stress human development, not the establishment of functional relationships to the economic system. Scientific, technical, and vocational education are likely to become increasingly important in such a society, but not at the expense of training in law, art, and the humanities.

Regardless of the political persuasions of the national leaders, education is clearly regarded as "the key that unlocks the door to modernization." Not only does education have a direct impact upon development, but also it has an indirect effect through its influence on factors such as natural resources, markets, the ratio between people and human resources, political stability, social and cultural institutions, and leadership. Moreover, although education is likely to play an important role in the growth of national income, it is important to recognize that the particular type of education and training system is probably as important as the amount of education. In other words, at a given stage in economic development some kinds of education and training are likely to be more important than other kinds. For example, increasing expenditures on art, humanities, and law when a country needs more scientists and technicians is not likely to promote economic development, and as countries develop, the percentage of national income for HRD is likely to rise everywhere.

Building an Industrial Labor Force

Kerr and his colleagues identify four interrelated processes in building an industrial labor force. The first of these processes is *recruitment,* either through compulsory or voluntary means. Examples of compulsory recruitment are slavery and peonage. In modern times, however, only the communist countries have relied extensively on compulsory recruitment of labor—partly because "compulsory methods generally have proved to be unreliable as a permanent means of building an industrial labor force."[4] Fortunately, as industrialization proceeds and the amenities of industrial jobs become clearer to workers, the recruitment process is relatively easy. This is not due entirely to the attractiveness of industrial jobs but to the benefits that are much greater than those available to the workers in agriculture. Because the recruitment process tends to be relatively easy, labor shortages are likely to be mitigated fairly rapidly during the process of industrialization.

The second process, *commitment,* tends to be much more difficult. The "committed worker is one who stays on the job and who has severed all his major connections with the land." The process of commitment takes place in four stages—the uncommitted worker, the partially committed worker, the generally committed worker, and the specifically committed worker—the degree of commitment varying with the stage of economic development. The uncommitted worker takes an industrial job for a particular purpose with the intention of returning to the land when this limited purpose or objective is achieved. The partially committed worker takes an industrial job but maintains his rural connections. The generally committed worker has completely severed rural connections and has become committed to employment with a particular firm. Specific commitment is particularly important in Japan, where workers have strong commitments to particular employers and where employers are likely to view some workers as lifetime employees. It is also significant in Italy, France, and England and may become more important in the United States as a result of seniority systems and employers' heavy investment in the education and training of their employees.

Environmental factors, of course, may speed or retard the process of commitment. In large urban areas commitment is more easily achieved than in more isolated communities. Cultural factors such as religious and ethical valuations, the family system, class, and race all have a bearing on commitment, but, in one way or another, workers are uprooted from the old order and relatively soon become generally or specifically committed to the new.

The lack of worker commitment during early stages of industrialization might have positive as well as negative effects. The tensions generated by the industrial routine probably are relieved by occasional visits to a worker's village. Low labor productivity is an important deterrent to economic development during the initial stages of industrialization, but it is not a very serious problem once industrialization gets under way.[5]

The third process is *advancement*, which means developing the skills and attitudes necessary for industrial production. This is a most critical process in building industrial work forces. Advancement may be carried out by workers themselves, by company training programs, or by governmental or community programs. However, in modern times, increasing education and skill requirements make it difficult for workers to train themselves. As a consequence, a very large part of industrial training must take place on the job. Besides, on-the-job training imparts to workers not only skills but also attitudes conducive to industrial efficiency.

Because skill acquisition requires formal education as well as OJT, formal schools have an important role to play in the advancement process. During the early stages of industrialization, schools are not likely to be particularly well suited to turning out efficient work forces. Hence developing nations must draw their skilled manpower from other countries. But as the country develops, education becomes more closely related to economic institutions. In advanced industrial societies workers are required to have considerable formal education; and because education is likely to have social as well as individual benefits, governments tend to expand their role in education and training.

The fourth process is *maintenance*, which involves providing for the general welfare and security of the population. Industrialization invariably gives rise to the need for unemployment insurance, compensation for accidents, maintenance of people during their old age, and other forms of social security. Public maintenance increases in importance because the family ceases to be the primary producing unit and workers become dependent on their work for a livelihood. Provisions must be made, therefore, for people who either cannot or should not work. However, maintenance systems frequently are closely related to the other steps in the development of an industrial work force—because the level of maintenance depends upon the productivity of the whole work force and because various incentive systems might be developed to facilitate the entry of people into productive work rather than relying on welfare for maintenance.

THE RELATIONSHIP OF EDUCATION AND TRAINING TO ECONOMIC GROWTH

The relationship between the amount of educated manpower and economic growth has not been clearly established. No one is as yet able to assert that a large pool of scientists has a positive and direct impact on output and growth—even though theoretically such expenditures are considered as investment in educational capital and should raise productivity and output per person.

Harbison and Myers constructed an index of HRD consisting of (1) the number of teachers at the elementary and secondary levels per 10,000 population, (2) the number of engineers and scientists per 10,000 population, (3) the number of pupils enrolled in elementary school as a percentage of total possible enrollment, and (4) several other measures of development in education. They finally arrived at a composite index—the total of

> enrollment at the second level of education (secondary equivalent) as a percentage of the age group 15–19, adjusted for length of schooling and enrollment at the third level of education (higher education) as a percentage of the age group, multiplied by a weight of 5 (reflecting a greater weight for the influence of higher education).[6]

Using per capita GNP in U.S. dollars and percentage of population engaged in agriculture as indexes of economic output, Harbison and Myers found a significant correlation (+0.89) between their index and GNP per capita. There was negative correlation between the index and the percentage of population engaged in farming occupations (−0.81). But these quantitative relationships, the authors caution, do not establish causal relationships. In some cases (such as Japan), however, a claim of causality between an educated labor force and economic growth seems to be supported by the evidence. Japan has made a heavy investment in its educational system, which certainly has contributed to later rapid economic growth.

Although Harbison and Myers are cautious about assigning causal relationships between education and economic growth, other economists have not been as reluctant. There is, however, increasing skepticism about the large role some economists have assigned education as a factor in economic growth. Clearly, these relationships are not linear and homogeneous. At early stages of development general literacy is important in modernization. Moreover, the development of technicians and skilled workers also is important as the economy develops and becomes more technical. However, the relationship becomes more difficult to determine at later stages of economic development. Nevertheless, a relationship between education and individual incomes can be established because employers use education as a screening device.

EMPLOYMENT AND TRAINING
PROGRAMS AND REGIONAL DEVELOPMENT

Economic development is significant for regions and smaller economic sub-divisions as well as for nations. The development problems of regions derive from the fact that many areas have stagnant or depressed economies. Consequently their residents suffer unemployment, underemployment, and incomes far below national averages. In the United States, government and private agencies have been anxious to develop these areas. A basic question is whether the area development approach is more sound for improving per capita real income than moving people from those areas to jobs in places with greater economic potential.

The development of places is not necessarily incompatible with the development of people, but it can be. For example, creating marginal jobs might not be in the best interest of the younger, adaptable, better-educated people, who could compete successfully for the jobs. Subsidizing industry to locate in a depressed area could be particularly disadvantageous because a town's costs for public services are likely to rise faster than its revenue, thus depriving the town of funds to improve education, training, health, and other necessary investments in its people. Policies to improve mobility from such places to others might be in most people's best interest. (But marginal jobs might be in the best interest of *some* of the people in the depressed area.)

Even when industrial recruitment efforts are successful, such efforts are likely to attract low-wage, labor-intensive enterprises with dead-end jobs that will improve real incomes only marginally. High-wage firms are not likely to be as attracted by the blandishments of cheap labor and tax incentives as by the existence of skilled workers, adequate markets and resources, or external economies found in many locations. Because industry adapts to the kinds of resources available, higher-paying extramarginal industries have been attracted when a region upgraded its resources through education and training.

Indeed, the need for HRD programs in lagging areas is suggested by the fact that many former residents, whose education and skills enabled them to migrate, often return when jobs open up—leaving those without education and training still unemployed. Lagging regions, therefore, could more easily attract higher-paying industry by making investments in human resources than by giving locational subsidies directly to firms.[7]

Regional Development Policy in the United States

The basic U.S. policy for assisting lagging areas was established by the Public Works and Economic Development Act of 1965. This act is administered by the Economic Development Administration (EDA), which has attempted to aid development districts (defined largely in terms of high levels of unemployment and low income) by providing job opportunities in nearby growth centers to which migrants can be channeled through job information, resettlement assistance, and training.[8]

Although this program has made some important contributions, it has several limitations. First, the EDA has not had adequate funds to produce significant economic development in many areas. Second, the cities selected were generally too small to provide significant growth prospects. Third, the development centers selected by the EDA also ignored cities outside the lagging areas, which might have had greater growth potential. Finally, greater attention to investment in health, education, and training of the labor forces in lagging areas probably would be more effective than investing in sewer and water lines.[9]

Another regional development program was the Appalachian Regional Commission (ARC) created by the Appalachian Regional Development Act of 1965. Three of every five dollars allocated to ARC during its first 15 years went for highway construction, and the remaining outlays were for vocational and technical education, higher education, health facilities and components, water pollution control, and land reclamation. Appropriations for 1980 amounted to $300 million.

Although it is difficult to evaluate ARC's impact on Appalachia, it is clear, in the first place, that the scope of ARC's funding levels is not adequate to do much about many of the problems it seeks to redress. Secondly, ARC has attempted to influence the development policies of the states in the region. In this it has had some successes and some failures. On the positive side, ARC was sufficiently successful in developing and implementing a coordinated child development program so that the Department of Health, Education, and Welfare has requested the commission to coordinate technical assistance in child development for all 50 states. Also ARC apparently has been successful in strengthening the often weak executive branches in the Appalachian states.

In other areas the commission has been less successful. It has encouraged the development of multicounty local development districts, but these organizations have not done very much to facilitate intercounty or county-state cooperation, usually because these districts serve mainly in an advisory capacity. Perhaps the greatest problem with ARC—a problem that perhaps is compounded by inadequate resources—has been the commission's tendency to become more preoccupied with bureaucratic matters than with substantive programs.

Marginal Economic Activities

While the long-run desirability of capital-intensive industry and skill-upgrading programs for lagging regions is generally conceded, there are cogent reasons for arguing that HRD programs should also include a strategy for developing labor-intensive activities, at least in the short run. For one thing, labor-intensive jobs, especially in rural areas, are needed for people whose educations and experience have not prepared them for high-wage occupations. Many of these people are likely to work in marginal enterprises or receive welfare wherever they live. Limited public resources might be more effectively utilized in subsidizing marginal enterprises in rural areas than in income maintenance. Measures are especially needed to improve the position of small farmers by making it possible for many of those who wish to remain in agriculture to do so. With adequate technical assistance and loan programs many small farmers could switch from capital-intensive crops to such labor-intensive ones as vegetables and livestock production. It is possible that the ascendancy of large farms has resulted, in part, from federal agricultural policies, which favor large-scale activities, as well as from economies of size or comparative economic advantages that large farmers enjoy. The long overdue reform of American agricultural policies might slow down the displacement of small farmers.

Although cooperatives and other labor-intensive activities might be marginal economic enterprises, they could have significant noneconomic advantages that would have long-run beneficial implications for HRD. For example, significant actions against discrimination, poor education, unwise agricultural policies, and inadequate health and welfare services are unlikely without political pressures. Marginal economic enterprises might, therefore, form bases to generate pressures for improving the productivity of the rural poor and their children as well as providing minimum income bases for those who wish to remain in rural areas. Marginal enterprises also make it possible to slow the deterioration of many rural communities. In addition to marginal enterprises, public service employment programs have been launched in lagging regions to give jobs to persons with limited education or nonagricultural work experience.

RURAL DEVELOPMENT

Rural HRD is an important problem because many rural people are not prepared by education or work experience for many jobs available in urban centers or smaller communities. In some cases, for lack of HRD, rural people have not had access to emerging job opportunities in growing areas, allowing an inflow of more qualified workers from urban industrial areas. In other cases, people who could work in rural areas, and prefer to do so, are forced to migrate because of inadequate rural job opportunities, and therefore contribute to urban unemployment and underemployment. In addition, this is an important national problem because rural people suffer from some very serious HRD problems that cannot always be solved with the approaches adapted to urban environments.[10]

Despite its importance for domestic policy, a number of factors have caused neglect of rural HRD:

1. Perhaps most important is the invisibility of rural areas in a society in which the news media are mainly urban and, therefore, concentrate on urban problems.
2. Except for agribusiness, many rural groups have been disorganized and powerless, a condition aggravated by the declining financial bases of many small towns and the outmigration of people in the more productive age and education groups.
3. Many people have minimized rural problems because of the mistaken belief that rural populations were declining. This error was caused by equating *agricultural* with *rural* populations. It is true that the agricultural population has declined rapidly and is now a small, relatively stable amount, but, after remaining fairly constant between 1960 and 1970, total rural population has been growing.
4. Finally, HRD activities have been severely restricted in rural areas for a variety of reasons, including lack of interest in this topic by agribusiness, the absence of organizations to represent workers and small farmers, and the special problems involved in serving sparse populations.

Changes in Rural America

The wholesale displacement of farm populations has been one of the most dramatic developments since World War II and has created some serious HRD problems. The proportion of farm residents to the total population declined from about 25 percent in 1940 to about 3.7 percent in 1978, and the farm population declined from 30.5 million to 8.0 million during this period. The displacement of the rural black population was particularly dramatic. In 1950 blacks and other minorities constituted 16 percent of the farm population as compared with only 6.5 percent in 1978.

Labor requirements in agriculture have declined mainly because of rising productivity. In the decade following World War II, farm output per hour increased three times as fast as nonfarm output. Although some crops, such as cotton, have been fairly thoroughly mechanized, many technological breakthroughs in the production of tobacco, fruits, and vegetables have been estimated to have caused considerable displacement of labor during the 1970s.

These technological developments have increased the nation's agricultural output, but they have also created many problems for those displaced because these workers have inadequate education and training for nonagricultural jobs. Additional problems for rural development are created because the best-educated and most adaptable part of the rural population tends to move to urban areas, leaving behind many people who are unable to compete either with larger agribusiness or for rural jobs. By the end of the 1970s one of every four rural persons aged 25 years and older had 8 years or less of education compared with one of six people in metropolitan areas. Moreover, about five-eighths of all black farm residents had an education of 8 years or less. Rural populations also have relatively fewer people of working age. In 1977, 37 percent of the rural and 40 percent of the metropolitan population fell in the prime working-age group of 18- to 44-year-olds.

These factors have caused some significant changes in rural employment patterns. For one thing, large numbers of small farmers and tenants became agricultural laborers. The distinctions between farm and nonfarm workers also are diminishing. Improved roads and better communication made it possible for farm residents to commute to nonfarm jobs and for urban residents to commute to farm jobs.[11]

Rural Problems

The main problems for HRD in rural areas are widespread underemployment and poverty. In 1978 the poor constituted 12 percent of farm, 14 percent of central city, and 12 percent of metropolitan populations. Unemployment rates are very poor measures of the looseness or tightness of rural labor markets because these rates do not count part-time employment or those who are not actively seeking jobs. In other words, hidden unemployment would be a much more significant measure, although there are no precise measures of this condition.

The pattern that emerged in American agriculture by the early 1970s was one of considerable mechanization, growing farm sizes, and rising incomes for some rural residents but low incomes and underemployment for many others. Moreover, the people remaining in rural areas seemed to have many disadvantages for HRD purposes: They were old or very young, had larger families, had less and inferior education, or were minorities. In addition, they tended to be economically and politically disorganized and powerless, causing public policies that vitally affect them to ignore their interests. Finally, rural people suffer because their geographic dispersion makes it difficult to deliver employment and training services to them with traditional approaches, which often were developed for urban populations.

The problems of rural areas are not solving themselves. The following statistics for 1978 indicate the dimensions of various rural groups:

	MILLIONS
Rural population	51.6
Rural workforce	31.7
Employed persons in non-metropolitan areas	29.8
Agricultural workforce	3.3
Self-employed farmers	1.6
Wage and salary agricultural workers	1.4
Unpaid family farm workers	0.3
Seasonal farmworkers	1.0
Migrant farmworkers	0.2

Given that agricultural employment is a small part of the total rural work force, and hired farm labor is less than half the agricultural work force, the major problems for rural HRD derive from the necessity to prepare the rural population for employment opportunities in the nonagricultural industries and occupations to overcome labor surplus situations.

Many economic development experts believe that migration is the most effective remedy in many rural areas for the problems of labor surplus. Migration is necessary, according to this view, because continuing technological change in agriculture reduces jobs faster than industrialization creates them. Consequently, there has been substantial outmigration from rural areas, especially during periods of full employment in the national economy. Migration varies inversely with age, and the potential gains of the typical mover who remains in urban areas apparently outweigh the pecuniary costs of moving. However some migrants suffer income losses when they move, causing many of them to return to rural areas. Most important is the finding that natural massive outmigration from rural areas since 1940 has not by itself improved significantly the relative labor incomes of farm workers or reduced the income inequality within agriculture.

Because natural migration patterns have not been sufficient to reduce surplus populations in many rural areas, many consider relocation programs as superior alternatives to fruitless attempts to attract industry to rural areas with little economic potential, to transfer payments, or to a continuation of the economically irrational migation patterns based mainly on friends, relatives, and other not necessarily knowledgeable contacts. Those who favor growth center strategies advocate programs to rationalize the labor market by moving people to these growth centers rather than leaving workers free to migrate to congested urban areas.[12]

Most rural income and employment problems have come about because of the displacement of people from agriculture who have not always been prepared for nonfarm jobs. Although nonfarm employment has been growing, it has not been sufficient to close rural-urban income gaps or to provide jobs for all of those who have been displaced from farms and have not migrated to urban areas. Employment and training programs should play a larger role in helping find solutions to all of these problems. However, if this is to be done, the states with the assistance of the federal government must adopt rural employment and training policies, develop innovative programs geared to local realities, and provide support for more adequate human resources in rural areas. More specifically, rural employment and training could promote a rural HRD strategy by:

1. Facilitating rural industrialization by providing better labor market information and helping to upgrade available work forces.
2. Helping people relocate from labor-surplus to labor-shortage areas.
3. Providing better job information and job training to rural youth through schools or employment and training providers.

4. Providing outreach programs to deliver employment and training services to groups who have not had equal access to these services (the extension service, private organizations, or other entities could be used for this purpose).
5. Providing public employment in a variety of public service areas that could simultaneously provide jobs and training while supplying important needs such as improved health and recreation facilities, nursing homes, nutrition and food supply, and day-care programs.
6. Encouraging cooperative and other organizations to represent disorganized rural groups.[13]

The Role of Employment and Training Programs for Rural Development

There are a number of obstacles to effective manpower planning for rural areas, including: program inflexibility, which causes the unique needs of rural people to be ignored; a preoccupation with perpetuating a bureaucracy rather than encouraging innovation, which often produces inappropriate attempts to fit urban models to rural situations; and poor coordination, which causes interagency coordination often to be characterized by lip service instead of meaningful action. Another obstacle is insufficient funding because employment and training expenditures, like most other social outlays, have had an urban bias. Rural areas receive a less-than-proportional share of human resource program funds, except for elementary and secondary education.[14] In part, this is due to the greater visibility of urban problems and the greater administrative capacity of urban governments.

The Comprehensive Employment and Training Act of 1973 perpetuated the disadvantages of rural areas in the allocation of funds. This was done both through the allocation formula, which gave heavy weight to unemployment, and through "hold-harmless" clauses, which guaranteed prime sponsors that their funds would not be reduced too much below past allocations. As a result, for example, federal outlays in fiscal year 1976 to metropolitan counties were $47 per capita compared to $21 per capita going to nonmetropolitan areas. Unemployment statistics discriminate against rural areas because they do not reflect the larger rural needs—needs that arise from the large proportion of the rural population not working because of the relatively fewer jobs available, the relatively large numbers of people working part time, and the higher incidence of poverty. Formulas that gave greater weight to these factors rather than to unemployment would be better for rural areas. Under the 1978 CETA amendments, employment and training resources have become better targeted to low-income persons, and rural areas have received a more equitable share of the funding. However, an equitable formula would be difficult to devise, and it would probably be too complex to be readily understood. Perhaps then it would be better practice to simply have separate parts of major legislation deal with the unique employment and training, health, and other human resource problems of rural areas.

A measure that would allocate funds under a formula which would consider income as well as employment would be helpful in designing a fair formula for allocation of CETA and other funds to rural areas. The U.S. Department of Labor has recommended the formulation of such measures.[15]

National employment and training programs have evolved to the point where state and local governments have an opportunity to fashion effective HRD strategies for rural and small community populations. Program elements include (1) better information about labor markets, career options for rural youth, and specific job opportunities, (2) basic skill training, either institutional or on-the-job, (3) upgrade training, (4) retraining and relocation assistance, (5) outreach and antidiscrimination activities, and (6) public service employment. In addition, certain states have extended collective bargaining rights to agricultural workers, while recent legislation has increased the capital available to cooperatives.

Through the Job Service and CETA program operators, both existing and prospective employers and employees enjoy better rural labor market information. Although the Rural Manpower Service has been terminated, the Job Service is placing renewed emphasis on providing equity of access to farmworkers and other rural workers.

State and local governments control the prime sponsor system which administers the bulk of the CETA programs. The balance of state prime sponsors, the rural CEPs (concentrated employment programs), and certain state-wide and county consortia constitute the system operating in rural areas.

Aside from expanding the quantity of employment and training opportunities, new programs have been introduced to improve the quality of employment and training opportunities. In addition, there has been a major expansion in special national programs for migrant and seasonal farmworkers, Native Americans, older workers, women, and other special population segments which augmented the employment and training options available to rural persons.

As noted earlier, essential economic problems of rural areas are how to provide income or employment for the unemployed or underemployed and how to facilitate the movement of people from labor-surplus areas to areas where jobs are more plentiful. Employment and training programs should play an important role in both the process of industrialization and the movement of people to where job opportunities exist. Employment and training programs should facilitate industrialization by providing potential employers with information about local labor markets, helping employers train their work forces, and providing training for unemployed workers or upgrading training for those who are employed.

If private industrialization does not soak up that part of the potential work force that is unemployed or underemployed, full employment could only be achieved through outmigration, public employment, or welfare payments to those who cannot work. It might be also good to use public funds to subsidize marginal firms partially, many of which might have considerable growth potential. Agricultural as well as nonagricultural enterprises could be encouraged. These activities are not likely to produce high incomes, but they could provide supplementary family incomes that might significantly improve the conditions of the rural poor.

CONCLUSION

The strong presumptive relationship among education and manpower programs and economic development has been explained. It is presumptive because many aspects of the causal relationships between these activities and economic development remain to be established. For example, no clear relationship has been discovered among expenditures on education, economic productivity, and incomes. Lack of precision in establishing these relationships is attributable both to the complexity of our problem and to the fact that education has noneconomic as well as economic objectives, and its effects are difficult to measure.

Nonetheless, considerable support exists for several conclusions. Fundamental is the realization that the development (recruiting, commitment, advancement, and maintenance) of industrial work forces is a prerequisite to economic development.

Second, the particular HRD strategy depends to some extent on the stage of economic development; for example, the emphasis on science and technology varies directly with the level of economic activity. However, at advanced stages, noneconomic objectives become relatively more important because economic problems are less acute and people are concerned with the quality of life rather than with the struggle for survival. During this stage, the consumption aspects of education assume greater importance. Education in the arts and humanities again becomes important, as it was during the preindustrial period—with the difference that it is now available to the masses, not only the elite. Before this stage is reached, however, there are likely to be urgent demands for equalizing the incomes of different groups and regions that have lagged during the industrial process. Minority groups are apt to demand that discrimination be ended and economic opportunity be enlarged, and people in low-income areas are apt to demand programs to reduce the gap between their incomes and those of more affluent regions. HRD can play important roles in all of these objectives. Measures will be demanded to provide jobs in lagging geographic and industrial areas and reduce shortages of skilled labor in the faster growing areas. This will require programs to create public or private employment opportunities in underdeveloped rural or urban areas. Moreover, it will be necessary to prepare people for expanding job opportunities and redirect the flows of people to growth centers. Proper mixes of private and public programs also will be needed to facilitate the retraining and upgrading of people who already are in the labor force but whose skills have been made obsolete or those who want to acquire the necessary skills and education to upgrade themselves.

DISCUSSION QUESTIONS

1. What is meant by human resource development (HRD)? Why is HRD a fundamental prerequisite for economic growth and development?
2. How can education and training programs speed up the economic development process?
3. Explain why some regions of the U.S. are more "developed" than others. What public policies are presently on the books to assist these less-developed areas? Are they successful?
4. "The basic factors of production—land, labor, capital, and entrepreneurship—are all important. But capital formation is the true engine of growth. Because it increases productivity the most, capital formation must be encouraged." Discuss.
5. Rural areas are a special case. The decline of agriculture and the inherent immobility of the rural population has created a situation requiring particular policies. What initiatives do you recommend for dealing with the peculiar problems of rural areas?
6. Who should assume the most responsibility for human resource development programs: government or business? Discuss the role played by these and other institutions in an HRD strategy.
7. "With economic growth and capital intensive industrialization, the production process and economic life in general have become less personal. Individuality is no longer an integral part of a product, and workers have less pride in what they produce. The very fabric of the production process is undermined, and consumers pay the price for an inferior product." Discuss.

Notes

1. Clark Kerr et al., *Industrialism and Industrial Man* (Cambridge, Mass.: Harvard University Press, 1960), p. 35.
2. Frederick Harbison and Charles A. Myers, *Education, Manpower, and Economic Growth* (New York: McGraw-Hill, 1964).
3. Max Lerner, "Humanistic Goals," in Paul R. Hannah, ed., *Education: An Instrument of National Goals* (New York: McGraw-Hill, 1962), p. 103.
4. Kerr et al., op. cit., p. 167.
5. Walter Galenson, *Labor and Economic Development* (New York: Wiley, 1959), p. 3.
6. Harbison and Myers, op. cit., pp. 31–32.
7. Ray Marshall, *Rural Workers in Rural Labor Markets* (Salt Lake City, Utah: Olympus Publishing Company, 1974), pp. 117–118.
8. Sar A. Levitan and Joyce K. Zickler, *Too Little But Not Too Late: Federal Aid to Lagging Areas* (Lexington, Mass.: Lexington Books, 1976).

9. Niles Hansen, "Growth Centers, Human Resources, and Rural Development," a paper written for the Rural Labor Market Strategies Project, the University of Texas, 1971.

10. Gene S. Leonardson and David M. Nelson, *Rural Oriented Research and Development Projects: A Review and Synthesis,* U.S. Department of Labor, R & D monograph 50 (Washington, D.C.: GPO, 1970).

11. Claude C. Haren, Ronald W. Holling, and M. F. Petrulis, "Growth Patterns in Nonmetro-Metro Manufacturing Employment," Rural Development Research Report no. 7, Economics, Statistics and Cooperative Services, U.S. Department of Agriculture, January 1979, in Richard E. Lonsdale and H. L. Seyler, eds., *Nonmetropolitan Industrialization* (Washington, D.C.: V. H. Winston & Sons, 1979); and Calvin L. Beale, "The Revival of Population Growth in Nonmetropolitan America," ERS-605, U.S. Department of Agriculture, December 1976.

12. Brian Rungling, Lewis H. Smith, Vernon M. Briggs, and John F. Adams, *Employment, Income and Welfare in the Rural South* (New York: Praeger, 1977), chapters 8, 9.

13. Ray Marshall, *Rural Workers in Rural Labor Markets* (Salt Lake City, Utah: Olympus Publishing Co., 1974); and Southern Regional Council, *Increasing the Options,* A Report of the Task Force on Southern Rural Development, Atlanta, Georgia, March 1977.

14. J. Norman Reid, W. Maureen Godsey, and Fred K. Hines, "Federal Outlays in 1976: A Comparison of Metropolitan and Nonmetropolitan Areas," Rural Development Research Report no. 1, Economics, Statistics and Cooperative Services, U.S. Department of Agriculture, August 1978.

15. U.S. Department of Labor, *Interim Report of the Secretary of Labor on the Recommendations of the National Commission on Employment and Unemployment Statistics,* March 3, 1980, p. 9; and Sigurd R. Nilsen, "Employment and Unemployment Statistics to Nonmetropolitan Areas," Background Paper no. 33, National Commission on Employment and Unemployment Statistics, April 1979.

EPILOGUE

Chapter 26
Issues for
the Next Decade

What will be the critical human resource issues in the foreseeable future? Crystal-ball gazing is a hazardous pursuit. For example, few foresaw the increasing importance of female workers over the past three decades, the population explosion that followed World War II, and the more abrupt decline in birth rates that occurred during the 1960s and 1970s. Nonetheless, social institutions and trends are to a large extent shaped by past events. This review provides at least a tentative basis for pinpointing some of the major issues and indicating future directions of human resource development in the United States.

SCARCITY AND THE MALTHUSIAN SPECTER

From a broad perspective human resources and labor markets are influenced by world population growth and movements. Of concern is the absolute size of the population, its characteristics, and its geographic distribution. The need to provide the knowledge and means to limit population growth has become a worldwide necessity because of the pressure of population on resources and living space. Experts estimate that the world's food supply must double during the next generation just to maintain present nutrition levels. Present levels are far from adequate for most of the world's people, and given existing technology, it is not at all clear that food production can be expanded to meet projected population growth. High-energy and capital-consuming techniques used in the United States are being limited by environmental concerns as well as energy shortages.

Our perspective must and will be modified during the 1980s and beyond to deal with the economic realities the world faces. The major long-run problem of the 1970s and 1980s is likely to be economic shortages, not surpluses. Moreover, national economic policy must pay more attention to measures to overcome scarcities and increase productivity. We must be concerned with developing adequate technologies to deal with the food, energy, and environmental problems.

Moreover, a major theme of this book has been that national economic policy can no longer assume homogeneous labor markets. Monetary and fiscal policies must be supplemented by labor market policies geared to the unique characteristics and problems of particular labor markets. For example, inflation can arise outside labor markets (as with shortages of food and energy), and unemployment can be the product of structural changes not necessarily related to prices and the general level of economic activity.

Traditional microeconomic theory must be reexamined in the light of the problems of the 1970s and 1980s. Much human resource policy has been based on neoclassical economic reasoning, which has serious limitations when applied to social problems. The neoclassical framework is useful when examining *individual* behavior, but it offers less guidance for group and community activity. We have noted the theoretical and practical limitations in applying the human capital concept (which grows directly out of the marginal productivity theory) to human resource development. Moreover, reliance on profit- or utility-maximizing concepts provides inadequate guides to public policy. For example, preoccupation with individual profit maximizing in farming has tended to maximize the profits and incomes of those farmers who survive, but it pays no attention to those who are displaced in the process and has not counted the direct public costs involved in promoting agribusiness interests through direct subsidies and the land grant college system. A preoccupation with *private* benefits may exaggerate the efficiency of the system and ignore social costs.

PREPARING FOR WORK

In regard to the United States alone, the declining rate of population growth is likely to be sustained. Concern with ecological balance, improved birth-control technology, the desire of women to opt for careers outside their homes, and the erosion of mores that hinder effective family planning will continue to reduce birth rates, conceivably to the point of stabilizing the population. In fact, U.S. birth rates are already below the zero population growth rate. The population continues to grow only because extraordinarily high numbers are currently, but temporarily, in the child-bearing ages. With an increasing proportion of the voting population beyond the child-bearing and child-rearing age and a large proportion of childless couples, there will be less political pressure to pour money into education. Nevertheless, it will remain true that those who gain their high incomes from their personal knowledge and talents will be concerned about gaining for their children the credentials and skills for similar earnings. These two trends will likely combine for a slowed growth rate for total educational expenditures but a rising per capita investment in education. More resources will be available for the development of each child, and radical changes are likely in the way this smaller number of American children are reared and educated.

Educational facilities have been hard pressed during this century to expand as rapidly as population and the demand for higher education. Consequently, institutional arrangements for children until they reach the normal school-entry age have been delayed, and many communities still lack organized provisions for children under age five. Despite the continuing and almost exclusive reliance upon home and mother to take care of children prior to their entering kindergarten, the number of working mothers continues to grow. They are likely to demand that society provide day care for their children. The experience of other countries that have grown to rely upon female labor has been to expand preschool child-care facilities, as the United States did during World War II. The government already provides some facilities, particularly for the poor under the antipoverty programs, and the more affluent purchase nursery care for their children; but expanded public coverage is needed. Child-care arrangements also might include educational and training components. This would involve the expansion of government-supported educational facilities to age three or possibly earlier. In all likelihood, child care, whether in school facilities or in specially designed institutions, will expand in the years ahead.

At the other end of the school-age spectrum the continued growth of longer education during the past century is likely to be arrested. Already, nearly nine of every ten young Americans are enrolled in schools until their 18th birthdays, and one of five continues for four or more years. The need, wisdom, and practicality of prolonging school attendance is being increasingly questioned; too frequently, the added school years have little relation to preparation for work or for life. Education throughout one's work life will probably emerge rather than further prolongation of the exclusively preparatory period during one's childhood, youth, and early adulthood. Changing technology and skill needs are likely to induce an increasing number of persons to undergo specific training periodically throughout their lifetimes.

While mature and committed workers may occasionally turn to the educational system to recharge their intellectual batteries or their manual skills, youth and young adults may combine experience beyond their school walls with educational pursuits. This may lead to a restructuring of both educational facilities and labor market institutions to provide flexibility for the student-worker to enter and leave school to work. As greater specialization is required and more of one's lifetime is spent in school, greater attention to counseling and exposure to work options will be necessary to facilitate successive occupational choices during the work career. Too often, career decisions are now being made on the basis of scholastic aptitude alone. Combining work experience with school attendance may lead to sounder career choices.

Career education is a significant development in preparation for the job market. It signals the recognition that work values and attitudes with an impact on the entire career have more basic importance than immediate job skills. The conceptual challenge is to fit all phases of education and training that are relevant to preparation for employment into a work-career framework. With the voting weight and political attention shifting to people in the older age brackets, it may be concluded that education is too important to be wasted on the young—that is, the preparation for employment that begins in childhood must be available throughout a lifetime as sought and needed. Europeans call this periodic career upgrading "recurrent education."

WORK ATTITUDES

Less tangible than the changing institutional arrangements for job preparation, but potentially of no less significance, will be the continued transformation of attitudes toward work. Much has been made of the alleged loss of pride in craftsmanship and the deterioration of the quality of services. These developments presumably reflect not only widespread job dissatisfaction but also a general antipathy to work, forsaking the traditional work ethic. Among youth, in particular, there is claimed to be a widespread rejection of the work ethic as the incentives of material rewards are becoming less important. To a large extent, these may be only youthful manifestations, and exaggerated at that. It is likely that the addiction to creature comforts that "hooked" their elders is also going to take hold of the current young as the responsibilities of family life, even if they may sometimes be postponed, induce them to maximize their incomes.

Rising affluence and educational attainment during the 1950s and 1960s brought real changes in attitudes toward work and the social unrest that followed threatened to accelerate those changes. However, the virulent inflation, falling living standards, and economic insecurities of the more recent period have increased the value of job security and, at least temporarily, stifled clamor for job restructuring. Still, it is evident that workers are becoming increasingly concerned with the qualitative aspects of work—not only with wages, hours, and benefits but also with opportunities, responsibilities, and freedom on the job. Inflation may be only delaying the inevitable. If real wages once again increase, income may become a less potent incentive and other motivating forces will be needed to ensure discipline in the work place. If economic prosperity and growth are sustained, the work ethic is likely to weaken as a generation of workers that has experienced nothing but relative affluence and job security takes its place. But until prices stabilize and unless productivity growth, which is the only source of per capita real income, increases, American workers are more likely to concentrate on keeping their earnings abreast of rising prices.

ADEQUACY OF EMPLOYMENT

Other changes have been occurring in the labor market. The growth of income-supported programs has provided many workers with more than one basic source of income. One-eighth of total personal income is the product of transfer payments, and a significant proportion of the population experiences periods of idleness cushioned by government programs. Nonetheless, the availability of jobs, as measured by the unemployment rate, is not a true indication of the *adequacy* of employment.

Low wages are a serious and persistant problem deserving at least as much attention as forced idleness. Raising the minimum wage is one possible policy, but the income gains for some may result in increased unemployment at the end of the labor queue. An alternative is a wage subsidy for low-income family heads. A reevaluation of employment and earnings inadequacy also might turn policy makers' attention to nonmetropolitan areas, where at least one-third of the needy are located but which have been shortchanged by federal employment programs.

WORK AND WELFARE

The inevitable growth of public income-support efforts will continue to erode the distinction between work and welfare. As the welfare floor is raised to help those nominally unable to work because of old age, infirmity, child-care responsibilities, or lack of jobs, and as supplements are extended to those who work but earn less than a socially acceptable minimum income, then increasing numbers may opt for welfare instead of economic self-reliance.

The challenge is to develop adequate work incentive schemes to ensure that those who can support themselves will do so. But work incentives are of no help to the millions of poor who are unable to find or hold jobs. The need, therefore, is to thus maintain a low guaranteed income and to encourage the poor to supplement their welfare by earnings, providing for a system that would guarantee those who work receive a higher income than those who depend only on welfare.

EMPLOYMENT AND TRAINING PROGRAMS

As the overlap between welfare and work increases, employment and training programs will have an expanded role. Opportunities must be provided for all individuals who will work but are unable to earn an adequate income. Artificial credential barriers can be broken down through subsidies, employer education, and governmental fiat; upgrading can be assisted through supplemental education and training; the employability of participants can be improved by training, counseling, education, and related services. However, those who believe that employment programs can substitute wages for welfare are likely to be disappointed. Only a minority of all welfare recipients can become self-supporting; employment and training programs may have to maintain the more modest aim of helping some recipients to supplement their welfare income.

In many cases, however, employment and training programs offer a second chance to those who failed in, or were failed by, the educational system and for those whose skills have been eroded by technological change. As more knowledge is gained about the needs of particular individuals and about the effectiveness of particular services or combinations of services in meeting these needs, the training programs may become an alternative for those who do not succeed in the regular school system. The experience gained from these programs may also help the regular school system to avoid many mistakes.

Employment and training programs have been consistently treated as a separate remedial system for a separate clientele. They have rarely been viewed as a component of a broader human resource development system. Their resources have always been minor in the total scheme of public and private efforts to prepare and maintain human resources. In fact, most such preparation is private, occurring in the homes and the employing establishments. Schools, churches, neighborhoods, and the entire community are involved in the process. Certainly, employment and training programs are limited efforts that can make sense only in a broader labor market/human resource context, but there is hope that the emergence of local labor market planning may encourage the integration of job creation, training and other human resources programs.

EQUAL EMPLOYMENT OPPORTUNITY

Employment and training programs are closely related to combating discrimination in employment. On the one hand, employment and training programs are frequently needed to help train the victims of discrimination in order to help them compete for available employment opportunities. On the other hand, training programs can be effective only if discrimination in employment is eliminated. Civil rights legislation and employment and training programs have contributed to the substantial gains of blacks;

pressures from women's liberation groups and action under civil rights legislation opened some doors for women; the problems of Hispanics, Indians, and other minorities also have been documented, and some efforts have been made to alleviate them. Nevertheless, discrimination remains a persistent and festering disease in the American economy.

It is naïve to assume that progress toward equal employment opportunity is guaranteed or that freedoms achieved in the past will necessarily persist. Other labor market problems may demand priority, or opposition may increase from those who are challenged by the gains of minorities. Also, if positive steps are not taken, the situation may deteriorate because of adverse developments in the labor market. An increasing number of educated women, blacks and other minorities will demand entrance into better-paying or more responsible positions, while the value of a college education is declining as a guarantee of choice jobs. Constant vigil must be kept, therefore to ensure that progress continues to be made.

It is the prime goal of employment and training policy to ensure that all human resources are fully developed and utilized. As long as discrimination exists and certain minorities are given fewer opportunities, assistance must be concentrated among these minorities. Therefore, employment and training policy must continue to focus on the victims of discrimination. Education must be improved, occupational training provided, and discriminatory barriers broken down. Both a push and a pull are required if those who are discriminated against are to get an equal chance in the work force.

THE ROLE OF GOVERNMENT

To achieve the expanded goals of human resource development, the government will have to assume an ever-increasing responsibility. In recent years the government's role in education and other human resource development programs expanded dramatically. At the same time, there is a heightened awareness of the effect that a wide range of government actions has upon the development and utilization of our human resources. No longer viewed separately and in isolation, these actions more and more are being examined and evaluated for their labor implications.

One example has been military manpower policies. During wartime, youth who were more likely to be unemployed were siphoned off, thereby easing unemployment pressure. And as the troops came home, the reverse situation became painfully evident. Another example is the role of government as a civilian employer. In the past neither the federal government nor the many state and local governments have acted as model employers. Pressures to eliminate discriminatory practices, to remove arbitrary credential barriers, and to expand training and advancement opportunities for the disadvantaged have resulted in some changes in governmental employment and training practices. Yet much remains to be done, especially at the state and local levels, to make governments equal opportunity employers.

The government also plays a major role through such regulatory functions as the enforcement of antidiscrimination laws and wage-and-hours regulations. Perhaps most significantly, the federal government has assumed responsibility for the maintenance of a favorable economic climate. But because high employment is not the only goal, the Employment Act of 1946 and the Full Employment and Balanced Growth Act of 1978, which made it the policy of the federal government to sustain maximum employment and to advance tight labor markets, remain largely exhortations. The consensus among economists, politicians, and informed citizens is that the unemployment rate can be lowered or raised almost at the public will. The problem is to achieve high employment without undue inflation, and thus the key issue is the tradeoff between unemployment and inflation. At least in the short run we can choose whatever employment level or price stability we are willing to pay for, but we cannot have both high employment and stable prices. In time, training programs and other structural measures such as aid to depressed areas may help to improve the terms of trade-off, but there is no indication that both full employment and stable prices can be achieved in the immediate future. Given this dilemma, experience dictates measures that will cushion the negative effects of inflation in order to sustain a high-employment economy. The progress made during the past three or four decades justifies optimism that increasingly sophisticated designs will ease the choice between inflation and unemployment.

PRODUCTIVITY, PRICES, AND EMPLOYMENT

Every advanced industrial economy operating within the context of political democracy wrestles with the continued problem of achieving high levels of employment while maintaining stable prices. The citizenry tends to use government to achieve guarantees of economic security and rising standards of living. In doing so, the people often demand from the economic system more than it can deliver. Only rising productivity can produce a higher per capita living standard. But productivity growth requires both investment and worker effort that frequently conflict with desires for greater consumption and leisure. "There ain't no free lunch" remains the first principle in economics.

In the United States recent growth in productivity was impeded by low savings, an influx of inexperienced workers, and a change in the industry mix shifting a greater proportion of employment from relatively high productivity manufacturing to lower productivity services and government. The population, accustomed to an annual average increase of nearly 3 percent in its standard of living over a quarter century, found achievement of price stability in face of declining growth in productivity an elusive goal. The overreliance on foreign energy sources made us vulnerable to international pricing pressures resulting in a declining rather than rising real living standard. Our unwillingness to accept that inevitability combined with our fruitless competitive pursuit of money income raises to offset the declining real income put us on an impossible treadmill.

Little of the inflationary pressure had emerged from our labor markets but every known device for stifling inflation had its negative impacts there. Probably the key labor market challenge of the 1980s will turn out to be reducing our excessive reliance on foreign oil, finding equitable means of sharing scarcity and restoring productivity growth so that the American standard of living *and* its ability to defend itself in a dangerous world can once again grow along a parallel path. This is only in part a human resource and labor market challenge, but it will have to be dealt with with the other key elements in any successful resolution of a most complex set of problems.

THE EMERGENCE OF HUMAN RESOURCE POLICY

According to dictionary definitions, no policy for human resources now exists. At the federal level most efforts have been a reaction to the special problems—real or imaginary—that caught public attention. Federal aid to elementary and secondary schools was initiated to help financially troubled areas, with little emphasis on educational innovations. Grants and loans to students were largely motivated by the Sputnik-induced fears of a technology gap and later to aid students needing financial assistance. Employment and training were funded in a haphazard fashion, in response to perceived needs. Monetary and fiscal policies were geared to affect normal economic activity with little consideration of their impact on special groups or their relation to programs that focused on special needs.

It is not at all clear, however, that the impact of human resource programs would be more salutary if a definite policy was selected to guide decision. What would be the nature and scope of such a policy? From our examination of past and present developments, we cannot answer this vital question, but we can define the ingredients and objectives of a human resource policy. Such a policy must be capable of identifying problems, setting goals, designing programs, marshaling resources, and mounting activities encompassing the entire labor market. To achieve the dual objectives of efficient allocation of labor resources and optimum choice of participants in the work force, the system should allow each individual to plan a working career in full awareness of individual abilities and the alternatives open to each person. A high and sustained level of economic activity is necessary to provide opportunities of sufficient number and range. Restrictions unrelated to productivity or equity—such as overcredentialization and discrimination based on age, race, or sex—must not be allowed to interfere with access to, and rewards for, these opportunities. The distribution of jobs must be open and flexible: Only the lack of potential competence should restrain preparation and access to individual occupational choice; lateral and upward mobility should be maintained; help in adapting to economic and technological change should be available. The reward structure—income, status, and job satisfaction—should be similarly unencumbered. All those able and willing to work should thus find both opportunities and rewards in the production of goods and services favored by society as reflected in the marketplace and the ballot box.

To what degree should policy be directed toward the achievement of these objectives? The supply of social energy is always limited and should be conserved for high-priority efforts. Interrelated with the development of human resources, as we have noted, are fiscal, monetary, education, housing, transportation, welfare, health, defense, and myriad other economic and social problems. Such linkages should be noted, and policy makers in each arena should act consistently, but no single policy can comprehend all the others. Indeed, experience suggests the wisdom of leaving to unguided individual choice all those decisions that will cause no serious problems in the aggregate, for centralized decisions are not necessarily wiser; and if they are short-sighted, they may cause more damage than a series of unwise individual decisions.

Public intervention is, in some cases, appropriate, but its limits must be understood. First, programs concerned with development of human resources can hope to solve only problems related to unemployment and earnings. A job creation or training program can contribute to the solution of poverty only for those families with present or potential workers; it can solve social discontent only for those whose problems relate to the lack of meaningful employment. Employment and training policies are likely to affect only marginally problems connected with family breakups, pollution, congestion, and other ills of a complex urban society. Second, public policy has only two sources of leverage: dollars and votes. Policies that do not affect the distribution of either are only pious declarations and have little influence.

Finding appropriate techniques to evaluate social programs is a pervasive constraint. Cost-benefit techniques provide very limited bases for a program evaluation. Aside from conceptual shortcomings, cost-benefit analysis may fail to raise the right questions. For example, in connection with welfare programs, we should be more concerned about our ability to redistribute available resources rather than whether a dollar spent on the poor adds a dollar to GNP. Evaluation is elusive because value judgments cannot be avoided.

Despite these limitations, important strides have been made toward more conscious and comprehensive action in human resource development. Insights have been gained by improved data and measurement techniques; one result has been a "cross-fertilization" showing the interdependence of problems and programs that had previously been dealt with independently. Educators are growing more aware of the need to prepare students for work, while human resource policymakers realize the difficulty and high cost of providing remedial attention where the schools have failed the first time around. The need to maintain full employment has been stressed by labor market analysts and the possibility of making monetary and fiscal policies more effective through employment and training programs has received increasing scrutiny. Interdependence of equal employment opportunity for minorities with education and employment and training policies is clearly recognized; the relation of all these policies to overall economic growth is also being examined.

Recognizing the interdependence of various aspects of human resource development is a far cry from articulating a comprehensive human resources policy. But it is not clear that such a policy is necessary or even desirable. The importance of various problems fluctuates as priorities change; public policy is hammered out step by step; the full consequences of existing programs and newly discovered concerns unfold slowly. Hence the trial-and-error approach may, in the long run, prove as effective as the most elaborate planning, possibly even more so. A comprehensive human resource policy may not be compatible with a pluralistic society such as ours, and perhaps the best that we can hope for is fragmented approaches to complex problems. The judgment of history may be that the search for a comprehensive human resource policy is in line with the search for the Holy Grail.

RESPONDING TO CHANGE

Some of the probable directions of change have been outlined and their implications identified. But there is no certainty that these will come about or that, even if they do, they will be the most significant developments of the coming years, for the only certain prediction about the future is that it will be different from the past. Clearly, changes lie ahead, and our policies and practices must be able to adapt.

Several steps can be taken to increase adaptability. Perhaps the most important is to expand the flow and currency of information. Data and evaluative techniques must be improved, and the knowledge that is gained must be widely disseminated. This will facilitate the recognition of changing circumstances and the rapid replication of successful techniques for dealing with them.

Another ingredient of adaptability is experimentation. Research and development have been important components of employment and training programs. Old approaches must be reexamined in the light of changing circumstances and improved accordingly; new ideas must be generated and tested; the future must be projected and its implications incorporated as plans are developed. In the evolution of policy one of the most difficult tasks is developing more orderly means of eliminating programs and practices that are no longer effective and of weeding out ideas and theories that have lost their relevance. But change for change's sake must be discouraged, and constant attention must be given to retaining what is useful from the past.

Finally, one of the most critical prerequisites to adaptability is an understanding of the historical context of change. Problems may gain sudden visibility, though they usually emerge gradually and are long undetected. To understand the present and to be able to cope with the future we need to know what has gone before. In this sense, the knowledge contained in this volume will, hopefully, serve as a basis for more comprehensive analysis and action so that we can make more effective and rewarding use of our human resources.

DISCUSSION QUESTIONS

1. What is the outlook for population growth in the United States? What are the factors behind the projections, and what effect will the growth rate have on economic development?
2. "The growth of public income-support programs will continue to erode the distinction between work and welfare so that soon there will be very little incentive among the disadvantaged to work." Discuss.
3. "The government must assume an ever-increasing responsibility for all aspects of economic life, particularly human resource development. As a result, the government must become the employer of last resort." Discuss.
4. "Under a basically competitive economic system, it is impossible to achieve both high levels of employment and stable prices. Alternative economic systems, however, are able to reconcile these conflicting goals." Discuss, with reference to the experiences of particular countries.
5. What role does productivity play in the U.S. economic system? What are some ways to increase productivity, assuming it is a desirable thing to do? What is the current outlook for trends in future productivity growth?
6. "The United States is moving from a free enterprise society to a welfare state." Do you agree?
7. What are the strengths and limitations of cost-benefit analysis as a tool for evaluating employment and training programs?

Bibliography

Adams, Arvil V., Garth L. Mangum, et al. *The Lingering Crisis of Youth Unemployment.* Kalamazoo, Mich.: The W. E. Upjohn Institute for Employment Research, 1978.

Topics covered include postwar trends and current outlook of youth unemployment, prospects over the next decade, the school-to-work transition, and the relationships between early work experience and future employability. The authors' policy recommendations are also included.

Anderson, Bernard E., and Isabel V. Sawhill, eds. *Youth Employment and Public Policy.* Englewood Cliffs, N.J.: Prentice-Hall, 1980.

A collection of five papers on various dimensions of the problem of high unemployment among youth and an overview by the editors on policy approaches for the years ahead. Richard Freeman analyzes its causes; Michael Wachter highlights the complexities of the problem; Elijah Anderson discusses black youth employment problems; Ernst Stromsdorfer assesses the effectiveness of current youth programs; and Beatrice Reubens reviews the experience of other industrial countries with youth unemployment.

Ashenfelter, Orley, and Albert Rees, eds. *Discrimination in Labor Markets.* Princeton, N.J.: Princeton University Press, 1973.

A collection of papers on discrimination in wages based on race and sex. Following a general economic theory of discrimination are papers devoted to consideration of education and trade unions. The final topic is an examination of public policy and discrimination.

Becker, Gary. *Human Capital.* New York: National Bureau of Economic Research, 1964.

The author first constructs a general theoretical framework within which investment in human capital can be analyzed and then illustrates the effect of human capital upon economic variables such as earnings and employment by a systematic analysis of on-the-job training. The second half of the book examines the empirical relationship between productivity and investment in human capital. Emphasis is on rates of return from investment in high school and college education in the United States.

Berg, Ivar. *Education and Jobs: The Great Training Robbery.* New York: Praeger, 1970.

The author argues that education in the United States is becoming a formalized credentialing procedure that acts as a barrier to the advancement of the poor. He analyzes the educational requirements of jobs along with Census Bureau reports on educational levels of the workforce by occupation. The study examines the relationship between educational achievement and workers' performance and promotion expectations.

Bok, Derek Curtis, and John T. Dunlop. *Labor and the American Community.* New York: Simon & Schuster, 1970.

A comprehensive overview of the present state of the American labor movement, which explores the public attitude toward labor, reviews the growth of trade unions and assesses their internal government, and discusses the changing nature of collective bargaining and the political impact of labor.

Borus, Michael E. *Measuring the Impact of Employment-Related Programs: A Primer on the Evaluation of Employment and Training, Vocational Education, Vocational Rehabilitation, and Other Job-Oriented Programs.* Kalamazoo, Mich.: The W. E. Upjohn Institute for Employment Research, 1979.

A how-to-do-it book for measuring the impact of employment-related social programs. The primary emphasis is on basic techniques of evaluation, with references to numerous theoretical and conceptual issues.

Bowen, Howard R. *Investment in Learning: The Individual and Social Value of American Higher Education.* Washington, D.C.: Jossey-Bass Publishers, 1977.

This volume is a comprehensive synthesis and analysis of the enormous studies available on the benefits of American higher education. The author's own optimistic views on the future of higher education are based on careful examination of the economic and noneconomic aspects of education.

Bowen, William G., and T. Aldrich Finegan. *The Economics of Labor Force Participation.* Princeton, N.J.: Princeton University Press, 1969.

A comprehensive and detailed analysis of the factors determining who is in the labor market and who is not working or seeking work. The effects on labor force participation of many individual characteristics and labor market conditions are analyzed for specific population groups. Also analyzed is the sensitivity of participation rates to the tightness of labor markets. Extensive appendices.

Briggs, Vernon M., Jr., Walter Fogel, and Fred Schmidt. *The Chicano Worker.* Austin: University of Texas Press, 1977.

An analysis of the factors affecting labor market experiences of Mexican-

American workers. The authors describe the major employment patterns of the Chicano labor force and discuss the historical and institutional factors determining these patterns.

Carnegie Council on Policy Studies in Higher Education, *Giving Youth a Better Chance: Options for Education, Work, and Service.* **Washington, D.C.: Jossey-Bass Publishers, 1979.**

The study examines the problems of transition from school to work, and appraises the existing policies and programs both within the school system and in the work environment related to this transition. Emphasis is placed on developing greater equality of opportunity for all youth entering the labor market. The study contains a series of recommendations by an advisory committee.

Chiswick, Barry R., and June A. O'Neill, eds. *Human Resources and Income Distribution: Issues and Policies.* **New York: W. W. Norton, 1977.**

Focusing on the Council of Economic Advisers' analyses, this volume includes discussions and analyses on the measurement of poverty, characteristics of the poor, income differentials among various demographic groups, factors influencing income inequality with particular attention paid to the role of unemployment, and relevant government programs and policies.

Doeringer, Peter, and Michael Piore. *Internal Labor Markets and Manpower Analysis.* **Lexington, Ma.: Heath, 1971.**

Examines the nature of labor markets within which the pricing and allocation of labor are governed by administrative rules and procedures. Part I develops theoretical concepts of the internal labor market. In part II these concepts are applied to a number of topics that are often of interest to human resources policymakers: human resources adjustment to labor market imbalances, technological change, racial discrimination, and the relationship of low-income employment to the disadvantaged labor force.

Douty, H. M. *Employment and the Wage Bargain.* **Baltimore, Md.: Johns Hopkins University Press, 1980.**

An historical and institutional review of the nature and outcome of the wage determination process. The volume includes a nontechnical summary of fluctuations in the supply and demand for labor, an analysis of wage differentials for skilled and unskilled workers, comparisons of direct wages and wage supplements, and a discussion of the relationship between wages and prices.

Freedman, Marcia K. *Labor Markets: Segments and Shelters.* **Montclair, N.J.: Allanheld, Osmun, 1976.**

A study of the American job structure in 1970, based on an occupational matrix developed for the study, which ranks jobs in terms of both average annual earnings and demographic variables. In addition to examining the segmentation of the labor market according to the data, the study explores the structural factors that distinguish the status of jobs. The concluding section of the book develops the concept of job shelters and presents the future research and public policy implications of the study.

Freeman, Richard B. *The Over-Educated American.* **New York: Academic Press, 1976.**

Discusses the causes and the consequences of changes in supply and demand for college graduates from the booming market of the 1960s to the depressed

1970s. Half the book is concerned with specific professions and demographic groups. The author concludes the analysis with the projection that labor market conditions for college graduates will improve in the 1980s.

Ginzberg, Eli. *Career Guidance: Who Needs It, Who Provides for It, Who Can Improve It?* New York: McGraw-Hill, 1971.

A broad study of the role of both occupational and educational guidance in enhancing the ability of people to make optimum use of their options in acquiring an education and in pursuing a career. After establishing the social dimensions of career guidance, the author examines the institutions through which it operates. Recommendations are offered for the guidance professional and the public, and likely developments during the 1970s are discussed.

Ginzberg, Eli. *The Manpower Connection: Education and Work.* Cambridge, Ma.: Harvard University Press, 1975.

The first of the three sections of this volume argues against a reliance on human capital theory as a basis for the development of education policy. A discussion follows on work and its discontents in the context of changing labor market and labor reform. In the final section of the book, the author expresses his views on the utility and the limits of public employment policy.

Ginzberg, Eli. *The Human Economy.* New York: McGraw-Hill, 1976.

The purpose of this book is to analyze the principal institutions and mechanisms which shape the development and utilization of human resources. First, an analytic framework is constructed which includes the differences between human resources and other resources, the relation between social theory and social action with reference to the human resources arena, and the interactions among the principal components of the human resources system. Next, the processes are analyzed through which people acquire skills and competencies in developed and developing nations, focusing on three basic institutions: family, school, and employing organizations.

Ginzberg, Eli. *Good Jobs, Bad Jobs, No Jobs.* Cambridge, Ma.: Harvard University Press, 1979.

An examination of the evolving U.S. job markets and parallel changes that are underway in the characteristics of jobseekers. The subjects covered in the 20 essays included in this volume range from military human resources policy to welfare in New York City to full employment in the United States. The author stresses the need for equity in the job market, offering recommendations leading to the achievement of this goal.

Ginzberg, Eli, ed. *Employing the Unemployed.* New York: Basic Books, 1980.

Eleven contributors in the field of human resources and employment policy discuss the various issues related to youth and minority programs, the supported-work experiment, and public service employment, along with other employment and training efforts, and appraise actual performances versus professed objectives.

Gordon, R. A. *The Need to Disaggregate the Full Employment Goal.* Washington, D.C: National Commission for Employment Policy, January 1978.

The author argues that less emphasis should be placed on a single figure for the full employment goal, and, instead, disaggregated targets should be formulated for different segments of the labor force. The discussion includes an examination of changing patterns of unemployment in the last 20 years, the factors contributing to the lengthening of unemployment duration, and the need to design measurements that link employment with income.

Grasso, John T., and John R. Shea. *Vocational Education and Training: Impact on Youth.* Berkeley, Calif.: The Carnegie Foundation for the Advancement of Teaching, 1979.

Based on an analysis of national longitudinal data, this report examines occupational education offered in high school, and its impact on eventual educational attainment, postschool training, and labor market experience following the first few years after leaving school.

Harbison, Frederick H. *Human Resources as the Wealth of Nations.* New York: Oxford University Press, 1973.

In contrast to the traditional view of development, which relies on the growth of GNP as the sole measure of progress, the author argues for human resources as a measure of a nation's wealth. He analyzes problems in developing the fullest utilization of the skills and capacities of the labor force. The human resources problems of developing countries are emphasized.

Harbison, Frederick, and Charles A. Myers. *Education, Manpower, and Economic Growth.* New York: McGraw-Hill, 1969.

The authors, both economists, argue that human resource development is the most important determinant of economic growth. Seventy-five countries are ranked on the basis of a composite human resource development index and then grouped into four levels of development ranging from underdeveloped to advanced. Each level is analyzed qualitatively, and appropriate development strategies are suggested.

Haveman, Robert H., ed. *A Decade of Federal Antipoverty Programs: Assessments, Failures, and Lessons.* New York: Academic Press, 1977.

Seven papers review the policies and progress of the antipoverty efforts between 1965 and 1975. In an overview chapter the editor speculates on the future course of social policy in the next decade. The authors of the other seven chapters and their subjects are: Lawrence Friedman—political and social origins of the war on poverty; Lawrence Lynn—income maintenance; Henry Levin—education and training; Karen Davis—health; Paul Peterson and David Greenstone—community action; Ellen Jane Hollingsworth—legal services; and Phyllis Wallace—equal opportunity in housing and employment.

Kalachek, Edward. *Labor Markets and Unemployment.* Belmont, Calif.: Wadsworth, 1973.

A study of the functioning of modern labor markets. The author combines a review of labor market theory with a discussion of empirical research on mobility and unemployment problems. The effects of education on the quality of labor and the impact of technological change on the labor market receive special emphasis.

Kolberg, William H. *Developing Manpower Legislation: A Personal Chronicle.* Washington, D.C.: National Academy of Sciences, 1978.

A study of the development and passage of employment legislation between 1973 and 1977, centering on the politics that led to the Comprehensive Employment and Training Act. The story is told from the personal view of a government official who played a major role in shepherding CETA and related programs through the executive and legislative branches of government.

Levitan, Sar A. *Programs in Aid of the Poor for the 1980s,* 4th ed. Baltimore, Md.: Johns Hopkins University Press, 1980.

A review of the nation's antipoverty programs. The author appraises income-maintenance programs, efforts to supply goods and services to the poor, programs to prevent youth from falling into poverty, and aid to the working poor. He concludes with an exploration of feasible approaches for future attacks on poverty.

Levitan, Sar A., and Belous, Richard S. *More Than Subsistence: Minimum Wages for the Working Poor.* Baltimore, Md.: Johns Hopkins University Press, 1979.

This study reviews the general role of the minimum wage in the welfare state. It traces the history of the wage floor from the turn of the century through 1979, critically examining the different research methods that have been employed and the findings reached in representative major studies.

Levitan, Sar A., and William B. Johnston. *Indian Giving: Federal Programs for Native Americans.* Baltimore, Md.: The Johns Hopkins University Press, 1975.

This book sketches the economic conditions on reservations and outlines the scope of federal aid to the Native American population residing on or near reservations. An underlying theme of the study is that reservation residents must be freed from federal dominance, no matter how well intentioned, and that Indian tribes and individuals must have more control over the development of their lives and institutions.

Levitan, Sar A., William B. Johnston, and Robert Taggart. *Still a Dream: Changing Status of Blacks During the Past Decade.* Cambridge, Ma.: Harvard University Press, 1975.

An analysis of the changes in the socioeconomic status of blacks in the United States. Separate chapters are devoted to income, occupations, education, family status, health, housing, and political power. In addition, the volume assesses the federal programs with the greatest impacts on blacks, including income support, in-kind assistance, education and training, and equal employment opportunity efforts.

Levitan, Sar A., and Garth L. Mangum. *Federal Training and Work Programs in the Sixties.* Ann Arbor: University of Michigan Press, 1968.

The authors trace the development of programs for training the unemployed and the disadvantaged: the Manpower Development and Training Act, the Job Corps, the Neighborhood Youth Corps, the vocational education and rehabilitation programs, and the federal-state employment service. They describe and evaluate the major programs and recommend improvements in administration for more effective delivery of services.

Levitan, Sar A., Martin Rein, and David Marwick. *Work and Welfare Go Together.* Baltimore, Md.: Johns Hopkins University Press, 1976.

The authors trace the growth and change in composition of the AFDC program and development of strategies to promote self-help, emphasizing the Work Incentive Program and social services. Analysis of WIN's initial impacts reveals limited success in curtailing the growth of welfare or removing enrollees from welfare rolls but suggests some benefits in increased earnings and reduced dependency of the participants. They conclude that future policies should recognize the growing interdependence of work and welfare.

Levitan, Sar A., and Robert Taggart. *Employment and Earnings Inadequacy: A New Social Indicator.* Baltimore, Md.: Johns Hopkins University Press, 1974.

The authors formulate and analyze an employment and earnings inadequacy index that considers individual and family income levels as well as employment status to measure the extent of labor market pathologies. Data from the 1968–1972 Current Population Survey are used to compare and contrast the new index with government unemployment statistics. Cross-sectional and longitudinal analyses indicate how the components of the new index vary by race, sex, family status, and area of residence.

Levitan, Sar A., and Robert Taggart. *The Promise of Greatness.* Cambridge, Ma.: Harvard University Press, 1976.

Examines the major programmatic components of the Great Society and assesses their combined effects on the primary target groups. The theme is that the policies and programs had an overwhelmingly beneficial impact. The underlying assumptions and standards of judgment are spelled out to be accepted or rejected by the reader.

Levitan, Sar A., and Gregory K. Wurzburg. *Evaluating Federal Social Programs: An Uncertain Art.* Kalamazoo, Mich.: The W. E. Upjohn Institute for Employment Research, 1979.

This study assesses the current state of the art of both process and impact evaluation, with emphasis on the limitations of evaluation tools currently in use. The authors have also provided an analysis of the federal government's institutional arrangements for evaluating social programs.

Mangum, Garth L. *The Emergence of Manpower Policy.* New York: Holt, Rinehart and Winston, 1969.

A brief history of U.S. human resources policies to 1960 and a summary of the changing goals and methods of government human resources policies in the 1960s. Mangum discusses the relative success of the Job Corps, Neighborhood Youth Corps, and other training programs. The final chapters recommend changes in the administration and structure of federal human resources programs.

Mangum, Garth L. *Employability, Employment, and Income: A Reassessment of Manpower Policy.* Salt Lake City, Utah: Olympus, 1976.

Focusing on human resource policy, the author examines labor market operations to which any effective human resource policy must accommodate. Recommendations are made for a series of policy changes.

Mangum, Garth L. *Career Education and the Comprehensive Employment and Training Act.* Office of Career Education. Washington, D.C.: Government Printing Office, 1978.

The Office of Career Education and the Comprehensive Employment and Training Act (CETA) serve a population overlapping in concept but little in practice. This review is offered to give a better understanding of CETA and its predecessors. It also presents recommendations for linking career education to current youth employment policies.

Mangum, Garth L., James Morlock, David Snedeker, and Marion Pines. *Job Market Futurity,* Salt Lake City, Utah: Olympus, 1979.

A how-to-do-it manual on planning and management for improving the functions of local labor markets, set in the context of the Comprehensive

Employment and Training Act. It traces the legislative background of CETA, describes the role and functions of the labor markets, provides a basic planning model, and presents a discussion, along with examples, of program design, implementation, and management.

Mangum, Garth L., and Seninger, Stephen F. *Coming of Age in the Ghetto: A Dilemma of Youth Unemployment* **(a report to the Ford Foundation). Baltimore, Md.: Johns Hopkins University Press, 1978.**

The authors examine the root causes of teenage unemployment in the ghetto emphasizing the social and psychological conséquences of unemployment. Life styles and career-development patterns among middle-class and ghetto youth, and job search behavior among teenagers are compared within the context of the city and ghetto economic structure.

Mangum, Garth L., and John Walsh. *A Decade of Manpower Development and Training.* **Salt Lake City, Utah: Olympus, 1973.**

Traces the accomplishments, problems, and limitations of the first ten years of the Manpower Development and Training Act of 1962. Identifies lessons that can be used to improve the quality of all adult occupational education.

Marshall, Ray. *Rural Workers in Rural Labor Markets.* **Salt Lake City, Utah: Olympus, 1974.**

In providing a factual and analytical basis for more effective development policies, the book discusses the major issues of affecting rural workers and rural labor markets, including analyses of labor relations in the agricultural sector, protective labor laws for agricultural workers, issues related to rural nonfarm employment, and economic development trends in the rural South.

Marshall, Ray, and Robert W. Glover. *Training and Entry into Union Construction.* **Manpower R & D Monograph 39, U.S. Department of Labor. Washington, D.C: Government Printing Office, 1975.**

This study of building trades in nine cities provides evidence that apprenticeship training gives construction craftspersons considerable advantage over those informally trained. Recommendations include upgrading apprenticeship programs, more union cooperation in education, and better record-keeping systems.

Marshall, Ray, Allan King, and Vernon Briggs, Jr. *Labor Economics: Wages, Employment, and Trade Unionism,* **4th ed. Homewood, Ill.: Richard D. Irwin, 1980.**

This text on labor economics provides the reader with the theoretical tools needed to understand labor market operations, while setting a framework for the role of empirical research as a method to evaluate the merits of conflicting theories. After a brief introduction to the study of labor economics, the three remaining sections discuss the historical development of the labor movement, wage and employment determination, and public policy issues concerning trade unions and labor markets.

Marshall, Ray, and Richard Perlman, eds. *An Anthology of Labor Economics: Readings and Commentary.* **New York: Wiley, 1972.**

A selection of articles covering both the theory and practice of labor economics. It also includes many of the classical articles in labor market theory, changes in the labor force, unemployment, and wage structure as well as readings that discuss collective bargaining, human resource development, poverty, and income. The editors provide commentary on each article and suggest related readings on the various topics.

National Commission for Employment Policy. *Labor Market Intermediaries.* **Washington, D.C.: Government Printing Office, 1978.**

Eleven papers examining the several different organizations and institutions, in both the private and public sector, that assist the labor market exchange process. In addition, these papers discuss how the various intermediaries can improve the overall operation of labor markets, thereby benefiting job-seekers, employers, and the nation as a whole.

National Commission on Employment and Unemployment Statistics. *Counting the Labor Force.* **Washington, D.C.: Government Printing Office, 1979.**

An analysis of labor market information. A congressionally mandated review of concepts and definitions, information gaps, and the methods employed in data gathering and statistical estimation. The report includes 88 formal recommendations and additional suggestions of the commission to improve the available labor market data. The three-volume appendix to the report contains 33 background papers prepared for the commission and reprints which review in detail the various topics discussed in the report.

Patten, Thomas H. *Manpower and the Development of Human Resources.* **New York: Wiley, 1971.**

The author, previously an industrial relations executive with the Ford Motor Company, examines, in nonmathematical terms, human resource planning and development within businesses and organizations. Separate chapters are devoted to particular types of training apprentices, salespersons, foremen, and executives. Other chapters deal in general terms with the objectives and organization of human resource planning.

Schiller, Bradley R. *The Economics of Poverty and Discrimination,* **3rd ed. Englewood, Cliffs, N.J.: Prentice-Hall, 1980.**

Emphasizing the complexity of the social, economic, and political aspects of poverty and discrimination, this volume offers an initial statement of the problem, a detailed analysis of possible causes, and a review of present and potential policies.

Smith, Ralph E., ed. *The Subtle Revolution.* **Washington, D.C.: The Urban Institute, 1979.**

A collection of papers on the impact of increased labor force participation on the part of women. Among the topics examined are the occupations and earnings and career opportunities of women, the relationship of female employment to marriage and family life, and the policy problems posed by these changes. Among the issues explored are female employment and its impact on the social security system and the federal income tax.

Snedeker, Bonnie B., and David M. Snedeker. *CETA: Decentralization on Trial.* **Salt Lake City, Utah: Olympus, 1978.**

A description and analysis of the first few years of local experience in the implementation of the Comprehensive Employment and Training Act based on observations of the authors in 45 prime sponsorships and analyses of other available research and data on CETA. The study concludes with a summary of the major problems that appeared in CETA's first years along with the authors' recommendations on how to improve the program.

Somers, Gerald G., ed. *Collective Bargaining: Contemporary American Experience.* Madison, Wisc.: Industrial Relations Research Association, 1980.
A detailed description and analysis of contemporary collective bargaining in ten major industries. Each study uses a common framework to facilitate a comparative analysis of collective bargaining in leading industries.

The Task Force on Education and Employment, National Academy of Education. *Education for Employment: Knowledge for Action.* Washington, D.C: Acropolis Books, 1979.
An analysis of the relationship of education and the changing labor market conditions. The study examines changing demographic and employment trends, the economic returns of education, the role of curriculum options in high schools, as well as work-education programs, guidance counseling and career development, and issues related to adult recurrent education, federal employment and training programs, and occupational licensure. The conclusions and resulting recommendations are directed toward students, parents, schools, unions, and government agencies.

Thurow, Lester. *Investment in Human Capital.* Belmont, Calif.: Wadsworth, 1970.
Emphasizes the need to integrate the concept of human capital into the main body of economic theory. Although much of the analysis is carried out within the framework of traditional investment theory, care is taken to describe the many peculiarities that differentiate human from physical capital. After dealing with the production and measurement of human capital, Thurow discusses investment decisions at the individual, firm, and government levels.

Appendix

EMPLOYMENT AND TRAINING ABCs

AFDC	Aid to Families with Dependent Children
AFDC-UP	Aid to Families with Dependent Children—Unemployed Parent segment
AFL-CIO	American Federation of Labor-Congress of Industrial Organizations
ARC	Appalachian Regional Commission
AVA	American Vocational Association
BAT	Bureau of Apprenticeship Training, U.S. Department of Labor
BCTD	Building and Construction Trades Department, AFL-CIO
BIA	Bureau of Indian Affairs, U.S. Department of Interior
BLS	Bureau of Labor Statistics, U.S. Department of Labor
CAA	Community Action Agency
CAMPS	Cooperative Area Manpower Planning System
CAP	Community Action Program
CBO	Community-based organization
CEA	Council of Economic Advisers
CEP	Concentrated Employment Program
CETA	Comprehensive Employment and Training Act

CIJC	Construction Industry Joint Conference
CLMS	Continuous Longitudinal Manpower Survey
CPI	Consumer Price Index
CPS	Current Population Survey
CSA	Community Services Administration
CWBH	Continuous Wage and Benefit History
CWHS	Continuous Work History Sample
CWT	Community Work and Training Program
DOL	Department of Labor
DOT	Dictionary of Occupational Titles
EDA	Economic Development Administration, U.S. Department of Commerce
EEA	Emergency Employment Act
EEOC	Equal Employment Opportunity Commission
EOA	Economic Opportunity Act
ERA	Equal Rights Amendment
ES	Employment Service, U.S. Department of Labor
ESARS	Employment Security Automated Reporting System
ESEA	Elementary and Secondary Education Act
ESL	English as a second language
ETA	Employment and Training Administration, U.S. Department of Labor
FAP	Family Assistance Plan
FEPC	Fair Employment Practices Commission
FLSA	Fair Labor Standards Act
GED	General education development
GNP	Gross national product
HRD	Human resource development
HRDI	Human Resource Development Institute, AFL-CIO
IHS	Indian Health Service, U.S. Department of Health and Human Services
INS	Immigration and Naturalization Service
ITA	Industrial Training Act of 1964 (in Britain)
JAC	Joint apprenticeship committee
JAV	Job analysis vocabulary
JBSS	Job Bank and Screening System
JIS	Job information service
JOBS	Job Opportunities in the Business Sector Program
LEA	Local education agency
LES	Limited English-speaking
LFPR	Labor force participation rate
LINCS	Labor Inventory Communications System
LMA	Labor Market Area
LMI	Labor Market Information
MAPC	Manpower Advisory Planning Council
MDTA	Manpower Development and Training Act

MIG	Manpower institutional grant
MIS	Management information system
NAACP	National Association for the Advancement of Colored People
NAB	National Alliance of Business
NLRB	National Labor Relations Board
NLS	National Longitudinal Survey
OECD	Organisation for Economic Co-operation and Development
OEO	Office of Economic Opportunity
OFCC	Office of Federal Contract Compliance, U.S. Department of Labor
OIC	Opportunities Industrialization Center
OJT	On-the-job training
OMB	Office of Management and Budget
OYP	Office of Youth Programs, U.S. Department of Labor
PBJI	Program for Better Jobs and Income
PEP	Public employment program
PIC	Private industry council
PIG	Private interest group
PSC	Public service careers program
PSE	Public service employment
PSIP	Private Sector Initiative Program
R & D	Research and development
RTP	Recruitment and Training Program
SAC	State apprenticeship council
SAT	Scholastic Aptitude Test
SER	Service, Employment, Redevelopment Program
SIPP	Survey of Income and Program Participation
SMSA	Standard metropolitan statistical area
SSI	Supplemental Security Income
SYEP	Summer Youth Employment Program
TJTC	Targeted jobs tax credit
UC	Unemployment compensation
UI	Unemployment insurance
USES	U.S. Employment Service, Department of Labor
VISTA	Volunteers in Service to America
WDL	Workers Defense League
WET	Work Experience and Training program
WIN	Work Incentive program
WPA	Work Projects Administration
YACC	Young Adult Conservation Corps
YCC	Youth Conservation Corps
YCCIP	Youth Community Conservation and Improvement Projects
YEDPA	Youth Employment and Demonstration Projects Act
YETP	Youth Employment and Training Programs
YIEPP	Youth Incentive Entitlement Pilot Projects
YOC	Youth Opportunity Center

INDEXES

Name Index

Subject Index

Accelerator concept, 181
Additional-worker hypothesis, 32, 103
Administrative statistics, 76, 81, 82
Affirmative action, 352, 356. *See also*
    Equal employment opportunity
    planning for, 385, 391
Age, and labor force participation, 27,
    72
Age Discrimination in Employment
    Acts, 286
Agricultural employment, decline in,
    60
Agricultural Establishment Survey, 81
Agricultural labor
    Chicanos in, 249–251, 254
    data sources for, 81
    income protection for, 254
    occupational mobility of, 21
    occupational forecasts for, 92
    and productivity, 72
    work-life expectancy of, 14, 56
Agricultural productivity, 70, 490
Agriculture
    effects of WWII, 308
    human resource development in,
        489
    Native Americans in, 261, 265
    seasonal unemployment in, 37, 41,
        53, 54
    technological change in, 490, 492
    youth in, 57
Aid to Families with Dependent Chil-
        dren, 319, 327–334
    additional benefits, 340
    compared to work, 329
    eligibility for, 330

in employment and training pro-
    grams, 334–341
and Medicaid, 328, 340–341
and PBJI, 343
and public employment service, 476
and Social Welfare Reform Amend-
    ments, 344
unemployed-parent component 328,
    329, 332, 341, 344
and WIN, 338
Aid to the Blind and Totally Disabled,
    319
American Federation of Labor-Con-
        gress of Industrial Organizations
    Appalachian Council, 454
    Building trades councils, 351
    and discrimination in apprentice-
        ship programs, 193
    and employment and training pro-
        grams, 453–454
    formation of, 431
    Human Resources Development In-
        stitute, 351
    withdrawal from, 442
American Society for Personnel Ad-
        ministration, 385, 386, 464
American Society for Training and
        Development, 464
American Telephone and Telegraph,
    349
American Vocational Association, 159,
    163
Antidiscrimination policy, effect of,
    233–234
Appalachian Regional Commission,
    488